Native Languages of the Americas

Volume 2

Native Languages of the Americas

Volume 2

Edited by Thomas A. Sebeok
Research Center for Language and Semiotic Studies
Indiana University
Bloomington, Indiana

PLENUM PRESS · NEW YORK AND LONDON

Library of Congress Cataloging in Publication Data

Main entry under title:

Native languages of the Americas.

Includes index.

1. Indians–Languages. I. Sebeok, Thomas Albert, 1920-

PM108.N3 497 76-28216

ISBN 0-306-37158-8 (Vol. 2)

A Division of Plenum Publishing Corporation

227 West 17th Street, New York, N.Y. 10011

Most of the material in this volume was previously published by Mouton & Co., in the series *Current Trends in Linguistics.* The chapters by Barthel, Grimes, Longacre, Mayers, and Suárez first appeared in Volume 4: *Ibero-American and Caribbean Linguistics;* the chapter by McClaran in Volume 10: *Linguistics in North America;* the chapters by Kaufman and Rensch in Volume 11: *Diachronic, Areal, and Typological Linguistics;* "North American Indian Languages," by Landar in Volume 10: *Linguistics in North America;* and "Historiography of Native Ibero-American Linguistics," by Landar in Volume 13: *Historiography of Linguistics* (©1968, 1973, 1975, Mouton & Co., N.V., Publishers, The Hague).

Printed in the United States of America

FOREWORD

The publishing history of the eleven chapters that comprise the contents of this second volume of *Native Languages of the Americas* is rather different from that of the thirteen that appeared in Volume 1 of this twin set late last year. Original versions of five articles, respectively, by Barthel, Grimes, Longacre, Mayers, and Suárez, were first published in Part II of *Current Trends in Linguistics*, Vol. 4, subtitled *Ibero-American and Caribbean Linguistics* (1968), having been commissioned by the undersigned in his capacity as editor of the fourteen volume series which was distributed in twenty-one tomes between 1963 and 1976. McClaran's article is reprinted from Part III of Vol. 10, *Linguistics in North America* (1973) and the two by Kaufman and Rensch were in Part II of Vol. 11, *Diachronic, Areal, and Typological Linguistics* (1973). There are three contributions by Landar: earlier versions of two appeared in Vol. 10 ("North American Indian Languages," accompanied by William Sorsby's maps of tribal groups of North and Central America), and in Vol. 13, *Historiography of Linguistics* (1975); however, his checklist of South and Central American Indian languages was freshly compiled for this book.

Generous financial support for preparing the materials included in this project came from several agencies of the United States government, to wit: the National Endowment for the Humanities and the National Science Foundation, for Vols. 10 and 13, and the Office of Education, for Vols. 4 and 11; in addition, the Canada Council gave partial aid for Vol. 10. Full particulars of these grants and contracts are given in my Introductions to the four books mentioned.

As related previously, the *Current Trends in Linguistics* series was a long-term venture of Mouton Publishers, of The Hague, under the imaginative in-house direction of Peter de Ridder. Various spin-offs were foreseen, many of them happily realized by alert publishers all over the world. The demand for pulling together all the contributions dealing with the native languages of the Americas was particularly insistent; accordingly, I am grateful to the present management of that publishing house I had been associated with until 1974 for having graciously yielded this important undertaking to Plenum.

Each of the authors was given an opportunity to correct, update, or otherwise alter his or her article; a few seized this oportunity even to make major revisions. Thus at least some of the texts in this book are by no means identical with those published earlier under the same or a corresponding title, so that, as a whole, it may be viewed as a reasonably up-to-date and comprehensive panoptic conspectus of the field in the last quarter of our century.

The earlier volume and this one both contain separate indexes of personal names mentioned in that tome. These were compiled by May Lee. Landar's checklists, together covering all the native languages of the Western Hemisphere, embody years of assiduous application to insure that this work will be used as an invaluable reference tool by a public significantly wider than a strictly academic readership. The substantive articles comprising the rest are the most authoritative to be found anywhere, and unlikely to be soon superseded.

My personal experience in the field covered in the compass of this volume is regrettably sparse, although I did have a brush with Aymara grammar and lexicon in the 1950s and even managed to produce fairly extensive materials for a dictionary of that language a quarter of a century ago. After the conquest of the area by emissaries of the Spanish Crown, "the priests of the Church began serious study of the indigenous languages spoken there," in the words of Norman A. McQuown, "in order to be able to preach the gospel, to convert and educate the heathen, and to provide the civil authorities with a linguistic vehicle to facilitate local government." For Aymara, the tongue that I know best, and which is still spoken by more than 600,000 people in Bolivia and Peru, Father P. Ludovico Bertonio, laboring at the turn of the sixteenth century, produced a stunning grammar (1603), followed by an equally magnificient vocabulary (beginning in 1610). Although his grammar is superficially based on a Latin model, it is of inestimable worth for our knowledge of this language at the moment when it was still free of Spanish contamination and as a base line for its post-Conquest development. Bertonio's books are so subtle, so profound that neither has as yet been equaled. I emphasize these enduring values to underline the slow rate of progress in linguistic studies, especially in this area, and in the hope that contemporary students may approach such past masters of the art, now largely blended into the tapestry of that era of evangelism, in a becoming spirit of humility all too rare in my profession.

Bloomington, October 8, 1976

THOMAS A. SEBEOK

CONTENTS
Volume 2

PART TWO: CENTRAL AND SOUTH AMERICA

PART THREE: CHECKLISTS

CONTENTS
Volume 1

PART ONE: NORTH AMERICA

General Chapters

Areal Groupings

LIST OF ABBREVIATIONS

1. JOURNALS AND BOOKS

AAA-M	*American Anthropological Association.* Memoirs (Menasha, Wisc.).
AAAS-P	*Proceedings of the American Association for the Advancement of Science* (Washington, D.C.).
AAcadAS-M	*American Academy of Arts and Sciences.* Memoirs (Boston).
AAcadAS-P	*American Academy of Arts and Sciences.* Proceedings (Boston).
AAOJ	*See* AmAnt.
AAUP Bulletin	*American Association of University Professors.* Bulletin (Washington, D.C.).
Acta Salamanticensia	*Acta Salamanticensia iussu senatus universitatis edita.* Filosofia y Lettras (Salamanca).
AD	*American Documentation* (Washington, D.C.).
ADD	*American Dialect Dictionary.*
AES-M	*American Ethnological Society.* Memoirs (Seattle).
AES-T	*American Ethnological Society.* Transactions (Seattle).
AFS-M	*American Folklore Society.* Memoirs (Philadelphia).
AGI	*Archivio Glottologico Italiano* (Florence).
AGR	*American German Review* (Philadelphia).
AIAK	*See* PICAm.
AJPh	*American Journal of Philology* (Baltimore).
AJSoc	*American Journal of Sociology* (Chicago).
AL	*Acta Linguistica Hafniensia.* International Journal of Structural Linguistics (Copenhagen).
ALF	*L'Atlas linguistique de la France.* By Gillérion and Edmont. (1902-1912).
ALH	*Acta Linguistica Academiae Scientiarum Hungaricae* (Budapest).
AmA	*American Anthropologist* (Menasha, Wisc.).
AmAnt	*American Antiquarian* (Boston, Mass.).
AmAntiquity	*American Antiquity* (Salt Lake City).
AMCIA	*See* PICAm.
América Indígena	*América Indígena* (Mexico, D.F., Mexico).
AMNH-M	*American Museum of Natural History.* Memoirs (New York).
Anglia	*Anglia.* Zeitschrift für englische Philologie (Tübingen).
AnL	*Anthropological Linguistics* (Bloomington, Ind.).
Anthropologica	*Anthropologica.* Centre Canadien de Recherches en anthropologie (Université d'Ottawa).

Anthropos	*Anthropos*. Revue internationale d'ethnologie et de linguistique/Internationale Zeitschrift für Völker- und Sprachenkunde (Freiburg, Switzerland).
AR	*Anthropological Record* (University of California Press, Berkeley and Los Angeles).
Archivum	*Archivum*. Revista de la Facultad de Filosofia y Letras (Universidad de Oviedo, Oviedo).
ArchL	*Archivum Linguisticum*. A review of comparative philology and general linguistics (Glasgow).
ArchSSL	*Archiv für das Studium der Neueren Sprachen (und Literatur)* (Braunschweig).
AS	*American Speech*. Quarterly of Linguistic Usage (New York).
ASR	*American-Scandinavian Review* (New York).
ASNS	*Archiv für das Studium der Neueren Sprachen* (Brunswick).
AvglPhon	*Archiv für Vergleichende Phonetik* (Berlin).
BAAS-R	*British Association for the Advancement of Science*. Annual Report (London).
BAE-B	*Bureau of American Ethnology*. Bulletin (Washington, D.C.).
BAE-R	*Bureau of American Ethnology*. Annual Report (Washington, D.C.).
BCLC	*Bulletin du Cercle Linguistique de Copenhague* (Copenhagen).
BHS	*Bulletin of Hispanic Studies* (Liverpool).
BIA	*Bilingualism in the Americas*. A bibliography and research guide, by Einar Haugen. PADS 26.
BS	*Behavioral Science* (Ann Arbor, Mich.).
BSL	*Bulletin de la Société de Linguistique de Paris* (Paris).
CAnthr	*Current Anthropology*. A world journal of the science of man (Chicago).
CAIL	*Conference on American Indian Languages*. Conference held in conjunction with annual meetings of the American Anthropological Association.
CE	*College English* (Chicago).
CEACritic	*CEA Critic*. College English Association (Fullerton, Calif.).
ChiLing	*University of Chicago Publications in Anthropology*. Linguistic Series (Chicago).
CJL/RCL	*Canadian Journal of Linguistics/Revue Canadienne de Linguistique* (Toronto). (Formerly JCLA.)
CNAE	*Contributions to North American Ethnology*. Department of the Interior, U.S. Geographical and Geological Survey of the Rocky Mountain Region. Edited under the direction of J. W. Powell (Washington, D.C.).
CSlP	*Canadian Slavonic Papers* (Montreal).
CTA Journal	*California Teachers Association Journal* (San Francisco).
CTL 3	*Current Trends in Linguistics*. Volume 3: Theoretical Foundations, ed. by Thomas A. Sebeok (The Hague, Mouton & Co., 1966).
CTL 4	*Current Trends in Linguistics*. Volume 4: Ibero-American and Caribbean Linguistics, ed. by Thomas A. Sebeok (The Hague, Mouton & Co., 1968).
CTL 9	*Current Trends in Linguistics*. Volume 9: Linguistics in Western Europe, ed. by Thomas A. Sebeok (The Hague, Mouton & Co., 1972).
CUCA	*Columbia University Contributions to Anthropology* (New York).
DA	*Dictionary of Americanisms on historical principles*. Ed. by M. M. Mathews (Chicago, 1951).
DAb	*Dissertation Abstracts*. A guide to dissertations and monographs available on microfilm (Ann Arbor, Mich.).
DAE	*Dictionary of American English on historical principles*. Ed. by Sir William Craigie and J. R. Hulbert (Chicago, 1938-1944).
Daedalus	*Daedalus*. Journal of the American Academy of Arts and Sciences (Boston).
DARE	*Dictionary of American Regional English*. Ed. by F. G. Cassidy. Forthcoming.
DC	*Dictionary of Canadianisms on historical principles*. Ed. by W. S. Avis (Toronto, 1967).
DN	*Dialect Notes*. Volume I (Boston), Volumes II-VI (New Haven).
EDD	*English Dialect Dictionary*.
EE	*Elementary English*. A magazine of the language arts. National Council of Teachers of English (Champaign, Ill.).
EETS	*Early English Text Society* (London).

EJ	*English Journal* (Urbana, Ill.).
ES	*English Studies*. A Journal of English Letters and Philology (Amsterdam).
ETC.	*ETC*. A review of general semantics (Chicago).
Ethnohistory	*Ethnohistory*. Devoted to the original research in the documentary history of the culture and movements of primitive peoples and related problems of broader scope. American Society for Ethnohistory (Lexington, Ky.).
Ethnology	*Ethnology*. International Journal of Cultural and Social Anthropology (Pittsburgh).
ExSI	*Explorations and Field Work of the Smithsonian Institution* (Washington, D.C.).
FdaM	*Le Français dans le Monde* (Paris).
FL	*Foundations of Language*. International Journal of Language and Philosophy (Dordrecht, The Netherlands).
FLing	*Folia Linguistica*. Acta Societatis linguisticae Europaeae (The Hague).
Florida Anthropologist	*Florida Anthropologist* (Florida State University, Department of Anthropology, Tallahassee, Fla.).
Florida FLR	*Florida Foreign Language Reporter* (Tallahassee, Fla.).
FR	*The French Review* (Baltimore).
GK	*Gengo Kenkyū*. Journal of the Linguistic Society of Japan (Tokyo).
GL	*General Linguistics* (Lexington, Ky.).
Glossa	*Glossa* (Simon Fraser University, Burnaby, B.C.).
HAIL	*Handbook of American Indian Languages* 4 Vols: 1 (1911) and 2 (1922) are BAE-B 40. Vols 3 and 4 (1940) published separately (J. J. Augustin, New York).
Hispania	*Hispania*. A journal devoted to the interest of the teaching of Spanish and Portuguese (Appleton, Wisc.).
HMAI	*Handbook of Middle American Indians*. Robert Wauchope, General Editor, Norman A. McQuown, editor of Vol. 5, Linguistics (Austin).
HO	*Human Organization*. Society for Applied Anthropology (Lexington, Ky.).
Homme	*L'Homme*. Revue française d'anthropologie (Paris and The Hague).
HUAIL	*Harvard University, Papers from the seminar in American Indian Linguistics* (Cambridge, Mass.). Mimeographed.
ICA	*See* PICAm.
ICSL	*International Conference on Salish Languages*.
IJAL	*International Journal of American Linguistics* (Baltimore).
IJSLP	*International Journal of Slavic Linguistics and Poetics* (The Hague).
IRAL	*International Review of Applied Linguistics in Language Teaching/Internationale Zeitschrift für angewandte Linguistik in der Spracherziehung* (Heidelberg).
IUPAL-M	*Indiana University Publications in Anthropology, [Folklore] and Linguistics*. Memoirs (Bloomington, Ind.).
IUP-LSM	*Indiana University Publications, Language Science Monographs* (Bloomington, Ind.).
JAbSocPsy	*Journal of Abnormal and Social Psychology* (Washington, D.C.).
JAcS	*See* JASA.
JAF	*Journal of American Folklore* (Philadelphia).
JanL	*Janua Linguarum*. Series maior, minor, practica, critica (The Hague, Mouton & Co.).
JAOS	*Journal of the American Oriental Society* (New Haven, Conn.).
JASA	*Journal of the Acoustical Society of America* (Lancaster, Pa. and New York).
JCLA	*The Journal of the Canadian Linguistic Association/Revue de l'Association canadienne de Linguistique* (Edmonton, Alberta).
JEGP	*The Journal of English and Germanic Philology* (Urbana, Ill.).
JEL	*Journal of English Linguistics* (Bellingham, Wash.).
JL	*Journal of Linguistics* (London).
JNH	*Journal of Negro History* (Washington, D.C.).
JSHD	*Journal of Speech and Hearing Disorders* (Ann Arbor, Mich.).
JSI	*Journal of Social Issues* (Ann Arbor, Mich.).
JSocAm	*Journal de la Société des Americanistes* (Paris).
JSocI	*See* JSI.
JVLVB	*Journal of Verbal Learning and Verbal Behavior* (New York).

JWAS	*Journal of the Washington Academy of Sciences* (Seattle).
KASP	*Kroeber Anthropology Society Papers* (Berkeley).
KDVS	*Det Konelige danske Videnskabernes Selskab. Hist.-Filo. Meddelelser* (Copenhagen).
Kybernetika	*Kybernetika* (Prague).
LANE	*Linguistic Atlas of New England.*
LenC	*Lenguaje y Ciencias* (Trujillo, Peru).
Lg	*Language.* Journal of the Linguistic Society of America (Baltimore).
Lingua	*Lingua.* International Review of General Linguistics/Revue internationale de linguistique générale (Amsterdam).
Linguistic Inquiry	*Linguistic Inquiry* (Toronto).
Linguistics	*Linguistics.* An International Review (The Hague).
Linguistique	*La Linguistique.* Revue internationale de linguistique générale (Paris).
LL	*Language Learning* (Ann Arbor, Mich.).
LPosn	*Lingua Posnaniensis.* Czasopiśmo poświęcone językoznawstwu porównawczemu i ogólnemu (Poznań).
L & S	*Language and Speech* (Teddington, Middlesex).
Man	*Man.* A Record of Anthropological Science (London).
META	*META.* Formerly *Journal des Traducteurs* (Université de Montréal).
MKAW	*Mitteilungen der kaiserlichen Akademie der Wissenschaften in Wien* (Vienna).
MLJ	*Modern Language Journal* (Ann Arbor, Mich.).
MLN	*Modern Language Notes* (Baltimore).
MLQ	*Modern Language Quarterly* (Seattle).
MLR	*The Modern Language Review* (Cambridge).
MPhil	*Modern Philology* (Chicago).
MPhon	*Le Maître Phonétique.* Organe de l'Association Phonétique Internationale (London).
MSLL	*Monograph Series on Language and Linguistics* (Georgetown University, Washington, D.C.).
MT	*Mechanical Translation* (Cambridge, Mass.).
Names	*Names.* Journal of the American Name Society (Berkeley).
NARN	*Northwest Anthropological Research Notes* (Moscow, University of Idaho).
NMC-B	*National Museum of Canada.* Bulletin (Ottawa, The Queen's Printer).
NoB	*Namn och Bygd.* Tidskrift för nordisk ortnamnsforskning (Uppsala).
Nph	*Neophilologus* (Groningen).
NPhM	*Neuphilologische Mitteilungen.* Bulletin de la Société neophilologique de Helsinki (Helsinki).
NRFH	*Nueva Revista de Filologiá Hispánica* (Mexico).
NTS	*Norsk Tidsskrift for Sprogvidenskap* (Oslo).
OED	*Oxford English Dictionary.*
OL	*Oceanic Linguistics.* Special Publication (Pacific and Asian Linguistic Institute, University of Hawaii, Honolulu).
Onomastica	*Onomastica.* Piśmo poświecone nazewnictwu geograficznemu i osobowemu (Wrocław).
Orbis	*Orbis.* Bulletin international de documentation linguistique (Louvain).
OSlP	*Oxford Slavonic Papers* (London).
OSUWPL	*Ohio State University Working Papers in Linguistics* (Columbus).
PADS	*Publications of the American Dialect Society* (Gainesville, Fla. and University, Ala.).
PAES	*Publications of the American Ethnological Society* (Seattle and Leiden).
PAPS	*Proceedings of the American Philosophical Society* (Philadelphia).
Phonetica	*Phonetica.* Internationale Zeitschrift für Phonetik/International Journal of Phonetics (Basel and New York).
PhQ	*Philological Quarterly* (Iowa City).
PIAcadS	*Proceedings of the Indiana Academy of Sciences* (Indianapolis).
PICAm [3, 35, etc.]	*Proceedings of the* [*Third, Thirty-Fifth, etc.*] *International Congress of Americanists.*
PICL [7, 9, etc.]	*Proceedings of the* [*Seventh, Ninth, etc.*] *International Congress of Linguists.*

PICPS 4	*Proceedings of the Fourth International Congress of Phonetic Sciences, held at the University of Helsinki, 4-9 September, 1961.* Edited by Antti Sovijärvi and Pento Aalto (The Hague, Mouton, 1962).
PJE	*Philippine Journal of Education* (Quezon City).
PJL	*Philippine Journal of Language Teaching* (Quezon City).
Plateau	*Plateau* (Northern Arizona Society of Science and Art, Flagstaff, Ariz.).
PNQ	*Pacific Northwest Quarterly* (Seattle).
PMLA	*Publications of the Modern Language Association of America* (New York).
Poetics	*Poetics.* International Review for the Theory of Literature (The Hague).
POLA	*Project on Linguistic Analysis* (The Ohio State University Research Foundation, Columbus).
PRS[IHS]	*Prehistoric Research Series* (Indiana Historical Society, Indianapolis).
PSLM	*Publications de la Section de Linguistique, Faculté des Lettres, Université de Montréal.*
QJSp	*Quarterly Journal of Speech* (Columbia, Missouri).
RCAFL-P	*Publications of the Research Center in Antropology, Folklore and Linguistics* (Bloomington, Ind.).
RCB & B	*Royal Commission on Bilingualism and Biculturalism.* Preliminary Report + 4 vols. (Ottawa). 1965–.
RDialR	*Revue de dialectologie romane.* Société de dialectologie romane (Hamburg).
RFE	*Revista de Filología Española* (Madrid).
RHiM	*Revista Hispánica Moderna* (New York).
RJb	*Romanistisches Jahrbuch* (Hamburg).
RLing	*Revue Roumaine de Linguistique* (Bucharest).
Romania	*Romania* (Paris).
RomPh	*Romance Philology* (Berkeley and Los Angeles).
RTE	*Research in the Teaching of English* (National Council of Teachers of English, Champaign, Ill.).
SA	*Scientific American* (New York).
Saga och Sed	*Saga och Sed.* Gustav Adolfs Akademiens årsbok (Uppsala).
SAS-P	*Sacramento Anthropological Society.* Papers (Sacramento, Calif.).
SCA	*Smithsonian [Institution] Contributions to Anthropology* (Washington, D.C.).
Science	*Science.* American Association for the Advancement of Science (Washington, D.C.).
SCK	*Smithsonian [Institution] Contributions to Knowledge* (Washington, D.C.).
ScS	*Scandinavian Studies.* Publication of the Society for the Advancement of Scandinavian Studies (Menasha, Wisc.).
SEEJ	*Slavic and East European Journal* (Bloomington, Ind.).
Sefarad	*Sefarad.* Revista del Instituto Arias Montano de Estudios Hebraicos y Oriente Próximo (Madrid and Barcelona).
SG	*Studium Generale* (Berlin, Göttingen and Heidelberg).
SIL	*Studies in Linguistics* (Buffalo, N.Y.).
SJA	*Southwestern Journal of Anthropology* (Albuquerque, N.M.).
SL	*Studia Linguistica.* Revue de linguistique générale et comparée (Lund).
SMC	*Smithsonian [Institution] Miscellaneous Collections* (Washington, D.C.).
SocSciI	*Social Science Information/Information sur les sciences sociales.* International Social Science Council (Paris).
Southern FL Quarterly	*Southern Folklore Quarterly* (University of Florida, Gainsville, Fla.).
Sprache	*Die Sprache.* Zeitschrift für Sprachwissenschaft (Vienna).
SPh	*Studies in Philology* (Chapel Hill, N.C.).
Style	*Style* (University of Arkansas, Fayetteville).
SWES	*Selected Writings of Edward Sapir in Language, Culture and Personality.* Ed. by David G. Mandelbaum (University of California Press, Berkeley and Los Angeles, 1949).
TAPA	*Transactions and Proceedings of the American Philological Association* (Ithaca, N.Y.).
TAPS	*Transactions of the American Philosophical Society* (Philadelphia).
TCLC	*Travaux du Cercle Linguistique de Copenhagen* (Copenhagen).

TCAAS	*Transactions and Collections of the American Antiquarian Society.*
TENES	*A Survey of the Teaching of English to Non-English Speakers in the United States.* By H. B. Allen (1966).
Thesaurus	*Thesaurus.* Boletin del Instituto Caro y Cueva (Bogotá).
TKAS	*Transactions of the Kansas Academy of Science* (Topeka).
TPhS	*Transactions of the Philological Society* (London).
TSLL	*Texas Studies in Language and Linguistics* (Austin).
UAS	*Uralic and Altaic Series.* Indiana University Publications (Bloomington, Ind., and The Hague).
UCPAAE	*University of California Publications in American Archaeology and Ethnology* (Berkeley and Los Angeles).
UCPL	*University of California Publications in Linguistics* (Berkeley and Los Angeles).
UHWPL	*University of Hawaii Working Papers in Linguistics* (Honolulu).
UNM-B	*University of New Mexico.* Bulletin (Albuquerque, N.M.).
UNM-PA	*University of New Mexico Publications in Anthropology* (Albuquerque, N.M.).
UPMAP	*University of Pennsylvania Museum Anthropological Publications* (Philadelphia).
UWPA	*University of Washington Publications in Anthropology* (Seattle).
VFPA	*Viking Fund Publications in Anthropology.* Wenner-Gren Foundation for Anthropological Research, Inc. (New York).
V & L	*Vie et Langage* (Paris).
VJa	*Voprosy Jazykoznanija* (Moscow).
WF	*Western Folklore* (California Folklore Society, University of California Press, Berkeley).
Word	*Word.* Journal of the Linguistic Circle of New York (New York).
WP-LBRL	*Working Papers, Language Behavior Research Laboratory* (University of California, Berkeley).
WSURS	*Washington State University Research Studies* (Pullman).
YFS	*Yale French Studies* (New Haven, Conn.).
YUPA	*Yale University Publications in Anthropology* (New Haven, Conn.).
ZDA	*Zeitschrift für Deutsches Altertum und deutsche Literatur* (Wiesbaden).
ZDPh	*Zeitschrift für deutsche Philologie* (Berlin).
ZEthn	*Zeitschrift für Ethnologie.* Organ der Deutschen Gesellschaft für Völkerkunde (Brunswick).
ZMaF	*Zeitschrift für Mundartforschung* (Wiesbaden).
ZPhon	*Zeitschrift für Phonetik, Sprachwissenschaft und Kommunikationsforschung* (Berlin).
ВЯ	*See* VJa.

2. OTHER ABBREVIATIONS

ADS	*American Dialect Society.*
ATESL	*Association of Teachers of English as a Second Language* (= *English Language Section of NAFSA*).
BIA	*Bureau of Indian Affairs.*
CAL	*Center for Applied Linguistics.*
CEA	*College English Association.*
CLA	*Canadian Linguistic Association.*
ERIC	*Educational Resources Information Centre* (London).
IEEE	*Institute of Electrical and Electronics Engineers.*
NACTEFL	*National Advisory Council on the Teaching of English as a Foreign Language.*
NAFSA	*National Association of Foreign Student Advisors.*
NCTE	*National Council of Teachers of English.*
TESL	*Teaching English as a Second Language.*
TESOL	*Teachers of English to Speakers of Other Languages.*
TOEFL	*National Council on the Teaching of English as a Foreign Language.*

PART TWO

CENTRAL AND SOUTH AMERICA

CLASSICAL LANGUAGES

JORGE A. SUAREZ

0.1. The absence of a clearly defined group of Indian languages to which the term 'classical' unquestionably applies is the first lacuna we meet in the literature on classical Indian languages. Nor has it been explicitly stated what characteristics, of time or others, some old period of an Indian language should have in order to qualify as classical. The term is firmly established for Nahuatl texts of chiefly the sixteenth century, but it is not universally applied to other languages. A few examples will suffice.

In the general introduction to Amerindian languages of *Les langues du monde*[1] we find only the expression 'langues de civilisation', applied to Quechua, Nahuatl, and Tupi-Guarani. But in the pertinent sections, apart from 'Aztec classique' (1058), the adjective is added only to Yucatec (1071) — somewhat hesitantly, to judge by the quotation marks enclosing it. McQuown[2] gives the name of Classical Yucatec to the language of the fifteenth century down to the middle of the seventeenth century. The cautious use of the term reappears for the Quechua of Cuzco: Trimborn[3] resorts also to including 'classical' between quotation marks, whereas Rowe[4] refers to sixteenth-century Cuzco Quechua, 'for convenience', as Classical Inca (but most of his sources belong, in fact, to the seventeenth century). On the other hand, no mention of Classical Quechua is to be found in the introduction of Rivet and de Créqui-Montfort's bibliography,[5] and when the designation appears, only once, in the complete alphabetic index, it is with reference to the paper by Rowe already mentioned. Cadogan speaks in various places[6] of Classical Guarani, meaning the Guarani of the seventeenth century, as attested by Ruiz de Montoya. For other languages in a

[1] A. Meillet and M. Cohen (ed.), *Les langues du monde*[2] 602 (Paris, 1952).

[2] Norman A. McQuown, *An Outline of (Classical) Yucatec*, in Robert Wauchope and Norman A. McQuown (eds.), *Handbook of Middle-American Indians*, V: *Linguistics* (Austin, 1967) pp. 201–47.

[3] Francisco de Ávila, *Dämonen und Zauber im Inkareich*, aus dem Khetschua übersetzt und eingeleitet von Dr. Hermann Trimborn. *(Quellen und Forschungen. Geschichte der Geographie und Völkerkunde*, vol. 4) 15 (Leipzig, 1938).

[4] John H. Rowe, 'Sound patterns in three Inca dialects', *IJAL* 16. 137-48 (1950).

[5] P. Rivet and G. de Créqui-Montfort, *Bibliographie des langues aymará et kičua*, 4 vols. (Paris, 1951-6).

[6] E.g. in León Cadogan, 'En torno al bilingüismo en el Paraguay', *Revista de Antropología* 6.24 (São Paulo, 1958).

similar situation, the term 'old' is used instead of 'classical': Old Quiche[7] or Old Tupi,[8] for example.

Apparently, neither the type of available texts nor the period in which they were written are determinants, as especially a comparison between Nahuatl and Guarani may illustrate. In the case of the former, a great amount of texts, which reflect the indigenous culture, were written by, or collected from, native speakers in the sixteenth century. In the case of Guarani, most of the texts were written by Spanish missionaries and, even when they were not, all have the same Catholic content; of those texts, grammars and vocabularies are from the seventeenth century, while all the extensive texts belong to the following century.

The criteria for setting the limits, within each language, of the period to be considered classical are not always explicitly stated and, in any case, appear to vary widely. For Nahuatl and Yucatec, the designation is restricted in such a way as to cover only those texts that are freer from the influence of European culture. But in the case of Quechua the same criterion would yield only a handful of short texts of pre-Hispanic origin and perhaps an isolated work by Francisco de Ávila, belonging in the seventeenth century.[9] The extension of the term to all the literature of the seventeenth century and part of the following century appears, therefore, to depend exclusively on the use of the language as a literary medium. For Guarani, in turn, the classical period corresponds to the years of Jesuit missionary work, and comes to an end together with the end of the missions.

Notwithstanding so many dissimilarities, it is possible to discover certain common traits which some indigenous languages share, at least partially, and which show that the common designation of 'classical' may be applied to them in not as arbitrary a way as our remarks above may lead to infer. Those traits are the following: a large body of texts; the use of the language as a literary medium; the development of a literary style; a special form of the language, characteristic of the higher strata of native culture (e.g. Nahuatl); local identification (e.g. Cuzco Quechua), and freedom from heavy Spanish or Portuguese borrowing (e.g. the Guarani of the missions, contrasted for its 'purity' to that spoken elsewhere).

0.2. For want of a standard accepted list, our selection of the languages to be considered classical for the purpose of the present survey has obeyed exclusively a practical consideration: that of including only those on which some significant or systematic work has been published during the period we intend to cover; namely, Nahuatl, Yucatec, Quiche, Quechua, Tupi, and Guarani. The addition of Cakchiquel to this list is intended as an example of an undoubtedly classical language for which investigation has been so far virtually nonexistent.

[7] E.g. Johannes Friedrich, *Kurze Grammatik der alten Quiché-Sprache im Popol Vuh. AAWL* No. 4 (1955).

[8] E.g. A. Lemos Barbosa, *Curso de Tupi antigo*[2] (Rio de Janeiro, 1956).

[9] Cf. fn. 3: *Dämonen* 3 and 13.

As the point of departure for this survey we have chosen 1940, a date somewhat removed, mainly because of the relatively slow rate of production in this field; but also because around that date some important collections of texts began to appear. In addition, we have found it convenient to include as well a few significant works that were published in the late thirties.

In a field such as this, in which amateurish work is so abundant, a great part of the total production had perforce to be left out. But the line was not easy to draw consistently, because it is difficult in some cases, due precisely to the relative scarcity of contributions, to consider any one of them as completely worthless.

1.0. *Editions and textual criticism.* It is obvious that one prerequisite of linguistic study in this field is the availability of the relevant sources — not only texts, but also old grammars and vocabularies. The editorial activity so far carried out for making them accessible has not been meager, and it is precisely in the edition of texts where the total output has been greater. Though, on the whole, the rate of publication is only moderate, nevertheless it is significant that a number of collections which are or have recently been under way show both system and continuity.[10] These collections, together with other less systematic efforts, have increased considerably in recent years the number of available texts. Of course, 'availability' in this connection does not only mean that previously unpublished documents have been published, but also that texts known so far only in rare or poor versions have been re-edited in a reasonably accurate way.

As it is to be expected, not all the languages have been equally favored. Thus the number of Nahuatl texts that have been published and translated in recent years is larger than that of any other classical language, and some of them have had more than one edition. Owing to its importance, Sahagún's work has been the most favored. We may especially mention the edition by Dibble and Anderson[11] of the manuscript known as *Florentine Codex*; the partial editions of the other manuscript (the *Matritensis*) made by Schultze Jena;[12] an edition based on both manuscripts, in course of publication under the direction of Garibay;[13] another text by Sahagún edited by

[10] *Corpus* (1942-); *Quellenwerke* (1938-); *Fuentes* (1958-); *ELTG* (1939-56).

[11] Bernardino de Sahagún, *Florentine Codex. General History of the Things of New Spain.* Translated from the Aztec into English, with notes and illustrations, by A. J. O. Anderson and C. E. Dibble. 12 vols. (Santa Fe, New Mexico, 1950–70).

[12] *Wahrsagerei, Himmelskunde und Kalender der alten Azteken*, aus dem aztekischen Urtext Bernardino de Sahagún's übersetzt und erläutert von Dr. Leonhard Schultze Jena. *Quellenwerke* No. 4 (1950). *Gliederung des alt-aztekischen Volks in Familie, Stand und Beruf*, aus dem aztekischen Urtext Bernardino de Sahagún's übersetzt und erläutert von Dr. Leonhard Schultze Jena. *Quellenwerke* No. 5 (1952).

[13] Miguel León-Portilla, *Ritos, sacerdotes y atavíos de los dioses. Fuentes (Informantes de Sahagún* No. 1, 1958). Ángel María Garibay K., *Veinte himnos sacros de los nahuas. Fuentes (Informantes de Sahagún* No. 2, 1958). Ángel María Garibay K., *Vida económica de Tenochtitlán I. Pochtecayotl* (*'Arte de traficar'*). *Fuentes* (*Informantes de Sahagún* No. 3, 1961). Alfredo López Austin, *Augurios y abusiones. Fuentes* (*Informantes de Sahagún* No. 4, 1969).

Lehmann and Kutscher;[14] and texts referring to medicine edited by López Austin.[14a] Some of the most important historical documents in Nahuatl, such as the *Historia tolteca-chichimeca*,[15] the *Códice Chimalpopoca*,[16] the *Anales de Tlatelolco*,[17] and the historical works of Chimalpahin[18] and Tezozomoc,[19] have been published in facsimile and/or paleographic versions. An extensive corpus of Nahuatl poetry has been edited by Schultze Jena and by Garibay.[20] This

[14] *Sterbende Götter und christliche Heilbotschaft.* Wechselreden indianischer Vornehmer und spanischer Glaubensapostel, 'Colloquios y doctrina christiana' des Fray Bernardino de Sahagún aus dem Jahre 1564. Spanischer und mexikanischer Text mit deutscher Übersetzung von Walter Lehmann. Aus dem Nachlass herausgegeben von Gerdt Kutscher. *Quellenwerke* No. 3 (1949).

[14a] 'De las enfermedades del cuerpo humano y de las medicinas contra ellas', *Estudios de Cultura Náhuatl* 8.51–122 (1969); 'De las plantas medicinales y de otras cosas medicinales', *Estudios de Cultura Náhuatl* 9.128–30 (1971); 'Textos acerca de las partes del cuerpo humano y de las enfermedades y medicinas en los Primeros Memoriales de Sahagún', *Estudios de Cultura Náhuatl* 10.129–54 (1972); 'Descripción de medicinas en textos dispersos del libro xi de los códices matritense y florentino', *Estudios de Cultura Náhuatl* 11.45–135 (1974).

[15] *Historia Tolteca-Chichimeca.* Die mexikanische Bilderhandschrift Historia Tolteca-Chichimeca. Die Manuskripte 46-58bis der Nationalbibliothek in Paris. Übersetzt und erläutert von Konrad Theodor Preuss und Ernst Mengin. Teil I: Die Bilderschrift nebst Übersetzung, *Baessler Archiv*, Beiheft 9 (1937); Teil II: Der Kommentar, *Baessler Archiv* 21.1-66 (1938). *Historia Tolteca-Chichimeca.* Liber in lingua nahuatl manuscriptus picturisque ornatus, ut est conservatus in Bibliotheca Nationis Gallicae Parisiensi sub numeris XLVI-LVIIIbis, edidit Ernst Mengin. *Corpus* vol. 1 (1942).

[16] *Die Geschichte der Königreiche von Colhuacan und Mexico.* Text mit Übersetzung von Walter Lehmann. *Quellenwerke* No. 1 (1938). *Códice Chimalpopoca. Anales de Cuauhtitlán. Leyenda de los Soles*, edición fototípica y traducción de Primo Feliciano Velázquez. Instituto de Historia, Universidad Nacional (México, 1945).

[17] *Unos Anales históricos de la Nación Mexicana.* Die manuscrits mexicains Nr. 22 und 22bis der Bibliothèque Nationale de Paris übersetzt und erläutert von Ernst Mengin. Teil I: Die Handschrift nebst Übersetzung; Teil II: Der Kommentar. *Baessler Archiv* 22.67-168 (1939); 23.115-39 (1940). *Unos Annales históricos de la Nación Mexicana.* Liber in lingua nahuatl manuscriptus paucisque picturis linearibus ornatus, ut est conservatus in Bibliotheca Nationis Gallicae Parisiensi sub numero XXII. Archetypum. Ejusdem operis exemplum aetate posterius nonnullisque picturis linearibus ornatum, ut est conservatum in Bibliotheca Nationis Gallicae Parisiensi sub numero XXIIbis, edidit Ernst Mengin. *Corpus* vol. 2 (1945).

[18] *'Diferentes historias originales de los reynos de Colhuacan, y México, y de otras provincias'. El autor de ellas dicho Don Domingo Chimalpahin.* Liber in lingua mexicana manuscriptus, ut est conservatus in Bibliotheca Nationis Gallicae Parisiensi sub numero LXXIV, edidit Ernst Mengin. *Corpus* 3:1-3 (1949, 1950, 1952).

Das Memorial Breve acerca de la Fundación de la Ciudad de Colhuacan, und weitere ausgewählte Teile aus den 'Diferentes Historias Originales' von Domingo de San Antón Muñon Chimalpahin Quauhtlehuanitzin. Aztekischer Text mit deutscher Übersetzung von Walter Lehmann und Gerdt Kutscher. *Quellenwerke* No. 7 (1958).

Günter Zimmermann (ed.), *Die Relationen Chimalpahin's zur Geschichte México's. Teil I: Die Zeit bis zur Conquista* 1521. *Teil II: Das Jahrhundert nach der Conquista (*1522-1615*).* Universität Hamburg, *Abhandlungen aus dem Gebiet der Auslandskunde*, vols. 68, 69, series B: *Völkerkunde, Kulturgeschichte und Sprachen* vol. 38, 39 (Hamburg, 1963, 1965).

[19] Fernando de Alvarado Tezozomoc, *Crónica Mexicayotl.* Paleografía y traducción directa del náhuatl por Adrián León. Publicación del Instituto de Historia, Primera Serie No. 10, Universidad Nacional Autónoma de México (México, 1949).

[20] *Alt-Aztekische Gesänge.* Nach einer in der Biblioteca Nacional von Mexico aufbewahrten Hand-

incomplete list[21] represents only the works of widest compass, but there have also been numerous publications of shorter documents, many of them due to the untiring activity of Garibay.[22] It is apparent, therefore, that even if there still are many unpublished texts, the Nahuatl corpus available is quite considerable.

For the Mayan languages the picture is somewhat different. The additions have been significant but few: the *Popol Vuh*[23] and indigenous chronicles,[24] for Quiche; the *Memorial de Tecpán Atitlán*,[25] for Cakchiquel, the Books of Chilam Balam for Yucatec.[25a] As it has been recently pointed out by E. Mengin,[26] the key elements for analyzing these sources, i.e., grammars and dictionaries, are for the most part still in manuscript or in unreliable editions. The gap is very great for some of the languages: as against the publication of a short *Confesionario*,[27] and of the *Memorial* already mentioned, a recent survey by Sáenz de Santa María[28] lists for Cakchiquel twelve vocabularies, five grammars, and six collections of sermons.

For Classical Quechua we have had editions of Jurado Palomino,[29] of Francisco de Ávila[30] (although some parts of his work are still unpublished[31]), of the dramas *Usca*

---

schrift übersetzt und erläutert von Dr. Leonhard Schultze Jena. Nach seinem Tode herausgegeben von Gerdt Kutscher. *Quellenwerke* No. 6 (1957). Angel María Garibay K., *Poesía Náhuatl I, II, III*, Universidad Nacional Autónoma de México, Instituto de Historia, México, 1964, 1965, 1968.

21 Cf. Concepción Basilio, 'Bibliografía sobre cultura náhuatl 1950-58', *Estudios de Cultura Náhuatl* 1.125-66 (1959); 'Bibliografía sobre cultura náhuatl 1959', *ibid.* 2.209-17 (1960).

22 Cf. the bibliography in *Estudios de Cultura Náhuatl* 4.20–6 (1963). For sources and studies in Classical Nahuatl, cf. Ascensión H. de León-Portilla, 'Bibliografía lingüística nahua', *Estudios de Cultura Náhuatl* 10.404–41 (1972).

23 *Popol Vuh. Das Heilige Buch der Quiché-Indianer von Guatemala.* Nach einer wiedergefundenen alten Handschrift neu übersetzt und erläutert von Dr. Leonhard Schultze Jena. *Quellenwerke* No. 2 (1944).

24 Adrián Recinos, *Crónicas indígenas de Guatemala* (Guatemala, 1957).

25 *Memorial de Tecpán-Atitlán (Sololá). Historia del antiguo reino del Cakchiquel dicho de Guatemala.* Liber in lingua cakchiquel manuscriptus, ut est conservatus in Bibliotheca Musei Universitatis Pennsylvaniensis Philadelphiae sub Br. 498.21/CAr15, edidit Ernst Mengin. *Corpus* vol. 4 (1952).

25a Alfredo Barrera Vázquez and Sylvanus Griswold Morley, *The Maya Chronicles.* Carnegie Inst. of Washington, *Contributions to American Anthropology and History* No. 48 (Washington, D.C., 1949).

26 'Die wichtigste Ergebnisse und Aufgaben der Maya-Sprachforschung', *AIAK XXXIV* 743-62 (1962).

27 Ernesto Chinchilla Aguilar, 'Un confesionario del siglo XVII, escrito por Fray Antonio del Saz, O.F.M.', *Antropología e Historia de Guatemala* 11.32-9 (1959).

28 C. Sáenz de Santa María, 'Una ojeada a la bibliografía lingüística guatemalteca', *Revista de Indias* 19:76.255-71 (1959).

29 Bartholomaei Juradi Palomini, *Catechismus Quichuensis.* Ad fidem editionis limensis anni MDCXLVI. Edidit, latine uertit, analysi morphologica synopsi grammatica, indicibus auxit Prof. Dr. Hippolytus Galante. Hispanice e latino reddedit Eliseus B. Viejo Olero. Consejo Superior de Investigaciones Científicas, Instituto Gonzalo Fernández de Oviedo (Madrid, 1943).

30 Francisci de Ávila, *De priscorum huaruchiriensium origine et institutis.* Ad fidem MSPTI 3169 Bibliothecae nationalis Matritensis edidit Prof. Dr. Hippolytus Galante. Consejo Superior de Investigaciones Científicas, Instituto Gonzalo Fernández de Oviedo (Madrid, 1942). See also fn. 3.

31 Hermann Trimborn, 'Ante una nueva edición del manuscrito quechua de Francisco de Ávila', *Letras* 49.233-9 (Lima, 1953).

paucar,[32] *El pobre más rico*,[33] and *Ollantay*.[34] There have also been various attempts at establishing the original text of the hymns collected by Cristóbal de Molina.[35]

A facsimile reimpression of a text by Nicolás Yapuguay[36] and six volumes of the collection *Etnografia e Língua Tupi-Guaraní* containing several 'Doctrinas' and 'Catecismos'[37] are the chief contributions, in this respect, to Classical Guarani, whose most important sources are, at least, not in manuscript. More has been done in Tupi: the most extensive text, Araujo's *Catecismo* whose first edition had become rare, has been re-edited in facsimile,[38] and important vocabularies have been published[39] as well as some studies on their relations to one another.[40] Other six volumes of *Etnografia e Língua Tupi-Guaraní* are devoted to Tupi texts; the publication of those by

[32] Teodoro L. Meneses, 'El "Usca Paucar", un drama religioso en quechua del siglo XVIII', *Documenta* 2.1-178 (Lima, 1949-50).

[33] Gabriel Centeno de Osma, *El pobre más rico, comedia quechua del siglo XVI* (Texto quechua y traducción castellana con reproducción facsimilar del manuscrito. Transcripción y traducción española de J. M. B. Farfán y Humberto Suárez Álvarez). Instituto Superior de Lingüística y Filología de la Universidad Nacional Mayor de San Marcos (Lima, 1938).

[34] J. M. B. Farfán, *El drama Quechua Apu Ollantay* (Lima, 1952). Hipólito Galante, *Ollantay*. Ad fidem codicis Pastor-Justinianiensis Archiuii Nationalis Limensis recensuit latine uertit integra codicis Sahuaraurensis lectione analysi morphologica grammatica indicibus dissertationibus scholiis auxit (Lima, 1938).

[35] John H. Rowe, 'Eleven Inca prayers from the Zithuwa ritual', *The Kroeber Anthropological Society Papers* (The Walter B. Cline Memorial Volume) 8-9.82-99 (Berkeley, 1953). Lucas Guerra, 'Traducción y comentario de una de las oraciones incaicas de Cristóbal de Molina', *Revista de la Sección Arqueología de la Universidad Nacional* 3.148-67 (Cuzco, 1946). J. M. B. Farfán, 'Textos y glosario quechua, anexo a "Las curaciones por las fuerzas del espíritu en la medicina aborigen" de Juan B. Lastres', *Revista del Museo Nacional* 14.72-6, (Lima, 1945).

[36] *Sermones y exemplos en lengua guaraní por Nicolás Yapuguay con direction de vn religioso de la Compañía de Iesús*. Edición facsimilar de la edición príncipe del año 1727 (Buenos Aires, 1953).

[37] *El Tesoro de la Doctrina Christiana en lengua Guaraní (Catecismos varios* I). Prólogo de Plinio Ayrosa. *ELTG* No. 24 (1952). *Doctrina Christiana por el P. Gaspar Astete, traducida en lengua guaraní por otro Padre de la misma Compañía (Catecismos varios* II*)*. Prefacio de Plinio Ayrosa. *ELTG* No. 27 (1953). *Catecismo por el P. M. Gerónimo de Ripalda, traducido en Guaraní por Francisco Martínez, con cuatro tratados muy devotos (Catecismos varios* III). *ELTG* No. 29 (1954). *Catecismo mayor o Doctrina Christiana clarissima y brevissimamente explicada... por un Padre de la Compañía de Jesús (Catecismos varios* IV*)*. *ELTG* No. 30 (1955). *Varias doctrinas en lengua guaraní, por el P. Simón Bandini, de la Compañía de Jesús (Catecismos varios* V*)*. *ELTG* No. 31 (1956). *Compendio de la Doctrina Christiana para niños, compuesto en lengua francesa por el R. P. Francisco Pomeij. Traducido en lengua guaraní por el P. Christoval Altamirano (Catecismos varios* VI*)*. *ELTG* No. 32 (1956).

[38] Antonio de Araujo, *Catecismo na língua brasílica*. Reprodução fac-similar da 1ª edição (1618) com apresentação por A. Lemos Barbosa. *Biblioteca da Língua Tupi* vol. 1 (Río de Janeiro, 1952).

[39] Carlos Drumond, *Vocabulário na língua brasílica*, 2ª edição revista e confrontada com o Ms. fg. 3144 da Biblioteca Nacional de Lisboa. *ELTG* Nos. 23, 26 (1952, 1953). Plinio Ayrosa, *Vocabulário Português-Brasílico*. *ELTG* No. 21 (1951).

[40] Maria de Lourdes de Paula Martins, *Notas sôbre relações verificadas entre o Diccionário Brasiliano e o Vocabulário na língua Brasílica*, *ELTG* No. 7 (1945); 'O Diccionário Brasileiro Português e o Ms. 11481 da Biblioteca Nacional', *Boletim bibliográfico da Biblioteca Pública Municipal de São Paulo* 6.69-83 (1946); 'Notas referentes ao Diccionário Portugês-Brasiliano e Brasiliano-Português', *ibid.* 12.121-47 (1949); 'Vocabulários Tupis. O problema do Vocabulário na Língua Brasílica', *ibid.* 13.59-93 (1949).

Anchieta, here and elsewhere, has been especially in charge of M. de Paula Martins.[41]

1.1. If we consider all this work from the point of view of philological technique, its degree of achievement appears disparate. We shall comment on some of these editions only, taking each of them as representative of a group. Although we will not consider mere reproductions of earlier editions or of manuscripts, we want at least to make special mention of the excellent ones in facsimile made by E. Mengin.[42]

As far as formal philological technique is concerned, i.e., technical description of manuscript, information on the difficulties of certain readings, indication of interpolations, of improper linking of words, etc., variants—when more than one source is available—and critical notes in support of emendations and/or the translation, the *Quellenwerke* are on the whole the most satisfactory. Also of high standards are Meneses's edition of *Uscar paucar,*[43] and López Austin's editions of Sahagún's texts.[44] The most ambitious work on this line is the edition of Mayan Chronicles by Barrera Vázquez and Morley,[44a] where a text is reconstructed on the basis of three different sources.

In numbers 2 and 19 of *Etnografia e Lingua Tupi-Guaraní*,[45] Plinio Ayrosa does not give the text in facsimile, but only in the transcription adopted throughout the whole collection (a transcription based on an unexplained phonetic interpretation of the old texts). Number 3 of the same collection[46] is representative of the editorial practice of Paula Martins (also that of Ayrosa in number 17[47]) to offer either the facsimile or the paleographic version, followed by the transcription with corrections — the reasons for those emendations are given in notes, together with numerous, rather unsophisticated, linguistic remarks. In the two volumes edited by C. Drumond[48] it is impossible to know with certainty what parts come from one or other of the manuscripts utilized

[41] Plinio Ayrosa, *Poemas Brasílicos do Pe Cristóvão Valente S. J. ELTG* No. 2 (1941); *Orações e dialogos da Doutrina Cristã na lingua Brasílica. Mss. do século XVIII transcritos e anotados por ... ELTG* No. 17 (1950); *Nomes dos membros do corpo humano e outros designativos na linguá Brasílica. Mss. do século XVIII transcritos e anotados* por ... *ELTG* No. 19 (1950). Maria de Lourdes de Paula Martins, 'A "Cantiga por o sem ventura" do Pe. José de Anchieta', *Revista do Arquivo Municipal de São Paulo* 72.201-14 (1940); 'Literatura Tupi do Padre Anchieta', *ibid.* 79. 281-85 (1941); *Contribuição para o estudo do teatro Tupi de Anchieta: Diálogo e Trilogia (segundo manuscritos originais do século XVI), ELTG* No. 3 (1941); *Poesias Tupis (Século XVI), ELTG* No. 6 (1945); 'Teatro Tupi. Restituição de uma peça de Anchieta', *Revista do Arquivo Municipal de São Paulo* 114.223-51 (1947); *Auto representado na festa de São Lourenço (de José de Anchieta). Peça trilingue do sec. XVI.* Museu Paulista (São Paulo, 1948); *José de Anchieta, S.J.: Poesias, ms. do sec. XVI em Português, Latim e Tupi.* Transcrição, traduções e notas da ... Museu Paulista (São Paulo, 1954).

[42] *Cf.* fn. 10: *Corpus.*

[43] *Cf.* fn 32.

[44] *Cf.* fn. 14a.

[44a] *Cf.* fn. 25a.

[45] *Cf.* fn. 41: *Poemas Brasílicos* and *Nomes dos membros.*

[46] *Cf.* fn. 41: *Contribuição.*

[47] *Cf.* fn. 41: *Orações.*

[48] *Cf.* fn. 39.

(unless we check on a previous edition by Ayrosa[49]), nor what are the 'minor' corrections introduced by the editor. Notwithstanding their many apparent shortcomings, a very positive aspect in the editions made by Ayrosa and Paula Martins is that they pay predominant attention to linguistic problems in the notes, and that they frequently bring in their support evidence from old grammars, vocabularies, and other texts.

In his edition of Francisco de Ávila[50] H. Galante gives the facsimile reproduction of the manuscript, the emended text, and the critical apparatus; but that the latter is insufficient appears clearly from a comparison of the facsimile with the emended text, in which many of the changes have been introduced without any indication at all. The editor's decision of transcribing the text in González Holguín's 'classical' orthography is a rather bold step for which no reasons are adduced: the three stop series of Classical Quechua are not distinguished in Avila's manuscript, and this might be due to dialectal differences of which Galante seems to be entirely unaware. Even less satisfactory is his edition of Jurado Palomino.[51] It reproduces the original edition of 1649 and also includes the emended text, but this time with no critical apparatus. It is necessary to compare both texts word by word in order to become aware of the changes made by the editor. In the two editions the original is translated directly into Latin, and the Spanish version made after it. It is difficult to see the reason for this; certainly not because of Latin being less removed — at least lexically — from Quechua than Spanish is.

In his edition of Sahagún[52] Garibay utilizes mainly the Madrid manuscript, with mention of the variants found in the *Florentine Codex*; but not of all of them, 'o por ser vulgares, o por ser sin importancia' (10). However the relation between both manuscripts is not agreed upon (18-9), and their respective evaluation appears not to depend on internal comparison as much as on chronological arguments. Garibay's edition of another text collected by Sahagún[53] contains detailed information on the manuscript; the notes include an account of the emendations, of the reasons that led the editor to disagree in many points with Seler's translation, and a detailed justification of the translation here presented; but the numerous corrections made upon the manuscript of its crossings-out, repetitions, wrong separation of words, and so on are only partially accounted for (14).

In his edition of *Ollantay*[54] Farfán explicitly disclaims its being a work of textual criticism, but nevertheless several variants are mentioned, and the text is a mixture of different manuscripts with emendations introduced by the editor; on the other hand, the orthography is that of modern Cuzco Quechua. T. Meneses,[55] in his fitting criti-

[49] *Vocabulário na língua Brasílica.* Manuscrito português-tupi do século XVII coordenado e prefaciado por Plinio Ayrosa. *Coleção do Departamento de Cultura,* vol. 20 (São Paulo, 1938).
[50] *Cf.* fn. 30.
[51] *Cf.* fn. 29.
[52] *Cf.* fn. 13: *Vida económica.*
[53] *Cf.* fn. 13: *Veinte himnos.*
[54] *Cf.* fn. 34.
[55] 'En el primer centenario de la publicación del códice dominicano del Ollantay', *Documenta* 3.141-54 (1951-55).

cism of this edition, has pointed out that the author does not even follow, as regards the manuscripts he in fact utilizes, what he claims in the introduction. Meneses's critique concerning the exuberance of historical-literary studies, as well as translations, of the *Ollantay* at a time in which 'la etapa filológica no ha sido debidamente cumplida' (145), applies also to most Quechua sources, especially those of pre-Hispanic origin. And, to a great extent, it may serve to characterize as well the situation for other classical languages.[56]

As for the mentioned attempts at reconstructing the original text of the Quechua hymns,[57] Rowe has justly pointed out the principal weakness of his predecessors — which also applies to L. Guerra, unmentioned by him: the treatment of the language as if it had not undergone any changes, which leads to establishing the text in modern Cuzco dialect. Rowe's attempt, on the other hand, is sound in its conservative assumptions concerning the origin of the copyist's errors, the reliability of Molina's translation, and the tools for interpreting sixteenth-century Quechua. Aside from the emended text he also gives its transcription in his own phonemicization of Classical Inca[58] and his English translation. But for simplicity's sake he omits giving the critical apparatus necessary for checking on the emendations (there have been several edited versions of the manuscript, not available in facsimile), which are only sparingly explained. A similar attempt by Plinio Ayrosa to reconstruct a text in Old Tupi[59] has been the object of severe criticism by A. Lemos Barbosa:[60] his principal objection, which is undoubtedly right, refers to the fact that Ayrosa has not kept Tupi and Guarani properly differentiated in establishing the text. On the other hand, his opinion that the reconstruction of the text in question is a hopeless task is surely overpessimistic.

1.2. It is apparent, therefore, that textual criticism has followed very different principles and criteria, and that the results have varied a great deal. The philological problems encountered are possibly never so complex as the ones found in Greek or Latin philology. Most texts are available only in one manuscript or edition, so that problems of collation are few. In spite of this, inaccuracies in, or total disregard for, currently accepted philological procedures and technique are only too common. The standard format of text editions is ignored in most cases; the consequence is that the reader cannot pass judgment on them until he has remade for himself the work the editor was supposed to do. There is a tendency in some editors to obliterate the difference between a paleographic and a critical edition because, so it appears, of the notion that some kinds of mistakes (?) in the manu-

56 *Cf.* Norman A. McQuown, *AmA* 62.319 (1960).

57 *Cf.* fn. 35; see J. H. Rowe, *Eleven*, 85.

58 *Cf.* fn. 4.

59 P. Ayrosa, 'Colóquio da entrada ou chegada ao Brasil entre a gente do pais chamada Tupinambá e Tupiniquin, em lenguagem Brasílica e Francesa', in Juan de Léry, *Viagem à terra do Brasil*, tradução integral e notas de Sergio Millet (São Paulo, 1941).

60 Estudos de Tupi. *O 'Diálogo de Léry' na restauração da Plinio Ayrosa* (Rio de Janeiro?, 1944). It is a reprint of three papers that appeared in *Revista Filológica* (Rio de Janeiro) Nos. 16, 19, 25.

script are trivial.[61] But it is at least doubtful whether at this stage of philological work there are in fact any emendations that may be considered obvious. Sometimes this tendency is carried to an extreme, as in the case of J. Hasler's article entitled 'Paleografía',[62] in which two parallel texts — one of them otherwise still in manuscript — are given only in an unexplained modern orthography. The linguistic notes as well often fall short of accuracy but, as we shall see in the next section, this is in part due to the lack of any standard re-elaboration of old grammars, and references to them are sporadic.

The general impression one gets is that the seeming 'triviality', or directly the absence of philological problems is mainly due to cursory research, when not merely to the lack of all critical apparatus: in contrast to the frequent absence, in the editions, of all references to difficulties in reading the manuscripts, as soon as philological criticism becomes more detailed in the comparison of different readings, many points of divergence immediately appear, and problems begin to emerge.[63] A comparison of Schultze Jena's and of Garibay's editions of the *Cantares Mexicanos* reveals serious differences in the reading of the manuscript, in the emendations and in the interpretation (to the extent that sometimes the reader of the translations would suspect a different original); the former's analysis can be checked through the analytical vocabulary included, but this is not the case with Garibay's translation, and in some instances neither interpretation can be justified grammatically on the basis of the available information for Classical Nahuatl; one has to assume that either the text is corrupt or the translation inexact or the language had grammatical phenomena proper to poetry which have never been described.

As for other aspects of the philological content of these works, such as historical and bio-bibliographical ones, they are usually well covered. Yet we must regret the lack of compact manuals in which all the scattered information contained in the editions could be brought together. Much information on Nahuatl is to be found in Garibay's *Historia de la literatura náhuatl*,[64] but not systematically presented, since the fundamental purpose of the book is literary, not philological.

2.0. *Linguistic studies.* The specifically linguistic contributions have been so few, general, and diverse in their nature or subject, that it seems preferable to discuss them following an order of scope, rather than to classify them according to language or subject matter. Therefore, they will be distributed more or less consistently into full grammars, (structural) outlines, and monographic studies.

[61] So, for example, Garibay (*Poesía Náhuatl II*, p. liv) criticizes Schultze Jena's paleographic version on the grounds that it follows the manuscript too closely(!).

[62] Juan Hasler, 'Paleografía', *Archivos Nahuas* 1.303-23 (1958).

[63] *Cf.* e.g. A. Lemos Barbosa, 'Traduções de poemas tupis', *Revista do Arquivo Municipal de São Paulo* 128.27-44 (1949); A. M. Garibay K., 'Magnum Opus', *Cuadernos Americanos* 17:98.127-38 (1958).

[64] A. M. Garibay K., *Historia de la literatura náhuatl*, 2 vols. (México, 1953-54).

2.1. Jakob Schoembs[65] has tried to give 'eine möglichst umfassende Darstellung des Aztekischen' (7), but it is obvious that the book has fallen short of this claim. In the first place, and due to the scarcity of previous studies, a complete grammar would have had to offer detailed philological support, and this is not so in the present case. The phonemics is confusingly handled, with more concern for the orthographic practice than for its interpretation and analysis. The list of sentences (66-9), however useful for analysis it may be, with the corresponding translations, cannot be regarded seriously as a syntax; nor, in a language such as Nahuatl, can the page and a half devoted to stem composition be considered an adequate treatment of the topic. On the other hand, the rest of the morphology is extensively treated; but the description is far from clear, and neither inflection and derivation, nor free and bound forms, are kept properly distinct.[66] Especially useful is the vocabulary to the appended Book XII of Sahagún, with many cross-references to the grammar and including the bound morphemes.

In spite of its title, J. Friedrich's *Kurze Grammatik*,[67] on the contrary, is one of the most complete and detailed grammars of any of the classical languages so far available. Derivation and inflection are thoroughly treated, and in the case of verb inflection exhaustive information is given on the forms actually occurring in the *Popol Vuh* — with regard not only to inflection, but also to the underlying verb stems. The general plan of the book is not entirely satisfactory, in that it reflects a paradigmatic approach somewhat influenced by Indo-European categories. This gives rise to unnecessary complications and repetition and, in the last instance, obscures the general lines of the morphological system. But the discussion of each particular point is, in every case, thorough and clear. In the treatment of inflection and of particles, some syntactic information is implicitly contained, but except for a few sections (such as those on nominal phrases, 28-9; on the copula-like forms, 85-6; on 'absolute' verbs, 93-6; on verb sequences, 112-6), syntax is not independently handled. This omission results in some doubt as to the status of certain forms: it is not clear, for example, whether some forms which the author considers nominal (like the 'participle' in *-m*, 431, or the expression of 'superlative', 127) are in fact so rather than verbal. Phonology is cursorily treated. The section on orthography (12-5) lists with considerable detail the variant spellings, but with no clear distinction between mispellings and morphophonemic or phonological alternations. As it is explicitly admitted in the title, the only source for this grammar was the *Popol Vuh*; this may seem an arbitrary restriction, but due to the scarcity of other edited Quiche sources, it is unlikely that the author could have done otherwise. What seems unjustified is the total neglect of modern Quiche (7), notwithstanding the changes that the language may have undergone. But, on the whole, any shortcomings that this grammar may have are more than enough offset by the copious exemplification, as well as by the systematic cross-references to the text.

[65] *Aztekische Schriftsprache* (Heidelberg, 1949).
[66] For criticism of special points see the review by Walter Krickeberg, *ZPhon* 5.358-62 (1951).
[67] *Cf.* fn. 7.

The *Curso de Tupi antigo*[68] has been conceived, as the title indicates, as a textbook rather than as a descriptive grammar. That the author has done so is regrettable, for several reasons. In the first place, and apart from the fact that the book is remarkably complete, detailed, and serviceably indexed, those sections in which the discussion is more purely descriptive (392-419) show beyond doubt that the author is much more linguistically sophisticated than one might infer from the rest of the book. In the second place, the introduction makes it clear that he is perfectly aware of the best way in which a grammar of Old Tupi could be philologically grounded, though he undoubtedly felt that the practical character of the book made the task unnecessary: not only does the bibliography attached to each section not conform to the philological requirements he himself set forth, but one even gains the impression (a thorough checking would mean a virtual remaking of the book) that he may have extrapolated a good deal. It is also the pedagogic nature of the book which has led Lemos Barbosa both to dismember the materials in the traditional way — which seems to offer a reasonable graduation of complexities — and to approach the language through its equivalents of Portuguese categories — which is not even justified from the didactic point of view. Finally, we may reasonably ask whether the nature of extant Tupi texts is such as to attract a number of persons so forcibly that they may want to acquire a practical knowledge of the language. Notwithstanding all this, the book is an important contribution to Tupian studies, and it would be unfair, given its acknowledged aim, to insist on defects that the author has purposely incurred. All the more because in spite of the fact that the general plan is, as we have said, foreign to the language, the discussion of each particular point is not irreparably distorted. Yet it ought to be mentioned that inefficient treatment does not always derive from the author's pedagogic slant, but from the erroneous underlying analysis: e.g. a somewhat inconsistent orthography; also the treatment of morphophonemics, 34-42, and of the subject of predicative 'verbs', 87-9. Lemos Barbosa rightly stresses the fact that the study of Classical Tupi is fundamentally of a philological type, but, as in the case of Friedrich's Quiche grammar examined above, he is probably mistaken in wholly disregarding modern dialects.[69]

A comprehensive grammar of Nahuatl, which also has a pedagogical aim is the work of Andrews,[69a] until now the most complete treatment of this language. It is presented within an informal transformational model richly exemplified in a traditional orthography but marking, whenever the sources allow, vowel quantity and glottal stops. Various original analyses are proposed in the derivational and inflectional systems which appear well founded. The syntactic sections are the first extensive study of this aspect of the language based on a direct analysis of the texts—

[68] *Cf.* fn. 8.

[69] The reader should be warned, because of the misleading title, that Adaucto Fernandes, *Gramática tupi, histórica, comparada e expositiva*[2] (Rio de Janeiro, 1960) is totally devoid of any merits whatever.

[69a] J. Richard Andrews, *Introduction to Classical Nahuatl*, Austin, 1975; *Introduction to Classical Nahuatl: Workbook*, Austin, 1975.

chiefly those gathered by Sahagún—but the presentation is somewhat obscured and is rendered more complicated than necessary because, we think, of an erroneous interpretation of certain nominal expressions as predicative in more inclusive constructions. It is to be regretted that the examples are not cross-referred to the sources because, especially when dealing with word order, the author seems to have extrapolated for the sake of clarity.

Garibay's *Llave del náhuatl*[70] is neither a full grammar nor a structural sketch, since it has been conceived as a grammatical guide to the accompanying anthology. Nevertheless, even if less complete than Schoembs's grammar, and with a more superficial treatment of orthography and phonetics, it includes a better exposition of morphology: it is concise and clear, and contains a separate section on syntax (80-113). The author outlines a division in periods of the history of the language (313-27) which, though couched in somewhat vague and impressionistic terms, is likely to offer a valuable framework for future research, backed as it is by the author's thorough familiarity with the texts.

Anderson's adapted translation of the grammar by Clavigero (an unedited manuscript)[70a] together with the exercises he added can be useful as a pedagogical tool.

2.2. The first attempt at a structural sketch of Classical Nahuatl was an unpublished dissertation by Croft[71] where phonemics is fully discussed in relation to orthography, to the statements of old grammarians, and to the phonology of Spanish and of modern dialects. Morphology was handled more in outline form, although observed morpheme sequences were given in detail; syntax is not included. The major shortcoming of Croft's analysis is that it is based on a too limited corpus: among the grammars only Olmos and Molina—which are the less specific for certain phonemic points—were taken into consideration, together with the dictionary by the latter. This work has been superseded by Newman's compact but informative sketch[71a] based on the most important ancient sources. Phonemics, morphophonemics, and morphology are systematically covered using throughout a phonemic transcription (the first in marking vowel quantity), the mechanics of word formation being highlighted by the four structural types of stem differentiated by the author. Syntax is only cursorily dealt with but in his rightly sympathetic appraisal of the grammars of the friars the author, in pointing out that syntax was

[70] A. M. Garibay K., *Llave del náhuatl*². Colección de trozos clásicos, con gramática y vocabulario, para utilidad de los principiantes (México, 1961). The grammar occupies pp. 19-118.

[70a] Arthur J. O. Anderson, *Rules of the Aztec Language. A Translation by [. . .]*, Salt Lake City, Utah, 1973. *Grammatical Examples, Exercises, & Review [. . .]*, Salt Lake City, Utah, 1973.

[71] Kenneth Croft, *Matlapa and Classical Nahuatl: with comparative notes on the two dialects.* Univ. Microfilms Publ. 5858 (Michigan, 1953).

[71a] Stanley Newman, 'Classical Nahuatl,' in Robert Wauchope (ed.), *Handbook of Middle American Indians* 5.179–99 (Austin, 1967).

rather neglected, stated opportunately that 'the body of Classical Nahuatl texts still remains to be analyzed syntactically' (181), a task that has begun to be fulfilled only recently.

N. McQuown, in his structural sketch of Classical Yucatec,[72] avails himself of the little change undergone by Yucatec, which allows him to deal simultaneously with both the classical and the modern dialect. The language is described under the headings of Phonology and Morphology. Morphophonemic variations are described under the corresponding morphemes. Syntax is not treated independently, but syntactic information is given in the course of the discussion of morphology. (In the particular case of the 'verbal complex', the limit between morphology and syntax is not trenchant, and clitics are classified along with affixes according to their positions around the verbal core.) The phonological system here established is the same for both the classical and the modern stage, and, in the case of the former, is correlated with the orthography of the missionaries (which was under-differentiated). Special sections are devoted to allophones, to phonemic distribution, and to (high and low) tone sequences, the latter mostly intended as a frame of reference for further investigation. Very much detailed is the treatment of phonemic shapes of morphemes. These are classified morphologically into verbs, nouns, and particles, with syntactic subclassification of the latter. Derivation is covered under each morpheme class, and more extensively than is usual in sketches. All mentions of classical forms are referred to the Motul dictionary, and the exemplification is abundant. The wording is terse, with a straightforward presentation that allows for the inclusion of plenty of material notwithstanding the relative brevity of the outline. One only misses some information about sentence types — a fact which gives rise to some doubts as to the use of certain forms.

The comments above also apply to the sketch of Classical Quiche by Edmonson[72a] who followed McQuown's organization closely. It is also a concise description including much information on phonology and morphology. It constitutes a useful addition to Friedrich's grammar, having the advantage of a wider basis and a clearer presentation.

In 1969 the Seminario de Escritura Maya (afterward renamed Centro de Estudios Mayas) of the Universidad Nacional Autónoma de México started the publication of a series of monographs dealing with various aspects of Mayan languages which has maintained a good rate of publication and an adequate level of quality. Of direct interest to this survey are the studies of the language of a Mayan chronicle by Alvarez[73] where besides the structural description an effort is made to

[72] *Cf.* fn. 2.

[72a] Munro S. Edmonson, 'Classical Quiche,' in Robert Wauchope (ed.), *Handbook of Middle American Indians* 5.249–67 (Austin, 1967).

[73] María Cristina Alvarez, *Descripción estructural del maya de Chilam Balam de Chumayel.* (Seminario de Estudios de la Escritura Maya, Cuaderno 1), México, 1969. *Textos coloniales del Libro de Chilam Balam de Chumayel y textos glíficos del códice de Dresde.* (Centro de Estudios Mayas, Cuaderno 10). México, 1974.

pinpoint the grammatical peculiarities of the text and the linguistic analysis of an old Chontal text by Smailus.[73a] Although because of the language analyzed it would fall outside the limits of this survey, it is of interest that one of the conclusions drawn by the author is that the language is considerably closer to classical Yucatec than modern Chontal. Moreover, the presentation is excellent: the paleographic version, the emended text marking morpheme boundaries and a literal translation are given in successive lines followed by the Spanish translation contained in the original text and another one by the author. To this follows a lexico with parallels in various Mayan languages and a description of the morphology.

The outline of Quechua grammar which Galante included in his edition of Jurado Palomino[74] has escaped the risk of forcing the language into foreign molds only at the expense of depriving it almost completely of structure. Fundamentally he presents a list of suffixes, among which only those expressing 'person' offer a glimpse of organization. There is some report on canonical shapes, but they depend on a highly suspicious analysis of roots and stems.

2.3. Dávila Garibi has produced a book on Nahuatl orthography[73] which is informative in many respects, and contains some judicious remarks. But it is more an external account of the changes in graphic representation than of the underlying phonological problems. This approach results in a rather casual interpretation of the statements in old grammars. Besides, the book is not well planned.[75] Elsewhere[76] the author has attempted to classify Nahuatl verbs according to the ways in which they form the past tense, but the attempt is not successful because of its exclusive dependence on the orthography. Also several of the subclasses of 'irregular' verbs should be eliminated.

In Classical Nahuatl, stress has been usually assumed to fall on the penultimate syllable of the word, except for certain forms like the vocative. Starting from certain statements in Schoembs's grammar, and with the support of Rincón's grammar and, above all, of a minimal pair found in Molina, W. Barrett[77] has assumed instead a free accent and suggested the possibility of multiple stress in a word. The principal merit of this paper is to have called attention to the problem; its originality lies in the

[73a] Ortwin Smailus, *El maya-chontal de Acalan. Análisis lingüístico de un documento de los años 1610–1612.* (Centro de Estudios Mayas, Cuaderno 9). México, 1975

[74] *Cf.* fn. 29: *op.cit.* 447-73. It is fundamentally the same as that included in his edition of *Ollantay* (Lima, 1938), which has been reissued in Spanish translation: *Gramática quechua (del Ollantay)*, traducida del latín por Fernando Tola y Santiago Erik Antúnez de Mayola; 2ª ed. ampliada y corregida por Teodoro L. Meneses. Publicaciones del Inst. de Filología de la Fac. de Letras de la Univ. Nac. Mayor de San Marcos, *Gramática* No. 1 (Lima, 1959).

[74a] J. Ignacio Dávila Garibi, *La escritura del idioma náhuatl a través de los siglos* (México, 1948).

[75] The useful data have been summarized by Croft in his review, *IJAL* 16.103-6 (1950).

[76] J. I. Dávila Garibi, 'Clasificación del verbo náhuatl en grupos afines', *Estudios de Cultura Náhuatl* 4.61-72 (1963).

[77] Westbrook Barrett, 'The phonemic interpretation of "Accent" in Father Rincón's "Arte Mexicana"', *GL* 2.22-8 (1956).

hypothesis of multiple-stressed words. The problem was re-examined by W. Bright.[78] In his article Rincón's and Carochi's systems of accents are carefully analyzed (with quotation and interpretation of the pertinent passages), and found in agreement with each other. From this the author infers that stresses and pitches were always associated, inside the word, with differences in quantity, whereas the latter seems to be the same as in modern dialects. Bright's conclusion is that only quantity is likely to have been phonemic in Classical Nahuatl, stress and pitch having been subordinated to it.[79] This paper organizes into a coherent system the statements and examples of early grammarians, only we find it dubious that the association of stress with the penultimate syllable would have been a later development (the same association is found in other modern dialects whose differentiation antedates surely the epoch of Classical Nahuatl). The existence of phonemic quantity poses the problem of whether it played any role in poetry whose structure has been assumed by Garibay[80] to depend on penultimate stress; but his interpretation although it has some consistency is wholly speculative since the *Cantares* are written without any stanza structure in the manuscript.[81]

On the basis of statements by early grammarians, of fluctuations in the orthography, of the testimony of modern dialects, and, recently, of comparative evidence,[82] it has been generally assumed that Classical Nahuatl had a vowel system /i e a o/, with [o], [u] as allophones of /o/. Croft suggested in his sketch[83] the possibility of complementary distribution (though the passages in Olmos and Molina he quotes would rather point to free variation[84]), and Schoembs,[85] even if not within a clearly phonological framework, assumed the existence of a high *o*, represented by either ⟨o⟩ or ⟨u⟩, and a low *o* represented nearly always by ⟨o⟩. This is Seiler and Zimmermann's point of departure in their study of the ⟨o, u⟩ fluctuation.[86] In order to ensure dialectal uniformity they restrict their sources to Molina's dictionary, which is known to have been composed on the basis of only one informant. They assume, in the first place, that Molina heard the Nahuatl sounds consistently in terms of his own Spanish phonemic system, and that the ⟨o, u⟩ fluctuation represents [ʊ], while ⟨o⟩ represents [o]. They then look for the basis of complementation, and find it in the structure of the syllable: the

[78] William Bright, '"Accent" in Classical Aztec', *IJAL* 26.66-8 (1960).

[79] For a detailed study of a living dialect, *cf.* Dow F. Robinson, 'Puebla (Sierra) Nahuat Prosodies,' in *Aztec Studies I* 15–32 (Norman, 1966); this paper surveys also the problems in other dialects.

[80] *Cf.* fn. 64: *op. cit.* 1.60–4.

[81] It would be desirable to eliminate the widespread practice of quoting Nahuatl poetry and its translation, both in learned and popular books, with a stanza organization and without warning the reader of its hypothetical nature.

[82] C. F. and F. M. Voegelin, and Kenneth L. Hale, *Typological and Comparative Grammar of Uto-Aztecan: I (Phonology)* 36. Indiana University Publications in Anthropology and Linguistics. Memoir 17 of the *IJAL* (Baltimore, 1962).

[83] *Cf.* fn. 71: *op.cit.* 10.

[84] *Cf.* fn. 71: *op.cit.* 19.

[85] *Cf.* fn. 65: *op.cit.* 14.

[86] Hansjakob Seiler and Günter Zimmermann, 'Studies in the phonology and morphology of Classical Nahuatl: I. Orthographic variation o/u; its phonological and morphological implications', *IJAL* 28.243-50 (1962).

higher allophone would have occurred in checked syllables, and the lower allophone elsewhere. But this interpretation is dependent on the previous acceptance of the authors' characterization of checked syllables in Classical Nahuatl: not only CVC, but also C_1VC_2V where C_2 is a continuant; among the continuants, /č/, /λ/ and, presumably, /c/ are classified. They also consider that the type of consonant C_1 is, is relevant to the definition of the checked syllable. The impression we get from all this is that if some sort of complementation existed, it was more in terms of preceding and following consonants than in terms of a suspicious 'checked syllable'.[87] Quite apart from the main argument of the paper, the authors make some remarks on the correlation they assume between type of morpheme and [o] vs. [u] quality. But these remarks are not always easy to reconcile with the hypothesis of the checked syllable: e.g. the observation that the passive prefix /no/ is [no-], since such a prefix will surely occur attached to stems beginning with /č/. The authors also mention the fact that some other sources present ⟨o⟩ in every case, but this problem is left for further treatment. Finally they call attention to other pending problems of Nahuatl phonology, such as the 'saltillo' and the fluctuation between ⟨i⟩ and ⟨e⟩, ⟨e⟩ and ⟨a⟩. Independently of the degree of conviction the authors' interpretation may carry, this paper, based on a painstaking examination of the sources, is a careful study presenting explicit assumptions and a full discussion of the problems involved.

G. Zimmermann has also contributed to the field with a study on stylistics.[88] It is a general setting of the problems of Nahuatl style, focussing on the materials furnished by Sahagún's Book VI. The author states that in speeches we find the intensification of procedures also found in other types of texts — such as metaphors, twin-forms, fixed formulas, as well as some grammatical features: use of the vocative and of special forms of honorifics. He notes the sporadic use of rhetorical 'self-abasement', and suggests that its introduction was due to Spanish influence. Finally he studies the greeting formulas, and for some of them he establishes their precise meaning through observing their uses in the texts. (This paper continues, after a long interval, previous studies by Hölker that fall outside the scope of the present survey.[89])

In two recent papers[90] Langacker deals with problems of Classical Nahuatl from

[87] This is the conclusion of a careful presentation of the o–u variation in a modern Nahuat dialect, which should be compared with Zimmermann-Seiler's paper, *cf.* Carl Wolgemuth, 'Isthmus Veracruz (Mecayapan) laryngeals,' in *Aztec Studies I* 1–12 (Norman, 1969).

[88] Günter Zimmermann, 'Über einige stereotype Wendungen und Metaphern im Redestil des Aztekischen', *Baessler Archiv* N.F. 3.149-68 (1955).

[89] Georg Hölker, 'Dvandvaähnliche Wortkuppelungen im Aztekischen', *Wiener Beiträge zur Kulturgeschichte und Linguistik* 1.349-58 (1930); 'Einige Metaphern im Aztekischen des P. Sahagúns', *Anthropos* 27.249-59 (1932).

[90] Roland W. Langacker, 'Possessives in Classical Nahuatl' *IJAL* 38.173–86 (1972); 'Relative Clauses in Classical Nahuatl,' *IJAL* 41.46–68 (1975). I have not been able to see three papers by Jane M. Rosenthal which should have been commented on at this point: *The Omnipresent Problem of Omnipresent 'in' in Classical Nahuatl,* M.A. thesis, Chicago, 1971; 'On the Relative Clauses of Classical Nahuatl,' in P. M. Peranteau *et al.* (eds.), *Which Hunt, Papers from the Relative Clause Festival* 246–55 (Chicago, 1972); 'Some Types of Subordinate Clauses in Classical Nahuatl,' in Claudia Corum *et al.* (eds.), *You Take the High Node and I'll Take the Low Node, Papers from the Comparative Syntax Festival* 23–32 (Chicago, 1973).

a transformational point of view. Both are detailed and sophisticated analyses but the one on possessives, due to the nature of the problem, is more interesting as a contribution to grammatical theory and does not add much to the knowledge of the language. The paper on relative clauses, instead, clarifies not only the structure of that structure in Classical Nahuatl—a chief contention being that neither λein nor a·kin are relative pronouns—but also touches upon several points concerning subordinate clauses and the particle *in*. The corpus analyzed is rather small, as the author admits, but the argumentation is adequately exemplified and use is made of evidence from comparative Yutoaztecan (but not from modern Nahua dialects) and from grammatical typology. A query about this paper is why the author has represented vowel quantity by doubling the vowel.

As for Maya, it is worth mentioning Knorozov's hypothesis[91] that hieroglyphic Maya differs considerably from the classical dialect. Naturally this claim depends on the success of his decipherment, whose evaluation corresponds to a different section of this volume.

So far the only significant study of Classical Quechua has been Rowe's paper on the phonemic system.[92] His sources for the reconstruction are the statements by old grammarians, combined with the internal examination of their orthography, and the phonemic systems of modern Cuzco and Ayacucho Quechua. The system he finally establishes for Classical Quechua agrees in the number and kinds of contrasts with the modern Cuzco dialect, but with the Ayacucho dialect only in certain allophonic details. Two fricatives, represented by ⟨ç, z⟩ and ⟨s,ss⟩ respectively, are assumed, tentatively, on the basis of some consistency in González Holguín's orthography and agreements with the same words in Ecuadorian Quechua. But the author leaves the point as hypothetical, pending further comparative work which may also throw more light on the exact nature of the phonetic content of the fricatives (there is an explicit testimony that Cuzco Quechua had no equivalent for the Spanish ⟨x⟩, i.e. [š]). Rowe purposely dismisses the first Quechua grammar, written by Domingo de Santo Tomás, on the suspicion that it did not reflect Cuzco Quechua. This turns on the problem of dialectal variation, to which only slight consideration has so far been given. In commenting above (§ 1.1) on Galante's edition we mentioned the fact that Ávila's manuscript does not differentiate more than one series among the stops: on the basis of biographical data and of the occurrence in that text of certain nonclassical linguistic forms, Trimborn has suggested[93] that it reflects the dialect referred to by old grammarians as Chinchasuyu. In a later work, on the other hand, Ávila not only used the classical orthography, but also made statements that show he was aware of more than one stop series[94] (and Rowe uses this work among his sources for Classical Quechua).

[91] Y. V. Knorozov, 'La lengua de los textos jeroglíficos mayas', *Actas del 33 Congreso Internacional de Americanistas* 2.573-9 (San José, Costa Rica, 1959).

[92] *Cf.* fn. 4.

[93] *Cf.* fn. 3: *op.cit.* 15-6; also 'El manuscrito quichua inédito de Francisco de Ávila', *Actas del* 27 *Congreso Internacional de Americanistas* 1.223-5 (Lima and México, 1939).

[94] *Cf.* fn. 3: *op.cit.* 16.

Rowe also advances the rather bold hypothesis — given the time elapsed and the differences that the dialects show at present — that modern Quechua dialects do not continue the dialectal differentiation of pre-Inca times, but that they stem from a kind of 'koiné' based on Classical Cuzco Quechua. (On the other hand, there have been no attempts to establish the relation between the divergences called dialectal in the old sources and the modern dialects, nor between these and the old 'nonclassical' features.)

Comparatively, monographic studies in the field of Tupi-Guarani have been quite numerous. Aryón Dall'Igna Rodrigues has devoted separate papers to studying several aspects of Old Tupi morphology: composition, reduplication, voice.[95] He has also studied the phonology, but has so far only published the phonemic chart.[96]

Lemos Barbosa has described the system of demonstratives,[97] which he finds may be classified according to the categories of proximity and visibility. He has concerned himself too with one problem of Tupi-Guarani morphology which has attracted disproportionate attention: the alternation of initial consonants in noun stems, as shown e.g. by ⟨tape⟩ 'road', ⟨xe rape⟩ 'my road', ⟨sape⟩ 'his road'.[98] Some of the entries in the *Vocabulário na língua brasílica* give him cause for the assumption that the initial consonant was a class prefix, dividing nouns into a 'superior' and an 'inferior' class. The original paper has not been available to us, but judging from his discussion of this problem in his *Curso de Tupi antigo*[99] we must conclude that his argument does not carry enough conviction. The same facts have been studied by Ayrosa.[100] Due to his diffuse style, and to the amount of irrelevant digressions, it is difficult to see clearly which points he wants to prove. But it seems that his interpretation is that of ⟨t-⟩ as a determinative, and of ⟨r-, s-⟩ as indicating the noun is possessed. It must be pointed out that it is very questionable whether these alternations can be accurately analyzed other than as morphophonemic variations, and that any reconstruction of a former morphological status should better await the results of comparative work, in view of the parallel complex alternations of other Tupian languages.[101]

In the same paper Ayrosa also touches upon another trite point of Tupian grammar, to which F. Edelweiss has devoted a whole monograph:[102] the fact that the same set of prefixes express, according to the class of the following stem, possession, subject, or object. The unawareness of both authors of the widespread character of this phenomenon, added to a total incomprehension of the difference between unstressed prefixes

[95] Aryón Dall'Igna Rodrigues, 'A categoria da voz em Tupi', *Logos* (Curitiba) 2:6.50-3 (1947); 'A composição em Tupi', *ibid.* 6:14.63-70 (1951); 'Analise morfológica de um texto tupi', *ibid.* 7:15.55-7 (1952); 'Morfologia do verbo tupi', *Letras* (Curitiba) 1.121-52 (1953). These papers have not been available to me.

[96] Wanda Hanke, Morris Swadesh and Aryón Dal'Igna Rodrigues, 'Notas de fonología mekens', *Miscellanea Paul Rivet Octogenaria Dicata* 2.187-217 (México, 1958).

[97] A. Lemos Barbosa, 'Nova categoria gramatical tupi', *Verbum* (Rio de Janeiro) 4:2.67-74 (1947).

[98] A. Lemos Barbosa, 'Os índices de classe no tupi', *O Estado de São Paulo* (25-VIII-40).

[99] *Cf.* fn. 8: *op.cit.* 105-14, 294-301.

[100] *Dos índices de relação determinativa de posse no tupi-guarani. ELTG* No. 1 (1939).

[101] *Cf.* Perry N. and Anne M. Priest, and Joseph E. Grimes, 'Simultaneous orderings in Siriono (Guarani)', *IJAL* 27.335-44 (1961).

[102] Frederico G. Edelweiss, *O caráter da segunda conjugação tupi* (Bahía, 1958).

and stressed pronouns, prevent them from making in their respective studies any positive contribution to the description of these facts — and even give to both their papers an amateurish touch. In fact, the real problem here involved — namely, the attributive or predicative function of some nominal (?) stems, sometimes coupled with variations in the stem and, probably, with double stem affiliation — is left not only unsolved but not even well posed. Although the treatment is also unsatisfactory, this problem can be better understood in the exposition made by Lemos Barbosa in his book.[103] The monograph on the particle ⟨haba⟩, by C. Drumond,[104] also exhibits an extremely elementary linguistic technique, but it may be useful as a collection of examples.

In spite of the fact that phonology is the aspect of classical languages of which we at present have a clearer picture, there are still many dubious points of phonemic and phonetic detail. Obviously all the information that may be derived from the study of sixteenth-century Spanish or Portuguese is very helpful for the solution of those points, and many of the papers we have surveyed have profited from that information (usually Canfield and Menéndez Pidal). But for some years past a great many studies have been made, especially on the phonemic system of Spanish, which have modified in several ways the views formerly held on these matters. Yet none of the recent knowledge has so far contributed to the study of classical languages — nor, for that matter, to the study of any other Indian language, since the same problems obviously prevail in the interpretation of all the missionaries' grammars of the sixteenth and seventeenth centuries.

2.4. Notwithstanding their reduced number and their various shortcomings, we believe that the works we have just mentioned can, as a whole, be considered signs of a renewal of interest in the linguistic study of classical languages. The majority were published after 1950, and the philological and linguistic technique of some of them is sound enough. The extent of their significance cannot be wholly appreciated unless we bear in mind that we must go as far back as 1921 (Tozzer) for Yucatec, 1884 (Tschudi) for Quechua, or 1876 (Almeida Nogueira) for Tupi-Guarani to find works of real importance for the points covered by them.

3. *Dictionaries.* The most important contribution in this field, which has been scarcely explored, has been the vocabulary inserted by Schultze Jena in his edition of the *Popol Vuh.*[105] In the first place, because the old vocabularies for Quiche are still in manuscript. But also, what is more important, because the entries include the original spelling with the variants found in the manuscript, the editor's phonetic transcription, cross-references to the text and to some other manuscripts used by the author, and grammatical comments, while not so thorough as the one commented, special men-

[103] *Cf.* fn. 8: *op.cit.* 144-5.
[104] *Da particula hába do tupi-guarani. ELTG* No. 12 (1946).
[105] *Cf.* fn. 23.

tion has to be made of the glossaries included in his other editions.[106]

Another most important contribution is Edmonson's Quiche dictionary[107] which, while less philological than Friedrich's vocabulary, is based on all available sources: vocabularies as well as texts, edited or in manuscript, old and modern; it includes also proper names with tentative translations. Where the word is attested in only one source this is given, otherwise it is classified into three dialect regions; included too is a glottochronological code indicating which other Mayan languages share a cognate. The stated aim of the book is 'to arrive at an approximation to the minimal extension of the use of the root in space and time' (vii). In addition to being a much welcomed source of lexical information for Classical Quiche, it is the first attempt we know of a kind of historical dictionary for an Amerindian language.

Guided by his interests in language comparison Swadesh conceived the plan of analytical dictionaries where the lexicon of a language is represented by the most irreducible elements, and produced, in collaboration, one for Classical Nahuatl and another for Classical Yucatec.[107a] They include some grammatical information, list of affixes, and indications for its use in reading classical texts. This kind of work is undoubtedly very useful for comparative linguistics and for recognizing the elements in a Classical Nahuatl word, but not for a true understanding of the texts. The reading of classical texts, be it for linguistic, historic or literary purposes, requires the knowledge of the exact meaning of the word in a given context, and this cannot be arrived at on the basis of a mechanical analysis of words plus guesses at their meaning, as seems to be suggested in the introductions to these dictionaries.

H. Galante's above mentioned books[108] contain full Quechua glossaries. Their merits are not lexicographic, since only the most general meaning of each entry is given, but lie in the fact that for each root or stem several derived or inflected forms are presented, with cross-references to the text; in this sense they constitute a very useful tool for grammatical and lexical research.

Some other lexicons are also useful, but of reduced scope. E.g. a list of specific domains by Farfán,[108a] or the philosophical vocabulary assembled by León-Portilla.[109]

[106] *Cf.* fns. 12 and 20.

[107] Munro S. Edmonson, *Quiche-English Dictionary*, Publication 30, Middle American Research Institute, Tulane University, New Orleans, 1965.

[107a] Mauricio Swadesh y Madalena Sancho, *Los mil elementos del mexicano clásico. Base analítica de la lengua nahua.* Universidad Nacional Autónoma de México. Instituto de Investigaciones Históricas. (Serie de Cultura Náhuatl, Monografías 9), México, 1966. Mauricio Swadesh, María Cristina Alvarez, Juan R. Bastarrachea, *Diccionario de elementos del Maya Yucateco Colonial.* Seminario de Estudios de la Escritura Maya (Cuaderno 3). Unam, México, 1970.

[108] *Cf.* fns. 29, 30, and 34.

[108a] J. M. B. Farfán, 'Glosario patológico quechua de la "Crónica" de Guaman Poma y un breve vocabulario patológico quechua', *Revista del Museo Nacional* 10.157-64 (Lima, 1941).

[109] Miguel León-Portilla, 'Breve vocabulario filosófico náhuatl', in *La filosofía náhuatl estudiada en sus fuentes*[2] 325-45 (México, 1959).

The paper by Porras Barrenechea[110] is general, and rather rash in drawing conclusions, but in it the author rightly insists on the necessity of studying more closely the first lexicons for the sake of their cultural content.

L. Cadogan has dealt specifically[111] with the problem of important Guarani words which are buried in the entries of Ruiz de Montoya's *Tesoro*, and has shown the necessity of re-elaborating that dictionary. It is a very apposite paper, as it clearly illustrates the inconveniencies of ancient dictionaries in general (Zimmermann[112] mentions similar difficulties in Molina's dictionary), and its plea could be applied to all the classical languages.

4. *Conclusion.* It may be observed that studies on Tupi-Guarani, as well as all the philological work in this field, are in general more linguistically slanted — whatever their quality — than in the other classical languages. We do not believe this to be casual. Due to the nature and subject-matter characteristics of extant Old Tupi and Guarani texts, it would indeed be difficult to see how they could awake other than a linguistic interest. On the other hand, it is only natural that Nahuatl and Maya texts have attracted attention by their cultural contents, and only in an indirect way by their linguistic aspects. As a result, and in spite of the fact that certainly many more people are able to handle a classical text in Maya or Nahuatl than in Tupi, the total output of linguistic studies is comparatively more reduced in the former than in the latter.

The survey by E. Mengin[113] may be taken to a great extent as illustrative of this state of affairs: it is manifest that all the emphasis is placed on editions with TRANSLATIONS whereas, although listed in the bibliography, no special mention is made of Friedrich's grammar, which is undoubtedly the most important linguistic contribution to Quiche. Clearly, the best delineated trend so far in the study of classical languages has been translation, and, in keeping with it, there is also the tendency to write grammatical outlines chiefly as a practical guide for reading classical texts. Of course, every translation presupposes a certain linguistic analysis of the original text — and in this respect they are also useful. But the linguistic knowledge they require remains implicit and, to a great extent, noncumulative. Exceptions are Schultze Jena's already mentioned glossaries appended to his editions where the entries contain all the forms actually occurring in the text, with hyphens marking the boundaries between the component elements.

This situation is not surprising. Linguists working in Indian languages are for the most part chiefly interested in living languages, whereas scholars interested in the classical languages usually have interests other than merely linguistic ones. Nevertheless, the dates of some of the works we have commented on show signs — at least for

110 Raúl Porras Barrenechea, 'El primer vocabulario quechua', *Letras* 49.217-28 (Lima, 1953).

111 León Cadogan, 'Registro de algunas voces internas del Tesoro de la Lengua Guaraní del P. Antonio Ruiz de Montoya', *BFS* 41:8 (*TILAS* 3) 517-32 (1963).

112 *Cf.* fn. 89.

113 *Cf.* fn. 26.

some of the languages — of an increasing activity of mainly linguistic orientation. Within this activity, research tends — logically, we think — either to descriptive outlines or to the treatment of specific grammatical points (and, surprisingly enough, it is in these papers that the results tend to be better supported philologically than for the rest); an important consequence is that, in some cases, specific problems have begun to take shape. But the points that still need treatment of this sort are so numerous, for each and every language, that it would be useless to attempt their enumeration.

On the whole, we believe the philological aspect is still the weakest: not only because of the shortcomings of most editions, but also because in most works of strictly linguistic nature there is no systematic use of concrete data — from old grammars, texts, or vocabularies — in support of arguments and conclusions. Translations are seldom philologically justified, and the general procedure is to present side by side text and version, with no other comments than those based on the translator's familiarity with the classical language. As for the most advanced and refined stage of philological work, namely the truly critical edition, we believe it would mean, in the present circumstances, a veritable tour de force on the part of some one individual.[114]

If the term 'classical' is taken in its full implication and if, consequently, research in the Old World classical languages is taken as the standard point of reference, it is obvious that what has been done so far in indigenous languages is not much more than preliminaries. There seems to be a long way ahead before we can have standard reference grammars, philological guides, dictionaries with Authorities, and good critical editions.

There are still other aims to pursue. It is obvious that these languages have a privileged position among Indian languages in that they present multiple problems, some of which can at present be but enumerated: the emergence of a written language, its relations with the spoken language and with later dialects, its adaptation to the needs of expressing a different cultural content, the influence of a foreign literary language, the comparison of texts written by native speakers to those written by Europeans, and the control of old descriptions that those texts afford. The solutions to these problems go far beyond the linguistic interest for each particular language, and may represent a significant contribution to general linguistics.

[114] The importance of the philological approach cannot be overemphasized: there is the danger that efforts be wasted in linguistic analyses on the basis of poor sources or, as in the case of Nahuatl, that these efforts tend to concentrate on a restricted corpus, namely Sahagún's texts.

WRITING SYSTEMS

THOMAS S. BARTHEL

None of the native writing systems in the New World has reached the stage of a 'complete writing system' capable of fully mirroring a language. We are dealing with all levels of 'partial writing systems', that is to say, with incomplete systems which attempted in various ways to graphically set down segments of a richer oral transmission. This is the reason for its weakness as compared to the fully developed writing systems of the Old World and the reason for an absolute limitation of knowledge in this field of research, but at the same time it stimulates the task of analytically grasping the early phases and stages in the development of complete writing systems.

This presentation of the current status of research is within the geographic framework of this volume. Thus we are *not* discussing the primitive writing systems of the North American Indians (although they definitely belong to the great process of development of writing systems in the New World), although, on the other hand, we refer to Chile's Easter Island with its inscribed tablets (in spite of the fact that these relics are undoubtedly Polynesian). Our resumé starts with the South American pieces of evidence, moves on to the Mexican material and finally reaches its climax as to extent and intensity of coverage with the Maya hieroglyphs. The deciphering of these hieroglyphs is currently provoking vehement differences of opinion. For all details and further questions please refer to the bibiography. The period covered by this paper is not narrowly restricted in time, but does, however, concentrate mainly on the last 20 years.

I

There is no proof today as to whether or not any partial writing systems existed in the pre-Colombian Andes. The use of knotted strings (Quipus) other than in a mathematical-statistical context has not been attested by concrete pieces of evidence. Nevertheless, a minimum of objective information could be established by the different colors of the strings and special shapes of the knots. The mnemonic principle of such knotted strings is an almost insurmountable barrier for the comprehension of quipus discovered in archeological findings. Only in such cases where astronomical measurements (cycles and calendar units) are to be ascertained can an objective statement be made as to the intended meanings.

Larco Hoyle's suggestion that the Mochicas had an ideographic system has not evoked a positive response. The depictions of beans with extremely varied markings, especially on ceramics but also found on textiles, should be understood rather as gambling counters (analogous to the use by recent Chaco tribes). The interpretation of the rich iconography of ancient Peruvian vessels and textiles or of elaborate stone reliefs can be taken as a legitimate task of Peruvian Studies, but is not within the range of tasks involved in the research on a writing system. The possible hints at older pictographic documents (Cristoval de Molina, Sarmiento de Gamboa) also belong to such studies. The question remains unanswered as to the value of Montesino's report about a pre-Inca writing. Several investigators have postulated possible (genetic?) relationships with the Easter Island writing system, since in both cases it has been reported that banana leaves were used as writing material. Inasmuch as not a single piece of evidence of the 'Montesino writing system' is available, it seems to us that a precept of the most elementary prudence is not to argue *e silento*.

The fact that pictographic representations of Christian-religious texts existed in the southern area of the Andes has been known at least since von Tschudi. But it was not until the modern investigations had been made, especially by Ibarra Grasso, to whom we are indebted for the standard work on such material, that it became evident that this is a problem of interest in the field of writing theory. From a formal point of view, the documents produced by the Aymara and Quechua Indians constitute a pictography: the signs are not standardized, they differ per se and from place to place, they resemble certain rock pictures in their realistic configuration, and their inventory can be expanded at any time by random ad-hoc ingenuity. The writing material went through a certain development; for one thing, animal skins painted with the juices of plants or mineral pigments gave way to paper; for another thing, the grouping of clay figurines (human figures or objects) on a stationary disc gave rise, as it were, to a three-dimensional means of communication. Their purpose is a mnemonic device for illiterates and consists of Catholic prayers (the Lord's Prayer, catechism, etc.). Now that the proper sounds of the words of the appertaining Indian language have been established, it is possible to determine the precise function of the seemingly equivalent 'pictograms'. Thus it turns out that we are dealing with a 'mixed system': the majority of the pictograms are naturalistic reproductions of persons (also scenes, gestures) and objects, that is to say 'picture-writing' in the literal sense of the word. Elliptical spellings (pars-pro-toto method) are not found. A second group of signs comprises symbols, that is, it makes use of ideographic means of expression. The great surprise, however, is that about 20% of them operate according to a rebus procedure. Homophones are used as well as puns, with the latter allowing quite some latitude in the similarity of the sounds. Not only entire words but also parts of words can be transcribed 'quasi-phonetically' in this manner. In other words: what outwardly appears to be merely a pictography contains the multiple ways of expression used in a partial writing system! There is not always a one-to-one correspondence between a sign and a word and there are even instances in which considerably fewer signs occur than the actual words of the prayer being depicted. This is a case, then, of text condensation with the aid of cues; here the mnemonic goal is especially obvious. Now the question is whether we are dealing with an invention of the colonial period (possibly because of missionaries working with an illiterate people), or whether it is to be accepted that we are dealing with pre-Columbian roots ('Andean Proto-Writing'). The second possibility is not to be ruled out entirely, since the direction in which such texts are read (various types of boustrophedon or in a spiral reading inwards) are suggestive not of European models but rather of Amerindian creations. It is conceivable that a pan-American 'pictographic horizon' extended from Bolivia to North America.

The so-called 'Cuna Writing' could also belong to this category. Its thorough investigation is an accomplishment of the 'Göteborg School' which — following the pioneering analyses of Nordenskjöld — in close cooperation with Cuna informants collected and worked out detailed pictographs with their matching songs. The outward appearance of a picture-writing, which gets additional properties through the use of colors and which obviously follows autochthonous Indian patterns in its utilization of boustrophedon types, leads here also to an underestimation of the basic communication system. As a matter of fact, two principles can be seen at work: the simpler type is strictly pictographic, that is to say, it depicts in imagery the situation which is described in detail in the song. The more developed type (which at present seems to be on the decline) attempts to fix separate words or even parts of words. To do this, the entire range of rebus techniques (homophony, homeophony, a partial sound allusion, especially for the initial syllables) is used. Pictograms can be used ambiguously. Combined forms usually are used to express longer textual statements. There are instances of hybrid systems, when, for example, a pure pictorial element is coupled with a form which is functioning as an indicator of an initial sound. Contrary to the example of the Andean pictographs, the topic matter is autochthonous (songs and prayers of the medicine men in their healing rites and other rituals). Although there is no standardized inventory of obligatory forms, still in all, the differences between the forms used by the various 'schools' is not insurmountable. The function is based upon the mnemonic role of fixing long song texts and narrations by means of 'cues'. But the graphic notation per se seems to enhance the magical appreciation of the oral tradition. The illustrations from the Cuna writings demonstrate the fact that there is a strict barrier to comprehension at the lowest level of partial writing systems: as soon as we know the original text in its complete oral version, we can see right through the multiple expressions of an alleged 'pictography'. As long as we have only the effigy signs before us for consideration, a definitive decipherment is not possible; the rules governing the sound indicators, the condensation of cues, and so on, cannot be understood through the pictograms themselves. Strictly speaking, it's a matter of highly developed mnemonicons for one's personal information, not a matter of objectified information, that is to say, 'messages' which can be reproduced by strangers. The 'Cuna Writing' is the sole existing form of an ancient Indian 'writing' that is still used today in Latin America and is for that reason valuable as a prototype.

Various authors have sought to establish a connection between the Easter Island writing system and the American partial writing systems. These conjectures, however, must be regarded as obsolete, ever since the principal features of the structure, contents, and origin of the Easter Island writing system have been clarified through the work of the present writer. His 'Grundlagen zur Entzifferung' (i.e. Basic Principles for a Decipherment) has been further strengthened and broadened during the course of the last decade. According to those principles the following synthesis of that writing system which was still in use less than a hundred years ago on Easter Island can now be stated:

The classical Easter Island writing, in contradistinction to pictographic systems, comprises a corpus of standardized and conventional signs, which fixed the outlines of the natural or geometric models according to definite rules. Its inventory of about 120 basic graphemes can be combined with each other according to traditional and obligatory rules, resulting in up to 2,000 different composite forms. The texts are normally incised in boustrophedons on both sides of flat wooden tablets; it can be proven, however, that the very 'first writing' was done on fresh banana leaves, that is to say, that the very first writing material was perishable. Thus it is very likely that this writing, which was brought to Easter Island in the fifteenth century A.D. by a wave of Polynesian immigration, has left no evidences of its former existence in the area in which it originated, namely the area of Raiatea-Huahine (the Windward Islands, west of Tahiti). The deciphering of place names and names of deities as well as other bits of graphic evidence prove at any rate that this writing was not invented locally on Easter Island itself. The remote possibility has to be taken into account that the creation of the Central Polynesian protoform of the Easter Island writing is due to a 'stimulus diffusion' from Asia. From a linguistic point of view, the writing on the Easter Island tablets includes various stages of development of the Polynesian language. During the course of 400 years older Central Polynesian words were replaced on Easter Island to some extent by local regionalisms. Therefore, it is necessary in the deciphering work to try to bring in other East Polynesian languages for comparison with the Rapanui vocabulary.

The Easter Island writing merits theoretical interest because of its principles of internal structure. As a rule a grapheme corresponds to the fixed sound value of a radical. Occasionally a polyvalence is noted: in such instances it's a matter of related concepts, which can be concatenated with the pictorial quality of a sign functioning in a like manner. Some associations between the form of the sign and the spoken equivalent are obvious: color values are rendered by objects which are typical of the color in question; at times other properties are expressed pictorially by the shape of the sign itself; supernatural powers can be represented by their prominent characteristics or external features (pars-pro-toto or symbolic signs). Poetic circumlocutions or figurative phraseology are rendered, so to speak, as 'written metaphors'. Since the wealth of homonyms in the Polynesian language is cleverly exploited to its full extent, the nature of the phoneticization is crucial for an understanding of the inscriptions. In the rebus procedure the writers worked not only with homonyms but also with homeophonous elements (within precisely defined rules of sound similarity). Two factors, however, considerably complicate the situation: The first one is the fact that the Easter Island writing system was not able to reproduce a complete spoken sentence but was only able to use its graphic system as cues to the main ideas embodied in the sentences. Thus the profusion of the original oral transmission is reduced to a sort of telegraphic style which naturally causes considerable difficulties for the present day decipherer (with his quite different cultural milieu). Added to this difficulty is the fact that the writer was satisfied more often than not with a 'partial sound indication', that is, for example, with representing in writing only parts of a polysyllabic word. As with all partial writing systems, this then creates an 'information decrease' which is far more serious than, say, the lack of grammatical particles or the intricate variety of the poetic expressions in the Easter Island writing system. As seen from the point of view of the present day decipherer, the cue type inscriptions present a meager 'exteriority'; it is only when we can completely reveal the corresponding 'interiority' through other kinds of ethnographic sources that the original richness of the traditional culture is disclosed. The sequence of signs, through which the songs were transmitted in a fixed structure, had above all a complementary value for the Polynesian writer, the one who was qualified and knowledgeable to read them, whether they were mnemonicons or whether they were a normative means of standardization. Inasmuch as the Easter Island writing system was not constructed, properly speaking, as an autonomous communication system but merely as the auxiliary carrier of the traditions of their culture, it presents a paradox: It is a highly developed stage of mnemonics and a nascent early writing system at one and the same time.

The range of themes dealt with on the inscribed tablets are first and foremost of a ritualistic character revolving about deities, mythical events, and festivals. This results in a considerable yield for a deeper understanding of the Old-Polynesian religion. Sociology and history are harder to understand due to the technique of stereotyped circumlocutions. But even here some light is thrown on the former social functions and especially on the earlier migrations in eastern Polynesia. Even the archeological problems of Easter Island itself, such as the giant stone figures and the cult sites, are at least dealt with indirectly. The task today for research is to interpret and provide commentaries on the structures of the motifs in the long, interrelated texts on the tablets and to specify the linguistic change in the Easter Island writing system. The prospects for doing this may be considered to be favorable.

II

Teotihuacán, the northernmost of the great cult centers during the Meso-American classical period, apparently had a ritual calendar although the majority of the signs for the days have not yet been identified. Hasso von Winning has especially distinguished himself in his attempts to identify the signs. There is a complete lack of longer texts. For this reason an interpretation of the isolated symbols, which occur for the most part on ceramic ware, runs up against considerable difficulties. Regardless of the recalcitrance of the subject matter, individual studies are indispensable for future progress in this field since there are significant cross-connections leading from Teotihuacán to the sign inventories of other classical centers.

Xochicalco can well serve as an example of such cross-connections. Not long ago Sáenz dug up three stelae which, according to the iconography of their deities and their calendar data as well as the concomitant non-calendaric hieroglyphs, can pass as a proto-example of a late classic syncretism. And, last but not least, additional solutions would have a favorable effect on the investigation of the Zapotec hieroglyphs.

We probably reach the greatest time depth in Meso-America with the written monoliths at Monte Alban. The most important name connected with this research is that of Alfonso Caso. Although his first compendium of the Zapotec stone inscriptions (1928) was just restricted to a chronologically non-differentiated presentation which merely discussed the calendaric hieroglyphs, his second synthesis (1947) has brought us, however, quite a distance forward. Monte Alban I presents us with what is to all appearances the oldest Meso-American writing already completely developed without any recognizable preliminary stages. The calendar, starting with a ritual calendar of 260 days, already contains computations as to the year and probably also positions of the months. The signs for the days can be interpreted at least partially from their shapes. Hieroglyphs without concomitant numerals appear singly or in compounds and constitute short inscriptions. An analysis of the shapes of the forms yields three groups: anthropomorphic and zoomorphic heads, hand-forms (apparently for actions), and stylized objects of the material culture. Calendar and non-calendaric statements are already intermingled. The iconography of the figures plays a very important role, i.e. the characteristics of the costume and ornamentation provide essential additional information. Typical structures of the texts can be recognized in Monte Alban II. Such characteristic inscriptions taken from the 'Montículo J' have the following general structure:

1. A reversed human head with death-eyes, individualized especially by the headdress;
2. The hieroglyph 'mountain' with variable additional elements;
3. Dates (year, month, day);
4. Possibly other non-calendaric supplementary signs.

This sequence can be interpreted as 'substantive expression—location information—time information—(further elucidation)', and we can accept Caso's explanation that these are inscriptional proclamations of conquests (defeated opponent—location of the event — date of the triumph), i.e. political history. Hieroglyphic texts of this period occur in double columns, a fact that is familiar in Maya epigraphy. Only attempts at interpretation of the inscriptions of Monte Alban I and II are under consideration. Readings in the literal sense of the word are out of the question since the linguistic connection to Zapotec in the early period is rather problematic. The research suffers especially from a lack of Zapotec codices and of early colonial period commentators (of the level of a Sahagún or a Landa) and is therefore restricted to an inner analysis based on archeology, with at the most an insight — based on shapes — into written elements of other classical cultures. The extremely scanty number of 'Olmec' inscriptions have not yet been subjected to writing system research. Interest is concentrated mainly on questions of a calendar nature, especially the role of the 'Long Count' dating and the order of seniority precedence vis-à-vis the early classical Maya monuments.

The studies concerning the pre-Spanish codices have progressed disproportionately. There are essentially two groups of themes: codices of a religious (ritual and mantic) character and codices with a historical and genealogical content. The first group was the main subject of research at the turn of the century; the art of interpretation reached an apogee that has never been attained since then, especially with the commentary by Edward Seler on the manuscripts of the Codex Borgia-Group. More advanced ideas and methods are found in Novotny and Spranz. Novotny postulates a judicious separation between 'elucidation' and 'interpretation' of this paleographic material. While Novotny accepts Seler's elucidations of the effigies in the codices of the Codex Borgia-Group as appropriate and reliable, many of the earlier 'interpretations' seem to him to be dubious. This is mainly true in regard to the topics concerning astronomy and myths of nature in which there is a reflection of a vogue in the history of science. The re-interpretations which are required today must support the considerations of function, such as the role of the priestly rituals and the techniques of divination. The cataloguing of the manuscripts according to calendaric arrangements and to internal cross-connections creates an objective frame of reference. Another method of analysis is one of a precise and detailed study of the iconographic material. The painted designs on the faces and bodies, hair styles, clothing and ornaments characterize the images (deities or representations of priests as deities) and make it possible to recognize positions which are parallel and substitutable elements. Thus success has been achieved in grouping the deities solely according to their iconographic features, not biased by premature interpretations or conclusions drawn from analogies to sources of the Spanish colonial period. In this manner it is possible to reconstruct in a novel way the arrangement of the pantheon (of deities) according to the time horizon of the Mixteca-Puebla culture. The analyses which have just been outlined are not, strictly speaking, within the narrow scope of writing systems research, but they do show at the same time how a breadth of methods of investigation is essential when dealing with ancient Mexican picture writings. It is absolutely out of the question to talk of a real 'reading' of the codices mentioned above.

A stroke of luck has resulted in a decisive break-through in the Mixtec codices of the historical type. After a series of Anglo-American researchers had already begun to operate with the historicity of such documents (as opposed to the German scholars who had been advocating the thesis of mythological topics), Caso was successful in getting convincing proof that this material consisted of a record of the genealogies of the rulers. The key to the success, in some respects a Mexican 'Rosetta Stone', was a colonial document, a map of Teozacoalco drawn up in about 1580. It contains, along with other information, particulars of historical and genealogical nature about Mixtec kings who were then able to be identified in a number of preserved pre-Spanish codices by the iconographic and calendaric data. With this as a starting point, it was possible to interrelate and make sense out of the contents of longer passages. Thc genealogies of the Mixtec rulers can be traced back as far as the end of the seventh century and then followed, with a number of genealogical overlappings, up to the sixteenth and seventeenth centuries. What is interesting about the contents is the knowledge of which facts were considered to be 'worthy of noting down'. Given the present status of research, the main things which can be ascertained are birthdates and various types of cognominations the kings were given, their blood relatives (parents, siblings, and progeny) and marital ties, prominent events (enthronement, meetings of assemblies, trips or migrations, and especially military actions, conquests, and sacrificial acts) and, finally, the dates of their deaths. The codices either deal with genealogies of a single locality (e.g. the Codex Vindobonensis Verso provides the genealogy of Tilantongo) or with histories of a number of Mixtec rulers with information covering many localities (e.g. the Bodley Codex); it is possible to set up a number of concordances. The insight gained into this subject matter proves that a true consciousness of history existed in Meso-America. With the pictographic and calendaric system it was possible to pinpoint events temporally and spatially and thus pass them down to their descendants. At any rate an extract, and outline of cues, which called for the far more comprehensive oral treatment, could thus be written down. The main contribution of Caso's pioneering works, from the point of view of writing as a system, is in his determination of the graphic and typological forms for names. The names of persons (the 'nicknames' that signify rank as contrasted to the plain 'calendaric names' indicating the date of birth) and the names of places and localities are the components of the Mixtec codices which can be interpreted and thus make true readings possible. Hence it follows that the Mixtec language is the basis of the writing system (as contrasted to the Aztec speech medium of other Old-Mexican codices) and that, secondly, it involves a phoneticization by means of a rebus procedure. Pictorial elements are sometimes utilized for their phonetic value when it is necessary to differentiate homophonous words. Future research, especially toponymy, will be able to provide further insights into the construction principles of the Mixtec partial writing system; there is no significant difference between this writing and the possibilities of expression of the Aztec era. This also holds true for the usages of ideograms or symbolic graphemes scattered throughout the texts. Neither one of them have hieroglyphic texts which render complete sentences of a spoken language.

Of basic importance for a theoretical understanding of the Meso-American partial writing systems are Novotny's new analyses (1959, 1963) of the hieroglyphs in the Mendoza Codex. As is well known, this is a document from the early period of Spanish colonization in which the pictorial symbolizations (based on Aztec models) were explained by modern commentaries in order to make the document comprehensible. Thus, although no literal decipherment is given, still, thanks to the commentary, it is possible to take exact stock of structural symbolic characters, especially the locality hieroglyphs. It is evident that two-thirds of the hieroglyphs in the Mendoza Codex are clearly 'word pictures', i.e. that the name of the represented object provides the sound value. Further distinctions are introduced with the aid of 'inherent elements', that is to say through the addition of colors, ornaments, or changes in position. Hieroglyphic elements can be polymorphic (several signs can represent the same Aztec base word) or polyphonic (a sign can have several phonetic values). Hieroglyphic elements can be repeated several times for esthetic considerations without causing a corresponding repetition of the sounds. There is a relatively low proportion of 'elliptical writings' based on the pars-pro-toto principle and a relatively restricted inventory of true 'phonetic writings' based on rebus principles. Certain reading aids are used to make up for the ambiguity of the Aztec partial writing system. Hieroglyphs which are similar to each other or polyphonic are made precise by the use of 'double writings', and these double writings are repetitions of the first syllable or of the entire word. Pleonastic writings place the emphasis mainly on the beginning of the word. One can agree with Novotny that the Old-Mexican picture writings are not 'written texts but rather pictograms with interspersed pictures of words'. The heuristic value of such studies, let us say for the deciphering of the Maya hieroglyphs, is based on the fact that Meso-America is invested with a knowledge of hieroglyphic and calendaric means of expression which are structurally related and historically connected.

We will disregard the numerous detailed works covering questions about the Ancient Mexican calendar system since these are relevant only for writing system research proper where the beginnings of both of the two traditions are involved. At any rate the writing system and the calendar system have been closely united with each other in Meso-America since the pre-classical periods; in fact, this connection can be regarded as nothing less than the defining criterion of Ancient Mexico.

III

The endeavors to decipher the Maya writing system are being directed at the present time by a small number of scholars who are unfortunately very widely scattered. If we disregard the founding of the Seminario de Cultura Maya at the National University of Mexico, there has been no institutional center for such research on an international basis since the dissolution of the Department of Archeology of the Carnegie Institution. Those concerned are either former colleagues of the Carnegie Institution or are members of universities and academies. Occasional cooperation usually doesn't involve anything more than two partners in research or casual correspondence; instead of cooperation there have arisen controversies that have, now and then, reached deplorable heights of animosity. Unfortunately this latter situation, just like the lack of cooperation on Maya linguistic research, slows down and impedes progress in this field.

The key figure in efforts at deciphering the Maya heiroglyphs is indubitably Eric

Thompson. Not enough time has elapsed yet for an objective historical and scientific evaluation to be made of his accomplishments and shortcomings. It is incontrovertible that Thompson opened up a way (recognized since 1944) out of the blind alley of mere calendar and astronomical studies during the period between the two World Wars, and once again made the 'texts' themselves, consisting of non-calendaric hieroglyphs, the goal of the main research offensive. To work without his *opus magnum* (1950), a landmark of this new development, is inconceivable, although it is not free of errors, contradictions and illogical reasonings. A broad knowledge of the sources, placed against the broader Meso-American perspective, serves as a background for tracking down the entangled religious and ritual traces of the written elements. The deciphering work itself is occasionally in danger of being overshadowed by an emotional feeling for the intellectual history of the Maya culture. Kelley accepts approximately half of the new interpretations and new readings of the hieroglyphic elements; but even when more rigorous objections are made — we estimate that some 30 to 40% of Thompson's suggestions will be solidly substantiated — his 'quota of successes' is, still in all, considerably higher than all of the other works on the Maya writing system that are known to us. Thompson's articles on his deciphering ideas which have appeared in the last few years are somewhat less convincing than his major work; but we concur in the broad insights as to the character of the Maya hieroglyphs, especially as regards the role of the rebus readings and his observation about the 'pictorial synonyms and homonyms'. Thompson might make a further decisive breakthrough if the way were not blocked, in our opinion, by an overinterpretation of the Yucatec material that is based on Roy's work.

Tatiana Proskouriakoff and Heinrich Berlin succeeded in discovering political and dynastic events in the classical inscriptions and were thus able to bring real history into the discussion once again. This 'breakthrough to historicity' deals with the recognition of two things: 'emblem' hieroglyphs pertaining to specific localities and texts containing the biographies of rulers. The emblem hieroglyphs are for very definite cult centers and consist of individual main signs which occur, as a rule, only in that locality or in neighboring dependencies; they are coupled with ordinary affixes which, as a rule, can be identified throughout the entire area of the classical southern region. These affixes apparently indicate the lineage and rank of individuals while the main signs are surrogates for the various city-states. The biographies of the rulers contain hieroglyphic statements about births, enthronements or changes of official position, successful military actions and so on. The arrangement by dates makes it possible to draw up individual personal histories for particular Maya rulers (e.g. in Yaxchilan). Then too, the not inconsiderable role of female personages in certain inscriptions is starting to become evident. These new realizations have just reached the status of 'interpretations', and there are still considerable advances and refinements to be expected in this field. Nevertheless the basic principles discovered by Proskouriakoff can already be certified as valid today.

The so-called 'Hamburg School' has structural and functionalist methods which are related to those of the researchers named above, but it focuses more on studies of the interpretations and readability of single hieroglyphs. This then is a continuation of the Seler tradition which carefully judges the phenomena of the Maya culture against the larger background of Ancient Mexico and pays stronger attention to the symbolic means of expression and basic ideas they had in common. Only parts of the studies in the paleographic field have been published so far; further results will be forthcoming for the Madrid Codex (Zimmermann) and the Dresden Codex (Barthel). An investigation of worthwhile epigraphic targets (Chichen Itza, Tikal, Palenque) and also an analysis of the hieroglyphic writing present on Maya ceramic artifacts are under way at present in Tübingen.

There is a group of researchers, separated as to location but related in their theoretical position as to the writing system, who could be called, somewhat overstated perhaps, 'the phoneticians'. Knorosov, Kelley and Cordan are following a line of investigation which reflects an old tradition, even if not a too successful one, in the study of Maya hieroglyphs, a tradition that started with the so-called 'Landa alphabet'. The phonetic conception accounts to a considerable degree for the use of syllables or purely alphabetic values, i.e. this principle goes beyond a mere 'word sign writing'. According to this version, hieroglyphic compounds oftentimes consist of sound blends or instances of acrophony. The new readings which have been suggested so far, however, have to be considered as overwhelmingly controversial. The so-called 'Mérida System' approach signifies a step forward, since it deliberately attacks the problem through the philological reconstruction of a Proto-Maya language (that is to say, the spoken form of the language of the period during which the Maya writing system was invented). This approach is, on principle, necessary and most welcome, even if one, like the present writer, views most of the results attained so far with scepticism. The logical incorporation of Maya languages of the non-Yucatec group should undoubtedly open up new perspectives, especially for the epigraphy expert.

The experiment undertaken by the Siberian Academy of Science to decipher the Maya codices with the aid of electronic computers has to be considered as an attempt that failed. The criticism of the specialists is of one voice in the rejection of this attempt. It failed because the original premise was wrong, namely that of equating the lexical material of the Motul dictionary and of the Chilam Balam books *eo ipso* with the graphemes of the Maya paleography and wanting to undertake a schematic transference according to statistical rules. This mechanistic arrangement broke down, moreover, due to an inadequate theoretical grasp of the system of a partial writing mode such as the one represented by the Maya hieroglyphs. The decisive feats of deciphering will still have to be accomplished by researchers using their brains and not by machines in the foreseeable future.

Let us now proceed to a detailed report on the situation: The status of the sources has continued to develop unevenly. A new edition of the Dresden Codex, which is probably on a par with the Förstemann issues, has been published in the field of paleography. The new facsimile editions of the Paris Codex and of the Madrid Codex which have been announced will help facilitate their utilization on a broader basis. Publications on the Maya ceramic artifacts, whose iconography and concomitant hieroglyphic writings are of great heuristic value, are still fragmentary. There is no comprehensive opus of the type done by Gordon and Mason in which the objects scattered out through many private collections are inventoried. The same type of dispersal has to be taken into account when dealing with inscriptions on bones, shells, obsidian and greenstone, although these, as a group, are quite disparate as to subject matter and are less promising of success. The inscriptions of the classical period are still the basic material for epigraphic research, since our future understanding of the history, social structure and religion of the golden age of the Maya theocrats is dependent on their decipherment. Longer inscriptions, especially in the leading cult centers of Tikal and Palenque, have recently been uncovered. The discovery of stele 31 at Tikal has given us an early classical piece of evidence on which are shown influences from Teotihuacán; the iconography and text of this relic both hold out a promise for an approach with a successful solution. New important material is available in Palenque with the discoveries at the palace (Tablero de El Palacio, Tablero de los Esclavos) and in the crypt of the Temple of Inscriptions (sarcophagus texts). The discovery of new sites has provided the epigraphy experts with additional research possibilities of which only a fraction has been exploited so far. These include, among others, Bonampak, Caracol, and the cult centers in the basin of the Río Pasión (Aguateca, Dos Pilas, Machaquilá and Tamarandito). It is discouraging to report that the editing technique used in these and many other classical inscriptions is far inferior to the standard set by Maudslay at the close of the nineteenth century. An urgent list of desiderata for research is headed by a need for publication of larger and clearer photographs of the epigraphic material together with reliable and detailed re-drawing of the hieroglyphic passages. The decipherer lacks a handy working aid at the very beginning of his investigations unless he has adequate volumes of plates, arranged according to site and time depth, in which all of the inadequately covered as well as the unpublished inscriptions are systematically inventoried. Unfortunately even that preparation of series of hieroglyphic texts, for which Beyer established a model with the inscriptions from Chichen Itza, has come to a dead halt. Many of the cult centers have their own typical sequences of hieroglyphs (so-called 'clauses') which deal with expanded versions, abbreviated versions and modified versions of certain topics restricted to a specific locality. By arranging such texts in parallel sets it is possible, at least, to structurally divide an inscription which has not yet been deciphered and determine the possible substitutions in the sets of affixes, main signs, and combinations of signs. H. Berlin has recently begun to reveal such structural arrangements in at least a few of the Palenque texts.

The second step, after an inventory and presentation of the hieroglyphic texts that is justified by the facts, is to catalogue the attested elements of the writing system. The frequencies of occurrence of the individual main signs and affixes, the manner of their association, and the distribution in time and space reveal objective data before the deciphering work proper even begins. Thus a catalogue is not only a proof of the occurrences but as a result of the way in which it is prepared, also contains quantitative indices as to the possible types of writing. Zimmermann's catalogue (1956) is a precise and well thought out working aid that is available when working with the hieroglyphs in the three preserved Mayan manuscripts. Of the original stock of hieroglyphs in the paleographic texts the Madrid Codex has preserved 90%, the Dresden Codex about 85%, but the Paris Codex only about 30%. The main signs and the affixes are in a proportion of about 47 to 53 in the construction of the 5,770 hieroglyphs composed of a total of 14,230 construction elements. But if, from a statistical point of view, the main signs and affixes are almost equally divided, the picture shifts when one looks into the number of basic forms participating in the construction of this writing. There is a maximum of 230 main signs as compared to a stock of some 90 affixes in the paleography. Or in other words: affixes generally occur more frequently in the composition of compound hieroglyphs. Thus a study of the affixation facilitates a deeper penetration into the rules of construction of the Maya writing system, can indirectly connect isolated hieroglyphs, and, finally, can give rise to a sort of 'syntax' of hieroglyphic passages. It is here that one of the main thrusts of future research will be focused. Zimmermann's catalogue uses registration numbers for individual hieroglyphic sub-elements which are differentiated and grouped according to affixes or main signs of anthropomorphic, zoomorphic and geometric types. The manner in which the writing elements are combined in the formation of the hieroglyphs is indicated by dots or dashes between the registration numbers.

Unfortunately this catalogue, which is so satisfactory paleographically, has been pushed into the background by a further catalogue by Thompson (1962) which has the advantage of incorporating most of the epigraphic material. This unification was purchased, however, at the price of a completely new system of registration numbers for which a concordance list with the Zimmermann nomenclature gives no comfort, inasmuch as no decipherer can retain two completely different systems of enumeration of hieroglyphic elements in his memory at one and the same time. Furthermore, Thompson's catalogue is incomplete; the evidences for the occurrences of the important group of portraits of the deities is missing and the totality of the affix attestations can be revealed only indirectly. Controversies about the justification of 'splitting and lumping' of hieroglyphic sub-elements should disappear as the epigraphic research is refined further. Catalogue supplements for new inscriptions are indispensable and could be coupled with the elaboration of a real Corpus Inscriptionum Mayarum. Urgently needed, in addition, is access for all researchers to the texts in which the registered hieroglyphs are located. Even if Thompson's catalogue, despite the many years of work expended on it, has not yet achieved the desired completeness and precision, still it has proven to be exceedingly helpful even in the current stage of research for the rapid examination of textual cross-connections, and for a judgment as to the regional (but unfortunately not the temporal) dispersion as well as for a quantitative estimate covering the entire writing system of the Maya culture. Thompson enumerates a total figure of 862 hieroglyphic construction elements, including those types which are dubious. There are said to be 370 affixes with the main signs exceeding this by 30%. The number of main signs will probably exceed 500 when further anthropomorphic and zoomorphic portrait-glyphs, as well as forms which have not yet been inventoried – discovered at the new sites – are taken into consideration. Then, too, there is a part of the signs, no less limited, which occur only a single time. If such 'odd examples' are disregarded (some 80 affixes and 130 main signs), the total number still always works to be at least 650 hieroglyphic elements occurring in various constructions. This limit cannot be lowered any further and thus proves per se that the Maya writing cannot be an alphabet (requiring 20 to 40 signs) nor a syllabary (80 to 160 signs) but has to belong to the category of a 'word sign writing system'.

The constituent elements of the Maya writing system are divided into main signs and affixes. We call the smallest meaningful formal unit a 'grapheme'. A grapheme can have a certain amount of variation in its shape but does exist in a system of relationships to other graphemes. The graphemes follow certain rules of combination and arrangement, a fact that was already obvious from the formal analysis of the Maya hieroglyphs. Any further decomposition of a 'grapheme' into graphic sub-elements of signs generally destroys the semantic content of the grapheme and leads the decipherer away from the integral writing system into a 'world of subhieroglyphic forms'. Hermann Beyer, for example, has been taken in by this temptation for atomism.

The occurrence and distribution of the graphemes yield a statistical picture of the frequencies, favorite positions, and characteristic possibilities of substitution. A comprehensive 'study of the affix' — that is to say, an adequate investigation of the small signs in both the paleographic and the epigraphic material — has not been done, but such a study would afford considerable pre-orientation and clarification for the decipherment proper.

The solving of the Maya writing system is taking place at several levels of understanding. A basic distinction has to be made between 'interpretations' and 'readings'. 'Interpretations' are to a certain degree 'decipherings in the rough' established for a grapheme or compound hieroglyph by the analyst in a certain frame of reference. The degree of interpretation is variable: A good example of this is provided by the so-called 'positional meaning scheme' developed by Zimmermann which has been of value especially in paleography so far but which should be productive even for epigraphy. Sequences of hieroglyphic texts in the codices are often constructed according to a recurring pattern. In the first position in the 'sentence' are the so-called 'thematic hieroglyphs' which often correspond to a predicate. In the second position are the so-called 'nominal hieroglyphs' which designate the subject. The first position is occasionally expanded by the addition of hieroglyphs which give the object of the action or its setting. The second position can be supplemented by hieroglyphic titles or attributives. As for the latter of these, a group of 'attributive hieroglyphs' can be singled out which are often placed systematically at the end of a hieroglyphic sentence, unless this position is filled by a ritualistic expression (sacrifice offering hieroglyphs).

Thus it is often possible for the paleographer to obtain a first interpretation for the category just from the characteristic position in a hieroglyphic sentence. It appears, furthermore, that the graphemes are not distributed according to a choice of thematic, nominal, or attributive hieroglyphs but rather that they often display definite preferences. For example, the hand forms occur predominately as main signs in the first category and head variants in the second category. Also, with the aid of the 'positional meaning scheme', the framework of a rudimentary 'hieroglyphic syntax and grammar' can already be seen at an early stage of investigation. There are certain small signs which are always regulated by either thematic hieroglyphs or by nominal hieroglyphs. In the first instance, there is a limited number of frequently documented affixes (with prefixes occurring more frequently than suffixes) which can be interpreted as verbal formants and which serve to indicate a grammatical connection with the following hieroglyph. In the second instance, we are more likely to come upon affixes with a limited spread of occurrence which are occasionally so closely bound to the main sign of the nominal hieroglyphs that they can be taken as small signs serving as nominal indicators for a person or a deity. And, lastly, the logical exploitation of the positional meaning scheme makes it possible to differentiate the 'primary' and 'secondary' small signs from each other. A 'primary affix' is indispensable in the construction of compound hieroglyphs in which a new idea is thereby created or expressed. In other words: If a primary affix is detached from the other graphemes participating in the construction of a hieroglyph, then the meaning of the whole is lost. A 'secondary affix' on the other hand is not required inasmuch as its absence does not affect the core of the hieroglyphic statement. There are two reasons for this. It may be a matter of reflexes of a linguistic nature which can be interpreted as grammatical elements. Or it may be a matter of additions of artistic writing which function as 'reading aids' but whose use is absolutely facultative.

There is a distinct polarization of meanings in the group of the so-called 'attributive hieroglyphs'. One subgroup of attributive hieroglyphs appears exclusively in textual passages in association with the nominal hieroglyphs of the 'favorable' deities, while a second subgroup is always linked to 'unfavorable' deities. Thus we are able to differentiate the 'positive attributive hieroglyphs' from the 'negative attributive hieroglyphs' in the codices even at the stage of first interpretations before any kind of attempts at a reading are started. In addition, there is another less sharply distinguishable group that belongs here, one which is based not so much on a contrast between qualities as it is on a theme of an agrarian and meteorological nature.

The largest part of the paleographic material can be schematically grouped for the future 'reading' stage by a logical application of the so-called principles of arrangement and of interpretation. Some passages in the codices offer a certain resistance to the process and remain there, like erratic blocks, awaiting a solution. It seems as if it is a matter of expressions of some other topic, as is usually the case in the epigraphic material. A position scheme is applicable to the inscriptions whenever it is a matter of typical sequences of the 'thematic hieroglyph — nominal hieroglyph' type. Further principles of arrangement (clustering of titles, designations of place and kinship relationships, artifact and cult hieroglyphs, etc.) still have to be worked out laboriously in the field of epigraphy. The prospects for this can be said to be favorable.

Most of the specialists in this field probably agree on what has been covered up to this point in the analysis, namely on what we can call the 'structural interpretation process.' The difficulties and controversies start with the diverse suggestions proposed for the 'reading' proper, that is, for the replacement of graphemes by their oral equivalents.

Here we will have to differentiate some of the various complexes of problems and bring out some of the most important questions that are involved in the controversy:

1. Do the hieroglyphic components correspond to whole words, to simple syllables, or do they constitute an alphabet?

2. In compound hieroglyphs which consist of two or more graphemes:

a. Are the oral equivalents strung in a row without any sound loss?

b. At the points of connection is there any sort of fusion or overlapping, that is to say, a partial mutation (alteration or loss) of a final sound or of an initial sound?

c. Is there a system of abbreviation, corresponding to an acrophonic process, whereby only the initial sounds stand for something?

3. For compound hieroglyphs which consist of two or more graphemes, in which order are they read?

a. Does the order of reading correspond to the well known structuring of blocks of hieroglyphic texts from left to right (that is to say, prefix before main sign, or main sign before postfix) and from top to bottom (that is to say, superfix before main sign, or main sign before suffix)?

b. Does the order of reading start off with a main sign with the order based on the sequence of the affixes?

c. Is the order of reading 'arbitrary'; in other words, does the arrangement of the graphemes reflect some traditional, esthetically formal pattern which has nothing whatsoever to do with the order in which the spoken equivalents are uttered?

4. Is an ensemble of graphemes in a compound hieroglyph to be read always as purely 'additive', that is to say, as an accumulation of all the individual oral equivalents, or does one also have to take ideographic processes into account in which the graphemes form a sort of 'Gestalt'? In an 'integrative' reading two or more graphemes are not combined according to their individual sound values but rather express in combination an idea or situation with a new semantic value (example T 561 (544):526, 'sun' interpolated between 'heaven' and 'earth' does not result in an 'addition' of *kin* plus *caan* plus *caban* but rather results in 'integrating' the situation as 'the sun appears between earth and heaven', i.e., 'sunrise' *hatzcab*).

5. With which approach can the system of Maya hieroglyphs in general best reflect the language which forms its basis? The affixes which can be interpreted as grammatical particles are numerically far fewer than the prefixes or suffixes that are

in fact used in the Maya languages. The graphemes also do not occur in those frequencies and permutations which would soon be obvious even on an early analytical level in a syllabic system or an alphabetical system. If one accepts as a general rule that the normal spoken equivalent to a grapheme is a word, and if, furthermore, one brings into account the technique for a rendering of sounds which we call a 'rebus' process, then all of the homophones of the underlying language can be expressed. A strict homophony, by the way, has been authenticated in none of the Old World early writing systems which proceeded from picture to sound with the aid of a rebus process; they always admitted a certain degree of mere 'sound similarity' rather than a rigorous 'identical sound'. The field of possible relationships of meaning is thus broadened to that of 'homeophony'. We do not know a priori what degree of divergence in sound similarities the Maya writer felt was permissible. Puns from Maya texts of the post-Columbus period give a first inkling of the breadth possible in their homeophony. Partial writing systems, which imply a degree of permissible homeophony, are suitable for use as long as they function in passing down and commenting on the cultural pattern to which they owe their creation. For the present-day decipherer, such an obfuscation and paucity of the oral reflex naturally presents a considerable handicap since modern research can be enticed so easily into a morass of possible puns.

6. The question as to which stage of the language the Maya hieroglyphs are to be considered as coordinate is a paleolinguistic problem.

The first problem relates to time depth and the region of origin. Then too a portion or model from non-Maya languages would have to be taken into consideration for the moment of the creation and in the development of the writing system. Furthermore, one has to test the mutation or perseverance of language forms which are portrayed by specific graphemes, as well as the possible reflexes of local designations in the hieroglyphs that are confined to a specific subarea. A fundamental problem to be reckoned with is the growth of contradictions between the graphic forms and the linguistic content over the course of at least 1,200 years of hieroglyphic history. A key to the problem apparently lies in the spatial displacement of the use of hieroglyphs from an older center (Guatemala: Highlands/Pacific Coast) into the region of the classical golden age (the axis Palenque-Copan) and finally to a marginal province (Yucatan) where there was an encounter with Mexican foreign influence and a resultant syncretist decadence. From the point of view of incipient Maya research it was doubtless justified to start at first with the ethnolinguistic findings in Yucatan where a Maya culture using the writing system was still functioning at the time that the Spaniards arrived. But the greatest part of the possibilities contained in such source material have apparently been fully used and exhausted. Today we can state with confidence that Yucatan was NOT the area of origin of the Maya writing system but rather a late and historically accidental repository. Ethnolinguistic data ranging from the Chiapas tribes to the Chorti are coming more and more to the forefront as more worthwhile for new starts. The possibilities of obtaining readings of hieroglyphic components from the Maya languages of the uplands of Guatemala also appear noteworthy.

There still exists, however, at the current stage of investigation the danger of an inadmissible contamination from two different paths of research. It is important now to work hard with the aid of historical and comparative linguistic research to obtain the linguistic base of the Maya languages at a time depth of about 2,000 years in order to use reconstructed forms to tackle a correct time and place reading of the Maya hieroglyphs in the early stage of their invention and development. It is equally important that the epigraphic analysis should remain painstakingly separated from the linguistic analysis. According to our view, one should not start out with hypothetical attempts at reading the graphemes which then lead to the establishment of series of drifts right across the Maya languages, but rather first of all the linguistic reconstruction should be made, based on its own organic autonomies. The decipherer can then test out protoforms in the inscriptions. Of course, such reconstructed material is insufficient to probe the entire breadth of play of possible rebus readings, that is to say, the representation of identical sounding words or similar sounding words by a given grapheme. An etymological, semasiological comparative dictionary of the Maya languages is valuable in itself for its objective and beneficial contents, and its value in the hands of the decipherer working on a solution of the Maya writing system cannot be estimated too highly. Thus while 'interpretations' can be done independently by a researcher on writing systems with a knowledge of the techniques of writing analysis and a knowledge of the historical background of the ethnography and culture, he needs to work in close cooperation on specific systems with linguists in order to attain the goal of proper decipherment, i.e. correct 'readings'.

7. Partial writing systems can only be an extraction from the stream of tradition, and, thus, there is a need for additional sources of information. While the oral teachings in the Maya schools for priests and for scribes are forever lost to us (except for chance bits of isolated information in the ethnological material), we do have available an exceedingly valuable aid in the shape of the pictorial and iconographic representations. A hieroglyphic text never occurs in complete isolation in paleography, and seldom so in epigraphy. As a rule it is coupled with pictorial bits of evidence. The research on the codices, especially, has shown that this is not a simple parallelism between writing and pictures — wherein exactly the same information was merely repeated on two different levels — but rather a display of reciprocal interlocking and supplementation. In other words, the sequences of hieroglyphs are 'backed up' by expressions of imagery and the pictures are 'made clear and decreed' by the accompanying writings. Of course the image is oftentimes more than a mere 'illustration': It is frequently nothing less than a 'painted metaphor'. Figurative locutions from the language medium permeate the representations in the codices to a quite considerable extent. If, however, even the paleographic pictorial material is to be 'read' as pictorial homonyms and synonyms, this shows the compulsion there was to pass down meaningful and additional data that was beyond the capacity of the weaknesses

inherent in the Maya hieroglyphic system and shows furthermore a basic relationship in the techniques of expression. In other words: In the intimate coupling of imagery and writing we see a simple proof of the fact that the Maya hieroglyphs never attained that degree of sophistication required by a syllabic or entirely alphabetic writing system which alone would have allowed for an autonomous and complete representation of the transmission of speech.

8. A complete 'reading' of a hieroglyphic text is the prerequisite for a really profound interpretation. The Maya writing seems to be imbedded in a sort of priest language according to the results which have been achieved so far. There are serious obstacles blocking the real 'understanding' of the system due to the richness of metaphors and the techniques of paraphrasing and cover names. It reminds one of the so-called 'Language of Zuyûa', a knowledge of which was nothing less than a criterion for the right to inherit one of the positions of leadership. Even when we will have succeeded some day in reading the major portion of the Maya hieroglyphs, the investigation of the semantic content, of the ambiguities, and of the esoteric references will still be an especially difficult task.

9. The next task for the current stage of development in deciphering is to clarify whether or not the Maya writing shows evidences of multiple values or redundances, that is to say, pleonasms. Or more precisely:

a. Do we have to take polymorphy into account? That is, can various graphemes be identified which express the same sound value? In the Landa alphabet we are confronted with an apparent polymorphy (three graphemes for 'a', two graphemes for 'b', etc.), but it appears that the justification for the superficially similar arrangement of sound value and grapheme in this document has not been absolutely proven. Suggestions for decipherment which contain examples of polymorphy (e.g., Thompson's conjectures for affixes 'te 1', 'te 2' and 'te 3') apparently haven't met with much favor. On the other hand, there is one unique instance of polymorphy which can be characterized as the identifying property of the Maya writing system, namely the analogous possibilities of usage of geometrical signs and portraiture hieroglyphs.

b. Do we have to take redundancy into account? That is, is the multiple placement of a grapheme in a hieroglyphic construction to be understood as a repetition of the sound value of the same single grapheme, whether it be 'additive' or 'integrating' at a new level of meaning? Or does it retain the original simple communicative value with the multiple placement merely fulfilling a formal function, that is, some sort of graphic composition technique? Or does the first of the aforementioned apply only to the main signs, and the second only to the small signs? This group would also have to take into account graphemes which are utilized but which are not to be read with the proper sound value. The function of such 'reading aids' would probably consist in helping to make the proper selection when polyphonous main signs were involved. There are even other types of 'pleonastic writings' which cannot be excluded a priori when one thinks about the Aztec examples.

c. Do we have to take polyphony into account? That is, are there graphemes which have various sound values (over and beyond plain homeophony) which are demonstrable in various compositae? Suggestions for polyphonous readings pertain first and foremost to the main signs which function on the one hand especially in the make up of calendaric hieroglyphs and on the other hand in the non-calendaric hieroglyphs. Is such a polyphony historically conditioned (a frozen sound value dating from the beginning stage of development of the Maya hieroglyphs plus another sound value introduced later for other functions within the further developed writing system) or is it an obligatory part of the system itself? It is evident that there is a lack of suggestions concerning the polyphony of affixes. What also has to be tested out is where the boundary of a given postulated polyphony is situated, that is to say, whether clues exist to indicate that there are *more than two* different sound values for the same main sign.

Despite the dangers inherent in making scientific predictions, one dares, even in a most sober assessment of the state of research, to look forward with justified optimism to further advances in the decipherment of the Maya hieroglyphs. The situation has changed greatly since 1945 when Paul Schellhas, after a lifetime devoted to studies of Maya, stated that the Maya hieroglyphs are an insoluble problem. A painstaking re-evaluation of past achievements, a critical separation of the controversial integrations, and improvements in new methods and tools all promise, during the next decade, to bring into sharper focus the way of thinking of the Ancient American world.

BIBLIOGRAPHY

I. *South American Writing Systems*

Barthel, Thomas, 'Bemerkungen zu einem astronomischen Quipu aus Südperu', *Ethnos* 16.153-70 (1951).

——, 'Zwei problematische Schrifttafeln von der Osterinsel', *Z Ethn* 81.287-92 (1956).

——, 'Neues zur Osterinselschrift', *Z Ethn* 84.161-72 (1959).

——, 'Vorläufige Ergebnisse bei der Entzifferung der Kohau-Rongorongo von der Osterinsel', *PICAm* 32. 500-07 (1956). (= 'Resultados preliminares del desciframiento de las Kohau-Rongorongo de la Isla de Pascua', *Runa* 7.233-41 (1956)).

——, *Grundlagen zur Entzifferung der Osterinselschrift* (Hamburg, 1958).

——, 'Diskussionsbemerkungen zu einem Rongorongo-Text', *AEH* 12.65-83 (1963).

——, 'Rongorongo-Studien (Forschungen und Fortschritte bei der weiteren Entzifferung der Osterinselschrift)', *Anthropos* 58.372-436 (1963).

Butinov, N., 'Predvaritel'noe soobščenie ob izučenii pis'mennosti ostrova Pashi', *Sov Ethn* 4.77-91 (1956).

——, 'Ieroglifičeskie teksty ostrova Pashi-Rapanui', *Vestnik istorii* 3.69-80 (1959).

Butinov, N. and Knorozov, Yuri, 'Preliminary report on the study of the written language of Easter Island', *JPS* 66.5-17 (1957).

Heine-Geldern, Robert, 'La escritura de la isla de Pascua y sus relaciones con otras escrituras', *Runa* 8.5-27 (1956-57).

Heyerdahl, Thor, *American Indians in the Pacific* (London, 1952).

Holmer, Nils, Miranda Rivera, Porfirio and Ryden, Stig, 'A modelled picture-writing from the Kechua Indians', *Ethnos* 16.171-84 (1951).

Holmer, Nils and Wassén, Henry, *The complete Mu-igala in picture writing. A native record of a Cuna Indian medicine song* (= *Etnologiska Studier* 21) (Göteborg, 1953).

——, *Dos Cantos Shamanísticos de los Indios Cunas* (= *Etnologiska Studier* 27) (Göteborg, 1963).

Ibarra Grasso, Dick, 'La escritura indigena Andina', *AnnLat* 12.9-124 (1948).

——, 'La escritura jeroglífica de los indios andinos', *CA* 15.157-72 (1956).

Lanyon-Orgill, Peter, 'A catalogue of the inscribed tablets and other artifacts from Easter Island', *JAS* 1.20-39 (1956).

——, 'Addenda to the catalogue of the inscribed tablets and other artifacts from Easter Island', *JAS* 2.15-17 (1958).

Nordenskiöld, Erland, *Picture-writings and other documents by Nele, Paramount Chief of the Cuna Indians, and Ruben Perez Kantule, his Secretary* (= *Comparative Ethnographical Studies*) 7:1 (Göteborg, 1928).

——, *Picture-writings and other documents by Nele, Charles Slater, Charlie Nelson, and other Cuna Indians* (= *Comparative Ethnographical Studies* 7:2) (Göteborg, 1930).

Nordenskiöld, Erland and Wassén, Henry, *An historical and ethnological survey of the Cuna Indians* (= *Comparative Ethnographical Studies* 10) (Göteborg, 1938).

Rowe, John, 'Inca culture at the time of the Spanish Conquest'', *HSAI* 2.183-330 (1946).

Wassén, Henry, *Contributions to Cuna ethnography* (= *Etnologiska Studier* 16) (Göteborg, 1949).

II. *Mexican Writing Systems*

Barlow, Robert and MacAfee, Byron, *Diccionario de elementos fonéticos en escritura jeroglífica* (*códice mendocino*) (Mexico, 1949).

Burland, Cottie, 'Einige Bemerkungen über den Codex Vindobonensis Mexic. 1', *Arch V* 2. 101-07 (1948).

——, 'Town foundation dates and historical cross references in Mixtec codices', *AIAK* 34.665-69 (1962).

Burland, Cottie and Kutscher, Gerdt, *The Selden Roll* (= *Monumenta Americana* 2) (Berlin, 1955).

Caso, Alfonso, *Las estelas zapotecas* (Mexico, 1928).

——, 'Calendario y escritura de las antiguas culturas de Monte Albán', *Obras completas de Miguel Othón de Mendizabal* (Mexico, 1947).

——, 'El mapa de Teozacoalco', *CA* 8.145-82 (1949).
——, 'Explicación del Reverso del Codex Vindobonensis', *Memoria de El Colegio Nacional* 5:5.1-46 (1951).
——, 'Base para la sincronología mixteca y cristiana', *Memorias de El Colegio Nacional* 6:6.49-66 (1952).
——, *Interpretacion del Códice Gomez de Orozco* (Mexico, 1954).
——, 'Comentario al Codice Baranda', *Miscellanea Paul Rivet octogenario dedicata* 1.372-93 (Mexico, 1958).
——, 'El calendario mexicano', *Memorias de la Academia Mexicana de la Historia* 17.41-96 (1958).
——, 'Glifos teotihuacanos', *RMEA* 15.51-70 (1959).
——, 'Nuevos datos para la correlación de los años aztecas y christiano', *Estudios de Cultura Nahuatl* 1.9-25 (1959).
——, 'Valor histórico de los códices mixtecos', *CA* 19.139-47 (1960).
——, *Interpretacion del Códice Bodley* 2858 (Mexico, 1960).
——, 'Calendario y escritura en Xochicalco', *RMEA* 18.49-80 (1962).
——, 'Los Señores de Yanhuitlan', *ACIA* 35:1.437-48 (1964).
Dark, Phillip, *Mixtec ethnohistory: A method of analysis of the codical art* (Oxford, 1958).
——, 'Evidence for the date of painting and provenience of Codex Selden and Codex Bodley', *ACIA* 33 :2.523-29 (1959).
——, 'El antiguo sistema de escritura en México', *RMEA* 4.105-28 (1940).
——, *Códice Xolotl* (= *Publicaciones del Instituto de Historia* 22) (Mexico, 1951).
——, 'Spanish influence of the Aztec writing system', *Homenaje a R. Garcia Granados* 171-77 (Mexico, 1960).
——, 'Glifos fonéticos del Códice Florentino', *Estudios de Cultura Nahuatl* 4.55-60 (1963).
Franco, José Luis, 'La escritura y los códices', *Esplendor del México Antiguo* 1.361-78 (Mexico, 1959).
Kirchhoff, Paul, 'Calendarios tenochca, tlatelolca y otros', *RMEA* 15.257-67 (1954-55).
Kubler, George and Gibson, Charles, *The Tovar Calendar* (= *Memoirs of the Connecticut Academy of Arts and Sciences* 11) (New Haven, 1951).
Mengin, Ernst, 'Commentaire du Codex Mexicanus nos. 23-4', *JSAm* 41.387-498 (1952).
Miles, Suzanne, 'Sculpture of the Guatemala-Chiapas Highlands and Pacific slopes, and associated hieroglyphs', manuscript prepared for *Handbook of Middle American Indians.*
Nicholson, H. B., 'The Mesoamerican pictorial manuscripts: Research, past and present', *AIAK* 34.199-215 (1962).
Novotny, Karl, 'Erläuterungen zum Codex Vindobonensis (Vorderseite)', *Arch V* 3.125-200 (1948).
——, 'Der Codex Becker II', *Arch V* 12.172-81 (1957).

——, 'Die Bilderfolge des Codex Vindobonensis und verwandter Handschriften', *Arch V* 13.210-21 (1958).

——, 'Die Hieroglyphen des Codex Mendoza. Der Bau einer mittelamerikanischen Wortschrift', *Mitteilungen, Museum für Völkerkunde Hamburg* 25.97-113 (1959).

——, *Tlacuilolli. Die mexikanischen Bilderhandschriften, Stil und Inhalt* (= *Monumenta Americana* 3) (Berlin, 1961).

——, 'Der Bau der mexikanischen Hieroglyphen', *VIe Congrès International des Sciences Anthropologiques et Ethnologiques* 451-55 (Paris, 1963).

Robertson, Donald, *Mexican manuscript painting of the early colonial period: The metropolitan schools* (New Haven, 1959).

——, 'Los manuscritos religiosos Mixtecos', *ACIA* 35:1.425-35 (1964).

Ruz Lhuillier, Alberto, 'La escritura indígena', *México Prehispánico* 685-93 (Mexico, 1946).

Sáenz, César, 'Las estelas de Xochicalco', *ACIA* 35-2.69-84 (1964).

——, 'Tres estelas en Xochicalco', *RMEA* 17.39-66 (1961).

——, *Xochicalco. Temporada 1960* (= *Instituto Nacional de Antropología e Historia, Informes*, No. 11) (Mexico, 1962).

Spinden, Herbert, 'Indian manuscripts of southern Mexico', *Smithsonian Institution Annual Reports* 429-51 (1933).

Spranz, Bodo, *Göttergestalten in den mexikanischen Bilderhandschriften der Codex Borgia-Gruppe* (= *Acta Humboldtiana, Series Geographica et Ethnographica* Nr. 4) (Wiesbaden, 1964).

Sydow, Eckart von, 'Studien zur Form und Form-Geschichte der mexikanischen Bilderhandschriften', *Z Ethn* 72.197-234 (1941).

Thompson, Eric, *Dating of certain inscriptions of non-Maya origin* (= *Theoretical Approaches to Problems* 1) (Carnegie Institution, Washington, 1941).

Winning, Hasso von, 'Teotihuacan symbols: The reptile's eye glyph', *Ethnos* 26.121-66 (1961).

III. *Maya Hieroglyphic Writing*

Andrews, Wyllys, 'The Maya supplementary series', *PICAm* 29:1.123-41 (1949).

Araujo, R., Rodríguez, M. and Solis, H., *I Chol Kin* (Mérida, 1965).

Barrera Vásquez, Alfredo, 'Investigaciones de la escritura de los antiguos mayas con máquinas calculadoras electrónicas: Síntesis y glosa', *Estudios de Cultura Maya* 2.319-42 (1962).

Barthel, Thomas, *Studien zur Entzifferung astronomischer, augurischer und kalendarischer Kapitel in der Dresdener Mayahandschrift* (Dissertation, Philosophische Fakultät, Universität Hamburg, 1952).

——, 'Maya epigraphy: Some remarks on the affix "al"', *PICAm* 30.45-9 (1952).

——, 'Der Morgensternkult in den Darstellungen der Dresdener Mayahandschrift', *Ethnos* 17.73-112 (1952).

——, 'Regionen des Regengottes', *Ethnos* 18.86-105 (1953).

——, 'Versuch über die Inschriften von Chich'en Itzà Viejo', *Baessler-Archiv N.F.* 3.5-33 (1955).

——, 'Die gegenwärtige Situation in der Erforschung der Maya-Schrift', *JSAm* 45.219-27 (1956). (= *PICAm* 32.476-84 (1956)). 'El estado actual en la investigación de la escritura Maya', *Boletín del Centro de Investigaciones Antropológicas de México* 4.19-28 (1957).

——, 'Die Stele 31 von Tikal', *Tribus* 12.159-214 (1963).

——, 'Comentarios a las inscripciones clásicas tardias de Chich'en-Itzá', *Estudios de Cultura Maya* 4.223-44 (1964).

——, 'Gedanken zu einer bemalten Schale aus Uaxactun', *Baessler-Archiv N.F.* 13.131-70 (1965).

Berlin, Heinrich, 'El glifo "emblema" en las inscripciones Mayas', *JSAm*47.111-19 (1958).

——, 'Glifos Nominales en el Sarcófago de Palenque', *Humanidades* 2:10.1-8 (1959).

——, 'Actualidades de la Epigrafía Maya', *Antropologia e Historia de Guatemala* 14.32-7 (1962).

——, 'The Palenque Triad', *JSAm* 52.91-9 (1963).

——, 'The inscription of the Temple of the Cross at Palenque', *AA* 30.330-42 (1965).

Berlin, Heinrich and Kelley, David, 'The 819-day count and color-direction symbolism among the classic Maya', *Middle American Research Institute* 26.9-20 (1961).

Beyer, Hermann, *Studies on the inscriptions of Chichen Itza* (= *Carnegie Institution Washington Publication 483*, *Contribution 21*) (Washington, 1937).

Coe, Michael, 'Cycle 7 monuments in Middle America: A reconsideration', *AA* 59.597-611 (1957).

Cook de Leonard, Carmen, 'Dos extraordinarias vasijas del Museo de Villa Hermosa (Tabasco)', *Yan* No. 3.83-104 (1954).

Cordan, Wolfgang, *Götter and Göttertiere der Maya* (Bern-München, 1963).

——, *Introduccion a los Glifos Mayas* (*Sistema de Mérida*) (Mérida, 1963).

——, *La Clave de los Glifos Mayas* (Mérida, 1964).

Cordy, Napoleon, 'Examples of phonetic construction in Maya hieroglyphs', *AA* 108-17 (1964).

Evreinov, E., Kosarev, Y. and Ustinov, V., *Primenenie elektronnyx wytschiliteljnix maschin b issledowanij pijsmennosti drewnyx Maia*, 3 Vols. (Akademija Nauk CCCR-Sibirskoje otedelenie) (Novosibirsk, 1961).

Genet, Jean, 'Les glyphes symboliques dans l'écriture maya-quichée. Le glyph symbolique de la guerre', *REMQ* 1.23-7 (1934).

——, 'L'écriture maya-quichée et les glyphes phonétiques', *REMQ* 1.37-63 (1934).

Graham, John, 'Sobre la escritura maya', *Desarrollo Cultural de los Mayas* 243-54 (Mexico, 1964).

Kelley, David, 'Fonetismo en la escritura Maya', *Estudios de Cultura Maya* 2.277-317 (1962).

——, 'Glyphic evidence for a dynastic sequence at Quirigua, Guatemala', *AA* 27.323-35 (1962).

——, 'A History of the decipherment of Maya script', *AnL* 4. 1-48 (1962).

Knorozov, Yuri, 'Drevnaja pis'mennost' Central'noj Ameriki', *Sov Etn* 3.100-18 (1952). (= 'La antigua escritura de los pueblos de America Central') (Mexico, 1954).

——, 'Pis'mennost' drevnih Maija (opyt rasšifrovki)', (= *Ancient Maya writing; attempt at decipherment*) *Sov Etn* 1.94-125 (1955).

——, *Sistema pis'ma drevnih maija* (= *La escritura de los antiguos Mayas*) (Moskau, 1955).

——, 'New data on the Maya written language', *JSAm* 45.209-16 (1956). (= *PICAm* 32.467-75 (1956)).

——, 'The problem of the study of the Maya hieroglyphic writing', *AA* 23.284-91 (1958).

——, 'La lengua de los textos jeroglíficos mayas', *ACIA* 33:2.571-79 (1959).

——, *Pis'mennost' indeizev Maija* (Moscow, 1963).

——, 'Aplicación de las matematicas al estudio lingüistico', *Estudios de Cultura Maya* 3.169-85 (1963).

Lizardi Ramos, Cesar, 'Los jeroglíficos Mayas y su descifración', *Esplendor del México Antiguo* 1.243-62 (Mexico, 1959).

Long, Richard, 'Maya and Mexican Writing', *Maya Research* 2.24-32 (1935).

——, 'Maya writing and its decipherment', *Maya Research* 3.309-15 (1936).

Makemson, Maud, *The Maya Correlation Problem* (Vassar College Observatory, Publications V) (Poughkeepsie, 1946).

——, *The miscellaneous dates of the Dresden Codex* (Vassar College Observatory, Publications VI) (New York, 1957).

Maler, Teobert, *Researches in the central portion of the Usumatsintla Valley* (Piedras Negras, Chinikiha, etc.) (= *Memoirs of the Peabody Museum of Harvard University* 2:1) (Cambridge, 1901).

——, *Researches in the central portion of the Usumatsintla Valley* (*Memoirs of the Peabody Museum of Harvard University* 2:2) (Cambridge, 1903).

Maudslay, A. P., *Archaeology. Biologia Centrali-Americana*, 5 Vols. (London, 1889-1902).

Morley, Sylvanus, *The inscriptions at Copán* (= *Carnegie Institution Washington Publication* 219) (Washington, 1920).

——, *The inscriptions of Petén* (= *Carnegie Institution Washington Publication* 437, 5 Vols.) (Washington, 1937-1938).

Proskouriakoff, Tatiana, 'Historical implications of a pattern of dates at Piedras Negras, Guatemala', *AA* 25.454-75 (1960).

——, 'Portraits of women in Maya art', *Essays in pre-Columbian art and archaeology* 81-99 (Cambridge, Mass., 1961).

——, 'The lords of the Maya realm', *Expedition* 4:1.14-21 (1961).

——, 'Historical data in the inscriptions of Yaxchilan. Part I: The reign of Shield-Jaguar', *Estudios de Cultura Maya* 3.149-67 (1963).

——, 'Historical data in the inscriptions of Yaxchilan. Part II: The reigns of Bird-Jaguar and his successors', *Estudios de Cultura Maya* 4.177-201 (1964).

Sächsische Landesbilbiothek Dresden, Ed., *Maya-Handschrift der Sächsischen Landesbibliothek, Dresden* (Berlin, 1962).

Sáenz, César, *Exploraciones en la pirámide de la Cruz Foliada* (= *Instituto Nacional de Antropologia e Historia Informes*, No. 5) (Mexico, 1956).

Satterthwaite, Linton, *Concepts and structures of Maya calendrical arithmetics* (Philadelphia, 1947).

——, 'The dark phase of the moon and ancient Maya methods of solar eclipse prediction', *AA* 14.230-34 (1949).

——, 'Moon ages of the Maya inscriptions; The problem of their seven-day range of deviation from calculated mean ages', *PICAm* 29:1.142-54 (1949).

——, 'Radiocarbon dates and the Maya correlation problem', *AA* 21.416-19 (1956).

——, 'Five newly discovered carved monuments at Tikal and new data on four others', *Museum Monographs, Tikal Reports*, No. 4 (Philadelphia, 1958).

——, 'Early "uniformity" Maya moon numbers at Tikal and elsewhere', *ACIA* 33:2.200-10 (1959).

——, 'An appraisal of a new Maya-Christian calendar correlation', *Estudios de Cultura Maya* 2.251-75 (1962).

——, 'Note on hieroglyphs on bone from the tomb below Temple I, Tikal', *Expedition* 6.18-19 (1963).

——, 'Calendrics of the Lowland Maya', Manuscript prepared for *Handbook of Middle American Indians.*

Satterthwaite, Linton and Ralph, E. K., 'New radiocarbon dates and the Maya correlation problem', *AA* 26.165-84 (1960).

Schellhas, Paul, 'Die Entzifferung der Mayahieroglyphen ein unlösbares Problem?' *Ethnos* 10.44-53 (1945).

Smith, Robert, *Ceramic sequence at Uaxactún, Guatemala* (Middle American Research Institute, Tulane University Publication 20, 2 vols.) (New Orleans, 1955).

Termer, Franz, *Die Mayaforschung* (Nova Acta Leopoldina Board 15, No. 105) (Leipzig, 1952).

Thompson, Eric, *The fish as a Maya symbol for counting and further discussion of directional glyphs* (= *Theoretical Approaches to Problems* 2) (Carnegie Institution, Washington, 1944).

——, *Maya hieroglyphic writing*: *Introduction*, Publication 589 (Carnegie Institution, Washington, 1950).

——, 'Aquatic symbols common to various centers of the classic period in Meso-America', *PICAm* 29:1.31-6 (1951).

——, 'La inscripción jeroglífica del Tablero de El Palacio, Palenque', *AnINA* 4.61-8 (1952).

——, Review of Knorozov's 'La Antigua Escritura de los pueblos de America Central', *Yan* 2.174-78 (1953).
——, 'Research in Maya hieroglyphic writing', in Willey, Gordon, *Middle American anthropology* 43-52 (Washington, 1958).
——, 'Symbols, glyphs, and divinatory almanacs for diseases in the Maya Dresden and Madrid codices', *AA* 23.297-308 (1958).
——, 'Systems of hieroglyphic writing in Middle America and methods of deciphering them', *AA* 24.349-64 (1959).
——, 'A blood-drawing ceremony painted on a Maya vase', *Estudios de Cultura Maya* 1.13-20 (1961).
——, *A Catalog of Maya Hieroglyphs* (University of Oklahoma Press, Norman, 1962).
——, 'Pictorial synonyms and homonyms in the Maya Dresden Codex', *Tl* 4.148-56 (1963).
——, 'Algunas consideraciones respecto al desciframiento de los jeroglificos Mayas', *Estudios de Cultura Maya* 3.119-48 (1963).
Ulving, T. 'A new decipherment of the Maya glyphs', *Ethnos* 20.152-58 (1954).
Voegelin, C. F., and F. M., 'Typological classification of systems with included, excluded, and self-sufficient alphabets", *AnL* 3.55-96 (1961).
Whorf, Benjamin Lee, *The Phonetic value of certain characters in Maya writing* (= *Papers of the Peabody Museum of American Archaeology and Ethnology* 13:2) (1933).
——, 'Maya writing and its decipherment', *Maya Research* 2.367-82 (1935).
——, 'Decipherment of the linguistic portion of the Maya hieroglyphs', *Annual Report* 479-502 (Smithsonian Institution, Washington, 1942).
Zimmermann, Günter, *Kurze Formen- und Begriffssystematik der Hieroglyphen der Mayahandschriften* (= *Beiträge zur mittelamerikanischen Völkerkunde I*) (Hamburg, 1953).
——, 'Notas para la historia de los manuscritos Mayas', *Yan* 3.62-4 (1954).
——, *Die Hieroglyphen der Maya-Handschriften* (Hamburg, 1956).
——, 'La escritura jeroglífica y el calendario como indicadores de tendencias de la historia cultural de los Mayas', *Desarrollo cultural de los Mayas* 229-42 (Mexico, 1964).

DESCRIPTIVE LINGUISTICS

JOSEPH E. GRIMES

When Franz Boas introduced the first volume of the *International Journal of American Linguistics* he had to write: '... it is not saying too much if we claim that for most of the native languages of Central and South America the field is practically *terra incognita*. We have vocabularies; but, excepting the old missionary grammars, there is very little systematic work. Even where we have grammars, we have no bodies of aboriginal texts.'[1] The first number of *IJAL* contains a brief but systematic description by Boas himself,[2] and the first two volumes contain four more contributions of the kind Boas asked for.

Since then descriptive linguistics in Latin America has flourished. Vocabularies continue to be produced; grammars in whole or in part are common; entire text collections have been published for numerous languages. This florescence of descriptive studies can be attributed to the vigorous efforts of national institutions, such as the Instituto Nacional de Antropología e Historia of Mexico, the Comisión Indigenista of Venezuela, the Museu Nacional of Brazil, and similar institutions associated with the ministries of education of other nations. International organizations like the Summer Institute of Linguistics and the Instituto Indigenista Interamericano, which sponsor field work in a number of countries, have been an important factor in this growth in the field. Several North American universities have carried on research programs that touch indigenous languages of the area, notably California, Chicago, Cornell, Indiana, Pennsylvania, and Texas.

Periodicals in which descriptive statements on Latin American languages appear include not only *IJAL*, which specializes in such statements, but also *Acta Linguistica, American Anthropologist, América Indígena, Anales del Instituto Nacional de Antropología e Historia* (Mexico), *Anthropological Linguistics, Archivum Linguisticum, Boletín Indigenista, Boletín Indigenista Venezolano, Investigaciones Lingüísticas, Journal de la Société des Américanistes, Kroeber Anthropological Society Publications, Language, Lingua, Lingua Posnaniensis, Linguistics, El México Antiguo, Miscellanea Phonetica, Phonetica, Proceedings* of the International Congresses of Phonetic Sciences, of the International Congresses of Linguists, of the International Congresses of Americanists, *Revista Colombiana de Antropología, Revista Mexicana de Estudios Antropológicos,*

[1] *IJAL* 1.1-8 (1917).

[2] 'El dialecto mexicano de Pochutla, Oaxaca', *IJAL* 1.9-44 (1917).

Studies in Linguistics, Southwestern Journal of Anthropology, Tlalocan, Word, and *Zeitschrift für Phonetik, Sprachwissenschaft und Kommunikationsforschung.* Many universities, museums, and Indian institutes issue bulletins from time to time that contain descriptive material. The *Summer Institute of Linguistics Publications in Linguistics and Related Fields* is a series of monographs almost exclusively dedicated to descriptions made in Latin America; with it is associated a *Serie de Vocabularios Indígenas 'Mariano Silva y Aceves'*. For bibliographic reference the annual *Bibliographie linguistique publiée par le Comité International Permanent des Linguistes* gives coverage in a section on 'Langues Américaines', and the occasional *Bibliography of the Summer Institute of Linguistics* (latest edition dated February 1964) gives a cumulative list of all publications of the Institute's members. *Dissertation Abstracts* contains abstracts of all doctoral dissertations from a number of North American universities, including some on Latin American languages; *Linguistics* also reports dissertations occasionally.

In discussing the current status of descriptive linguistics and the trends the field is taking, then, there is no longer any need to sound as forlorn about the state of things as Boas did in 1917. On the contrary; the problem now is to maintain reasonably complete coverage of the field. In this chapter there is no attempt to mention every descriptive work published on an indigenous language of Latin America, but only to evaluate trends and emphases, citing works that are representative of schools of thought.

The kind of descriptive work done most recently in Latin America has varied in emphasis, depending partly on the end for which the studies were done and in even greater part on the theoretical interests at the moment of the analyst and his circle of colleagues. Thus, a number of descriptive studies have taken shape during the pursuit of some formulation of linguistic theory, while others during the course of field research have brought to light phenomena that required a revision of existing theory in order to account for them. Even these studies, however, reflect the Boasian bias toward getting on record all the data possible from as many languages as possible. Many other studies are routinely Boasian; they do not purport to form part of the continuing debate on the nature of human language, but only to report what the field worker hears and sees. A few studies have been made as preliminary to other linguistic work: preparation of language teaching materials, for example, or comparative linguistic studies.

I. PHONOLOGICAL THEORY

Theories concerning the nature of phonology and its relationship to the rest of language have been tested extensively on Latin American languages. At the same time, some developments in phonological theory have been required by the nature of some of the language systems observed, so that previously unnoticed phenomena could be described adequately.

The best illustration of this interplay between the growth of a theoretical position and the empirical requirement that all languages studied be adequately described is the work of Pike and his associates. The first attempted description in phonology by this group was McIntosh's 'Huichol phonemes', which appeared in 1945, prepared under Pike's guidance.[3] The approach to phonology used there and in subsequent papers from the same period was substantially the one embodied in Pike's *Phonemics* of 1947, a sequentially oriented approach to phonemicizing on the basis of relationships among neighboring phonetic segments.[4] Many descriptions of phonological systems were made using this approach, not only by members of the Summer Institute of Linguistics but also by linguists such as Hildebrandt in Macoita and Hawkins in Waiwai.[5]

A year after *Phonemics*, Pike set forth in *Tone Languages* a methodology that proved helpful in investigating systems of tonal contrasts in a number of languages.[6] He included in this book not only an exposition of his method but also two monograph-length appendices that describe in detail the phonology and the tonal morphophonemics of two Mexican languages. With Eunice V. Pike he also published 'Immediate constituents of Mazateco syllables',[7] which became the model for the development of a hierarchical view of phonological structure. Hockett, although disagreeing vigorously with Pike concerning what the latter insisted were 'grammatical prerequisites to phonemic analysis',[8] took up the hierarchical model in his *Manual of Phonology*,[9] which itself became the basis for several descriptions of phonological systems of Latin American languages.[10] Pike attempted to integrate a hierarchical view of phonology with a general theory of linguistics in 1954.[11] The first description of a Latin American phonological system produced under the impact of his general theory was the McArthurs' 'Aguacatec (Mayan) phonemes within the stress group', in which stress

[3] John B. McIntosh, 'Huichol phonemes', *IJAL* 11.31-5 (1945).

[4] Kenneth L. Pike, *Phonemics: a technique for reducing languages to writing* (Ann Arbor, 1947).

[5] Martha Hildebrandt, *Sistema fonémico del Macoita* (Caracas, 1958). W. Neill Hawkins, *A fonologia da língua uáiuái* (São Paulo, 1952).

[6] Kenneth L. Pike, *Tone languages: a technique for determing the number and type of pitch contrasts in a language, with studies in tonemic substitution and fusion* (Ann Arbor, 1948).

[7] 'Immediate constituents of Mazateco syllables', *IJAL* 13.78-91 (1947).

[8] Kenneth L. Pike, 'Grammatical prerequisites to phonemic analysis', *Word* 3.155-72 (1947). Charles F. Hockett, 'Two fundamental problems in phonemics', *SIL* 7.29-51 (1949). Pike, 'More on grammatical prerequisites', *Word* 8.106-21 (1952). In perspective it appears that both Pike and Hockett were reacting to high level phonological phenomena without recognizing them as such at the time. Now that they are explicitly taken into account in phonological analysis, this debate has lost most of its significance.

[9] Charles F. Hockett, *A manual of phonology* (=Memoir 11 of the International Journal of American Linguistics, Part I of *IJAL* 21:4) (Baltimore, 1955).

[10] Frank E. Robbins, 'Quiotepec Chinantec syllable patterning', *IJAL* 27.237-50 (1961). Robbins, 'Palabras nasales sin vocales fonéticas en el chinanteco de Quiotepec', *A William Cameron Townsend en el Vigésimoquinto Aniversario del Instituto Lingüístico de Verano* 653-6 (México, 1961). Joseph E. Grimes, 'Huichol tone and intonation', *IJAL* 25.221-32 (1959).

[11] Kenneth L. Pike, *Language in relation to a unified theory of the structure of human behavior* (Glendale, Part 1, 1954; Part 2, 1955; Part 3, 1960). Part 2 is especially concerned with phonology.

group boundaries, rather than grammatical word boundaries, were recognized as a conditioning environment for allophonic variation.[12]

In the analysis of some Indian languages of Peru, in which teams of field investigators worked intensively for several months under Pike's personal guidance, problems came to be recognized concerning the nature of peak and boundary phenomena at higher phonological levels: the possibility that complex foot nuclei consisting of several syllables might have to be recognized in Campa,[13] problems in locating syllable boundaries in Huitoto,[14] and a previously unreported kind of contrast — ballistic versus controlled feet — in Arabela.[15] Not long after this, Crawford, while studying under Pike, attempted to combine certain refinements in Pike's phonological theory with a descriptive dissertation, *Totontepec Mixe phonotagmemics*.[16]

The approach to phonology pioneered by J. R. Firth in Great Britain has been applied in the field of Latin American linguistics in a limited way, notably by Callow in Apinayé and by Bendor-Samuel in Terena.[17] The Terena data have also been discussed from within the Pike-Hockett tradition by Ekdahl and Grimes.[18]

Of other theoretical trends in phonology that are reasonably easy to identify and label, the generative theories of Chomsky are only beginning to be applied to indigenous languages of Latin America. To date nothing has appeared in print.

New linguistic phenomena have turned up in the process of field work in Latin America. They have had a tendency to stretch existing views of language in one direction or another, with the result that any workable linguistic theory must now be able to span a wider typological range than formerly. Among these phenomena can be mentioned the five-way pitch contrasts of Trique and Ticuna,[19] the five-way contrastive system of nasals in Pehuenche,[20] the complex structure of the foot in Shiriana,[21] the influence of syntactic as well as morphological factors in tonal morphophonemics in Huave and Northern Tepehuan,[22] phonetically atypical but distributionally plausi-

[12] Harry and Lucille McArthur, 'Aguacatec (Mayan) phonemes within the stress group', *IJAL* 22.72-6 (1956).

[13] Kenneth L. Pike and Willard Kindberg, 'A problem in multiple stresses', *Word* 12.415-28 (1956).

[14] Eugene Minor, 'Witoto vowel clusters', *IJAL* 22.131-7 (1956).

[15] Kenneth L. Pike, 'Abdominal pulse types in some Peruvian languages', *Lg* 33.30-5 (1957).

[16] John Chapman Crawford, *Pike's tagmemic model applied to Totontepec Mixe phonology* (University of Michigan doctoral dissertation, 1959), reissued as *Totontepec Mixe phonotagmemics* (Norman, Oklahoma, 1963).

[17] John Campbell Callow, *The Apinayé language: phonology and grammar* (University of London, 1962). John T. Bendor-Samuel, 'Some problems of segmentation in the phonological analysis of Terena', *Word* 16.348-55 (1960). Bendor-Samuel, 'Stress in Terena', *Transactions of the Philological Society* (1962), 105-23.

[18] Muriel Ekdahl and Joseph E. Grimes, 'Terena verb inflection', *IJAL* 30.261-8 (1964).

[19] Robert E. Longacre, 'Five phonemic pitch levels in Trique', *Acta Linguistica* 7.62-81 (1952). Lambert Anderson, 'Ticuna vowels with special regard to the system of five tonemes', 76-119 *Publicações do Museu Nacional* (Rio de Janeiro, 1959).

[20] Jorge A. Suárez, 'The phonemes of an Araucanian dialect', *IJAL* 25.177-81 (1959).

[21] Ernest Migliazza and Joseph E. Grimes, 'Shiriana phonology', *AnL* 3:6.31-41 (1961).

[22] Kenneth L. Pike and Milton Warkentin, 'Huave, a study in syntactic tone with low lexical functional load', *A William Cameron Townsend en el Vigésimoquinto Aniversario del Instituto Lingüístico de Verano* 627-42 (México, 1961). Burton Bascom, 'Tonomechanics of Northern Tepehuan', *Phonetica* 4.71-88 (1959).

ble variants of phonemes in Amuesha and Maxakalí,[23] three contrastive vowel lengths in Coatlán Mixe,[24] and simple patterns underlying complex consonant sequences in Chatino.[25] As spadework of this kind continues, it is probable that the yield of novel phenomena that have to be fitted into phonological theory by one means or another will increase before it levels off.

II. GRAMMATICAL THEORY

As in phonology, the clearest illustration of the interplay between problems encountered in the description of Latin American indigenous languages and the development of linguistics as a discipline is Pike's development of the so-called tagmemic theory of grammar. Just as his hierarchical view of phonology grew from an attempt to handle data in Mazateco and Mixteco, so his view of grammar was in part molded by the way in which Mixteco refused to fit neatly into a model that assumed a priori a distinction between morphology and syntax, or that required agreement between phonological and grammatical boundaries.[26] The theoretical framework he has developed over the last decade or so leaves open the possibility, therefore, that a language may be treated without reference to a clearcut distinction between levels, or rather (as explicated by Longacre[27]) may be treated with reference to a number of different levels of grammatical configuration. The extreme instance of the kind of phenomena that operate across levels in Mixteco is probably Rosbottom's analysis of Bolivian Guaraní, in which functional elements that form a small closed class, tense markers, are shown to fit into the grammatical system at widely different levels.[28]

Soon after Pike published his general statement of tagmemic theory he had opportunity in Peru to work with a team of field investigators to apply it in a variety of systems; it has since been put to use in many workshop situations. The third number of Volume 23 of *IJAL* (July, 1957), for example, is devoted exclusively to studies made as a test of Pike's theory as applied to five different American Indian languages.[29] Although the entire collection suffers from the ponderous style of Pike's *Language*, and the reader often bogs down in terminological and formulaic apparatus, the papers in it are remarkably thorough demonstrations that Pike's theory is applicable to natural language. More recent papers in the same tradition (for example, Lind's on

[23] Mary Ruth Wise, 'Diverse points of articulation of allophones in Amuesha (Arawak)', *Miscellanea Phonetica* 3.15-21 (1958). Sarah Gudschinsky, paper on Maxakalí presented to the summer meeting of the Linguistic Society of America (Bloomington, 1964).

[24] Searle Hoogshagen, 'Three contrastive vowel lengths in Mixe', *ZPhon* 12.111-5 (1959).

[25] Howard P. McKaughan, 'Chatino formulas and phonemes', *IJAL* 20.23-7 (1954).

[26] Kenneth L. Pike, 'Analysis of a Mixteco text', *IJAL* 10.113-382 (1944). Pike, *Language* 3.28,70.

[27] Robert E. Longacre, *Grammar discovery procedures: a field manual* (The Hague, 1964). This book contains a number of examples of linguistic structures in languages of Latin America viewed tagmemically.

[28] Harry Rosbottom, 'Different-level tense markers in Guaraní', *IJAL* 27.345-52 (1961).

[29] Doris Cox, 'Candoshi verb inflection', *IJAL* 23.129-40 (1957). Helen Long Hart, 'Hierarchical

Sierra Popoluca[30]) have become much more transparent, largely through the introduction of paradigm and matrix presentation of related phenomena and the simplification of formulas. Monograph-length examples of tagmemic analysis by Pike's students are Pickett on Isthmus Zapotec and Waterhouse on Oaxaca Chontal.[31]

The British structure-function approach to grammar, like Firthian phonology, is represented in the work of Callow on Apinayé and Bendor-Samuel on Jebero and Terena.[32] Bendor-Samuel's dissertation on Jebero was the first on an American Indian language to be presented at the University of London.

Pittman introduced a Hjelmslevian note into Latin American linguistics with his grammar of Tetelcingo Náhuatl,[33] but his example was not followed further. Studies made from the point of view of generative or transformational grammar have not been published on languages of Latin America.[33a] The transformation has, however, been used as a descriptive device within a different framework by Gudschinsky and Grimes.[34]

The notion of a morphology-syntax division is still under discussion by linguists who work in Latin America. Hoff deals with it in Carib and Clark finds it not completely relevant in Sayula Popoluca.[35]

Types of grammatical phenomena recently brought to light in languages of the hemisphere include the complex grammar and morphophonemics associated with stem initial position in Otomí reported by Wallis,[36] the discrepancies between morphophonemic domains and grammatical constructions reported by Priest, Priest, and Grimes in Siriono,[37] the compound affixes found by Pike in Ocaina.[38]

structuring of Amuzgo grammar', 141-64. Marvin Mayers, 'Pocomchi verb structure', 165-70. Martha Duff, 'A syntactical analysis of an Amuesha (Arawak) text', 171-8. Olive A. Shell, 'Cashibo II: grammemic analysis of transitive and intransitive verb patterns', 179-218.

30 John O. Lind, 'Clause and sentence level syntagmemes in Sierra Popoluca', *IJAL* 30.341-54 (1964).

31 Velma Bernice Pickett, *The grammatical hierarchy of Isthmus Zapotec* (Baltimore, 1960). Viola Waterhouse, *The grammatical structure of Oaxaca Chontal* (Bloomington, Indiana, 1962).

32 See also Footnote 17. John T. Bendor-Samuel, *The structure and function of the verbal piece in the Jebero language* (University of London doctoral dissertation, 1958), reissued as *The verbal piece in Jebero* (Monograph 4, Supplement to *Word* 17), 1961.

33 Richard S. Pittman, *A grammar of Tetelcingo (Morelos) Nahuatl* (Language Dissertation No. 50, Supplement to *Lg* 30), Baltimore, Linguistic Society of America (1954).

33a Since this chapter went to press, John Paul Daly's *Generative Syntax of Mixteco* (Indiana University doctoral dissertation, 1966) has appeared.

34 Sarah C. Gudschinsky, 'Mazatec kernel constructions and transformations', *IJAL* 25.81-9 (1959). Joseph E. Grimes, *Huichol syntax* (Cornell University doctoral dissertation, 1960), reissued as *Huichol syntax* (The Hague, 1964).

35 B. J. Hoff, 'The nominal word-group in Carib: a problem of delimitation of syntax and morphology', *Lingua* 11.157-64 (1962). Lawrence E. Clark, 'Sayula Popoluca morpho-syntax', *IJAL* 28.183-98 (1962).

36 Ethel E. Wallis, 'Simulfixation in aspect markers of Mezquital Otomi', *Lg* 32.453-9 (1956).

37 Perry N. Priest, Anne M. Priest, and Joseph E. Grimes, 'Simultaneous orderings in Siriono (Guarani)', *IJAL* 27.335-44 (1961).

38 Kenneth L. Pike, 'Compound affixes in Ocaina', *Lg* 37.570-81 (1961).

III. SEMANTICS

Mathiot's work on the form of a dictionary for Papago and Cowan's notes on a Mazateco text[39] are the most extensive attempts at a theoretically oriented description of semantics yet undertaken in languages of Latin America. Landar made a semantic componential analysis of Tequistlatec kinship terminology; Grimes and Grimes did the same for Huichol.[40] More restricted studies in the field of semantics include those by Pottier, Ramírez, Aschmann, and Wiesemann.[41]

IV. BASES FOR COMPARATIVE STUDIES

A number of linguistic descriptions seem to be made with the primary motivation of providing data for comparative linguistic studies to be made later. This seems to be a focus (though by no means the limit) of interest for a number of Mexican linguists, particularly those who worked with Swadesh.[42] Others such as Fernández de Miranda and Weitlaner, who were not directly associated with Swadesh, agree with his group in this orientation toward descriptive work for comparison's sake.[43] Rodrigues in Brazil has similar interests.[44]

V. DIALECTOLOGY

While no extensive work in the dialectology of Indian languages has been carried out, small projects are reported from several places, and there appears to be continuing interest.[45] John Crawford is directing an extensive set of field surveys in Mexico but has not yet prepared materials for publication.

39 (Mathiot, reference unavailable.) George M. Cowan, *Some aspects of the lexical structure of a Mazatec historical text* (Norman, Oklahoma, 1965).

40 Landar, Herbert J., 'Semantic components of Tequistlatec kinship', *IJAL* 26.72-5 (1960). Joseph E. Grimes and Barbara F. Grimes, 'Semantic distinctions in Huichol (Uto-Aztecan) kinship', *AmA* 64.104-14 (1962).

41 Bernard Pottier, 'Catégories linguistiques et expérience en guarani', *BFS* 39.329-32 (1962), Félix C. Ramírez, *Semántica y mecanismo de construcción de la lengua Phurhembe (Tarasca o Michoacana)* (México, 1955). Herman P. Aschmann, 'Totonac categories of smell', *Tl* 2.187-9 (1946). Ursula Wiesemann, 'Semantic categories of good and bad in relation to Kaingang personal names', *RMPaul*, n.s. 12.177-84 (1960).

42 For example, Roberto Escalante H., 'El Pima Bajo', *AnINA* 14.349-52 (1962), and similar studies by Manrique and Arana.

43 María Teresa Fernández de Miranda, *Diccionario Ixcateco* (Instituto Nacional de Antropología e Historia, Dirección de investigaciones antropológicas, Publicación 7, México, 1961). Roberto J. Weitlaner, 'El Otomí de Ixtenco, Tlaxcala', in *Estudios antropológicos publicados en homenaje al doctor Manuel Gamio*, 693-6 (México, Universidad Nacional Autónoma, 1956).

44 Arion Dall'Igna Rodrigues, 'Morphologische Erscheinungen einer Indianersprache', *MSS* 7.79-88 (1955).

45 Jacob A. Loewen, 'Dialectología de la familia lingüística Choco', *RCA* 9.9-22 (1960). Marvin K. Mayers, 'The linguistic unity of Pocomam-Pocomchí', *IJAL* 26.290-300 (1960). Bernard Pottier,

VI. PRESERVATION OF DISAPPEARING LANGUAGES

In some areas, notably the southern part of the Amazon basin and the Chaco, a number of languages have but recently gone out of existence, and others seem to be headed for extinction. Rather than allow these languages to be lost, linguists have made a special effort to record them. Much of the work of Nimuendajú had this effect.[46] Sargent and Peeke made a special project of recording Záparo and Shimigae.[47] Fernández de Miranda's Ixcateco field work was done under similar circumstances.[48]

VII. SUMMARY

In the field of descriptive linguistics in Latin America there has been interaction between theoretical development and on-the-spot analysis, particularly in the case of Pike's linguistic theories, and to a lesser extent in the case of the British structure-function school. New types of linguistic phenomena continue to come to light even in the case of routine investigations made without reference to refining any particular theory of language. While little was known about any of the indigenous languages of Latin America thirty to fifty years ago, enough work is now completed, in progress, or planned to insure eventual thorough coverage of the area from a descriptive point of view. [1964]

'Problèmes de dialectologie dans le domaine du tupi-guaranai', *Orbis* 10.31-34 (1961). Sarah C. Gudschinsky, 'Mazatec dialect history: A study in miniature', *Lg* 34.469-81 (1958). Juan A. Hasler, 'La posición dialectológica del Pipil como parte del Nahua del Este', *América Indígena* 18.333-9 (1958).

[46] Curt Nimuendajú, 'Reconhecimento dos Rios Içána, Ayarí, e Uaupés, março a julho de 1927. Apontamentos linguísticos', first part in *Revista del Instituto de Etnología de Tucumán* 2.590-618 (1932), second part in *JSAm* 44.149-78 (1955).

[47] Mary Sargent, 'Vocabulario Záparo', in *Estudios acerca de las lenguas Huarani (Auca), Shimigae y Zápara*, 43-8 (Publicaciones científicas del Ministerio de Educación del Ecuador, 1949). Catherine Peeke, 'Structural summary of Záparo', *Studies in Ecuadorian Indian languages I*, 125-216 (Publication 7 of the Linguistic Series of the Summer Institute of Linguistics of the University of Oklahoma, 1962). Catherine Peeke, 'Shimigae, idioma que se extingue', *Perú Indígena* 5.170-8 (1954), reprinted in *Estudios acerca de las lenguas Huarani (Auca), Shimigae y Zápara* 18-28 (1959). Catherine Peeke and Mary Sargent, 'Pronombres personales en Andoa', *Perú Indígena* 5.103-12 (1953), reprinted as 'Pronombres personales en Shimigae', *Estudios acerca de las lenguas Huarani (Auca), Shimigae y Zápara* 29-42 (1959).

[48] María Teresa Fernández de Miranda, *Fonémica del Ixcateco* (Instituto Nacional de Antropología e Historia, Publicación 3), México, 1959). See also Footnote 43, *Diccionario*.

AREAL LINGUISTICS AND MIDDLE AMERICA[1]

TERRENCE KAUFMAN

1. MIDDLE AMERICA AS A CULTURE AREA

Middle America (also called Mesoamerica, henceforth MA), as a product of the culture area concept, is only one of the approximately 35 areas into which most anthropologists (and others) interested in the concept would divide the pre-Columbian New World. MA is of special interest in that (a) 'civilization' — by whatever definition — first appeared in the New World in MA, and (b) in political terms MA is divided between just two[2] contemporary nations — Mexico and Guatemala — both of them officiall using Spanish as the national language.

1.1 Several scholars have contributed to the definition of culture areas in the New World and in MA in particular: Kirchoff (1943), Kroeber (1939), Driver and Massey (1957), and Driver (1961) have made the most useful (to me) studies towards defining MA. From Kirchoff I list some of the cultural features which define MA:

1. a certain type of digging-stick (*coa*)
2. cultivation of the century plant (*maguey*) for its juice (*aguamiel*)
3. cultivation of cacao
4. grinding of corn softened with ashes or lime
5. pyrite mirrors
6. sandals with heels
7. step pyramids
8. stucco floors
9. ball courts with rings
10. hieroglyphic writing
11. year of 18 'months' of 20 days, plus 5 additional days
12. good and bad omen days
13. the flying game or ritual (*juego del volador*)
14. drinking the water in which the deceased relative has been bathed

[1] Given Emeneau's justly famous article on India (1956), I would not dare use the title 'Middle America as a Linguistic Area' unless I had made an equally incisive study for Middle America.

[2] A third unit, the colony of British Honduras (or Belice) (which is claimed by Guatemala), contains some MA Yucatecs, and some non-MA Black Caribs.

15. ceramics
16. cultivation of corn, beans, squash, sweet cassava, chile, pineapple, avocado, papaya, zapote, 'plums' (*jobos*)
17. confession
18. cultivation in the hands of men
19. markets
20. domestication of duck, fattened voiceless dog
21. underground ovens; steam bath

1–14 are, according to Kirchoff, exclusively Meso-american; 15–21 are shared with some groups outside Mesoamerica.

1.2 What I accept as MA is fairly conservative: it does not include Northern Mexico or any Central American country but Guatemala; the geographical coordinates are approximately 106°W (western boundary), 88°W (eastern boundary), 23°N (northern boundary), and 13°N (southern boundary). In this paper MA will be defined by enumeration of the languages, and frontier areas under MA linguistic influence will also be defined by enumeration.

Languages and families of MA are:[3] Tequistlatecan, Tlapanecan, Otomanguean,[4] Huave, UtoAztecan: Cora-Huichol plus Aztecan only, Cuitlatec, Xincan, Mayan, MixeZoque, Tononacan, and Tarasco.

Language groups of northwestern Mexico which fall under MA influence are Piman and Yaquian, both UtoAztecan.

Languages of northeastern Mexico which fall under MA influence are all extinct, but include the following, for which we have some data: Coahuilteco and Comecrudo.

Languages and families of Central America which fall under MA influence are Lencan, Paya, and Jicaque.

2. CIVILIZATIONS IN MIDDLE AMERICA

Such cultural unity and distinctiveness as MA possesses — in an area of wide ecological diversity — is largely the result of historical processes and events associated with the successive and frequently contemporaneous civilizations which arose there, starting around 1500 B.C. with the beginnings of Olmec civilization — although the domestication of certain indispensable plants (like maize) and the beginnings of cultivation are prior to this.

[3] A listing of all the individual languages of MA would greatly increase the length of this paper› since it would commit me to a specific classification scheme for each family and group; and since unanimity in subgrouping of MA families is by no means frequent, the tiresome process of comparing my classification with that of other scholars and evaluating the whole thing would have to be gone through.

[4] Otomanguean is a stock or phylum including several families; one Otomanguean family, Manguean, has an outlier, Mangue or Chorotega, in Nicaragua.

A general familiarity with the language of MA, their distributions and genetic groupings, as well as the application of measures like glottochronology, makes it apparent that a great deal of the linguistic diversity of MA antedates 1500 B.C.; indeed, most of the families of MA had long since been in MA (wherever they ultimately came from) by this date: a probable exception is UtoAztecan; possible exceptions are Lencan and Paya; less probable are Tequistlatecan, Tlapanecan, and Jicaque. If these latter groups are Hokan, and if Hokan is recessive in the face of later immigrations, then they have probably been in MA longer than 3500 years. Given their distributions, they do indeed seem to have been shoved into corners by more recent invasions.

There is a great deal of diversity of linguistic type in MA, and whatever linguistic unity there is — other than genetic — is due primarily to the small number of linguistic families and to the spreading of linguistic features (phonological, lexical, morphological, syntactic, and semantic) along with jewelry, pots, patterns of social organization, and more perishable artifacts — among the successive civilizations there.

In the spreading of linguistic features which have contributed to a kind of linguistic unity in MA, certain specific languages and language groups have been of greater influence than others, as the following remarks on the successive and coexisting cultures of MA will suggest. (For more bibliography see Coe 1968.)

2.1 *Olmec Civilization*
(1300–400 B.C.; southern Veracruz coast)

In the area of the former Olmec civilization, mostly MixeZoque (henceforth MZ) languages are now spoken. The glottochronological time depth of MZ is 3500 years (as calculated both by Swadesh 1959, 1962a, *and* by Kaufman (ms.)) or 1500 B.C., which correlates with the first glimmerings of Olmec civilization. MZ languages have provided loans into Otomian, Zapotecan, Mayan, Xincan, and Lencan languages, among others. Olmec trade routes penetrated to Central Mexico (where Otomian is spoken), crossed the Isthmus of Tehuantepec (contacting Zapotecan), and spread down the Pacific coast from Tehuantepec to El Salvador (contacting Mayan, Xincan, and Lencan). I would claim that at least some of the Olmecs were MZ speakers.

2.2 *Zapotec Civilization*
(400 B.C.–700 A.D.; Oaxaca)

The rise of 'Zapotec' civilization (mainly at Monte Albán) follows on the decline of Olmec civilization. The Zapotecan family has some 2400 years time depth (Swadesh 1967) and includes Zapotec (several languages, with about 1700 years time depth), Papabuco, and Chatino. The presence of Zapotecan loans in the Mayan languages

Huastec and Yucatec indicate contact between the two families, probably in the Isthmus, and suggests a wider extension for Zapotecan 2000 years ago than at present.

2.3 *Teotihuacán Civilization*
(100–600 A.D.; Central Mexico)

Teotihuacán civilization arose in Central Mexico after the decline of Olmec civilization. Except for the obviously intrusive and fairly late Aztec language, the languages of Central Mexico are Otopamean, more specifically Otomían (= Otomí dialects plus Mazahua). Otomían has a time depth of 1600 years (Swadesh 1967), and the dialect diversification of Otomí itself is about 850 years (Swadesh 1967). Aztecan (including Pochutec) has a time depth of about 1400 years (Swadesh 1959, 1962a, 1967; Hale 1959). We can assume that the Teotihuacán civilization was Otomían-speaking, with the beginnings of diversification setting in about 400 A.D., 200 years before their civilization was destroyed by outsiders. These outsiders we can identify as Aztecans, who around 600 A.D. entered Central Mexico from the west (say Jalisco), occupying the favorable parts of Central Mexico, and sending out a branch to Pochutla in Oaxaca. Otomían loans in other MA languages have not yet been sought. Some Aztec traditions state that Teotihuacán was built by Totonacs, a possibility which should also be investigated. There is significant Teotihuacano influence in Highland Guatemala.

2.4 *Toltec Civilization*
(850–1100 A.D.; Central Mexico)

Two or three centuries after the end of Teotihuacan civilization, Toltec civilization arose in Hidalgo and Central Mexico. It sent out people into southern Mexico and Central America as early as 900–1000 A.D. The 'Pipil' varieties of Aztec found in the Mayan area an dfurther south have the appropriate time depth from Central Mexican Aztec. The Toltecs were presumably Aztec-speaking, and Aztec loans are found in most MA languages, although some of these are undoubtedly due to Tenochtitlán (two paragraphs further on) and not Toltec influence.

2.5 *Maya Civilization*
(pre-Classic: 100 B.C.–300 A.D.; Classic: 300 A.D.–950 A.D.; Chiapas, Yucatán, and Guatemala)

Pre-Classic Maya civilization arose in the Mayan linguistic area after the decline of Olmec civilization. The Mayan family began to break up as early as 42 centuries ago (Kaufman, ms.) and no correlation can be drawn between the beginnings of Maya civilization and the beginning of Mayan linguistic diversification. Distributions and subgroupings, however, suggest that Yucatecans have been in Yucatán since about 1000 B.C. In 900–1000 A.D. Central Mexican ('Toltec-Pipil') influence and conquest occurred in Yucatan. The time depth of the Yucatecan group is not more than1000 years (Kaufman, ms.). This suggests that Yucatecan maintained linguistic uniformity for many centuries, constantly reabsorbing a dleveling changes, until cultural unity was finally destroyed by Toltec invasions. Mayan loanwords are found in Xincan, Lencan, Jicaque, and Paya among others.

2.6 *Tenochtitlán Civilization*
(1250–1519 A.D.; Mexico City)

Tenochtitlán civilization arose in Mexico City around 1250, was Aztec-speaking, and in control of most of Central Mexico by the time of the Spanish conquest. In 1519 the Aztecs were the most powerful people in MA, and given another century or two to themselves might have unified MA politically; after that, with anything like the Inca model, MA might eventually have become largely Aztec-speaking. Since Aztec was used as a language for keeping records during the early colonial period, it is clear that some loans from Aztec in MA languages may post-date the conquest; others have entered indigenous languages via Spanish.

3. TYPOLOGICAL FEATURES OF MIDDLE AMERICAN LANGUAGES

To date there has been virtually no investigation of the languages of MA with a view to establishing a list of MA areal linguistic features (if it is possible) or for any other areal or typological purpose. That is to say, there is almost no literature to be cited or reviewed. I am not in a position to attempt either a pioneering work or a synthesis in this area, but it is possible to state some of the problems, indicate places to look for data, and suggest what are some of the conclusions that might be drawn from fuller data and deeper studies.

3.1 In comparing languages typologically we may look at the following sub-systems:

Phonology:	[a] elementary units and oppositions (or contrasts)
	[b] pronounciation and allophonics
	[c] morphophonemic rules
Lexicon:	[d] roster of morphemes
	[e] derivational patterns
Syntax:	[f] word order
	[g] inflexional patterns
Semantics:	[h] grammatical categories
	[i] types of metaphor used in lexeme formation

What we can do to investigate MA typologically and areally is to look at available data. One good way to get a reasonable sample would be to have data from at least one language in every major branch of every universally-accepted genetic group as well as from each language isolate.

For the investigations of [a] and [b] we need phonologies, or at least phonemic statements. Phonemic statements are hard to evaluate outside the context of a phonology or in the absence of an extensive wordlist.

For the investigation of [c] we need phonologies; in fact whole grammars, dictionaries, and collections of texts are desirable here, since the phonologies produced by different investigators are so non-uniform in their theoretical base and thus distribution of crucial facts.

For [d] we need dictionaries.

For [e] and [i] — which are interrelated — we need dictionaries and grammars.

For [f] and [g] we need syntactic descriptions.

For [h] we need grammars.

3.2 The bulk of descriptive linguistic work done in MA has been by Americans, either academic linguists or missionary linguists (the latter primarily members of the Summer Institute of Linguistics = Wycliffe Bible Translators). Compared to New Guinea, Australia, and South America, the languages of Middle America have been reasonably well worked on, although much work has yet to see print.

3.3 I will discuss in varying degrees of detail four areas in which conclusions can be drawn, or in which investigation is perfectly feasible, given the current state of descriptive studies. The first is *phonological elements and pronunciation*; the second is *grammatical categories and morphological patterns*; the third is *metaphor in lexeme formation*; the fourth is *morpheme roster* (*lexical borrowing*). Only the first category will be gone into at length.

4. PHONOLOGICAL ELEMENTS AND PRONUNCIATION[5]

For the investigation of phonological patterns with a view to establishing areas of relative uniformity and cross-influence, we may examine the following languages — the last being selected from available (mostly published) sources and observing the principle outlined above of one language for each genetic group or major subgroup, including isolated languages: protoTequistlatec; Tlapanec; protoOtomí, protoPopolocan, Mazatec, protoMixtecan, Mixtec, Amuzgo, Chatino, protoZapotec, Chinantec, Chiapanec; Huave; Huichol, Aztec; Cuitlatec; Xinca B; protoMayan, Tzeltal, Huastec; protoMixeZoque; protoTotonacan; Tarasco; Coahuilteco; Comecrudo; Cáhita, Chilanga Lenca.

[5] Phonemes occurring in loans from Spanish have been systematically excluded.

Paya and Jicaque, for which it would be desirable to have data, are not well-attested phonologically. †Chiapanec, †Comecrudo, and †Coahuilteco data are interpretable with some guesswork, and Tlapanec, Xinca, and Lenca data are pre-structural but probably sound. Some protolanguages have been included as standing for whole families or groups, and as well making clear the difference between original diversity and subsequent assimilation (and vice-versa).

4.1

There follows a listing of the phonological elements for each of the languages named above. The symbols used are not those of the original sources, but are those currently being used by me for the keypunching of lexical and textual materials in various New World languages. The symbols are the letters, numerals, and punctuation signs found in the minimal keypunch symbology. Values are here cited for those symbols not used in accordance with current Americanist usage. Some symbols stand for segments, others for features, others for accentual phenomena.

Feature symbols are

V labialization (raised *w*)
J palatalization (haček/wedge or raised *y*)
$ retroflexion (underdot)
: vowel length (raised dot)
' glottalization (apostrophe)
" 1) aspiration (raised *h*)
2) devoicing
5 lateral spirant articulation; thus barred *l* = *S5*, lamda = *Z5*, and barred lamda = *C5*

Accent symbols are

* 1) stress
2 marked member of a two-way tone opposition
3) high (± falling) tone
/ 1) mid-tone
2) rising (± high) tone
+ low tone

Segment symbols are

7 glottal stop
C voiceless affricate
Z voiced affricate
8 theta
9 1) eng/angma

2) vowel nasality
3) consonant prenasalization

3 barred *i* (in presence of contrast with schwa/caret)
6 1) schwa/caret
2) barred *i* (in absence of contrast)
2 open *o*/turned *c*
4 1) aesc/digraph
2) open *e*/epsilon

Note: phonetic beta and *v* are structurally either *b* or *w*.

In use the symbols look as follows:

P	*T*	*C*	*K*	*9*	*7*	*1*	*3*	*U*
B	*D*	*Z*	*G*			*E*	*6*	*0*
F	*8*	*S*	*X*		*H*	*4*	*A*	*2*
M	*N*		*9*					
	L							
	R							
W		*Y*						

labialization	*KV*
palatalization	*CJ*, *SJ*
retroflexion	*C$*, *S$*
laterality	*C5*, *S5*
glottalization	*T'*, *CJ'*, *K'*, *KV'*, *A'*
aspiration	*T"*, *CJ"*
devoicing	*W"*, *M"*, *A"*
vowel length	*A:*, *E:*
stress, etc.	*A**, *A:**
mid-tone, etc.	*A/*, *A:/*
low tone	*A+*, *A:+*
nasalized vowel	*A9*, *A:9**
prenasalized consonant	*9T*, *9K*

4.2 *Middle American Languages*

ProtoTequistlatecan [pTeq] (Turner 1969): *b d g*, *p t c k*; *f' c5' c' k'*; *f s5 s (sj?)*; *7 h* (or *x*); *m n* ; *w y*; *l* (voiceless *w* and *n* are either *w"*, *n"* or *wh*, *nh*); *i e a o u*; stress (*).

Tlapanec [Tlp] (Radin 1933; Schulze-Jena 1938; interpreted by Kaufman): *p t c cj k*; *b d z zj g*; *s sj x*; *m n nj 9*; *l r*; *w y* ; *7*; *i a 2* (write *o*) *u*; vowel length (:); vowel nasality (different from *9*?; same as *n*?); several tones; prenasalized consonants are clusters.

ProtoOtomí [pOtm] (Newman and Weitlaner 1950; and Bartholomew 1959, 1960, also in Longacre 1967:127–129, 154–155): *p t c k kv*; *b d z g w*; *y*; *s*; *m n*; *7 h*; *i e 4 3 6 a u o 2*; nasal vowels *i9*, *e9*, *a9*, *o9*, *u9*; three tones (*[high], /[rising], +[low]); aspirated, glottalized, and prenasalized consonants are clusters.

ProtoPopolocan [pPop] (Gudschinsky 1959; also in Longacre 1967:126–127): *t tj c cj k kv*; *s sj h hv*; *n nj m*, (*l*?) *y w*; *7*; *i e a* (*o*?) *u*; vowel nasality (*9*); three tones (*[mid-high], /[mid-low], +[low]), one per syllable; aspirated, glottalized, and prenasalized consonants are clusters.

Mazatec of Huautla de Jimenez [Maz] (E. Pike 1967:312–313): *t c cj c$ k*; *sj*; *7 h*; *m n nu nj*; *w l y*; *r* (rare); *i e a o*; (vowel nasality is analyzable as syllable-final *n*); three basic tones (as in proto-Popolocan); aspirated, glottalized, and prenasalized consonants are clusters; *m n nj* may be analyzed as *w l y* respectively before nasal vowel, or *n* before consonant.

Proto Mixtecan [pMxt] (Longacre 1967:125–126): *t k kv*; *8 x xv*; prenasalized *d g gv* which I analyze *nt nk nkv*; *n*; *m* (which is rare before vowels); *y w*; *l* (of limited distribution); *i e 6 a u o*; three tones (*[mid-high], /[mid-low], +[low]), one per syllable.

Mixtec of San Miguel el Grande [Mix] (Kaufman 1968): *t cj k kv*; *s sj h*; *l y w*; *r*; *7 n*; *i e 6 a o u*; vowel nasality is analyzed as syllable-final *n*; prenasalized stops are *n* + *t c k*; there are initial clusters of *s* + *t c k kv* and *sj* + [n] [nj] *l r* (or *nt*); phonetic [m] [n] [nj] are *w l y* respectively before nasalized vowel; there are three tones (*[high], /[mid], +[low], one per syllable; there are long vowels which are analyzed as geminates.

Amuzgo [Amz] (Longacre 1966; Bauernschmidt 1965): *t tj c cj kj k kv j s sj*; prenasalized *9p*, *9t*, *9tj*, *9k* (*; t cj* etc. may be preceded by *n*); *7 h*; *m n nj*; *w l y*; *r*; *i e 4 a 2 o u*; vowel nasality with non-high vowels (*9*); three tones (*[high], /[mid], +[low]), one per syllable.

Chatino of Yaitepec [Cht] (Pride 1965; Upson and Longacre 1965): *t tj c cj kj k kv*; *s sj hj h hv*; *7*; *m n nj l lj y w*; *i e a o u*; vowel nasality (*9*; occurs with *a* only in Zenzontepec); vowel length (*:*); four tones — only on word-final syllables. Pride analyzes *sj* as a unit, *c* and *cj* as *t* plus spirant (*s* or *sj*) and otherwise writes *j* as *y* and *v* as *w*.

ProtoZapotec [pZap] (Swadesh 1947; and Fernández:Longacre 1967:129–130; interpreted by Kaufman): consonants which may be doubled fortis): *p t* (*c*?) *cj k s sj n l* ; consonants which may not be doubled: *w y r*; fortis clusters: *ty*, *kw*; *nl*; *nw* (pronounced fortis *m*; Swadesh writes *np*, Fernandez reconstructs *mm*); proto-Zapotec tones as per Swadesh are not convincing; vowels *i e a u*/*o*; Isthmus Zapotec has three tones (*[high], /[rising], +[low]), one per syllable, though prefixes mostly have no inherent tone.

Chinantec of Palantla [Chn] (Merrifield 1968): *p t c k*; *b d z g*; *s h*; *7*; *m n 9*; *r l*; *w y*; *i e 3 6 a u o*; vowel nasality is analyzed as syllable-final *n*; three tones (*[high], [mid], +[low]]); *7 h* may preceed and *y w* follow other consonants in syllable-initial clusters.

Chiapanec [Chp] (Fernández and Weitlaner 1961; interpreted by Kaufman): *p t cj k*; *s h*; *m n*; *l r*; *w y*; *i e a u*; possibly vowel length (:), word-final glottal stop (*7*), several tones. *n* + *p t c k* produces voiced prenasalized stops; *h* clusters with following *m* and *w* (the latter case varying with bilabial *f* phonetically); *ny* occurs, and phonetic *sj* which is rare is either *hy* or *sy* phonemically.

Hauve [Hve] (Warkentin 1947, 1952; interpreted by Kaufman): *p t c k*; *s h*; *m n*; *l r*; *w y*; *i e a o 6*; *c* and *s* are *e- cj* and *sj* respectively next to front vowels (*i e*); *p t c k* are voiced after nasal, and V*h*C# becomes V:C_{voiced}; the accentual system is not completely analyzed, but lexical tone seems absent.

Huichol [Hui] (Grimes 1964): *p t c k kv*; *s$* (write *s*); *7 h*; *m n*; *r*; *y w*; *i e a u 6*; vowel length (:); pitch and/or stress is distinctive but not fully described.

Aztec of Cuatlamayán [Azt] (Kaufman 1969, ms.): *p t c5* (write *t5* since related to *t*) *c cj k kv*; *s sj*; *l*; *l*; *y w*; *m n*; *r* (rare); *i e a o*; vowel length (:), intervocalic and syllable-final *h*. PROTO-AZTECAN has *t* for *t5*, *7* or *w* for syllable-final *h*, and *7* for intervocalic *h*, and five vowels — *i e a o/u 6*; otherwise it is identical with Cuatlamayan.

Cuitlatec [Cui] (McQuown 1941; Hendrichs 1946; Escalante 1962): *p t cj k kv*; *b d g*; *s5 sj*; *7 h*; *m n*; *l*; *y w*; *i e a o u 6*; stress (*).

Xinca [Xin] of Chiquimuilla probable phonemes (Schumann 1967, McQuown 1949, Kaufman 1970) : *p t c cj k*; *p' c' cj' k'*; *s sj*; *7 h*; *m n5*; *w y*; *l r*; *i e a o u 6*; vowel length (:); stress (*).

Proto Mayan [pMay] (Kaufman, ms.): *p t tj c cj* (*kj?*) *k q*; *b' t' tj' c' cj'* (*kj'?*) *k' q' 7*; *s sj x h*; *m n 9*; *l r w y*; *i e a o u 6*; vowel length (:).

Tzeltal of Bachajon [Tze] (Kaufman, ms.): *p t c cj k*; p' *t' c' cj' k' 7*; *b'*; *s sj x h*; *m n*; *l r* (marginal); *w y*; *i e a o u*.

Huastec diasystem [Hua] (Kaufman, ms.): *p t tj c k kv*; *b t' tj' c' k' kv' 7*; *8 sj h*; *m n*; *l*; *r* (marginal); *y w*; *i e a o u*; vowel length (:).

ProtoMixeZoque [pMZ] (Kaufman, ms.): *p t c k 7*; *s h*; *m n*; *y w*; *i e a o u 6*; vowel length (:).

ProtoTotonacan [pTot] (Arana 1953) = Totonac of Villa Juarez: *p t c cj c5 k q*; *s sj s5 x*; *m n*; *l*; *w y*; *i a u*; vowel length (:); vowel glottalization (').

Tarasco [Tar] (Foster 1969; Friedrich 1969): *p t c cj k*; aspirated *p"t"c"cj"k"* (if not clusters); *s sj*; *m n 9*; medial *r* (in complementary distribution with *h*); medial *r$* (in CD with *y*); *h* (initial only), *y* (initial only) *w*; *i e a o u 6$* (write *6*). *c c"* and *s* are retroflex before *6*. Friedrich writes *w y* as *u i* respectively, and Foster writes *h* as *x*.

4.3 *Languages under Middle American Influence*

Coahuilteco probable phonemes [Coa] (Garcia in Swanton 1940; interpreted by Kaufman): *p t c cj k kv*; *p' t' k' kv'*; *s sj x xv*; *m n*; *l*; *y w*; *i e a o/u*; vowel length (:) and/or stress (*).

Comecrudo [Com] probable phonemes (Gatschet in Swanton 1940; interpreted by

Kaufman): *p t c k kv*; *s h hv*; *m n*; *l*; *y w*; *i a u*; maybe stress (*) and/or length (:); initial clusters of stop plus *l* occur.

Cáhita [Cah] (Johnson 1962; Collard and Collard 1962; interpreted by Kaufman): *p t cj k bv* (from original *kv*); *s*; *7 h*; *b* (spirant); *m n*; *l r*; *y w*; *i e a o u*; vowel length (:); there is a two-way pitch contrast (high:low) on short vowels only.

Lenca of Chilanga [Len] (Lehmann 1920; interpreted by Kaufman): *p t s sj k*; *m n*; *l r*; *w y*; *7*; occasional non-predictable ultimate vowel stress before a resonant (*m n l r*). obstruent + *7* is glottalized; medially *7*+ obstruent or resonant yields a voiceless consonant, while postvocalic consonants are uniformly voiced.

4.4

Now that the phonological elements of the sample have been laid out, certain generalities will be abstracted, and a few additional pieces of relevant data will be cited.

In order to facilitate and abbreviate citations of language names, MA plus areas under MA influence will be divided into *batches* of languages. That the division is not quite arbitrary will become apparent as the discussion proceeds.

Batch A EASTERN

Southeastern

1. Lenca
2. Xinca
3. Mayan (a) + Tzeltal (b)

Northeastern

4. Huastec
5. Coahuilteco
6. Comecrudo

Marginal Southern

7. Tequistlatecan

Marginal Eastern

8. Totonac(an)

Batch B WESTERN

Northwestern

9. Cáhita
10. Huichol
11. Aztecan (a) + Aztec (b)
12. Cuitlatec

Southern

13. MixeZoque

Marginal Western

14. Tarasco

Batch C CENTRAL

North Central
15. Otomí(an)
16. Popolocan (a) + Mazatec (b)
17. Mixtecan (a) + Mixtec (b)
18. Amuzgo

Marginal Central
19. Chinantec
20. Chatino

South Central
21. Zapotec
22. Chiapanec
23. Huave
24. Tlapanec

4.5

The following chart presents some of the more salient widespread features.

Column 1 labial stops
2 glottalization
3 aspiration
4 prenasalization
5 vowel nasality
6 accent phenomena (S = stress; PA = pitch accent, T = tone)
7 presence of labial spirant (implies labiovelar stop)
8 *l*'s and *r*'s (blank implies *l* is found)
9 number of vowels ± length

Blanks mean absent; ? means not known; ( ) means marginal.

Language	1	2	3	4	5	6	7	8	9
1. Len	p	C7				(S)		+r	5
2. Xin	p	C′				S		+r	6
3a. pMay	p	C′						+r?	6+L
3b. Tze	p	C′						(+r)	5
4. Hua	kv,p	C′						(+r)	5+L
5. Coa	kv,p	C′				?	xv		4(+L?)
6. Com	kv,p	?				?	hv		3
7. pTeq	p	C′				S	f		5
8. (p)Tot	p	V′							3+L
9. Cah	bv,p	V7				PA		(+r)	5+L
10. Hui	kv,p	V7				PA		−l,+r	5+L
11. (p)Azt	kv,p	V7							5→4,+L

12.	Cui	kv,p	V7				S			6
13.	pMZ	p	V7						−l	6+L
14.	Tar	p(,kw)		C″			(S)		−l,+r,+r$	6
15.	pOtm	kv,p	C7	Ch	nC	V9	T		−l	9
16a.	pPop	kv	C7	Ch	nC	V9	T	hv	l?	4
16b.	Maz	kv → ku	C7	Ch	nC	V9	T			4
17a.	pMxt	kv			nC	V9	T	xv	l?	6
17b.	Mix	kv			nC	V9	T			6
18.	Amz.	kv			nC	V9	T			7
19.	Chn	p				V9	T		+r	7
20.	Cht	p → kv				V9	T	hv		5
21.	pZap	p(,kw)	V′?		C_1C_1		T		+r	4
22.	Chp	p			nC		T	(hw)	+r	4
23.	Hve	p			nC		?		+r	5
24.	Tlp	p			nC		T		+r	4

4.6 *Generalities about MA languages*

1. *rarities*

Voiced spirants: are missing from all MA languages. Some analyses of Zapotec analyze the lenis/non-geminate series as voiced and the fortis/germinate series as voiceless, thus implying the existence of [z] and [ž].

Voiced stops and affricates: are rare in MA but occur in pTeq (7), Tlp (24), pOtm (15), Chn (19), Cui (12), Xin (2); in the cases of Tlp and Xin, they may be allophonic. In the cases of pOtm and Chn, they have developed out of other things. In a number of languages voiced stops and affricates occur as phonetic realizations of consonants not marked for voice; for example, stops are voiced after nasals in pMxt, Mix, Totonac, Chp (not Mangue), Chiapas Zoque (not other MZ), Tar, and Hue.

Lateral spirant (*s5*): is found in a random geographical distribution in pTot (8), Cui (12), and pTeq (7).

Velar nasal (*9*): is found in a random distribution in Tar (14), pMay (3), and (maybe allophonically) Tlp (24).

Velar spirant (x) contrasting with glottal spirant (h): is found only in pMay (3a).

Postvelar stop (p): is found in pTot (8) and pMay (3a), non-contiguously.

Lateral affricate (*t5* or *c5*): is found in pTot (8) and some dialects of Azt (11b); these are contiguous.

2. *widespread features*

Phonetically aspirated stops and affricates: occur in Tar (14), pOtm (15), pPop (16a), and Maz (16b). In 14 they are at least partly derived from spirant + stop; in 15–16, they are clusters. The language groups in question form a continuum.

Initial prenasalized consonants (which in all cases may be analyzed as *n* + consonant): occur in 15–18, 22–24, all (except 24) Otomanguean languages. In pZap (21) C_1C_1 seems to correspond to *nC* of the other languages, and Cht (2) which is genetically close to 21 has neither prenasalization nor gemination/fortition, nor does Chn (19), which is also Otomanguean.

Nasalized vowels (in some cases analyzable as $V + n$): occur in 15–20, all Otomanguean languages; Zap (21) has no nasalized vowels, though Cht (20) does; 21 has presumably lost nasality in contact with 7, 23, 13.

No nasal consonants: It is possible, and indeed preferable, to analyze Maz (16b), Mix (17b), and Cht (2) as having no nasal consonants, but specifying that *w l y* are pronounced [m][n][nj] before nasal vowels. Nasality is definable in these languages — which are roughly contiguous — as an element, *n*, which may occur before consonants, or after vowels, but not elsewhere. The Siouan language family in North America, and several South American languages have a similar lack of underlying nasal consonants.

Tones: are found in 15–24, with 23, Hve, remaining uncertain. All are Otomanguean except 24 (Tlp). Some of these languages have only two tones (21, 15?), some have three (16–19), while with others the facts remain uncertain. Some other languages of MA not included in the present sample also have two-way tone systems; in almost all cases they can be shown to be historically secondary. They may be secondary in Otomanguean as well, but synchronically 15–24 form a solid bloc of tone languages at the present time.

Distinctive stress (*): is found only in pTeq (7), Cui (12), Xin (2), Tar (14) (mostly predictable), Len (1) (mostly predictable), and maybe Coa (5) and Com (6). Xin and Len are contiguous, Cui and Tar are contiguous, and Coa and Com maybe were contiguous. Distinctive stress is mutually exclusive with tone.

Labiovelar stops (*kv*): are common in northern and central MA. In northeastern, northwestern, and central Mexico, *p* and *kv* usually contrast (4–6, 9–12, 15). In 16–18, only *kv* occurs; in 20, *p* has become *kv* under the influence of 18. In the rest of MA (1–3, 7–8, 13–14, 19–24) only *p* occurs.

Glottalization: 1–7 have glottalized consonants; in 1 these consonants are analyzable as clusters. 15–16 also have clusters of obstruent + glottal stop. Tot (8) has glottalized vowels, unique for MA, and rare in the world generally. 9–13 (as well as 3) have syllable canons allowing vowel plus glottal stop to be followed by a consonant. In Zap (21) glottal stops seems to be suprasegmental. 1–3 from a continuum, as do 4 and 5, although 4 is displaced from 1–3 in the first place. Teq (7) is isolated geographically, 9–12 form a continuum, but 8 and 13 are isolated again.

4.7

Having stated the more salient phonological phenomena shared by blocs of languages, we may proceed to play the game of setting up an average-type phonological system for MA and show how various languages an dgroups diverge from it.

The typical MA consonant system is

p	*t*	*c*	*k*	*7*
		s		*h/x*
m	*n*			
	l			
w			*y*	

The typical MA vowel system is

i		*u*
e		*o*
	a	

The typical syllable canon is

CV

Variations from the norm are as follows:

(a) different phonetics

kv but no *p*: 16–18, 20
r but no *l*: 10
8 but no *s*: 4, 17a
6 but no *u*: 10, 11a, 23
2 but no *a*: 24

(b) reductions

no *c*: 1, 17a
no *7*: 5?, 6?
7 only as a satellite: 1, 8, 11, 17, 21
no *h*: 11, 21
h only as a satellite: 15
[m n] = /w l/ before nasalized vowel; therefore /n/ is a satellite element: 16b, 17b, 20, and probably others [old][6]
no *l*: 13–15
no *e*: 6, 8
no *o/u* contrast: 5, 6, 8, 10, 11b, 16, 21, 22, (24)

(c) amplifications

features	
consonant glottalization:	2–7 (1; 15–16 clusters) [old]
vowel glottalization:	8, 21 (9–13 clusters) [old]
vowel nasality:	15–20 [old]
consonant prenasalization:	15–18, 22–24 [old]
consonant aspiration:	14 (secondary), 15–16 (clusters) [old]
resonant devoicing:	(7)
vowel length:	3a, 4, 5?, 8, 9, 10, 11, 13
tone:	15–24 [old]

[6] [old] means the fact has already been mentioned in a previous section.

palatalization of consonants other than *s*, *c*:	
(i) of *n*:	16b, [17b], [22], 24
(ii) of *t* and/or *k*:	3a, 4, 16a, 18, 20
stop/affricate voicing:	2, 7, 12, 15, 19, 24 [old]
stress:	(1), 2, 7, 12, (14) [old]
segments	
c5	8, 11b [old]
c AND *cj*:	11, 14, 16, 18, 20, (21?), 24
kv:	4, 5, 6, 9 (bv), 10, 11, 12, 15 [old]
q:	3a, 8 [old]
s5:	7, 8, 12 [old]
s/8 AND *sj*:	4, 5, 8, 11, 14, 16, 17b, 18, 20, 21, 24
h AND *x*:	3a, 3b [old]
xv/hv/f (always implies *kv*):	5, 6, 7, 16, 20 (secondary), 22 (cluster)
b:	4, 9
p' AND *b'*:	3b
9 (velarnasal):	3a, 14, 19, 24 [old]
r:	1–2, 3a?, 19, 21–24
6:	2, 3, 12, 13, 17
3 AND *6*:	15, 20
4 AND *2*:	15, 18

4.8 *Summary and Conclusions*

To summarize and draw some conclusions from the data discussed, we may make the following observations:

1. languages of northern MA tend to have a *kv/p* contrast; those farther south do not. Hua acquired *kv* and *kv'* from non-Mayan sources.

2. there is a Central batch of languages (15–24), largely Otomanguean, but with great time depth, that share a large number of typological features, some of which are probably diffused or triggered by outside influences: e.g. $p \rightarrow kv$ in Cht; $kv \rightarrow ku$ in Maz, V → V in Zap.

3. languages with glottalized consonants occupy peripheral areas in northeast Mexico (4–6), southeast MA (1–3) and Oaxaca (7).

4. languages with 'glottalized vowels' are largely in northwest Mexico (9–12), with Tot (8), and MZ (13) lying elsewhere.

5. at the southeast boundary of MA with the circum-Caribbean area, there is a fairly clear division between Mayan, Xincan, and Lencan on the one hand, and Paya, Sumu, and Matagalpan on the other, the latter having rather simple sound systems reminiscent of MixeZoque or Chinantec. Jicaque phonology is unknown. North-easterly, there is not much similarity between Otomanguean and the languages of

northeast Mexico (Coahuilteco) (Comecrudo) other than the presence of *kv*, found also in Uto-Aztecan and Yuman, both of them originally foreign to MA, the latter still so.

6. three of the simplest sound systems in MA form a continuum: Chn, MZ, and Hve.

5. GRAMMATICAL CATEGORIES AND MORPHOLOGICAL PATTERNS

An ambitious typological study of the languages of North America has been carried out as a doctoral thesis by Joel Sherzer (1968). The data examined by Sherzer is both phonological and of the kind that falls under the present rubric. Sherzer lays out in advance the categories that he intends to seek in each language, and the list for grammatical features is fairly long.

I have not been able to devote the time to an investigation as elaborate as Sherzer's, but I have been able to check out Sherzer's categories in a number of MA languages, as well as think up a few of my own independently. On some reflection, it seems that the following categories (at least) might be of typological relevance, both in setting off MA languages from others, and in subdividing MA languages typologically. The categories are put as queries:

5.1 *Possible Typological Categories*

5.1.1 *Nominal categories*:

1. Do nouns have cases? If so, are they prefixes or suffixes?
2. Do nouns have subclasses according to the way they are possessed? If so, is the subcategorization semantically motivated or not?
3. Are nouns subdivided by 'gender' agreement that other word classes share with them?
4. Is there a definite article?
5. Is there an inclusive: exclusive contrast for 'we'?
6. What is the contrast system for deictics/demonstratives? 2-way, or 3-way, or other?
7. How is the numeral system structured?
8. Are there numeral classifiers?
9. Are locative notions [parallel to English prepositions] expressed by prefixes, suffixes, prepositions, or post-positions, or *other* means? And if so, what?

5.1.2 *Verbal categories*:

10. Is there incorporation of noun objects (and intransitive subjects)? If so, preverbal or postverbal?
11. Is the subject of a transitive verb prefixed, suffixed, or independent?

12. How is the object of a transitive verb marked?
13. How many morphologically marked verb classes are there?
14. Do verbs have instrumental prefixes?
15. How is tense/aspect marked?
16. How are direction and location of action [parallel to English adverbs and verb prefixes] indicated?

5.1.3 *Other categories*:

17. Are there honorific or special respect forms that are morphologically marked?
18. Is reduplication found? If so, what functions does it fill?
19. How is plurality marked — On nouns? On pronouns? On verbs?
20. Is there consonantal or vocalic ablaut? If so, what does it indicate?

One would naturally check out all of the universals and general tendencies that J.H. Greenberg has pointed out.

5.2

Since the languages I have asked these questions of (as contrasted with the phonological survey just past) are not a systematic sample, no systematic conclusions will be drawn, other than to repeat my belief that these 20 questions will provide useful data for typologizing. I will make a few informal observations.

to question 1: Some UA languages, MZ (13), and Tar (14) all have suffixed cases. This tends to provide a grammatical basis for the *Western* Batch outlined by phonological criteria.

to question 7: Virtually all MA languages, as well as Coahuilteco, have vigesimal enumeration, in that '20' is a basic unit and that all higher numerals are expressed as multiples of '20' plus a remainder. There is usually a special morpheme for '400' (20×20 or 20^2) and at the time of the Spanish Conquest most languages had special morphemes for '8000' ($20 \times 20 \times 20$) or 20^3); some had even higher special numbers as for 20^4, 20^5, 20^6, etc. Except for this common feature of enumeration above 20, there is a good deal of variety in the structure of numerals between one and twenty, some languages having only 1–4 and 10 as single morphemes (the rest being composite), others having 5 as a single morpheme, and others having 1–10 as units. The first is a quaternary system, the second quinary, and the third decimal. All MA languages except Coahuilteco formed 11–19 on 10 plus 1–9. The contrast between a vigesimal enumeration on the one hand and frequently subdecimal enumeration on the other hand — all in a single language — indicates that vigesimal enumeration spread fairly recently — probably it was invented by the Olmecs.

to question 8: Mayan languages, Tar (14), and Tot (8) have numeral classifiers, and others may as well.

to question 9: In UA, Mayan, and MZ languages — and others as well — locative notions parallel to English prepositions are expressed by 'relative nouns' — morphologically always possessed — the posesssing pronoun being what in English is the 'object', and the relational nouns can be translated as 'surface' (= on), 'interior' (= in), 'exterior' (= out of), 'back' (= behind), 'face' (= before), 'side' (= beside).

to question 10: In most MA languages, aspect is a primary category of the verb (phrase); tense is secondary or entirely unmarked.

6. METAPHOR IN LEXEME FORMATION

There is another area in which MA languages seem to show a great deal of similarity, and that is in the area of the use of specific metaphors in forming lexical items. In general, MA languages show a high level of lexico-morphological economy — that is, a large number of lexical items are formed from a modest number of root morphemes and productive derivational affixes. So for example, while a dictionary of a typical Mayan language may contain thousands of lexical entries, there may be no more than 1500 to 2000 roots plus 50 to 75 derivational morphemes (exclusive of borrowings and arcane vocabulary which may violate the phonological canons of ordinary vocabulary).

Thus, in most Mayan languages, 'door' is 'mouth of house', 'soot' may be 'nose of firewood', 'fruit' is 'eye of tree', 'bark' is 'skin of tree' or 'back of tree', 'vein' may be 'road of blood', 'bladder' may be 'house of urine', 'thumb' will be 'mother of hand'.

Such patternings of lexical structuring are widespread in MA languages and should be investigated; they probably will provide bases for typologically classifying the present languages as well as suggest specific historical contracts no longer implicit in the current language distributions.

7. MORPHEME ROSTER (LEXICAL BORROWING)

Under this rubric we may mention the sole substantive work dealing with MA in any of the possible ways outlined in the paper — Benjamin Lee Whorf's *Loanwords in Ancient Mexico* (1943 and 1947). Whorf treats borrowing from Aztec into Tepecano, Cora, Huichol, Tequistlatec, Huastec, Yucatec, Quiche and Cakchiquel.

One of the words Whorf thinks is Aztec, namely /tomi:n/ 'money' is really from Spanish *tomin*. The Aztec *mizton*, *miztli* 'cat, wild-cat' is believed by some to be of Spanish origin, but, as Whorf mentions, Hopi *mosa* allows a UA reconstruction **musa* which may have referred to a small wild cat. At least one of the items that Whorf thinks Yucatec borrowed from Aztec, namely *a:k*' 'roofing straw, thatch' from Aztec *aaka-t5* 'reed', is probably a misjudgment, since a proto-Mayan *^{7}*a:q*'can be reconstructed with the meaning 'grass, straw'.

Whorf refers to a Huichol vocabulary collected by one Lumholtz which contains a word *aina*, 'crocodile'. Whorf compares the Hui word to Mayan **76hi:n*, and assumes Hui borrowed the word from Mayan. Actually the word is Hui *7aina* = Cora *haihina*, and means 'crab'.

Whorf discusses a form *tu*^{x}*koro* ~ *tu*^{x}*kori* meaning 'owl' in a large area of MA and the western U.S. The form is so ancient that it may be part of proto-UA. It has been diffused into several Mayan languages, but it is difficult to state from what specific language.

He devotes a section to 'supercognates', word-forms of a similar shape shared by UA and Mayan languages, which he assumes are not borrowings but cognates within a superstock he calls proto-Penutian (and later called Macro-Penutian).

Whorf draws a number of tentative conclusions about the earlier distributions of Aztec, Cora-Huichol, and Mayan languages in MA. They seem rather fanciful in that they take no account of where Totonacan, Otonamguean, and MixeZoque languages may have been at the time, and are partly based on incorrect equations and guesses.

7.2

As mentioned earlier, we would naturally expect to find a certain number of loanwords radiating out from the areas of each of the several successive civilizations of MA. In the next few lines some of these are indicated.[7]

7.3 *MixeZoque into other languages*
[Olmec civ.]

	MixeZoque	Mayan	Mixtec	Zapotec	Otomian	Lenca	Xinca	Aztec	Jicaque
♮ *toto*	paper		X	X					
♮ *koya*	rabbit	X			X				
♮ *yuku*	mountain		X						
♮ *ciwa*	squash					X			
ij *pom*	incense	X					X		
♮ *cima*	calabash	X			X				X
♮ *kakawa*	cacao	X						X	
♮ *kuku*	turtledove	X	X						
♮ *hahcuku*	ant		X						

The 'sharp' sign before a word means that the form is found in some language in the family, and is similar to the form that was diffused, or is similar to the proto-form.

7.4 *Zapotecan into other languages*
[Zapotec civ.]

	Zapotecan	Huastec	Yucatec	Paya
pi^{7}kku^7	dog	X	X	X
picjinja	deer/large animal	X		
taa	woven mat	X		
pisjiicju7	coatimundi	X		
mani7	horse (< deer)		X	

7.5 *Mayan into other languages*
[Maya civ.]

	Mayan	Xinca	Lenca	Jicaque	Sierra Popoluca
cjenek'	bean	X	X	X	
muy	chicle tree	X			
pokok	toad	X			
sinaq	scorpion	X			
pop	woven mat	X			
kok	turtle	X			
k'ucj	buzzard	X	X		
k'ay	to sell	X			
c'uc'um	honey bear	X	X		
petak	prickly pear				X
xul	hole, cave			X	
sjocj'	screech owl			X	
til	tapir			X	
huhcj'	possum			X	

7.6 *Aztec into other languages*
[Toltec, Tenochtitlan civ.]

	Aztec[8]	Lenca	Xinca	Huichol	Tzeltal	Comecrudo	Coahuilteco
tequetl	work	X					
teopan	church	X		X			
tepoztli	'iron'	X		X			
matzahtli	pineapple	X					

[8] Aztec forms are cited in 'classical' 16th century orthography.

cuauhtlan	forest	X					
chiquihuitl	basket	X	X	X			
miztontli	cat	X	X	X			
tenextli	lime (calx)		X				
chocolatl	chocolate			X			
xihuitl	year	X					
xicalli	calabash	X					
tentzontli	goat				X		
tenamitl	fortress				X		
yeyi	three					X	
nahui	four					X	
macuilli	five					X	
chicuacen	six						X
comitl	kettle					X	

8. AREAL PHENOMENA AND LINGUISTIC DIFFUSION

We look at MA with a view to seeing if there are notable areal phenomena because we know that the kinds of historical developments that have been going on there in the last 3– to 400 years logically could foster such a situation. MA has not yet been subjected to a systematic investigation; once this is done, the result should be compared with and if possible integrated with Sherzer's work. A look at MA data suggests that indeed there are many features uniting now one part, now another part of MA; what remains unclear is whether there is a notable break between MA and North America, and — since our attestation of languages of the circumCaribbean area is poor — how significant is the typological break between MA and the circumCaribbean.

8.1

There are other parts of the New World that may be looked at from this viewpoint besides the obvious case of the Andes. Levi-Strauss' work on South American myths leads him to make the following observations on pp. 8–9 of *The raw and the cooked* (1969):

> ... I ask the historian to look upon Indian America as a kind of Middle Ages that lacked a Rome: a confused mass that emerged from a long-established, doubtless very loosely textured syncretism, which for many centuries had contained at one and the same time centers of advanced civilization and savage peoples, centralizing tendencies and disruptive forces .... [It is] certain that a [myth] set, such as the one studied here, owes its character to the fact that in a sense it became crystallized in am already established semantic environment, whose elements had been used in all kinds of combinations .... Such an interpreta-

tion ... is obviously based on historical conjecture: it supposes that tropical America was inhabited in very early times; that numerous tribes were frequently in movement in various directions; that demographic fluidity and the fusion of populations created the appropriate conditions for a very old-established syncretism, which predeced the differences observable between the groups; and that these differences reflect nothing or almost nothing of the archaic conditions but are in most cases secondary or derivative.

The study of areal phenomena and linguistic diffusion will allow inferences about the past culture history of the New World in a complementary way to those reached by the study of genetic relationships.

REFERENCES

Arana Osnaya, Evangelina. 1953. Reconstruccion del proto-Totonaco in Huastecos, Totonacos y sus vecinos, 123–30.

Bartholemew, Doris. 1959. Proto-Otomi-Pame. Master's thesis.

——. 1960. 'Some revisions of Proto-Otomi consonants. IJAL 26.317–29.

——. 1965. The reconstruction of Otopamean (Mexico), Ph.D. dissertation, University of Chicago.

Bauernschmidt, Amy. 1965. Amuzgo syllable dynamics. Lg. 41.471–83.

Coe, Michael D. 1968. America's first civilization: Discovering the Olmec. Washington, D.C. Smithsonian Library Series.

Collard, Howard and Elizabeth. 1962. Vocabulario Mayo. Serie de vocabularios indígenas Mariano Silva y Aceves 16. Mexico.

Driver, Harold E. 1961. Indians of North America. Chicago, University Press.

Driver, Harold E., and William C. Massey. 1957. Comparative studies of North American Indians. TAPS 47.165–460.

Emeneau, M.B. 1956. India as a linguistic area. Lg. 32.3–16.

Escalante Hernández, Roberto. 1962. El Cuitlateco. AnINA 9.

Fernández de Miranda, M.T. and R.J. Weitlaner. 1961. Sobre algunas relaciones de la familia Mangue. AnL 3/7.1–99.

Foster, Mary LeCron. 1969. The Tarascan language. UCPL 56.

Friedrich, Paul. 1969. On the meaning of the Tarascan suffixes of space. IUPAL Memoir 23.

Grimes, Joseph E. 1964. Huichol syntax. JanL, series practica 11.

Gudschinsky, Sara C. 1959. Proto-Popotecan: A comparative Study of Popotocan and Mixtecan. IUPAL Memoir 15.

Hale, K. 1958–9. Internal diversity in UtoAztecan. I. IJAL 24.101–07. II. IJAL 25.114–21.

Hendrichs Perez, Pedro R. 1946. Por tierras ignotas. Vol. 2, 139–246.

John, Jean Bassett. 1962. El idioma Yaqui. AnINA 10.

Kaufman, Terrence. 1968. Review of Dyk and Stoudt: Vocabulario Mixteco de

San Miguel el Grande. IJAL 33.257–8.
——. 1969. Ms: notes on Cuatlamayán Aztec.
KIRCHOFF, PAUL. 1943. Mesoamerica: Its geographic limits, ethnic composition and cultural characteristics. Ancient Meso-america: Selected readings, ed. by John A. Graham, pp. 1–14. Palo Alto, Peek.
KROEBER, A. L. 1939. Cultural and natural areas of Native North America. UCPAAE 38.1–242.
LEHMANN, WALTER. 1920. Zentral-Amerika, Teil I, 668–722.
LÉVI-STRAUSS, CLAUDE. 1969. The raw and the cooked (Introduction to a science of mythology: I). New York, Harper and Row.
LONGACRE, ROBERT E. 1966. On linguistic affinities of Amuzgo. IJAL 32.46–49.
——. 1967. Systemic comparison and reconstruction. HMAI 5.117–60.
MCQUOWN, NORMAN A. 1941. La fonémica del Cuitlateco. El México Antiguo 5.239–54.
——. 1949. Xinca fieldnotes.
MERRIFIELD, WILLIAM R. 1968. Palantla Chinantec grammar. Serie Científica 9, Museo Nacional de Antropología. Mexico, Instituto Nacional de Antropología e Historia.
NEWAN, S., and WEITLANER, R. J. 1950. Central Otomian I. Proto-Otomi reconstructions. II. Primitive Central Otomian reconstructions. IJAL 16.1–19, 73–81.
PIKE, EUNICE V. 1967. Huautla de Jimenez Mazatec. HMAI 5.311–330.
PRIDE, KITTY. 1965. Chatino syntax. Publications in Linguistics and Related Fields 12. Norman, Okla. Summer Institute of Linguistics of the University of Oklahoma.
RADIN, PAUL. 1933. Notes on the Tlappanecan language of Guerrero. IJAL 8.45–72.
SHERZER, JOEL. 1968. An areal-typological Study of North American Indian languages north of Mexico. Philadelphia, University of Pennsylvania dissertation.
SCHULTZE-JENA, LEONHARD. 1938. Indiana, III. Jena, Gustav Fischer.
SCHUMANN GÁLVEZ, OTTO. 1967. Xinca de Guazacapán. Mexico, Universidad Nacional Autonoma de México (thesis).
SWADESH, MORRIS. 1947. The phonemic structure of Proto-Zapotec. IJAL 13.220–30.
——. 1959. Indian linguistic groups of Mexico. Mexico, Escuela Nacional de Antropología e Historia.
——. 1961. Interrelaciones de las lenguas mayenses. AnINA 13.231–67.
——. 1962a. Afinidades de las lenguas amerindias. AIAK 34.729–38.
——. 1962b. Nuevo ensayo de glotocronología Yutonahua. AnINA 15.263–302.
——. 1967. Lexicostatistic classification. HMAI 5.79–116.
SWANTON, JOHN R. 1940. Linguistic material from the tribes of Southern Texas and Northeastern Mexico. BAE-B 127.
TURNER, PAUL R. 1969. Proto-Chontal phonemes. IJAL 35.34–37.

UPSON, B.W. and ROBERT E. LONGACRE. Proto-Chatino phonology. IJAL 31.312–322.

WARKENTIN, MILTON and CLARA. 1947. Diccionario Huave. Mexico.

——. 1952. Vocabulario Huave. Mexico.

WHORF, B.L. 1943. Loan words in ancient Mexico. Tulane University, Middle American Research Institute, Pub. 11, no. 1. Also 1947. SIL 5/3.49–64.

A fair amount of additional work on areal features (especially lexical diffusion) in Middle America has been done since the first publication of this article. New works by Kaufman and by Campbell and Kaufman are listed below. For grammatical features see Kaufman 1974a, 1974b, Campbell and Kaufman 1976 ms. For lexical diffusion see Kaufman 1974a, 1974b, 1976a, Campbell and Kaufman 1976, 1976 ms. For notational systems see Kaufman 1976b.

1976 CAMPBELL, LYLE and TERRENCE KAUFMAN. A linguistic look at the Olmecs. American Antiquity, January 1976. 41.80–89.

1976 ms CAMPBELL, LYLE and TERRENCE KAUFMAN. Linguistic diffusion in Meso-America. ms.

1974a KAUFMAN, TERRENCE. Meso-American Indian Languages. Encyclopaedia Britannica, Macropaedia 11.955-963.

1974b KAUFMAN, TERRENCE. Idiomas de Mesoamérica. Guatemala, Seminario de Integración Social Guatemalteca, Publicación No. 33, 126 pp.

1976a KAUFMAN, TERRENCE. Linguistic and archaeological correlations in Mayaland and associated areas. World Archaeology 8.1.101–118.

1976b KAUFMAN, TERRENCE. Proyecto de alfabetos y ortografías para escribir las lenguas mayances. Guatemala, Ministerio de Educación 161 pp.

INDIGENOUS DIALECTOLOGY

MARVIN K. MAYERS

Dialect studies in broad perspective have to do with any linguistic study that involves structural or comparative consideration of dialect. Dialectology, or dialect studies more narrowly conceived, involves those linguistic studies that indicate dialect distinction or definition. The goal of such research is to establish a sound base from which to project further structural and historical linguistic studies. Effective dialectology is dependent on two main factors: the provision of extensive diagnostic linguistic materials,[1] and the confirmation of results from various related and supporting disciplines such as geography, anthropology, psychology and sociology.[2] Linguistics has an adequate technique for providing the materials for such study in the dialect survey.[3] Since, however, dialect surveys can be carried out ineffectively as well as effectively, the following paper will attempt to present an ideal approach to dialect survey, and with this as background, discuss a number of attempts to do dialect studies in Ibero-America in light of their successes and shortcomings. It is quite obvious, from a study of the literature, that very little dialectology has been done in this area of the world. That which has been done is of a preliminary nature and itself needs amplification and extension before its validity can be fully established and evaluated.

An ideal approach to dialect studies would involve a careful geographical consideration of the area of interest, with mapping undertaken following the general knowledge of a given language area as provided by government personnel, business interests, missionaries, nationals, etc. Political boundaries need to be kept in mind as well,

[1] There is no intention here of becoming involved in the argument of whether a mass of material is needed to prove genetic relationship, i.e. by eliminating the chance factor, or whether in fact, a single innovation may constitute the entire phonological evidence for proving the unique common history of a given subgroup. The information called for here is all the defining and supporting evidence necessary to convincingly establish dialect boundary.

[2] Linguistics has long recognized the need for adequate geographical orientation to dialect research. Uriel Weinreich in *Languages in contact* (The Hague, 1963) indicates the need for psychological and sociocultural stimuli to structural (or linguistic) stimuli which help to determine linguistic interference, and he also warns that 'the linguist who makes theories about language influence but neglects to account for the sociocultural setting of the language contact leaves his study suspended, as it were, in mid-air'. Further, quoting Haugen, he suggests that 'talk of substrata and superstrata must remain stratospheric unless we can found it solidly on the behavior of living observable speakers'.

[3] Hans Kurath, *Handbook of the linguistic geography of New England*, 48-50, (Providence, R.I., 1939) gives some excellent instruction for field work. New techniques are being developed with the wider usage of the tape recorder, but little is in print describing these techniques.

so that both urban and rural areas might be included in the study. Lines of communication and transportation throughout the area would be plotted since migration is generally effected along lines of easy access.

The survey itself is best carried out in multiple stages, where possible. The initial stage would be a sociolinguistic shallow survey involving sociocultural[4] data; a linguistic word list such as the Swadesh 100 diagnostic word list;[5] a supplementary word list prepared for the local area in mind, to be appended to the basic word list and used as a control for evaluating the results of the 100 list; and a questionnaire involving details of the community involvement for every political unit, i.e. every town, city, etc. in the language area to provide broad background knowledge.[6] Observations made by the field investigators of a sociocultural nature not specified on the various questionnaires would also be noted. The linguistic and sociocultural questionnaires would ideally be elicited from at least two individuals from every distinct geographical or political division within the potential language community. Where the population is larger, or the geographical or political entity more extensive or diversified, more questionnaires[7] would be completed as a safeguard.

During the carrying out of the shallow survey or following its completion, all materials would be processed in a consistent way prior to instituting the second stage. Processing would involve first of all a lexicostatistical analysis of the diagnostic word lists.[8] The purpose of the lexicostatistical study would be primarily synchronic rather than diachronic, in that all the linguistic features would be submerged within the whole, and specific details of the languages would only be projected onto the gross lexicostatistical results.[9] This would be effected by the preparation of a linguistic-geographical map,[10] which would be used as a base map for dialect geography map-

4 The term 'sociocultural' will be used to include details of social organization, cultural information, and physiological information of both individual and society.

5 Any word list could serve so long as it represented 'cultural' items and 'noncultural' items and was recorded systematically and consistently throughout the area of the survey. The Swadesh 100 diagnostic list is satisfactory for this purpose and in fact to be desired as a base list, since it has been used in a wide variety of situations and thus can serve as a 'standard' word list, eliminating the proliferation of word lists with only local impact.

6 As a check on the coverage of the survey, a question such as: 'Are there any towns or villages in this area where the people do not speak exactly as you do?' should be asked of each informant in the survey.

7 Because of the factors of time and finances, it is seldom possible to effect a 'statistically' valid selection of participants in the survey. A survey, however, executed according to the above plan will turn up enough diagnostic details for the preliminary determination of dialect boundary and will be far superior to the 'hit and miss' method employed in dialect survey at the present time.

8 See Sarah C. Gudschinsky, 'The ABC's of lexicostatistics (glottochronology)', *Word* 12.175-210 (1956), and David Henne, 'Quiche dialect survey', ms. Summer Institute of Linguistics (Guatemala, 1965), for two ways of processing the lexical material of the survey.

9 This particular aspect of lexicostatistical method, which is a shortcoming in diachronic studies, becomes a distinct asset in synchronic studies.

10 By permuting columns and rows on a traditional lexicostatistical chart until there was an overall gradation of percentage of shared retention from high to low on the rows and columns, there would result clusterings of similar numbers at the point of intersection of rows and columns. Such clusterings of similar numbers are interpreted as dialect cores. These dialect cores would then be spread on a

ping as well as for other sociolinguistic plotting. Such a map is the base map used in Norman A. McQuown, *Measures of dialect-distance in Tzeltal-Tzotzil*,[11] and Marvin K. Mayers, 'The linguistic unity of Pocomam-Pocomchi'.[12] Isoglosses drawn on a linguistic geographical base map have been found to produce a clearer profile of dialect unity or separation than those drawn on a strictly geographical map. A preliminary attempt should be made at this time also, to correlate sociocultural information with linguistic usage.

Once the shallow survey had been completed, and the results known, a second survey would be planned making maximal usage of the processed data of the first. This would be a depth survey and would be carried out ideally with representatives of the resultant dialect areas selected on the basis of the shallow survey. Approximately one-tenth[13] of the initial participants in the original survey would thus be revisited and restudied. A new word list would be compiled, based on the first and including as many new items as would appear to be fruitful for a comparative study of the dialects. A more extensive sociocultural questionnaire would be prepared involving daily schedules, year cycles, diets, as complete kinship data as possible, etc. A tape recording would be made for each informant and each recording played to the other for mutual intelligibility check, and all played for specialists in the language where these are available. The speech of each individual in the survey would be structurally analyzed as fully as possible in the time available. This would involve not only phonological analysis of the traditional segmental type but also of phonological units more complex than those of the segment, such as the syllable, word, and others. Grammatical structures would also be analyzed for all levels of grammatical analysis.[14] Lexical-semantic analysis should be undertaken as well to the limits of theory, though at present, technique of such analysis follows far behind that of the phonological or grammatical techniques. If possible, psychological tests could also be applied.[15]

A third stage of ongoing linguistic and cultural studies would follow the processing of the material of stage two. Two or more representative speakers of the language whole would be selected to enter into full scale language and cultural analyses in preparation for multi-language diachronic studies in the language family involved, and from this into a multi-family comparison.

---

geographical map and the two be made to coincide with the least amount of distortion of either the linguistic data or of the geographical information.

[11] University of Chicago (1958).

[12] *IJAL* 26.290-300 (1960a).

[13] This percentage would be adjusted in keeping with the extensiveness of the survey.

[14] Once analysis is in hand for this aspect of the linguistic whole, any one of the descriptive techniques of the stratificational, tagmemic, or transformational approaches can be applied to the analysis for structural presentation and the phonology oriented to the grammar in the final description. The main requisite is that the material be handled consistently and compared consistently.

[15] McQuown, in his *Indian and ladino bilingualism: sociocultural contrasts in Chiapas, Mexico*, mimeo (Chicago, 1964), made use of the conventional T.A.T. as well as a photo test for cultural perception devised especially for the Chicago Chiapas project.

No one study, however carefully made, produces the final answer in language classification.[16] Such a careful preparation for further comparative work, however exhausting and time consuming, will insure more effective results than we are now achieving. The program, further, is totally within the realm of possibility for Ibero-America with the extensive research programs of various universities and of the Summer Institute of Linguistics.

In 1958, McQuown[17] presented some of the linguistic results of the ongoing Chicago project among the Tzeltal and Tzotzil Indian peoples of Chiapas, Mexico. The survey team consisted of a geographer, a botanist, an archaeologist, two social anthropologists and a linguist. The initial survey made use of Swadesh's 100- and 200-word 'basic' vocabulary lists coupled with a list of 400 'cultural words'. To these 600 words were added, in a few instances, more specialized vocabularies covering the geography and the flora and fauna. The purpose of this initial survey was 'to work out a minimal questionnaire of maximally contrastive items for a saturation study of the dialect variation in the project transect'. An intensive dialect distributional survey was planned for the summer of 1958 and was expected to include the social differentiation dimension, as well as the geographical dimension; in this survey it was intended that informants would be so chosen as to represent both 'horizontal and vertical dimensions'.

The processed material, as presented, included a geographical map of the transect, the lexicostatistical results ordered first with an arbitrary geographical ordering and then following an ordering based on the permutation of columns and rows of the geographical chart, until clusters of like numbers (of sameness-difference) appeared at the point of intersection of rows and columns; a geographical linguistic map; and four presentations of dialect geographical studies including two of normalized phonemic isoglosses, and one each of phonetic and lexical isoglosses. The isogloss presentations utilized the geographical linguistic map as a base map.

Further materials, reporting on the survey in depth and its significance, are continuing to appear. McQuown[18] reported on the attempt to correlate linguistic materials with the results of cultural projection tests and sociocultural census information. Though the purpose of the paper was to study bilingualism, it gives invaluable background for proper evaluation of the language contact problem in dialect studies.

Nicholas A. Hopkins[19] has submitted a paper to the Boletin of the Instituto Nacional Indigenista in which he reports on sociocultural aspects of linguistic distributions in the Tzeltal Tzotzil area. He attempts to describe briefly the varieties of Tzeltal and

[16] Though we do agree with Gudschinsky, 'Mazatec dialect history', *Lg* 34.474 (1958), that 'for establishing linguistic subgroups, lexical isoglosses are less reliable than phonological isoglosses. ...' and thus would rank aspects of the total study in terms of 'more helpful, less helpful'; 'more reliable, less reliable' etc.

[17] Norman A. McQuown, *op. cit.* (1958).

[18] Norman A. McQuown, *op. cit.* (1964).

[19] Hopkins, 'Sociocultural aspects of linguistic distributions: a preliminary study of Tzeltal and Tzotzil dialects', ms. (1965).

Tzotzil and the geographical distributions of these varieties; to relate these geographical distributions to social factors which underlie them; to place the contemporary linguistic varieties in the perspective of their historical development; and to draw inferences about the historical development of the indigenous communities themselves. Hopkins finds each community relatively homogeneous internally with some phonological, morphological, or lexical features shared by no other community. Likewise, clusters of geographically contiguous communities share features not found outside the cluster. 'It is suggested that this situation results from a series of splits in speech communities, the single, homogeneous, Proto-Tzeltal-Tzotzil speech community having split into two divisions, the ancestors of Tzeltal and of Tzotzil, each of these further split into several speech communities, the progenitors of the modern dialect clusters, which in turn developed into the modern individual dialects.'

The materials by McQuown and Hopkins are the first of a wealth of material coming from the Chiapas area and in effect set the standard for dialect studies in the Americas. There will be no question in the mind of the reader nor of the scholar who makes use of the material for comparative work as to the representativeness of the data, nor are there likely to be significant dialects left out of major language studies, produced in the area.

Gudschinsky has presented a 'precise analysis, in miniature, of successive dialect splits and of the effects on these splits of the disturbing factors of shift in the boundaries of speech communities'.[20] The analysis is further supported by a high correlation with the word geography of the area and with what is known of the political history of the Mazatecs. Being both a careful comparativist and a thorough field worker, the scholar is not too concerned that he must accept Gudschinsky's word that the material she utilizes is complete as far as diagnostic detail is concerned, representative of the language,[21] and true to each dialect in the languge; but her approach in the hands of a lesser scholar could seriously affect the usefulness of the results.

In 1960[22] I undertook a dialect survey of one of the Mayan languages of Guatemala, first to understand the internal dialect picture of the language and second to prepare a base from which the language itself could be effectively compared with other languages, both within and without the Mayan family of languages. The survey was undertaken in two stages: in the first I made use of few materials with a sampling of fifty individuals. In the second stage, I made use of extensive materials with nine individuals. The purpose of the first stage of the research was to select the individuals who would be most representative of their particular cultural and linguistic subgroup so that I

[20] Sarah C. Gudschinsky, *op. cit.* (1958).

[21] We are informed at the end of the article that 'the earlier study was able to draw on data from only six dialects instead of the present ten', which in itself would be no problem except that because of this, 'the unity of the high dialect was not apparent'. The question naturally arises, are there further dialects that could modify the picture presented in this later article or are we to await new information after further dialects are studied?

[22] Marvin K. Mayers, *The Pocomchi: a sociolinguistic study*, University of Chicago (1960b abstract).

could proceed with depth studies. The purpose of the second stage of the research was to prepare a preliminary phonology, grammar, and lexicon that would be as much as possible representative of the language itself, and to attempt to understand a) the way language interacts with culture and b) the way culture confirms dialect groupings or indicates further dialect divisions based on sociolinguistic criteria. It is with this basic linguistic and sociocultural information that the language itself can be compared beyond the borders of the language, i.e. with other Mayan or non-Mayan languages.

The structural studies produced two distinct dialects,[23] i.e. two dialects, with one having two divisions within the Pocomchi language, based on the phonology and grammar. Only one dialect with three subgroups resulted on the basis of the lexicostatistical counting.[24] Geographical and cultural divisions within this ethnic linguistic group bear out the division into three groups. As might be expected, the group dialects are mutually intelligible, and the dialect division is based on the clustering of features, rather than as a result of any neat break in a scale of sameness-difference.

I took with me into the field three basic tools of research: a linguistic word list, a sociocultural census, and a tape recorder. The linguistic word list consisted of the Swadesh diagnostic one-hundred-word list to show minimum difference between informants and to be the basis for lexicostatistical counts. It also included an additional one-hundred-and-fifty-word list that was intended to show maximum difference between informants. Both word lists were designed to provide phonological, lexical, and grammatical information, which, in turn, would contribute toward descriptive analysis of the speech of these informants. It was further planned that specific linguistic features, isolable in the material in the word lists, would form the basis for dialect distributional studies.

The sociocultural census included one hundred and twenty-six questions designed to give information regarding the person of the informant, his family, his social and civic responsibilities, his occupation and wealth, his religion and religious responsibilities, and the degree of his assimilation into the Latin culture. It also attempted to indicate his preference for dress, for his living situation, i.e. house type and location, and in what relationship to his neighbors he considered himself in terms of wealth, social class, and prestige. The census was to provide the basis for a descriptive statement of the sociocultural placement of the informants. Finally, the results of the census were to be placed side by side with those of the word list, in an attempt to observe whatever correspondences[25] there might be between the two, and to determine just how language indexes culture.

[23] The San Cristobal and the Tactic-Tamahu dialects.

[24] In initial interpretations two subdialects resulted, but final interpretations of the results of the counting showed the necessity for having three groupings of speakers with the Tactic-Tamahu core splitting.

[25] 'Correspondences', as used here, simply refers to the observation that the group of informants utilizing a linguistic feature is the same as, or almost the same as, i.e. corresponds to, the group of informants characterized by a specific sociocultural feature. There was no attempt made to do a statistical evaluation of these correspondences.

The word lists were tape recorded to provide a check on the phonetic transcription by hand of the linguistic materials, to provide material for future research in areas of interest involving linguistic and paralinguistic structures, and to enable the investigator to check on variations within the speech patterns of any particular informant. Ethnographic text material was recorded, whenever possible, to provide material for future research in linguistic and paralinguistic structures, for content analysis studies, and to provide sociocultural information needed for a more complete understanding of the sociocultural census.

I was prepared, in a few intensive studies of selected informants,[26] to add to the basic tools of the first stage of survey a second word list, to provide additional material for a preliminary phonemic and grammatical analysis of the informant's speech; a genealogy, a life history, day schedules, and daily diets. These items of information were sought (1) to provide more information on a smaller number selected from among the same informants, (2) to provide for sociolinguistic comparisons in depth, and (3) to provide, in addition to further text material, the needed background for the interpretation of the results of the survey.

The tools of research, mentioned above, were used in three municipalities or townships in Guatemala. These townships were Tamahu, Tactic, and San Cristobal, all in the department of Alta Verapaz. The predominant ethnic group occupying these three townships is named Pocomchi.[27]

Processing the data provided the following:

1. Assurance that all the major dialects and most of the minor dialects were represented in the survey.

2. Assurance that individuals who were chosen for in-depth studies were representative of their dialects, and that those chosen for ongoing comparative work were representative of their language.

3. Lexicostatistical results coincided basically with structural results, the difference being, as Gudschinsky found, one of 'detail and supporting evidence'.[28]

[26] Informants were selected for the depth studies on the basis of the results of the lexicostatistical counts. Once the counts for a town were completed, and the reordering of the informants on the basis of relative distance were complete, one informant was selected from the first of the list, one from the middle of the list, and one from the bottom of the list. It was hoped in this way to be able to work with an informant who diverged only a little from the others, one who diverged a little more from the others, and an informant who diverged a great deal linguistically from all the others. It was not always possible, however, to arrange to work with an informant so chosen, though it was possible to find a cooperative informant from the same relative position in the count results.

[27] Conservative estimates of the Pocomchi population living in Alta Verapaz, as well as in Baja Verapaz and Quiche, would indicate about 37,500 Pocomchi speakers. Of this number, 3,500 live in the township of Tamahu; 7,000 live in the township of Tactic, and 13,000 live in the township of San Cristobal. The township is an area of jurisdiction over a geographically centrally located town, and any number of rural villages. The majority of the population lives in the rural districts. Only about 300 inhabitants occupy the town of Tamahu; about 1,200 occupy the town of Tactic; and about 3,000 occupy the town of San Cristobal. The remainder of the population lives in three other centers in the same geographical area. A preliminary survey carried out in the six townships of the Pocomchi in 1954 set the stage for the survey carried out in the three representative townships.

[28] Gudschinsky, op. cit., p. 481 (1958).

4. The linguistic-geographical map enabled clear presentations of the detail of linguistic divergence and indicated that the phonemic isoglosses produced the clearest picture of language boundaries, followed by lexical isoglosses, then grammatical isoglosses, and finally phonetic isoglosses.

5. Dialect geographical studies, projected on the linguistic-geographical map, revealed dialect boundaries, confirming again both the lexicostatistical and structural studies.

6. Sociocultural results made it possible to sort out inconsistencies in the handling of the linguistic material, to confirm results of the linguistic studies, and to eliminate, up to a point, chance responses and the possibility of accidental influences in language relationships.

7. These latter results again gave clear indication that culture is indexed by language, though such a process is seen to be highly selective in the case of the Pocomchi.

The Pocomchi study complements another one,[29] placing Pocomchi in a larger frame of reference by relating it to Pocomam. The techniques of lexicostatistics, the comparative method, and dialect geography were utilized to gain an understanding of the relationships existing between the dialects of these languages. The results of the various studies reflect the close relationships of the two languages and indicate the possibility that the San Cristobal dialect of the Pocomchi language is in reality as close to, if not closer to the San Luis dialect of Pocomam than it is to other dialects of the Pocomchi. Unfortunately, a completely new synchronic study of the two languages was not undertaken in preparation for the study and though the results are gratifying, a more thoroughgoing research program, undertaken in the same amount of elapsed time, could have provided even more adequate results.

Bridgeman and Gudschinsky[30] have produced a plan for the study of the Tupi languages in Brazil. The suggestion is advanced that classifications have previously been made on the 'basis of geographical or ethnological factors or in the distribution of given morphemes'. These have been criticized correctly as being inadequate indicators of dialect when taken alone.[31] However, the lexicostatistical technique suffers under the same criticisms when taken as the sole basis for language division, as is pointed out by Bridgeman and Gudschinsky when evaluating an article by Aryón D. Rodrigues on the 'Classification of the Tupi-Guarani'. They propose to follow up Rodrigues' study by doing research in the living languages and to 'verify, by the method of comparison, the validity (or lack of validity) of the groupings made by Rodrigues; and 2) to prepare complete descriptive studies, at least of the most representative languages, in the major groups, in accord with what the results of the inspection, i.e.

[29] Marvin K. Mayers, op. cit. (1960a).

[30] Loraine Bridgeman and Sarah Gudschinsky, 'A plan for study of the Tupi languages', ms. (Brazil, 1965).

[31] Psychological, geographical, or sociocultural materials prove nothing of linguistic groupings when taken alone. They provide, rather, clues to follow in the study of language divergence as well as provide supporting evidence for linguistic conclusions and confirm or suggest further study to confirm division.

analysis or study, may indicate, and on the basis of these results proceed with a definitive and complete reconstruction of the Proto-Macro-Tupi and distribute (or classify) the various languages by subgroups'.[32]

The program of research is being carried out to produce more than just a 'series of little lists'. Because of restrictions in time and money, a special 'Standard or pattern for Tupi Research' has been developed as a supplement to the 'Standard Questionnaire for the Study of the Indigenous Brazilian Languages' organized by the National Museum of Brazil. It contains two parts, the first of which has 'as its goal a rapid verification of phonemic contrasts with each series of words illustrating a phonemic contrast, or the occurrence of important allophones in Guarani; and the second part shows lists of categories of affixes which pertain to Kaiowá to give a reasonably complete picture of the grammatical structure of the dialect being examined'. In spite of the obvious advantage in determining linguistic groups on the basis of linguistic information alone, features of control of representation as well as of verification appear to be missing from this otherwise excellent plan for field survey.

A number of studies have been made dealing with mutual intelligibility as one technique for determining dialect boundaries. Bruce Briggs has utilized such a technique among the Yuman speakers of California and has thus set a pattern that could be followed in Spanish America. 'Briefly, the technique involves asking an informant to respond in the investigator's language to a tape recording of a text in a language different from, but related to the informant's own language. The response is scored against a master translation, and the result expressed as an index of the degree of intelligibility. This is checked with lexicostatistical counts. It is evident that the higher the degree of linguistic similarity, the more likely there is to be a one-to-one correlation of cognate percent and intelligibility percent. The lower the degree of linguistic similarity the more likely the intelligibility percent will fall below the cognate percent.'[33]

The Mexican Branch of the Summer Institute of Linguistics is also carrying on mutual intelligibility testing of the Indian languages of Mexico, directed by John Crawford. This is being effected by the use of questionnaires and tape recordings, though at the moment no material has reached the publication stage.

David Henne has utilized tape recordings to determine mutual intelligibility borders in the Quiche area of Guatemala.[34] He recorded the materials in a 'shallow' survey of the Quiche area, and as he moved from town to town, he would play the tapes and take reaction of informants in an informal way. When he had all the tapes recorded, he worked with a companion who had been studying the Quiche language for twelve years and together they grouped recordings into like groups on the basis of impressionistic reactions to phonological and grammatical features. These coincided almost completely with studies made focusing first on similar features in the language and then focusing on variations in the responses of informants. He derived by this means

[32] *IJAL* 24.231-234 (1958).
[33] Bruce Briggs, 'Testing intelligibility among Yuman languages', *IJAL* 23.57-62 (1957).
[34] Henne, op. cit. (1965).

a three-way verification of dialect boundaries and will be adding a fourth, i.e. dialect geography.

Perhaps the greatest threat to dialect studies in the twentieth century is the possibility that efforts will not be coordinated. With the Summer Institute of Linguistics actively engaged in field research in the majority of the countries of Spanish America, and with some of the greatest Universities of the world now engaged in field research in this area, the future for dialect studies has never been so bright. If there could be (1) basic tools utilized in initial survey so that a broad base could be laid for future work, and (2) if the results of this preliminary survey work, as well as further materials as it became available, could be archived in some accessible, interested University or center, dialect studies and further comparative studies based on the dialect studies could produce research sources and research such as has never been achieved in any other area of the world. Such studies are not foreign to the basic goals of the various institutions working in the area, nor for that matter of the governments sponsoring or cooperating in the research. Dialect studies are vital to the researcher interested in the professional field, in order to enable him to place his work in a broad linguistic framework, as well as a broad cultural and geographical framework. They are necessary to the members of the Summer Institute of Linguistics, since a given Scripture translation should be representative of a given dialect to be utilized effectively; and further, since scientific knowledge must be at hand, indicating need for separate translation projects and in decisions regarding assignment of personnel to a given field. Governments should be vitally interested in (1) the spread of dialects; (2) a field worker's careful estimate of the number of speakers; and (3) the mutual intelligibility. of the dialects. Business interests now using the dialects for their public advertisements need to become apprised of their effectiveness in a given dialect area, or the need for restating the 'ad' in the 'idiom' of the area. Cooperation in this area of linguistic activity is therefore valuable and could result in many side benefits.

Besides the need for standardized research materials and for a center for archiving such materials, the materials that are available in various files, both institutional and individual, should be made available to the rest of the scholastic world (perhaps in a mimeographed form as a publication of the archives), as research is accomplished and later in established journals when there has been time for summarization and synthesis. Unfortunately, at the present time, there is little being produced, and this is either not being published or is finding its way into relatively unknown journals.[35]

[35] The lack of theoretical orientation, its physical bulk and the need for phonetic script that is difficult to reproduce in conventional type is likely keeping this type of material out of the more scholastic journals.

COMPARATIVE RECONSTRUCTION OF INDIGENOUS LANGUAGES

ROBERT E. LONGACRE

0. For many years the accomplishment of Indo-European comparative reconstruction has stood in lonely splendor without a serious rival (in depth and scope) in other linguistic stocks. Current work in Latin America and the Caribbean is, however, now going forward at such a pace that in the near future it will no longer be possible to equate comparative linguistics with Indo-European studies. In Mesoamerica comparative reconstruction is reaching a very mature stage — especially in the Otomanguean and Mayan stocks and in the Mixe-Zoque family. Proto-Otomanguean, embracing some thirty languages grouped into seven component families, is currently on the drawing boards. Meanwhile, phonologies of component families have either been worked out as of several years ago or are currently being completed. Etymological dictionaries — sizeable bodies of cognate sets — will soon be available for component families and the stock as a whole. Current work in the Mayan stock is also very promising with a proven link of Mayan to one South American language. Mixe-Zoque is shaping up well. Good work has been done recently in Utoaztecan but we still lack an etymological dictionary of adequate size for that stock. Less advanced are available comparative studies in Totonac-Tepehua (not to mention the vexed question of 'Mexican Penutian': Mayan, Totonac-Tepehua, Mixe-Zoquean) and in Yuman (Hokan).

In South America and in the Caribbean, comparative projects are at early stages. Arawakan, Tupi-Guaraní, Chibchan, and Carib are scarcely begun. Nevertheless, in Quechua-Aymara and in Pano-Tacanan mature projects with sizeable ensembles of reconstructed forms will soon be forthcoming. A significant beginning has been made in Gê.

A sine qua non of careful comparative reconstruction is adequate synchronic data. It is probably no accident that comparative reconstruction is at an advanced stage in Mesoamerica, where investigators of the Summer Institute of Linguistics are currently working in approximately 100 languages and dialects, and where that organization began work in 1935. In as much as the same organization has been at work in Peru since 1946, Ecuador since 1953, Bolivia since 1955, Brazil since 1956, and Colombia since 1962 (with projected expansion into yet other countries), the descriptive data needed for sound comparative work on an extensive scale are either available already or will be available shortly.

This article does not pretend to be either exhaustive or encyclopedic. I have concentrated on reporting comparative projects that seemed to me to be genuinely significant. Articles which are essentially collations of word lists from two or more languages (or dialects) without application of the comparative method have usually not been mentioned. Such articles, if they contain reliable data, are sources for comparative projects but not themselves such projects. By the same token, the rather extensive literature of lexico-statistics (glottochronology) has been bypassed. Many such articles have been written without application of the comparative method or with a minimum use of that method. Such articles deal with resemblant forms rather than with cognates. Nor have I been concerned to report the varying linguistic classifications found in the literature. Greenberg's and McQuown's classifications have proved useful for providing frames of reference (and occasionally a convenient whipping-boy).

In that some of the most significant comparative work is still unpublished — some even in non-final form — this article cites a much higher proportion of unpublished works than is customary. My defense for this unorthodox procedure is that the sketch would have been most impoverished otherwise. Colleagues of the Summer Institute of Linguistics have been cooperative in providing unpublished materials and letting me quote from them — as have also María Teresa Fernández de Miranda, Terrence Kaufman, and José Rona (who lent me the unpublished Ferrario manuscript on Charruan). Naturally, the citation of so many unpublished works is inevitably accompanied by failure to cite other such works unknown to me.

Current progress in comparative reconstruction throughout Latin America and the Caribbean — along with the prospect of increased momentum in such studies during the immediate future — offers promise of payoff in the following domains: (1) Cultural analysis of reconstructed vocabularies and evidence of past cultural contacts; (2) evidence of past migrations and locations of original homelands of some language groups; (3) scope for application of dialect geography (e.g. Mixtec, Mazatec, Zapotec, Chinantec in Mexico); (4) fresh examination of substratum theory (e.g. Aymara substratum in Quechua); (5) study of late spread of certain languages as linguae francae (Quechua, Tupi-Guarani) vis-a-vis tribal languages on the one hand and Spanish or Portuguese on the other hand; (6) classification of languages and dialects.

The last point needs to be underscored. Consider, e.g. 'Macro-Otomanguean' as set up by Greenberg and predecessors. In this classification, the whole phylum has been divided into the following stocks: Otomanguean, Mixtecan, Chinantecan, Zapotecan. Within Otomanguean stock the following families have been posited: Otomian, Popolocan, Mazatecan, Trique, Chorotegan (Chiapanec-Manguean). The Mixtecan stock is said to contain the Mixteco family: Mixtec, Cuicatec, Amuzgo. Such a classification reflects intuitive groupings, guesses made before adequate descriptive data were available, and before serious comparative work was undertaken in various branches of the phylum. However, it is now evident (see section 6 below) that Popolocan contains Mazatecan (as its most divergent member), that Trique belongs within Mixtecan, and that Amuzgo is not Mixtecan but a separate family in the stock or phylum. Furthermore, the very grouping 'Otomanguean' within 'Macro-Otomanguean' can no longer be justified. Popolocan within 'Otomanguean' shared important developments with Mixtecan which is not in this grouping. Although it is probable that Chorotegan shares developments with Mixtecan-Popolocan, there is no evidence as yet that Otomian is any nearer to these two families than, say, to Zapotecan or Chinantecan. The old Mixtecan-Zapotecan grouping may not be entirely irrelevant. In brief, it is best at present to posit an Otomanguean phylum or stock (discarding the term 'Macro-Otomanguean') with seven component families: Otomian (or better, 'Otopamean'), Popolocan, Mixtecan, Amuzgoan, Chorotegan (or better, 'Chiapanec-Manguean'), Zapotecan, Chinantecan. These are the main pieces. How they mutually relate will be decided when Proto-Otomanguean is published. It will then be possible to trace not only isoglosses as such but shared innovations versus shared retentions. In that shared innovations are crucial to genetic grouping (cf. 4.2 below) it should be possible to make some mature judgments regarding groupings within Otomanguean.

Special mention should be given to those obliged to work with often poorly recorded data of extinct languages in an effort to use such data for comparative reconstruction and language classification. María Teresa Fernández de Miranda and Roberto Weitlaner's comparative reconstruction of Proto-Chiapanec-Manguean (6.3) and Benigno Ferrario's treatment of the scanty data for Charruan (9) are exemplary in this regard.

1. Wonderly's reconstruction of Proto-Zoquean[1] was based on the comparison of Zoque (4 dialects), Tapachulteco, Sierra Popoluca, and Mixe. The Tapachulteco data, characterized by Wonderly as 'scanty and not too reliable', are all we can expect to have in that the language is either already extinct or very close to extinction. In an important little note Nordell[2] presented evidence to show that the Zoquean family does not consist of three branches, Zoque, Popoluca, and Mixe, but basically of two: Zoquean and Mixean. The 'Popolucan' dialects may be parcelled out on one side or the other. In this judgment Kaufman has now concurred and has placed Tapachulteco on the Mixean side as 'Chiapas Mixe'. Kaufman's unpublished study, *Mixe-Zoque diachronic studies*[3] replaces all former work in its detail and scope.

Wonderly set up the phonemic system for Proto-Zoquean (Table 1):

[1] William L. Wonderly, 'Some Zoquean phonemic and morphophonemic correspondences', *IJAL* 15.1-11 (1949).

[2] Norman Nordell, 'On the status of Popoluca in Zoque-Mixe', *IJAL* 28.146-9 (1962).

[3] Terrence Kaufman, unpublished manuscript.

*p	*t	*c	*k	*k^w	*ʔ
	*s				*h
*m	*n			*ŋ	
*w	*y				
		*i	*ʌ	*u	
		*e		*o	
		*ä		*a	

Table 1

Of the phonemes in Table 1 (a) *k^w is set up on the basis of the correspondence Zoque and Popoluca k^w ~ Tapachulteco and Mixe p in but one set; (b) *ŋ is set up only in word final; (c) *ä is set up to account for Mixe-Zoque-Popoluca a ~ Tapachulteco e.

Kaufman does not reconstruct these three phonemes. In common with Wonderly, he finds the correspondence Zoque and Popoluca k^w ~ Mixe p in but one set where he posits a Proto-Mixe-Zoque cluster *kw which went to common Mixe p. An allophone *[ŋ] of Proto-Mixe-Zoque *w is considered to have become phonemic in common Zoquean. Concerning Wonderly's posited *ä Kaufman suggests: 'more data on Tapachulteco would probably show the correspondence Tap./e/: other MZ /a/ to be the result of a secondary development in Tap. For instance, if we assume this correspondence to go with MZ *a, we can account for the Tap. forms by the following rules ...' (42).

One of the most marked features of Mixe-Zoque is its complicated morphophonemics: palatalization, metathesis, assimilation, loss or gain of laryngeal (ʔ or h); lengthening or shortening of vowel. One can proceed neither synchronically nor diachronically in this family without attending to such processes. Wonderly's article was significantly entitled 'Some Zoquean phonemic and morphophonemic correspondences'. Kaufman's careful consideration of the morphophonemics is matched by his care in reconstructing affixes both derivational and inflectional; and patterns of word, phrase, and clause structure. In one respect Kaufman was handicapped, however: no published modern description of Oaxaca Mixe was extant when he wrote. A major breakthrough has now been scored in understanding the grammar of Oaxaca Mixe. The clause system described for Tlahuiltoltepec Mixe[4] is in some ways strikingly different from that found in any previously described Mixe-Zoquean dialect. Thus, while Kaufman describes two sets of person markers for verbs, Tlahuiltoltepec Mixe has eight partially similar but functionally distinct sets of such markers.

2.1. The comparative reconstruction of Próto-Mayan has been under way by McQuown for many years. His sketch of 1955[5] (revised somewhat in 1956)[6] outlines a phonemic

[4] Shirley Lyon, 'Tlahuiltoltepec Mixe clause structure' *IJAL* 33.25-33 (1967). A similar analysis is followed in unpublished materials of Searle Hoogshagen and John Crawford for two other Oaxaca Mixe dialects.

[5] Norman McQuown, 'The indigenous languages of Latin America', *AmA* 57.501-70 (1955).

[6] Norman A. McQuown, 'The classification of the Mayan languages', *IJAL* 22.191-5 (1956).

system for Proto-Mayan but cites data only from Mam and Huastec. Kaufman, with access to McQuown's data, has published recently[7] an ensemble of 532 reconstructed forms classified according to semantic domains and accompanied by a chart of the phonemic system. Olson's article on the genetic relation of the Chipaya of Bolivia to Mayan contains a sketch of Proto-Mayan.[8] None of these materials are adequate at present. Kaufman's sketch, the best of the three, needs to be amplified into an etymological dictionary; it cites no actual language forms but gives only reconstructions. Olson's sketch (to which I contributed) is based on a more meager file of reconstructions than is Kaufman's — although some sets have fuller representation and spread. Furthermore, in Olson's article, only those Proto-Mayan sets are given for which Chipaya cognates exist. Olson is able, however, to state in some detail reflexes of Proto-Mayan phonemes in the various Mayan languages. His description of Proto-Mayan reflexes is based on the total corpus of sets, published and unpublished, which Olson and I assembled.

McQuown's inventory of Proto-Mayan phonemes (1955 modified by 1956) follows in Table 2:

*p	*t	*c	*č	*ç̌	*k	*ḳ	
*p'	*t'	*c'	*č'	*ç̌	*k'	*ḳ'	*ʔ
		*s	*š		*x		*h
*m	*n				*ŋ		
*w			*y				
	*l						
	*r						
*i	*ï	*u					
*e	*a	*o					

Two tones 'and`; Clusters $C_1 C_2$ in which C_1 = any except bilabials, liquids and semivowels; and C_2 = semivowels *y and *w.

Table 2

Kaufman's inventory of phonemes is much the same as McQuown's except (1) that he does not reconstruct retroflexed *ç̌ and *ç̌'; (2) he does not reconstruct *r; and (3) he posits a threefold contrast among the bilabials: *p, *p', and *b.

Olson's inventory of phonemes includes *t̯ and *t̯' as well as *k̯ and *k̯' — all of which McQuown handles as clusters of *t, *t', *k, and *k' with *y. Likewise, Olson reconstructs $*h^w$ and $*x^w$ which McQuown handles as clusters of *h and *x plus *w. Olson also includes a full series of retroflexed affricates and sibilants (ç̌, ç̌', and ş̌). Olson, like McQuown, posits a simple two-way contrast of bilabials (*p versus *b)

[7] Terrence S. Kaufman, 'Materiales lingüísticos para el estudio de las relaciones internas y externas de la familia de idiomas mayanos', Evon Z. Vogt and Alberto Ruz L., eds. *Desarrollo cultural de los Mayas* 31-136 (Mexico City, 1964).

[8] Ronald D. Olson, 'Mayan affinities with Chipaya of Bolivia I: correspondences', *IJAL* 30.313-24 (1964) and 'Mayan affinities with Chipaya of Bolivia II: cognates', *IJAL* 31.29-38 (1965).

and of liquids (*l and *r). As in McQuown's 1955 sketch, he posits five vowels rather than six.

Olson summarizes as follows the sound correspondences on which the threefold distinction among the Proto-Mayan affricates (*c, *č, *ç̌) is based: '*c regularly has reflex c in most languages. ... In M this reflex occurs only root finally. Root initially the M reflexes are č in the environment of high vowels ... and t in the environment of low vowels ... Under obscure conditions, reflex s occurs in P and K ... as well as in C and Tz. Similarly obscure is t ... versus Ø in H.

*č has reflex c in A, Q, C, P, Pm, K, Ch, Chr, Chl, and Tz ... Root initially it has č before front vowels and ç̌ elsewhere in I, Ag, Mm, and J ... Root finally, č occurs in Ag, Mm, and J, but c in I and M.

*ç̌ has reflex č in A, Q, C, Pm, K, Ch, Chr, Chl, Tz, M, and H... ; it has reflex č in I, Ag, Mm, and J before front vowels ... it has reflex ç̌ in I, Ag, M, and J in other environments' (318).

In brief, *c is based on correspondence of c ~ c throughout the languages with occasional reflex s under conditions as yet not understood; while *ç̌ has reflex č in languages which have no retroflexed affricate but is ç̌ in languages having this phoneme (aside from fronting to č before front vowel). A further affricate *č is reconstructed on the basis of the correspondence c ~ ç̌ (~ č), i.e. the phoneme *č merged with reflexes of *c in some languages and with those of *ç̌ in others.

Olson's reconstruction of *r is based on the correspondence r(A, Q, C, P, Pm, K) ~ y (J, Ch, Chr, Chl, Tz, Mop, H), ~ (with weaker witness) č (I,M) ~ ç̌ (Ag). In words where Olson and I reconstructed *r, Kaufman reconstructed *y — for which Olson posits uniform reflex y in all languages. However, Olson's reconstructions of *y are all contiguous to vowel *a. In that *r — which has wider distribution — also occurs contiguous to *a there is apparent contrast. Here, however, Kaufman reconstructs vowel *ë. Thus, where Olson posits **par* or **pahar* 'skunk' Kaufman posits **pahëy*; and where Olson posits **raş* 'green' Kaufman posits **yëš*. A phonemic contrast must be posited here somewhere in the Proto-Mayan forms. Olson accounts for the contrast by positing *r (versus *y); Kaufman, by positing *ë (versus *a).

It is impossible at present to evaluate Kaufman's three-way contrast among bilabials. McQuown and Olson reconstruct only *p versus *b. The phoneme b, which is a reflex of the latter in contemporary Mayan languages, is usually accompanied by glottal friction or closure. In some languages it has a variety of allophones. Thus, in Tzotzil[9] the phoneme varies from [b], to [ʔb], to [ʔm] to [ʔM]. In that Kaufman reconstructs *p' presumably he has found sets of correspondences which justify his assuming that b in contemporary Mayan has two different sources. The slender file of comparative Mayan sets which Olson and I assembled is not sufficient to check this out. All etymons in our present data are forms where Kaufman reconstructs either

[9] Nadine Weathers, 'Tsotsil phonemes with special reference to allophones of B', *IJAL* 13.108-11 (1947).

*p or *b; we do not have sets containing the (relatively few) etymons for which Kaufman reconstructs *p'.

One of the most commendable features of Kaufman's work is his careful attention to the geographical distribution of cognates which do not occur in the entire family. He sets up the following subgroupings in Mayan: (1) Huastecan; (2) Yucatecan; (3) Cholan; (4) Tzeltalan; (5) Tojolabal; (6) Chuj; (7) Kanjobalan (includes Jacaltec); (8) Motocintleco (extinct); (9) Mamean (includes Aguacatec and Ixil); (10) Quichean (includes Kakchiquel, Tzutujil, and Achi); (11) Kekchian (includes Pocoman-Pocomchi).

Excluding Huastecan (which is geographically noncontiguous) Kaufman sets up (2)-(11) as a dialect chain along which certain cognates, not found in the whole family, occur in continuous areas. In this way he is able to group (2)-(5) as a lexical area distinguishable from (6)-(7); and from (8)-(11). Other cognates, which have less than family-wide distribution may reflect sporadic survival of competing Proto-Mayan forms. In the above dialect chain, (2), (4), and (7) are especially singled out as centers of lexical innovation.

Kaufman closes his article with a consideration of extra-Mayan contacts as reflected by the presence of 11 loans from Mixe-Zoque; one from Zapotec; and three from Utoaztecan.

2.2. By far the most interesting feature of Olson's paper is the evidence that it presents that the Uru-Chipaya of the Bolivian altiplano is related to Mayan.[9a] One hundred twenty-one cognate sets are presented in which reconstructed Proto-Mayan forms are given along with Chipaya forms and reconstructed Proto-Mayan-Chipaya forms. Both the present day phonemic system of Chipaya and the reconstructed Mayan-Chipaya system are quite similar to that posited for Proto-Mayan.

The phonemic system of Proto-Mayan-Chipaya follows (Table 3):

*p	*t̯	*t	*c	*č	*ç̌	*k̯	*k		*ḳ	*ʔ
*p'	*t̯'	*t'	*c'	*č'	*ç̌'	*k̯'	*k'		*ḳ'	
*v			*s	*š	*ş̌		*h^{w}	*h	*x	*x^{w}
*m		*n					*ŋ			
		*l								
		*r								
*w		*y								
*i	*ʌ									
*e	*a	*o								

Table 3

It is interesting to note in Table 3 that three bilabials are reconstructed (cf. Kaufman's reconstruction of three bilabials in Proto-Mayan); a full set of retroflexed alveopalatals

[9a] Cf. Eric Hamp, 'On Maya-Chipayan', *IJAL* 33-74-76 (1967).

(cf. Olson's Proto-Mayan); *r versus *y (cf. Olson's Proto-Mayan); and six vowels (cf. Mc Quown 1956 and Kaufman). In the above *v deserves special comment. The reflexes in Chipaya are: zero in root-initial; w in root-final in certain special phonemic environments; elsewhere: l after high vowels and r after low vowels. The Proto-Mayan reflex is, according to Olson, *b. It would be interesting to see if Kaufman's reconstruction of *p versus *b corresponds in any sets with Olson's Proto-Mayan-Chipaya *p' versus *v.

The Mayan-Chipaya link undoubtedly will not stand as an isolated example of demonstrated linguistic relationship between Mesoamerica and South America. Indeed, the Mayan-Chipaya tie cannot in itself be evaluated without broader context. It has been assumed that Mayan, Mixe-Zoquean, and Totonacan are related.[10] The day when Mayan and Mixe-Zoquean can be seriously compared should be near, in that both language families are subjects of serious comparative study. When etymological dictionaries of the two families are available, serious comparison of the two will be greatly facilitated.

Olson summarizes the problem of the relation of Uru-Chipaya to these three families as follows: 'At least four solutions are possible. These solutions imply varying estimates of the relative recency of migration to South America. In order of relative recency of migration these four possibilities are:

(1) Is Uru-Chipaya the farthest extension of the Mayan stock, the Tocharian of Mayan?

(2) Does Uru-Chipaya form a sub-grouping with either Mayan, Zoquean, or Totonacan as against the other two, or does Uru-Chipaya form a subgrouping with any two of the three as against the third?

(3) Are Uru-Chipaya, Mayan, Zoquean, and Totonacan all coordinate on the same horizon?

(4) Does Mayan-Zoquean-Totonacan form a grouping against Uru-Chipaya?' (29).

3. Evangelina Arana has reconstructed Proto-Totonacan-Tepehuan on the basis of three Totonac dialects and one Tepehua dialect.[11] She reconstructs the following phonemes (Table 4):

[10] After this article went to the editor I received from Terrence Kaufman some mimeographed sheets which present the first solid evidence yet assembled to demonstrate the affinities of these three linguistic families. He has 131 cognate sets plus sixteen further sets that he regards as possible diffusions. Of the 131 sets, 51 are Mayan and Mixe-Zoquean; 31 are Mayan and Totonacan; 28 are Mayan, Mixe-Zoquean, and Totonacan; and 21 are Mixe-Zoquean and Totonacan. Cognates and reconstructed forms are not given. The catalogue consists rather of a set of English glosses with indications of presence of cognates in the two or three families involved in each set. In that Kaufmann is conservative in what he terms 'cognate' we may feel assured that published evidence regarding 'Macro-Mayan' is forthcoming.

[11] Evangelina Arana O., 'Reconstrucción del Protototonaco', Ignacio y Eusebio Davalos Hurtado Bernal, eds. *Huastecos, Totonacos y sus vecinos*, 123-30 (Mexico City, 1953).

*p	*t	*c	*č	*tl	*k	*ḳ	*ʔ
		*s	*š	*ł	*x		
*m	*n						
*w		*y					
	*l						
*i	*i·	*u	*u·				
	*a	*a·					

Table 4

Initially, certain clusters of spirant plus stop occurred: *sk, *šk, *st, *sḳ, *łk, *łt. Medially, syllable final consonants (*t, *k, *s, *n, *y) followed by the syllable initial consonants and consonant clusters constituted clusters of two or three members.

Proto-Totonacan-Tepehua was characterized by regular morphophonemic alternation among the members of the following sets of consonants: *k/*ḳ; *c/*č/*tl; *s/*š/*ł. Notice that these morphophonemic alternations involve contiguous pairs or triplets of consonants within the stop or spirant series.

While *ʔ is included in the stop series, Arana actually reconstructs glottalized vowels in preference to either a glottal stop or a series of glottalized consonants. The role of the Proto-Totonac-Tepehua laryngeal thus forms an interesting comparison and contrast with laryngeals in other reconstructed languages (cf. Proto-Mayan, Proto-Chipaya-Mayan, and Proto-Mixe-Zoque).

Phonological developments from Proto-Totonacan-Tepehua to the various daughter languages show a minimum of split and merger. Presumably the dialects involved have not diverged far from each other. The Totonac dialect of San Pedro Octlacotla seems to display evidence of borrowing from the adjacent Tepehua.

4.1. For Proto-Utoaztecan we have an early sketch of Whorf's (1935)[12] and the recent work of the Voegelins and Hale (1962).[13] These may be supplemented by an unpublished study of Burton Bascom on the Piman group.[14]

Whorf reconstructed the following phonological entities for Proto-Utoaztecan (Table 5):

*p	*t	*c	*ḳ	*k	*kʷ	*ʔ
*m	*n	*ⁿs	[ñ]	*ŋ	*ŋʷ	
*v	*r	*s				
*w	*l	*y				
	*i			*u		
	*e	*a	*a·	*o		

Table 5

[12] Benjamin L. Whorf, 'The comparative linguistics of Uto-Aztecan', *AmA* 37.600-8 (1935).

[13] C. F. and F. M. Voeglin, and Kenneth L. Hale, 'Typological and comparative grammar of Uto-Aztecan: I (phonology)', Indiana University publications in anthropology and linguistics memoir 17 of *IJAL* 28 (Jan., 1962).

[14] Burton William Bascom Jr., 'Proto-Tepiman', unpublished manuscript, (University of Washington, 1965). I have had access only to an abstract prepared by Bascom.

The Proto-Utoaztecan phonemic inventory of the Voegelins and Hale is somewhat simpler (Table 6):

*p	*t	*c	*k	*k^w	*ʔ
*m	*n		*ŋ		
		*s			*h
*w	*r	*y			
	*l				
*i	*ï	*u			
	*a	*o			

Table 6

Whorf's reconstruction of k̯ was based on the contrast of k̯ and k in Hopi. The Voegelins and Hale trace this development in Hopi to preceding high vowel versus preceding low vowel: 'Accordingly, we argue that UA *k descends as [Hopi] /k/ when preceded by a high vowel and followed by *a, but as /q/ when preceded by a low vowel and followed by *a. This argument can be extended — if restricted to examples descended from reconstructable forms — to account for the Hopi reflection of *k in all environments: UA *k>/k/ when contiguous to a high vowel; *k>/q/ when initial before a low vowel and when medial and flanked by low vowels, i.e. when not contiguous to a high vowel' (51).

Certain other features of Whorf's reconstruction possibly reflect Hopi bias: (1) *ñ (a reconstruction of which Whorf himself is doubtful) is probably based on Proto-Utoaztecan *ŋ >Hopi /ŋ^y/ after a high vowel. (2) *ŋ^w is based on Hopi reflex of *w in a special morphophonemic environment discussed below. Whorf's *^{n}s and his *p versus *v also involve us in Hopi and Utoaztecan morphophonemics.

Whorf's six vowel system is awkward and off balance with respect to the occurrence of only one long vowel. The Proto-Utoaztecan vowel system of the Voegelins and Hale is more plausible.

Whorf, impressed by the p/v and w/ŋ^w alternations in Hopi, tried to outline a theory to account for these and other alternations: (1) The stop-spirant alternation p/v reflects a stage in which spirant allophones occurred intervocalic and stop allophones elsewhere; (2) Some Utoaztecan stems which contain stops resistant to spirantization probably witness to a lost consonant which occurred in cluster before the nonspirantizing stop; (3) Other Utoaztecan stems, which contain non-spirantizing stops associated with a nasalizing influence, witness to medial clusters of nasal plus stop. Thus *w alternating with *ŋ^w really was originally *w versus nw (or *mw?). For the lost consonants of (2), Whorf suggested '*l, *r, possibly no more' (606).

Whorf seemed to believe that the canonical pattern *CVCVC occurred as well as *CVCV and that final consonants were nasals, *l, and *r. Occurrence of one of these syllable finals accounted for a further *CVCCV pattern. While Whorf's choice of *r and *l as syllable finals is probably a poor choice, his theory of a syllable final consonant (or consonants) is worth serious consideration.

The most regrettable feature of Whorf's study is its brevity. The article is especially deficient in having no catalogue of cognate sets appended to it. However, as an example of careful logic and good writing, the article is still quite relevant.

4.2. The study of the Voegelins and Hale takes account of the following languages in the U.S. and Mexico: Papago, Hopi, Huichol, Cora, Tarahumara, Zacapoaxtla Nahuat, Pochutla Nahuat, Nahuatl, Tübatulabal, Southern Paiute, Comanche, Mono, Bannock, Luiseño, Cahuilla, and Yaqui-Mayo. The varying quality of their sources causes them to treat some languages more fully than others. In their own words 'In our procedure, we have reconstructed where we had evidence to reconstruct, typologized whether or not reconstruction was possible, and quantified rather casually wherever quantification promised to be interpretable' (7). Phonemic systems are typologized, given numerical ratings, and compared with each other. Glottochronology — with a disavowal of interest in dates — is applied along with Grimes-Agard quantifying.[15] Nevertheless, proto forms are reconstructed, phonological developments traced in various Utoaztecan languages, and various horizons carefully distinguished.

Besides Proto-Utoaztecan, the authors also reconstruct Proto-Aztec, Proto-Shoshonean, Proto-Sonoran. The evidence for Proto-Aztec is clear: loss of initial *p and of the laryngeals *h and *ʔ; *s and *c splitting to s, š and c, č; and *l remaining l (instead of at least some allophones becoming n or r). While the split of *s to s, š is shared by a secondary development in Luiseño and that of *c to c, č is shared by Southern Paiute, this does not greatly weaken the argument. Aztec stands out, at all events, as a well-defined group within Utoaztecan — as indeed no one is inclined to doubt.

Proto-Shoshonean (really beyond the scope of this paper) is not so well attested; it is united by shared phonological retentions rather than by shared innovations, while the morphophonemic innovations are not universally shared. The one exclusive universally shared phonological innovation in Shoshonean is medial *l>n.

Although the Voegelins and Hale reconstruct 'Proto-Sonoran', they are unable to cite one exclusive, universally shared innovation in support of the grouping. Thus, while *n and *ŋ merge into /n/ in all Sonoran, they also so merge in Aztec, and in the following Shoshonean languages: Shoshone, Comanche, Mono, and pre-Bannock; in brief this development is found in all branches of Utoaztecan. The merger of morphophonemic $*V^n$ and $*V^u$ is found in all Sonoran and in Aztec. Complete merger of the morphophonemes $*V^s$, $*V^n$, and $*V^u$ is found in Taracahitan (Tarahumara, Yaqui-Mayo, and possibly a number of extinct languages). Other developments are given; none seem to point conclusively to the reality of the Sonoran

[15] Joseph E. Grimes and Frederick B. Agard, 'Linguistic divergence in Romance', *Lg* 35.598-604 (1959).

grouping. On the other hand, merger of $*V^n$ and $*V^u$ in Sonoran and Aztec cannot be cited in favor of the 'Aztecoidan' (Aztec, Cora-Huichol, and extinct languages) in that this development is found in Taracahitan and in Piman as well.

All in all the evidence suggests that the surviving 'Sonoran' languages might better be considered to constitute three branches of Utoaztecan: Taracahitan; Cora-Huichol; and Piman.[16] The first has at least one solid, exclusive, and universally shared innovation to support it. It is no final objection that 'shared cognates are no more numerous between Tarahumara and Yaqui-Mayo than those between Papago and Yaqui-Mayo, for example' (130).[17] It would be interesting to see whether Varohio (or Guarajio), still spoken by a few bilinguals, is also 'Taracahitan'. Regarding the closeness of Cora-Huichol no one is prepared to object but they scarcely share enough of the characteristic Aztec developments to be called 'Aztecoidan'. Finally, regarding the unity of Piman (Upper Piman, Lower Piman, Northern Tepehuan, Southern Tepehuan) there can be no doubt — as will be presented below.

The Voegelins and Hale treat Utoaztecan morphophonemics very thoroughly. They set up $*V^s$ on a broader basis than did Whorf (and Sapir): '$*V^s$ is written when a vowel preceding a stop may suspend the stopness of the stop, and when preceding a nasal may suspend the nasal articulation. ... In Sapir's terminology, V^s 'spirantizes'; but we use a more general term, since 'suspending' extends all the way from a replacement within the stop series (plosive stop by affricate stop) to a replacement of a consonant by zero. ...' (82). They set up $*V^n$ 'when a vowel precedes a consonant which is reflected either by a change of the consonant, or by addition of a nasal in consonant cluster with the unchanged consonant' (82). They wisely choose to write $*V^u$ when there is enough data to show that neither of the above takes place.

One who has carefully read Whorf's sketch of Utoaztecan immediately begins to thumb through the Voegelins-Hale monograph to see if their sketch can be shown either to support or to disprove Whorf's theory that Utoaztecan stems, whose medial consonant neither spirantizes nor nasalizes, really contained medial consonant clusters. Does anything in the Voegelins-Hale description bear out this theory of 'lost' or 'ghost' consonants which occurred as first members of medial *CC clusters? Whorf speculated that the ghost consonants may have been *l and *r. Of this there is no hint in the data more recently presented. There is, however, some slight support that other consonants, possibly laryngeals, did occur as first members of medial clusters. The evidence must be sought in stems where the Voegelins and Hale mark the first vowel as $*V^u$ — since here was where a 'lost' consonant would have prevented both spirantization and nasalization. It is intriguing to note that in Southern Paiute, -xC- clusters (C=stop) occur after $*V^u$, while in Comanche -hk- clusters also occur

[16] Swadesh has analyzed the available scanty material on the extinct Tamaulipeco language in the south of the state of Tamaulipas. He concludes that Tamaulipeco was an independent division within Utoaztecan. 'El Tamaulipeco', *RMEA* 19.93-104 (1963).

[17] Comparative linguistics, as developed on the terrain of Indo-European studies, has not considered percentages of shared cognates to be decisive of genetic grouping. On the contrary, the principle of shared innovations has been held to be the criterion. See Eric Hamp as quoted in 4.3.

after $*V^u$ (85-6). Yaqui-Mayo have a gemination of medial consonants: 'Under certain morphophonemic conditions involving stress and length alternation, medial consonants are doubled (geminated)' (75). It is interesting to note that this gemination occurs only twice after $*V^s$, while after eleven examples of $*V^s$ no gemination occurs. After $*V^u$ the data are evenly divided: 5 examples of gemination versus 5 examples of single consonant. In brief, Yaqui-Mayo gemination is rare after $*V^s$ but not uncommon after $*V^u$. It is possible, therefore, that this gemination has its origin in old laryngeal plus consonant clusters which are reflected as Yaqui-Mayo geminates. The Southern Paiute -xC- clusters and the Comanche -hk- cluster may be direct witness to the existence of such Proto-Utoaztecan clusters. That Proto-Utoaztecan syllables were closed with a laryngeal is not improbable in view of the occurrence of such syllables in some of the language: 'Some of these, as Comanche and Cora, permit a laryngeal consonant final, /h/ or /ʔ/ or both, but no other final consonant' (96). If Proto-Utoaztecan *cvʔ and/or *cvh syllables occurred, then canonical patterns *CVLCV and *CVLCVL (ʔ or h = L) also occurred. The $*V^u$ posited by the Voegelins and Hale would be a first syllable vowel which occurred in either of these canonical patterns, while $*V^s$ would be a vowel that occurred in the first syllable of *CVCV and *CVCVL. Possibly, $*V^n$ was a first syllable vowel which occurred in *CVnCV and *CVnCVL — to reinstate bodily this part of Whorf's 1935 reconstruction. Further work on Utoaztecan morphophonemics is needed to test these hypotheses.[18] The Voegelins and Hale assumed no consonant clusters and no final consonants in Utoaztecan. It may be somewhat whimsically asserted, however, that no reconstruction project of any scope and depth can be engaged in without encountering a laryngeal problem. Perhaps Utoaztecan is no exception?

The Voegelins and Hale give 171 cognate sets. This needs to be expanded with addition of further data. Ultimately we need an etymological dictionary of Utoaztecan, both for further work within the stock and comparison with other stocks.

4.3. Burton Bascom's recent study *Proto-Tepiman* reconstructs Piman or Piman-Tepehuan on the basis of Upper Piman, Lower Piman, Northern Tepehuan, and Southern Tepehuan. The terminology is misleading in that there apparently is no Piman versus Tepehuan division. Rather, according to Bascom 'There seems to be no clearcut grouping among the Tepiman languages'. Four unique universally shared innovations define 'Tepiman'; $**k^w > *b$; $**y > *d$; $**w > *g$; and $**c > *s$ (double asterisk for Proto-Utoaztecan; single asterisk for Proto-Tepiman). The first three innovations yield a new series of consonants in Proto-Tepiman. In no other subgrouping in Utoaztecan is Hamp's dictum regarding the crucial relevance of exclusive shared innovations so well exemplified: 'The only criterion for genetic proximity consists in the recognition of a decisive set, whether in number or in structural place-

[18] Cf. e.g. Hansjakob Seiler, 'Accent and morphophonemics in Cahuilla and in Uto-Aztecan', *IJAL* 31.50-9 (1965).

ment, of shared structural innovations; and these must be innovations by addition or replacement, rather than by loss.'[19]

A further interesting detail of Bascom's reconstruction is best stated in his own words: 'Probably the most satisfying result of our research was the ability to demonstrate the derivation of Northern Tepehuan tone from Proto-Tepiman stress. This development has resulted, at least in part, from the loss of laryngeals and the resultant vowel clusters with contrastive pitch patterns. In certain environments a Proto-TP contrast in syllable types, *'CVV versus *'CVʔV, has merged into a single syllable in NT. The contrast between proto-syllables, however, has been maintained in NT by the contrasting tone patterns which they manifest, NT CVV́-versus CV́V respectively.'

Bascom's array of 473 Proto-Tepiman cognates might well form the nucleus for a Proto-Utoaztecan etymological dictionary.

5. Recently Alan Wares has made a good beginning towards the systemic comparison of the Yuman languages.[20] Wares characterizes his study as follows: 'The Yuman languages, with which this study deals, are spoken by some four to five thousand Indians living in the southwest United States and the northwest of Mexico ... The corpus of language data that forms the basis for this study covers material in Havasupai, Walapai, Yavapai, Mohave, Maricopa, Yuma, Cocopa, Diegueño, Tipai, Paipai, and Kiliwa ... On phonological and lexical grounds, four groups of languages are posited: (1) Northern Yuman (Havasupai, Walapai, Yuvapai, and also Paipai which, although spoken in Lower California near the southern limit of Yuman speech, exhibits features in common with the other languages in this group); (2) Central Yuman (Mohave, Maricopa, Yuma); (3) Delta-California (Cocopa, Diegueño, Tipai); and (4) Kiliwa ... Chapter XIII deals with a reconstruction of Proto-Yuman phonemes — chiefly consonant phonemes — on the basis of sets of correspondences found in this comparative vocabulary. No attempt has been made here to reconstruct entire forms. ... A comparative vocabulary of 501 cognate sets (some 3000 individual items) concludes the paper.'

While it is evident that the study here summarized is only a beginning, it appears nevertheless to be a good beginning. The size of the comparative vocabulary is gratifyingly large.

6. In published or unpublished form extensive, detailed reconstructions are now completed for all language families considered to belong to the Otomanguean stock of Mesoamerica. Furthermore, Calvin Rensch has now completed the reconstruction of Proto-Otomanguean itself. The publication of this study will give us one language stock of the western hemisphere in which systemic reconstruction has been carried out on a scale somewhat comparable to the scope and depth of Indo-

[19] Eric P. Hamp, 'Protopopoloca internal relationships', *IJAL* 24.151 (1958).

[20] Alan Campbell Wares, 'A comparative study of Yuman consonantism', unpublished manuscript (University of Texas, 1965). I have had access to an abstract prepared by Wares. cf. also Mary R. Haas, 'Shasta and Proto-Hokan', *Lg* 39.40-59 (1963).

European studies — although with a fraction of the manpower involved in the latter.

Some thirty native languages of Middle America are probably included in Otomanguean. The central mass of Otomanguean languages is found in the Mexican state of Oaxaca, and in surrounding areas of Puebla, Veracruz and Guerrero. To the west within this general area are found the Mixtecan (Mixtec, Cuicatec, and Trique), Popolocan (Popoloc, Ixcatec, Choco, and Mazatec), and Amuzgoan (one language) branches. To the east within the central mass lie Chinantecan and Zapotec- Chatino. While Chinantecan and Zapotecan have been spoken of as each consisting of but one language they are in reality complexes of at least six or seven languages each.

The northern outliers of Otomanguean constitute the Otopamean branch (Otomí, Mazahua, Pame, Chichimeco-Jonaz, Matlatzinca, and Ocuilteco); these languages are found in the Mexican states of Hidalgo, México, Queretaro, Guanajato, and San Luis Potosí. Pame lies north of the cultural boundary of Mesoamerica as defined by Kirchhoff in 1943.[21] Two extinct languages, Chiapanec and Manguean, which are southern outliers, constitute the Chiapanec-Manguean branch of Otomanguean. Chiapanec was spoken until fairly recently in and around the town of Chiapa de Corzo in Chiapas, Mexico. Mangue, which became extinct in the late nineteenth century was spoken along the Pacific coast of Central America in Honduras, Nicaragua, Costa Rica, and El Salvador with some extensions into the interior. Chiapanec and Mangue appear to have been very similar. Evidently they comprised a group which emigrated southward from the central mass of Otomanguean. The Chiapanecs stopped off in Chiapas while the Mangue continued to disperse further southward where they formed the southermost continuous extension of Mesoamerica as a cultural area.

Swadesh wrote a brief but suggestive sketch of Proto-Zapotecan in 1947.[22] In 1950, Stanley Newman and Robert Weitlaner published two articles which pioneered in the reconstruction of Proto-Otomi and Proto-Otomi-Mazahua.[23] The first detailed full scale reconstruction of a branch of Otomanguean was my 1957 Proto-Mixtecan.[24] This was followed in 1959 by Sarah Gudschinsky's triple piece of reconstruction (Proto-Mazatec, Proto-Popolocan, and Proto-Popolocan-Mixtecan).[25] In 1961 María Teresa Fernández de Miranda and Robert Weitlaner published a monograph which reconstructed Proto-Chiapanec-Mangue on the basis of extant data from those two

[21] Paul Kirchhoff, 'Mesoamerica', *Acta Americana* 1.92-107 (1943).

[22] Morris Swadesh, 'The phonemic structure of Proto-Zapotec', *IJAL* 13.220-30 (1947).

[23] Stanley Newman and Robert Weitlaner, 'Central Otomian I: Proto-Otomí reconstructions' and 'Central Otomian II: primitive central Otomian reconstructions', *IJAL* 16.1-19 and 73-81 (1950).

[24] Robert E. Longacre, 'Proto-Mixtecan', *IJAL* part III (1957). For an alternative reconstruction of Proto-Mixtecan (based on a narrower empirical base) see Evangelina A. Osnaya, 'Relaciones internas del Mixteco-Trique', *AnINA* 12.219-73 (1960).

[25] Sarah C. Gudschinsky, 'Proto-Popotecan' Indiana University publications in anthropology and linguistics memoir 15 of *IJAL* 25 (April, 1959). Paul Kirk, with access to an enlarged corpus of Mazatec dialect material, has recently completed a more definitive and detailed reconstruction of Proto-Mazatec (Proto-Mazatec Phonology, unpublished dissertation, University of Washington, 1966).

extinct languages, and tied them in convincingly to Proto-Mixtecan, Proto-Popolocan, and Proto-Popolocan-Mixtecan.[26] Rensch's as yet unpublished *Proto-Chinantec phonology* was completed in 1963.[27] Doris Bartholomew published a revision of the Newman-Weitlaner line-up of Proto-Otomian consonants (1960);[28] she has now completed *The reconstruction of Otopamean.*[29] Fernández de Miranda's reconstruction of Proto-Zapotecan is all but complete.[29a] I have argued in several articles that Amuzgo, traditionally considered to Mixtecan, is in reality a separate branch of Otomanguean.[30]

On the basis of Proto-Mixtecan, Proto-Popolocan, and Amuzgo (with a side-glance at Proto-Chiapanec-Mangue), I hazarded a preview of Otomanguean in 1964.[31] The following consonants seemed indicated (Table 7):

*t	*tʸ	*k	*kʷ	*ʔ
*θ	*θʸ	*x	*xʷ	
*n			*[m]	
	*y		*w	

Table 7

In that Proto-Chiapanec-Mangue, Proto-Zapotecan, and Proto-Otopamean all contain *p, the absence of this phoneme in the above scheme, shows an evident bias towards Mixtecan-Popolocan-Amuzgoan. *[m] was an allophone of *n in that *m occurred preposed and postposed while *n occurred in roots.

For a vowel system I guessed six vowels, perhaps *i, *e, *ï, *a, *o, *u.

Taking a clue from Gudschinsky it seemed to me very certain that Proto-Otomanguean had a system of postposed elements that reconstructed as follows (Table 8):

*-m	
*-xm	-*xV
-*xmʔ	-*xVʔ
-*ʔm	-*ʔ/ʔV

Table 8

I considered that postposed elements contained either a syllabic *m or a repeat of the

[26] María Teresa Fernández de Miranda and Roberto J. Weitlaner, 'Sobre algunas relaciones de la familia Mangue', *AnL* 3:7.1-99.

[27] Calvin Ross Rensch, 'Proto-Chinantec phonology', unpublished thesis, (University of Pennsylvania, 1963).

[28] Doris Bartholomew, 'Some revisions of Proto-Otomi consonants', *IJAL* 26.317-29 (1960).

[29] Doris Bartholomew, 'The reconstruction of Otopamean (Mexico)', unpublished dissertation, (University of Chicago, 1965). I have had access only to an abstract prepared by Bartholomew.

[29a] This is fortunate in view of the untimely death of our colleague. Plans have been initiated for posthumous publication of her work.

[30] 'On Linguistic Affinities of Amuzgo', *IJAL* 32.46-49 (1966); 'The Linguistic Affinities of Amuzgo', *Homonaje a Roberto Weitlaner* (Mexico City, 1967); 'Progress in Otomanguean reconstruction', *Proceedings of the Ninth International Congress of Linguists, Cambridge, Mass.*, 1962, 1017-19 (The Hague, 1964).

[31] Longacre, 'Progress in Otomanguean reconstruction', 1016-25.

stem vowel, and that the only other elements involved were laryngeals. I could not, however, fully account for the distribution and development of laryngeals even in Mixtecan.

Calvin Rensch's work in Otomanguean reconstruction indicates rather clearly that several cherished assumptions stated above are either doubtful or wrong. Rensch is challenging the palatal series of consonants, reducing the vowels to four, and reducing to a minimum the posited system of postposed elements. It is possible, however, that the four-level tone system which I reconstructed for Proto-Mixtecan, and Gudschinsky for Proto-Popolocan-Mixtecan, may be a rather primitive feature.

At all events, this is the worst of all times to speculate as to the details of Proto-Otomanguean. When Rensch's study appears — itself based on the work of many predecessors — it will merit careful scrutiny from all those familiar with given branches of Otomanguean. Out of the foment that is certain to ensue, an even better picture of Proto-Otomanguean will be obtained than can be hoped for from Rensch's initial treatment — as brilliant an accomplishment as that is.

Brief reports on the reconstruction of various branches of Otomanguean follow:

6.1. My Proto-Mixtecan reconstructions demonstrated that Trique belongs to Mixtecan properly conceived.[32] Subsequent study has shown that Amuzgo does not belong to the Mixtecan family. There are 279 cognate sets with reconstructions of consonants, vowels, glottal stop, initial consonantal alternations, tone patterns, and postposed elements. Proto-Mixtecan consonants were (Table 9):

*t	*k	*k^w	*ʔ
*θ	*x	*x^w	
*^{n}d	*^{n}g	*^{n}g^w	
*n	*ñ	*m	
*l(?)	*y	*w	

Table 9

Of the above (Table 9) *ñ was eliminated in a joint paper with Mak.[33] While seven vowels were reconstructed, *ɔ was eliminated in a subsequent article of mine.[34] Four tones were reconstructed in fourteen tone couplets, eight of which occurred in basic forms and six only in tone sandhi variants. The highest tone level was apparently restricted to sandhi variants. Especially characteristic of Proto-Mixtecan is its prenasalized series.

The joint paper with Mak was a brief sketch of Proto-Mixtec based on a scattering of data collected from 28 points in the Mixtec-speaking regions of Oaxaca, Puebla,

[32] Cf. the isoglosses considered in my article, 'Swadesh's Macro-Mixtecan hypothesis', *IJAL* 27.9-29 (1961).

[33] Cornelia Mak and Robert Longacre, 'Proto-Mixtec phonology', *IJAL* 26.23-40 (1960).

[34] Robert E. Longacre, 'Amplification of Gudschinsky's Proto-Popolocan-Mixtecan', *IJAL* 28.227-42, especially 231-4 (1962).

and Guerrero. Besides establishing that *ñ and the anomalous *tn cluster were both unnecessary in Proto-Mixtecan and Proto-Mixtec, this brief study (some 100 cognate sets) also revealed that Proto-Mixtecan *i and *e probably never completely merged in Proto-Mixtec *i but remained separate in a few environments. In brief, it showed the relevance of a mass of dialect material in one language to the reconstruction of a language family. The paper also revealed that Mixtec dialect geography will be an engrossing and rewarding study when it can be undertaken.

6.2. Gudschinsky's Proto-Popolocan followed an earlier sketch of Fernández de Miranda which brought together Popoloc, Chocho, and Ixcatec.[35] Gudschinsky first reconstructed Proto-Mazatec on the basis of four dialects and then went directly to the reconstruction of Proto-Popolocan (356 sets). In her own words, 'I have bypassed the fuller reconstruction of PP (Proto-Popoloc), however, and proceeded directly to PPn (Proto-Popolocan). It remains for others to fill in the detail of development in PP and its exact position within the family'[36](2).

Proto-Popolocan consonants are (Table 10):

*t	*t^y	*k	*k^w	*ʔ
*c	*č			
*s	*š	*h	*h^w	
*n	*ñ		*m	
*l(?)	*y		*w	

Table 10

Especially characteristic of Popolocan is its alveopalatal order, and the proliferation of sibilants and affricates. Five oral vowels are reconstructed, *i, *e, *a, *o, *u, as are their nasalized counterparts. While Proto-Mazatec tone is reconstructed in detail with four tones, Proto-Popolocan tone could not be reconstructed in detail because adequate synchronic sketches of present day tone systems were not available. Certain preposed and postposed elements were posited.

For 113 of Gudschinsky's Proto-Popolocan sets she was able to suggest etymologies with Proto-Mixtecan. I subsequently added some seventy further etymologies (1962).[37] Thus, we now can give Proto-Popolocan-Mixtecan etymologies for approximately half of the Proto-Popolocan reconstructions. In the same article in which I proposed these etymologies I suggested a few refinements in the comparative phonology of the two language families.

6.3. The Fernández-Weitlaner reconstruction of Chiapanec-Mangue was based on poorly phonemicized materials recorded by various people before these two languages

[35] María Teresa Fernández de Miranda, 'Reconstrucción del Protopopoloca', *RMEA* 12.61-93 (1951).

[36] Cf. fn. 25.

[37] 'Amplification of Gudschinsky's Proto-Popolocan-Mixtecan', 237-42.

became extinct.[38] They were able to compile some 286 Chiapanec-Mangue sets. For 64 of these sets they suggest etymologies with Proto-Mixtecan, for 75 sets, etymologies with Proto-Popolocan. My inspection of their materials convinces me that more such etymologies could be posited.

The consonants of Proto-Chiapanec-Mangue are (Table 11):

*p	*t	*k	
	*s	*h	*h^{w}
*^{m}b	*^{n}d	*^{n}g	
*m	*n(ñ?)		*M[hm]
*w	*y		
	*l/r		

Table 11

Chiapanec-Mangue, unlike Proto-Mixtecan and Proto-Popolocan, had a labial order. The absence of a labiovelar may, however, indicate some relation of Proto-Popolocan-Mixtecan *k^{w} to Proto-Chiapanec-Mangue *p and *^{m}b. Like Proto-Mixtecan, Proto-Chiapanec-Manguean has a prenasalized series. Reflexes of *n and *ñ overlap as do those of *l and *r. Five vowels are reconstructed: *i, *e, *ɨ, *a, *u. Three further vowels are reconstructed in the comparison of Proto-Chiapanec-Mangue with Proto-Mixtecan and Proto-Popolocan. Possibly at least two of these vowels can be eliminated in similar fashion to my elimination of *ɔ from Proto-Mixtecan and both *ë and *ɔ from Proto-Popolocan-Mixtecan.[39] Postposed elements containing nasals and the laryngeal h (ʔ was not recorded) are clearly witnessed to.

6.4. Fernández de Miranda's as yet unpublished reconstruction of Proto-Zapotecan (some 300 sets) gives the following system of consonants; all consonants not in italics have a fortis (or according to Swadesh, a geminated[40]) counterpart (Table 12):

*p	*t	**t^{y}*	*k	**k^{w}*	*ʔ
*c					
	*s	*š			
**m*	*n				
	*l				
	*r				**R*
**w*	**y*				

Table 12

[38] Cf. fn. 26.
[39] 'Amplification of Gudschinsky's Proto-Popolocan-Mixtecan', 231-2.
[40] 'The phonemic structure of Proto-Zapotec', 221.

Swadesh[41] did not reconstruct *m for Proto-Zapotec. While Fernández de Miranda reconstructs *m it is a very rare phoneme and does not have a fortis (or geminated) counterpart. According to my tentative sketch of Proto-Otomanguean (based on Mixtecan, Popolocan, and Amuzgo), *[m] was an allophone of *n and was restricted to preposed and postposed elements. Possibly the scarcity of *m in Proto-Zapotec and the origin of the geminates are related. As I have already suggested: 'Preposed *m, however, could conceivably have coalesced with a following consonant to form a geminate which in time came to pattern as a fortis consonant. I suggest, therefore, that PZ fortis consonants hark back to Proto-Otomanguean *mC clusters while PZ lenis consonants hark back to consonants without the preposed *m.'[42]

Proto-Zapotecan *R was apparently restricted to postposed elements. It is attested somewhat obliquely by divergent developments in a few Zapotecan languages. Apparently it had an uvular or velar quality. In other branches of Otomanguean a velar spirant is found in certain postposed elements.

The contrast of *p and *k^w is noteworthy (only *k^w in Proto-Mixtecan and Proto-Popolocan; only *p in Proto-Chiapanec-Mangue).

Of some relevance here is Chatino and the extinct Papabuco. Upson and I reconstruct the following consonants for Proto-Chatino[43] (Table 13):

	*t	*t^y	*k	*k^y	*k^w	*ʔ
	*c	*č				
	*s	*š				
	*n	*n^y				
	*l	*l^y				
*w	*y		*h	*h^y	*h^w	

Table 13

The extinct Papabuco is considered to be simply a further Chatino dialect. The Papabuco does display, however, rather divergent reflexes from those found in the other Chatino dialects. Fernández de Miranda has pointed out that some of the Papabuco reflexes agree with those posited for Proto-Zapotec. Thus, the commonest Papabuco reflex of Proto-Chatino *k is b which corresponds to *b (lenis p, or ungeminated p) in reconstructed Zapotec forms. Likewise, the commonest Papabuco reflex of Proto-Chatino *t is s — which often corresponds to Proto-Zapotec s. Fernández would, therefore, place Papabuco on the Zapotec, rather than the Chatino side of Zapotec-Chatino.

Two hundred fifty-one sets have been assembled for Proto-Chatino. Papabuco forms, painfully culled from Belmar (1901)[44] are found in only 84 of the sets.

41 'The phonemic structure of Proto-Zapotec', 223.
42 Longacre, 'Progress in Otomanguean reconstruction', 1023.
43 Bill Upson and Robert Longacre, 'Proto-Chatino phonology', *IJAL* 31.312-22 (1965).
44 Francisco Belmar, *Breve reseña histórica y geográfica del estado de Oaxaca* (Oaxaca City, 1901).

6.5. Bartholomew's recently completed reconstruction of Proto-Otopamean was preceded by the Newman-Weitlaner Otomi-Mazahua reconstruction (1950)[45] and by Bartholomew's own revision of their consonantal reconstructions for Proto-Otomi-Mazahua.[46] She is able to reduce the consonant inventory from 20 to 16 by eliminating *č, *s, *ñ, *r. Her present reconstruction of Proto-Otopamean consonants is starkly simple [47](Table 14)

*p	*t	*c	*k	*ʔ
	*s			*h
*m	*n			

Table 14

Fortis and lenis forms of the above were environmentally conditioned: Lenis forms occurred intervocalic; fortis forms elsewhere. Nasal influence as well as weakening resulted from addition of an *m/nV- prefix. Clusters of laryngeals (*ʔ or *h) with the above occurred as well.

The vowel system is also the simplest reconstructed for any Otomanguean language yet: *i, *e, *a, *o, and their nasalized counterparts. Vowel clusters *ao, *oa, *ai, *ia, *io, *oi, *eo, and *oe occurred. Reconstruction of these clusters involving *i and *o presumably obviated the need for reconstructing *w, *y, $*k^w$, and $*h^w$.[48]

Six tones are reconstructed: high, low, falling, and rising, plus two further contours falling plus low, and high plus falling.

Characteristic of Otopamean is the structure: prefix plus root syllable plus stem formative. The latter two are reconstructed in detail; the first only sketchily.

There are 700 cognate sets of which about half contain cognates from the two largest subgroups, Otomian and Pamean. Other languages cited are: Mazahua, Matlatzinca, Ocuilteco, and Chichimeco. A good amount of paradigmatic material is included in the sets. The tone correspondences are based on 147 sets.

Bartholomew's work is of special interest in that she follows the model of generative phonology.

6.6. Rensch's reconstruction of Proto-Chinantec is at once sufficiently important — and unavailable — to require fuller treatment than we have given any of the reconstructed languages above.[49] The reconstructions (773 sets) are based on material from 23 points in the Chinantec language complex. Synchronic descriptions of the present day Chinantec languages (Rensch nowhere attempts to distinguish language from dialect and would probably not be prepared to sustain the thesis that all 23 points on

[45] Cf. fn. 23.
[46] Cf. fn. 28.
[47] Cf. fn. 29.
[48] Cf. Longacre, 'Progress in Otomanguean reconstruction', 1023.
[49] Rensch's work was preceeded by Roberto Weitlaner and Paul Smith, 'Detalles de la fonología del idioma Proto-Chinanteco', unpublished manuscript (Mexico City, 1957).

his map represent separate languages) is followed by a presentation of the phonemic system of Proto-Chinantec.

The consonants of Proto-Chinantec are (Table 15):

*p	*t	*k	*k^w	*ʔ
*b	*z	*g	*g^w	
	*s			
	*l			
*w	*r	*y		

Table 15

Clusters of consonants included *ʔ or *h plus *b, *z, *g, or *l.

Somewhat startling in Table 15 is the absence of nasals. Rensch explains this: 'The sets of correspondences that witness to *[b] reconstruct only with oral vowels. In all Chinantec languages nasals appear only before nasalized vowels and, therefore, sets of correspondences that witness to nasal proto-segments reconstruct only with nasalized vowels. It follows, then, that the sets of correspondences that witness to *[b] and *[m] are in complementary distribution and may be grouped together under the same symbol, say *b. The same may readily be done for sets witnessing *[g] and *[ŋ] in the same way. However, no *[d] and thus, no oral counterpart to *[n] is available. There are, however, three other correspondence sets which are reconstructed only before oral vowels, *g^w, *z, and *l. Because of the supposed labiovelar articulation of *g^w it would seem a poor choice, but either *[z] or *[l] could well be matched with *[n] as the oral allophone of the voiced stop in the dental-alveolar area. *[z] has been selected for reasons of clustering with *h and *ʔ which will be discussed in a subsequent section, but the choice is somewhat arbitrary. In summary, then, apart from *g^w, three voiced stops are postulated for Proto-Chinantec *b, *z, and *g with allophones *[b], *[z], and *[g] respectively before oral vowels and allophones *[m], *[n], and *[ŋ] respectively before nasalized vowels. Phonetically, the oral allophones may have been prenasalized as they are to varying degrees in a number of the modern Chinantec languages' (32-3).

The Proto-Chinantec vowels are (Table 16):

*(i)	*ɨ	*u
*(e)	*ʌ	*a

Table 16

Rensch comments: 'Clusters of vowels include *i plus each of the vowels shown outside the parentheses. The vowels *i and *e correspond to the clusters **iɨ and *iʌ respectively. ... However, since the evidence indicates that they were probably articulated as phonetic units and since the distribution of these correspondence sets is broader than that of the other *iV clusters, these are treated as special members of the inventory of single vocalic elements' (24). In brief, the evidence points to a period (perhaps pre-Proto-Chinantec?) when a four vowel system was extant: (cf. Otopamean above, and Rensch's hypothesis of four vowels for Otomanguean and his desire to reduce Proto-Mixtecan vowels to four).

A consonant, a vowel, and a tone pattern were essential to a Proto-Chinantec syllable. In addition, the syllable could: (a) have ballistic articulation; (b) be lengthened; (c) be checked with *ʔ; (d) have a prepeak vowel *i; (e) be nasalized; and (f) be closed with *z. I have arranged these schematically as follows (Table 17):

		(/)			
		T			
C	(i)	V	(·)	(ʔ)	(z)
		(N)			

Table 17

The diagram — in which optional elements are in parenthesis — implies that all possible combinations of optional elements with obligatory elements occur. More will be said about this later.

The ballistic articulation is described by Rensch as 'sharp, ballistic, fortisly articulated'; syllables without this feature are 'smooth, controlled, lenisly articulated'. The phonetic description is based, of course, on the phenomenon as observed in several Chinantec languages.

In that ballistic versus controlled articulation, length, and glottal closure are all independent variables, this yields eight syllable patterns: *CV, *CV́, *CV·, *CV́·, *CVʔ, *CV́ʔ, *CV·ʔ, *CV́·ʔ (103).

Apparently, prepeak *i may occur with any of the above also; although it is for example, very rare with *CV́ʔ and *CV·ʔ.

It is of special interest that nasalization and postposed *z appear to be independent variables — since postposed *z is also a source of nasalized vowels in some Chinantec languages. The phoneme *z, as was stated above, belongs to a series of three phonemes (*b, *z, *g) which have nasal allophones (*m, *n, *ŋ) before the phonemically nasalized Proto-Chinantec vowels. Furthermore *z had an allophone *y in cluster with *h or *ʔ before oral vowels. In the various languages the reflexes of postposed *z range from postposed i or y to n, to ŋ, to nasalization, to affecting of vowel quality in various ways.

Rensch reconstructs a system of three level tones (*1, *2, *3 from high to low) and four sequences: *32, *23, *21, and *131.[50] Tone reflexes are radically affected by occurrence of Proto-Chinantec ballistic versus controlled syllables. Further sets of correspondences not fitting in the above scheme are conscientiously listed.

[50] As this goes to press Rensch informs me that he now posits a Proto-Chinantec tone system with two register tones and the following tone sequences: high-low, low-high, and high-low-high.

Although the study is called *Proto-Chinantec phonology*, Rensch gives summary information regarding the Proto-Chinantec verb — even to the point of giving a Proto-Chinantec verb paradigm. Only those who have tried to rationalize the structural vagaries of the verb in any Chinantec language can appreciate Rensch's accomplishment.

Rensch's work is a model in respect to good craftsmanship, carefully reasoned logic, and scope of detail. We can only hope that it will be published soon.

6.7. Swadesh has repeatedly urged that Huave (an unclassified language of Mexico) be considered to be related to Otomanguean.[51] Notwithstanding my initial skepticism, I now am inclined to believe that Swadesh may be correct. Swadesh's flat horizon approach to reconstruction — without taking account of particular developments in the several language families composing Otomanguean — vitiates many of his reconstructions. He sets up, among other features, more alveolar and alveopalatal sibilants and fricatives than the data warrant, and imposes his theory of geminates versus singles (Zapotec bias) on Otomanguean. I have taken his Huave-Otomanguean sets, restated some of them along the lines of the phonology more congenial to me, and added a few sets of my own. The results are not implausible. Possibly, as Swadesh suggests, Huave witnesses to original *p versus *k^w which have been merged into one phoneme or the other in some traditional Otomanguean languages (e.g. in Mixtecan, Popolocan, Amuzgoan, and Zapotecan).

6.8. Reconstructed vocabularies may be subjected to cultural analysis in an effort to reconstruct past cultural horizons. Some of the obvious dangers of this approach can be obviated by reconstructing cultural complexes rather than isolated items. Millon and I examined[52] the vocabulary of reconstructed Proto-Mixtecan and noted six cultural complexes witnessed to by various reconstructed vocabulary items: (1) agricultural; (2) maize; (3) masa preparation; (4) palm; (5) maguey; (6) weaving. Comparing Amuzgo with the above, all complexes except (4) reconstructed. Recent archeological investigations square well with the linguistic reconstruction.[53]

McQuown in three and a half pages[54] succinctly summarizes probable features of Proto-Mayan culture as reflected in reconstructable forms. The resulting picture is typically Mesoamerican. Noteworthy is the variety of cultivated plants: maize (with

[51] 'The Oto-Manguean hypothesis and Macro-Mixtecan', *IJAL* 27.9-29 (January, 1961). 'Interim Notes on Oaxacan phonology', *SJA* 20.168-89 (Summer, 1964). 'Algunos problemas de la lingüística Otomangue', *Anales de antropología* 1.91-123 (1964).

[52] René Millon and Robert E. Longacre, 'Proto-Mixtecan and Proto-Amuzgo-Mixtecan vocabularies: a preliminary cultural analysis', *AnL* 3:2.1-44 (1961).

[53] Richard Stockton MacNeish, 'First' and 'Second annual reports of the Tehuacan archeological-botanical project' (Andover, 1961) cf. MacNeish and Antoninette Nelken, 'Le Mexique et les débuts de l'agriculture au Nouveau Monde', *L'Anthropologie* 65:349-53 (1961).

[54] Norman McQuown, 'Los orígenes y la diferenciación de los Mayas segun se infiere del estudio comparativo de las lenguas Mayanas', *Desarrollo cultural de los Mayas* 49-80, especially 77-80 (Mexico City, 1964).

terms for green ear, dry ear, and cob), squash, sweet potatoes, chile, avocado, maguey, cotton, and cacao. Other terms are suggestive of cooking, weaving, housmaking, and other techniques. Still others suggest nature deities (water, sun, wind), and religious ceremonies (incense, mask).

Without attempting reconstructions of linguistic forms as such, Howard Law had some success in obtaining a sketch of Proto-Yuman culture.[55] In that the Yuman languages have not diverged too radically from each other and most sound correspondences are quite regular, Law was able to proceed somewhat surely in identifying cognates. His attention to culture complexes (in which various items mutually reinforce each other as witnesses) helped him scale his results in terms of probability. The reconstructed horizon is more shallow than for Proto-Mixtecan or Proto-Mayan. Nevertheless, the cultural sketch reveals a culture still largely dependent on hunting but with developing agriculture. Again, the picture is a plausible one.

The reconstruction of Proto-Maya has advanced far enough to invite inquiry as to the homeland of the Mayas. A. R. Diebold, Jr. in an article concerned with the application of migration theory,[56] makes out a plausible argument that the homeland of the Mayas was the Central Guatemalan highlands. Migration theory, as thus exemplified, is based on comparative reconstruction. The latter gives a measure of the closeness of the linguistic relationships. This consideration, taken together with that of the distribution of present day languages, makes possible probability judgments as to original homeland of a language family and migrations from that homeland.

Comparative reconstruction within a family or stock may also yield evidence of past cultural contacts between population groups speaking diverse languages. This is possible in that careful application of the comparative method facilitates recognition of loanwords as opposed to inherited items. Kaufman's summary and analysis of Mixe-Zoque loans in Mayan (cf. 2.1) is suggestive of what can be done. The fact, moreover, that Mixe-Zoque seems to have had more cultural influence on early Mayan than either Zapotecan or Utoaztecan is in itself significant. On a lesser scale my tracing of a few Mixtec loans in Trique is of some interest.[57] In that the Mixtec loans are words referring to pathological states it is possible that the presence of these loans is another evidence of Mixtec cultural domination over the Triques. In this case we infer a situation involving Mixtec shamans and Trique clients.

Isoglosses within Mixtecan are traced in my 1961 article.[58] Shared innovations between Mixtec and Trique are relatively weak while those between Mixtec and Cuicatec, and between Cuicatec and Trique are relatively strong. There is some relevance to culture history and even migration theory here: ... 'Mixtec and Cuicatec

[55] Howard W. Law, 'A reconstructed proto-culture derived from some Yuman vocabularies', *AnL* 3:4.45-57 (1961).

[56] A. Richard Diebold, Jr., 'Determining the centers of disposal of language groups', *IJAL* 26.1-10 (1960).

[57] Longacre, 'Systemic comparison and reconstruction of Middle American Indian languages', to appear in McQuown, ed. *Handbook of Middle American Indians* 5.

[58] 'Swadesh's Macro-Mixtecan Hypothesis', 12-19.

have apparently been in unbroken contact since the common Proto-Mixtecan period. By contrast, Cuicatec-Trique have not been in contact in historical times, while an argument can well be made in favor of the thesis that Mixtec-Trique (now found in contact) were out of contact for a significant period of time. The paucity and weakness of shared Mixtec-Trique innovations versus the comparative wealth and strength of Cuicatec-Trique shared innovations seem to indicate that Cuicatec-Trique, although now not in contact, were actually in longer early contact than were Mixtec-Trique. Apparently Trique moved off from Mixtec during the period of early dialect differentiation (but retained contact for some time with Cuicatec) only to be engulfed on all sides by Mixtec during the later period of Mixtec expansion' (12).

It is apparent that serious linguistic reconstruction has much to offer to the student of culture history. This is evident, e.g. in the recent symposium volume: *Desarrollo cultural de los Mayas*[59] — where articles of linguists McQuown and Kaufman make a crucial contribution.

In a classic article dealing with Mazatec dialect history,[60] Gudschinsky brings together insights of dialect geography with those of comparative reconstruction. Basing her arguments on exclusively shared phonological innovations she traces successive dialect splits and constructs a genealogical tree of the Mazatec dialects. She then considered 'word geography', i.e. lexical innovation versus retention. She then compares her results with what is known or conjectured regarding Mazatec history (480-1). Two periods of dialect development are distinguished before 'the period in which a lowland nation first flourished'. A third period is posited 'in which Low Mazatec developed its characteristic phonological and lexical features'; this period is probably that of the 'Lowland Mazatec Nation'. The fourth period — possibly a period of domination by some non-Mazatec people — saw the development of a 'Valley dialect', and subsequent split into 'Northern Valley' and 'Southern Valley' dialects. The fifth period (possibly 1300-1456) saw the development of a High Mazatec dialect in that both highland and lowland Mazatec kingdoms flourished at this time. One village, which had belonged to the Lowland kingdom and dialect in period three, now was absorbed into the highland kingdom with consequent dialect adjustments. The sixth and seventh periods (Aztec and Spanish domination) have seen further dialect developments.

7. The possible genetic affinity of the highland Andes languages, Quechua and Aymara, has been debated since 1888 when Steinthal affirmed that the two languages 'were genetically related and mutual exchange of loans was secondary'.[61] This has been controverted by others, such as Mason, who, while admitting phonological and morphological parallelism of the two languages, denied genetic affinity. Mason held

[59] cf. fns. 7 and 54.

[60] Sarah C. Gudschinsky, 'Mazatec dialect history, a study in miniature', *Lg* 34.469-81 (1958).

[61] Heymann Steinthal, 'Das verhältniss, das zwischen dem Keschua und Aymara besteht', 7 *Congreso Internacional de Americanistas,* 462-4 (Berlin, 1888).

that 'the lexical roots seem to have little in common, except a large number, perhaps as much as $^1/_4$ of the whole, obviously related and probably borrowed by one or the other language'.[62] Both these contrary evaluations find present day adherents. What is needed is a careful assessment of the dialect situation in Quechua itself (with careful attention to the history of Quechua-Aymara contacts and present dialect geography) plus the culling out and evaluation of resemblant forms between the two languages.[63]

7.1. Benigno Ferrario published a very important article concerning Quechua dialectology.[64] He argued that a basic division must be made between Quechua dialects that are in direct descent from Proto-Quechua and dialects that represent a late spread of Quechua, first as the language of the Inca empire, and secondly as a lingua franca for Spanish administrators and the missionary friars. Thus, he considers Ecuadorian, Colombian, and Argentine Quechua to be largely irrelevant to the reconstruction of Proto-Quechua. To distinguish the lingua franca of these areas from the most relevant dialects he terms the former 'Neo-Quechua' and the latter 'Runa-simi' (i.e. 'the people's language' in Quechua).

Within the dialects of 'Runa-simi' Ferrario recognized a further dichotomy: '... dialetti derivati dalla Proto Runa-simi, ossia: a) le parlate delle popolazioni che circondavano il luogo dove sorse, di poi, il Cuzco; b) quelle dei Chinchas (che già erano una nazione potente, a base federale, quando gli Inca ancora erano occupati a consolidare il loro piccolo Stato locale, nucleo del futuro impero) cioè le varietâ di Ancash, di Huánuco, di Cajamarca ed altri luoghi' (136).

The dialect division posited by Ferrario within 'Runa-simi' was considered to be more relevant to phonology than to morphology. The salient phonological difference is that Cuzco type dialects (including those of Bolivia) have aspirated and glottalized series of stops as well as a simple series, while other dialects have only the latter.

Ferrario argued cogently that the aspirated and glottalized stops of Cuzco Quechua were due to Aymara substratum. He presented two maps. In the first, which represents the linguistic situation in the sixteenth century, the Aymara speaking region of Peru is shown to extend up to the 11° parallel south and to include a fingershaped strip of territory running up to the north of Lima; this region also includes most of Huancavelica, parts of Ayacucho, and Arequipa and extends about half way from Lake Titicaca to Cuzco. On the second map, reflecting the present linguistic situation, the former Aymara region of Peru is shown to be largely Quechua speaking, with Aymara

[62] J. Alden Mason, 'The languages of South American Indians', ed. Julian H. Steward, *Handbook of South American Indians*, 6.157-317 (Washington, 1950).

[63] The Haquearu language of west central Peru (which Ferrario considered to be simply an Aymara dialect) should also be included in the sphere of investigation: cf. José M. Farfán, 'Diccionario conciso Castellano-Haquearu-Quechua', *Revista de Museo Nacional* 30.19-40 (1961).

[64] Benigno Ferrario, 'La dialettologia della Runa-Simi', *Orbis* 5.131-40 (1956). I am indebted to Miss Yolanda Lastra and Mr. Alfred Pietrzyk of the Center for Applied Linguistics (Washington, D.C.) for securing for me copies of this and other articles which were hard for me to obtain under field conditions.

confined to a narrow region north and west of Lake Titicaca (plus of course the Altiplano of Bolivia). Ferrario further argued that many of the placenames of Peru can be shown to be Aymara, while the Haquearu enclave in central Peru can be shown to be a remnant of the original Aymara-speaking population. Ferrario concludes: 'Il gruppo dei dialetti di tipo 'Cuzqueño' rappresenta, invece, una Runa-simi aymarizzata, e non solo foneticamente, ma altresì nel lessico, dovuto alla convivenza, sopra un medesimo territorio, di gente parlante Aymara e Runa-simi, già in epoca preincaica' (139-40).

It is probably somewhat inconsistent of Ferrario to draw such a sharp line between his Quechua or 'Neo-Quechua' (as a lingua franca) and dialects of 'Runa-simi' properly constituted. The data that he presents regarding displacement of Aymara by Quechua would indicate that many Quechua-speaking areas of southern Peru represent a recent spread of that language — even as the Quechua dialects of Ecuador, Colombia, and the Argentine. At any rate, Ferrario concludes that the dialects of greatest relevance to Proto-Quechua are the dialects now spoken in Ancash, Húanuco, and Junin.

The current studies of Gary Parker[65] seem to substantiate Ferrario's conclusion. Parker distinguishes Quechua A (including Cuzco, Ayacucho, Bolivia, and Ecuador-Ucayali) from Quechua B (Ancash, Húanuco, and Junin). While Ferrario had argued that all dialects of Quechua were quite similar morphologically, Parker contrasts the two major groups of Quechua dialects in respect to postpositions on nouns, person markers, and verb inflection. He also delineates certain isoglosses that separate the various dialects in each of the two large divisions. Phonologically, Ayacucho in Quechua A is more similar to Quechua B. While the Cuzco and Bolivian dialects have both aspirated and glottalized stops, and central Ecuador-Ucayali dialects have aspirated stops (and one phoneme which is a reflex of a former glottalized stop), Ayacucho has no trace of either aspirated or glottalized stop.

Parker, like Ferrario, considers the aspirated and glottalized stops of Quechua A to be by way of influence from Aymara: 'Aunque se ha presumido que éstas son originales del Quechua, el autor prefiere considerarlas como que fueron prestadas del Aymara, tanto sobre la base de la distribución geográfica como del relativamente bajo rendimiento funcional de estos componentes en el Quechua' (248). He points out the interesting fact that in Quechua no more than one laryngealized (aspirated or glottalized) consonant may occur per word. Possibly of greater relevance is the fact that the laryngealized stops are limited to roots in Quechua while they are also found in affixes in Aymara.

Parker reconstructs Proto-Quechua A, Proto-Quechua B, and Proto-Quechua. Since he groups Ayacucho in 'Quechua A' and does not reconstruct glottalized and aspirated stops in that dialect, the phoneme inventories of the three do not markedly differ.

[65] Gary Parker, 'La classificación genética de los dialectos Quechuas', *Revista del Museo Nacional* 32.241-52 (1963).

The phonemes of PQA are as follows (Table 18):

*p	*t	*č	*k	*ḳ
	*s	*š	*x	
*m	*n	*ñ		
	*l	*l^y		
*w	*r	*y		
		*i	*u	
		*a		

Table 18

PQB differs only by virtue of the presence of a further affricate: c. Proto-Quechua is considered to have the phoneme inventory of PQB, plus the phoneme š based on the correspondence: PQA s ~ PQB x in some sets.

Parker considers that the 1560 lexicon of Domingo de Santo Tomás (the first printed work in Quechua) is an early dialect witness to Quechua A. He believes that this was a coastal dialect. Ferrario's description of the linguistic situation in the sixteenth century leaves no room for a 'coastal' dialect of Quechua; in southern Peru the Aymara-speaking strip separated the Quechua region from further languages spoken on the coast. The orthography of Santo Tomás gives no hint of aspirated or glottalized stops, nor of the contrast k:ḳ. While Parker concludes that the dialect in question is obviously QA, (on the basis of morphology?) he admits that the accentual system is that of Quechua B. Presumably, this is a link in his argument for eliminating aspirated and glottalized stops from PQA. Ferrario and Rowe seem to locate Santo Tomás' Quechua dialect in Apurimac — where it would have been contiguous to Ayacucho. Presumably, both the dialect of Santo Tomás and Ayacucho — granting that both can be classified morphologically as Quechua A — are phonologically like Quechua B.

By contrast, the classic 'Inca' dialect ('court dialect' of Cuzco) which Rowe posits on basis of early 17th century documents[66] clearly had aspirated and glottalized stops. Ecuador-Ucayali dialects, some of which preserve aspirated stops and partial witness to existence of a glottalized series, presumably are developments from such Cuzco dialects on spread of the latter northwards.

7.2. The question of Quechua-Aymara genetic affinity is complicated by the undoubted prolonged historical contact of the two peoples and the presence of Aymara substratum in a large area of southern Peru.

In an unpublished study Carolyn Orr has assembled some 300 Proto-Quechua sets of which a bit under 50% can be shown to have resemblant forms in Aymàra of Bolivia.[67] These tentative Quechua-Aymara cognate sets include some body parts

[66] John Rowe, 'Sound patterns in three Inca dialects', *IJAL* 16.137-48 (1950).

[67] Since submitting this article, Orr and I have further studied the Quechua-Aymara problem. Our joint paper, 'Proto-Quechumaran', is committed to the thesis that the two languages are genetically related. We now reconstruct glottalization and aspiration as Proto-Quechua features.

(*fist/joint*, *knee*, *finger/toenail*, *skin/hide/back*, *goiter/mumps/Adam's apple*), kinship terms (*father*, *man's brother*, *woman/wife*, *child/baby*, *sister/daughter-in-law*, *relative*, *brother/son-in-law*, and other items (*carry*, *put/give*, *be*, *want*, *cut*, *ripen*, *gather*, *walk*) that are usually less suspect of being loans from one language to the other. On the other hand, other items (*money*, *gold*, *write*, *two*, *three*, and *ten*) might well be loan-words from one of the languages into the other. Furthermore, Orr's sets do not include on the Quechua side, dialect witness from Ancash, Húanuco, and Junin — which according to Ferrario are less 'Aymarized' dialects of Quechua. If, on addition of material from these dialects, it is found that most of the presumed Proto-Quechua forms can be witnessed to in these cruical dialects, then a case can be made for the genetic affinity of Quechua-Aymara.[68] The case will rest heavily on the argument that a form disseminated homogeneously throughout Quechua dialects is not likely to be a loan from Aymara. Loans of this sort should tend to be statistically most frequent in dialects contiguous to Aymara (including Ucayali-Ecuador, if these are derived from Cuzco Quechua) and less frequent in other dialects (Ancash, Húanuco, Junin).

In brief, if — as generally admitted — the two languages are quite similar morphologically, and not so dissimilar phonologically (aside from extra series of aspirates and glottalized consonants in Aymara), and if cognate sets with plausible geographical spread can be assembled from vocabulary domains not highly suspect of containing loans, and if a viable phonology can be reconstructed based on systemic sound correspondences, then there would seem to be little point in continuing to doubt the genetic affinity of the two languages.

8. Olive Shell has made a good beginning at the reconstruction of Proto-Panoan,[69] while Mary Key has completed a sketch of Proto-Tacanan.[70] The two stocks have been assumed to be related (e.g. in Greenberg's Macro-Panoan).[71] This relationship is confirmed by the present studies.

8.1. Olive Shell's unpublished study is based primarily on seven Pano languages for which extensive lexical materials as well as phonological and grammatical analyses exist: Cashinahua, Shipibo, Capanahua, Amahuaca, Marinahua, Cashibo, and Chacobo. The first six are spoken in Peru, the last in Bolivia. Shell describes her procedure as follows: '... the comparative method was applied to data from seven Pano languages in current investigations to obtain a tentative reconstructed primitive Pano. Reversing the process of reconstruction, rules of historical change were noted

[68] Since writing this, I have received from Helen Larsen (Summer Institute of Linguistics) a word list in the Quechua dialect of Ancash. Larsen has only recently begun her studies of Ancash Quechua and has incomplete lexical materials. Nevertheless, for almost one half of the Quechua-Aymara sets she readily found cognates in Ancash Quechua.

[69] Olive A. Shell, 'Pano reconstruction', unpublished monograph.

[70] Mary Ritchie Key, 'Comparative phonology of the Tacanan languages', unpublished dissertation (University of Texas, 1963).

[71] Sol Tax, 'Aboriginal languages of Latin America', *CAnthr* 1.430-8 (1960) (reproduces Greenberg's classification of 1956).

which enabled the investigator to predict forms in the daughter languages. By applying these rules and making comparisons with further word lists found in the literature, the latter were evaluated, their symbolization interpreted, and the findings utilized in modifying the first construction' (1). Besides the seven control languages, Shell also had word lists from current investigations in the following Pano languages (all but the first are spoken in Brazil): Isconahua, Marobo, Yaminahua, Chaninahua, Mastanahua. Published word lists of varying quality (many nineteenth century) were available for: Atsahuaca, Yamiaka, Cakobo, Pakaguara, Karipuna, Culino, Mayoruna, Arazaire, Canawary, Poyanawa, Tutxiunaua, Pano, Wariapano, and Nokaman.

Although the published word lists of earlier investigators enter only indirectly into Shell's studies, they enable her to make a careful evaluation (6-39) of previous classifications. This admirably demonstrates the relevance of careful, detailed comparative reconstruction for the classification of languages. It is not necessary that the careful, detailed work embrace the entire family or stock but enough must be done — and done well — to provide a solid core around which other material can nucleate.

Even the mutual classification of the seven Panoan languages entering directly into Shell's study is of considerable interest. The grouping is done on the basis of shared phonological innovations with some attention to shared lexical innovations as well (131-6). On this basis (1) Shipibo-Conibo is first grouped with Capanahua, then (2) these, with (3) Chacobo. (4) This grouping is more or less coordinate with Amahuaca and Cashinahua-Marinahua. Finally, (5) Cashibo ties in on a still earlier horizon. By contrast McQuown[72] groups as follows: (1) Shipibo and Conibo. (2) These, in turn, group with Cashibo (all sub-divisions of his QIA) (3) The preceding comprise a branch roughly coordinate with those branches represented by Capanahua (his Capanahuan is QIC) by Amahuaca (his Amahuacan is QID), and by Marinahua (in his Panoan QIF). Most distantly related of all is Chacobo (QIIIAa of Southwest Panoan QIII). Greenberg's classification — here, as in other places — is geographic rather than linguistic. Chacobo as 'South east Panoan' is separated from the other six languages which are classified as 'Central Panoan'. A glance at the striking difference in the classifications (e.g. Cashibo ties in on the earliest horizon in Shell's classification; Chacobo, in McQuown's) suffices to emphasize the difference between tentative classifications and those coming about as a by-product of the comparative method. Shell modestly entitles her reconstructions 'Reconstructed Panoan' instead of 'Proto-Panoan': 'The reconstruction is not claimed to be final. Further research in Bolivia and Brazil may provide data for a more primitive Pano than can be reconstructed from present data' (2). Needless to say, 'proto-languages' have been posited by other comparativists on a much more slender basis. Granting the inevitable subsequent revision of any pioneer piece of linguistic reconstruction, there is no reason why Shell's reconstructions should not be considered to be for all practical purposes 'Proto-Panoan'.

[72] Norman McQuown, 'The indigenous languages of Latin America', *AmA* 57.501-70 (1955).

After a careful presentation of current phonemic systems in the seven languages, Shell presents the phonemes of 'Reconstructed Panoan' (Table 19):

*p	*t			*k	*kʷ	*ʔ	
	*c	*č					
*ƀ	*s	*š	*ṣ̌				
*m	*n						
	*r			*i	*ï	*į	*į̈
*w	*y			*a	*o	*ą	*ǫ

Table 19

In a series of charts Shell presents the developments from Reconstructed Pano to each daughter language. There is a minimum of split and merger among the consonantal reflexes in the various languages. The nasals, however, condition nasalized reflexes of vowels in certain environments. The patterns of split and merger involving *b, *w, and *y vary in interesting fashion among the seven languages. Vowel reflexes are fairly consistent from language to language except for (1) loss of final vowels under certain conditions varying in degree and kind from language to language; (2) merging of oral and nasalized vowels in varying degree and under varying conditions; and (3) other miscellaneous developments too detailed to mention here. Development (2) is of special interest in that while it reflects a tendency to lose nasalized vowels, such vowels are developed in all the languages except Chacobo on loss of nasal consonants in third syllable (with nasalization of all second syllable vowels — although vowel nasalization is considered to be an allophone of nasal consonant in Capanahua).

Of the seven Pano languages under consideration, in two a two-way stress contrast is posited; in four a two-way tone contrast; and in one a complex stress-tone contrast. A two-way tone contrast is reconstructed. Shell comments: 'The RP high toneme was probably accompanied by strong stress, except when affected by over-all rhythm patterns' (116).

The Pano languages are very complex morphologically. Shell is able to reconstruct certain morphological features of RP. In current Pano languages there is a difference in the form of the noun when subject of a transitive verb and when either subject of an intransitive verb or object of a transitive — although this is expressed in different ways in the various languages. Shell reconstructs three-syllable forms for the nouns as subjects of transitive verbs versus two syllable forms either as subjects of intransitives or objects of transitives. In two-syllable Reconstructed Pano nouns, she posits a morpheme of high tone and nasalization on the last syllable of forms that were subjects of transitive verbs.

Shell lists 512 cognate sets. Forms from the seven languages on which the study is based are given when extant and available. At the bottom of each page additional cognates are given for languages other than the seven on which the reconstruction is primarily based. We thus have for Proto-Panoan an etymological dictionary of no mean proportions. This should greatly facilitate further comparison of Panoan with Tacanan (see below) and with Macro-Guaycuruan — if Greenberg's Macro-Panoan grouping (Panoan-Tacanan with Macro-Guaycuruan) can be verified.

8.2. Mary Key's *Comparative phonology of the Tacanan languages* is based on three languages of Bolivia: Tacana, Cavineña, and Chama. For these three languages phonological, lexical, and (to some degree) grammatical materials are available, whether published or unpublished. Mary Key herself did some field work in the first two. These data are supplemented by Reyesano and Huarayo word lists recorded phonetically on short field trips. Reyesano may be the same language as that referred to as 'Maropa' by earlier investigators and still occurring as such in McQuown's and Greenberg's classifications: 'Both Armentia (1905) and Cardus (1886) identify the Maropa as the tribe which formed the mission of Reyes. If this is true, Maropa would be the dialect which is known today as Reyesano' (6). On the basis of phonological isoglosses Key feels that Reyesano is closer to Tacana, and Huarayo to Chama. She then posits that Chama-Huarayo, Cavineña, and Tacana-Reyesano, are more or less coordinate on the same horizon of reconstruction.

Current phonemic systems are duly presented, followed by the phonemic system of Proto-Tacanan (I have rearranged Key's chart and changed a few symbols in the interest of consistency with the format followed for the phonemes of Proto-Pano) (Table 20):

*p	*t			*k	*ʔ(?)
*b	*d				
	*c	*č	*č̣		
	*s	*š	*ṣ̌	*x	
*m	*n				
	*r	*ř			
*w	*y				
		*i	*o		
		*e	*a		

Table 20

Aside from the inevitable 'obscure reflexes' and 'unexplained residues' which to varying degrees plague all comparativists, the reflexes of Proto-Tacanan phonemes are straightforward with a minimum of split and merger. One outstanding problem is Chama t: 'The status of Chama t is not satisfactorily explained. While it is a fairly common phoneme in the language it is found in only a few cognates. The limited material shows reflex t only occurring after the morpheme e — (which indicates an unidentified possessed form) in stem initial position. ... The conditioning factor cannot be e alone since s also occurs in that circumstance' (54). A further problem is posed by the systemic interchange of certain phonemes in Chama. The problem affects not only Chama but the reconstruction of Proto-Tacanan: 'In almost all of the instances of specific fluctuations listed, corresponding problems are found in the comparative data. Either the sounds involved are proved reflexes of a sister language or remain as unexplained residues in one of the sister languages' (58). Key suggests dialect borrowing as at least a partial explanation of these 'fluctuations'. She adds a rather puzzling comment: 'Often the Panoan languages clarify the Chama problems better than do the Tacanan languages' (58).

Key's cognate sets, for which she gives Proto-Tacanan reconstructions, number about 200. Along with sets of this nature she presents many further sets with obviously resemblant forms among two or three of the languages, but for which she does not attempt specific reconstructions. The entire ensemble of sets are not numbered, but are arranged alphabetically according to English glosses. Forms answering to the glosses are added from various Panoan languages — whether or not the forms are cognate or even resemblant. No reconstructed Proto-Tacanan-Pano forms are given. On casual glance I would say that some 70 of the sets contain Pano forms that would seem to be very plausible cognates with the Tacanan languages.

8.3. Prospects seem bright for reconstruction of Proto-Tacanan-Pano in the near future. The extensive array of materials presented by both Shell and Key will greatly facilitate the task of bringing the two language groups together.

The reconstructed phonemic systems of the two language families are gratifyingly similar. Both have: four stops (*p, *t, *k, *ʔ), a voiced bilabial (Panoan *ƀ; Tacanan *b), five affricates and sibilants (*c, *č, *s, *š, *ş), two nasals (*m, *n), one vibrant (*r), two semivowels (*w, *y) and four vowels (*i, *ï, *a, *o in Panoan; *i, *o, *e, *a in Tacanan). In addition, Proto-Pano has the further stop *kʷ and four nasalized vowels. Proto-Tacanan has a further voiced stop (*d), a further affricate (*ç̌), a further vibrant (*ř), and a velar spirant (*x). This resemblance is all the more remarkable in that neither Shell nor Key had access to the materials or conclusions of the other while carrying out her reconstructions. In brief, the converging of the two reconstructions is dictated by the data. The phonemic systems of the two language families are similar, and this similarity is undoubtedly based on linguistic kinship.

9. Benigno Ferrario, in an as yet unpublished manuscript,[73] treated exhaustively the question of the genetic affinity of three extinct languages of Uruguay: Chana, Güenoa, and Charrúa. He believed these languages to have been related to the Matacan

[73] Benigno Ferrario, 'Las lenguas indígenas del Uruguay', unpublished manuscript, 160 handwritten pages.

Antonio Tovar has written two articles on Matacan, but I was not able to obtain access to them in the limited time available before submitting this paper: 'El grupo mataco y su relación con otras lenguas de America del Sur', Congreso Internacional de Americanistas *Actas y memorias* 2.439-52 (1964); 'Relación entre las lenguas del grupo mataco', *Homenaje a Fernando Márquez-Miranda*, 370-7 (Madrid-Sevilla, 1964).

languages of Paraguay and the Argentine (cf. Greenberg's Macro-Guaycuruan, which in turn belongs along with Panoan and Tacanan in his Macro-Panoan).[74]

The extant data are pitifully restricted: 90 words and 26 expressions in Chana; 19 expressions in Güenoa; and 50 words in Charrua. For a fourth language Minuana (presumed to have been related) but one word (a place name) has survived. This small corpus Ferrario analyzed morpheme by morpheme in masterful fashion.

Ferrario had first to dispose of other suggestions regarding the affinities of the 'Charruan' family (listed as 'unclassified' under Macro-Guaycuruan by Greenberg). He does this incisively with cutting criticism of those who confuse social entities and linguistic families, of those who 'leaf through vocabularies' and latch on to superficial resemblances — comparing parts of words willy-nilly and discarding the rest without regard to the morphological structures involved; and of the cavalier handling of data and the semantic confusions found in some so-called 'comparative work'. Specifically he examines and rejects claims of affinity with Tupi-Guarani, Guaycuru, Kaingang (Gê), and Arawakan. These claims are not superficially dismissed; on the contrary, available evidence is painstakingly examined. The Tupi-Guarani claim is seen to be based on place names resultant on spread of Tupi-Guarani as a lingua franca. Assumed Charruan cognates with Guaycuru and Kaingang are laid in the balances and found wanting. Especially sharp is his criticism of Sixto Perea y Alonso's suggestion that Charruan is Arawakan.[75]

Ferrario's positive argument for Matacan affinities cannot be based on systematic sound correspondences supported by an imposing array of cognate sets — the data are too fragmentary to permit this. He showed, however, that certain basic morphological features of Charruan — and certain specific morphemes — are very similar to those of such Matacan languages as Nocten, Vejoz, Choroti and Mataco. The resemblances are not superficial. Ferrario was especially interested in archaic and non-productive features rather than in features which may reflect recent analogical spread. Affixes such as first person singular, first person plural, second person common, and pluralizer are examined with care in Charruan and Matacan. Ferrario had the material well in hand. His methodology was sound and his arguments convincing.

10. Comparative Arawakan is scarcely begun as yet.[76] In the words of Douglas

[74] José Pedro Rona, *Nuevos Elementos acerca de la Lengua Charrúa*, (Montevideo, 1964). In this 28-page work, Rona first analyzes some proper names (found in the Jesuit mission records of the town of São Borja, Rio Grande de Sul, Brazil) for names of possible Charruan origin. The restricted nature of extant data on the Charruan languages necessitates efforts of this sort. The second section of the article presents comparative evidence that Charruan pertains to the Lule-Vilelan subdivision of Macro-Guaycuruan rather than to the Matacan sub-division.

[75] Sixto Perea y Alonso, *Filología comparada de las lenguas y dialectos Arawak* 1 (Montevideo, 1942). Reproduces his earlier work 'Apuntes para la prehistoria indígena del Rio de la Plata y especialmente de la banda Oriental del Uruguay, como introducción a la filología comparada de la lengua y dialectos Arawak', *BFM* 1.217-45 (1937) cf. Olaf Blixen, *Acerca de la supuesta filiación Arawak de las lenguas indígenas del Uruguay* (Montevideo, 1958).

[76] After this article went to the editor the following monograph appeared: G. Kingsley Noble,

Taylor: 'No serious work on comparative Arawakan can be undertaken until we have adequate descriptions of some of the more typical Arawakan languages. Recent work on such languages as Amuesha, Campa, Tereno, etc. are little help, as these languages are very far indeed from the type represented by Arawak, Achagua, Goajiro, or the Rio Negro group. It seems to me that in order to make a beginning in any comparative work, one must have reasonably reliable descriptions of at least several languages showing a moderate amount of likely cognates. Outliers can be dealt with only at a later stage' (private correspondence).

Robert Shafer has assembled some 125 sets from some sixty Arawakan languages.[77] Certain languages enter, however, into only a few sets (e.g. Amuesha, which Greenberg considers to be 'unclassified' Arawakan, occurs in only two sets). The data are assembled from published sources which required some interpretation of the phonetically recorded data. Thus, Shafer felt it safe to consider that any given Arawakan language has but one set of stops whether voiced or voiceless. At any rate his sources did not record consistently any such differences if they were contrastive in the data. It now turns out that in at least one of the languages of his sources — Arawak proper — there is an opposition of aspirated and unaspirated consonants.[78] This opposition includes two of the stops (t versus t^h; k versus k^h;) and the lateral (l versus l^h). Thus, in the Arawak word for 'moon' where Shafer's source recorded katti, the tt was not an inconsistency of recording but a way of indicating the aspirated stop (kat^hi). Difficulties of this sort in his sources naturally limit the scope of Shafer's work.

Shafer reconstructed the following consonants (he does not reconstruct vowels): *h, *k, *t, *p, *n, *m, *t', *ś, *ts (doubtful), *d, *y, *w, *r. It is difficult to arrange these in any sort of orderly array. The phoneme *h is a major problem since Shafer's sources indicate a variety of reflexes: h, ø, k, s, z, and t. Maybe it was a fronted k which palatalized to č/c and thereby gave the latter three reflexes. By contrast, *k and *t have fairly consistent reflexes. Aspirated p occurs as a reflex of *p in some sets, while plain p occurs in others. Shafer believed these sets to be in complementary distribution, but the data are fragmentary. For phoneme *n, a puzzling reflex n^h occurs in several languages of one set. The occurrence of *d — one lone voiced stop

'Proto-Arawakan and its Descendants', *IJAL* (July, 1965) (Part II). As the author admits 'The sources of data have often been rather inexact transcriptions. Sometimes, they have represented compilations of several, often unobtainable primary sources' (113). In addition, the book tries to cover an immense area linguistically. Not only is Arawakan proper included, but Uru-Chipayan is assumed to be Arawakan (on the basis of some twenty sets) and included in the line-up along with Tupian and Chapacuran, for which data are given on the assumption that they are related to the Arawakan stock. A brief sketch of Goajiro is included as a control. Nevertheless, the overall result is almost as diffuse as Shafer's brief sketch described in this section. Noble, however, pays some attention to morphological features and to shared innovations — whether phonological, grammatical, or lexical. In this way he obtains a family tree for Arawakan and related languages. It needs to be emphasized, however, that without a detailed reconstruction of a proto-language shared innovations are not surely distinguished from shared retentions. Some use is made of glottochronology.

77 Robert Shafer, 'Algumas equações fonéticas em Arawakan', *Anthropos* 54.542-62 (1959).

78 H. C. van Renselaar and J. Voorhoeve, 'Rapport over een ethnologische studiereis door Mata', *BijdrTLV* 3.328-61 — probably 1959).

— is difficult to systematize. In two-thirds of the languages cited initial *d gives zero; in others, d or t (h in Yukuna). While Shafer labeled *ts as doubtful, the data for the reconstruction of *t′ are even scantier. The doubtful status of *ts is due, however, to the fact that in all but two of the thirteen sets where it is posited it occurred before vowel i (probably Proto-Arawakan *i). While Shafer reconstructs only *r, his sets may possibly indicate three phonemes, say, two varieties of r, and an l.

Douglas Taylor has compared (Surinam) Arawak with Island Carib (the language is Arawakan in spite of the name) as culled from historical sources and as now spoken by the 'Black Caribs' of Central America.[79] Taylor is encouraged by the comparative Arawak data to interpret his historical sources as indicating a contrast of aspirated and unaspirated consonants in the stops, nasals, and liquids. He symbolized the consonant systems of Dominican Island Carib (17th century) and Vincentian Island Carib (spoken until 1920) as follows (Table 21):

	DIC:			VIC:	
m	n		m	n	
	n^h			(?)	
b			b	d	g
	t	k		c	
p^h	t^h	k^h		t^h	k^h
	s	h	f	s	h
	r,l				r,l
	l^h				

Table 21

In VIC, as in Arawak, the f phoneme is probably a development from earlier p^h. DIC, which has no f, has a p^h.

Although Taylor's study is on a narrow front, it may have significance for Arawakan in general. Shafer's n^h residue and apparent contrasts among reflexes of his r might be explained by some such scheme as the above. In current Arawak and in the 17th century DIC, there were three contrasting phonemes: r, l, l^h. Notice also Shafer's sets which witness to *[p^h] in possible contrast with *[p]. Furthermore, in that the contrast — if it existed — could have been fortis-lenis in Proto-Arawakan, Shafer's *h versus *k could be lenis versus fortis velar, while his *d may also have been a lenis alveolar. It is futile to speculate further. As reliable synchronic data become available, the serious reconstruction of Proto-Arawakan will become possible.

11. Irvine Davis' unpublished sketch of Proto-Gê[80] is brief but fulfills many of the

[79] Douglas Taylor, 'Surinam Arawak as compared with different dialects of Island Carib', *BijdrTLV* 3.362-73 (1959?) cf. earlier article 'Some problems of sound correspondence in Arawak', *IJAL* 24. 234-9 (1958).

[80] Irvine Davis, 'Comparative Jê phonology', unpublished manuscript, Brazilian branch of the Summer Institute of Linguistics (1964).

requisites of a good comparative study: (1) presentation of current phonological systems; (2) reconstruction of an earlier phonological system; (3) careful tracing out of reflexes in daughter languages; (4) attention to apparent irregularities of a quasi-systemic sort; (5) presentation of a significant number (112) of cognate sets, and English indexing of cognates.

Davis' Proto-Gê is based on: Apinaye, Canela, Suyá, Xavante, and Kaingang. While the choice of languages was partially dictated by availability of data, the languages chosen are nevertheless well representative of Gê. Thus: 'Apinaye in its relationship to Proto-Jê, is in most respects representative of the Northern Kayapó dialects. ... Most of the facts concerning Canela outlined in the paper are apparently also true of the other members of the Eastern Timbira subgroup. ... So far as it is known, Suyá constitutes in itself a subdivision of Jê lacking other members, while Xavante with its several dialects plus Xerente forms another distinct subgroup' (3).

Regarding Kaingang, Davis says 'For the purposes of phonological reconstruction Kaingang belongs more logically within the Jê family than as a separate family within the Macro-Jê stock. It is obviously more closely related to the traditional Jê languages than are other Macro-Jê languages such as Maxakalí, and in many respects it shows closer conformity to Proto-Jê phonology than does Xavante, an undisputed member of the Jê family' (2). With Kaingang Davis groups Xokleng as 'either a somewhat divergent Kaingang dialect or a separate but closely related language' (2). Ursula Weisemann unhesitatingly places Xokleng (which she spells Xokreng) as a fourth Kaingang dialect (along with Paraná, South Kaingang, and Saõ Paulo).[81]

Davis reconstructs Proto-Gê phonemes as follows (Table 22):

Consonants				*Oral Vowels*			*Nasal Vowels*		
*p	*t	*c	*k	*i	*ɨ	*u	*į	*ɨ̨	*ų
*m	*n	*ñ	*ŋ	*e	*ə	*o	*ę	*ą	*ǫ
*w	*r	*z		*ɛ	*a	*ɔ			

Table 22

The phonetics of the Gê languages is anything but straightforward. In current languages the phonemes symbolized as nasals 'vary from voiced stops or affricates to prenasalized or postnasalized stops, to nasal continuants depending on the environment and on the language' (4). Phonemes transcribed as w/v and y/z vary from non-syllabic vocoids to fricatives. In some languages vowel length, possibly even consonant length, are phonemic. Current phonemic systems are variations on Proto-Gê. Thus, Apinaye adds glottal stop to the consonants and a tenth oral vowel (and seventh nasal vowel). Canela (tentative phonemicization) adds two laryngeals, ʔ and h, and an aspirated velar k^h. The vowel system is identical with that of Proto-Gê. Suya (even more tentatively phonemicized) adds one laryngeal h, a spirant s, two

81 Ursula Weisemann, 'Notes on Proto-Kaingang: a study of four dialects', unpublished manuscript, Brazilian branch of the Summer Institute of Linguistics.

aspirants, t^h and k^h, and a further vowel (as in Apinayé). Xavante eliminates phonemes corresponding to *n and *z, but adds one laryngeal, h. The glottal stop ʔ occurs instead of the velar k. The system of oral vowels is identical to Proto-Gê, but one nasal vowel is eliminated.

Kaingang raises a few problems due to the uncertainty of phonemic analysis in present-day Kaingang dialects. Weisemann (in what appears to be an early paper) states that possibly some Kaingang dialects and Proto-Kaingang had a voiced obstruent series b, d, g. Since, however, Weisemann collaborated somewhat with Davis in his recent reconstruction, it appears that her more recent thinking would not lead to positing such a series. Davis indicates that, as in the traditional Gê languages, voiced obstruents are allophones of the nasals.[82] Even if the obstruents are phonemic in one or more current Kaingang dialects their sub-phonemic status seems probable in Proto-Kaingang. We may assume, then, that relative to Proto-Gê, Kaingang eliminates one stop *c, adds two laryngeals ʔ and h, and two spirants f and š. The system of oral vowels corresponds to that of Proto-Gê, while one nasal vowel has been eliminated.

Phonological developments — granting the above range of allophonic variation in certain phonemes — are, as a whole, consistent and straightforward. Conditioned sound changes and unexplained residues often involve vertical shunting within an order of consonants. Thus *p is, on occasion, reflected as m or w in certain languages; *m, on occasion as p. Similarly *t is, on occasion, reflected as n or r; *n, on occasion, as t. By conditioned sound change *c splits to c/y in Canela, and ñ/y in Kaingang. Less parallel is the velar order, but even here Kaingang has a few unexplained reflexes ŋ of *k. While these are by no means the only conditioned sound changes and unexplained residues in the reflexes in current Gê languages, nevertheless the parallelism of the above is scarcely fortuitous. It is puzzling that the vertical shunting is neither wholly conditioned by sound change nor wholly irregular and sporadic. If the latter were the case, we could posit Proto-Gê consonantal alternation — possibly marking one or more grammatical categories. Some sort of morphophonemic alternation — partly phonologically conditioned — is nevertheless indicated.

12. Proto-Tupi-Guarani is, like Proto-Arawakan, more of a promise than a reality at present. We have, nevertheless, a phonological sketch by Hanke, Swadesh, and Rodrigues of the Mekens language along with (1) a sketch of the phonology of Tupinambá and Cocama; (2) a page of Proto-Tupi phonemes along with reflexes in thirteen languages; and (3) a Mekens word-list with a scattering of cognates from various other languages.[83]

[82] Cf. Weisemann, Notes on Proto-Kaingang (2,3): 'According to the phonemic analysis now established for Paraná dialects as spoken at Rio dos Cobras however, [b], [d], and [g] do not have phonemic status. They occur only contiguous to homorganic nasals. ...' It is possible that this analysis could also be established for some of the other dialects if sufficient data were available.

[83] Wanda Hanke, Morris Swadesh, and Aryón D. Rodrigues, 'Notas de fonología Mekens', *Miscellanea Paul Rivet octogenario dicata* (Mexico City, 1958).

Although they divided the Tupi stock into seven component families as did Rodrigues, 1958[84] (except that the Tupari family is rechristened Mekens), no attempt is made to distinguish Proto-Tupi as such from Proto-Mekens, nor to proceed step-wise by reconstruction of the phonologies of component families, then of the stock as a whole. The table of reflexes in thirteen languages tabulates reflexes of eight languages of Tupi-Guaraní proper, one of the Yuruna family, one of the Ariken family, two of the Mekens family, and one of the Monde family. Typologically Mekens is compared directly with Tupinamba and Cocama (both of Tupi-Guarani proper) with the comment 'Podemos, pois, ter uma idéia geral de qualquier idioma tupí, examinando o Tupinamba é o Kokama. ...' (192).

The reconstructed consonants are plausibly similar to those found in Tupinambá, Cocama, or Mekens — except for two oddities $*t^y$ and *g (the latter is the only voiced obstruent posited and is very poorly attested). Six oral vowels are reconstructed as against four in Tupinamba and five in Mekens.

In a student paper at Indiana University[85] Loraine Bridgeman lines up comparative data in the following Tupí languages: Urubu, Kamayura, Assurini, Guajajara, and Satare (all Tupi-Guaraní proper). She suggests a few sound correspondences (each one attested in at least five sets involving four or five languages), but does not reconstruct forms. Some 75 sets are given with forms in five languages, some 48 sets with forms in four languages; and some 65 sets with forms in two or three languages.

In a four-page article Bernard Pottier[86] suggests a few sound correspondences in the following Tupi languages: Xeta, Chiriguano, Izozo, Guarayo, Siriono, Guayaki, Cocama, Emerillon, Oyampi, and Tembe (all Tupi-Guarani proper). He proposes a division within Tupi-Guarani (corresponding to the first of Rodrigues' seven main divisions of the Tupi stock) in which the 'South-West' group (Xeta, Guayaki, Chiriguano, Izozo, Guarayo, Siriono) is distinguished from the 'North and East' group (Tupi, Tembé, Oyampi, Emerillon, Cocama) on the basis of certain phonological isoglosses. In that Rodrigues' slightly different grouping within Tupi-Guarani is based on lexical-statistics, while Pottier's is based on phonological isoglosses, the two articles form an interesting comparison.

13. Bruce Moore has compared two Chibchan languages, Colorado and Cayapa, spoken in the Ecuadorian coastal jungle.[87] Sound correspondences are carefully sorted out and classified according to Moore's stated purpose: 'The present study attempts to explain all the differences between 207 cognate pairs' (273). Although Moore never gives the phonemic system which he reconstructs for 'South Barbacoan Chibchan' —

[84] Aryón D. Rodrigues, 'Classification of Tupi-Guaraní', *IJAL* 24.231-4 (1958).

[85] Loraine I. Bridgeman, 'Preliminary notes on a comparative study of five Tupi-Guaraní languages' (1965).

[86] Bernard Pottier, 'Problemes de dialectologie dans le domaine du Tupi-Guaraní', *Orbis* 10:1.31-4 (1961).

[87] Bruce R. Moore, 'Correspondences in South Barbacoan Chibcha', Benjamin Elson, ed., *Studies in Ecuadorian Indian Languages I:* 270-89, (Norman, 1962).

nor a reconstructed form for each of his sets — the following phonemes occur in reconstructed forms scattered through the article (Table 23):

*p	*t	*t^{y}	*k	*ʔ			
*b	*d	*d^{y}					
*f	*s	*š		*h			
	*c	*č					
*m	*n	*ñ					
	*l	*l^{y}					
	*r				*i		*u
*w		*y			*e		*o
						*a	

Table 23

In addition, there occurs an *N which was a syllable final nasal element whose reflexes are vowel nasalization and nasal consonants. An *S is reconstructed to account for two irregular cognate pairs.

The only syllable final elements were *N and *h.

14. Comparative Carib is yet to be initiated. Desmond Derbyshire, however, has written briefly concerning three mutually intelligible dialects of Brazilian Carib: Hiskaryana, Katxhuyana, and Waiwai.[88] Internal reconstruction is employed within each dialect with attention to differences in phoneme inventories, restrictions in distribution of certain phonemes, and the distribution of allophones. On this basis the three dialects are reduced to the same inventory of phonemes. This yields a system considered to be that of the common stage lying back of the three dialects. The comparative method is not employed. Some lexical and grammatical comparisons are given — especially in respect to the structure of verbs.

Without engaging in comparative reconstructions, Jacob Loewen presents several isoglosses dividing the Choco languages of Panama and Colombia (in Greenberg's 'Northwestern Cariban').[89] It is, however, impossible to distinguish shared innovations from shared retentions without prior application of the comparative method. And, to refer again to Hamp's dictum (4.3), shared innovations are the sine qua non of genetic groupings.

[88] Desmond Derbyshire, 'Comparative notes on three Carib dialects', *Boletim do Museu Paraense Emílio Goeldi, nova série, Anthropologia* 14 (1961).

[89] Jacob A. Loewen, 'Chocó I: introduction and bibliography', *IJAL* 29.239-63 (1963).

MEXICO

MARLYS McCLARAN

1. INTRODUCTION

For Mexico, as part of Meso-America and Ibero-America, there are two recent reference works (McQuown 1967a (= *HMAI* 5); Sebeok 1968 (= *CTL* 4)) with bibliographies of linguistic materials and studies which are virtually exhaustive through the mid-sixties. Therefore, it has seemed appropriate in this article to try to highlight the cumulative results of studies in this area rather than to duplicate bibliographical coverage. The sixth *Bibliography of the Summer Institute of Linguistics* (Wares 1968) is to be noted as well as recent bibliography in Bartholomew (1969b). There have also been some notable articles and monographs of very recent appearance.[1]

From an areal point of view Mexico is an ideal linguistic laboratory. Diebold 1962 has made a good case for Mexico as a laboratory for studying language contact, but in the more general sense it offers documentation situations appropriate to every conceivable linguistic subdiscipline and cross-discipline. It is also relatively accessible, in both political and geographical terms, even to the most remote hamlet. This is not the case for many areas of equal linguistic diversity in today's world. In most other areas of North America where non-European languages are still spoken, the original cultural setting of these languages has been severely distorted, or, where only a few speakers remain, it has ceased to be viable altogether. By contrast, most of Mexico's diverse linguistic communities thrive in corresponding, diverse cultural settings, at various stages of acculturation with respect to the national life, and are not likely to lose their uniqueness soon. There are presently about three million speakers of indigenous languages (based on the 1960 census), or about twelve percent of the population.

Mexico's more than two-hundred languages have received varying kinds and amount of attention from linguists and other language-oriented investigators. I will attempt to survey the kinds of information that exist about the languages and language families ordered in a roughly north to south sequence. For an inventory of names of languages the reader is referred to Bright 1967 and to McQuown 1955. The latter locates languages by latitude and longitude. There is also a map in Longacre 1967 (following

[1] The contributions of Lyle Campbell to this article are gratefully acknowledged. Any errors of omission or fact are the author's responsibility.

page 120), showing language affiliations based largely on Frederick Johnson's earlier map (1940) and on McQuown 1955.

The investigative typology which I have in mind while reviewing these results is one which considers studies in three categories: 'straight' linguistic, including descriptive and historical reconstruction; sociolinguistic, which considers language phenomena in relation to facts of people within social structure, succession of generations and in contact with other groups; and ethnolinguistic, which considers language in the semantic aspect of its cultural context. Of course these categories overlap to a considerable degree. Characterization of a study as primarily linguistic, sociolinguistic or ethnolinguistic is only an indication of where its major import seems to lie.

The three major language families of Mexico, considering both number of speakers and amount of study directed toward them are Uto-Aztecan, Otomanguean and Mayan. They have all been the object of descriptive and historical investigations. A Uto-Aztecan language, Nahuatl, was the medium for a large body of literature of valuable ethnographic content dating from the post-Conquest 'Classical' period. Consequently, there is a sizeable amount of descriptive material on both classical and modern dialects. Comparable classical texts exist in the Mayan language of Yucatan. Both the Otomanguean and Mayan families have been the objects of a concerted and systematic effort at reconstruction. An Otomanguean language, Mazatec, has been studied in a sociolinguistic context with some interesting results for dialectology. The Mayan languages of Chiapas in southern Mexico have yielded data in both sociolinguistic and ethnolinguistic contexts with implications for both of these subdisciplines. A language isolate, Tarascan, has been the subject of a recent ethnolinguistic article that makes a contribution to the linguist's inventory of language phenomena. In the pages that follow, I will try to show in greater detail the developments in the study of these and other languages which seem to have implications either for the greater understanding of Mexico as a linguistic area or for advancements in the various investigative disciplines.

The Estados Unidos de México is the largest single political area within the Meso-American culture region as defined by Kirchhoff (1943). The northern border of Mexico and the United States lies north of the Meso-American culture area itself, whose limits extend jaggedly from east to west through the states of Tamaulipas, San Luis Potosí, Zacatecas, Durango and Sinaloa, or roughly where the central highlands give way to the more arid north. Most of the Otomanguean languages are within the borders of Mexico and the Meso-American area; the Uto-Aztecan languages are found both within and out of the area, as well as north of the Mexican border in California and the American Southwest. The Hokaltecan languages, the first to be considered below, also have representatives north and south of the international border, and within the Meso-American area. The Mayan languages, centered in Guatemala and Southeastern Mexico, define the southern limit of the Meso-American area. This southern border can be pictured as running north to south through Honduras, Nicaragua and Costa Rica. Thus, while this article will deal mainly with the languages found within the national borders of Mexico, it will be necessary to refer, if only in passing, to the Hokaltecan and Uto-Aztecan affiliates to the north, to the Mayan languages to the south, and even to far-flung southern outliers of Uto-Aztecan, Hokaltecan and Otomanguean.

2. HOKALTECAN LANGUAGES

Most of the northern border region, because of its harsh, semi-arid climate, has always been sparsely populated. In ancient and historical times its inhabitants were primarily hunting and collecting tribes. The eastern section, identified as the Northeast Mexico-Texas culture area (Willey 1966; Driver 1961) includes approximately the territory of Tamaulipas, Nuevo León, Coahuila, and Chihuahua, as well as southern Texas. This coincides with a linguistic grouping, Coahuiltecan, including Coahuilteco, Comecrudo, Tamaulipec, Karankawa, Cotoname and Tonkawa. Most of these languages were extinct by the end of the eighteenth century; all are now extinct.

Except for Tonkawa of Texas (Hoijer 1933, 1946), our knowledge of them consists principally of wordlists. In two papers Sapir proposed the Coahuiltecan grouping which he connected, first (1920) with the Hokan languages, and later (1925) with Subtiaba in Nicaragua, now extinct, and Tlappanec of Guerrero. Tlappanec is reported to have about 18,000 speakers (Marino Flores 1967) at the present time, but has received scant attention from linguists (see items in Bright's 1967 bibliography).

Sapir's articles mentioned above, Sapir 1917, and Kroeber's study (1915) of Serian, Tequistlatecan and Hokan form the classic core of work on the proposed Hokan and Hokan-Coahuiltecan grouping. Brinton's early classification (1891) here, as elsewhere, came close to the mark, but Kroeber's paper was the first to present evidence. Also, the Jicaque language of Honduras has been proposed as a Hokan language (Swadesh and Greenberg 1953). However, Hokaltecan, or Hokan-Coahuiltecan, as a stock is probable; but its internal groupings must remain somewhat uncertain for lack of data (Bright 1956).

The westernmost languages of this stock are separated from the Coahuiltecan group by the great wedge of Uto-Aztecan languages. Along the lower Colorado River live speakers of Cocopa (Cucupa). The Baja California peninsula, from an ethnologic point of view, is an interesting cul-de-sac. Few speakers of indigenous languages remain, but archaeological and ethnohistorical studies (Massey 1966:38–50) suggest three layers of migration south from California, which is supported by the available linguistic evidence. At the tip of the peninsula the Guaicura-Pericú languages, now extinct, presumably represented the oldest populations. Their wider affiliations are unknown. The middle layer, the Peninsular Yuman languages, include Cochimí and Laymon, no longer spoken. There were no doubt others. Their territory, according to the 18th century missionaries, lay between Loreto and the 30th parallel.

The most recent layer corresponds to the California Yuman group of languages:

Diegueño, Paipai or Akwaʔala, Kiliwa, Kamia and Ñakipa in the older literature. A more recent classification of the Yuman group is made by Judith Joel (1964:99–105). Her paper also contains information on the location of the few remaining speakers of these languages. She constructs an ethnohistory of the Yuman area on the basis of the linguistic classification. Progress in the reconstruction of Proto-Yuman has been furthered by the publication of Wares 1968. A review of this work by Langdon (1970) adds informative detail based on her own work on Yuman. A paper by Law (1961) draws conclusions about the Yuman proto-culture on the basis of comparison of vocabularies.

Finally, with regard to these northern Hokaltecan languages, a recent sociolinguistic study by Crawford (1970) on Cocopa baby talk compares the reduced consonantal inventory resulting from rules of consonantal ablaut, used in addressing babies and young children, with the reconstructed Proto-Yuman consonantal system.

Morris Swadesh (1967:100–15), by way of demonstrating the lexicostatistic procedure in its new form, defined a Coahuilan group of languages with a maximal internal divergence of 88 minimum centuries. This group, as he defined it, includes some of Sapir's Hokan-Coahuiltecan languages plus Jicaque and Guaicura. The group is considered to present one of the more difficult problems of comparison, and for that reason serves to illustrate the conditions taken into account both in obtaining a score and weighing its validity. Since its inception this procedure has seen a constant refinement and a movement away from being considered an hypothesis about rate of language change to be accepted or falsified, to its present status as a useful heuristic. Swadesh, whose untimely death in 1967 deprived linguistic science of one of its most gifted practitioners, will be remembered for the development of the glottochronologic method and some of the daring relationships based on it, among many other accomplishments. Although the method and the groupings which Swadesh put forth were sometimes not without critics, the point was, after all, to refine the method whenever one had independent historical or prehistorical controls, and to project it where one needed it most.

The Yuman languages were early included in the Hokan grouping (Dixon and Kroeber 1913). Kroeber's 1915 article, mentioned above, showed Seri and Chontal to be related to Yuman. Seri is spoken in Sonora on the Gulf of California coast. Descriptive materials are not plentiful (for lexicon and phonology cf. Bright 1967; for texts and literacy material, Wares 1968). Chontal of Oaxaca, or Tequistlatec as it is also called, is one of the best described languages of Mexico. About 9,000 people speak a coastal dialect, Huamelula or Lowland Chontal, plus a mountain dialect or group of dialects. The Lowland Chontal is principally associated with the work of Viola Waterhouse (1962, 1967). Recently, Turner has described Highland Chontal (1967a, 1968a, 1968b). On the basis of comparison of the phonemic systems of the two dialects, Turner 1969 reconstructs the Proto-Chontal phonemic system. Waterhouse 1969 in general supports this reconstruction, but uses cognates rather than comparison of phonemic systems. Turner 1967b, in a rather startling paper aimed at refutation of Kroeber 1915, attempts to show that Seri and Chontal are not related — that, indeed, if one of these languages is Hokan then the other cannot be. His evidence, based on lack of correspondence between systems and inventories, is not conclusive, but suggests that the internal groupings of the Hokaltecan stock may not be definitive. An opposing view is presented by Bright (1971).

Viola Waterhouse reported a sociolinguistic phenomenon in "Learning a second language first" (1949), which at that time was unique in the literature but which has since been reported for at least one other language (Foster 1969). Children are addressed exclusively in Spanish; only when they enter the adult community do they begin to learn Chontal, which is their principal language as adults. This fact is shown to be related to certain morphophonemic phenomena.

3. OTOMANGUEAN LANGUAGES

The Otomanguean languages, at the time of the Conquest, were distributed in three groups: the central concentration in Oaxaca, homeland of the Zapotecs and Mixtecs; the northern group, whose languages are spoken principally in San Luis Potosí, Guanajuato, Hidalgo and Querétaro; and the Southern outliers, in Chiapas and along the Pacific coast of Central America. Both the Chiapanec of Chiapas and the Mangue of Central America are now extinct.

The Oaxaca group of languages presently includes Mixtecan, Popolocan (including Ixcatec, Chocho, and Mazatec), Chinantec, and the Zapotec-Chatino languages. Amuzgo is a fifth coordinate branch surrounded by Mixtecan. The present State of Oaxaca is almost co-extensive with the cultural-archeological sub-area of that name, whose center was the Monte Albán civilization. While archaeologists will not speculate about the linguistic affinities of the earlier horizons at Monte Albán, the Zapotecan occupancy of the area can be projected backward from historical times. The Mixtec, descending from the northwestern part of the area during the period from 1000 A.D., challenged the hegemony of the Zapotecs. Their center, Mitla, probably dates from this period. Glyphic writing, which exists for both Zapotecan and Mixtecan, has made it possible to trace the genealogy of Mixtec kings back to the seventh century A.D. (Willey 1966:164–5). Both groups were engaged in their resistance to the Aztec expansion at the time of the Conquest. Most of the Oaxacan languages of the Otomanguean stock are still viable. At mid-century there were reportedly some 35,000 speakers of Chinantec, 225,000 speakers of Zapotec (which includes at least six or seven different languages all referred to as 'Zapotec'), 13,000 speakers of Chatino, 185,000 speakers of Mixtec, 17,000 speakers of Popoloca and 80,000 speakers of Mazatec (Marino Flores 1967:22). Trique and Cuicatec of the Mixtecan group, and Ixcatec and Chocho of the Popolocan group have fewer speakers. Papabuco, thought to be a dialect of Chatino, is probably recently extinct (Harvey 1968). Descriptive materials on these languages are listed in Bright's bibliography (1967) and in the S.I.L.

bibliography (Wares 1968). A model tagmemic sketch of Isthmus Zapotec is that of Pickett 1967. Some more recent studies include Earl 1968 on Zapotec; Upson 1968 on Chatino; Pike and Cowan 1967, Merrifield and Stoudt 1967, and Hunter and Pike 1969 on Mixtec; and on Popoloca, Williams and Longacre 1967, Karlstrom and Pike 1968, and Williams and Pike 1967.

At least some of the Otomanguean languages exhibit tonal contrasts and have received much close attention in this regard. Pike's (1948) treatise on *Tone languages* is heavily illustrated with examples from these languages. George Cowan (1948) has an article describing the singular ability of Mazatecos to carry on whistle conversations based on the four tones of the language.

The languages of the Otopamean branch are found north of Mexico City between about the 21st and 22nd parallel. This group includes Pame, Chichimeca-Jonaz, Otomí, Mazahua, Matlatzinca and Ocuilteco. Otomí has over 180,000 speakers and Mazahua over 84,000 (Marino Flores 1967:22). The rest are weaker. South Pame is reported nearly extinct (Manrique 1967). These languages show great internal diversity (Manrique 1958), suggesting a time depth greater than Indo-European. It has been suggested that the languages of the inhabitants of the Valley of Mexico before the invasion of the Aztecs were Otopamean. Between these languages and those of the Oaxacan group Swadesh finds a measure of 49 minimum centuries of divergence (Swadesh 1967:93, comparing Mazahua and Ixcateco).

Recent treatments of Otopamean languages include Bernard 1967, 1970; Lanier 1968 on Mezquital Otomí; and Bartholomew 1969 on comparative Otopamean numerals.

The southern outliers of the Otomanguean stock were Chiapanec, spoken until recently around Chiapa de Corzo, and Mangue of coastal El Salvador, Honduras, Nicaragua, and Costa Rica, which became extinct toward the end of the last century. Together they constitute the Chorotegan family. Bibliography of the scant materials can be found in Bright 1967. These two languages form the basis for comparison with the Oaxacan languages in a work by Fernández de Miranda and Weitlaner (1961), which is an example of judicious use of limited materials on extinct languages.

For the practice of historical linguistics Otomanguean offers much promise. Those who work in this area believe they will soon have the systemic reconstruction of a language stock 'somewhat comparable to the scope and depth of Indo-European studies — although with a fraction of the manpower involved in the latter' (Longacre 1968:333–4). For a sketch of the developments in Otomanguean reconstruction, two articles by Longacre (1964, 1968) are useful; and Longacre himself is responsible for much of the work. Among other contributions, his paper on Amuzgo (1966) served to establish that the language is coordinate with Mixtecan and the other branches, not a Mixtecan language as had been believed. Other linguists particularly associated with this effort are Sarah Gudschinsky, María Fernández de Miranda, and Doris Bartholomew. Most recently, the comprehensive work on Otomanguean reconstruction of Calvin Rensch is, at this writing, in press.

Gudschinsky's work on Mazatec dialects (1955, 1958) presents an outstanding example of the historical conclusions which can be drawn by a convergence of techniques carefully applied. She is able to integrate the results of lexicostatistic counts on the present-day dialects with the history of hypothesized sound changes from reconstructed Proto-Mazatec, deriving a history of dialect development and contact among dialects to give a picture of linguistic history which is reconcilable with historical record.

Ethnolinguistic work on these languages also includes a preliminary reconstructed cultural vocabulary for Proto-Mixtecan and Proto-Amuzgo-Mixtecan (Millon and Longacre 1961). Merrifield 1966 uses place names to generate hypotheses about Chinantec prehistory.

Otomanguean linguistics owes much to Robert J. Weitlaner (1883–1968). As Foster 1970 points out in his obituary article about the Austrian engineer-turned-ethnolinguist, his major linguistic contributions were made in the Otomanguean languages. His ethnographic accomplishments are fittingly represented in the recently published volume 7, *Ethnology*, of the *Handbook of Middle American Indians*.

4. UTO-AZTECAN LANGUAGES

At the time of the Spanish Conquest a Uto-Aztecan language, Nahuatl or Aztec, was the language of the rulers of Mexico. However, at that time the Aztecs were but recent arrivals from the North. Their hegemony, which reached out from the Valley of Mexico, dates only from the mid-fifteenth century. Although it is uncertain how far back the legendary history of the Aztecs can be taken to identify tribes speaking Uto-Aztecan languages, it is clear that successive waves of peoples, dissociating themselves from the 'barbarian' hunter-gatherers of the northern desert — called 'Chichimecs' by the Aztecs — made incursions into the agricultural Meso-American area, sometimes established great centers, and reached as far south as Guatemala, Costa Rica, and Panama. The great Teotihuacan of the Classic period, 'place of the gods' to the later Aztecs, may have been inhabited by Nahua speakers. The Tolteca of later Tula were more surely a Nahua-speaking tribe or group of tribes. Then, with the rise of Tenochtitlan-Tlatelolco as center of the Aztec Empire, the language of the Aztecs became a lingua franca over most of central Mexico and as far south as present-day Chiapas.

Soon after the Conquest, Spanish priests began the study of many indigenous languages for the purposes of conversion, education and government. In many cases, during the early period, Indians were taught to write their own language in Latin orthography. Consequently, for the politically important language of the Aztecs we have texts, grammars and dictionaries. All the early grammars (or 'artes') and dictionaries are listed by Bright 1967 and by McQuown 1967b. Of the texts, both religious and secular, the most famous are the Nahuatl 'ethnographies' collected by Fray

Bernardino de Sahagún, forming the basis for this *General history of the things of New Spain* (1577). The history of textual criticism and analysis of this and other texts is to be found in León-Portilla 1967 and Suárez 1968. In connection with Sahagún, one must single out for particular attention recently the ongoing work of Anderson and Dibble in translating and publishing the Florentine Codex. The Mexican scholar Angel María Garibay Kintana (1892–1967) devoted over thirty years to the study of Nahuatl language and culture and was a founder of the Seminario de Cultura Nahuatl of the National University of Mexico, whose publications reflect the great interest and progress in Nahuatl studies (especially *Estudios de cultura Nahuatl*, volumes 1–8 to date). A sketch of Classical Nahuatl by Newman has also been recently published (1967).

At the present time the speakers of Nahua dialects number about 640,000. For the most part they are found in central Mexico. Hasler 1961 identifies four dialects on the basis of some ten diagnostic characteristics. Earlier studies had recognized three on the basis of the phoneme corresponding to the 'classical' /λ/, viz. /t/ or /l/, and this gave rise to the labels Nahuatl, Nahuat or Nahual. The name Pipil refers to Nahua dialects of Central America. The 'Alagüilac' of Brinton 1887 was a Nahua dialect of Guatemala. An important volume of descriptive studies since Bright's bibliography is the collection of Robinson 1969.

The other Uto-Aztecan languages of Mexico are found in the northwestern part of the country, from the border to Nayarit. Papago is spoken in northern Sonora on the United States border, Pima Alto in southeastern Sonora, Pima Bajo or Yecora in south-eastern Sonora and Chihuahua, Northern Tepehuan in southern Chihuahua near Durango, Southern Tepehuan in southern Durango near Nayarit, and Tepecano in Jalisco. The Cáhita languages, Yaqui and Mayo, are spoken in southern Sonora on the Gulf coast and in southern Sonora-Sinaloa, respectively. There are about 3,000 speakers of Yaqui in Mexico, and 31,000 speakers of Mayo (Marino Flores 1967). Tarahumara is spoken by 18,000 in southwestern Chihuahua. Varohío or Guarijío is spoken, if at all, in Moris, Chihuahua (Olivera and Sánchez 1965). Yet another group consisting of Cora (3,000) and Huichol (3,000 in Marino Flores 1967, 7,000 in Grimes 1964) is spoken in Nayarit. Many more languages of the Uto-Aztecan group which were spoken by the peoples of the arid northern zone and the Southwest United States and California are now extinct. Except for the Nahua languages or dialects mentioned above, Uto-Aztecan falls mainly outside the Meso-American area.

Bibliographies of the Middle American Uto-Aztecan languages are to be found in Bright 1967, and for the U.S. languages in Bright 1964. Recent descriptive studies are found in the *Estudios de cultura Nahuatl*, already mentioned. Woo 1970 gives a feature analysis of tone in Northern Tepehuan, with discussion of implications for Proto-Tepiman. Bascom's work on Proto-Tepiman is summarized by Longacre 1968; McMahon 1967 sketches the phonemic system of Cora.

Language in an ethnographic context has been considered by Crumrine 1968 for styles of Mayo speech; Price 1967 considers an ethnobotanical taxonomy in Huichol.

Language contact has been studied by M. Miller 1970 in terms of Pima-English and Spanish bilingualism. The study of loanwords involving Uto-Aztecan languages has been important in partial reconstructions of ethnohistory, particulary with regard to layers of borrowing; an example of such investigation is Bright and Thiel 1965. Campbell 1970 uses Uto-Aztecan loanwords in Quichean languages to suggest that the origin of the borrowings is in Gulf Nahua dialects.

Comparative Uto-Aztecan has a long and significant history. A comprehensive summary of the identification and classification of the Uto-Aztecan languages is by Lamb 1964. Sapir's articles of 1913–19 on Southern Paiute and Nahuatl will remain the classics in this field. They were, as Lamb says (p. 121), 'the first extensive application of the comparative method to a group of American languages'. The reconstruction of a phonological system for the proto-language was accomplished by Whorf in the mid-30s. A full typological and comparative treatment of some fifteen languages, together with their reconstructions of Proto-Uto-Aztecan, Proto-Aztec, Proto-Shoshonean, and Proto-Sonoran constitute an important monograph by Voegelin, Voegelin and Hale (1962). Although the unity of the Uto-Aztecan languages is beyond question, their internal relationships remain in dispute. The older tradition postulated the unity of the three subgroups, Shoshonean, Sonoran, and Nahuatlan, largely on a geographical basis. Voegelin, Voegelin and Hale seem to believe that their comparisons and lexocostatistic counts support this grouping within a genetic model. Other investigators, such as Whorf, Kroeber, and Lamb, have found the internal relationships within the stock to be otherwise. The Shoshonean problem is outside the scope of this paper, but a review of this material can be found in Hopkins 1965 and in Lamb's article mentioned above. The so-called Sonoran languages, which really straddle the Mexican-United States border, may conservatively be considered, after Lamb 1964, to consist of Pimic (Pima-Papago and Tepehuan) and Taracahitic (Tarahumara and Cahitan, including Yaqui-Mayo, Varohío, and the extinct Ópata) as coordinate families within the Uto-Aztecan stock. The closely related languages Cora and Huichol, sometimes considered Sonoran, were grouped with Nahuatlan by Mason 1940. Lamb, on the basis of lexicostatistics, views them as a coordinate family within Uto-Aztecan. The Nahuatlan or Aztekic languages or group of dialects constitute the southernmost family within the stock.

The most engaging problem in reconstructing Proto-Uto-Aztecan thus far is morphophonemic. The problem was first carefully elaborated by Sapir in his description of Southern Paiute where the alternation of stem forms involves spirantization, nasalization, or gemination as synchronic phenomena. Whorf's 1935 reconstruction of Proto-Uto-Aztecan included a theory to account for these alternations, based on an earlier stage where the 'spirantizing' resulted from an intervocalic allophone, the non-spirantizing and gemination from a reduced consonant cluster where a stop was lost, and the nasalization from a nasal plus stop consonant cluster. Longacre (1968:328–32) compares this theory with Voegelin, Voegelin and Hale's treatment of the problem (1962, Ch. 3, 'Interphonemic specifications'), concluding that the latter partially supports Whorf's theory. The problem also involves vowel length and stress patterns. An overall explanation is still lacking, at least in published form, but recent studies, such as Seiler 1967 and Hill and Hill 1968 indicate that the problem continues to be studied. Voegelin, Voegelin and Hale's study has 171 cognates. To this can now be added Wick Miller's (1967) Uto-Aztecan cognate sets, and the additional material in Bright's review (1968).

5. MAYAN LANGUAGES

The Mayan languages are spoken over a continuous area of the Yucatan peninsula, Southern Mexico, British Honduras, Honduras, and Guatemala (except for Huastec of Veracruz and San Luis Potosí — the 'Huasteca' region). As was the case with the Aztecs of Central Mexico, the Spanish invaders found a high civilization, considerably factionalized but exhibiting those cultural traits later considered characteristic of the Middle America area, such as religious art and ritual, hieroglyphic writing, complex calendrics, an agricultural system, and a stratified society.

Geographically and culturally the Mayan-speaking peoples are usually considered in terms of three areas: the Huastec or northeastern region, the Maya Lowlands, and the Maya Highlands. The first group is within Mexico proper, but the territory of the last two is about equally divided between Mexico and adjacent countries, which makes a discussion of the Mayan languages of Mexico arbitrary in certain respects. In fact, the Guatemalan highlands are considered to be the location of Proto-Mayan unity, an area which today, considering its territorial extent, has a considerable diversity of mutually unintelligible Mayan languages (McQuown 1964; Diebold 1960).

Huastec is spoken in Northern Veracruz and eastern San Luis Potosí by 67,000 people (Marino Flores 1967). Chontal is the Mayan language of Tabasco (not to be confused with Chontal of Oaxaca, a Hokaltecan language). The State of Chiapas is linguistically a highly diversified area. The principal languages are Tzeltal (50,000, Marino Flores) and Tzotzil (75,000, Marino Flores). Other Mayan languages of this state are Chol, Maya (Lacandón), Mam, and Tojolabal (according to Marino Flores), and also Kekchí, Ixil, Chuj, Jacaltec, Quiché, and Motozintleco on the Guatemalan border, according to Olivera and Sánchez 1965. Kaufman 1969 reports a Mayan language Teco, closely related to but distinct from Mam, and clarifies the linguistic situation of this border area.

The jungle of the Petén region of Guatemala is more or less uninhabited, although an island in Lake Petén, Itzá, was the last holdout among the Mayan kingdoms of the Lowlands, falling to the Spaniards in 1697.

North of the Petén, the Yucatan peninsula is an extensive area of relatively homogeneous speech, Yucatec or Maya proper. Speakers number over 300,000. While there are pronounced regional varieties, speech all over the peninsula is mutually intelligible. Lacandón of the Chiapas-Guatemala border along the Usumacinta River (Tozzer 1921), as well as the Mopan of San Luis Petén and Punta Gorda, British

Honduras (Ulrich and Ulrich 1965), are sufficiently similar to Yucatec to raise the question of whether they should be considered Yucatecan dialects.

For Huastec, descriptive materials are listed in Bright 1967 and Wares 1968. For the Guatemalan languages, some of which are spoken in Chiapas, the most extensive recent source of grammatical sketches is Mayers 1965. This volume contains information on Achí, Quiché, Pocomchí, Kekchí, Ixil, Aguacatec, Mam, Jacaltec, Chuj, Chortí, and Mopan. For Tzeltal and Tzotzil, sketches are listed in Bright and in Wares. Other more recent sketches of Tzotzil are Colby 1966, Hopkins 1967, and Cowan 1969. Blair's dissertation (1964) is a description of Yucatec noun and verb morphology. The pedagogical grammar *Spoken Yucatec Maya* by him and Vermont-Salas (1965) is a valuable aid to training for ethnolinguistic fieldwork in Yucatan as well as a useful textual source in itself. Baer and Merrifield (1967) give a sketch of the Lacandón pronominal system.

As in the case of the Aztecs of Mexico, post-Conquest priests in Yucatan taught the use of Latin orthography for writing Maya to a few native speakers, and they used it themselves to compile dictionaries, and to compose 'artes' or grammars and religious materials. The texts of this early period represent Classical Yucatec. McQuown (1967b) gives a review of this literature, as well as a sketch of Classical Yucatec (1967c). Another comprehensive listing of source is found in Tozzer's (1921) Maya grammar. Among the indispensable aids to reading texts the foremost is the Motul dictionary, first published in Merida in 1929 (Martínez Hernández, ed.). This edition also carries the Arte of Fray Juan Coronel. Notable among the natively composed texts are the Books of Chilam Balam, containing rituals, chronicles and other traditional materials. They are named after the place of composition or discovery. The Chilam Balam of Chumayel, translated by Ralph Roys, was published in a critical edition in 1933. The reading of these texts presents a certain amount of difficulty, both because of the highly metaphorical style of language use and because of the inadequacies of the Latin-Spanish alphabet to render the phonemic distinctions of Maya. Scribes reliably differentiated the glottalized from the unglottalized stops; but the syllabic distinctions of length, glottalization and tone are rendered either unreliably or not at all.

An exciting part of Mayan studies is the ongoing work with the hieroglyphic materials. Primarily from Yucatan, but also from the Petén region, there are stone inscriptions and paper codices, the best known of these being the Dresden codex. Despite the effort of many years, the greater part of the work of decipherment remains to be done. A recent summary and bibliography is by Barthel (1968), who is himself among the foremost investigators. The first international conference on the Mayan glyphs met in Mexico City in 1966. Groups in Germany (Barthel and Zimmerman), Mexico (The Comisión para el Estudio de la Escritura Maya), and in the United States (David Kelley and others) are at work. The Russian study by J.V. Knorozov et al. is thought to have been concluded; their solutions seem to be generally rejected, however. Criticism is directed toward their language data and their hypotheses about linguistic change. A summary of what is generally conceded about the glyphs is as follows. They represent early Yucatec and possibly some other languages around the edge of the glyph area (Chol at Palenque, Kekchí or Chortí at Quirigua). There appears to be some evolution from a more ideographic writing in the early inscriptions to a more phonetic or syllabic writing in later inscriptions. Some phonetic or syllabic values of various glyphs have been generally agreed to work in all or most contexts by many of the present investigators. The basis of these identifications is the same as that for the few grammatical affixes which have been identified, namely, the distributional constraints which the glyph is observed to obey. From that is deduced the value it would need to have according to the hypothetical values of the glyphs of its environment. The method is the circular but pragmatic one of familiar linguistic analysis.[2] The most recent volume of *Estudios de cultura Maya* (volume 7, 1968) contains some of the latest published work on glyph decipherment and methodology.

The classification of the Mayan languages and the reconstruction of Proto-Mayan, and now some of the intermediate groupings, has absorbed the effort of scholars since the mid-nineteenth century. Historically, the most important of these are Stoll (1884), Seler (1887), Kroeber (1939:112–14), Halpern (1942), and McQuown (1956). Knowl edge of Mayan is accumulating rapidly, owing partly to increasing numbers oı students entering the field. Consequently, much important work is not yet published. The most extensive study over the last few years is that of Terrence S. Kaufman, much of which is unpublished. Part of the results of his work appears in his article of 1964, which together with McQuown 1964 gives a reasonably up-to-date overview of language development and associated culture history. Kaufman's article on Teco, a Mamean language (1970), contains a summary of the latest classification. (Cf. also his article in *Current Trends*, vol. 11, "Areal linguistics and Middle America", 1973.)

In addition to descriptive and historical studies of the Mayan languages, there is an important and growing amount of sociolinguistic and ethnolinguistic research, which owes its impetus mainly to Norman A. McQuown and the Chiapas Project which began in the late fifties. Although comprehensive reports of this work are unpublished (McQuown 1959; cf. 1962), a convenient summary of the research designs and kinds of data obtained is to be found in Gudschinsky 1967. Later ethnolinguistic studies by Berlin (1964, 1968) deal with the semantics of numeral classifiers — a striking characteristic of certain noun phrases in the Mayan languages. This is also treated by Hopkins 1970. The Mayan Ethnolinguistics Symposium held during the 1969 meetings of the American Anthropological Association in New Orleans attests the growing depth and breadth of Mayan studies. And most recently (1970), the *Papers of the Sixth Regional Meeting of the Chicago Linguistic Society* has a section on Mayan linguistics. The field has broadened greatly since the time when Kluckhohn could accuse those involved in Middle American studies of being 'but slightly re-

[2] I am indebted to Nicholas A. Hopkins for some information on glyph research.

formed antiquarians', in 'realms where there seems a great deal of obsessive wallowing in detail of and for itself' (1940:42).

6. MIXE-ZOQUE

The languages comprising the Zoquean or Mixe-Zoque family are spoken in eastern Veracruz and Oaxaca, and in northern Chiapas. The northernmost dialect, Sierra Popoluca (not to be confused with Popoloca, an Otomanguean language) is spoken by ten to twelve thousand people in southeastern Veracruz (Elson 1967). Sayula Popoluca is spoken in the Veracruz town of that name by about 4,000 (Clark 1961). Mixe is spoken by 46,000 people (Marino Flores 1967) in Oaxaca; and Zoque, primarily in Chiapas but also in Oaxaca, by 18,000 (Marino Flores 1967). The Tapachulteco dialect, although within the Zoquean area of Chiapas, is rather a Mixean dialect (Nordell 1962; Kaufman 1964).

William Wonderly is closely associated with the reconstruction of Proto-Zoquean (1949; Wonderly and Elson 1953). More recently the work of Terrence Kaufman (1964 and unpublished manuscripts) has carried the reconstruction beyond the phonemic system to include affixes and syntax. The Wonderly and Elson article reconstructed the system of personal prefixes. As for classification, it seems to be the consensus that there are only two main branches of the family, Mixean and Zoquean, and that the Popolucan dialects do not constitute a unity but are either Mixean or Zoquean. Longacre 1968 summarizes work in Mixe-Zoque, pointing out that complicated morphophonemic processes are characteristic of the family.

Elson 1967 gives a sketch of Sierra Popoluca. Other recent sketches (since Bright's 1967 bibliography) are of Mixe clauses (S. Lyon 1967) and Mixe verbs (D. Lyon 1967).

7. TOTONAC-TEPEHUA

The Totonac, from their center of Cempoala, were the first to become allies of Cortez when he disembarked on the coast of Veracruz and set out to conquer Mexico. The city, soon left in ruins, was reported to have twenty to thirty thousand inhabitants.

There are presently well over 130,000 speakers of Totonacan dialects in Veracruz and Puebla. The internal diversity among the three Totonac dialects and Tepehua is not very great. Swadesh 1967 estimates the Totonac-Tepehua divergence at 26 minimum centuries. Perhaps for this reason there is a lack of published material on reconstruction, and instead, attention is focused on the place of Totonacan in the proposed Macro-Mayan grouping (see below).

The only detailed reconstruction is that of Arana 1953. Aschmann has published a number of descriptive papers. The few major studies since Bright's bibliography are

Reid's 1967 tagmemic description of discourse, Bower and Erickson's 1967 sketch of Tepehua, and Herzog's (forthcoming) discussion of the Tepehua verb in *Linguistics*.

8. LANGUAGE ISOLATES: TARASCAN AND HUAVE

The Tarascan language, sometimes called Porepecha (or a variant spelling), is spoken by 40 or 50 thousand people in the State of Michoacan. Its linguistic relationships are unknown, not for lack of descriptive materials but for lack of demonstrable affinities with other languages.

The Tarascans were empire builders in historic times — if not rivalling the Aztecs, at least withstanding their dominion. The post-Conquest language was studied to a certain extent. In addition to the general bibliographies referred to, a summary of the early materials can be found in Swadesh 1969, a posthumous publication dealing with the morphology and lexicon of old Tarascan. Mary Foster (1968, 1969) has been working on the contemporary language.

Three ethnolinguistic studies by Friedrich (1969a, 1969b, 1970) probe and analyse the semantics of Tarascan derivational morphology and grammatical processes, particularly the 'body-part' affixes so characteristic of Tarascan. This work (especially 1969 and 1970), reported in the eloquent tradition of Sapir, is important, not only for the understanding of Tarascan, but also in adding to the universal inventory of language phenomena from which linguistic theory is formulated.

Huave, like Tarascan, is a language whose genetic affiliation is unknown, notwithstanding several attempts at demonstrating relationships. Its speakers are estimated to number 7,000 in five communities on the Pacific coast of Oaxaca (Diebold 1961).

Diebold has studied the sociological and linguistic factors involved in bilingualism in one of these communities. Part of this work, in which he isolates a stage of language contact which he has called incipient bilingualism, is reported in the 1961 article.

A recent detailed descriptive sketch of the Huave verb is by Stairs and Erickson 1969.

9. WIDER GROUPINGS

There have long been attempts to group the more or less demonstrated families and stocks mentioned above, together with the isolates, into larger families and 'super' stocks. Some of these proposed groupings, such as Uto-Aztecan and Tanoan (Whorf and Trager 1937) are generally accepted. Others, such as Macro-Mayan (e.g. McQuown 1942), including Mayan, Mixe-Zoque and Totonac-Tepehua, are accepted by many. Still others, such as Macro-Penutian (generally following Sapir 1929) are more controversial. Finally, some, such as Hokaltecan with Malayo-Polynesian or with Quechuaymara, or Tarascan with Quechua, are regarded as fanciful. A conservative attitude would characterize the business of linguistics as being to demonstrate the relationship. Where the time depth involved is so great as to render the relationship beyond the capabilities of the present techniques of demonstration (the comparative method), a synthesis of archaeological and linguistic data of another kind (e.g. lexicostatistic) may compensate for the inapplicability of the comparative method. A good example of such a synthesis is Hopkins' hypothesis concerning Uto-Aztecan and Great Basin prehistory (1965).

The recent use of comparison to attempt the demonstration of the relationship of Maya to Uru-Chipaya (Olson 1964, 1965; Hamp 1967) is a notable beginning for the establishment of linguistic relationships between Middle America and South America, which undoubtedly exist, but are vacuously postulated in the absence of reconstructions and rules for deriving the attested languages (or reconstructed intermediate languages) from the reconstructions.

REFERENCES

ARANA OSNAYA, EVANGELINA. 1953. Reconstrucción del proto-totonaco. Revista Mexicana de Estudios Antropológicos 13.123 30. Mexico.

BAER, PHILLIP, and WILLIAM R. MERRIFIELD. 1967. Restatement of the pronominal series in Maya (Lacandon). IJAL 33.206–8.

BARTHEL, THOMAS S. 1968. Writing systems. CTL 4.275–301.

BARTHOLOMEW, DORIS. 1969a. Los numerales uno a diez en los idiomas Otopameanos. El Simposio de Mexico (Programa Interamericano de Lingüística y Enseñanza de Idiomas). México, Universidad Nacional Autónoma de México.

——. 1969b. Boletín informativo sobre idiomas indígenas de Latinoamerica. América Indígena 29.515–28.

BERLIN, BRENT. 1968. Tzeltal numeral classifiers: A study in ethnographic semantics. JanL, series practica 70.

BERLIN, BRENT, and A. KIMBALL ROMNEY. 1964. Descriptive semantics of Tzeltal numeral classifiers. AmA 66.70–98.

BERNARD, H. RUSSELL. 1967. The vowels of Mezquital Otomi. IJAL 33.247–8.

——. 1970. More on nasalized vowels and morphophonemics in Mezquital Otomi: A rejoinder to Bartholomew. IJAL 36.60–3.

BLAIR, ROBERT W. 1964. Yucatec Maya noun and verb morpho-syntax. Indiana University dissertation. Ann Arbor, University Microfilms.

BLAIR, ROBERT W., and R. VERMONT-SALAS. 1965. Spoken (Yucatec) Maya. Chicago.

BOWER, BETHEL, and BARBARA ERICKSON. 1967. Tepehua sentences. AnL 9/9.25–37.

BRIGHT, WILLIAM. 1956. Glottochronologic counts of Hokaltecan material. Lg 32.42–8.

——, ed. 1964. Studies in Californian linguistics. UCPL 34.

——. 1967. Inventory of descriptive materials. HMAI 5. 9–62.

——. 1968. Review of Miller 1967. IJAL 34.56–9.

——. 1971. On linguistic unrelatedness. IJAL 36.288–90.

BRIGHT, WILLIAM, and ROBERT A. THIEL. 1965. Hispanisms in a Modern Aztec dialect. RomPh 18.444–52.

BRINTON, DANIEL. 1887. On the so-called Alagüilac language of Guatemala. PAPS 24.366–77.

——. 1891. The American race. New York.

CAMPBELL, LYLE. 1970. Nahua loan words in Quichean languages. Papers from the 6th Regional Meeting of the Chicago Linguistic Society 1–13.

CLARK, LAWRENCE. 1961. Sayula Popoluca texts. Linguistic series 6. Norman, Oklahoma, Summer Institute of Linguistics.

COLBY, LORE. 1966. Esquema de la morfología Tzotzil. Los zinacantecos, ed. by Evon Vogt, pp. 373–95. Colección de antropología social 7. México, Instituto Indigenista Nacional.

COWAN, GEORGE. 1948. Mazateco whistle speech. Lg 24.280–6.

COWAN, MARION M. 1969. Tzotzil grammar. S.I.L. publications in linguistics, 18. Norman, Okla., Summer Institute of Linguistics.

CRAWFORD, JAMES. 1970. Cocopa baby talk. IJAL 36.9–13.

CRUMRINE, LYNNE S. 1968. An ethnography of Mayo speaking. AnL 10/2.19–31.

DIEBOLD, A. RICHARD. 1960. Determining the centers of dispersal of language groups. IJAL 26.1–10.

——. 1961. Incipient bilinguialism. Lg 37.97–112.

——. 1962. A laboratory for language contact. AnL 4/9.41–51.

DIXON, R.B., and A.L. KROEBER. 1913. Relationship of the Indian languages of California. Science 37.225.

DRIVER, H.E. 1961. Indians of North America. Chicago, University of Chicago Press.

EARL, ROBERT. 1968. Rincon Zapotec clauses. IJAL 34.269–74.

ELSON, BENJAMIN. 1967. Sierra Popoluca. HMAI 5.269–90.

FERNÁNDEZ DE MIRANDA, MARÍA TERESA, and ROBERT J. WEITLANER. 1961. Sobre algunas relaciones de la familia mangue. AnL 3/7.1–99.

FOSTER, GEORGE M. 1970. Robert J. Weitlaner 1883–1968. AmA 72.343–5.

FOSTER, MARY LECRON. 1968. Componential analysis of grammar: The Tarascan verb. IJAL 34.259–68.

——. 1969. The Tarascan language. UCPL 56.

FRIEDRICH, PAUL. 1969a. Metaphor-like relations between referential subsets. Lingua 24.1–10.

——. 1969b. On the meaning of the Tarascan suffixes of space. IUPAL Memoir 23. (=IJAL 35/4/2, pp. 1–48).

——. 1970. Shape in grammar. Lg 46.379–407.

GRIMES, JOSEPH E. 1964. Huichol syntax. The Hague, Mouton.

GRIMES, JOSEPH E., and BARBARA F. 1962. Semantic distinctions in Huichol kinship. AmA 64.104–14.

GUDSCHINSKY, SARAH C. 1955. Lexico-statistical skewing from dialect borrowing. IJAL 21.138–49.

——. 1958. Mazatec dialect history: A study in miniature. Lg 34.469–81.

——. 1967. Environmental correlational studies. HMAI 5.161–6.

HALPERN, A.M. 1942. A theory of Maya tš-sounds. Carnegie Institute of Washington, Notes on Middle American Archeology and Ethnology 13.

HAMP, ERIC. 1967. On Maya-Chipayan. IJAL 33.74–6.

HARVEY, H.R. 1968. Chatino and Papabuco in the historical sources. IJAL 34.288–89.

HASLER, JUAN A. 1961. Tetradialectologia Nahua. A William Cameron Townsend, pp. 455–64. México, Instituto Lingüístico de Verano.

HAY, C.L., et al., eds. 1940. The Maya and their neighbors. New York, Appleton-Century. (Reprinted, Salt Lake City: Univ. of Utah Press, 1940.)

HERZOG, DOROTHY L. Forthcoming. Person–tense–number markers in the Tepehua verb. Linguistics.

HILL, JANE H., and KENNETH C. 1968. Stress in the Cupan (Uto–Aztecan) languages. IJAL 34.233-41.

HOIJER, HARRY. 1933. Tonkawa, an Indian language of Texas. HAIL, part 3, pp. 1–148.

——. 1946. Tonkawa. Linguistic structures of native America, pp. 289–311. VFPA 6.

HOPKINS, NICHOLAS A. 1965. Great Basin prehistory and Uto-Aztecan. AmAnt 31.48–60.

——. 1967. A short sketch of Chalchihuitan Tzotzil. AnL 9/4.9–25.

——. 1970. Numerical classifiers in Tzeltal, Jacaltec, and Chuj (Mayan). Papers from the Sixth Regional Meeting of the Chicago Linguistic Society, 23–35.

HUNTER, GEORGE G., and EUNICE V. PIKE. 1969. The phonology and tone sandhi of Molinos Mixtec. Linguistics 47.24–40.

JOEL, JUDITH. 1964. Classification of the Yuman languages. UCPL 34.99–105.

JOHNSON, FREDERICK. 1940. The linguistic map of Mexico and Central America. *In* Hay 1940:88–116.

KARLSTROM, MARJORIE R., and EUNICE V. PIKE. 1968. Stress in the phonological system of Eastern Popoloca. Phonetica 18.16–30.

KAUFMAN, TERRENCE S. 1964a. Materiales lingüísticos para el estudio de las relaciones internas y externas de la familia de idiomas mayanos. *In* Vogt and Ruz (eds.) 1964:81–136.

——. 1964b. Mixe–Zoque subgroups and the position of Tapachulteco. Actas del XXXV Congreso Internacional de Americanistas (1962), 403–11. México.

——. 1969. Teco—a new Mayan language. IJAL 35.154–74.

——. 1973. Areal linguistics and Middle America. CTL 11.

KIRCHHOFF, PAUL. 1943. Mesoamérica: Sus límites geográficos, composición étnica y caracteres culturales. Acta Americana 1.92–107.

KLUCKHOHN, CLYDE. 1940. The conceptual structure in Middle American Studies. *In* Hay 1940:41–51.

KROEBER, A. L. 1915. Serian, Tequistlatecan, and Hokan. UCPAAE 11.279–90.

——. 1939. Cultural and natural areas of native North America. UCPAAE 38.1–242.

LAMB, SYDNEY M. 1964. The classification of the Uto-Aztecan languages: A historical survey. *In* Bright 1964:106–25.

LANGDON, MARGARET. 1970. Review of Wares 1968. Lg 46.533–44.

LAW, HOWARD. 1961. A reconstructed proto-culture derived from some Yuman vocabularies. AnL 3/4.45–57.

LEÓN-PORTILLA, MIGUEL. 1967. Language-in-culture studies. HMAI 5.369–84.

LONGACRE, ROBERT. 1964. Progress in Otomanguean reconstruction. PICL 9. 1017–19.

——. 1966. The linguistic affinities of Amuzgo. *In* Pompa y Pompa 1966:541–60.

——. 1967. Systemic comparison and reconstruction. HMAI 5.117–60.

——. 1968. Comparative reconstruction of indigenous languages. CTL 4.320–60.

LYON, DON. 1967. Tlahuiltoltepec Mixe verb syntagmemes. IJAL 33.34–45.

LYON, SHIRLEY. 1967. Tlahuiltoltepec Mixe clause structure. IJAL 33.25–33.

MCMAHON, A. 1967. Phonemes and phonemic units of Cora (Mexico). IJAL 33.128–34.

MCQUOWN, NORMAN A. 1942. Una posible síntesis lingüística Macro-Mayance. Mayas y Olmecas 2.37–38. México, Sociedad Mexicana de Antropología.

——. 1955. The indigenous languages of Latin America. AmA 57.501–70.

——. 1956. The classification of the Mayan languages. IJAL 22.191–5.

——, ed. 1959. Report on the 'Man-in-Nature' project of the Dept. of Anthropology of the University of Chicago in the Tzeltal-Tzotzil speaking region of the State of Chiapas, Mexico. Manuscript.

——. 1962. Indian and Ladino bilingualsm: Sociocultural contrasts in Chiapas, Mexico. MSLL 15.85–106.

——. 1964. Los orígenes y la diferenciación de los Mayas según se infiere del estudio comparativo de las lenguas Mayanas. *In* Vogt and Ruz (eds.) 1964:49–80.

——, ed. 1967a. Linguistics. Volume 5, Handbook of Middle American Indians (general editor, Robert Wauchope). Austin, University of Texas Press.

——. 1967b. History of studies in Middle American linguistics. HMAI 5.3–8.

——. 1967c. Classical Yucatec (Maya). HMAI 5.201–48.

MANRIQUE, C. LEONARDO. 1958. Sobre la classificación del Otomí-Pame. Acts of the 33rd International Congress of Americanists 2.551-9. México.

——. 1967. Pame. HMAI 5.331–48.

MARINO FLORES, ANSELMO. 1957. Bibliografía lingüística de la República Mexicana. México, Instituto Indigenista Interamericano.
——. 1967. Indian population and its identification. HMAI 6, Social anthropology, ed. by Manning Nash, 12–25. Austin, University of Texas Press.
MARTÍNEZ HERNÁNDEZ, JUAN. 1929. Diccionario de Motul. Mérida.
MASON, J. ALDEN. 1940. The native languages of Middle America. *In* Hay 1940: 52–87.
MASSEY, WILLIAM C. 1966. Archaeology and history of Lower California. HMAI 4: Archaeological frontiers and external connections, ed. by G.F. Ekholm and G.R. Willey, pp. 38–58. Austin, University of Texas Press.
MAYERS, MARVIN, ed. 1966. Languages of Guatemala. JanL, series practica 23.
MERRIFIELD, WILLIAM R. 1966. Linguistic clues for the reconstruction of Chinantec prehistory. *In* Pompa y Pompa 1966:579–95.
MERRIFIELD, WILLIAM R., and BETTY J. STOUDT. 1967. Molinos Mixtec clause structure. Linguistics 32.58–78.
MILLER, MARY R. 1970. The language and language beliefs of Indian children. AnL 12/2.51–61.
MILLER, WICK R. 1967. Uto-Aztecan cognate sets. UCPL 48.
MILLON, RENÉ, and ROBERT LONGACRE. 1961. Proto-Mixtecan and Proto-Amuzgo-Mixtecan vocabularies: A preliminary cultural analysis. AnL 3/4.1–44.
NEWMAN, STANLEY. 1967. Classical Nahuatl. HMAI 5.179–200.
NORDELL, NORMAN. 1962. On the status of Popoluca in Zoque-Mixe. IJAL 28.146–9.
OLIVERA, MERCEDES DE V., and BLANCA SÁNCHEZ. 1965. Distribución actual de las lenguas indígenas de México. México, Instituto Nacional de Antropología e Historia.
OLSON, RONALD D. 1964. Mayan affinities with Chipaya of Bolivia, I: Correspondences. IJAL 30.313–24.
——. 1965. Mayan affinities with Chipaya of Bolivia, II: Cognates. IJAL 31.29–38.
PICKETT, VELMA B. 1967. Isthmus Zapotec. HMAI 5.291–310.
PIKE, EUNICE V., and JOHN H. COWAN. 1967. Huajuapan Mixtec phonology and morphophonemics. AnL 9/5.1–15.
PIKE, KENNETH. 1948. Tone languages. Ann Arbor, University of Michigan Press.
POMPA Y POMPA, A., ed. 1966. Summa antropológica en homenaje a Roberto J. Weitlaner. Mexico, Instituto Nacional de Antropología e Historia.
PRICE, P. DAVID. 1967. Two types of taxonomy: A Huichol ethnobotanical example. AnL 9/7.1–28.
REID, AILEEN. 1967. Totonac: From clause to discourse. S.I.L. Publications in Linguistics 17. Norman, Okla., Summer Institute of Linguistics.
ROBINSON, DOW F. 1969. Aztec Studies I: Phonological and grammatical studies in modern Nahuatl dialects. S.I.L. Publications in Linguistics 19. Norman, Oklahoma, Summer Institute of Linguistics.
ROYS, RALPH L. 1933. The book of Chilam Balam of Chumayel. Carnegie Institu-

tion of Washington, publ. 438. [Reprinted, Norman, Univ. of Oklahoma Press, 1967.]

SAHAGÚN, BERNARDINO DE. 1577. Florentine Codex: General history of the things of New Spain. (Original Nahuatl texts and English translation by A. J. O. Anderson and C. E. Dibble. Salt Lake City, University of Utah. 1950—.)

SAPIR, EDWARD. 1915–19. Southern Paiute and Nahuatl: A study in Uto-Aztecan. AmA 17.98–120, 306–28; JSocA 11.433-88.

——. 1917. The position of Yana in the Hokan stock. UCPAAE 13.

——. 1920. Hokan and Coahuiltecan languages. IJAL 1.280–90.

——. 1925. The Hokan affinity of the Subtiaba in Nicaragua. AmA 27.402–35, 491–527.

SEBEOK, THOMAS A., ed. 1968. Current trends in linguistics, 4: Ibero-American and Caribbean linguistics. The Hague, Mouton.

SEILER, HANSJAKOB. 1967. Structure and reconstruction in some Uto-Aztecan languages. IJAL 33.135–47.

SELER, EDUARD. 1887. Das Konjugationssystem der Maya-Sprachen. Berlin.

STAIRS, EMILY F., and BARBARA ERICKSON. 1969. Huave verb morphology. IJAL 35.38–53.

STOLL, OTTO. 1884. Zur Ethnographie der Republik Guatemala. Zürich. (Spanish translation by Antonio Goubaud Carrera: Etnografía de la República de Guatemala. 2nd ed., Guatemala, 1958.)

SUÁREZ, JORGE A. 1968. Classical languages. CTL 4.254–74.

SWADESH, MORRIS. 1967. Lexicostatistic classification. HMAI 5.79–117.

——. 1969. Elementos del Tarasco antiguo. México, Univeridad Nacional Autónoma de México, Instituto de Investigaciones Históricas.

SWADESH, MORRIS, and JOSEPH GREENBERG. 1953. Jicaque as a Hokan language. IJAL 19.216–22.

TOZZER, ALFRED M. 1921. A Maya grammar. Papers of the Peabody Museum 9. Cambridge, Mass., Harvard University.

TURNER, PAUL. 1967a. Highland Chontal phrase syntagmemes. IJAL 35.282–6.

——. 1967b. Seri and Chontal (Tequistlateco). IJAL 33.235–9.

——. 1968a. Highland Chontal clause syntagmemes. Linguistics 38.77–83.

——. 1968b. Highland Chontal sentence syntagmemes. Linguistics 42.117–25.

——. 1969. Proto-Chontal phonemes. IJAL 35.34–6.

ULRICH, MATTHEW and ROSEMARY. 1966. Mopan Maya. *In* Mayers 1966:251–71.

UPSON, JESSAMINE. 1968. Chatino length and tone. AnL 10/2.1–7.

VOEGELIN, C. F., F. M. VOEGELIN, and KENNETH L. HALE. 1962. Typological and comparative grammar of Uto-Aztecan: I (phonology). IJAL Memoir 17.

VOGT, EVON Z., and ANTONIO L. RUZ, eds. 1964. Desarollo cultural de los Mayas. México, Seminario de Cultura Maya, UNAM.

WARES, ALAN C. 1968. Bibliography of the Summer Institute of Linguistics, 1935–1968. Santa Ana, Calif., S.I.L.

——. 1968. A comparative study of Yuman consonantism. JanL, series practica 57.

WATERHOUSE, VIOLA. 1949. Learning a second language first. IJAL 15.106–9.

——. 1962. The grammatical structure of Oaxaca Chontal. IUPAL 19. (=IJAL 28/2/2).

——. 1967. Huamelultec Chontal. HMAI 5.349–68.

——. 1969. Oaxaca Chontal in reference to Proto-Chontal. IJAL 35.231–3.

WHORF, BENJAMIN L. 1935. The comparative linguistics of Uto-Aztecan. AmA 37.600–8.

WHORF, B. L., and G. TRAGER. 1937. The relationship of Uto-Aztecan and Tanoan. AmA 39.609–24.

WILLEY, GORDON R. 1966. An introduction to American archaeology, volume one: North and Middle America. Englewood Cliffs, N.J., Prentice-Hall.

WONDERLY, WILLIAM L. 1949. Some Zoquean phonemic and morphophonemic correspondences. IJAL 15.1–11.

WONDERLEY, WILLIAM L., and BENJAMIN ELSON. 1953. El sistema de prefijos personales en las lenguas zoqueanas. Memoria del Congreso Científico Mexicano 12.207–13. México.

WOO, NANCY. 1970. Tone in Northern Tepehuan. IJAL 36.18–30.

OTOMANGUEAN ISOGLOSSES

CALVIN R. RENSCH

1. INTRODUCTION

During the past decade and a half vigorous activity in comparative linguistics has given us a picture of the phonology of a number of ancestor languages from which Middle American language families have sprung.[1] Much of this effort has been concerned with the several branches of the Otomanguean grouping and has made possible the reconstruction of an even more remote stage termed Proto Otomanguean. Only recently, however, has the work been extensive enough to make possible an informed discussion of the similarities and dissimilarities among the various branches of the Otomanguean group.

Before discussing phonological traits that are shared by some Otomanguean languages and not by others it is necessary to determine which languages constitute the Otomanguean grouping.

For over a century such groupings of Mexican languages as Mixtec-Zapotec, Otomi-Mazahua, and Mazatec-Chiapanec have been proposed.[2] Schmidt (1926) appears to have been the first to use the term Otomi-Mangue to designate a large grouping named for the languages spoken at the northwest and southeast extremities of the language area. This term was soon changed to Otomanguean (Sp. *otomangue*).

The set of languages considered in the early reconstruction of Proto Otomanguean (Rensch 1966) is that proposed by Longacre (Longacre 1961, 1962, and 1968). At that time seven branches of Otomanguean were recognized: (1) Mixtecan: Mixtec, Cuicatec, Trique; (2) Popolocan: Ixcatec, Chocho, Popoloc, Mazatec; (3) Amuzgo; (4) Chiapanec-Mangue: Chiapanec, Mangue (both extinct); (5) Otopamean: Otomi, Mazahua, Chichimeco Jonaz, North Pame, South Pame, Matlatzinca, Ocuilteco; (6) Zapotecan: Zapotec, Chatino; and (7) Chinantecan. Most of these languages are spoken in the Mexican state of Oaxaca and adjacent areas of the states of Puebla and Guerrero, except that the Otopamean languages are spoken west, north, and northeast of Mexico City. At the time of extinction Chiapanec was spoken in the Mexican

[1] Many of the published materials resulting from this activity are included in the references.

[2] For a fuller discussion of the various proposals for classification of the languages here under attention cf. Rensch 1966: chapter 1, and Rensch's "Classification of the Otomanguean languages and the position of Tlappanec" (ms).

state of Chiapas and Mangue along the Pacific coast of Nicaragua.[3]

Typologically, the Tlapanec language of the Mexican state of Guerrero is similar to many of its Otomanguean neighbors in that it exhibits a system of lexical tone, nasalized as well as oral vowels, and two laryngeals occurring in several positions in the syllable. The typological similarity between Tlapanec and a number of languages recognized to be Otomanguean was the first clue in the recognition of Tlapanec as an Otomanguean language. Further examination of Tlapanec forms has also revealed a sizeable number of cognates, permitting the establishment of sound corrospendences between Tlapanec and the other seven branches of Otomanguean (Rensch, "Classification of the Otomanguean languages and the position of Tlappanec", section 4). It should be noted, however, that Tlapanec and its neartwin Subtiaba have usually been considered members of the Hokan stock in accord with Sapir's assignment (Sapir 1925:403–4). The association of Tlapanec with Otomanguean raises the question of a possible link between Otomanguean and Hokan.

Swadesh proposed a grouping which rejects Chiapanec-Mangue but includes Huave (Fernández de Miranda, Swadesh, and Weitlaner 1959; Swadesh 1960 and 1964). This proposal is based largely on the reckonings of glottochronology, but in his 1964 study he compares some Huave data with forms from Zapotec, Mixtec, and Ixcatec and offers some correspondences to support his thesis. Longacre has stated that he is now inclined to believe that Swadesh's inclusion of Huave in Otomanguean is correct, although he does not join Swadesh in excluding Chiapanec-Mangue (Longacre 1968:6.7).

It remains, then, to investigate the proposal that Huave be included within the Otomanguean grouping and to substantiate such a proposal, if possible, with statements of sound correspondences validated by cognate sets. The results of the present investigation of Huave data do, as a matter of fact, support the conclusion of Swadesh and more recently that of Longacre. The following section reports the results of that investigation.

2. THE RELATION OF HUAVE TO OTOMANGUEAN

In the Otomanguean languages other than Huave the canonical shape of the stem, and sometimes the word, is typically CV or CVCV, ignoring for the moment laryngeals and tone. In Huave, however, a characteristic shape of the stem beginning at the onset of stress is CVC or CVVC, with the vowel cluster of the latter being either geminate or diverse.[4] It is not at first obvious how the Huave forms are to be compared with other Otomanguean forms of such different canonical shape. It has been proposed by Swadesh that the Huave word-final consonants were followed at an

[3] Cf. the linguistic map in Longacre 1967: Figure 15.

[4] In several dialects of Zapotec also words typically end with a consonant, but such forms are readily traceable from earlier forms ending in a posttonic vowel which has been lost.

earlier period by a vowel which was subsequently lost. Before this final vowel was lost, however, it affected the quality of the vowel of the preceding syllable, frequently diphthongizing the preceding vowel (Swadesh 1964:175). An examination of Huave borrowings from Spanish such as *ser* (Sp. *cera* 'wax') and *maril* (Sp. *amarillo* 'yellow') indicates that some Spanish final vowels have been lost in Huave. However, other borrowings such as *paneal* (Sp. *panela* 'raw sugar') and *permer* (Sp. *primero* 'first') indicate the some CV sequences have been permuted to VC sequences.[5] This evidence from Spanish loanwords is, of course, only supportive, and it indicates neither the conditions under which the final vowel was lost nor those under which the permutation took place. The comparative evidence, however, suggests that forms descended from Proto Otomanguean have undergone similar permutations in Huave and that a final **h may have been the environment in which the permutation took place, i.e., **CVCVh > CVVC.[6]

Given these interpretations of the Huave forms it is not difficult to identify among them numerous cognates relatable to Otomanguean sets. Usually, the final CV or VC of the Huave stem is cognate with the final CV of the stem of the sister languages and is relatable to the reconstructed **CV of Proto Otomanguean.

Several forms show a matching of the final CVC of the Huave form with an equivalent stretch in Isthmus Zapotec. However, although these forms appear at first to be promising cognates, they have been found in several cases to be Huave borrowings from their culturally dominant Isthmus Zapotec neighbors, e.g. Huave *pič* 'cotton seed', Isthmus Zapotec *biʔiǰiʔ* 'seed'.

The Proto Otomanguean ultima in its simplest form consisted of a consonant, a vowel, and a tone. In addition, it could invlude an initial or final laryngeal or both; the nasal **n, the palatal element **Y, or both, preceding the consonant; and the nasal following the vowel.

The single consonants of Proto Otomanguean have developed in Huave in a very straightforward manner. The only observed shift has been that of POM $**k^w > H$ *p*.[7] (Cf. the discussion of labial stops in section 3.)

The following cognate sets illustrate the development of the Proto Otomanguean consonants in Huave. For economy of space only a sampling of the available sets is presented here.

[5] The Spanish loanwords and the forms of Huave origin cited in this paper have been drawn largely from Warkentin and Warkentin 1952. I have also benefited from discussions with Glenn and Emily Stairs regarding several points of Hauve phonology.

[6] Cf. the fuller discussion of Huave reflexes of Proto Otomanguean syllables containing **h at the end of this section, p. xxx–xx.

[7] The following abbreviations have been used to indicate language names: POM Proto Otomanguean; PMn. Proto Mixtecan; PPn. Proto Popolocan; A Amuzgo; PCM Proto Chiapanec-Mangue; POP Proto Otopamean; PZn. Proto Zapotecan; PCh. Proto Chatino; IZ Isthmus Zapotec; PCn. Proto Chinantecan; Tl. Tlapanec; H Huave. Frequently the prefixed 'P' has been omitted, especially in the citation of cognate forms from the several branches. Tone has not been indicated in this section inasmuch as the tone of Huave is not here being considered.

**t: OP **thǫ-s*; Ch. **te·heʔ*; IZ *zidi*; H *nahtiš* 'salty' (POM 5).[8]

Pn. **tʸha-wa(ʔ)*; A *thąʔ* 'skin', *thą́* 'leather'; Tl. *šta*; H *otaag* 'skin, leather' (POM 47).

CM **naa-te* 'eye', **ⁿgi-ru-te* 'cheeks, face'; OP **te/ne* 'mouth'; H *tey* 'face' (POM 22).

OP **tʔa-m* 'to work'; Cn. **ta*; H *nahiit* 'work' (POM 43).

Mn. **yu-/ya-/tu/ta-ʔtu* 'tumpline'; A *cʔɔ* 'vine'; Ch. **hų* 'thread'; IZ *doʔo* 'rope'; H *šiit* 'string' (POM 93).

**k: Pn. **kha-ce* 'red'; CM **ⁿdi-/na-ku-me*; OP **kʔa-s-tʔ*; Ch. **ka·či* 'yellow'; H *nakants* 'red' (POM 121).

CM **ni-hú*; OP **khi*; H *kieh* 'blood' (new set).

Pn. **ki-ča* 'hard, metal'; A *ki* 'hard'; IZ *gie* 'stone'; Cn. **ŋį́* 'iron', **kų́·* 'stone'; Tl. *akī* 'strong, hard'; H *mančiik* 'iron' (POM 103).

**kʷ: PP **pe-nʔ/-k* 'wash clothes', **pe-ʔ-tʔ* 'wash (vegetables)'; IZ *rigiʔibiʔ* 'wash'; H *apeh* (*oniiag*) 'wash (the face)' (POM 158).

CM **ata-pa(me)* 'hard'; IZ *nadipaʔ* 'strong'; H *napak* 'hard, strong' (POM 199).

A *ckʷa* 'bark'; OP **si-pah-nʔ/-n* 'skin'; Cn. **kʷé·ʔ* 'bark'; H *opang* 'peeling, bark' (POM 204).

**s: CM **nuu-siʔ* 'cocoa beans'; Ch. **ku-ta/ti*; IZ *biʔiǰiʔ*; Tl. *sigaʔ*; H *osaab* 'seed' (POM 265).

Mn. **yam(h)/θamh* 'thorn'; Cn. **sių·ʔ*; Tl. *mīsuʔ* 'sharp'; H *sats* 'thorn' (POM 322).

Mn. **ⁿdi-θe(m)* 'roasting ear', **ye(m)(h)/θemh*; OP **-sa*; IZ *zeʔe* 'ear of corn'; Tl. *eši* 'corn'; H *as* 'roasting ear' (POM 285).

**n: OP **nʔi-m*; H *onih* 'meat' (new set).

**w: OP **hoi-t/-nʔ/-t* 'fan, blow'; Cn. **hwi*; H *awin* 'to whistle' (POM 354).

Mn. **ʔwa(m)* 'mouth, mouthful'; Pn. **cu-ʔwa*; Ch. **tu·ʔwa*; IZ *ruaʔa*; Cn. **ʔa·* 'mouth', **ʔa·(ʔ)* 'cry'; H *aw* 'say' (POM 394).

***y*: A *lhó* 'here'; CM **ya* 'today, now'; Otomi **nuya* 'now'; H *nganiy* 'today', *hogiy* 'here it is' (POM 402).

Pn. **ʔye* 'hear'; A *mantʔiaʔ*; CM **pe-ko-ñu/yu*; IZ *ruʔuyaʔ* 'see'; Cn. **yą·* 'know'; H *angeay* 'hear' (POM 413).

Trique *yąʔą* 'night', *aʔnï yąʔą* 'dream'; OP **ʔįah-nʔ/ø* 'sleep'; H *aimeay* 'dream' (POM 417).

As has happened also in the other branches of Otomanguean, the Huave reflexes of POM clusters of nasal plus consonant have in most cases remained distinct from those of the single consonants. The POM sequences of nasal plus stop have remained

[8] The numbers cited after each set indicate the Proto Otomanguean set in Rensch 1966 from which the data from the languages other than Tlapanec and Huave are drawn. Where a series of forms have the same gloss, the gloss is written after only the last of those forms.

such in Huave: **nt > *nd*; **nk > *ng*; **nk^{w} > *mb*. The nasal plus fricative cluster has become an affricate — occasionally prenasalized, probably by analogy with the prenasalized stops: **ns > *(n)ts*. No special development of **nn has been observed. The reflexes of the POM semivowels are not parallel, since the labial cluster has developed as a stop and the palatal cluster as a liquid: **nw > *p*; **ny > *l*. The POM cluster **nw occasionally shows a reflex *(m)b*. The nasalization and voicing have presumably developed by analogy with the reflexes of the POM clusters of nasal plus stop.

**nt: Mn. *^{n}*du-htum* 'egg, fruit, vegetable'; PCM *^{n}*du* 'gourd dipper'; IZ *ndoʔpaʔ* 'large gourd dipper'; Tl. *šndu* 'egg, ball'; H *ndop* 'gourd dipper' (possibly borrowed from IZ) (POM 89).

Pn. **ʔi-/na-ntaʔ* 'water, river'; CM **na-*^{n}*da* 'stream, lake'; OP *=*teh* 'water'; IZ *guǰa* 'dampness'; Cn. **ziá·* 'pool, lake'; H *ndek* 'sea' (the vowel is difficult to explain) (POM 67).

**nk: OP *=*ko* 'negative'; H *ngo* 'not' (POM 136).

Pn. **nki* 'under, earth'; H *otieng* 'stomach' (POM 99).

**nk^{w}: Mn. **ka-/θa-*^{n}*g*^{w}*a(m)(h)* 'twist, grind'; Chinantec of Lalana *gwənnq̧* 'I grind'; H *ambil* 'twist (thread)' (POM 224).

CM *^{m}*busu*, **pusu* 'run, escape'; Cn. **g*^{w}*u* 'you go'; Tl. *kamba* 'road'; H *amb* 'go' (POM 214).

**ns: Ch. **cǫ* 'to warm'; IZ *na'ǰaʔa*; Cn. **ziá·*; H *ntsan* 'warm' (POM 295).

Mn. **θa(mh)/*^{n}*dam* 'tamale, tortilla'; OP **chq̧o-nʔ* 'boiled corn'; H *ahtsah* 'corn dough' (POM 306).

Pn. **ceʔe* 'stomach, intestines'; A *cʔǫ (siʔ)* 'heart'; IZ *laǰi'doʔ* 'heart, stomach'; Cn. **zí*; H *ameaats* 'heart' (POM 278).

Mn. **yamʔ/ʔyam/*^{n}*damh* 'rope, cord, root'; Pn. **na-/mu-/ka-šaʔ/ncha* 'hair, blanket'; Ch. **ki·cą*; IZ *giča* 'hair'; H *ondeats* 'hair' (POM 324).

Mn. *^{n}*dah*; A *cháʔ*; Cn. **zia·* 'fiber of the century plant'; H *nčiiits* 'net' (POM 321).

**nw: Pn. **ča-/ču-hmi* 'person, male'; CM **ma-*^{n}*ge-me* 'lord, God, dominate'; OP **mhǫ-ʔ* 'owner, chief'; Cn. **hmį·* 'father'; H *nipilan* 'person' (POM 361).

Mn. **tam-/na(m)-ʔmim(H)* 'to converse, word'; Pn. **ca-/na-hmi/hmiʔ* 'fruit, tell, thing'; Ch. **ki·k*^{w}*iʔ* 'talk'; IZ *rabi* 'say'; H *apiing* 'say' (POM 365).

**ny: Pn. **ka-lihi/nt*^{y}*ihi* 'pasture, grass'; CM **ni-/nu-lú/lu*; Cn. **lį*; Tl. *riʔi* 'flower'; H *šiil* 'tree' (POM 396).

The POM clusters which include the preposed palatal element are not fully attested in Huave. The only Huave forms which have been so identified reflect clusters of the palatal element with POM apical obstruents, with and without the preposed nasal: **Yt > *(n)č*; **Ynt > *r*; **Ys > *š*; **Yns > *č*.

**Yt: A *kat*^{y}*ǫ* 'lizard'; IZ *gučačiʔ* 'iguana'; H *nčey* 'white lizard' (POM 28)

A *ntʸu* 'cane leaves'; H *nahčow* 'reed' (POM 80).

**Ynt: Trique *maru* 'black'; Cn. **t(i)u·* 'deaf mute, blind'; H *nambeor* 'black' (POM 94).

Pn. **tʸha-wa*; Cn. **tia·*; H *raan* 'white' (POM 46).

**Ys: Pn. **še*; Ch. **ši*; IZ *nanaši* 'sweet'; H *našiš* 'tasty' (POM 260).

IZ *giži*; Tl. *raša* 'hay'; H *soeš* 'grass' (POM 272).

**Yns: A *kačiʔ* 'mouse, rat'; H *čiy* 'mouse' (POM 243).

Pn. **n-či* 'little'; H *kičeeč* 'small' (POM 258).

Cn. **ziʔ* 'bitter'; H *načič* 'sour' (POM 269).

The Otomanguean cluster **hk was reduced to *h* in several branches of Otomanguean. A similar development seems to have taken place in Huave. However, the occurrence of some examples of the cluster *hk* in the Huave data makes such a development less than certain. Consider the following sets for possible reduction of this laryngeal cluster:

Pn. **ni-/na-nka*; A *ñhǫ* 'deep'; OP **hąi* 'difficult, deep'; CM **na-ku-ha/hí* 'cave, eye of needle, canyon'; IZ *geteʔ*; Cn. **hi·n* 'deep'; H *nahal* 'deep, long' (POM 114).

Pn. **kaha/kahaʔ*; Otomi **hą* 'carry'; IZ *riǰaʔaga* 'it is carried'; Cn. **ką* 'carry'; Tl. *kaye* 'bring'; H *ahan* 'bring people' (POM 126.

Proto Otomanguean was characterized by a series of consonantal alternations between obstruents, semivowels, and the nasal (Rensch 1966:2.1.3). In sets including the labio-velar stop, to cite one example, there is evidence of a four-way alternation among **k^w ~ **k ~ **w ~ **n. Huave, like the other branches of Otomanguean, gives evidence of such alternation patterns. The Huave evidence is of two sorts: (a) etymological doublets witnessing to pairs of consonantal alternants and (b) reflexes of a given POM consonant which agree with some sister branches and disagree with others that reflect a different member of the alternation set. The following pair of Huave forms, reflecting POM **k^w and **k respectively, is evidence of the first type: *ngwiy* 'no', *ngo* 'not'. The forms in the following sets witness to the four alternants of the **k^w alternation set in the various branches of Otomanguean:

(reflecting **k^w) CM **nii-ᵐbi* 'cloud'; (reflecting **k) Cn. **ŋį* 'smoke'; H *oik* 'cloud'; (reflecting **w) Pn. **š-/t-/yu-hwiʔ/hwi* 'clouds, fog'; (reflecting **n Cn. **hnį·* 'cloud' (POM 152).

(reflecting **k^w) A *tkʷi* 'dry'; (reflecting **w) IZ *žilu'eʔ* 'dry season'; H *nawaag* 'dry' (POM 187).

The four-vowel system of Proto Otomanguean is preserved in Huave with little shifting, apart from the lowering of **u to *o*. (The Huave vowel *u* occurs infrequently and principally in words borrowed from Spanish.) Also the POM vowel **a became *e* in Huave following the palatal cluster **Ys. Similarly, the vowel **e became *i* following the palatal clusters **Yt and **Yns. The Huave reflexes of the vowels **i, **e, **a, and **u are illustrated by the following sets:

**i: A *kačíʔ* 'mouse, rat'; Ch. *k^{w}itiʔn^{y}ąʔ* 'rat'; IZ *biziña* 'rat, mouse'; Tl. *sihni* 'mouse'; H *čiy* 'mouse' (POM 243).
Pn. *ča-/ču-hmi 'person, man'; CM *^{m}bu-/nu-h^{w}i, etc. 'husband, man, male'; Cn. *hmį·* 'father'; H *nipilan* 'person' (POM 361).
OP *nʔi-m; H *onih* 'meat' (new set).
**e: CM *naa-te 'eye'; OP *te/*ne 'mouth'; H *tey* 'face' (POM 22).
Trique *dumi*; Pn. *ša-ʔwe 'wasp'; OP *ʔǫe/*ʔoe/*ʔį 'worm, fly'; Cn. *mį·ʔ 'wasp, hornet'; H *mbel* 'wasp' (POM 170).
OP *oe-ʔt/-nʔ; Cn. *ʔmį(·); H *ambet* 'sew' (POM 376).
Trique *gačih* 'sneeze'; Pn. *the 'itch, cough'; OP *theʔ 'a cold', *he(h)/*the-(h) 'cough'; H *ahčiy* 'sneeze' (POM 19).
CM *ya-si; Ch. *til^{y}a; Cn. *zíʔ 'bitter'; H *načič* 'sour' (POM 269).
**a: Pn. *t^{y}ha-wa; Cn. *tia·; H *raan* 'white' (POM 46).
Mn. *k^{y}a-/xa-/ka-/^{n}da-x^{w}a(h) 'noisy, weep, scream'; A *šua* 'yell, scream'; CM *h^{w}a/ku 'say'; OP *paʔ-t/*ma-ʔ-t 'call, shout'; Cn. *hwa·ʔ 'speech'; H *apah* 'shout' (POM 198).
Mn. *yamʔ/ʔyam/θuʔ/^{n}dumh 'rope, cord'; Pn. *na /nu /ka-šaʔ/ncha 'hair, blanket'; CM *^{n}gi-sa 'beard'; Ch. *ki·cą; IZ *giča ike*; H *ondeats* 'hair' (POM 324).
Mn. *ka-hθa 'son-in-law'; Pn. *ča-/ču-hmi 'person, man'; A *saʔ* 'husband', *yusʔá* 'man'; Cn. *zá· 'male', *za(·) 'person'; H *našey* 'man' (POM 296).
**u: CM *^{n}gi-tuʔ; Cn. *tiu·ʔ; Tl. *aʔdu* 'breast'; H *onday* 'suck' (POM 81).
CM *aku 'no, not'; OP *=ko 'not'; IZ *koʔ* 'no'; H *ngo* 'not' (POM 136).
Mn. *ka-/xa-/tam-/xi-ʔnu(mʔ) 'break, cut'; Ch. *ši·ʔyu 'cut'; Cn. *yu· 'dig'; H *alood* 'pierce' (POM 426).

Where the POM nasal was postposed the result in Huave is that the preceding vowel was backed or raised; the front vowels are backed and the back vowels are raised. If one assumes that the Huave *ɨ* has been unrounded from an earlier *u, the well known rounding effect of the POM postposed nasal is quite evident in Huave (Longacre 1957:28). Thus, **in > *ɨ* except after *i* or before *č*, where it becomes *e*; **en > *a*; **an > *ɨ*; **un > *ɨ*. The following sets of cognates illustrate the development of the POM **Vn sequences in Huave:

**in: Pn. *ʔnt^{y}e 'earth, mud'; IZ *de* 'ash'; Cn. *tiu· 'pulp, shredded material'; H *iɨt* 'earth' (POM 9).
Mn. *ta-xi/xim/kim/ki 'send, give'; Proto Mazatec *-kįya 'lend'; H *angiy* 'pay' (POM 105).
A *chǫ́ ñhę*; Cn. *ku· 'money', *ŋį́; H *mančiɨk* 'iron' (POM 103).
CM *ni-/nu-lú/lu 'flower'; H *šiɨl* 'tree' (POM 396).
Mn. *ki 'stomach'; Pn. *nki 'under, earth'; A *nakiʔ* 'inside', *nakhé* 'under'; H *otɨeng* 'stomach' (POM 99).

Mn. **(ʔ)li(m)(h)* 'little'; IZ *piʔizi* 'small', *nabiuže* 'small, fine'; H *kičeeč* 'small' (POM 258).

Mn. **ka-/xa-/θa-/kʷa-θi(m)/yi* 'nurse, a drop, breast'; Pn. **chį* 'milk'; IZ *raǰi* 'nurse', *šiǰi* 'breast', *niʔiǰi* 'breast milk'; H *ačeč* 'nurse' (POM 261).

**en: Mn. **yam-/ya-te(m)* 'alligator, lizard'; A *katʸǫ* 'lizard'; H *pohtan* 'green iguana' (POM 28).

A *cʔǫ́ (siʔ)* 'heart'; OP **nia* 'stomach, liver'; Ch. **sęʔę* 'intestines'; IZ *laǰi'doʔ* 'heart, stomach'; H *omeaats* 'heart' (POM 278).

Mn. *ⁿ*di-θe(m)* 'roasting ear', **ye(m)(h)/θemh* 'ear of corn'; A *cąʔ* 'corncob'; OP *-*sa* 'ear of corn'; IZ *zeʔe* 'roasting ear'; H *as* 'roasting ear' (POM 285).

Pn. **ni-/na/-nka*; A *ñhǫ* 'deep'; OP **hǫi* 'difficul*t*, deep'; CM **na-ku-ha/hí* 'cave, eye of needle, canyon'; H *nahal* 'deep, long' (POM 114).

**an: OP **k(h)ǫ* 'to fish'; Cn. **ʔŋių* 'a type of fish'; H *kiet* 'fish' (POM 128).

Proto Mazatec **hau*; CM **hu/hau-mihi*; H *ihpiw* 'two' (POM 222).

Mn. **ka-/θa-ⁿgʷa(m)(h)* 'twist, grind'; Proto Mazatec **ʔwau* 'grind'; A *macikʷʔɔ* 'twist'; H *ambil* 'twist (thread)' (POM 224).

Trique *žutą*; Pn. **ku-či-/nči-se/sę/sęʔ* 'fly'; H *iis* 'flea' (POM 311).

**un: Pn. **ʔñuʔ/yuhų* 'rope'; A *taʔ hnǫ́* 'tumpline'; Ch. **hų* 'thread'; IZ *doʔo* 'rope'; H *šiit* 'thread' (POM 92).

All traces of Otomanguean **ʔ seem to have been lost in Huave. The laryngeal *h* occurs in Huave, but it is not certain that Huave *h* ever reflects POM **h alone. When *h* occurs at the beginning of a syllable or closing the ultima it reflects the old cluster **hk. However, in *h*C clusters, which occur internally, the *h* may reflect POM **h, though it is not clear at present from which POM sequences such *h*C clusters developed.

Otomanguean **h is also the source of the Huave vowel clusters. In this connection it is noteworthy that a Huave penult of the shape CV_1V_1C has an alternant of the shape CV*h*C when suffixed. Thus, the Huave sequence CV_1V_1C appears to have derived from the POM sequence **CVhCV. The final vowel of **CVhCV sequences has been lost as has the corresponding vowel in **CVCV sequences.

The Huave form *teat* 'father' is instructive for further analysis of the development of POM laryngeals. This form appears to be related to Amuzgo *tá*, Chiapanec-Mangue *ⁿ*guu-táʔ*, and Chinantecan **tiá*, meaning 'father', and all reflecting the POM laryngeal **h closing the syllable. This would suggest that Huave *teat* is derived from POM **tatah. In pre-Huave, as in at least some Mixtecan and Zapotecan languages, the placement of stress moved from the ultima to the penult with a resulting loss of the vowel of the now unstressed ultima. The only instance in which the vowel of the ultima was preserved in Huave is the CV_1V_2C sequence, presumably derived from POM and pre-Huave *CVCVh. This preservation is here attributed to the presence of final **h protecting the preceding vowel from loss.[9] Futhermore, the development in Mixtecan may be cited as roughly analogous: The POM ultima developed in Mixtecan as dissylabic rather than monosyllabic when closed by a laryngeal. The same ultima developed in Huave as syllabic rather than as a single consonant when closed by **h.

Thus, we may summarize the development of POM **h in Huave: **CVhCV > CV_1V_1C ~ CV*h*C-; **CVCVh > CV_1V_2C; **CVCV > CVC. The following cognate sets illustrate the development of sequences including **h:

**CVhCV: Pn. **tʸha-wa(ʔ)* 'skin'; A *thą́* 'leather'; H *otaag* 'leather, skin' (POM 47).

Mn. **θa-/ⁿda/na-ku(mh)*; A *tinkʷé*; H *nawaag* 'dry' (POM 187).

OP **sa-h-t* 'bathe oneself, another'; Cn. **láʔ* ~ *liaʔ*; H *ašeeb* 'bathe' (POM 286).

Pn. **čhųʔ* 'cotton, thread'; H *misoots* 'hair' (POM 336).

**CVCVh: Pn. **yuhų* 'rope'; A *taʔ hnǫ́* 'tumpline'; IZ *doʔo* 'rope'; H *šiit* 'string' (POM 92).

Mn. **tu(m)(h)/hnumh*; A *ntǫ́* 'black'; Tl *miruʔun* 'night'; H *nąmbeor* 'black' (POM 94).

Mn. **kamh* 'snake, lizard'; A *čkʷą́*; CM **puu-/naa-kúʔ* 'lizard'; H *ndiik* 'snake' (POM 231).

Mn. **ye(m)(h)/θemh* 'ear of corn', **yeh/yem/θem* 'corn cob'; A *cíǫ* 'ear of corn', *nną́* 'corn'; IZ *zeʔe* 'roasting ear'; Cn. **ʔnį* 'corn cob', **lá*; H *as* 'roasting ear' (POM 285).

3. SOUND CHANGES SHARED BY OTOMANGUEAN LANGUAGES

Having described the major features of Otomanguean phonology — apart from tone[10] — and having consequently accorded Huave a place as still another branch of the Otomanguean grouping, we turn now to the engaging question of subgrouping among the several branches of Otomanguean. For over a century those with some knowledge of these languages have believed that the relationship between this or that pair of languages is especially close. However, only in the present quarter century and especially in the past decade and a half has the study of the individual branches been sufficiently detailed to permit comparison of entire phonological systems.

In considering similarities and differences of development among the Otomanguean languages we must concern ourselves with sound changes in which more than one

[9] It may be that in syllables closed by **h the stress was not shifted. If that is so, the vowel of the ultima was preserved only when stressed. There is evidence from other branches of Otomanguean that position of laryngeals and the placement of a moveable stress may have been related phenomena at a very early period of development.

[10] For a fuller discussion of the POM phonological system, cf. Rensch 1966: chapter 2, and Rensch, Classification of the Otomanguean languages and the position of Tlappanec.

branch of Otomanguean has participated. Thus, in the succeeding paragraphs the various shared changes will be discussed and in section 4 a history of the changes will be proposed.

Changes in the consonantal system have principally to do with the POM clusters of nasal plus consonant, palatal plus consonant, and the laryngeal **h plus **k.

The POM clusters of nasal plus apical obstruent, **nt and **ns, have in some cases fallen together, giving prenasalized stop *^{n}d in Mixtecan and Chiapanec-Mangue, cluster nd in Tlapanec, and affricates *č in Zapotecan and *z in Chinantecan. Elsewhere these clusters have remained distinct. Compare the following sets which illustrate both of these apical clusters:

> Mn. *^{n}dam-/kam-^{n}da(m) 'water'; Pn. *ʔi-/na-ntaʔ 'water, river'; CM *na-^{n}da 'stream, lake'; IZ guǰa 'dampness'; H ndek 'sea' (POM 67).
>
> Pn. *ku-nt^{y}a(ʔ) 'fox, wolf, dog'; IZ beʔeǰeʔ 'mountain lion'; Cn. *zi· 'dog'; Tl. endiʔ 'wild cat' (POM 39).
>
> Pn. *čahu 'dust'; A cha 'ashes'; CM *lu-^{n}da 'sand'; Tl. hndaʔ 'dust' (POM 283).
>
> Mn. *yamʔ/ʔyam/θaʔ/^{n}damh 'rope, cord'; Pn. *na-/nu-/ka-šaʔ/ncha 'blanket, hair'; Ch. *ki·cą; IZ giča ike; H ondeats 'hair' (POM 324).
>
> Pn. *ceʔe 'stomach, intestines'; A cʔǫ́ (siʔ) 'heart'; IZ laǰi'doʔ 'heart, stomach'; Cn. *zí; H omeaats 'heart' (POM 278).

The POM cluster of two nasals **nn became *m in Popolocan, Chiapanec-Mangue, and Chinantecan. The labialization is explained by the fact that the preposed nasal probably closed the preceding syllable and was in that position phonetically labial. This may be assumed from its rounding effect on preceding vowels where it closes the POM ultima. The following set demonstrates the development of **nn:

> Pn. *n-ca-mi/me 'elbow, fist'; CM *^{n}gi-Mi 'elbow', *na-/^{n}gi-/^{n}gu-/^{m}ba-/pa-Miʔ 'knee'; Cn. *mį·ʔ 'elbow', *hnį 'knee' (POM 257).

The POM cluster **nw became a labial stop *k^{w} in Zapotecan and p in Huave, thus merging with the reflex of **k^{w}:

> Mn. *tam-/na(m)-ʔmim(H) 'word, conversation'; Pn. *ca-/na-hmi/hmiʔ 'fruit, tell, thing'; A ñʔǫ 'word'; Ch. *ki·k^{w}iʔ 'talk'; IZ rabi 'say'; H apiing 'say' (POM 365). p

The POM cluster **ny became *l in Mixtecan,[11] Popolocan, Chiapanec-Mangue, Zapotecan, Chinantecan, and Huave, and r in Tlapanec:

> Pn. *ka-lihi/nt^{y}ihi 'pasture, grass'; CM *ni-/nu-lú/lu; IZ gieʔ; Cn. *lí; Tl. riʔi 'flower'; H šiil 'tree' (POM 396).
>
> Trique yąʔą 'night'; OP *ʔįah-nʔ/ø 'sleep'; Ch. *tela; IZ geʔelaʔ 'night'; Cn. *ʔlá· 'afternoon' P(OM 417).

The POM clusters of preposed palatal plus consonant developed most extensively in Popolocan, Amuzgo, and Chinantecan. Fewer of the clusters are attested in Huave,

[11] For a discussion of the development of **ny in Mixtecan cf. Rensch, Classification of the Otomanguean languages and the position of Tlappanec, 2.1.2.

Tlapanec, Zapotecan, and Chiapanec-Mangue. Speciffically, the development of the palatal clusters is as follows: **Yt > t^y in Popolocan, Amuzgo and Zapotecan, > *ti in Chinantecan, and > *č in Tlapanec and Huave. **Ynt > *nt^y in Popolocan and Amuzgo, > *zi in Chinantecan, > ǰ in Tlapanec, > r in Huave. **Ys > *š in Popolocan, Amuzgo, Zapotecan, Tlapanec, and Huave, si in Chinantecan. **Yns > *č in Popolocan, Amuzgo, and Huave, > *zi in Chinantecan. **Yk > *č in Popolocan and Chiapanec-Mangue, > k^y in Amuzgo, > *ki in Chinantecan. Although some languages reflect a larger number of clusters than others, all branches except Mixtecan and Otopamean reflect some **YC clusters. The following sets may be taken as typical of those which reflect POM **YC:

IZ *giži*; Cn. **są·* 'hay'; Tl. *raša* 'hay, grass'; H *soeš* 'grass' (POM 272).

Pn. **šu-te* 'biol'; Cn. **siṹ·* 'toast, fry' (POM 331).

Pn. **če*; A *$k^w ik^y$é* 'ripen' (POM 149).

Mn. **θi-/^{n}di-/yi-ku*; A *$ntk^y u$*; Cn. **giá·* 'twenty' (POM 227).

The velar stop was lost from the POM cluster **hk in Popolocan, Amuzgo, Chiapanec-Mangue, Otopamean, and Huave, as illustrated by the following sets:

Pn. **ni-/na-nka*; A *ñhǫ* 'deep'; CM **na-ku-ha/hi* 'cave, eye of needle, canyon'; OP **hąi* 'difficult, deep'; Cn. **hį·n* 'deep, high'; H *nahal* 'deep, long' (POM 114).

Pn. **nahį/*šhą*; CM **ha-mihi* 'three' (POM 111).

The principal changes in the POM vowel system have affected the front vowels. The vowel **e was raised to *i in Mixtecan, Chiapanec-Mangue, Zapotecan, and Tlapanec and to *ɨ in Chinantecan.

OP **ca-h-te* 'mountain lion'; Cn. **zi·* 'dog'; Tl. *endiʔ* 'wild cat' (POM 39).

Mn. **θi(h)* 'tough'; A *cą́* 'strong, tough'; CM **^{m}ba-ya-si* 'strong, strength'; OP **=cai-t* 'strong'; Ch. **ti·hi* 'tough'; IZ *ǰiʔičiʔ* 'strong' (POM 277).

The front vowels were generally backed before the postposed nasal, but in Popolocan, Amuzgo, and Tlapanec **i was lowered before the final nasal. The particular developments were as follows:[12]

**in: Pn. *e; A e; CM *u; OP *o; Cn. *u; Tl. a; H ɨ

**en: Pn. *a; A a; CM *a; OP *a; Cn. *a; Tl. a; H a

**iHn: Pn. *į; A ę; OP *ǫ; Cn. *ų; Tl. ą

**eHn: Pn. *ą; A ą; OP *ą; Cn. *ą; Tl. ą

The following sets illustrate these vowel changes:

**in: Pn. **n-/h-teʔ* 'sandals'; CM **^{n}du* 'skin, drum, sandal' (POM 8).

Cn. **ku·* 'money'; H *mančiik* 'iron' (POM 103).

A *maweʔ* 'arrive there'; OP **poeHC-nʔ* 'go out' (POM 147).

Pn. **še* 'sweet'; Tl. *saʔ* 'nectar' (POM 260).

**en: CM **^{m}bari-/pari-ta*; OP **taʔ* 'cut'; Cn. **ta* 'scrape' (POM 29).

Pn. **h^waʔ/k^waʔ* 'snail'; CM **na-^{n}du-h^wa* 'armadillo' (POM 175).

12 For illustrations of the development of the POM vowel system in the various branches of Otomanguean, cf. Rensch 1966: 2.2.

A *chaʔ* 'ashes'; CM **lu-ⁿda* 'sand'; Tl. *hndaʔ* 'dust' (POM 283).

OP **-sa* 'ear of corn'; H *as* 'roasting ear' (POM 285).

**iHn: A *chɔ́ʔ ñhę* 'money'; Cn. **kų́·* 'stone' (POM 103).

Pn. **ni-čihį*; OP **(n)sǫ* 'woman' (POM 255).

**eHn: Cn. **kʷą·ʔ* 'hill'; Tl. *aʔhwan* 'slope, ascent' (POM 167).

POM initial **ʔ has been lost in at least some environments in Mixtecan, Popolocan Chiapanec-Mangue, Chinantecan, Tlapanec, and Huave. The particular developments are as follows: Initial **ʔ before a stop or spirant is lost in Mixtec, is shifted to initial position in the penult in Cuicatec, and is lost with some tone patterns and shifted to close the ultima with others in Trique. Initial **ʔ is lost in Popoloc before a sequence of nasal plus stop or affricate and is shifted to close the ultima if it would otherwise occur before a stop; it is lost everywhere in Chocho. Initial **ʔ is lost in in Tlapanec when it would be initial in the word but is preserved when protected by a preceding syllable. It is lost before obstruents in Chinantecan and is lost everywhere in Huave and perhaps in Chiapanec-Mangue.

Mixtec *ti-yaka, čaka*; Cuicatec *ʔyaaka*; Trique *žukwaha* 'fish'[13]; Cn. **ʔŋių* 'a type of fish' (POM 128).

Popoloc *kintana* 'husband of daughter'; Ixcatec *škaʔnda* 'spouse of child'; Proto Mazatec **haʔnta, *škaʔnta* 'wife of brother or son' (Popolocan set 263).

Popoloc *toʔ*; Ixcatec *tʔo*; Chocho *duu* 'gruel'; OP **tʔę-m* 'corn drink' (POM 23).

Tl. *yō* 'dust'; Mn. **ⁿda-/ta-ʔyu* 'mud, mud-hole'; Pn. **ʔntʸe-ʔtu* (POM 96).

Cn. **zí* 'heart'; Pn. **ceʔe* 'stomach, intestines'; A *cʔǫ́ (siʔ)* 'heart'; CM **ⁿgu-si* 'stomach' (POM 278).

The POM syllable-final **h developed as an interrupting glottal stop in Zapotecan and Tlapanec.

Pn. **ntʸihiʔ* 'pot, pitcher, bowl'; CM **naa-tí* 'pot'; Ch. **tę·ʔę* 'clay jar'; IZ *riʔi* 'water jug' (POM 11).

Mn. **tu(m)(h)/hnumh* 'black, soot'; A *ntǫ́* 'black'; Tl. *miruʔun* 'night' (POM 94).

In the original reconstruction of the Proto Otomanguean ultima (Rensch 1966: chapter 2) a unique laryngeal cluster **hʔ was posited in final position. Popolocan, Amuzgo, Chiapanec-Mangue, and Chinantecan witness to such a cluster. However, it now appears that the cluster was not a feature of the ancestor language but rather has developed in those languages in which POM final **h has shifted so that it no longer follows the vowel, thus permitting such a syllable with internal reflex of **h to be closed by the reflex of **ʔ. This change in analysis has been made because the laryngeal cluster was anomalous and because the grouping of languages which do not share this cluster is unique. If one were to propose that such a laryngeal cluster existed in Proto Otomanguean but was lost in Mixtecan, Otopamean, Zapotecan,

[13] For details of the development within Trique cf. Longacre 1957:84–7.

Tlapanec, and Huave, one would be confronted with a grouping of languages united by no other sound change. However, the languages which do suggest such a cluster are precisely those which share special developments of the clusters **Yk and **nn and also share a number of sound changes with other languages. Therefore, the development of the laryngeal cluster appears to have taken place after the Proto Otomanguean period. The following sets illustrate the reflexes of the non-initial laryngeals and the combinations of these which occur in the innovating languages:

PCM **naa-tí* 'pot'; Ch. **tę·ʔę* 'clay jar'; IZ *riʔi*; Cn. **tu·ʔ* 'clay pot'; Pn. **(n)tʸihiʔ* 'pot, pitcher, bowl' (POM 11).

Pn. **ntʸi-/tʸo-tʸhų*; A *ntʸúʔ* 'nose' (POM 95).

Mn. **θa-ta(h)* 'tortilla'; CM **táʔ* 'cooked corn' (POM 48).

Ch. **sa·ʔa* 'full'; A *macikatoʔ* 'fill'; Cn. **táʔ* 'put in, be in' (POM 71).

The reflexes of POM high tone (**1) and POM mid tone (**2) have fallen together in Popolocan, Amuzgo, Otopamean, and Chinantecan. It is certain that they have remained distinct in Mixtecan. Information is lacking for Chiapanec-Mangue, Zapotecan, Tlapanec, and Huave.

**1: Mn. **kʷa(m)-/xi-/ka-/^{n}da-^{n}de(m)*^{32} 'ripen'; OP **(n)=tą-ʔ (V)* 'cooked, ripe' (POM 27).[14]

Mn. **yam-/yu-Hta*^{42} 'river, valley, canyon'; Pn. **ʔı/na-ntaʔ*^{3} 'water'; A *hn^{t}a*^{1} 'river'; Cn. **ziá· (LH)* 'pool, lake' (POM 67).

**2: Mn. **tam(h)*^{43} 'a span (measure)'; Pn. **tʸha*^{3} 'hand, arm, shoulder'; OP **ʔai*, **nʔi-ai (V)* 'hand' (POM 73).

Mn. **hθam*^{3} 'deer, horse'; Pn. **ku-ceʔ*^{3} 'rabbit'; A *ka*^{2}*só*^{3} 'horse'; Cn. **sių́· (HLH)* 'temazate, a kind of deer' (POM 317).

Sequences of two or more tones on single syllables have developed in Popolocan, Amuzgo, Otopamean, and Chinantecan because of the shifting of the tone of the penult onto the ultima. Mixtecan, on the other hand, has retained the simpler Proto Otomanguean system of just one tone per syllable. In Otopamean a system of level and gliding tomes has developed. In contemporary Otopamean languages pitch typically is contrastive on only one syllable of the stem. Apparently the pitches of other syllables have shifted to the one syllable, in some cases creating gliding tones. Thus, POP tone *I, which is proposed as a falling-low tone, enters into the same tone correspondences as does tone *III, which is proposed as a low tone. Similarly, in Popolocan, Amuzgo, and Chinantecan, tone sequences enter into the same tone correspondences as do the final members of the sequences by themselves. Note the following sets in which the final tone of the tone sequences of the above mentioned languages is shown to be the relevant one for determining sound correspondences:

Pn. **š-khą*^{43}; A *ntkʸu*^{21}; Mn. **θi-/^{n}di-/yi-ku*^{23} 'twenty' (POM 227).

Pn. **yą*^{3} 'not'; Mn. **θam(h)*^{23} 'none, it isn't so' (POM 313).

[14] The following symbols are used in indicating tone in the several branches: numbers (with 1 as high) in Mixtecan, Popolocan, and Amuzgo; I (falling-low), II (high-falling), III (low), IV (rising), V (falling), VI (high) in Otopamean; and H (high) and L (low) in Chinantecan.

A *cą*^{1}; Mn. **ye(m)(h)/θem*^{23} 'hail' (POM 279).

Cn. *zí (LH)*; Mn. **ye(m)(h)*^{23}; A *cą*^{1} 'hail' (POM 279).

Cn. **za· (H)* 'sin, guilt'; Mn. **na(m)(h)/naʔ*^{23} 'ashamed, shame'; Proto Mazatec **ča*^{3}*ʔu*^{3} 'bad, wicked', Pn. **sa*^{3}*-waʔ/wa* 'ashamed' (POM 318).

OP **pa (I, falling-low)* 'hot'; Cn. **ʔmą́· (L)* 'tepid' (POM 136).

OP **coe (IIIǰ low)*; Cn. **g*^{w}*íʔ (L)* 'cold' (POM 141).

One question not yet considered here is that of the labial stop of Otomanguean. It has been assumed in previous discussions that Proto Otomanguean had a labiovelar stop **k^w, as reflected in Mixtecan, Popolocan, Amuzgo, Chatino, and Chinantecan, rather than a *p* as in Chiapanec-Mangue, Otopamean, Isthmus Zapotec, Tlapanec, and Huave. That the stop was labio-velar rather than bilabial is suggested by its alternation with **k and by the reduction of the sequence **k^{w}Vn to **ku* in some languages. However, the group of languages which share *p* is quite unlike any other grouping indicated by the shared sound changes. Nor, for that matter, is the group of those sharing *k*^{w} an especially promising grouping. However, the two groups do accord rather well with south and west as opposed to north and east geographical divisions. Consequently, it seems preferable to regard the *k*^{w}*/p* split as the result of a dialect difference already existing in Proto Otomanguean before the various sound changes discussed here took place.

	Mn.	Pn.	A	CM	OP	Zn.	Cn.	Tl.	H
(1) **nt, **ns	^{n}d			^{n}d		č	z	nd	
(2) **nn		m	n̩n	m			m		
(3) **nw						k^w			p
(4) **ny	l	l		l		l	l	r	l
(5) **Ys		š	š			š	si	š	š
(6)		č	k^y	č			ki		
(7) **hk		h	h	h	h		h		h
(8) **e	i			i		i	ɨ	i	
(9) **in		e	e	u	o		u	a	ɨ
(10) **iHn		į	ę		ǫ		ų	ą	
(11) **ʔC	C	C					C	C	C
(12) **Vh						VʔV		VʔV	
(13) **VH		hVʔ	V́ʔ	V́ʔ			V́ʔ		
(14) **1, **2		3	1/3		I, II III, VI		H		
(15) **CV^{T}CV^T		43	13, 21		IV, V		LH, HLH		

Fig. 1. Otomanguean Shared Changes

The shared sound changes which are considered in this study are displayed in Figure 1. From the tabulation of Figure 1 it may be readily observed that some branches of Otomanguean are more innovating than are others. Chinantecan and Popolocan are the most innovating since Chinantecan participated in 13 of the 15 sound changes and Popolocan in 11. On theo ther hand, Mixtecan and Otopamean are the most conservative since Mixtecan participated in only 4 sound changes and Otopamean in 5.

	Mn.	Pn.	A	CM	OP	Zn.	Cn.	Tl.	H
Mn.		2	0	3	0	3	4	4	2
Pn.			9	6	5	2	11	5	5
A				5	5	1	9	3	3
CM					2	3	8	4	3
OP						0	5	2	2
Zn.							4	5	3
Cn.								7	5
Tl.									4

Fig. 2. Number of changes shared by language pairs

It is possible, of course, for two language groups to be equally innovating but to have no change in common. Such is the case with Mixtecan and Otopamean, as seen from Figure 2. Mixtecan and Otopamean are almost equally conservative, but not one of those sound changes in which they did participate is shared by the two groups. On the other hand, the innovating groups — Chinantecan, Popolocan, and Amuzgo — share many changes. In fact, there are nine pairs of groups which share all the changes of the less innovating member of the pair: Chinantecan shares all the innovations of Mixtecan, Otopamean, Popolocan, Amuzgo, and Chiapanec-Mangue; Popolocan all those of Amuzgo and Otopamean; Amuzgo all those of Otopamean; and Tlapanec all those of Mixtecan. However, Mixtecan does not share any innovation with either Otopamean or Amuzgo, nor does Zapotecan with Otopamean; Zapotecan shares only one with Amuzgo.

Thus, it may be observed that Otopamean and Amuzgo are very unlike Mixtecan and Zapotecan. It may be observed further that Popolocan shares the innovations of Otopamean and Amuzgo, that Tlapanec shares the innovations of Mixtecan, and that Chinantecan shares the innovations of both groups and of Chiapanec-Mangue as well.

The preceding statements treat only those pairs of groups which share all the innovations of the less innovating member and, therefore, do not discuss the relationships of either Zapotecan or Huave. However, examination of those pairs of groups which share 80 to 90 per cent of the changes of the less innovating member of the pair not only shows Chinantecan to be aligned with Tlapanec but also shows Tlapanec to be aligned with Zapotecan and both Popolocan and Chinantecan with Huave.

4. HISTORY OF OTOMANGUEAN SOUND CHANGES

From an examination of the sound changes shared by the several branches of Otomanguean eight periods of development of the Otomanguean languages can be deduced.

Period I. During the first period these nine Otomanguean groups were in rather close contact. This period might be termed the Proto Otomanguean period.

Period II. By Period II the Mixtecan and Zapotecan groups had moved away from the main mass. Assuming that at the end of the common period the groups was located somewhere in central Mexico, one can surmise that the Mixtecan and Zapotecan groups may well have moved south and east by Period II, perhaps to southern Oaxaca.[15]

During this period a major reworking of the system of vowel-nasal sequences took place in the main mass (sound changes 9 and 10 of Figure 1). Popolocan, Amuzgo, and Tlapanec seem to have been in close contact, but somewhat separated from Otopamean, Chiapanec-Mangue, Chinantecan, and Huave. The groupings of Period II are indicated in Figure 3.

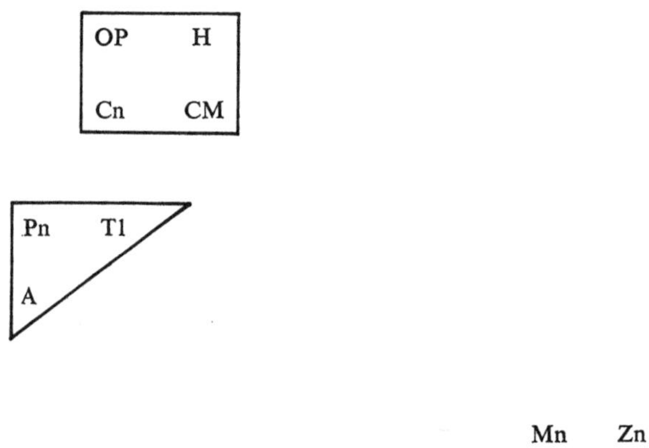

Fig. 3. Period II

In the Popolocan-Amuzgo-Tlapanec groups the front vowels were lowered before **n*: **in* > **ε*; **en* > **a*. Where followed by **Hn*, however, these vowels simply became nasalized: **iHn* > **į*; **eHn* > **ę*. Probably during this period each of the three languages carried out further changes in the low front area. Popolocan lowered **e* to **ε*, thus merging it with the development of **in*. Amuzgo lowered **e* to *ä* and **į* to *ę* and **ę* to *ą*. Tlapanec moved **ε* to *a*, thus merging it with the development of **a* and moved **į* and **ę* to *ą*. Since Period II seems to have been the period when the front vowels were reworked, it is assumed that these isolated changes in Popolocan, Amuzgo, and Tlapanec took place during this period; however, it is not possible to demonstrate that they did not take place at a later period.

In the group consisting of Chiapanec-Mangue, Otopamean, Chinantecan, and Huave the front vowels were backed before **n*: **in* > **u*; **en* > **a*; **iHn* > **ų*; **eHn*

[15] Any interpretation of Figures 3 through 8 in terms of specific geographic movements must be made, of course, on the basis of nonlinguistic factors such as present settlement patterns and inferences from archeological evidence; although shared phonological innovations can indicate that two groups were together during a given period, they do not indicate their specific location.

> **ą*. Apparently the shift from **en* to **a* was an independent parallel development in the two areas.

Period III. By Period III Tlapanec had moved off, probably to the southeast to join Mixtecan and Zapotecan, with which it clearly had considerable contact at a later period. Popolocan and Amuzgo moved again into contact with Otopamean, Chiapanec-Mangue, Chinantecan, and Huave. The grouping of Period III is indicated in Figure 4.

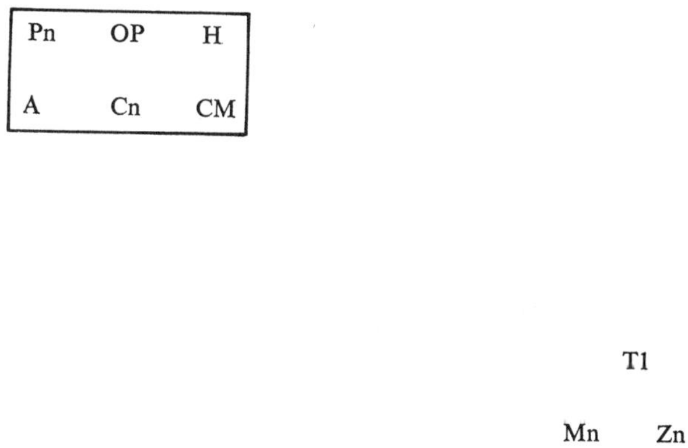

Fig. 4. Period III

During this period the changes in the tone system and the loss of **k* from the cluster **hk* took place (sound changes 7, 14, and 15 of Figure 1). However, since the development of tone in Huave, Chiapanec-Mangue, Tlapanec, and Zapotecan has not been studied, it can only be supposed at present that these languages shared the tone development of the others with which they were associated in sound change 7 of Figure 1.[16]

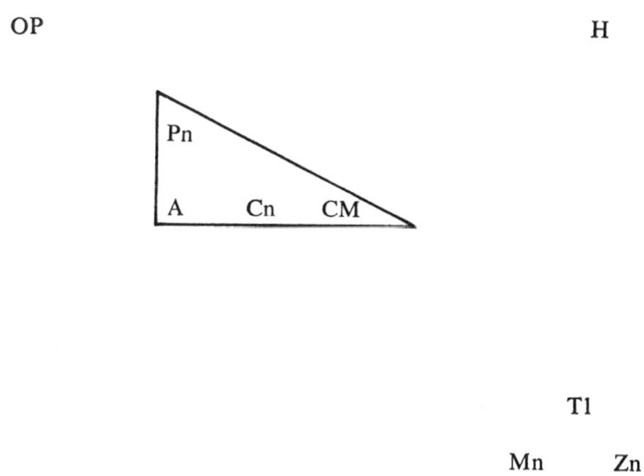

Fig. 5. Period IV

[16] Perhaps during this period when Chiapanec-Mangue and Huave were in contact they merged nasalized vowels with their oral counterparts. However, it is not certain that the loss of nasalization was not an independent parallel development; neither can we be sure from presently available data that nasalization was really lost in Chiapanec-Mangue.

Period IV. By Period IV Huave had moved away, perhaps to its present position on the south coast of the Isthmus of Tehuantepec. However, since during the next period Huave developed especially like Chinantecan and Amuzgo, it may be that it simply moved off east, rather than southeast to join the Tlapanec-Mixtecan-Zapotecan grouping. Also by Period IV the innovating group of Popolocan, Amuzgo, Chiapanec-Mangue, and Chinantecan had moved away from Otopamean — presumably along a path similar to that already taken by Mixtecan, Zapotecan, and Tlapanec, though it was not yet in contact with the latter groups. The grouping of Period IV is indicated in Figure 5.

During this period the earliest modification of the clusters of palatal plus consonant (sound change 6 of Figure 1) and of the clusters of nasal plus consonant (sound change 2 of Figure 1) occurred. Also, the combinations of non-initial laryngeals developed since by this time final **h* had moved to a position within the syllable (sound change 12 of Figure 1).

Period V. By Period V the innovating group, consisting of Popolocan, Amuzgo, Chiapanec-Mangue, and Chinantecan, had moved back into contact with Huave and also with Tlapanec and Zapotecan, but not with Mixtecan. It may be that Chiapanec-Mangue moved to the east of the grouping since it did not participate in the changes of this period. The grouping of Period V is indicated in Figure 6.

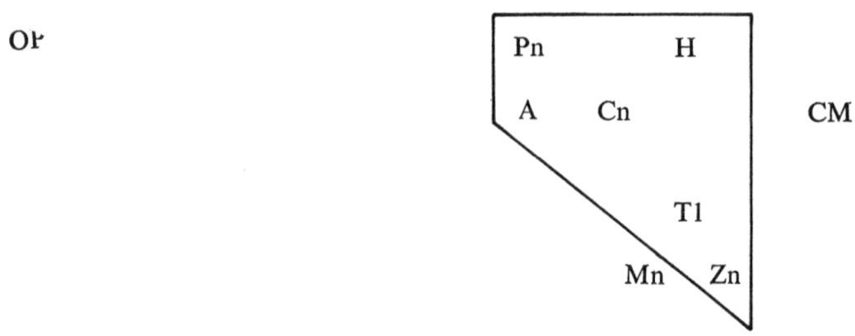

Fig. 6. Period V

During this period the clusters of palatal with **t* and **s*, with or without the preposed nasal, (sound change 5 of Figure 1) developed most fully in Popolocan, Amuzgo, Chinantecan, and Huave. The development of the palatal clusters with the preposed nasal was more restricted in Tlapanec and Zapotecan.

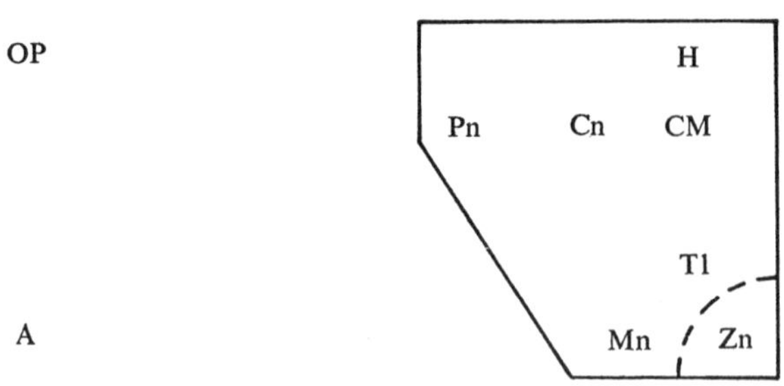

Fig. 7. Period VI

Period VI. By Period VI Amuzgo had moved off, perhaps to the Pacific coast in roughly its present location. During this period the grouping of the preceding period (minus Amuzgo) was again in contact with Chiapanec-Mangue and by now with Mixtecan. The grouping of Period VI is indicated in Figure 7.

During this period the development of the cluster **ny* as a liquid took place (sound change 4 of Figure 1). The loss of initial *ʔ (sound change 11 of Figure 1) probably took place during this period also. However, it is not certain that this change occurred in Chiapanec-Mangue; it did not take place in Zapotecan; it took place in only part of the Mixtecan and Popolocan areas; and it took place in only some environments in Mixtecan, Popolocan, Chinantecan, and Tlapanec. Thus, this is one of the poorest pieces of evidence here considered for determining periods of common development.

Period VII. By Period VII Popolocan had moved off. Assuming that the developments of Period VI took place in central Oaxaca, Popolocan may well have moved northward to approximately its present location. Huave was again out of contact with the innovating group by this time and may well have migrated to the south coast of the Isthmus of Tehuantepec if it was not already there (cf. Period IV). The grouping of Period VII is indicated in Figure 8.

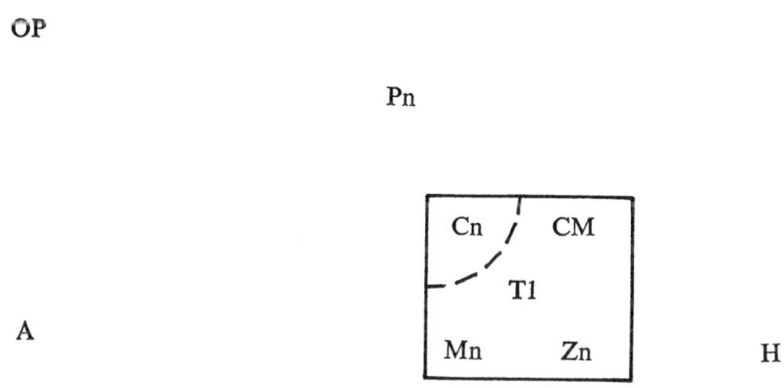

Fig. 8. Period VII

During Period VII the clusters **nt* and **ns* merged (sound change 1 of Figure 1) as a stop in Mixtecan, Chiapanec-Mangue, and Tlapanec and as an affricate in Zapotecan and in Chinantecan. It is possible that **nt* and **ns* merged as a stop in Zapotecan and Chinantecan also during this period, and that in the following period, during the Zapotecan expansion, Zapotecan and Chinantecan shifted the stop to an affricate. During the same period, the vowel **e* was raised to **i* in Mixtecan, Chiapanec-Mangue, Zapotecan, and Tlapanec, thus merging with **i*, and was raised to **ɨ* in Chinantecan (sound change 8 of Figure 1).

Period VIII. By the most recent period Chiapanec-Mangue had moved eastward, and perhaps Chinantecan had moved slightly eastward also. During this period the expansion of Zapotecan brought it into contact with Chinantecan (see above), Huave, Tlapanec, and perhaps Mixtecan. During the Zapotecan-Huave contact sound change 12 of Figure 1 took place. During the Zapotecan-Tlapanec contact sound change 3 took place, after which Tlapanec apparently moved somewhat westward, perhaps as a result of Mixtec expansion. A possible shared feature linking the Chatino side of Zapotecan with its Mixtecan neighbors is the occlusion of *s. Proto Zapotecan *s became *ǰt* in Proto Chatino, and Proto Mixtecan *θ became t before back vowels in Trique and d in Cuicatec.[17]

The position of the Otomanguean languages at present (or at the time of extinction in the case of Chiapanec-Mangue) is plotted in Figure 9.

Fig. 9

[17] The complex nature of the Cuicatec and Trique developments (Longacre 1957:150) leaves the question open as to whether they came about in connection with the Chatino shift.

REFERENCES

ARANA OSNAYA, EVANGELINA. 1960. Relaciones internas del mixteco-trique. AnINA 12.219–73.

BARTHOLOMEW, DORIS. 1960. Some revisions of Proto-Otomi consonants. IJAL 26.317–29.

——. 1965. The reconstruction of Otopamean (Mexico). Ph.D. dissertation, Univ. of Chicago.

FERNÁNDEZ DE MIRANDA, MARIA TERESA, MORRIS SWADESH, and R.W. WEITLANER. 1959. Some findings on Oaxaca language classification and culture terms. IJAL 25.54–8.

FERNÁNDEZ DE MIRANDA, MARIA TERESA, and R.W. WEITLANER. 1961. Sobre algunas relaciones de la familia mangue. AnL 3.7.1–99.

GUDSCHINSKY, SARAH C. 1959. Proto-Popotecan. A comparative study of Popolocan and Mixtecan. (Indiana University Publications in Anthropology and Linguistics, 15.) Bloomington.

HAMP, ERIC P. 1964. Toward the refinement of Chiapanec-Mangue comparative phonology. ACIAm XXXV.387–402.

KIRK, PAUL L. 1966. Proto Mazatec Phonology. Ph.D. dissertation, Univ. of Washington.

LONGACRE, ROBERT E. 1957. Proto-Mixtecan. (Indiana University Research Center in Anthropology, Folklore, and Linguistics, 5.) Bloomington.

——. 1961. Swadesh's Macro-Mixtecan hypothesis. IJAL 27.9–29.

——. 1962. Amplifications of Gudschinsky's Proto-Popolocan-Mixtecan. IJAL 28. 227–42.

——. 1964. Progress in Otomanguean reconstruction. PICL 9.1016–25.

——. 1966. The linguistic affinities of Amuzgo. Summa Anthropologica en homenaje a Roberto J. Weitlaner, ed. by Antonio Pompa y Pompa, 541–60. Mexico City, Instituto nacional de antropologia e historia.

——. 1967. Systemic comparison and reconstruction. Handbook of Middle American Indians, ed. by Norman McQuown, 5.117–59. Austin, Univ. of Texas.

——. 1968. Comparative reconstruction of indigenous languages. CTL 4.320–60. The Hague, Mouton.

MAK, CORNELIA, and ROBERT LONGACRE. 1960. Proto-Mixtec phonology. IJAL 26. 23–40.

RENSCH, CALVIN R. 1966. Comparative Otomanguean phonology. Ph.D. dissertation, Univ. of Pennsylvania.

——. 1968. Proto Chinantec phonology. (Serie cientifica, 10.) Mexico City, Museo nacional de antropologia.

——. ms. Classification of the Otomanguean languages and the position of Tlapanec.

SAPIR, EDWARD. 1925. The Hokan affinity of the Subtiaba in Nicaragua. AmA 27.402–35, 491–527.

SCHMIDT, P. WILHELM. 1926. Die Sprachfamilien und Sprachendreise der Erde. Heidelberg.

SWADESH, MORRIS. 1960. The Oto-Manguean hypothesis and Macro Mixtecan. IJAL 26.79–111.

——. 1964. Interim notes on Oaxacan phonology. SJA 20.168–89.

UPSON, B.W., and ROBERT E. LONGACRE. 1965. Proto-Chatino phonology. IJAL 31.312–22.

WARKENTIN, MILTON, and CLARA WARKENTIN. 1952. Vocabulario Huave. Mexico, Instituto Lingüístico de Verano.

WEITLANER, ROBERT J. and PAUL SMITH. 1962. Detalles de la fonología del idioma proto-chinanteco, un informe preliminar. RMEA 18.117–23.

HISTORIOGRAPHY OF NATIVE IBERO-AMERICAN LINGUISTICS

HERBERT LANDAR

THE FIRST WAVE

The first students of American Indian languages were missionaries. They were sent to the New World by the monarchs of Spain to propagate the Faith. Administrative and military personnel of the same monarchs relied upon the priests to facilitate operations which involved taxation and slavery, and when colonial avarice was opposed by clerical charity friction resulted, friction which in the case of the Jesuits led to their expulsion late in the eighteenth century.

The Jesuit reductions had been established in the southern part of South America as a model of clerical charity. Records of these reductions, places to which Indians came for settlement life, constitute our earliest substantial basis for inferences about the distribution and census of indigenous tribes. The most convenient place for the study of these records, perhaps, is the Archivo General de Indias in Seville. Here were sent reports and other records of the Spanish operations in the American colonies. Daniel G. Brinton, the cardinal linguistic historiographer of the Americas in the nineteenth century, drew upon colonial records (though not very thoroughly) in his survey of tribes and languages, *The American race* (1891). He remarks, for example, that the languages used in Jesuit missions of Apolobamba province (W. of Rio Beni, E. of the Cordillera, about 80 leagues from N.E. to S.W.) were Leco and Maracani. At the Chiquitos mission, Chiquito was the language used by the priests for forty-nine tribal groups, each with a distinctive language or dialect. For twenty-nine tribes at the Moxos mission, there were several sacerdotal languages, including Moxo, Mure, Mobima, Baure, Cayubaba, Ocorona, Maracani and Itonana, which served for communication with 30,000 converts (census of 1726) who spoke a total of fifteen languages (Brinton 1891:305).

Religious zeal and Hispanic administrative efficiency under ideal conditions produced large bodies of linguistic data. Early in the history of the American empire royal decrees insisted that priests learn the languages of their converts, not only for propagation of Christianity but also because with order and literacy (epitomized in the reductions) Indians could be tithed and taxed. The priests in the south and west were more successful in this enterprise, however, than those in the Spanish Main and other northerly regions. Capuchins among Caribs in the north were sufficiently distressed by the monarch's insistence that they master the language of each native tribe, to respond with reckless impertinence that the task was impossible.

Religious texts, supplemented by grammars and dictionaries prepared by priests mainly for new missionaries, were intended to be suppressed by the Spanish crown. The Jesuits returning to Europe were forbidden to carry with them books or notes. Of those which were smuggled into Europe, however, a large portion were acquired by Lorenzo de Hervas. Vatican librarian and encyclopedist, Hervas was the first major compiler of data on South American tribes and languages. The Jesuit expulsion probably resulted in the loss of much linguistic data; but for Hervas, intent on establishing similarities of languages of the world that for him reflected dissemination from the Tower of Babel, and intent on cataloguing all the languages of the world, the Jesuit records in Europe, assembled at his behest in Rome, were a windfall.

The Jesuit Order has carefully inventoried the American linguistic data which Hervas used; four Roman libraries now hold these materials, all the more interesting for having been used by Wilhelm von Humboldt, Prussian minister in Rome and perhaps the chief beneficiary, from a scholarly point of view, of what Hervas had assembled. Hervas was supplied in his cataloguing by many correspondents, including Clavijero, who intended to produce a book on Mexican languages but never did. The exasperation of Clavijero with carelessness on the part of Hervas, preserved in his correspondence, suggests that the encyclopedist was more blithe than diligent. The British historiographer Latham was not particularly critical of the quality of Hervas's work; the American historiographer Brinton, on the other hand, constantly calls some of the dicta of Hervas to question.

Early historiography for native Ibero-America, then, was problem oriented. Practical missionary activities and, especially from the turn of the nineteenth century, interest in exotic languages from a typological point of view (Humboldt was interested in evolutionary speculations as well as the value of language in the shaping of national character and world view), made the study of languages of Latin America vibrant.

Among nonclerical scholars three Prussians were prominent in the problem-oriented (as opposed to index-oriented) study of American Indian languages, Wilhelm von Humboldt, his brother Alexander, and Julius Klaproth. Klaproth was an orientalist with diplomatic experience in Asia; with Wilhelm's help, he was able to live in Paris with permission of the Prussian monarch. Permission extended over the period necessary for publication of his works; in effect, he was a resident of Paris for life. His *Asia polyglotta* (1823) shows a problem-oriented interest in American linguistic data. Alexander is famous for his travels in the Americas as a naturalist and explorer. His visit to the United States stimulated Albert Gallatin, who has, with some reason, been called the father of American linguistics. Though not a Sinologist like Klaproth, Alexander used linguistic and ethnographic data to contend that American Indians migrated to the New World from Asia; he brought to public attention the view that the calendars of Asia have been carried to Mexico and elsewhere, opening up a discussion which despite evidence to the contrary has not yet ceased.

Wilhelm von Humboldt came to linguistics from an interest in aesthetic philosophy. He was well favored; he moved in the highest aristocratic and intellectual circles in Berlin, Paris and London as well as in Rome. Brinton translated his study of the American verb, and summaries of his philosophy were published in German and English in the middle years of the nineteenth century; Gallatin secured handwritten translations of some of his pronouncements, before the Humboldtian vogue accelerated to the point of published critical evaluations; and Humboldt's views about the kinds of research which would be most fruitful in linguistics influenced contemporary research. Typological historiography began on the phonological level with Hervas, out to show that all languages came from Babel; on the morphological level if it did not begin with Humboldt it certainly was accelerated by his speculations and advice to scholars.

Humboldt thought that inflections marked a high point in the evolution of a language; pushing beyond the contemporary typology which clumsily separated monosyllabic languages from the polysyllabic, he claimed that the literature most pleasin g aesthetically has to be composed in inflectional languages, of which he esteemed especially Sanskrit and Greek; Chinese, an isolating language, debased by a lack of inflections, he rated at the opposite extreme. Of American Indian languages, he esteemed most the language of the Aztecs, whose verbs could have an aorist-like prefix reminiscent of that of the Greeks. His researches ranged over many of the languages of the world, Basque, Sanskrit, Chinese, American Indian languages (better known to him, through the Hervas collection, probably, than to any other European scholar of his time), and, at the last, Kawi, a language of Java. In the introduction to his description of Kawi, Humboldt summarized the major points of his philosophy; publication, unfortunately, was posthumous. Humboldt's style is rich in vague, romantic generalizations, difficult to find fault with as long as they are unexemplified. But in his writing one can find seeds later to be nurtured by B.L. Whorf, having to do with the power of individual morphemes of a word over perception and cognition. In characterizing the power of Tupian morphemes, Wilhelm helped to initiate philosophical and psychological investigations which, where not wild, are vibrant and interesting.

Colonial interests sometimes have shaped lines of investigation. French, British and Spanish concerns in Latin America, commercial au fond, gave impetus nevertheless to linguistic and ethnographic researches, not always divorced from those which were commercial; Dutch and Portuguese concerns have produced similar effects, to a lesser degree. Many expeditions to South and Central America and to Mexico particularly in the present and the last centuries led to publications indexing, as it were, tribes and languages along the exploratory routes. Of writers in the German language capitalizing on linguistic data thus made public special note must be taken of Adelung and Vater, whose *Mithridates* contains specimens of vocabulary, grammatical rules and short texts (such as the Lord's Prayer); the title probably refers to the *Mithridates* or linguistic catalogue of Konrad Gesner, who died in 1565, after establishing himself as a physician, naturalist and bibliographer without peer not only in his native Switzerland but also in the civilized world. Adelung's project did not reach American Indian languages until after his death; Vater edited the volume with American specimens; Friedrich Adelung later published an index of language names for the project. The project did not reflect the Humboldtian contributions to linguistic historiography, but, with the work of Hervas, it stood as an index-oriented monument of early nineteenth century labors.

The foremost specialist on American Indian languages in England during the middle years of the nineteenth century, building on the British colonial interests in North as well as South America, was Robert Gordon Latham. His historiographical efforts were problem oriented; unlike the efforts of Wilhelm von Humboldt, however, Latham's were directed largely at problems of subgrouping and migration analysis. In a sense, Latham's work anticipates the crowning achievement of Brinton in synthesizing and evaluating contributions of the nineteenth century; Latham, however, lacked the patience, I suspect, which enabled Brinton to master the field as far as he did; it took more than patience, of course, if we may permit ourselves a mild pun — both men were physicians, but while Latham resigned his medical appointments (keeping the M.D. for title pages) Brinton carried on a heavy medical practice while serving as the major ethnologist of the University of Pennsylvania.

Latham was born in 1812. After studies at Eaton and Cambridge he taught English at University College, London, for a decade. At the same time he studied medicine at the University of London; in 1844 he was elected assistant physician at Middlesex Hospital; but in 1849 he resigned in order to devote himself to ethnology. In the period 1850 to 1859 he published eleven volumes on ethnology; in 1860 he published a work in which he demonstrates his skill and interests regarding classification of languages of America, *Opuscula: Essays, chiefly philological and ethnographical*; but just in *Man and his migrations* (1851), at the start of his ethnological career, do we find the scholarly ingredients which enable us to distinguish him easily from Humboldt. After 1860, Latham's publications showed a catholicity of scholarly interests; like Emerson, he suffered in his last days from aphasia; he died in 1888.

Latham was a precursor of Brinton in style, with meticulous attention to earlier sources, evaluation of data afresh, and judgments based on rather flimsy, though by no means primitive, classificatory procedures: demonstrations of relationship or dissimilarity on the basis of little more than short vocabularies. And while lexicostatistical computations in subgrouping began in the eighteenth century, Latham was ahead of his time in his exploitation of such computations.

In *Man and his migrations* Latham opened by discussing philology as an instrument of ethnological investigation, reviewing the work of Hervas, Adelung, Klaproth and others. Methods he discussed in his third chapter. In the fourth chapter he took up tribes of the Americas by name and geographical location. He proposed that linguistic evidence spotlights common origin. He experimented with lexicostatistics: 'Out of 100 words in two allied languages, a percentage of any amount between 1 and 99 may coincide. Language then is a *definite* test, if it be nothing else' (Latham 1851:27).

Latham recognized Pigafetta (with the Portuguese commander Fernão de Magalhães) as the earliest collector of speciments of native languages. He traced a line of historiographers in short shrift: 'In 1801 Adelung's *Mithridates* appeared, containing specimens of all the known languages of the world; a work as classical to the comparative philologist as Blackstone's *Commentaries* (1765–69) are to the English lawyer. Vater's *Supplement* (1821) is a supplement to Adelung; Jülg's (1847) to Vater's' (Latham 1851:29).

Prichard's amateurish speculations in *Eastern origin of the Celtic nations* struck Latham as praiseworthy: Prichard, he said, was the first scholar to combine the arts of ethnography and philology. Thus did he cast aside centuries of clerical debate about the lost Israelites of *Esdras*, a debate sometimes weaving into whole cloth glittering fibers of linguistic data. In place of the Biblical theme, Latham proffered sensible evaluation of data, observing in his lexicographical speculations, indeed, that identification of genetic relationship on the basis of vocabulary, even on the basis of identity of language, is not absolutely certain, because sometimes words are borrowed, are accidentally similar, or are similar because of imitation of physical sounds or by nursery phylogeny (1851:85–6).

The French explorer D'Orbigny classified tribes of South America in *L'Homme américain*; following D'Orbigny (whom Brinton also studied closely) Latham tallied tribes with probably mutually unintelligible languages (1851:114); the list bears repeating here as an indication of the extent of mid-nineteenth-century erudition:

Yurakare
Mocéténè
Tacana
Apolista

In Missions:

Moxo
Movima
Cayuvava
Sapiboconi or Moxo

In Chiquitos:

Covareca
Curuminaca
Curavi
Curucaneca
Corabeca
Samucu

In Brazil:

Botocudo
Goitaca (called Coroados by the Portuguese)
Camacan

Kiriri and Sabuja
Timbira
Pareci
Mundrucu
Muru
Yameo
Maina
Chimano
Coretu
British Guiana:
Warow
Taruma
Wapisiana
Atúrai
Daúrai
Amaripas
Venezuela:
Salivi, including the Aturi
Maypure
Achagua
Yarura, allied to Betoi
Ottomaka
Central, Middle and North American:
Moskito
Carib
Astek [Aztec]
Maya
Natchez
Algonkin
Iroquois
Sioux
Eskimo
Athabascan
Kolúch
Ugalents or Ugyalyackhmutsi
Micmac

The contributions of Gallatin and Hale had not reached Europe, obviously, in a general sense, by the time of Latham's *Man and his migrations;* Gallatin had placed his classification of 1836 in the hands of his friend, Alexander von Humboldt, as soon as possible, but that was no help to Latham. (The presentation copy, in fact, found its way back to America, to the New York Public Library.) With Latham as with Hervas, the substantial body of information on American linguistics came from the more southerly parts of South America; in Hervas's case, his material for the *Catálogo* disappears almost entirely north of the Mexican area. In short, American Indian linguistic historiography began with and was essentially limited at first to native Ibero-America.

It is more convenient to refer here to Latham's speculations about non-Ibero-American populations than to take the matter up elsewhere. His interest reflects a transitional stage, I think, between the first wave of historiographical writing and the second, between writings based on dogmatic assumptions that truth could be determined by inspection of data, whether for indexing purposes or for the solution of philosophical problems, and writings of greater subtlety, truly academic writings founded on post-Victorian urbanity.

Latham tied the Eskimos to N.E. Asia by linguistic data, without supplying details. And he supposed that the Aleutians were connected either to the Kamskadales or the Curiles, his lexical comparisons being indecisive in the matter (1851:124). There is a hint of urbanity in the heavy qualification which serves as a frame for Latham's conclusions about the original homeland of the human race (1851:248):

> ... the evidence of the human family having originated in one particular spot, and having diffused itself from thence to the very extremities of the earth, is by no means absolute and conclusive. Still less is it certain that that particular spot has been ascertained. The present writer *believes* that it was somewhere in intratropical Asia, and that it was *the single locality of a single pair* — without, however, professing to have proved it. Even this centre is only *hypothetical* — near, indeed, to the point which he looks upon as the starting-place of the human migration, but by no means identical with it.

He closes (1851:250):

> That there is much in all existing classifications which requires to be unlearnt is certain. Lest anyone think this is a presumptuous statement, let him consider the new and unsettled state of the science, and the small number of the labourers as compared with the extent of the field.

INSTITUTIONALIZED HISTORY

It is a generalization widely advertised that each generation rewrites history in terms of contemporary perspectives. Problems of past centuries have led to descriptions and studies proper to those centuries; problems of the present have led to reevaluations as well as new, specialized concerns. Corridors of communication, once they have been institutionalized, whether by royal edict or by academic society, reinforce local concerns. The development of views on Indians as Hebrews took place mainly in religious corridors of communication; those on Indians as Welshmen, perhaps mainly among romantics, utopians, and Welshmen (as Southey's *Madoc* partly testifies). More to the point in this essay, a Parisian student of American Indian linguistics would in great likelihood, if he were a member of the Société d'Ethnographie, be taken up with problems put forward in the *Revue Orientale et Américaine*, problems of Aztec language and culture, in the main, than he would be with problems put forward in Berlin, London, Rome or New York.

Or Saint Petersburg. Much remains to be written about the academic circles of Europe in the earliest days of Americanist linguistic research. Among the listers, circulators of questions about Ibero-American (as contrasted with North American) languages, Catherine the Great of Russia must be accorded priority. She circulated vocabulary lists around the world, as well as requests to heads of state for linguistic data. The Marquis de Lafayette, for example, at her behest contacted George Washington, who responded by sending several vocabularies. Lafayette also procured from Guatemala a set of vocabularies the originals of which I believe are in Leningrad, and a copy of which I examined at the Archivo General de Indias. Pallas and Yankievitch edited her vocabularies; Friedrich Adelung celebrated her work in *Catherinens der Grossen Verdienste um die vergleichende Sprachenkunde*, appropriately published in Saint Petersburg. I take such projects as Catherine's, which require institutional procedures, as 'institutionalized history'.

Institutions need not be heads of state; they include learned societies, and journals produced by those societies; repositories like the Archivo General de Indias or the British Museum or the Bibliothèque Nationale, Paris; commercial serial publications, such as the Bibliotheque Linguistique Américaine with which Lucien Adam was associated; and national museums and bureaus. To the extent that any of these institutions has a special public, to that extent, I think, we can detect what I have called institutionalized corridors of communication. And among current trends in linguistics we can detect a trend to analyze in detail such corridors.

Their existence can be inferred from various documents, published and unpublished, as well as from other sources. And bibliographic and biographical materials, works such as Pilling's *Proof-sheets* (1885) [which, unlike his later productions, contains much Ibero-American material] or the G. K. Hall reproduction of the cards indexing the Newberry Library's Ayer Collection, are being made available to ever-wider publics. Computerized bibliographies are also being compiled, coded for rapid information retrieval. And newsletters such as the *Andean Newsletter* of Gary Parker and Louisa Stark as well as restricted conventions of specialists in particular linguistic families add to the evidence of an information explosion. With this basis for analysis we can expect many stimulating contributions to the study of the relationships of linguistic historiographers to institutions.

TYPOLOGY AND GENETIC GROUPINGS

We have seen how in the nineteenth century two major historiographical interests came into focus, the typological and the genetic. Wilhelm von Humboldt gave priority to typology and the study of evolution in language. Recent studies of color categories and Huichol and Tzeltal ethnobotanical methods of categorization, such as the investigations of Price, Berlin and Kay, have begun to color native Ibero-American historiography once more with typological priority; but these modern studies move in counterpoint to genetic advances rather than against them. Humboldt disregarded the fact that French and Sanskrit belong to a single family, the Indo-European, and that French, the linguistic vehicle of Prussian aristocracy, represents a level of civilization far in advance of that of Rome say in the time of Caesar. He refused to see that civilization is independent of linguistic structure.

Since Humboldt represents a certain type of historiographer, and since we have attempted here to identify past and current trends in Americanist historiography in terms partly of channels of communication (a typological gambit), and since, moreover, the position of Chomsky and other generative theorists which leads to praise of Humboldt for his recognition of "linguistic creativity" seems to have been made in ignorance of the peculiar slant on creativity which Humboldt took, I find justification for a brief sketch of Humboldt as personality and as theorist.

We note first his influence in the institutional matrix of his time. He was elected to the Prussian Academy in 1810. He presented papers to that body, for example, "On the comparative study of language and its relation to the different epochs of the development of languages" (1820) and "On the province of the historian" (1821). He read papers in Paris and London, too, for example "On the affinity of the pluperfect, the reduplicating aorist, and the Attic perfect of the Greek, with the tense-formations of the Sanskrit" (read to the French Institute, 1828) or "On the best means of ascertaining the affinities of Oriental languages" (read to the Royal Asiatic Society of London, 1828).[1] Humboldt's academic presence and his typological interests had an immediate effect on the nature and direction of Americanist studies conducted by Europeans in the nineteenth century.

John Pickering, an American attorney and man of letters, author of a proposal for uniform orthography for North American Indian languages (1818, 1820), of an article on "Indian languages of America" for Francis Lieber's new *Encyclopædia Americana* (1831, 1836), and of other Americanist studies, held the view that European publication was important. Perhaps there is a touch of rue in his letter of February 19, 1834, in which he asked Lieber:

> Do you think, if I should make up a *Mémoire* on the general subject of the American Languages, that they would publish it in the Transactions of the Berlin Academy, or any other Society of that kind? What would my "friend" Humboldt say to such a proposal?

Eventually Pickering's "Americana" article was printed in Leipzig, in 1834, translated by Mrs. T.A. Robinson as "Ueber die indianischen Sprachen". But it could not have been to Humboldt's taste.

For Humboldt, all languages are essentially identical in the mind, in an ideal way. As different nations try to realize that ideal they succeed or fail, each in its own way. The intellect pulls toward uniformity but phonetic substance pulls toward differentia-

[1] See G.J. Adler 1866, pp. 9, 12, and C. Brandes 1841–52.

tion and idiosyncracy. Both intellect and formal rules shape the individual language. The articulation of thought, however, varies from language to language. Different nations manifest different degrees of intellectual power, of imagination, and of feeling, just as individuals do, with resultant imperfections in language.

Typology for Humboldt, then, means measuring each language against the ideal language. One counts excellent devices such as inflections and one counts defects such as lack of inflections.

Language is at its highest perfection when there is a perfect union of thought and sound, of phonetic and intellectual elements. Only the languages which come closest to the perfect mixture of the two elements of speech are proper media for great art, which requires "a complete representation of the ideal in its material form."

When a language has reached its formal culmination the nation turns from synthesis to use of the language. Use, by poets, historians and grammarians no less than by the general population, then gives the language its character. Forms and meanings, synonyms and syntax, and use in poetry and prose, in verbal art, all give the language its character.

Humboldt's typology was based on years of reading grammars of languages of the world. Not given to psychological experimentation, working in the laboratory of his mind as philosophers are wont to do, he concluded that the way in which a language forms roots, words and constructions indicates how thought and sound are peculiarly united, and how much energy, intensity and depth of synthesis are involved. With grammatical forms especially we have the axis or key to the categorization of our thoughts, he concluded, and he suggested that there are three methods of categorization: (1) inflection, (2) isolation and (3) agglutination.

For Humboldt, inflection is the best method of expressing form and thought together, showing relations, either by ablaut or accretions (*Anbildungen*), illustrated by *sing*, *sang*, *sung*, *song* and *to* love, lov*ing*, lov*er*, lov*ed* — both processes of symbolization, in which a root is tagged.

When a root is insulated, in contrast, we have isolation. Then only radical thoughts and sounds can be linked: the synthetic power of the language goes no further. The grammar offers no phonetic clues about the form classes of words; the intellect must operate independently, as with Chinese. The mind relies upon a sort of *grammaire sous-entendue.*

Agglutination takes a halfway position between isolation and inflection, as with Turkish, where suffixes give a trail of additions rather than accretions.

In sentence construction we have a fourth category, incorporation, in addition to the first three. When incorporation is used, the sentence is treated not as tied up in strings of relations (inflection) or as framed by intonation, rules of word order and markers (isolation) but is made whole by everything being incorporated into a single sentence-word, as in Mexican and other American Indian languages, where there is no gradual build-up of discrete parts.

For Humboldt the key parts of speech to examine in typologizing languages are conjunctions, relative pronouns, and most of all, verbs. But any language has all typological elements in various mixtures. Humboldt saw Sanskrit, Gothic, Greek, Latin, German and Hebrew as touchstones; but he did not fail to see the typological basis for rejecting certain Indo-European languages as inferior, and he did not provide grounds within his own writings for the Whorfist construct of "SAE' or Standard Average European.

Humboldt declined to scale languages in evolutionary perspective, through lack of data. He thought too that an exhaustive classification of languages was beyond reach, and he was willing to settle for a limited classification, tentative, for a special purpose, based say on verb morphologies and their implications regarding intellectual activity.

He ventured to guess, however, from man's nature and the elements of his language, that a language has three stages in its history: (1) primitive formal organization, about which we know nothing except that essential forms evolved; (2) culmination to a point at which literary character appears and at which change would destroy the peculiar structure of the language; and (3) decadence, with some degree of disintegration, stagnation, corruption, even extinction, a stage of intellectual triteness or enfeeblement from which only the heroism of geniuses can rescue a nation.

Humboldt said that language originated instantaneously as an organism. It was unfinished, crude, but all of a piece. There was for him no justification, then, in assigning a chronological order to the invention of all of the parts of speech. But some parts of speech are more primitive than others, to judge by their intellectual necessity. Thus the personal pronouns must have been used from the start, while the less essential interjections and prepositions were invented later.

Bopp distinguished between subjective roots and objective roots. Subjective roots referred to emotional matters, our feelings and emotions, so they must be part of the most primitive level. Objective roots which denote motion and quality must have been needed for personal expression also from the start.

In his earlier work, before he wrote the 'Einleitung' of his study of the Kawi language, Humboldt speculated on these phases of stage one:

Phase 1. Isolation and Incorporation. Objects are designated by isolated words or by whole sentence-words, and the mind has to supply relations for lexical items (which do not belong to parts of speech yet). Relational particles and word order, however, were used from the start. [In a letter to Abel-Rémusat, Humboldt propagated a form of cultural relativism which was destined to spread to the writings of American historiographers such as Gallatin. He said that those destined to be the best of languages probably began with 'real grammatical forms' because of the national intellectual superiority and genius for language of certain groups of men. Chinese is a case of arrested development, because of national intellectual inertness as well as phonetic poverty.]

Phase 2. The arrangements are regularized and the relational particles are eroded in sound and lose independence.

Phase 3. Agglutination. Unity increases as relational particles become loosely bound affixes.

Phase 4. Inflection. Roots take paradigmatic (purely relational) affixes and each word now represents a certain part of speech and is 'purely grammatical.'

Evolution in all languages was from monosyllabic words to polysyllabic words by compounding and affixation. One can read national character, moreover, from syntax. If an inflecting language uses 'grammatical words' (auxiliary verbs, for example, or prepositions which replace inflectional suffixes) its character changes. Practicality replaces imaginativeness; ingenious but tangled webs of agreement are replaced by easy comprehension. There is a purely intellectual and moral element which preponderates in some languages and nations. In others, the preponderant element is external and practical.

The science of linguistics thus enables man to evaluate his intellect, to explore external forms by the method of natural history, and to explore inner forms too, as facts of intellectual teleology. Even the worst language of a savage group is a sort of species, to study as an example of the universal genus.

Humboldt influenced his contemporaries in the lines of their research, and European work on Ibero-American languages in the nineteenth century sometimes mirrors the intellectual climate which he helped to establish. He drew up a program of research, and scholars followed his lead. An important avenue of investigation today must be the tracing of his influence on the linguistic descriptions of such scholars as Grasserie, Charencey, Duponceau and Gallatin.

Humboldt called for monographs on different languages and for comparative studies of a given part of speech. The aim was to frame an outline of human speech, to see how thought could be comprehended in its universal medium, to see the extent of thought in this medium, to establish postulates and laws of language and to see how they could be applied. As for the exploration of intellectual teleology, that could be accomplished only if a nation has a literature: for only through a literature could a national type of thought and feeling be manifested in language.

The linguist, Humboldt said, should catalogue languages on a scale of progress. He should show how some languages best advance the intellectual life and the ideals of the human race, and how these better languages have come from better nations, whose own life has been enriched by these better languages. How far and how well has the ideal of language been seized by various nations? A study of literature and culture is needed as the linguist advances to answer this question. For the *Weltanschauung* or world view of a culture is a reflection of its 'essential differences of intellectual development', and that is what must be analyzed, in studying the ideal goals of all human beings.

To the extent that Humboldt's influence was institutionalized in European and American corridors of communication there was a demonstration of the generalization which opens the preceding section of this essay. A seminal author stimulates hundreds of studies all of which bear upon the problems which he has identified. In recent years, ethnographic semantics of the sort popularized by Frake, Conklin, Berlin, Stefflre, Williams, and many others has mined a new vein of ore in the study of Mayan and other languages of Latin America.

Another vein was opened, if I may put it that way, in psycholinguistics, several decades ago. John B. Carroll, Director of the Southwest Project in Comparative Psycholinguistics of the Social Science Research Council (1955–56), initiated Project experimentation in communicative efficiency on a cross-cultural basis. Suppose we suspend a ball on a string and twirl it so that it moves in a certain pattern. Will a Hopi describe the pattern more efficiently, in communicating the event to another Hopi, than say a Navaho to another Navaho? This question and the philosophical problems which it exposes promise to stimulate more Uto-Aztecanist research, and perhaps research involving other American Indian languages as well.

A new trend has been initiated also by Bever and Langendoen (1971), whose research shows the value of psychological experimentation when coordinated with linguistic analysis. These authors have demonstrated a principle and techniques which have not yet been applied to American Indian languages but which promise to be as seminal in our time as were the dicta of Humboldt in the nineteenth and early twentieth centuries. Bever and Langendoen have shown that children are constrained by nature to understand and learn certain grammatical structures (and not some others which adults have). As the child encounters new sentences he experiences a kind of linguistic evolution in which systematically constrained neologisms interact with 'an ontogenetically shifting filter'.

We have, then, several new views of linguistic evolution which have colored recent research. It might be better to say that there are now several evolutionary perspectives to be studied, not just one which will turn out to be the best. The perspective developed by Morris Swadesh (1971) involves comparative grammar and historical reconstruction. That developed by Paul Kay (1971) incorporates some of Swadesh's vision but integrates ethnographic semantic data. Kay notes (1971:6) that the direction of linguistic evolution 'is from a non-autonomous to an autonomous system of communication'. Autonomous means 'suited to the communication of novel, exact, emotionally neutral information to a unfamiliar addressee' (1971:3). Kay integrates the findings of Berlin and Kay (1969) and Berlin (1971) in this new synthesis.

CONCLUSION

While an enormous amount of work has been done on Ibero-American languages by individuals and institutions, directions of research which have determined the sorts of things investigators respond to seem to form a limited number of patterns. A distinction must be made between history, mere production of chronicle, and historiography, discovery of the motives of historians which have determined the ways in which they have written their histories.

In the essay on native American historiography north of Mexico I have reserved a place for discussion of some matters which might as readily have been made part of this essay. An enumeration of monuments and institutions, repositories of data and the like, significant in the history of native Ibero-American linguistic studies, would inflate our discussion needlessly. Yet something should be said about sources which will enable the reader to make independent judgments about the thematic strands just exposed.

Part of the job is done in the bibliography, where annotations may be found. Part must be done, however, in the remainder of this discussion. To measure the scope of institutional involvement one might turn first to the *International Directory of Anthropological Institutions* compiled by the editors of *Current Anthropology*. This organ was established in 1957 with the aid of the Wenner-Gren Foundation for Anthropological Research (established in 1941). In the *Directory* are listed various stations of the Summer Institute of Linguistics, each the repository of much as-yet-unpublished linguistic data.

The Summer Institute of Linguistics has developed into a major institution in linguistic research, with investigations of over 500 languages around the world as part of its program. It began on a relatively large scale in the 1930's with work in Mexico, some of which has been reported in the journal *Investigaciones Lingüísticas*. Outstanding in the field of ethnolinguistic surveying is Key and Key, *Bolivian Indian Tribes* (1967). The Summer Institute maintains a computerized bibliography (Wares 1968, 1971a, 1971b).

Among other sources of information on institutions is the series called *The World of Learning*. In the nineteenth edition, for 1968–69 (London, Europa Publications, 1969), p. 382, to take an example, one finds:

Société des Américanistes: Musée de l'Homme, place du Trocadéro, Paris 16e; f. 1895; 450 members; Pres. M. Bataillon; Gen. Sec. J. Lafaye; publ. *Journal de la Société des Américanistes* (biannual), *Bibliographie américaniste* (annual).

For maps and bibliographies as well as files of extracts from various sources one might turn to the Human Relations Area Files in New Haven. Murdock and others (see the journal *Ethnology*) have computerized data from these files, though not much in linguistics; there is a basis, nonetheless, for computerized typological surveys which may some day involve native American languages on a large scale. Murdock has done a North American bibliography; for South American see O'Leary (1963).

Particularly valuable for researchers in native languages of Ibero-America are certain libraries, of which I will mention two with remarkable Latin American collections, that of the University of Texas and that of Tulane University. G.K. Hall has published the card catalogue of the Latin American Collection of the former, one of a number of similar productions, some of which will be listed in my next essay. I have mentioned other important libraries above; the list if continued would extend the present volume by a second.

Each institution, in fact, invites the writing of a separate book. How much could be written about the International Congress of Americanists, for example, its roots in French scholarship in the second half of the nineteenth century, and its career since its establishment in 1875! A number of books probably are being written about linguists of the past, sensitive to motive and milieu; aside from a biography and bibliography of Alphonse Pinart, however, issued by the Southwest Museum, and deficient in linguistic detail, I know of nothing in print in this figure-centered genre.

One of Albert Gallatin's passions was the Mexican calendar. His interest led to an article on the semi-civilized tribes of Mexico, reflecting a mass of notes (archived by the New York Historical Society) indicative of the problems of data-collection in his day. More will be said about him in the next essay.

Clavijero brought Mexican history to a wide public in Europe (1780–81, 1789); he helped Hervas, too, with linguistic data. Bibliographic data were published by Beristáin (1816–21), Squier (1861), Brasseur de Bourbourg (1871), Pinart (1883), Brinton (1883), and others, and by such exquisitely sensitive specialists in books as Icazbalceta (1866, 1886) and José Toribio Medina, Chile's most distinguished historian. Lord Kingsborough, an eccentric scholar, ruined himself publishing monuments of Aztec culture (King 1830–48), which he connected to Hebrew origins.

Along with these annalists and quasi-theorists we have to mention James C. Pilling, whose *Proof-sheets* (1885), recently made available in a facsimile edition, is an excellent source of bibliographic data, distinguished above all others of its century in its value to linguists. Pilling's bibliographies of North American language families were based on the *Proof-sheets*. One hundred copies were printed for loan to correspondents; ten were printed on one side of the leaf only, for use by friends of Pilling's who were librarians and who wanted them for paste-ups.

Pilling suffered from a wasting nervous disease. To read his correspondence (archived at the John Carter Brown Library) is to sorrow at his ambitions to do a Mexican bibliography, aided by his friend Icazbalceta and his correspondent Nicolás Léon. Pilling was by turns stimulated and disheartened by the project. When he died, Major Powell gave his records to George Parker Winship, hoping that Winship would complete the Mexican bibliography. Winship never did.

Among important classifications of languages of native Ibero-America the following are richer than most: Pimentel (1862–65, 1875), Orozco y Berra (1864), Lehmann (1920), Mason (1950), McQuown (1955), and Tax (1960). Among important recent bibliographical compilations which include classifications and maps are Tovar (1961) and Loukotka (1968). These last two open doors to many other distinguished sources.

BIBLIOGRAPHY

ADELUNG, FRIEDRICH VON. 1815. Catherinens der Grossen Verdienste um die vergleichende Sprachenkunde. St. Petersburg.

——. 1820. Uebersicht aller bekannten Sprachen und ihrer Dialekte. St. Petersburg.

——. 1824. Prospetto nominativo di tutte le lingue note e dei loro dialetti, tr. by Francesco Cherubini. Milano.

ADELUNG, JOHANN CHRISTOPH, and JOHANN SEVERIN VATER. 1806–17. Mithridates oder allgemeine Sprachenkunde mit dem Vater Unser als Sprachprobe in bey nahe fünfhundert Sprachen und Mundarten. Berlin. 4 vols. [Vol. 3 contains vocabularies, grammatical notes and texts for numerous American Indian groups. See Pilling's index of these materials (1885:4–7). [Further references to Pilling are to 1885.)]

ADLER, GEORGE J. 1866. Wilhelm von Humboldt's linguistical studies. New York.

BERISTÁIN Y MARTIN DE SOUZA, JOSÉ MARIANO. 1816–21. Biblioteca Hispano-Americana. Mexico. 3 vols.

BERLIN, BRENT. 1968. Tzeltal numeral classifiers: A study in ethnographic semantics. Janua Linguarum, Series Practica, 70. The Hague.

——. 1971. Speculations on the growth of ethnobotanical nomenclature. Language-Behavior Research Laboratory Working Paper No. 39. Berkeley.

BERLIN, BRENT, and PAUL KAY. 1969. Basic color terms: Their universality and evolution. Berkeley.

BESTERMAN, T. 1935. The beginnings of systematic bibliography. Oxford.

BEVER, T.G., and D.T. LANGENDOEN. 1971. A dynamic model of the evolution of language. Linguistic Inquiry 2.433–63.

BLACKSTONE, SIR WILLIAM. 1765–69. Commentaries on the laws of England. 4 vols. London.

BRANDES, C., ed. 1941–52. Willhem von Humboldts Gesammelte Werke. 7 vols. Berlin.

BRASSEUR DE BOURBOURG, CHARLES ÉTIENNE. 1871. Bibliothèque Mexico-Guatémalienne. Paris. [A. Pinart purchased most of these works.]

BRINTON, DANIEL G. 1883. Aboriginal American authors and their productions; especially those in the native languages. A chapter in the history of literature. Philadelphia.

——. 1891. The American race: A linguistic classification and ethnographic description of the native tribes of North and South America. New York.

CLAVIJERO, FRANCISCO JAVIER. 1780–81. Storia antica del Messico, cavata da' migliori storici Spagnuoli, e da'manoscritti, e dalle pitture antiche degl' Indiani. Cesena. 4 vols.

——. 1789. Storia della California. Venezia. [On Baja California.]

GESNER, KONRAD. 1555. Mithridates: De differentiis linguarum, tum veterum, tum quæ hodie apud diversas nationes in toto orbe terrarum in usu sunt. Tiguri. [An account of 130 languages, with the first commercial collection of Lord's Prayers.]

GREENBERG, JOSEPH H. 1960. The general classification of Central and South American languages. Men and cultures, Selected papers of the Fifth International Congress of Anthropological and Ethnological Sciences, A.F.C. Wallace, ed., pp. 791–4. Philadelphia. [Greenberg's classification focuses on eight groups: Macro-Chibchan, Andean-Equatorial, Ge-Pano-Carib, Tarascan, Hokan, Penutian, Aztec-Tanoan and Otomanguean.]

HERVAS, LORENZO DE. 1778–85. Idea dell' universo che contiene la storia della vita dell'uomo. Cesena. [A series of 18 vols. was later extended to 22. Hervas's collections in Rome have been catalogued, annotated and indexed by Fr. Miguel Batllori, S.J. The materials are in the Archivo Romano de la Compañia de Jesús (*Opp. NN.* 342 [*olim* Jap. Sin. III.9]), the Biblioteca Apostolica Vaticana (*Vat. lat.* 9801, 9802, 9803), the Archivio di Stato (Ms. 229/14, ff. 312–29) [this and *Vat. lat.* 9803 have no American linguistics] and the Biblioteca Nazionale (Ms. gesuitico 1074).]

——. 1784. Catalogo delle lingue conosciute e notizia della loro affinità, e diversità. Vol. 17 of Idea dell'Universo. Cesena. [The languages have been indexed in Pilling 1885:337. This volume was enlarged to 6 vols., published in Spanish in Madrid, 1800–05.]

——. 1785. Origine, formazione, meccanismo, ed armonia degl'idiomi. Vol. 18 of Idea dell'Universo. Cesena. [Presents supposed evidence of diffusion of tribes from the Tower of Babel.]

——. 1786. Aritmetica delle nazioni e divisione del tempo fra l'orientali. Vol. 19 of Idea dell'Universo. Cesena. [Index of language and contents, Pilling 1885:338.]

. 1787a. Vocabolario poligloto con prolegomini sopra più di CL. lingue, ed utili all'antica storia dell'uman genere, ed alla cognizione del meccanismo delle parole. Vol. 20 of Idea dell'Universo. Cesena. [Only a few American Indian words passim.]

——. 1787b. Saggio pratico delle lingue con prolegomeni, e una raccolta di orazioni dominicali in più di trecento lingue, e dialetti, con cui si dimostra l'infusione del primo idioma dell'uman genere, e la confusione delle lingue in esso poi succeduta, e si additano la diramazione, e dispersione della nazioni con molti risultati utili alla storia. Vol. 21 of Idea dell'Universo. Cesena. [Index of languages and contents, Pilling 1885:339.]

——. 1800–05. Catálogo de la lenguas de las naciones conocidas, y numeracion, division, y clases de estas según la diversidad de sus idiomas y dialectos ... Volúmen I [-VI]. Lenguas y Naciones Americanas. Madrid. 6 vols.

HUMBOLDT, WILHELM VON. 1836–39. Ueber die Kawi-Sprache auf der Insel Java, ed. by J.C.E. Buschmann. Berlin. 3 vols.

ICAZBALCETA, JOAQUIN GARCÍA. 1866. Apuntes para un catálogo de escritores en lenguas indígenas de América. Mexico.

——. 1886. Bibliografia Mexicana del siglo XVI. Primera parte. Catálogo razonado de libros impressos en México de 1539 á 1600. Mexico. [The only part published. Icazbalceta (properly, García Icazbalceta) did a 16th century Mexican bibliography for Beristáin (1816), pp. 307–67.]

JÜLG, B. 1847. Literatur der Grammatiken, Lexica und Woertersammlungen aller Sprachen der Erde, Von Johann Severin Vater. Zweite völlig umgearbeitete ausgabe von B. Jülg. Berlin.

KAY, PAUL. 1971. Language evolution and speech style. [A paper based on one read to the American Anthropological Association, New York City, 1971.]

KEY, HAROLD, and MARY KEY. 1967. Bolivian Indian tribes: Classification, bibliography and map of present language distribution. Summer Institute of Linguistics Publications in Linguistics and Related Fields, No. 15. Norman.

KING, EDWARD (LORD KINGSBOROUGH). 1830–48. Antiquities of Mexico. London. 9 vols.

KLAPROTH, HEINRICH JULIUS VON. 1823. Asia polyglotta. Paris.

LATHAM, ROBERT GORDON. 1851. *Man and his migrations.* London.

——. 1860. Opuscula: Essays, chiefly philological and ethnographical. London.

LEHMANN, WALTER. 1920. Zentral-Amerika. Die Sprachen Zentral-Amerikas. Berlin. 2 vols.

LOUKOTKA, ČESTMIR. 1968. Classification of South American Indian languages. Latin American Center, UCLA, Ref. Ser., ed. by Johannes Wilbert, Vol. 7. Los Angeles. [The map is said to show 1,492 languages on a scale of 134.2 mi. =1 in. The bibliography has 2,201 references up to 1964 (346 of them to unpublished mss.), for 117 stocks and isolated languages.]

MASON, J. ALDEN. 1950. The languages of South American Indians. BAE-B 143, Pt. 6, pp. 157–317. Washington, D.C. [Attention to 65 families.]

MCQUOWN, NORMAN A. 1955. The indigenous languages of Latin America. AmA 57.501–70. [Attention to 17 large families, 38 lesser ones, and 682 unclassified.]

——. 1967. Handbook of Middle American Indians, Vol. 5. Austin.

O'LEARY, TIMOTHY J. 1963. Ethnographic bibliography of South America. New Haven.

ORBIGNY, ALCIDE DESALLINES D'. 1839. L'homme américain (de l'Amerique Méridionale), considéré sous ses rapports physiologiques et moraux. Paris. 2 vols. and atlas.

OROZCO Y BERRA, MANUEL. 1864. Geografía de las lenguas y carta ethnográfica de México, precedidas de un ensayo de clasificación de las mismas lenguas y de apuntes para las inmigraciones de las tribus. Mexico. [Contents enumerated by Pilling 1885, 559–60.]

PALLAS, PETER SIMON, 1786–89. Linguarum totius orbis vocabularia comparativa. Petropoli. [A word list with 286 items was used.]

PICKERING, JOHN. 1818. On the adoption of a uniform orthography for the Indian languages of North America. American Academy of Arts and Sciences 4(2). 319–60. Boston. [Issued separately, Cambridge, 1820.]

——. 1831. Indian languages of America. Encyclopaedia Americana 6.581–600. Philadelphia. [Issued separately in German: Leipzig, 1834; and in English: Philadelphia, 1836.]

——. 1834. Letter to Francis Lieber, Feb. 19, 1834. Ms., 2 pp., ALS, Huntington Library HM LI 2998. [The quotation is given from p. 1, with the kind permission of the Henry E. Huntington Library.]

PILLING, JAMES CONSTANTINE. 1885. Proof-sheets of a bibliography of the languages of the North American Indians. Washington, D.C. [Reprinted by Central Book

Co., Brooklyn, N.Y., 1966. For the major bibliographical sources of the period, see pp. xi-xxxvi.]

PIMENTEL, FRANCISCO. 1862–65. Cuadro descriptivo y comparativo de las lenguas indígenas de México. Tomo Primero [Segundo]. Mexico. [List of families by chapter heads, Pilling, 1885: pp. 587–8.]

——. 1875. Cuadro descriptivo y comparativo de las lenguas indígenas de Mexico, o tratado de filología Mexicana. Mexico.

PINART, ALPHONSE LOUIS. 1883. Catalogue de livres rares et précieux, manuscrits et imprimés, principalement sur l'Amerique et sur les langues du monde entier. Paris.

PRICHARD, JAMES COWLES. 1857. The eastern origin of the Celtic nations proved by a comparison of their dialects with the Sanskrit, Greek, Latin, and Teutonic languages. London.

RIVET, PAUL, and GEORGES DE CRÉQUI-MONTFORT. 1951–56. Bibliographie des langues aymara et kičua. Travaux et Mémoires de l'Institut d'Ethnologie, 51. Paris. [Vol. 1, 1540–1875; Vol. 2, 1876–1915; Vol. 3, 1916–40; Vol. 4, 1941–55.]

SALZMANN, ZDENĚK. 1970. Review of Classification of South American Indian languages, by Čestmír Loukotka. IJAL 36.70–2.

SOUTHEY, ROBERT. 1805. Madoc. London.

SQUIER, EPHRAIM GEORGE. 1861. Monograph of authors who have written on the languages of Central America, and collected vocabularies or composed works in the native dialects of that country. New York.

SWADESH, MORRIS. 1971. The origin and diversification of language, ed. by Joel Sherzer. Chicago.

TAX, SOL. 1960. Aboriginal languages of Latin America. Current Anthropology 1.430–6. Chicago. [McQuown's list amalgamated with Greenberg's classification.]

TOVAR, ANTONIO. 1961. Catálogo de las lenguas de America del Sud: Enumeración, con indicaciones tipológicas, bibliografía y mapas. Buenos Aires.

WARES, ALAN C. 1968. Bibliography of the Summer Institute of Linguistics, 1935–1968. Santa Ana.

——. 1971a. Bibliography of the Summer Institute of Linguistics. Supplement No. 1. Santa Ana.

——. 1971b. Bibliography of the Summer Institute of Linguistics. Supplement No. 2. Santa Ana.

YANKIEVITCH, FEODOR DE MIRIEVO. 1790–91. Comparative dictionary of all languages and dialects, arranged in alphabetical order. First [-fourth] part. St. Petersburg. [Title and text in Russian.]

PART THREE

CHECKLISTS

NORTH AMERICAN INDIAN LANGUAGES

HERBERT LANDAR

INTRODUCTION

This checklist is based largely on contributions of the Bureau of Ethnology of the Smithsonian Institution, particularly the bibliographies edited by James C. Pilling, the *Handbook of American Indians North of Mexico* (1907–10) edited by F. W. Hodge, and J. R. Swanton's *Indian Tribes of North America* (1952). These works should be consulted as a first step in cases where the present checklist fails to solve a given problem of identification.

More often than not, 'classifications' of languages have represented arbitrary or imaginary constructs justifiable in part as tags for programs of research rather than as reports on historical fact. I have felt free, therefore, to indicate in the directory of classifications superordinate constructs which conservative scholars might shrink from as claims about truth, but which they can have no qualms about accepting as estimates of range of interest. For that is all such terms as 'Hokan-Siouan' or 'Macro-Penutian' are intended to show, an estimate of range of interest. When *Yanan* is followed by *Hokan-Siouan* in the directory, no claim is made that a supposed Hokan-Siouan entity ever existed. All that is claimed is that if a scholar specializes in Yanan he will be more inclined to study languages called Hokan-Siouan, to vivify his attentiveness to his specialty, than languages which are not given under the Hokan-Siouan rubric.

In general, scholars have not taken pains to define the difference, in their usage, between 'language' and 'dialect'. In addition, classifications have been proposed with little support — we are rich in claims but poor in data. Support of claims with systematic information on phonological correspondences is rare. Such support by itself does not rule out borrowing as responsible for resemblances, and additional documentation, clinching data involving close semantic and morphophonemic resemblances, is essential. There are several reasons, then, for the policy I have adopted in the directory of classifications, of avoiding hyphens between names, and of using commas, semicolons and tiers of names as my own reaction to the views of others.

I have tried to use commas instead of hyphens in giving names under classificatory rubrics because hyphens can be ambiguous: *Mattole-Bear River* represents data on a single language (from a Mattole source and a Bear River source) while *Hokan-*

Siouan represents data on dozens of languages. When the situation permits, I drop hyphens, and produce such sequences as *Mattole, Bear River*. That a comma separates two terms means the difference between them is minimal, involving not much more than such lexical, morphological and semantic differences as can be mastered by a cross-comma speaker in a few weeks, given his pragmatic control of communicative situations. A semicolon indicates my guess that differences are more formidable.

In no case does the grouping of names constitute a claim that one family tree diagram is superior to another. Tree diagrams are convenient fictions, which prompt and guide research; sometimes they are less useful than other models. Krauss decries reification of trees by mythologists, a view properly stressed in this introduction, which anticipates a tree directory. I have included in this directory, as will be seen, classifications which belong to the history of American Indian linguistics and which therefore have special call upon our attention, issues of validity aside.

It is a pleasure to acknowledge, finally, support of the National Science Foundation and the John Simon Guggenheim Memorial Foundation in my collection of classifications and synonyms during bibliographic research. In recent years the setting for most of this research has been the Henry E. Huntington Library in San Marino, California. To the librarians, staff and fellow readers at the Huntington I owe a special debt of gratitude.

CLASSIFICATION

Adaizan. See Caddoan.
Algonquian.* Algonquian-Wakashan.
    Central-Eastern
        Central
            Cree, Montagnais, Naskapi
            Menomini
            Fox, Sauk, Kickapoo
            Shawnee
            Peoria, Miami, Illinois

* The classification shown represents an older tradition than that alluded to by Teeter in the present volume. It is always pleasant and exciting to learn of progress in comparative and historical studies, and we look forward to bibliographic and other clarifications which will resolve some of the difficulties offered the synonymist by the following list of Eastern Algonquian languages (from Teeter):
Eastern Abnaki
Western Abnaki
Carolina Algonquian
Connecticut, Unquachog, Shinnecock
Delaware
Loup
Mahican
Malecite, Passamaquoddy
Massachusett
Micmac
Mohegan, Pequot, Montauk
Nanticoke, Conoy
Narragansett
Powhatan

Potawatomi
Ojibwa, Ottawa, Algonquin, Salteaux
Delaware
Powhatan
Eastern
Natick, Narragansett, Wampanoag, Pennacook
Mohegan, Pequot, Wappinger, Montauk
Penobscot, Abnaki
Passamaquoddy, Malecite
Micmac
Western
Blackfoot, Piegan, Blood
Cheyenne
Arapaho, Atsina, Nawathinehena
Algonquian-Wakashan.[1]
Beothukan
Algonquian
Kutenai
Salishan
Wakashan
Chimakuan
Ritwan
Amuzgo. See Mixtecan.
Arawakan.[2]
Central American Carib
Asian-American. See Paleosiberian.
Athapaskan*. Na-Dene.
Apachean
Navaho, San Carlos, White Mountain, Chiricahua, Mescalero; Jicarilla
Lipan
Kiowa-Apache
Pacific Coast
Oregon
Euchre Creek, Coquille; Tolowa, Tututni, Chetco; Chasta Costa; Galice, Applegate
Umpqua
California
Hupa, Chilula, Whilkut
Wailaki, Kato; Mattole, Lassik, Nongatl, Sinkyone

[1] Sapir's rubric for the units shown. In 1951–60 Haas linked Algonquian and the Gulf languages and Tonkawa.
[2] A South American family represented in the Antilles and Central America by a language sometimes called Island Carib, Central American Carib or Black Carib.
* See also Addendum.

Northern

Tanaina (Outer Tanaina, Inner Tanaina); Ingalik (Anvik, Shageluk, Holy Cross, Middle Kuskokwim [Nikolai]); Nabesna; Ahtena (Outer Ahtena, Mentasta)

Koyukon (Inner Koyukon [Tanana Village, Stevens Village, Crossjacket, Kantishna, Roosevelt, Manley, Bearpaw], Outer Koyukon); Tanana (Upper Tanana, Central Tanana [Minto-Nenana]; Upper Kuskokwim [Nikolai]); Han; Tutchone (Northern Tutchone, Southern Tutchone, Snag, Kluane)

Kutchin (Ft. Yukon, Ft. McPherson)

Carrier (Stuart Lake, Babine, Ulgatcho [Lower Carrier]) .

Chilcotin (Alexis Creek, Anahim [?]); Nicola

Kwalhioqua; Tlatskanai

Western Canadian type

Kaska (Lower Post?), Tahltan, Tsetsaut; Tagish, Taku (?), Sekani (Ft. Graham [?], Ware [?])

Chipewyan type

Chipewyan, Hay River Slave, Yellowknife; Beaver, Sarsi, Mountain; Dogrib, Hare, Ft. Norman Slave, Bear Lake

Athapaskan-Eyak. Na-Dene.

Athapaskan

Eyak

Attacapan. Hokan-Siouan (?). See Gulf.

Atakapa

Aztec-Tanoan.[3] Macro-Penutian.

Uto-Aztecan

Kiowa-Tanoan (Tanoan-Kiowa)

Zuni (?)

Aztecan. See Nahuatlan.

Aztecoidan.[4] Uto-Aztecan.

Coran

Cora

Huichol

Nahuatlan

Nahuatl

Nahuat (incl. Pipil)

Pochutla

Beothukan. Algonquian-Wakashan.

Beothuk

Caddoan. Hokan-Siouan.

Caddo

[3] Sapir's rubric for the units shown.

[4] Mason's rubric for the units shown.

Caddo
Haina
Adai (?) [Powell's Adaizan]
Kitsai
Pawnee
Pawnee
Arikara
Wichita
Cariban.[5] Hokan-Siouan.
Karankawa
Paya (?)
Galibi
Chocoan (?)
Catawba. See Siouan.
Cayuse.[6] Penutian.
Cayuse
Chiapanecan. See Chorotegan.
Chibchan.[7] Macro-Chibchan.
Mason's picture:
Rama Corobici
Guatuso (incl. Corobici)
Rama
Talamanca (incl. Terraba, etc.)
Guaymi-Dorasque
Guaymi (incl. Penonomenyo)
Cueva-Cuna
Coiba
Cuna
Estrella type
Uren type
Voegelin's picture:
Eastern Chibchan (Central American type)
Rama
Western Chibchan
Guatuso
Gotane, Cocora (?)
Cuna
San Blas, Chicuna, Cueva

[5] Powell's Karankawan has been linked by Landar to Cariban, most of whose members are in South America.
[6] Powell following Hale used the rubric Waiilatpuan for Cayuse and Molale; Voegelin following Rigsby lists Cayuse and Molale as isolated languages.
[7] Chibchan is a cover-term for tenuously described and compared languages.

Talamanca
Bribri
Terraba
Boruca
Cabecar
Tucurrike-Orisa
Suerre
Guetar
Voto
Pacific Chibchan
Dorasque
Guaymi
Chimakuan. Algonquian-Wakashan.
Chimakum
Quileute
Chimarikan. Hokan-Siouan.
Chimariko
Chimmesyan. See Tsimshian.
Chinantecan. Oto-Manguean.
Chinantec
Chinookan. Penutian.
Lower Chinook
Clatsop
Lower Chinook
Upper Chinook
Wasco, Wishram
Cascades
Multnomah
Clackamas
Kathlamet
Chipaya-Uru.[8] Penutian.
Chipaya
Uru
Chitimachan. Hokan-Siouan.
Chitimacha
Chocoan.[9] Cariban or Chibchan.
Kimbaya
Choco
Northern Epera
Dabeiba, San Jorge, Rio Verde, Sambu

[8] Rivet tied these Bolivian languages to Arawakan; recently they have been tied to Mayan.

[9] Rivet linked Kimbaya and Choco as Cariban. Voegelin identifies Choco (of Panama, Colombia and Ecuador) as Chibchan.

Southern Epera
Saixa, Baudo, Rio Sucio, Tado, Chami
Waunana
Chorotegan.[10] Oto-Manguean.
Chiapaneco
Mangue
Dirian
Orotinan
Chumashan. Hokan-Siouan.
Purisimeño; Barbareño; Ynezeño; Ventureño
Island; Obispeño
Interior (?)
Coahuiltecan. Hokan-Siouan.
Coahuilteco
Comecrudo
Cotoname
Pakawa
Carrizo
Tamaulipec
Cochimi. See Yuman.
Coos. Penutian.
Hanis
Miluk
Copehan. See Wintun.
Costanoan. Penutian.
San Francisco
Santa Clara
Santa Cruz
San Juan Bautista (Mutsun)
Monterey (Rumsen)
Soledad
Saklan (?)
Cunan.[11] Cariban or Chibchan.
Cuna
Eskimauan. See Eskimo-Aleut.
Eskimo-Aleut. See Paleo-Siberian.
Aleut
Atka (Western Aleut)
Unalaska (Eastern Aleut)

[10] Thomas's rubric for the units shown was Chiapanecan. To these some have added Subtiaban despite Sapir's view of Subtiaba (Squier's Nagrandan) as Hokan; also added have been Orisi, Orotinya (same as Nicoya) and Cholutec.

[11] See Cuna under Chibchan. Thomas connected Cuna to Chibchan, Pinart to Cariban.

Eskimo[11a]
Yupik
Sirenik
Chaplino-Naukan
Pacific
Central
Inupiaq
Wales, King Island; Barrow, Inglestatt, Kotzebue Sound; Mackenzie River Delta, Coronation Gulf, Labrador; Thule, Greenland

Esselenian. Hokan-Siouan.
Esselen

Eyak. See Athapaskan-Eyak.

Galibi. Cariban.[12]
Carib (Galibi)
Kumanagoto
Tamanak
Chaima
Oyana
Palenke
Guaikeri
Upurui

Guaycuran. Hokan-Siouan (?).
Guaycura

Gulf.[13] Hokan-Siouan or Algonquian-Wakashan.
Muskogean
Natchez
Tunica
Chitimacha
Atakapa

Haida.[14] Na-Dene.
Skidegate

[11a] Eskimo dialects called Inupiaq have not yet been subgrouped; a geographical list of dialect labels includes Greenland: Ammassalik, East Greenland, Frederick VI Coast, Thule, West Greenland (including South Greenland); Labrador; Northern Alaska: Barrow, Inglestat, Seward Peninsula, Wales, King Island, Diomede (Kingingmiut, Bering Straits Innupiaq), Colville River, Kobuk River and Kotzebue Sound; Canada: Baffin Island, Caribou, Upper Kazan River, Coppermine or Copper Eskimo, Coronation Gulf, Kangerjuarmiut, Umingmaktormiut, Cumberland Sound, Herschel Island Eskimo (a trade jargon), Icy Cape, Iglulik, Inupiat or Inupiaq, Mackenzie (Chiglit or Mackenzie River), Melville Peninsula, Netsilik, Arviligjuaq, Simpson Peninsula, Ungava Bay.

Yupik covers (1) Sirenik; (2) Chaplino-Naukan (with Chaplino, including Chaplino of St. Lawrence Island; and Naukan); (3) Pacific Yupik (including Kodiak, Prince William Sound, Chugach, and Kodiak Aleut or Sugestun); and (4) Central Yupik (including Nunivak or Nunivarmiut, Nelson Island, Kuskokwim, and Mainland).

[12] These are South American languages relatable to Karankawa, and to other Hokan languages.

[13] The rubric of Haas for the units shown.

[14] Powell's Skittagetan.

Masset

Hokan.[15] See Hokan-Coahuiltecan and Hokan-Siouan.

- Shastan
  - Shasta
  - Achumawi, Atsugewi
- Chimariko
- Pomo
- Karok
- Yana
- Esselen
- Yuman
- Salinan
- Chumash
- Seri
- Tequistlatec
- Washo

Hokan-Coahuiltecan.[16] Hokan-Siouan.

Hokan-Siouan.[17]

- Hokan-Coahuiltecan
- Yuki
- Keres
- Tunican
- Iroquois-Caddoan
- Eastern Group
  - Siouan-Yuchi
  - Natchez-Muskogean

Huave. Penutian.

- Huave

Iroquoian. Hokan-Siouan.

- Northern Iroquoian
  - Mohawk
  - Oneida
  - Seneca, Cayuga, Onondaga
  - Wyandot
  - Tuscarora
- Southern Iroquoian
  - Cherokee

[15] The rubric of Dixon and Kroeber (1913–19) for the units shown.

[16] By 1920 Sapir had listed under this rubric the Hokan languages and the Coahuiltecan group. In 1925 he added Supanec (Subtiaba, Maribichicoa, Tlapanec). In 1953 Greenberg and Swadesh added Jicaque. In 1968 Landar assigned Karankawa, formerly supposed to be Coahuiltecan, to Cariban, adding Cariban to the Hokan list.

[17] Sapir's rubric for the units shown.

Iskoman.[18] Hokan-Siouan.
- Salinan
- Chumash

Jicaquean. Hokan-Siouan.
- Yoro
- Palmar

Kalapooian. See Kalapuyan.

Kalapuyan. Penutian.
- Santiam
- Yonkalla
- Tualatin

Karankawan. See Hokan-Coahuiltecan and Cariban.

Karok.[19] Hokan-Siouan.
- Karok

Keresan. Hokan-Siouan.
- Western Keresan
  - Acoma, Laguna
- Eastern Keresan
  - Cochiti, Zia, Santo Domingo, San Felipe, Santa Ana

Kiowa-Tanoan.[20] Aztec-Tanoan.
- Kiowa
- Tiwa
  - Taos, Picuris; Isleta, Sandia
- Tewa
  - San Juan, Santa Clara, San Ildefonso, Tesuque, Nambe, Hano
- Towa
  - Jemez, Pecos

Kitunahan. See Kutenai.

Klamath.[21] Penutian.
- Klamath
- Modoc

Koluschan. See Tlingit.

Kulanapan. See Pomo.

Kusan. See Coos.

Kutenai.[22] Algonquian-Wakashan.
- Kutenai

[18] In 1913 Dixon and Kroeber used this rubric for the units shown. In 1919 these units were added to the Hokan list.

[19] Powell's Quoratean.

[20] Powell listed Kiowan, represented by the Kiowa language, as a separate unit, and Tanoan as another. Harrington connected the two in 1910.

[21] Powell's rubric was Lutuamian. The rubric Klamath-Modoc has also been used for this group.

[22] Powell's rubric was Kitunahan. Also represented as Kutenaian.

Lencan.[23] Macro-Chibchan.
- Lenca

Lutuamian. See Klamath and Sahaptin.

Maidu.[24] Penutian.
- Nisenan (Southern Maidu)
- Northwest Maidu
- Mountain Maidu
- Valley Maidu

Macro-Chibchan.
- Chibcha
  - Chibchan
  - Misumalpan
    - Misumalpan
    - Paya (?)
    - Xinca
    - Lenca
  - Waican
- Paezan
  - Barbacoan
  - Choco (?)
  - Yunca-Puruhan
  - Jirajaran
  - Warao
  - Muran
  - etc.

Macro-Mayan.[25] (Mexican Penutian). Macro-Penutian.
- Mayan
- Zoquean
- Totonacan

Macro-Otomanguean.[26]
- Otomanguean
  - Otomian
  - Popolocan
  - Mazatecan
  - Triquean
  - Chorotegan
- Mixtecan
  - Mixtec

[23] Voegelin following Greenberg keeps Lenca and Xinca in separate families; others propose Xinca-Lencan with two languages, Xinca and Lenca.
[24] Powell's rubric was Pujunan.
[25] The rubric of Lehmann, McQuown and others for the units shown.
[26] Mason's rubric for the units shown just below. A more recent list follows.

Cuicatec
Amuzgo
Chinantecan
Chinantec
Zapotecan
Zapotec
Northern Mountains
Southern Mountains
Valleys
Chatino
Papabuco
Soltec
Revised:[27]
Otomanguean
Otopamean
Chinantecan
Zapotecan
Mixtecan
Popolocan
Chorotegan (Chiapanec-Mangue)
Amuzgo
Macro-Penutian.[28]
Penutian
Northern
Tsimshian
Sahaptian
Molale
Cayuse
Klamath
Coos
Yakonan
Oregon
Chinookan
Kalapuyan
Takelma
California
Wintun
Maidu
Costanoan
Miwok

[27] See *Handbook of Middle American Indians* [hereafter, *HMAI*], vol. 5, map facing p. 120.
[28] This rubric more than most indicates a range of special interest on the part of scholars, rather than well-documented genetic ties.

- Yokuts

- Aztec-Tanoan
  - Uto-Aztecan
  - Kiowa-Tanoan
  - Zuni (?)
- Mayan
  - Mayan
  - Chipaya-Uru
- Zoquean
- Totonacan
- Macro-Otomanguean

Manguean. See Chorotegan.
Mariposan. See Yokuts.
Matagalpan. See Misumalpan.
Mayan. Penutian.

- Huastecan
  - Huasteco
- Cholan
  - Chontal of Tabasco
  - Chol
  - Chorti
- Maya
  - Yucatec, Itza, Lacandone, Mopan
- Tzeltalan
  - Tzeltal
    - Bachahom, Highland Tzeltal, Lowland Tzeltal
  - Tzotzil
    - Chamula, Huixteco, San Andres, Zinacanteco
  - Tojolabal
- Chuh
- Kanjobalan
  - Jacaltec
  - Kanjobal, Solomec
- Motozintleco
- Mamean
  - Mam
  - Aguacatec [Aguacatec I]
  - Aguacatan, Chalchitan
- Ixil
- Tacaneco (?)
- Teco

Quichean

- Quiche

Cakchiquel
Tzutuhil
Uspantec
Rabinal (Achi)
Kekchian
Kekchi
Pocomchi
Pocomam
Mazatecan. See Popolocan.
Misumalpan (Mosumalpan). Macro-Chibchan.
Matagalpan
Matagalpa
Cacaopera (?)[29]
Mosquito (Miskito)
Tawira, Wanki, Honduran Miskito (Mam)
Sumo
Northern Sumo
Southern Sumo
Lencan[23]
Paya (?)
Xinca[23] (?)
Miwok.[30] Penutian.
Coast Miwok, Lake Miwok
Sierra Miwok
Southern, Central, Northern, Valley
Mixe-Zoque. See Zoquean.
Mixtecan.[31] Oto-Manguean.
Mixtec
Cuilapa, Cuixtlahuac, Mictlantongo, Montanyes, Nochiztlan, Tamazulaxa, Tepuzculano, Tlaxiaco, Xaltepec, Yanhuitlan
Cuicateco
Trique
Mizocuavean.[32] Penutian.
Mixe-Zoquean
Mixe (Mixe; Sierra Populuca, incl. Sayula)
Zoque (Zoque; Tapachultec I, Aguacatec II)
Huavean

[29] Thomas guessed that there were two dialects, following Sapper; Mason followed Thomas, but note that Heath calls Cacaopera a Sumo dialect.

[30] Powell's rubric was Moquelumnan.

[31] Amuzgo was deleted and Trique inserted by Longacre in 1966; but Voegelin includes both Trique and Amuzgo here. See Macro-Otomanguean.

[32] Mason's rubric for the units shown. See Longacre, *CTL* 4.322 (1968), however, and Tapachulteca in the Checklist.

Huave

Molala.[33] Penutian.

Molale

Cayuse

Moquelumnan. See Miwok.

Mosan.[34]

Wakashan

Salishan

Chimakuan

Quileute

Chimakum

Mosquitoan.[35] Macro-Chibchan. See Misumalpan.

Muskhogean. See Muskogean.

Muskogean.[36] Hokan-Siouan (?).

Western Muskogean

Choctaw, Chickasaw

Eastern Muskogean

Muskogee (Creek), Seminole

Hitchiti, Mikasuki

Alabama

Koasati

Mutsun.[37] Penutian.

San Juan Bautista

Carmelo (of the Eslenes)

Santa Cruz

La Soledad

Costano

Olamentke (Bodega Bay)

San Rafael

Talatui (Talantui)

Chokuyem (Tchokoyem)

Na-Dene.[38]

Haida

Continental Na-Dene

Tlingit

[33] Powell following Hale listed the units shown under the rubric Waiilatpuan. See Cayuse.

[34] Frachtenberg's rubric (1920) for the units shown. See Algonquian-Wakashan. Swadesh grouped Wakashan with Eskimo-Aleut in 1962.

[35] Adam refused to classify Mosquito as Cariban *or* Chibchan. Thomas saw Mosquito as either Cariban or weighted with Carib elements, from which fact Hokan affiliation is suggested.

[36] Grouping Alabama and Koasati as Coushatta is debated. Here we follow Haas, who has added Natchez, Tunica, Chitimacha and Atakapa and has connected Proto-Muskogean to Proto-Algonquian.

[37] Term used for languages now called Costanoan and Miwok. Gatschet in 1877 listed the units shown as Mutsun (or Rumsen or Runsien).

[38] Sapir's rubric for the units shown. Also spelled Nadene.

Athapaskan-Eyak

Nahuatlan.[39] Uto-Aztecan.

Acaxee
Aztec (Mexican, incl. Meztitlaneca, Cuitlateco, Tlaxcala)
Cazcan
Concho
Cora
Huichol (and Guachichil)
Lagunero (?)
Nio
Niquiran
Opata (Teguima)
Pima
Pipil (with Alaguilac and Tlaxcalteca)
Sigua
Tarahumare
Tepahue
Tepecano
Tepehuane
Yaqui (Cahita)
Zacateco
Zoe (Troe)

Natchesan.[40] Hokan-Siouan (?).

Natchez (Na'htchi)
Taensa

Olivean.

Olive

Oto-Manguean.[41] Macro-Otomanguean.

List One:
Proto-Popotecan (Proto-Popolocan-Mixtecan)
Popolocan
Mixtecan
Proto-Popo-Manguean
Popolocan
Mixtecan
Chiapanec-Manguean (Chorotegan)

List Two:
Otopamean

[39] Thomas's rubric for the units shown. These languages have been grouped since as Piman, Taracahitian and Aztecoidan.

[40] Powell's rubric for the units shown. In 1924 Swanton connected Powell's Natchesan and Muskhogean as Natchez-Muskogean. See Muskogean.

[41] The first list shows subgroups discussed by Longacre, *HMAI* 5.130–5. The second shows items given on the map facing p. 120 of Longacre's article.

            - Pame
            - Chichimeca-Jonaz
            - Otomi
            - Mazahua
            - Matlazinca
        - Chinantecan
        - Zapotecan
        - Mixtecan
        - Popolocan
        - Chorotegan
        - Amuzgo

Otomian.[42] Macro-Otomanguean.

- Thomas:
    - Otomi
    - Pame
    - Mazahua
    - Pirinda (Matlazinca)
- Voegelin:
    - Central Otomian
        - Otomi
        - Mazahua
    - Southern Otomian
        - Ocuiltec
        - Matlatzinca
    - Northern Otomian
        - Chichimeca-Jonaz
        - Pame

Otopamean.[43] (Otomi-Pame). Macro-Otomanguean.

- Central Otomian
    - Otomi
    - Mazahua
- Southern Otomian
    - Matlazinca
    - Ocuiltec
- Chichimec (Chichimeca-Jonaz)
- South Pame
    - Jiliapan, Pacula; Tilaco
- North Pame
    - Ciudad del Maiz, Alaquines, La Palma, Gamotes; Santa Maria Acapulco

Palaihnihan. Hokan-Siouan.

- Atsugewi

[42] Two lists for this rubric are shown, those of Thomas and Voegelin.

[43] Soustelle in 1937 did basic classificatory work. Manrique, *HMAI* 5.332–3, lists units which differ slightly from those given above under Oto-Manguean. We follow Manrique here,

Achumawi
Adjumawi, Atwandjini, Ilmawi, Hammawi
Paleosiberian.[44]
Western (Yeniseian)
Ket
Kot
Asan
Arin
Eastern
Luorovetlan
Chukchi
Koryak
Kamchadal
Yukaghir (incl. Chuvanets)
Gilyak
Pame. See Otopamean.
Payan. See Cariban and Macro-Chibchan.
Penutian. See Macro-Penutian.
Piman. Uto-Aztecan.
Pima Alto
Papago (incl. Pima)
Piato
Himeri
Pima Bajo
Nevome
Ure
Yecora
Tepehuan
Northern Tepehuan
Southern Tepehuan
Southern Tepehuan
Tepecan
Pomo.[45] Hokan-Siouan.
Southeastern
Southeastern Pomo
Eastern
Eastern Pomo
Northeastern
Northeastern Pomo
Western-Southern

[44] This group is not North American. It is listed because various scholars have suggested links with Eskimo-Aleut.

[45] Powell's rubric was Kulanapan.

Northern
Northern Pomo
Kashaya
Central Pomo
Kashaya (Southwestern Pomo)
Southern Pomo
Popolocan. Oto-Manguean.
Popoloc
Popoloca
Popoloca
Chocho
Ixcatec
Mazatec
Huatla de Jimenez
San Jeronimo Tecoatl
Mazatlan de Flores
San Miguel Soyaltepec
Popotecan.[46] Oto-Manguean.
Mixtecan
Amuzgo
Mixtecan
Mixtec
Cuicatec
Trique
Popolocan
Popoloc
Ixcatec
Popoloc
Chocho
Mazatec
Pujunan. See Maidu.
Queen Charlotte's Island. See Haida under Na-Dene.
Quichoid.[47] Mayan.
Mam-Aguacatec
Mam
Aguacatec I (Coyotin)
Quichil
Quiche
Quiche
Cakchiquel
Tzutuhil

[46] Gudschinsky's rubric (1959) for the units shown. See Popolocan.
[47] Mason's rubric for the units shown. See Mayan.

      - Uspantec
    - Ixil
  - Kekchom
    - Kekchi
    - Pokom
      - Pokomam
      - Pokonchi
- Quoratean. See Karok.
- Rama. Macro-Chibchan.
  - Rama
- Ritwan.[48] Algonquian-Wakashan.
  - Yurok
  - Wiyot
- Sahaptian.[49] Penutian.
  - Sahaptin
    - Northern Sahaptin
      - Northwest Sahaptin
        - Yakima, Klikitat, Kittitas, Upper Cowlitz, Upper Nisqually
      - Northeast Sahaptin
        - Walla Walla, Wanapam, Wawyukma, Peloos
      - Columbia River
        - Umatilla, Rock Creek, Tenino, John Day, Celilo, Tygh Valley
    - Nez Perce
  - Waiilatpu [see Cayuse above]
    - Molale
    - Cayuse
  - Lutuami
    - Klamath
    - Modoc
- Salinan. Hokan-Siouan.
  - Antoniano
  - Migueleño
  - Playano (?)
- Salishan. Algonquian-Wakashan.
  - Bella Coola
    - Bella Coola
  - Coast Salish

[48] Sapir's rubric for the units shown. Powell's rubrics were Weitspekan and Wishoskan. The term Ritwan suggests closer ties than have been demonstrated, but Yurok and Wiyot are generally recognized as Algonquian entities.

[49] In 1931 Jacobs united Powell's Shahaptian, Waiilatpuan and Lutuamian. In 1956 Swadesh used the rubric Lepitan for this group. Some scholars use the term Sahaptin instead of Sahaptian, for Plateau Penutian. Hale in 1846 used Sahaptin for the Nez Perce language, and Walawala as a rubric for Klikitat, Yəkima and Peloos. See Cayuse above.

North Georgia
Comox
Sechelt (Sishiatl)
Pentlatch
South Georgia
Squamish
Halcomelem (Halkomelem, Lower Fraser River)
Nanaimo, Cowichan, Chemainus, Musqueam, Kwantlen, Katzie, Sumas, Chehalis, Chilliwack, Tait
Lkungen (Straits)
Lummi; Songish; Clallam, Saanich, Semiahmoo, Samish
Nootsack
Puget Sound (Southern Puget Sound Salish)
Skagit, Duwamish, Snoqualmie, Snohomish, Nisqualli
Hood Canal
Twana
Olympic
Cowlitz, Upper Chehalis (Chehalis), Satsop
Lower Chehalis, Quinault
Oregon Salish
Tillamook, Siletz
Interior Salish
Lillooet (Chin)
Thompson; Shuswap
Okanagon, Colville, Sanpoil (Nespelim), Lake; Kalispel, Pend d'Oreille, Flathead, Sematuse, Plains Salish
Wenatchi, Columbia (Middle Columbia), Peshkwaus (Piskwaus)
Coeur d'Alene
Santa Barbara.[50] Hokan-Siouan.
Northern
San Luis Obispo
San Antonio
Southern
Santa Inez
Santa Barbara; Kasuá (Cieneguita)
Santa Cruz Island
Sastean. See Shastan.
Serian. Hokan-Siouan.
Seri
Guayma
Upanguayma

[50] Gatschet's rubric (1877) for Chumash languages.

Shahaptian. See Sahaptian.
Shastan.[51] Hokan-Siouan.
    Shasta
    New River Shasta
    Konomihu
    Okwanuchu
Shoshonean. See Uto-Aztecan.
Siouan. Hokan-Siouan.
    Mississippi Valley
        Dakota
            Sisseton, Wahpeton, Santee, Yankton, Yanktonnais, Teton; Assiniboin
        Winnebago
            Winnebago
            Chiwere
                Iowa, Oto, Missouri
        Dhegiha
            Omaha, Osage, Ponca, Quapaw, Kansa (Kaw)
    Missouri River
        Crow
        Hidatsa
    Mandan
        Mandan
    Ohio Valley
        Tutelo
        Ofo
        Biloxi
    Eastern
        Catawba
        Woccon
Skittagetan. See Haida.
Straits of Fuca. See Wakashan.
Supanec. See Hokan-Coahuiltecan.
Subtiaban. See Supanec.
Takelma.[52] Penutian.
    Takelma
Takilman. See Takelma.
Tamaulipecan.[53] Hokan-Siouan (?).
    Tamaulipec

[51] Powell's Sastean and Palaihnihan were connected by Gatschet. Dixon in 1905 assented, and the rubrics Shasta-Achomawi and even Palaihnihan were used for the enlarged group.

[52] Powell's rubric was Takilman. In 1969 Shipley, *IJAL* 35.226–30, put Takelma and Kalapuya (using Yoncalla, Santiam and Tfalati data) under the rubric Takelman.

[53] Thomas's rubric for the unit shown. Later scholars have assigned this unit (with an uncertain number of members) to Coahuiltecan.

Tanoan. See Kiowa-Tanoan.
Taracahitian.[54] Uto-Aztecan.
  Tarahumaran
    Tarahumare
  Cahitan
    Cahita
      Yaqui
      Mayo
    Tepahue
      Tepahue
      Conicari
    Tahue
    Guasave
    Varohio (?)
    Acaxee (?)
    Xixime (?)
    Ocoroni (?)
Tarascan.
  Tarascan
Tequistlatecan. Hokan-Siouan.
  Tequistlatec (Chontal of Oaxaca)
    Highland (Mountain Tequistlatec)
    Huamelultec
Timuquan.[55] Hokan-Siouan (?).
  Timucua
Tlapanecan. See Supanec under Hokan-Coahuiltecan.
Tlingit.[56] Na-Dene.
  Tlingit
Tonikan. Hokan-Siouan (?). See Gulf and Tunican.
  Tunica
Tonkawan.[57] Hokan-Siouan (?). See Algonquian-Wakashan.
  Tonkawa
Totonacan.[58] Macro-Penutian.
  Totonac
  Tepehua
Triquean. See Oto-Manguean.

[54] Mason's rubric for the units shown. *HMAI* lists 42 Taracahitian languages; all but four of these, however, are extinct, and data are lacking for most of them.
[55] Powell's rubric was Timuquanan. In 1929 Sapir suggested tentative assignment to Natchez-Muskogean.
[56] Powell's rubric was Koluschan.
[57] In 1967 Hymes connected Tonkawa to Penutian.
[58] Orozco y Berra assigned Totonacan to the Mayan group. See Macro-Mayan.

Tsimshian.[59] Penutian.

- Tsimshian, Niska, Gitksan

Tunican.[60] Hokan-Siouan (?). See Gulf.

- Tunica
- Atakapa
- Chitimacha
- Bidai
- Deadose
- Opelousa

Ulvan. See Sumo under Misumalpan.

Uchean. See Yuchi.

Uto-Aztecan.[61] Aztec-Tanoan.

- Voegelin:
  - Plateau Shoshonean
    - Mono
    - Bannock type
      - Bannock, Snake, Northern Paiute (Paviotso)
  - Shoshoni type
    - Shoshoni, Gosiute, Wind River, Panamint (Koso)
  - Ute type
    - Ute, Chemehuevi, Kawaiisu, Southern Paiute

Pueblo Shoshonean

- Hopi

Sierra Nevada Shoshonean (Kern River Shoshonean)

- Tubatulabal

Southern California Shoshonean

- Gabrieleño, Fernandeño
- Luiseño
  - Luiseño; Pauma, Rincón, Pala, Temecula; Juaneño (?)
- Cahuilla
- Cupeño
- Serrano

Sonoran

- Opata
- Cahita

[59] Powell's rubric was Chimmesyan.

[60] In 1917 Swanton used the rubric Tunican for Powell's Tonikan as well as his Attacapan and Chitimachan. In 1929 Sapir put Tunica and Atakapa into a subgroup as against Chitimacha. In 1950 Swanton listed the units shown under the rubric Tunican.

[61] In 1913–15 Sapir put under this rubric Powell's Piman and Shoshonean and also some languages of Mexico. In 1934 Kroeber identified six subgroups, to which he added a seventh group comprising unplaced languages; his first three correspond to groups now classified by some scholars as Shoshonean, Piman and Taracahitian, and his fourth, fifth and sixth correspond to Aztecoidan.

Mason in his Utaztecan has two groups called Aztecoidan, Coran and Nahuatlan.

Two lists are given here, that of Voegelin and that of Miller.

Pima-Papago
Pima Bajo (Nebome)
Yaqui-Mayo
Tarahumara
Cora
Huichol
Tepehuan
Tepecano
Northern Tepehuane
Southern Tepehuane
Aztec (Nahuatlan)
Nahuatl (Mexicano)
Tetelcingo, Matlapa, Milpa Alta, etc.
Nahuat
Zacapoaxtla, etc.
Mecayapan
Pochutla
Pipil
Miller:[62]
Numic (cf. Plateau Shoshonean)
Tübatulabal (cf. Sierra Nevada Shoshonean)
Takic (cf. Southern California Shoshonean)
Hopi (cf. Pueblo Shoshonean)
Pimic
Papago
Northern Tepehuan
Southern Tepehuan
Tarahumara
Tarahumara
Varohio (?)
Cahita
Mayo
Yaqui
Corachol
Cora
Huichol
Aztec (cf. Aztec or Nahuatlan above)
Waïcurian.[63] Hokan-Siouan (?).
Waïcuri
Pericu

[62] Miller following Lamb lists nine branches (*UCPL* 48.11).
[63] Thomas's rubric for the units shown. Thomas's evidence is so slim that the units must be considered extinct, unclassified entities.

Waiilatpuan.[64] Penutian. See Molale and Sahaptian.

Molale

Cayuse

Wakashan. Algonquian-Wakashan.

Nootka

Nootka

Nitinat

Makah

Kwakiutl

Kwakiutl

Bella Bella (Heiltsuk)

Kitamat (Haisla)

Washoan. Hokan-Siouan. See Hokan.

Washo

Weitspekan. See Ritwan and Yurok.

Wintun.[65] Penutian.

Wintun type

Wintun, Wintu

Patwin type

Patwin

Wishoskan. See Ritwan and Wiyot.

Wiyot.[66] Algonquian-Wakashan.

Wiyot

Xincan.[67] Macro-Chibchan. See Lencan and Misumalpan.

Xinca

Populuca of Conguaco (?)

Yakonan.[68] Penutian.

Yaquina

Alsea

Siuslaw

Kuitsh (Lower Umpqua)

Yanan.[69] Hokan-Siouan.

Kroeber:

Northern Yana (Gari'i) [Northeastern Yana]

[64] Powell's rubric for the units shown. Powell followed Hale, who had no notes on structure and who recognized that Molale and Cayuse were 'perfectly distinct' in vocabulary except for numerals and pronouns.

[65] Powell's rubric was Copehan.

[66] Powell's rubric was Wishoskan.

[67] Mason's rubric for the units shown.

[68] Powell's rubric for the units shown. Frachtenberg teased out Siuslaw; Wissler grouped the first two as against the second two; neither move was well-documented.

[69] Under this rubric Powell set the language of the Nozi tribe. In 1925 Kroeber listed four groups, with an alternative list based on geography. Bruce E. Nevin suggested the alternative shown under his name, at the Hokan Conference held at San Diego in 1970.

Central Yana (Gata'i)	[Northern Yana]
Southern Yana (Gata'i ?)	[Central Yana]
Yahi	[Southern Yana]

- Nevin:
    - Yaana
        - Northern Yaana
        - Southern Yaana
    - Yahi
        - Northern Yahi
        - Southern Yahi

Yokuts.[70] Penutian.

- Valley
    - Southern
        - Yawelmani, Tachi
    - Northern
        - Chauchila, Chulamni; second group, unnamed, unlocated
- Foothill
    - Buena Vista
        - Tulamni, Hometwoli, Tuhohi
    - Poso Creek
        - Paleuyami, Kumachisi (?)
    - Tule-Kaweah
        - Yawdanchi, Wükchamni, Bokninuwad, Yokod, Kawia
    - Kings River
        - Choinimni, Chukaimina, Entimbich, Toihicha, Aiticha, Kocheyali (?); Gashowu
    - Northern Foothill
        - Chukchansi, Dumna, Toltichi (?), Kechayi, Dalinchi

Yuchi.[71] Hokan-Siouan.

- Yuchi

Yukian. Hokan-Siouan.

- Yuki
    - Northeast Yuki; Ukhotnom; Huchnom
- Wappo

Yuman.[72] Hokan-Siouan.

- Yuman
    - Yuma (Colorado River)
        - Yuma
        - Mohave
        - Maricopa

[70] Powell's rubric was Mariposan.

[71] Powell's rubric was Uchean.

[72] Some writers use the term Cochimi for all Yuman languages of Baja California. Mason's view of Yuman with two main subgroups, Yuman and Cochimi, is adopted here.

Kavelchadom
Halchidom
Walapai (Upland Arizona)
Walapai
Havasupai
Yavapai
Northeastern Yavapai, Southeastern Yavapai, Western Yavapai, Wipukapaya; Paipai (Akwa'ala)
Cocopa (Colorado Delta)
Cocopa
Kohuana
Halyikwamai
Diegueño (California)
Northern Diegueño (Mesa Grande), Southern Diegueño (Baron Long, Viejas), Campo, Mexican Diegueño (Imperial Valley, La Huerta)
Cochimi
Cadegomo, San Javier, San Joaquin; Laimon
Yurok.[73] Algonquian-Wakashan. See Ritwan.
Yurok
Yurumangui. Hokan-Siouan (?).
Yurumangui
Zapotecan.[74] Macro-Otomanguean.
Thomas:
Mixteco
Chocho
Amishgo
Chatino
Trike
Mazateco
Cuicateco
Zapoteco
Chinantec
Peñafiel:[75]
[Valle (?)]
Miahuateco
Pochutla
Yautepec

[73] Powell's rubric was Weitspekan.

[74] Thomas's rubric for what Pimentel called the Mixteco-Zapoteco family. Thomas, however, did not follow Pimentel and Belmar in listing Chinantec. Compare Thomas's list with that given s.v. Macro-Otomanguean.

[75] In 1887 Peñafiel used lexical subgrouping to identify nine varieties of Zapoteco; he published names for only eight, shown here. He used Mexican census vocabularies; hopefully these will be found and used to evaluate his work.

Tehuano
Choapeño
Villalteco
Tanetze
Ocotlan
Revised:
Southern (Miahuateco)
Cuixtla
Coatlán
Central
Valle (Ocotlan)
Istmo (Tehuano)
Northern (Villalteco)
Serrano (Ixtlan)
Nejicho (Nexitzo)
Cajono
Bijano (Vijana)
Voegelin[76]:
Southern Mountain (Miahuatlan)
Miahuatlan, Cuixtla, the Coatlanes, the Mixtepecs
Valley (Valley-Isthmus or Central)
Mitla, Teotitlan del Valle, Tule, Tehuantepec, Ejutla, Ocotlan, Zaachila
Northern Mountain
Sierra de Juarez (Ixtlan or Serrano)
Ixtlan, Ixtepexi, Macultanguis, Xaltianguis
Sierra de Villa Alta (Yalálag or Rincón)
Yalálag, Yatzachi el Bajo
Zoquean (Mixe-Zoque).[77] Macro-Penutian. See Macro-Mayan and Mizocuavean.
Mixe
Northern Mixe, Southern Mixe
Zoque
Copainala, Ocotopec, Ostuacan
Sierra Popoluca (Popoloco of Puebla)
Texixtepec
Sayula
Oluta
Zuni.[78] Penutian.
Zuni

[76] Voegelin following De Angulo and Freeland describes Zapoteco as one language, coordinate under the rubric Zapotecan with Chatino. Contemporary field workers, however, count eight or nine Zapotecan languages. Voegelin's 'main dialects' are given here, with indication of localities.

[77] Extinct languages listed under this rubric are Tapachultec I or Tapachula, and Aguacatec II. Sapper considered his Tapachulteca as a dialect of Mixe.

[78] Powell's rubric was Zuñian.

CHECKLIST

Each entry other than a cross-reference consists of an entry word; when possible this item is followed by a superordinate term which can be found in the directory of classifications, and after that, by data on location and population. Every index item in the bibliographies of James C. Pilling has been considered for inclusion in this checklist. Such index items are tied clearly and distinctly to linguistic data, as labels of such data, and in an ideal checklist complete information would be given. But it has not been possible in the time available to determine the exact reference of each of Pilling's terms. In such cases, the entry is incomplete. A certain number of terms collected from Pilling, on the other hand, has been subjected to synonymic reduction. Where synonyms (exactly equivalent or not) of interest to the linguist (as distinct from the ethnographer or ethnohistorian) are available, they are listed in alphabetic order in a column following the opening matter of the entry. This method of presenting data has been chosen because it permits of economy and compactness, reducing printing costs. In some cases I have included the name of a band or tribe for which no linguistic data are available, following Swanton, Hodge or some other source; such cases, however, are rare, though they are not without appeal to a larger audience of anthropologists.

Abnaki. Eastern Algonquian; 50 St. Francis Abnaki in Quebec (1962).
- Abanaki
- Abenaki
- Abenakise
- Abenaqui
- Albinaquis
- Caniba
- St. Francis
- St. John
- Tarratine
- Wawenoc
- Wewenoc

Acadian. Algonquian.

Acala. Mayan; extinct.

Acasaquastlan. Nahuatl; Honduran Republic.

Acatlan. Nahuatl; Puebla.

Acaxee. Uto-Aztecan, possibly Taracahitian (so Swanton); Sinaloa and Durango; extinct.[79]
- Topia

Achastli. See Rumsen, Mutsun.
- Achastlien
- Achastlier

[79] Pimentel (1874) gave Sabaibo, Tebaca and possibly Xixime as dialects of Acaxee. Swanton, *Tribes*, p. 614, prefers the label Taracahitian. He lists as divisions: Acaxee, Sabaibo, Tebaca, Papudo and Tecaya.

Achi. Quichean; extinct.
Achire. Taracahitian; extinct.
Achumawi. Palaihnihan; 10 to 100 in California (1962).
    Achomawi
    Achomáwi
    Pit River
    Pit River Valley
    Pitt River
Achumawi-Atsugewi. See Palaihnihan.
Acolapissa. Muskogean; extinct, 100? (1739).
Acoma. Keresan; 600 or more in New Mexico (1970).
    Acuco
Acuera. Unclassified; a Florida group which became extinct perhaps in the seventeenth century.
Adai. Caddoan (?); extinct, 27 in Louisiana (1825).
    Adahi
    Adage
    Adaihe
    Adaize
    Addaise
    Natao
Adaizan. See Caddoan.
Admiralty Inlet. See Tununirusirmiut.
Ado. Cochimi? Baja California; extinct.
    = Adac?
Aglemiut. Eskimo; N.W. Alaska. See Kuskokwim.
    Aglemoute
    Aglegmut
Aguacatec. Mamean; 8,000 in Huehuetenango department, Guatemala (1965).
    Aguacatan No. I
    Aguacatec I
    Chalchitec
    Coyotin
Aguacatec. Zoquean (Zoque); Guatemala; extinct.
    Aguacatan No. II
    Aguacatec II
    Aguacateca
Ahantchuyuk. Kalapuyan; extinct, perhaps 200 or more in Oregon (1780).
    French Prairie
    Pudding River
Ahome. Taracahitian; extinct.
Aht. See Nootka.
Ahtena. Athapaskan; 250 in Alaska (1970).
    Ahtená

Ahtinné
Atna
Atnaer
Atnah
Copper Indians
Mednofski
Mednovskie
Midnooski
Yellowknife

Ahuachapan. See Pokomam.
Ahualulco. Aztecoidan; Tabasco.
Agualulco
Ahualalco

Ais. Muskogean(?); S. E. Florida; extinct, 250? (1650).
Jece

Aiticha. See Kings River Yokuts.
Aivillirmiut. Eskimo; Canada.
Aivitumiut. Eskimo; Canada.
Ajumawi. Achumawi.
Fall River

Akokisa. Atakapa; extinct, 250 in Texas (1812).
Accokesaw
Arkokisa

Akudnirmiut. Eskimo; Canada.
Akuharmiut. Eskimo; Canada.
Akwa'ala. See Paipai.
Alabama. Eastern Muskogean; 200 to 400 in Texas (1962).
Alaguilac. Pipil; E. Guatemala on Río Motagua.
Alagüilac

Alaquines. See North Pame.
Alaska. Geographical term.[80]
Aleut. Eskimo-Aleut; Western Aleut, 100 in Alaska and 400 (including some Eastern Aleut on the Commander Islands, U.S.S.R.; Eastern Aleut, 600 to 700 in Alaska (1962); all Aleut, 650 (1970). Krauss gives 35 Western, 115 Central, and 500 Eastern Aleut (1970).
Aléoute
Aleutskie
Aliyut

Algon-Ritwan. Group with Algonquian, Wiyot and Yurok.

[80] Pilling, *Proof-sheets*, No. 1558b, reference to languages which have borrowed Russian words [V. M. Golovnin, 1861]; and reference, *ibid.*, to G.H. von Langsdorff, *Voyages and travels* (1813–1814), vol. 2, pp. 1–144, 219–46: words and names of Alaskan Indians, not otherwise identified.

Algic
Algonkian-Ritwan
Algonkian-Wiyot-Yurok

Algonkin. Algonquian; Quebec and Ontario, under 1,550 in 1900. See Algonquin.

Algonquian. Algonquian-Wakashan.
Algic

Algonquian-Mosan. Group with Algonquian (and Beothuk) and Kutenai and Mosan.
Algonkian-Mosan
Algonkian-Wakashan
Algonquian-Wakashan

Algonquin. Algonquian. See Algonkin.
Algonchina
Algonkin
Algonkine
Algonkinska
Algonquian
Algonquine
Old Algonkin

Aliche. Eyeish.

Alikwa. Data lacking.

Alliklik. Ventureño; California; extinct.

Alsea. Yakonan; extinct, fewer than 9 in Oregon (1930).
Alséya

Alta California. Geographical term.[81]

Amikwa. Algonquian; N. shore of Lake Huron, coming perhaps from Lake Nipissing in the seventeenth century; extinct.
Amihouis
Nez-Percés

Amuzgo. Otomanguean; Guerrero and Oaxaca, 11,066 monolinguals (1960).
Amishgo
Amuchgo
Amusgo

Andastes. See Conestoga.

Andreanowski. See Atkan.

Antoniano. Salinan; California; extinct, 1,000? (1814). See Migueleño.
San Antonio
San Antonio (de Padua) Mission

Anvik. Athapaskan; 300 in Alaska (1965). See Ingalik.
Anvik-Shageluk

[81] Pilling, Nos. 3577 and 3578, Lord's Prayer from Duflot de Mofras in J.G. Shea, *History of the Catholic Missions* (1855).

Apache. Apachean. See Chiricahua, Cibecue, Jicarilla, Lipan, Mescalero, San Carlos, Tonto, and White Mountain.[82]

Apatch

Apatsche

Apatsh

Apachean. Athapaskan.

Southern Athapaskan

Apalachi. Eastern Muskogean; originally in Florida; extinct: a remnant of 50 was recorded in Louisiana (1814).

Apalachee

Apalachian

Appalachian

Apalachice

Apalachicola. Hitchiti; originally in Georgia, later in Florida, Alabama and Oklahoma; extinct; 239 (1832).

Apanec. Unclassified; extinct; Mexico (?).

Api. Mayan; Chiapas.

Apay

Apayac

Applegate Creek. Athapaskan; Oregon; probably extinct before 1914.

Dakubetede[83]

Nabiltse

Arapaho. Algonquian; 1,000 to 3,000 in Oklahoma and Wyoming (1962).

Arapahoe

Arapoho

Arapohoe

Arrapaho

Arawak. Arawakan.

Arawack

Great Antilles

Island Carib

Arctic Family. Eskimo (?).[84]

Argalaxamut. Eskimo.

Arikara. Caddoan; 200 to 300 in North Dakota (1962).

Arikare

Arickaree

[82] Apaches at various times ranged southward from Canada along the eastern flanks of the Rockies possibly as far as southern Mexico. Pimentel's Mexican list (1874) includes Lipan or Faraon, Mescalero, Mimbreño (Coppermine), Navajo, Pinaleño and Xicarilla (Jicarilla); Orozco y Berra mentions also the Toboso. Pilling in 1885 confused Yumans called Apaches with Athapaskans; by 1892 he had decided on the following terms for indexing: Arivaipa, Chiracahua [sic], Coppermine, Coyotero, Faraone, Jicarilla, Mescalero, Mimbreño, Pinaleño, and Sierra Blanca (White Mountain) Apache.

[83] Swanton lists the Dakubetede as a division of the Umpqua.

[84] Pilling, No. 2840. Pilling used 'Arctic' for Eskimo in 1887.

Arickkara
Pani
Ricara
Riccara
Riccaree
Riccari
Rickarie
Rikara
Ris

Arin. Western Paleosiberian.

Aripe. Guaycura; extinct; Baja California.[85]
Aripa

Arivaipa. Apachean.
Aravaipa

Arveqtormiut. Eskimo; Canada.

Arviligyuarmiut. Eskimo; Canada.

Asan. Western Paleosiberian.

Asiagmiut. Eskimo; Canada.
Asiagmut

Assiniboin. Dakota (Yanktonai); 1,000 to 2,000 in Montana, Alberta and Saskatchewan (1962).
Assineboin
Assinee
Assinepoetuc
Assiniboels
Assiniboinice
Assiniboire
Assinneboin
Poetuce
Rocky Mountain Stoney Indians
Stone
Stone Boiler

Astariwawi. Achumawi.

Atakapa. Gulf; Texas and Louisiana; Eastern Atakapa was extinct after 1835; Western Atakapa was extinct after 1908.
Akokisa
Atacapa
Attacapa
Attakapa
Han

Ateacari. Uto-Aztecan; data lacking.

[85] Aripe belongs in a group with Loretano, Cora and Uchitie in Baja California, and should not be confused with Arizpe (Arispe), an Opata pueblo in Sonora.

Ateanaca. See Cora.
Atfalati. Kalapuya; Oregon; extinct, 44 (1910).
Atfálati
Tfalati
Wapatu
Athabaska. Term used for (1) Chipewyan, at Lake Athabaska, or (2) Cree (1795).
Athapuskow
Athapaskan. Na-Dene.
Athabascan
Athabaskan
Athapasca
Athapaska
Athapasken
Dèné
Dèné Dindjie
Northern Indians
Tinne
Tinné
Atka. Term applied to Central Aleut (Atka) and Western Aleut (Attu) settled on Atka in 1945; 75? Atkans and 25? Attuans on Atka (1950).
Atkan
Andreanowski (Islands)
Atklan
Attuan
Western Aleut
Atlaiaca. Nahuatl; Guerrero.
Atlin. Tlingit.
Atna. Term used for (1) Shuswap (Salishan), (2) Carrier (Athapaskan) or (3) Ahtena (Athapaskan).
Atnaer
Atnah
Atsina. Algonquian; under 10 in Montana (1962).
Ahahnelin
Ahnenin
Fall Indians
Gros Ventre
Atsugewi. Palaihnihan; 4 in California (1962).
Atsuke. Atsugewi.
Hat Creek
Attacapan. Gulf.
Atakapa
Attu. Western Aleut. See Atka.
Atwamsini. Achumawi.

Atzacualoya. Nahuatl; Guerrero.
Auk. Tlingit; 279 in Alaska (1890).
Avoyel. Unclassified; Louisiana; extinct, 2 or 3 (1805).
 Avoyelles
 Little Taensa
 Tassenocogoula
Ayook. See Mixe.
Ayutla. Mixtec.
Aztec. See Nahuatl.
Aztecan. Uto-Aztecan.
 Aztekic
 Nahuatlan
Aztecoidan. Uto-Aztecan.
 Aztecoid
Aztec-Tanoan. Macro-Penutian.
 Azteco-Tanoan
 Nahua-Tanoan
Babine. Athapaskan. The Babine are a subdivision of the Carrier, q.v.
Bachahom. Tzeltal.
Baciroa. Taracahitian; Mexico south of the Conicari and between the Tehueco and the Mayo; extinct.
Baffin Bay. Eskimo.
Bagaz. Aztecoidan; Costa Rica; extinct.
 Bagaces
Baimena. Taracahitian; Sinaloa; extinct.
Bainoa. Arawakan (?); Haiti; extinct.
Baker Lake. Eskimo; W. Hudson's Bay, Canada.
 QaiRniRmiut
Bamoa. See Cahita.
Bannock. Plateau Shoshonean (Numic); range formerly S. E. Idaho, N. W. Colorado, N. Utah, W. Wyoming, S. W. Montana, and Oregon; fewer than 20? (1970).
 Bannack
 Diggers
 Northern Paiute
Barbacoan. Paezan.
Barbara. Unidentified.[86]
 Canal de Santa Barbara
Barbareño. Chumashan; California; extinct in 1965.
 Santa Barbara
Barrow. Eskimo; Alaska.
 North Alaska

[86] Pilling, No. 165: vocabulary of a language at Santa Barbara, California.

Basopa. Unclassified; Sinaloa; extinct.
Batemdakaii. Kato.
    Batemdakaice
Bathurst. Eskimo.
Baturogue. Unclassified; Sonora; extinct.
Baudó. Chocoan.
Bear Lake. Athapaskan; Mackenzie.
    Bearlake
Bear River. Term refers to (1) an extinct Athapaskan group of California, dialectically close to Mattole; 23 (1937), or (2) an extinct Algonquian group of North Carolina (also called Bay River Indians); 200? (1709).
Beaver. Athapaskan; 300 in British Columbia and Alberta (1962).
    Biber
    Castors
    Tsattine
Bella Bella. See Hailtsuk.
Bella Coola. Salishan; 200 to 400 in British Columbia (1962).
    Belacoola
    Belhoola
    Bellacoola
    Bellechoolo
    Bilechula
    Bilkula
    Billechoola
    Billechoula
    Billechula
    Bilqula
    Friendly Village
    Salmon River
    Tallion Nation
Beothuk. Beothukan; Newfoundland; perhaps extinct about 1827.
    Beothuc
    Bethuck
    Bethuk
    Newfoundland
    Red Indians
Beothukan. Algonquian-Wakashan.
Bering Island Aleut. Central Aleut.
Bidai. Attacapan (?); Texas; extinct, fewer than 100 (1850).
Bijano. Northern Zapotecan.
    Vijana

Biloxi. Ohio Valley Siouan; ranged in Mississippi, Louisiana, Texas and Oklahoma; 6 to 8 (1908), perhaps less than 8 in Rapides Parish, Louisiana (1950). Language extinct after 1934.

Blackfoot. Algonquian; 5,000 to 6,000 in Montana, Alberta and Saskatchewan (1962).
    Blood
    Blood Blackfoot
    Earchethinue
    Pedum-Nigrorum
    Pieds-Noirs
    Piegan
    Sastica
    Sastika
    Sastikaa
    Schwarzfüssige
    Siksika

Blanco. See Boribi.

Blood. Algonquian. See Blackfoot.
    Kainah

Bodega. Coast Miwok; 1 in California (1962).
    Bodega Bay
    Olamentke
    Olamentko

Bokninuwad. Tule-Kaweah Yokuts.

Boribi. Possibly Bribri, but data are lacking.[87]
    Blanco

Borique. Mayan (?); extinct.[88]

Borjeño. Cochimi; Baja California; extinct.
    Borjeno
    San Borgia
    San Borja
    San Francisco Borja
    San Francesco Borgia Mission
    San Francisco de Borgia

Boruca. Chibchan (Talamanca); S. E. Costa Rica.
    Bronka
    Brunca
    Brunka

[87] Pilling, No. 3617, Blanco numerals, and No. 3974a, a vocabulary published by Valentini.

[88] Identified by Pimentel (1874) as an extinct Mayan language. Probably not the same as Burica, a Chibchan language.

Bribri. Chibchan (Talamanca); Panama and Costa Rica.[88a]
Bristol Bay. Eskimo.
Brotherton. Term for various Algonquian refugee groups in New York, 1788–1833.
Brulé. See Dakota.
Brunka. See Boruca.
    Brunca
Brunswick. Data lacking.[89]
Buena Vista. Foothill Yokuts.
Burica. Chibchan (Dorasque); S. W. Panama and nearby Costa Rica.
Cabecar. Chibchan (Talamanca); inland E. Costa Rica.[88a]
Cacaopera. Matagalpan; N.E. El Salvador.
Cácari. Unclassified; Durango; extinct.
Cacoma. Unclassified; Mexico (?); extinct.
Cacunica. Unclassified; extinct.
Caddo. Caddoan; 300 to 400 in Oklahoma (1962).
    Caddoe
Cadegomeño. Cochimi.
    Cadegomo
Cahibo. Arawakan (?); N.W. Santo Domingo; extinct.
    Cibao
Cahita. Taracahitian; S.W. Sonora and N.W. Sinaloa.[90]
    Cáhita
    Cahitan
    Caita
    Cinaloa
    Sinaloa
    Sinalua
Cahokia. Data lacking.
Cahuilla. Southern California Shoshonean (Takic); 10 to 100 in California (1962).
    Cahuillo
    Kahweyah
    Kauvuya
    Kawia
Cahuimeto. Unclassified; Sinaloa; extinct.
Caizcimu. Arawakan (?); Santo Domingo; extinct.
Cajono. Northern Zapotecan.
    Cajonos

88a Brinton, *PAPS* 23.75 (1886): 'The Bri-Bri and Cabecar, although dialects of the same original speech, are not sufficiently alike to be mutually intelligible. The Cabecars occupied the land before the Bri-Bris, but were conquered and are now subject to them. It is probable that their dialect is more archaic.'

89 Pilling, No. 1860, vocabulary by J. House in *Phil. Soc. Proc.* 4.102–22 (London, 1850).

90 Pimentel said that Cahita had three major dialects, Yaqui, Mayo and Tehueco. To these Swanton added Bamoa, Sinaloa and Zuaque.

Vijana
Cajuenche. Yuman (Cocopa); Sonora and Arizona.
Cucapa
Jallicuamay
Cakchiquel. Quichean; in Chimaltenango, Sololá, Escuintla, Quiché and Sacatepéquez departments, Guatemala; 225,000 (1968).
Calapooya. See Kalapuya.
Caledonia Bay. Data lacking.[91]
California Penutian. Rubric for Yokuts, Maidu, Miwok-Costanoan, and Wintun.
Calusa. Muskogean (?); Florida; extinct, 1,000? (1839).
Carlos
Muspa
Calveras County. Data lacking.[92]
Cambridge Bay. Eskimo; Central Canadian Arctic. See Coppermine.
Iqaluktuttiaq
Camoteca. Unclassified; Guerrero; extinct.
Campo. Diegueño; N. Baja California; 185? (1960).
Tipai
Canada. See Huron.
Canadois
Canestoga. See Conestoga.
Conestogue
Canniba. Abnaki.[93]
Caniba
Caparaz. Unclassified; Florida; extinct, perhaps 100 (1674).
Capachequi (?)
Cape Fear Indians. Eastern Siouan; North Carolina and South Carolina; extinct, 30 (1800).
Cape Flattery. See Makah.
Carib. Term used for (1) Arawakan in the Antilles and Central America, or (2) Cariban languages.[93a]
Caraib
Caraibe
Caraibean
Caraibee
Caraiben

[91] Pilling, No. 2349, vocabulary from the Isthmus of Darien near San Blas, in *TAPA* 1873, pp. 103–9 (Hartford, 1874).
[92] Pilling, Nos. 755b and 2348.
[93] Canniba = Norridgewock, the type of Abnaki recorded by Rasles.
[93a] In 1675 the Bishop of Cuba, Gabriel Diaz Vara Calderón, wrote a letter to Queen Regent Mariana of Spain, describing tribes of Florida, including thirteen tribes of Caribs: (1) Surruquêses, (2) Aŷses, (3) Santalûces, (4) Geigas, (5) Jobêses, (6) Vizcaynos, (7) Matcumbêses, (8) Bayahondos, (9) Cuchiagâros, (10) Pojôyes, (11) Pineros, (12) Tocopâcas, (13) Carlos.

Caribbee
Caribe
Caribicé
Charaibe
Charibbean
Charibbee
Karaib
Karib
Karif
Veragua (?)

Cariban. Hokan-Siouan.
Caribe-Tamanaque. Data lacking.[94]
Caribou Eaters. See Mountain (Athapaskan).
Caribou Eskimo. Eskimo; Canada.
Caribou Indians. See Tutchone.
Carmel. Term for (1) Esselen, or (2) Rumsen, at the Carmel Mission in California.

Carmel Mission
Carmelo

Carolina. Data lacking.[95]
Carolina Algonquian. Algonquian. Perhaps the same as Pamlico.
Carrier. Athapaskan; 1,000 to 3,000 in British Columbia (1962).

Babine
Chin Indians
Nagailer
Nagalier
Naguiler
Nētcā'ut'in
Ntshaautin
Tacollie
Tacoullie
Taculli
Tacullie
Tahculy
Tahcully
Tahkali
Tahkoli
Tahkotinne (?)
Takulli
Ulkatcho

Carrizo. Coahuiltecan; near Camargo, Mexico; extinct.

[94] Pilling, No. 1978a: name of a language family, in L.-F. Jéhan, *Dictionnaire de Linguistique*, cols. 381–6 (1858).
[95] Pilling, Nos. 2224–7 (Lawson).

Cascades. See Kiksht.
Cascan. See Cazcan.
Caszan
Casdal. Unclassified; Chiapas; extinct.
Catawba. Eastern Siouan; North Carolina and South Carolina; 166 (1930).
Issa
Katába
Katahba
Ushery
Cathlamet. See Kathlamet.
Cathlapotle. Chinookan (Clackamas or Multnomah ?); Washington; extinct, 900 (1806).
Cathlascon. See Wasco.
Caughnawaga. See Mohawk.
Cochnewago
Cochnowago
St. Regis
Cayubaba. Data lacking.[96]
Cayuga. Iroquoian; New York, Ohio, Oklahoma (as 'Seneca'); 500 to 1,000 in Ontario (1962), 25 in Oklahoma (1974).
Cayiuker
Quengues
Cayuse. Penutian; Washington and Oregon; 6? speakers (1888); probably extinct as a language; population on Umatilla Reservation, 370 (1937).[97]
Cayus
Kayouse
Kayux
Wailetpu
Cazcan. Aztecoidan; Zacatecas and Jalisco; extinct.[98]
Cascan
Caszan
Cazcane
Cegiha. See Dhegiha.
Ȼegiha
Celilo. Columbia River Sahaptin.
Central Alaskan Yupik. Yupik.
Central Aleut. Aleut; 25 on Bering Island, in the Commander Islands, and 90 on Atka (1970). See Commander Island Aleut.
Commander Island Aleut

[96] Pilling, No. 2678: numerals. The name belongs to a language group of South America.
[97] Many Cayuse joined the Nez Perce before 1852, and the term 'Cayuse' has been used sometimes for the Nez Perce language.
[98] Divisions of the Cazcan tribe were: Cazcan, Coca, and Tecuexe.

Central Coast Salishan. Term used by Thompson for non-enclave Coast Salish languages other than Olympic.
Central Eskimo. Eskimo.
Central Otomian. Otomian.
Central Pomo. Pomoan; fewer than 40 in California (1962).
Central Siberian Yupik. Yuit.
Central Sierra Miwok. Sierra Miwok; fewer than 5 in California (1962).
Central Tanana. Athapaskan.
    Minto-Nenana
Central Tewa. A Kiowan-Tanoan group with speakers in San Juan, San Ildefonso, Nambe and Tesuque.
Central Zapotecan. Zapotecan.
    Valley Zapotecan
    Valley-Isthmus Zapotecan
Chaima. Cariban.
    Chayma
Chainslek. Data lacking.[99]
Chacahuaztli. A Totonac division in Veracruz.
    Chacahuaxtli
    Chaka Huaxti
Chalchitan. Aguacatec.
Chakchiuma. Muskogean; Mississippi; extinct, 150 (1722).
Chameltec. Unclassified; Mexico (?); extinct.
Chamí. Chocoan.
Champagne. Southern Tutchone; southern Yukon.
Chamula. Tzotzil.
Chañabal. Mayan; S.E. Chiapas. See Tojolabal.
    Chanabal
    Chaneabal
    Comiteco
    Jocolabal
    Toholabal
    Tojolabal
Chandalar River. See Natsit-Kutchin.
Changuena. Chibchan (Dorasque); W. Panama.
Chantaleno. Unclassified; Oaxaca; extinct.
Chapai. See Cocopa.
Chaplino. Central Siberian Yupik; 700 in Siberia and 850 on St. Lawrence Island, Alaska (1970).
    Uŋaziq
Chasta Costa. Athapaskan; Oregon; 30 (1937), extinct before 1960.
    Chastacosta

[99] Pilling, No. 1508: vocabulary.

Cista Kwusta
Shasta Costa
Shista-Kwusta

Chatino. Zapotecan; S.W. Oaxaca; over 20,000 total (1965) with over 10,000 monolinguals (1960).[100]
Papabuco

Chatot. Muskogean; Florida, S.W. Georgia, Alabama, Louisiana; extinct, fewer than 240 (1817).

Chauchila. Northern Valley Yokuts.

Chawasha. Chitimachan; Louisiana; extinct, 48? (1758).

Chehalis. Halcomelem; 150 in British Columbia (1962). See Upper Chehalis and Lower Chehalis.[101]
Checalish
Chekeeli
Chihalis
Chikeelis
Tsheheilis
Tsihalis
Tsihalish

Chemainus. Halcomelem; 300 in British Columbia (1962).

Chelan. See Wenatchi.

Chemainus. Halcomelem; 300 in British Columbia (1962).

Chemakuan. See Chimakuan.

Chemakum. See Chimakum.

Chemehuevi. Numic (Ute type Plateau Shoshonean); 100 to 200 in California and Arizona (1962).
Chemegue[102]
Chemuevi
Chimehuevi
Tantawaits
Tä'n-ta'wats

Cheraw. Siouan (?); South Carolina, North Carolina and Virginia; extinct, fewer than 60 (1768).
Saraw
Saura
Suali
Xuala
Xualla

[100] The name Chatino refers to three mutually unintelligible languages. They center at Taltaltepec, Yaitepec and Zenzontepec.
[101] Spier in 1927 used 'Lower Chehalis' for Chehalis. But the Upper Chehalis, the Lower Chehalis and the Chehalis are three different tribes. See Stalo.
[102] A group in Sonora.

Cherehuen. Data lacking.[103]

Cherokee. Iroquoian; Tennessee, Georgia, North Carolina, South Carolina, Alabama, Virginia; 9,000 in Oklahoma and 1,000 in North Carolina (1962).

Alligewi
Alleghany
Cerochese
Cheerak
Cheerake
Chel-a-ke
Cheleki
Chell-o-kee
Cherakee
Cheroki
Cherokie
Mountain Cherokee
Talligewi
Tcálke
Tcerokiéco
Tchálagi
Tscherokese
Tselogi

Chetco. Athapaskan; fewer than 5 in Oregon (1962).

Cheyenne. Algonquian; Minnesota, North Dakota, South Dakota, Nebraska, E. Wyoming, E. Montana, Oklahoma; 3,000 to 4,000 in Montana and Oklahoma (1962).

Chayenne
Northern Cheyenne[104]
Scheyenne
Sheyenne
Shienne
Shiyan
Shyenne[105]
Southern Cheyenne[106]

Chiaha. Hitchiti; Tennessee, Georgia, South Carolina; some in Florida were called Mikasuki from 1778; extinct, 381 (1833).[107]

Chiagmiut. Eskimo.

Chiapa. Data lacking.[108]

Chiapanec. Chorotegan; W. Chiapas and other areas in Mexico; extinct.

[103] Pilling, No. 547.
[104] Used since 1832 for contrast with Southern Cheyenne.
[105] Used by Gallatin (1836) for a Siouan vocabulary.
[106] Used since 1832 for contrast with Northern Cheyenne.
[107] In later times the Chiaha of Oklahoma spoke Muskogee. See Swanton, *Tribes*, pp. 106, 133.
[108] Pilling, Nos. 566a, 705, 2525, 3986. At least partly Mayan.

Chapanec
Chapaneco
Chiapaneca
Chiapanecan
Chiapaneco
Chiapanèque

Chibcha. Macro-Chibchan.
Chibchan

Chibchan. Macro-Chibchan.

Chichimec. This term refers to (1) any of a number of hunting and gathering tribes of N. E. Mexico and other parts of Mexico,[109] or (2) the Northern Otomian Chichimeca-Jonaz, at the Misión de los Chichimecas about 50 miles N. W. of Guanajuato, Mexico; 800 (1963).
Chichimeca
Chichimeca-Jonaz
Chichimeki
Chichimèque
Meco

Chickasaw. Western Muskogean (Choctaw); Mississippi, South Carolina, Georgia and other areas; 2,000 to 3,000 in Oklahoma (1962).
Chakchiuma
Chicasa
Chickasa
Chickasah
Chickesaw
Chikasah
Chikasaw
Chikasha
Chikkasah
Napochi

Chicomuceltec. Huastecan; extreme S.E. Chiapas.
Chicomulcalteca

Chicorato. Unclassified; Sinaloa; extinct.

Chihuahueño. No data.[110]

Chilac. Nahuatl; Puebla.

Chilcotin. Athapaskan; 1,000 or more in British Columbia (1974).
Tsilkotin

Chilkat. Tlingit (Yakutat); on Copper River, Alaska.
Čilkat

Chilkoot. Tlingit; on Lynn Canal, Alaska; 106 (1890).[111]
Chilcoot

[109] Listed by Driver and Driver, *IJAL* 29.2.2 (1963), pp. 4-5.
[110] Pilling, No. 836: Lord's Prayer.
[111] Hodge (*Handbook* 1.267) says that the Chilkoot are 'practically the same as the Chilkat'.

Chilliwack. Halcomelem; 150 in British Columbia (1962).

Chilluckittequaw. Chinookan; north side of the Columbia River from the Cascades to 10 miles below the Dalles; extinct, 2,200 (1806).

Chilula. Athapaskan; California; 12? (1950).

Chimakuan. Algonquian-Wakashan.

Chimakum. Chimakuan; Washington; extinct, 3 (1890).

Chemakum

Chimacum

Chimalapa. See Zoque.

Chimarikan. Hokan.

Chimálakwe

Chimariko

Chimariko. Hokan; California; extinct, 5? (1950).

Chimmesyan. See Tsimshian.

Chin. See Lillooet and Carrier.

Chinantec. Chinantecan; mostly in N. Oaxaca; also in Veracruz, Nuevo Leon, and Zacatecas; 23,066 monolinguals (1960), 50,000 speakers (1968).[112]

Chiananteco

Chinanteca

Chinanteco

Cinacanteca

Tzinacanteca

Tzotzlem

Zotzlem

Chinantecan. Otomanguean.

Chinarra. Taracahitian; Chihuahua; extinct. See Concho.

Chinipa. Taracahitian; Chihuahua; extinct. See Varohio.

Chino. Data lacking.[113]

Chinook (Lower Chinook). Chinookan; Washington; extinct about 1850, after political merger with the Chehalis. See also Upper Chinook.

Chenook

Chinuc

Chinuk

Coastal Chinook

Tchinoque

Tchinouc

Tchinouk

Tshinook

[112] C.R. Rensch, *Proto Chinantec phonology* (Mexico, 1968), lists 23 Chinantec languages: (1) Chiltepec, (2) La Alicia, (3) Lacova, (4) Lalana, (5) Latani, (6) Lealao, (7) Mayultianguis, (8) Ojitlán, (9) Ozumacín, (10) Palantla, (11) Petlapa, (12) Quetzalapa, (13) Quiotepec, (14) Rio Chiquito, (15) Sochiapan, (16) Temextitlán, (17) Teotalcingo, (18) Tepetotutla, (19) Tlacoatzintepec, (20) Usila, (21) Valle Nacional, (22) Yolox, (23) Zapotitlán.

[113] Pilling, No. 3702: some Chino words handwritten on a page of Soriano's *Arte* [a manuscript description of Pame and Otomi].

Tshinuk
Tsinuk

Chinookan. Penutian.

Chinook Jargon. Chinookan etc.; 10 to 100 in the Pacific Northwest (1962).

Chipaya. Chipaya-Uru.

Chipaya-Uru. Mayan (?), Arawakan. See Yunga.[114]

Chipewyan. Athapaskan; 3,000 to 4,000 in Alberta, Saskatchewan, Manitoba and Mackenzie (1962).[115] Krauss reports 5,000? (1970).
Chepewyan
Cheppewyan
Chipewayan
Chipewyan
Chippewyan
Chipwyan
Cold Lake
Fort Chipewyan
Montagnais
Mountain
Mountaineers
Yellowknife

Chippewa. Algonquian; 40,000 to 50,000 in Saskatchewan, Manitoba, Ontario, Quebec, Montana, North Dakota, Minnesota, Wisconsin and Michigan (1962).[116] See Saulteurs.
Algic
Bawichtigouek
Chipouais
Chippawa
Chippeway
Cypawais
Ochepwa
Ochippeway

[114] Rivet, *Les langues du monde* 2.1106 (1952): 'La langue *uru* n'est autre que le **Pukina*, signalé par les anciens auteurs comme une des 'lenguas generales' de l'ancien royaume du Pérou.'

[115] Swanton lists as subdivisions the Athabaska, Desnedekenade, Etheneldeli or Caribou Eaters, and Thilanottine.

Haas (1968) identified Li's Fort Chipewyan dialect as virtually the same as Goddard's Cold Lake Chipewyan; she identified Yellowknife as like the Fort Chipewyan dialect except for the Yellowknife shift of */t/ → /k/.

[116] The language of the Migichihilinious or Eagle Eyed Indians is thought by Hodge to be Chippewa, despite the Siouan identification of Dobbs.

The preferred term of linguists is Ojibwa. Dialects include Eastern Ojibwa, Northern Ojibwa and Western Ojibwa. Eastern Ojibwa has 1,000 to 2,000 speakers around Lake Huron, in S.E. Ontario, and in Michigan, Wisconsin and Oklahoma; a sub-dialect is Ottawa or Odawa, spoken especially on Manitoulin Island in Lake Huron. Northern Ojibwa (also called Cree-Saulteau) is spoken in the Island Lake area, central Manitoba; and in the Trout Lake-Round Lake area, N. Ontario. Western Ojibwa (also called Saulteau) is spoken in W. Ontario, S. Manitoba and N. Minnesota. Sub-dialects of Western Ojibwa are Western Chippewa in N. Minnesota, and Lake of the Woods Ojibwa, elsewhere.

Odjibwa
Odjibway
Odjibwe
Odschibwa
Ojeboa
Ojebwa
Ojibbewa
Ojibbeway
Ojibbwa
Ojibua
Ojibue
Ojibwa
Ojibwauk
Ojibway
Ojipue
Otchilpwe
Pillager
Saulteaux
Saulteurs

Chiquimula. Data lacking.[117]

Chiricahua. Apachean; 100 to 1,000 in Arizona and Oklahoma (1962). Some in Mexico?
Gileño
Jocome (?)
Mimbreño
Mogollon
Querecho (?)
Vaquero (?)
Warm Springs

Chitimacha. Chitimachan; fewer than 10 in Louisiana (1962).
Chetemacha
Chetimacha
Shetimasha

Chitimachan. Gulf.

Chiwere. Winnebago type Siouan.

Chizo. Taracahitian (Concho); Chihuahua; extinct.

Choapeño. Zapotecan.

Chochenyo. Costanoan.

Chocho. Popolocan; N. Oaxaca.
Canton of Choco
Chocha
Choco

[117] Pilling, No. 2877, referring to languages of Guatemala.

Chocho of Oaxaca[118]
Chocona
Choconate
Chota
Chuchon
Chuchona
Chucon
Popoloca
Popoloca of Oaxaca

Choco. Cariban (or Paezan or Chibchan)?

Chocoan. Cariban? Chibchan?

Choconate. Unidentified; Darien.

Choctaw. Western Muskogean; Mississippi, Alabama, and elsewhere; 10,000 in Oklahoma, Mississippi and Louisiana (1962).
Chacta
Chactaw
Chactawice
Chactawisch
Chahta
Chahta-Muskokee
Chaktaw
Chata
Chocktaw
Choktah
Choktaw

Choinimni. Kings River Yokuts.

Chokuyem. Miwok.
Chocouyem
Chocoyem
Chocuyem
Joukiousmé
Jukiusme
Tchokoyem

Chol. Cholan; Tabasco and E. Chiapas; 32,815 monolinguals (1960).[119]
Chol Lacandon
Cholti
Cholti
Mopan

[118] As opposed to Chocho of Puebla (Popoloca of Puebla).

[119] Swanton, *Tribes*, p. 618, gave two divisions, the Chol and the Chol Lacandon. Rivet saw the Chol (also called Cholti) as modern descendants of the Chol Lacandon. Mason's 'Chol' has six dialects: (1) Chol (Mason says Cholti is an extinct variety of this Chol), (2) extinct Chorti, (3) Chol Lacandon (which Mason does not call extinct), and perhaps the extinct (4) Acala, (5) Toquegua and (6) Manche.

Chol Lacandon. Cholan; E. Chiapas, along the Río Usumacinta; extinct?[120]
Cholan. Mayan.
Cholo. Choco (?) or Darien; S.E. Panama.
Choloteca. Nahuatl; Nicaragua.
Cholti. See Chol.
    Choltí
Cholutec. Chorotegan; S. Honduras; extinct.
    Choluteca
    Mangue
Chontal. Term (from a Nahuatl word for 'stranger') used for various groups. See Chontal of Guerrero, Chontal of Nicaragua, Chontal of Oaxaca, Chontal of Tabasco.
    Chondal
    Popoluca
Chontal of Guerrero. Unclassified; Guerrero; extinct.
Chontal of Nicaragua. Term for (1) Sumo, or (2) Matagalpa.
Chontal of Oaxaca. See Tequistlatec.
Chontal of Tabasco. Cholan; E. Tabasco.
Chopunish. See Nez Perce.
    Chopunnish
Chorotega.[121] Chorotegan.
    Choroteca
    Chorteca
    Chorotegan
    Diria
    Dirian
Chorotega de Nicaragua. See Tarascan.
Chorotegan. Otomanguean.
    Chiapanec-Manguean
Chorti. Cholan; E. Guatemala and nearby Honduras, about Copan; 25,000 in E. Chiquimula department, Guatemala (1965).
    Cholti
    Chorte
    Chortí
Chowanoc. Algonquian; N.E. North Carolina; extinct, 5 (1755).
Choweshak. Data lacking.[122]
Chuchon.[123] Otomanguean.
Chuckbuckmiut. Eskimo; Labrador.
Chugachigmiut. Eskimo; S. Alaska.
    Chugach

[120] Not to be confused with the Maya Lacandon.
[121] See note s.v. Tarascan.
[122] Pilling, No. 1501, vocabulary (of California?) by Gibbs in Schoolcraft, *Tribes* 3.434–40 (1853).

Chugátchigmūt
Chugatch
Mount St. Elias
Tchougatsche-Konega
Tschugazzen
Tshugazzi

Chuh. Mayan; 14,000 in Guatemala (1965).
Chuj
Chuje

Chukaimina. Kings River Yokuts.

Chukchansi. Northern Foothill Yokuts; 10 to 20 in California (1962).
Chuckchansi

Chukchi. Luorovetlan; N.E. Siberia; 12,000 (1936).
Aglegmiout
Aglemoute
Chugatchigmut
Chukch
Chukche
Chukchee
Konægen
Konega
Luoravetlany
Tchougatche
Tchouktche
Tchouktchi
Tchuktchi

Chuklukmut. See Yuit.
Chū'klūkmūt
Chūklū'kmut
Chukohukmute

Chulamni. Northern Valley Yokuts.

Chumash. Chumashan.[124]

Chumashan. Hokan-Siouan.
Chumash
Santa Barbara

Chumbia. Unclassified; Guerrero; extinct.

Chumteya. A Miwok term for Miwok people to the south; a geographical term.[125]
Chimteya
Chúmeto
Chumtéya

[123] In Pimentel's Mixteco-Zapotecan family (1874), with two dialects.

[124] Extinct subdivisions of California given by Swanton: (1) Barbareño, (2) Cuyama, (3) Emigdiano, (4) Island Chumash, (5) Obispeño, (6) Purisimeño, (7) Santa Ynez (Ynezeño) and (8) Ventureño.

[125] Pilling, No. 1440: a vocabulary recorded by Gatschet, *CNAE* 3.536–49 (1877).

Chutsinni. Haida (?).[126]
Chuvanets. Yukaghir.
Chwachamaju. Pomo around Fort Ross, California, during the Russian occupation.
    Chwachamajee
    Chwachamajul
    Khwakhamaiu
    Khwakhlamayu
    Northerners
    Severnovskia
Cibecue. Apachean; 1,000 in Arizona (1962). See White Mountain.
    Cibecue Apache
Ciboney. Unclassified; S.W. Haiti and W. Cuba; extinct.
Cinaloa. See Cahita.
Ciudad del Maiz. North Pame.
Clackamas. Chinookan; Oregon; extinct, fewer than 5 (1920).
    Clakama
Clallam. Lkungen; 100 in Washington and British Columbia (1962).
    Klallam
    Noosdalum
    Nusdalum
    Sklallam
Classical Nahuatl. Nahuatl.
Clatskanie. Athapaskan; Washington; extinct, 3 (1910).
    Clackstar
    Klatskanai
    Tlatskanai
Clatsop. Chinookan (Lower Chinook); Oregon; 26 (1910); language extinct ca. 1890.
    Klatsop
    Tlatsop
Clear Lake. Data lacking.[127]
Cloud Lake. Sekani.
Clowwewalla. Chinookan (Clackamas); Oregon; extinct, 13 (1851).
    Chahcowah
    Cushook
    Fall
    Nemalquinner
    Tumwater
    Willamette
    Willamette Falls
Coahuiltecan. Hokan-Siouan.[128]

[126] Pilling, No. 1507: a vocabulary by Gibbs, *CNAE* 1.135–42 (1877).
[127] Pilling, No. 367: a manuscript vocabulary by F. Berson, taken in 1851, 50 miles south of Clear Lake, California.
[128] Swanton, *Tribes*, pp. 309–11, lists about 220 names of 'Coahuiltecan' groups.

Coahuiltec

Coahuilteco. Coahuiltecan; Coahuila, Nuevo Leon, Tamaulipas; extinct.

Coahuiltec

Pajalate

Tejano

Texas

Coano. An extinct division of the (Aztecoidan) Cora.

Coaque. Karankawa; Texas; extinct.

Cokés

Coast Miwok. Miwok; 1 in California (1962).

Coast Salish. Salishan.

Coast Tsimshian. Tsimshian; over 1,000 in British Columbia (1962).

Coast Yuki. Yukian; N.W. California; extinct, 15 (1910).

Coastal Chinook. See Lower Chinook.

Coatlán. Southern Zapotecan.

The Coatlanes

Coca. Aztecoidan; Jalisco; extinct. A division of the Cazcan.

Cochimi. Yuman; Baja California; extinct.[129]

Borjeño

Cadegomeño

Cochetimi

Cochima

Cochimí

Cochimtee

Didiu

Laimon

Laymon

San Javier

San Joaquin

San Xavier

Cochin. Unclassified; Mexico (?); extinct.

Cochiti. Keresan; 500 in New Mexico (1962).

Coco. Sumo.

Cocomacague. Piman (Pima Bajo); extinct.

Cocomacaque

Cocomaricopa. See Maricopa.

Opa

Coconoon. Yokuts.

Coconom

Cocopa. Cocopa type Yuman; Baja California, later also in Sonora and Arizona; 300 to 400 mostly in Arizona (1967).

Chapai

[129] See entries for Borjeño, San José de Comondre, San Xavier, and Santa Gertrude Mission.

Cucupa
Hogiopas
Kwikapa
Cocora. Chibchan (?); S.E. Nicaragua.
Coeur d'Alene. Interior Salish; 100 in Idaho (1962).
Coeur d'Alêne
Schitsui
Skitsamish
Skitsuish
Skitswish
Coiba. Chibchan; Panama.
Colorado Delta Yuman. Yuman.
Cocopa Type Yuman
Delta-California Yuman
Colorado River Yuman. Yuman.
Central Yuman
River Yuman
Yuma Type Yuman
Colotan. Piman; Jalisco and Zacatecas; extinct.
Colotlan
Colouse. Patwin.
Korusi
Columbia. Interior Salish; 200 in Washington (1962).
Columbia-Wenatchi
Middle Columbia
Moses
Moses-Columbia
Sinkiuse
Sinkiuse-Columbia
Columbia River Sahaptin. Northern Sahaptin.
Columbian. See Columbia.
Colville. Interior Salish; Washington; 322 (1937). See Okanagon.
Basket People
Kettle Falls
Schwoyelpi
Shwoyelpi
Skoyelpi
Whe-el-po
Colville Lake. Hare.
Comanche. Shoshoni; Wyoming, Nebraska, Kansas, Oklahoma, Texas; 1,500 in Oklahoma (1962).
Allebome
Camanche

Ca-mán-chee
Comanch
Hietan
Jetan
Komanche
Komantsche
Llanero
Meco
Näuni
Nüma
Paduca
Snake
Yampa
Yampais

Comanito. Taracahitian; Mexico; extinct.

Comecrudo. Coahuiltecan; Tamaulipas; extinct.

Comiteco. See Chañabal.

Commander Island Aleut. Aleut; 50? in U.S.S.R. (1968).

Comopori. An extinct subdivision of the Guasave.

Comox. North Georgia Salish; E. Vancouver Island; 2 or 3 in British Columbia (1962). See Sliammon.

Catoltq
Comux
Komookhs
Komuk

Concho. Taracahitian; Chihuahua; extinct.[130]

Abasopalme
Concha
Julime

Concho. Guaycuran; Baja California; extinct.

Lauretano

Conestoga. Iroquoian; New York, Pennsylvania, Maryland; extinct about 1763.

Akhrakouaehronon
Andaste
Canestoga
Conestogue
Minckus
Minqua
Minque
Mynckussar
Mynquess

[130] Major divisions were the Chinarra and the Chizo.

Susquehanna
Susquehannock

Congaree. Siouan (?); South Carolina; extinct, 40 (1715).

Conguaco. Xincan or Lencan (?); S.E. Guatemala; extinct.
Popoloca
Popoloca of Conguaco
Popoluca
Pupuluca of Conguaco

Conicari. Taracahitian; Sonora; extinct.

Connecticut. Term used by Teeter for Quiripi [Quinnipiac] (an Algonquian pidgin) and related dialects.

Conoy. Algonquian (Nanticoke type?); West Virginia and Maryland; extinct, 150 (1765).
Canawese
Ganawese
Piscataway

Continental Na-Dene. See Na-Dene.

Cook's River. See Chugachigmiut.

Cookra. Data lacking.[131]

Coos. Penutian; 1 or 2 in Oregon (1962).
Hanis
Kusa

Coos Bay. Name of a Coos Bay village or tribe.
Anasitch

Copainala. Zoque.

Copalis. Coast Salish; Washington; extinct, 5? (1888).
Chepalis (?)

Copehan. See Wintun.

Copper Indians. Ahtena or Yellowknife (Athapaskan).

Copper Island Aleut. Western Aleut, heavily Russianized by 1963.

Coppermine. Eskimo; Central Canadian Arctic. See Cambridge Bay.
Qurluqtuq

Coquille. Athapaskan; Oregon; 1 or 2? (1962).
Mishikhwutmetunne
Upper Coquille

Coquille. Coos; Oregon; extinct.
Lower Coquille
Miluk

Cora. Aztecoidan; Sinaloa, Jalisco, Nayarit; 3,731 monolinguals (1960).[132]

131 Pilling, No. 217, 217a-b: a language of Honduras mentioned in H.H. Bancroft, *Native races*, vol. 3, ch. 12.

132 Swanton named as divisions of Cora the extinct Coano, Huaynamota and Zayahueco. Pimentel (1874) gave the dialects of Cora as Muutzicat, Teacucitzin and Ateanaca. Rivet reports that Totorame was very close to Cora.

Ateanaca
Chora
Chota
Coraice
Muutzicat
Teacuacitzia
Teacuaeitzica

Cora. See Pima.

Cora. A division of the Waicuri.

Coran. Uto-Aztecan.
Corachol

Coree. Iroquoian or Algonquian (?); North Carolina; extinct, 100? (1707).
Coranine
Cwarennoc
Narhantes
Raruta

Corobici. Chibchan; Costa Rica.

Coronation. Eskimo; Northwest Territories.
Coronation Gulf

Costaño. Costanoan; any of several groups formerly on the San Francisco Peninsula, California; extinct, 5? (1950).[133]
Ahwaste
Altahmo
Costanos
Costeno
Costeño
Olhon
Olhone
Romonan
Tulomo

Costanoan. Penutian.

Coto. Chibchan; Costa Rica.
Cocto

Cotoname. Coahuiltecan.

Coushatta. See Alabama and Koasati under Muskogean.

Cowichan. Halcomelem; 500 in British Columbia (1962).
Cowitchen
Kawichen
Kawitchen
Kawitshin

Cowlitz. Olympic Salish; 1 in Washington (1962).

[133] In Pimentel's Mutsun family (1874). Swanton lists as subdivisions: (1) Monterey, (2) Saclan, (3) San Francisco, (4) San Juan Bautista, (5) Santa Clara, (6) Santa Cruz, (7) Soledad.

Cowlitch
Kaulits
Kawelitsk
Kowelitz
Kuwalitsk
Noosoluph
Noosolup'h
Noosolupsh
Nū-so-lupsh
Nusulph

Coxoh. Mayan.[134]

Coyotero. Apachean.

Coyotin. See Aguacatec.

Cree. Algonquian; 30,000 to 40,000 especially in British Columbia, Alberta, Saskatchewan, Manitoba, Ontario, Quebec and Montana (1962). See Moose Cree, Plains Cree, and Swampy Cree.[134a]

Christenaux
Clistenos
Cri
Crianae
Crie
Cris
Crise
Ile à la Crosse
Iyiniwok
Kalisteno
Kenistenoag
Killisteno
Knisteneaux
Knisteneux
Kri
Krih
Kristinaux
Muskotawenewuk
Roundhead
Saskatchewan

[134] Listed by Pimentel (1874) as one of twenty groups called 'Maya'.

[134a] B. F. Grimes, *Ethnologue* (Huntington Beach: Wycliffe Bible Translators, 1974), distinguishes Eastern or Coastal Cree; Moose Cree with two dialects, West Shore or York Cree, and Swampy Cree; and Plains or Western Cree. Eastern Cree is spoken in Quebec, and in Newfoundland, E. of James and Hudson's Bays to and including the Naskapi of Schefferville. Moose Cree is spoken at the S. end of James Bay in Moosonee, Ontario, and in Ontario and Manitoba W. of James and Hudson's Bays. Plains Cree is spoken in British Columbia, Alberta, Saskatchewan, Manitoba, Montana and North Dakota. Grimes counts Tête de Boule as a separate Algonquian language "closely related to Cree."

Têtes de Boule

Creek. See Muskogee.

Crow. Missouri River Siouan; Montana, Wyoming; 3,000 in Montana (1962).

Absaraka

Absároke

Aubsároke

Belantsea

Corbeaux

Earchethinue

Mountain Crow

Upsároka

Upsaropa

Cuaima. See Seri.

Gayama

Cuahcomeca. Unclassified; W. Guerrero; extinct.

Cuauhcomec

Cuba. Data lacking.[135]

Cubana

Cubano. Mayan (?).[136]

Cuchan. See Yuma.

Cucharete. Unclassified; Mexico (?); extinct.

Cueva-Cuna. Chibchan.

Cuicatec. Mixtecan; Oaxaca; 2,553 monolinguals (1960).[137]

Cuiateca

Cuicateco

Cuilapa. Mixtec.

Cuitlatec. Classification disputed; Guerrero.[138]

Cuitlateco

Popoloca of Michuacan

Popoloco

Cuixtla. Southern Zapotecan.

Cuixtlahuac. Mixtec.

Cumberland Strait. Eskimo; Canada (Baffin Island?).[139]

[135] Pilling, No. 1318a: vocabulary in N. Fort y Roldan, *Cuba Indígena* (1881).

[136] Classed as 'Maya' by Pimentel (1874).

[137] Not to be confused with Cuitlatec, a language of Guerrero.

[138] Assigned by Pimentel (1874) to his Mixteco-Zapoteca family; he lists two dialects. Thomas, following Orozco y Berra, called Cuitlateco Nahuatlan.

R. Weitlaner, "Notes on the Cuitlatec language", *El Mexico Antiguo* 4.363–73 (1939), suggested a tie with Otomian (specifically Ocuiltec), but a closer tie with Hokan. He notes, p. 364: 'The majority of words in the two languages [Cuitlatec and Ocuiltec] show a marked similarity in the number of syllables. Morphologically, however, both languages seem to remain quite apart, Cuitlatec giving the impression of coming nearer to the Hokan than to the Otomian group. Lexically, however, Cuitlatec has very little in common with either Tlapanec or Subtiaba.'

[139] Pilling, Nos. 941 and 3778.

Cuna. Chibchan; Panama.
Bayano
Chicuna
Chucunaque
Cueva
Cunacuna
Darien
Mandinga
San Blas
Tule
Yule
Cupan. A Southern California Shoshonean subgroup composed of Cahuilla and Cupeño, and Luiseño.[140]
Luiseño-Cahuilla
Luisish
Cupeño. Southern California Shoshonean (Takic); fewer than 10 in California (1962). See Cupan.
Kupa
Cusabo. Muskogean; South Carolina; extinct, 535 (1715).[141]
Casapullas (?)
Coosaboys
Coosa
Coosah
Cosapuya (?)
Cuscatlan. Data lacking.[142]
Cushna. Southern Maidu.
Kushna
Cux. Central Yupik.
Cuyama. Chumashan.
Cuyumatec. Unclassified; Mexico (?); extinct.
Cuyusumateco. Unclassified; Guerrero; extinct.
Cuyutec. Unclassified; Jalisco; extinct.
Cuyuteca
Dabeiba. Chocoan.
Dakota. Mississippi Valley Siouan; Minnesota, Wisconsin, Iowa, South Dakota; 3,000 to 5,000 Dakota or Santee in Minnesota, North Dakota, South Dakota, Nebraska, Montana and Manitoba, 1,000 to 2,000 Yankton or Nakota in North Dakota, South Dakota and Montana, 10,000 to 15,000 Teton or Lakota in

[140] See Bright and Hill 1967:351–71.
[141] The tribe was composed of the Cusabo proper and the Coosa. The Cusabo called Coosa should not be confused with the Coosa or Abihka who were Upper Creeks, on the Coosa River. Some early writers mistakenly identify the (Siouan) Sewee and Santee as Cusabo.
[142] Pilling, No. 2877. Name of a province of the Audiencia de Guatemala.

South Dakota, Montana and Manitoba, 1,000 to 2,000 Stoney Assiniboin in Montana, Alberta and Saskatchewan (1962).[143]

Assiniboin
Brulé
Dacota
Dacotah
Dahcotah
Dahkotah
Hunkpapa
Hunkpatina
Lacotah
Lakota
Nadowess
Nadowessier
Nakota
Naoudoouessis
Naudoway
Naudowessi
Naudowessie
Ogallah
Ogallala
Oglala
Sansareh
Santee
Scioux
Sioune
Sioux
Sisseton
Teton
Teeton
Uncpapa
Yancton
Yanctonai
Yankton
Yanktong

Dakubetede. Applegate Creek.

Dalinchi. Northern Foothill Yokuts.

Darien. Cuna.

Bayano

[143] Swanton's Dakota subdivisions (1–4 are Santee): (1) Mdewakanton, (2) Wahpeton, (3) Wahpekute, (4) Sisseton; (5) Yankton, (6) Yanktonai (Upper Yanktonai and Lower Yanktonai or Hunkpatina), (7) Teton (Brulé, Hunkpapa, Miniconjou, Oglala, Oohenonpa or Two Kettle, San Arcs, and Sihasapa or Blackfoot).

Cholo
Savaneric
Toole
Yule

Davis Strait. Eskimo; N.E. Baffin Island (?).[144]

Deadose. Atakapa; Texas; extinct.

Dease River. Data lacking. Kaska?

Delaware. Eastern Algonquian; New Jersey, New York, Pennsylvania, Delaware; fewer than 100 in Oklahoma and Ontario, with fewer than 10 Munsee in Ontario (1962).[145]

Abnaki
Assunpink
Delewes
Lenape
Lenapee
Lenapi
Lennape
Lennappé
Lenni
Lenni Lenape
Lenni-Lenape
Linapi
Opuhnarke
Sankhican
Sankihani
Sankikani
Sankitani
Unami
Wabanaki

Déné Dindjié. Athapaskan.

Desaguedero. Aztecoidan; Costa Rica and Nicaragua at the mouth of the Río San Juan.

Desert Cahuilla. Cahuilla.

Dhegiha. Mississippi Valley Siouan.

Cegiha
₵egiha

Didú. Unclassified; Baja California; extinct.

Diegueño. Diegueño type Yuman; fewer than 500 (1962), with fewer than 100 in California (1967). See Southern Diegueño, Eastern Diegueño.

[144] Pilling, *BAE–B* 1.37 (1887): 211 words by Gibbs, in a Smithsonian manuscript.

[145] Swanton lists as major Delaware groups: (1) Munsee, (2) Unalachtigo, and (3) Unami. Brinton, *PAPS* 23.51 (1886), speaks of the Lenape Trade Jargon, a much-simplified 17th century Delaware jargon, used in the *Catechism* of Johan Campanius, Lingua Suecico-Americana or American-Virginiske Språket.

Campo
Cuneil
Diegano
Diegeño
Dieguina
Dieguiño
Dieguno
Kamia
San Diego (?)
San Diego Mission (?)
Santo Tomas

Dihai-Kutchin. Athapaskan; N.E. Alaska; extinct.

Dirian. See Chorotega.
Diria
Diría

Dixie Valley. Atsugewi.
Aporuke

Dogrib. Athapaskan; 800 in Mackenzie (1974).
Dog Rib
Rae
Thlingchadinne

Dorasque. Chibchan; Panama.

Dry Bay. Tlingit.

Dule. Matagalpan (?); Honduras.
Chato (?)

Dumna. Northern Foothill Yokuts.

Durango. Nahuatl; Durango.

Duwamish. Southern Puget Sound Salish; 1 or more in Washington (1962).
Dwamish

East Bay Costanoan. Northern Costanoan.
Chocheño

Eastern Abnaki. Algonquian (Penobscot, Canniba, and Androscoggin and Wewenoc of Quebec).

Eastern Aleut. See Unalaska.

Eastern Algonquian. A group of Algonquian languages from Canada to the Carolinas. See Teeter's list in the present volume.

Eastern Chibchan. Chibchan.

Eastern Diegueño. Diegueño type Yuman; Santa Catarina Mission, Baja California.
Kamia
Paipai

Eastern Miwok. Utian.

Eastern Muskogean. Muskogean.

Eastern Niantic. Algonquian; west coast of Rhode Island and Connecticut; extinct,

fewer than 16 (1910).
Nehantic
Nihantic

Eastern Paleosiberian. Paleosiberian.

Eastern Pomo. Pomoan.
Clear Lake Pomo

Eastern Siouan. Siouan.

Ecclemach. See Esselen.
Eclemanch

Edú. Unclassified; Baja California; extinct.

Eel River. Data lacking.[146]

Ehnek. Karok.
Amaikiara

Ejutla. Central Zapotecan.

Ekaluktogmiut. Eskimo.

Ekogmut. Eskimo; Alaska.
Ikogmiut

El Salvador. Nahuatl; El Salvador.

Emigdiano. Barbareño.

Eno. Siouan (?); South Carolina; extinct some years after 1743.
Haynokes

Entimbich. Kings River Yokuts.

Erie. Iroquoian; Ohio, Pennsylvania, New York, perhaps Indiana; extinct as a tribe in 1656 but with survivors joining other Iroquoian tribes. Some Erie may have reached Oklahoma as 'Senecas'. An Erie vocabulary was printed in 1798: see Erigas.
Cat Nation
Ehriehronnons
Erigas
Gaquä'gaono
Kakwas
Rhiierrhonons

Erigas. Erie.[147]

Esbataottine. See Sekani and Nahane.
Espatodena

Escoria. Unclassified; W. Panama.

Eskimo. Eskimo-Aleut; 13,000 to 14,000 Yupik or Western Eskimo in Alaska and 900 to 1,100 in N.E. Siberia; 40,000 to 50,000 Inupik in Alaska, Canada and

[146] Pilling, Nos. 217, 217a-b.
[147] Pilling, No. 298: vocabulary in B.S. Barton, *New views* (1798).

Greenland, about 10,000 of these in Canada, and 25,000 in Greenland (1967).[148]
Eskimau
Eskimo of Greenland
Eskimo of Labrador
Esquimaude
Esquimaux
Esquimaw
Esquimo
Innok
Innuit

Eskimo Point. Eskimo; W. Hudson's Bay, Canada.
ARviaq

Esselen. Esselenian; California; extinct, 500 (1770).
Carmel
Carmel Mission
Carmelo
Ecclemach
Eclemanch
Ecselen
Ensen
Escelen
Eskelen
Eslen
Eslene
Esseleneijan
Huelel
Soledad Mission

Esselenian. Hokan-Siouan.
Esselen

Estrella. Chibchan (Talamanca); N.E. Panama.

Etchaottine. See Slave, Fort Norman Slave.

Etchemin. Malecite.[149]
Echemin
Etchimi
Etechemin
Etechemine

[148] L.L. Hammerich (1970), p. 6, indicates there are four mutually unintelligible Western Eskimo dialects. The number of dialects or languages north of Unalakleet and eastward is uncertain. Names listed at this entry are mostly from Pilling's *Proof-sheets*. Passim and on the maps will be found a variety of local and band names, taken mostly from Smithsonian and Summer Institute of Linguistics sources. For estimates from Krauss see his paper in volume 1, pp. 175–281.

[149] Champlain's 'Etchemin' on the St. Croix River may be Passamaquoddy.

Etla. Zapotecan; Oaxaca.

Euchre Creek. Athapaskan; Oregon; extinct some time after 1934.

Eudeve. Taracahitian; an Opata division; extinct.
Batuco
Dohema
Dohme
Eudeva
Hegue
Hequi
Heve

Eufaula. A Muskogee division in Alabama; extinct.
Yufera (?)

Eyak. Athapaskan-Eyak; Copper River mouth and eastward along the coast of Alaska; 3 speakers in Alaska (1970). See Ugalakmiut.
Ougalentsi
Ugalent
Ugalentsi
Ugalenzen

Eyeish. Caddoan; Texas; extinct, about 800 merged with other Caddoans around 1828.
Aays
Aix
Aleche
Aliche
Háish
Yayecha

Fall Indian. Atsina.

Faraon. Apachean; Texas, Chihuahua; extinct. See Lipan.

Fernandeño. Takic (Southern California Shoshonean); N. of Los Angeles, California; extinct, fewer than 5? (1950).

Fitzhugh Sound. Data lacking.[150]
Fitz-Hugh Sound

Flatbow. Kutenai.
Arc-A-Plat
Lower Kutenai

Flathead. See Kalispel.
Tête-Plate

Floridan. Term used by Pickering and others of the early nineteenth century for Cherokee, Creek, Choctaw and other languages of the Southeastern United States.
Southern

[150] Pilling, Nos. 537 and 2205: numerals in Latham, *J. Eth. Soc.* 1.154–66 (London, 1848), perhaps repeated by Buschmann (1858).

Foothill Yokuts. Yokuts.
Fort Chimo. Eskimo.
Fort Good Hope. Hare.
Fort Graham. Athapaskan; central British Columbia on the Finlay River.
    Fort Grahame
Fort Liard. Slave.
Fort McPherson. Kutchin; N.W. Mackenzie, on Peel River near the mouth of the Mackenzie River.
Fort Nelson. Slave; N.E. British Columbia.
Fort Norman. Slave? Hare? W. Mackenzie.
Fort Providence. Slave; S.W. Mackenzie, W. of Great Slave Lake.
Fort Ross. Data lacking.[151]
Fort Simpson. Slave? Hare? S.W. Mackenzie.
Fort St. James. Carrier; E. end of Stuart Lake, central British Columbia; under 3,000 (1974).
Fort Yukon. Kutchin; N.E. Alaska.
Fox. Algonquian; Wisconsin, Michigan (?), Iowa, Kansas; 400? in Iowa plus 1,000 (including Sauk) in Iowa, Oklahoma and Kansas (1962).
Fox Channel. Eskimo.[152]
    Foxe Channel
    Sikosuilarmiut (?)
Fox Island. See Aleut.
Frances Lake. Kaska.
Friendly Village. Bella Coola.
Fuca. Makah.[153]
    Fuca Straits
    Straits of Fuca
Gabrieleño. Takic (Southern California Shoshonean); vicinity of Los Angeles, California; extinct, under 5? (1950).
    Gabrielino
    Kij
    Kīj
    Kizh
    San Gabriel Mission
    Tobikhar
Gaitchini. Data lacking.[154]
    Gaitchim

[151] Pilling, No. 3006i, vocabulary taken by Pinart of an informant born at Ft. Ross, California, in Pinart's possession in 1885.
[152] Pilling, *BAE-B* 1.42 (1887), citing C.F. Hall, *Narrative* (1879), p. 354: 50 place names, probably from the S.W. coast of Foxe Peninsula, Baffin Island.
[153] Pilling, Nos. 537, 538 and 2205; data from Tolmie published by Scouler, *J. Roy. Geog. Soc.* 11.215ff. (London, 1841).
[154] Pilling, Nos. 1425, 1426, 2305, 2307. Vocabulary by O. Loew in G.M. Wheeler, *Report* 7.424–65, 474–9 (1879).

Galibi. Cariban.
Carib
Cayenne
Galice. Athapaskan; Oregon; extinct since 1958.
Taltushtuntude
Gallinomero. Southern Pomo.
Gallinoméro
Gamotes. North Pame.
Gashowu. Kings River Yokuts.
Giamina. Southern California Shoshonean?
Gilyak. Eastern Paleosiberian.
Gitksan. Tsimshian; fewer than 1,000 in British Columbia (1962).
Kitksan
Gjoa Haven. Eskimo.[155]
King William's Land (?)
Natsiliŋmiut
Netsilingmiut
Utkusiksalingmiut
Gosiute. Numic (Shoshoni type Plateau Shoshonean); N. Utah; part of the Shoshoni total of 5,000 (1962). See Western Shoshoni.
Goshute
Gossi Ute
Kusiuta
Gotane. Chibchan (Rama-Corobici).
Grand Traverse Bay. Chippewa.
Grape Island, Bay of Quinte. Data lacking.[156]
Greenland. Eskimo.
Greenlandic
Groenland
Groenlandais
Groenlandice
Grönland
Grigra. Natchez (?); Mississippi; extinct, 240? (1725).
Gray Village
Gris
Gras
Gros Ventre. Term for (1) the Atsina, also called Gros Ventres or Minetarees of the Prairies, or (2) the Hidatsa, also called Gros Ventres or Minetarees of the Missouri.

[155] Gjoa Haven is a settlement on King William Island, south of Boothia Peninsula. Here S.I.L. records have been made of Netsilingmiut and Utkusiksalingmiut.
[156] Pilling, No. 3020.

Guacata. Unclassified; Florida; extinct, perhaps removed to Cuba in 1763.
Guaccaiarima. Unclassified; S. W. Haiti; extinct.
Guachichil. Aztecoidan; Coahuila, Nuevo Leon, San Luis Potosi, Zacatecas, Jalisco; extinct.
 Cuachichil
 Guachichile
Guaiame. Unclassified; Sonora; extinct.
Guaicura. See Waïcuri.
Guaikeri. Cariban.
Gualaca. Chibchan.
Guale. Muskogean; Georgia, later Florida and South Carolina; extinct, 600? (1715).[157]
Guanexico. Sumo (Woolwa).
Guarijío. See Varohio.
Guasapar. Taracahitian; Chihuahua; extinct.
Guasave. Taracahitian; Sinaloa.[158]
Guatajigiala. Subtiaba.
Guatinicamame. Popolocan (?).
Guatuso. Chibchan; Costa Rica.
 Corobici
Guaxabana. Unclassified; Guanajuato; extinct.
Guaycura. Guaycuran; Baja California; extinct.[159]
 Guaicura
 Monqui
Guaycuran. Unclassified. (Hokan-Siouan?).
Guayma. Serian.
 Guaymi
Guaymi. Chibchan; Panama.[160]
Guazacapan. Data lacking.[161]
Guazápare. Taracahitian; Chihuahua; extinct.
 Guasapar
 Guazapare
Guetar. Chibchan (Talamanca); Costa Rica; extinct, perhaps before 1865.
 Guetare
 Huetare

[157] A grammar of Guale is said to have been written by Domingo Augustin, S.J., after 1569 (Swanton, *Tribes*, p. 110).
[158] Swanton lists as subdivisions: (1) Achire, (2) Ahome, (3) Comopori, (4) Vacoregue.
[159] Pimentel's 'familia Guaicura' (1874) has: (1) Guaicura, (2) Aripa, (3) Uchita, (4) Cora, (5) Concho.
[160] Swanton's divisions: (1) Doleguas, (2) Move, (3) Muoi, (4) Murire, (5) Muite, (6) Pariza (?), (7) Penomeño [i.e., Penonomeño].
[161] Pilling, No. 2877: name of a province of the Audiencia de Guatemala.

Suerra (?)
Suerre (?)
Guichiovian. Mixe.
Guiluco. Unidentified; California; extinct.[162]
Huiluc (?)
San Francisco Solano Mission
Gulf. See Hokan-Siouan.
Haida. Na-Dene (?); mostly on Queen Charlotte Islands, British Columbia, with some in Alaska; 100 [fewer than 20 speaking Skidegate] (1962).
Haidah
Hyda
Hydah
Kaigani[163]
Queen Charlotte's Islands
Skiltageet
Skitaget
Skittagete
Skittegat
Hailtsuk. Kwakiutl; 100 to 1,000 in British Columbia (1962).
Bellabella
Haceltzuk
Haeeltzuk
Hailtsa
Hailtzuk
Hailtzukh
Millbank Sound
Wikenak
Wikeno
Haina. Caddoan.
Haisla. See Kitamat.
Haitiano. Mayan (?).[164]
Haitina (?)
Itis
Quitzqueja
Halchidom. Yuma type Yuman; Arizona; 1,000? (1770). Extinct (after joining the Maricopa some time after 1700).

[162] Costanoan? Pilling, No. 1101: Lord's Prayer in E. Duflot de Mofras, *Exploration* (1844), pp. 390–1.

[163] Name of the Haida on S. Prince of Wales Island, Alaska, after 1700.

[164] Listed as Mayan by Pimentel (1874). The names are from Pimentel, except for 'Haitina', which is from Pilling, No. 2682a: vocabulary in C.G. von Murr, *Reisen* (1785), pp. 403–8, from Oviedo, Peter Martyr, Acosta and others.

Halchidhoma

Halcomelem. South Georgia Salish; 1,000 to 2,000 in British Columbia (1962).[165]

Halkomelem

Lower Fraser River

Halyikwamai. Cocopa type Yuman; Arizona; extinct (after joining the Cocopa?), 1,000? (1775).

Kikima

Quicama

Hammawi. Achumawi.

Hammonasset. Wappinger.

Hammonassett

Han. Athapaskan; 60 in Alaska and Yukon (1962).

Hong Kutchin

Hancock Harbor. Data lacking. Nootka?[166] See Klaokwat.

Hancock's Harbor

Haneragmiut. Eskimo.

Haningayormiut. Eskimo.

Hanis. See Coos.

Hano. Tewa; 200 in Arizona (1962).

Hopi-Tewa

Hare. Athapaskan; 600 in Mackenzie (1962).

Colville Lake

Fort Good Hope

Kawchottine

Peau de Lièvre

Harvaqtormiut. Eskimo.

Hasinai. Caddo.

Assinay

Cenis

Hainai

Hatteras. Algonquian; North Carolina; extinct, fewer than 1,000? (1600).

Croatan (?)

Hauheqtormiut. Eskimo.

Havasupai. Walapai type Yuman; over 200 in Arizona (1962).

Coconino

Tonto

Hay River. Slave.

Henagi. See Tolowa.

165 Chafe's list (1962): Chehalis 150, Chemainus 300, Chilliwack 150, Cowichan 500, Katzie 50, Kwantlen 15, Musqueam 100, Nanaimo 150, Sumas 60, Tait 250.

166 Pilling, No. 4091: a manuscript vocabulary of 200 words taken about 1808 by A. Waters.

Haynarger
Heve. See Eudeve.
Hewisedawi. Achumawi.
Hewut. See Umpqua.
H'hana. Pomo.[167]
Khana
Hidatsa. Missouri River Siouan; 500 to 1,000 in North Dakota (1962).
Gros-Ventre
Gros Ventres of the Missouri
Minatarree
Minetare
Minetari
Minitaree
Minitari
Minnataree
Minnetahse
Minnetare
Minnetaree
Minnitaree
Mönnitarri
Highland Tequistlatec. Tequistlatec.
Highland Chontal
Mountain Tequistlatec
Highland Tzeltal. Tzeltal.
Himeri. Pima Alto (Pima); Sonora; extinct.
Hine. Xixime.
Hitchiti. Eastern Muskogean; Alabama, Georgia, Florida; 381 (1832).[168]
Apalachicola
Hecheta
Hitchitathli
Hitchita
Hitchiteco
Hitchitee
Hochelaga. Iroquoian.
Hochelagense
Hoh. Chimakuan; Washington; extinct, 62 (1905).
Hokaltecan. See Hokan-Coahuiltecan.
Hokan-Coahuiltecan. See Hokan-Siouan.

[167] Pilling, No. 282, vocabulary by J.R. Bartlett, *CNAE* 3.483–8, 504–8 (1877).

[168] Still spoken, presumably in Oklahoma, in 1940. Possibly extinct (1970). Most of the 'Seminole' in Florida before the Creek-American War (1813–1814) spoke Hitchiti.

Hokaltecan
Hokaltekan

Hokogian. Term proposed by Swadesh in 1954 for a subgroup of Hokan-Siouan with Yuki, Hok(an) and (Musk)ogian.

Holikachuk. Athapaskan; Grayling on Yukon; 50 (1970).

Holólupai. Maidu.
Hololopi
Hol-ó-lu-pai
Ololopa

Holy Cross. Ingalik.

Homalco. Comox.

Hometwoli. Buena Vista Yokuts.

Honduran Miskito. Mosquito.
Mam

Honniasont. Iroquoian; E. Ohio, West Virginia and W. Pennsylvania; extinct, a remnant perhaps having joined the Seneca; 3,200? (1662).
Black Minqua

Hood Canal Salish. Coast Salish.

Hoona. Tlingit.

Hootsnahoo. Tlingit.

Hopi. Pueblo Shoshonean; fewer than 4,800 in Arizona (1967).
Hopitu
Moqui
Shinumo

Hopi-Tewa. See Hano.

Houma. Muskogean (close to Choctaw); Mississippi, Louisiana; 947 in Terrebonne Parish, Louisiana (1930).

Housatonic. See Stockbridge.

H'taäm. Yuman.[169]
H'taän

Huajuapan. Mixteco.

Hualahuises. Unclassified; Nuevo Leon; extinct.

Hualapai. See Walapai.

Huamelultec. Tequistlatec.
Huamelula
Huamelultec Chontal

Huastec. Huastecan; Veracruz, San Luis Potosi and Oaxaca; 6,527 monolinguals (1960).[170]
Cuexteca

169 Pilling, Nos. 1354, 1358, 1430.
170 The dialects of Huastec are Potosino and Veracruzano.

Guasteca
Guasteco
Houastéque
Huasteca
Huastecae
Huastecan
Huasteco
Huastek
Huasteka
Huastéque
Huaxteca
Huaxteco
Huaxtèque

Huastecan. Mayan.

Huastuso. Undetermined; Costa Rica.[171]
Huasturos
Huatuso

Huatiquimane. Unclassified; Oaxaca; extinct.

Huautla de Jimenez. Mazatec; 30,000 in Oaxaca (1967).
Huautla
Huautla de Jiménez

Huave. Huavean; Oaxaca; 2,972 monolinguals in a total of about 7,000 (1960).
Guave
Guavi
Huavi
Huazonteco
Wabi

Huavean. Penutian or Mizocuavean (Mason).
Huave

Huaynamota. An extinct division of the Aztecoidan Cora.

Hubabo. Unclassified; N. Santo Domingo; extinct.
Ciguayo
Ciguana
Macoryzes

Huchnom. Yuki.
Redwoods

Hudson's Bay. Term refers to (1) Eskimo, or (2) Athapaskan.
Baie d'Hudson
Hudson Bay

[171] Pilling, Nos. 363n, 437a, and 1313a, all in the Berendt collection.

Huejotzingo. Nahuatl; Puebla.
Huichol. Aztecoidan; Jalisco, Nayarit, Durango and Puebla; 3,932 monolinguals (1960).
    Huichola
Huite. Taracahitian; Chihuahua (?); extinct.
Huixteco. Tzotzil.
Humboldt Bay. See Wiyot.
Hume. Term for (1) an extinct subdivision of the Taracahitian Xixime, or (2) a dialect of Chinantec.
Humptulips. Coast Salish; Washington; extinct, 21 (1904).
Hupa. Athapaskan; California; 12 (1970).
    Hoopa
    Hoopah
    Hopah
    Hupâ
    Nabiltse
    Natinnoh-hoi
    Trinity Indians
Huron. See Wyandot.
    Hurone
Hutshi. Southern Tutchone.
Ibitoupa. Muskogean (?); Mississippi; extinct, survivors probably joined the Chickasaw after 1730; 24? (1722).
Icafui. Timucuan; S.E. Georgia and Florida; extinct.
    Cascangue
Icaiche. Mayan.
Iglulirmiut. Eskimo.
Ignacieno. Cochimi.
    Ignacieño
Ika. Waïcurian (?); Baja California; extinct.
Ikogmiut. Eskimo.
Illinois. Algonquian; Illinois, Ohio, Iowa, Indiana and elsewhere; fewer than 10 (1962). See Mascouten.[172]
    Cahokia
    Illinese
    Illinice
    Illinoise
    Kaskaskia

[172] A shortened list of Illinois groups includes the Cahokia and Kaskaskia in Illinois, the Michigamea in Arkansas, the Moingwena and Peoria in Iowa. After 1860 the term Peoria came to include Kaskaskia and other Illinois groups in Oklahoma.

Mascouten
Michigamea
Moingwena
Peoria
Tamaroa
Tamarois
Ylinesa
Ilmawi. Achumawi.
Iluilirmiut. Eskimo.
Imaklik. Eskimo of Big Diomede Island. See Wales.
Imaklimiut. Eskimo.
Indian. An ambiguous term sometimes used as a label for data.[173]
Inezeño. See Ynezeño.
Ingalik. Athapaskan; 160 in Alaska (1970).[174]
Inkilek
Inkalik
Inkalit
Inkilek
Inkilik
Káiyuhkhatána
Tananá
Ulúkuk
Inglestatt. Eskimo.
Inkalik. See Ingalik.
Inkalit-Yugelmut. See Kuskokwim.
Inkalit-jug-elmut
Inkuluklates. Eskimo.
Innuit. See Eskimo.
Interior Chumash. Chumashan.
Interior Salish. Salishan.
Intibucat. See Lenca.
Inupik. Eskimo.[175]

[173] For several dozen references which invite study see Pilling, *Proof-sheets*, pp. 1015–6.

[174] In 1965 a split was judged by Irvine Davis, *IJAL* 31.346, to represent two languages, (1) Ingalik of Anvik and (2) Ingalik of Nikolai, with populations of 300 and 100 respectively. The latter is separated from the former by a range of mountains, the Kuskokwim Mountains, and it seems fair that Nikolai should be, as Krauss observes, more akin to Central Tanana (Minto-Nenana) to the northeast across relatively level country, than to Ingalik of Anvik.

The usage of early scholars in interesting. Buschmann's Inkalit-Kinai vocabulary perhaps is Tanaina. Dall in 1870 used the label 'In′galik' for three vocabularies: (1) Nūláto [Koyukon], (2) Ulū′kuk [Ingalik of Anvik], and (3) Tananá.

[175] There are two oppositions in use, Yupik versus Inupik and Iñupiat versus Inupik. In the former, Inupik covers dialects north and east of Unalakleet, Alaska. In the latter, Inupik covers areas east of Iñupiat.

Iñupiat. Eskimo.[176]
Inuvik. See Mackenzie River.
    UumaRmiut
Iowa. Chiwere; Iowa, Minnesota, Missouri and elsewhere; 100 to 200 in Kansas, Oklahoma and Nebraska (1962).
    Ioway
    Nadouessioux Maskoutens
    Nez Percés
    Pahodja
Ipai. Diegueño.
Ipapana. See Totonac.
Ircitila. Unclassified; Durango, Coahuila; extinct.
Iroquoian. Hokan-Siouan.
    Iroquois
Iroquois. Iroquoian.[177]
    Agoneasean
    Irivokoise
    Irokese
    Iriqois
    Mingwe
    Nadowa
Iroquois-Caddoan. Hokan-Siouan.
Irritila. See Lagunero.
Iskoman. Hokan-Siouan.
Island Chumash. Chumashan.
Island Comox. Comox.
Isleta. Kiowa-Tanoan; 2,000 in New Mexico (1967).
    Ysletta
Isleta del Sur. Town near El Paso, Texas, where rebellious Rio Grande Pueblo Indians were sent by Otermin in 1681. Others were sent to Senecú del Sur, Chihuahua. See Isleta.
Isthmus Nahuat. Nahuat.
Isthmus Zapotec. Central Zapotecan.
    Istmo
    Juchitan
    Tehuano
    Tehuantepec

[176] In recent S.I.L. reckoning, Inupik covers dialects from Gjoa Haven to Ponds Inlet and from Tuktuyatuk eastward, and Iñupiat covers the north coast of Alaska and part of Canada, from Unalakleet to the Mackenzie River, with an extension westwards from Inuvik.

[177] A general term covering the Mohawk, Oneida, Onondaga, Cayuga, Seneca, Huron (Wyandot), Neutral, Erie, Wenrohronon, Honniasont, Tuscarora, Cherokee and others. Pilling's use of the term as a label for linguistic data invites study.

Tehuantepecano

Ita. Eskimo.

Thule

Itivimiut. Eskimo.

Itsatawi. Achumawi.

Itza. See Maya.

Itzuco. Unclassified; N. Guerrero; extinct.

Izcuca

Izcuco

Ixcatec. Popolocan; Oaxaca; 300? (1952).

Ixcateco

Ixil. Mamean; N. Quiché department, N.W. highlands of Guatemala; 25,000 (1967).[178]

Ixtepexi. Northern Zapotecan.

Ixtlan. See Serrano (Northern Zapotecan).

Izalco. Pipil.

Jacaltec. Kanjobalan; Jacaltenango and Concepción, Huehuetenango department, N.W. Guatemala; 12,000 (1960).

Jacalteca

Jalisco. Aztecoidan; Jalisco.

Jalisciense

Mexicano de Jalisco

Jamaica. Mayan (?); extinct.

Janambre. Unclassified; Coahuila, Tamaulipas, Nuevo Leon; extinct.

Xanambre

Jeaga. Unclassified; Florida; extinct.

Jemez. Towa; 1,200 in New Mexico (1962).

Amayes

Ameias

Emeges

Gemes

Ha'-mish

Hae'-mish

Tu'-wa

Jicaltepec. Mixtec.

Jicaque. Jicaquean; N.W. Honduras.[179]

Xicaque

Jicaquean. Hokan-Siouan.

Jicarilla. Apachean; nearly 1,800 in New Mexico (1970).

[178] Ixil has three mutually-intelligible dialects: (1) Nebaj, (2) Chajul, and (3) Cotzal.

[179] Dialects listed by Swanton are (1) Yoro, (2) Palmar (also called Sula), and (3) Lean y Mulia.

Jicorilla
Llanero
Querecho
Vaquero
Xicarilla

Jiliapan. South Pame; 5 or 6 (1967).
Jirajaran. Paezan.
Jocolabal. See Chañabal.
John Day. Columbia River Sahaptin.
Jonaz. See Chichimec.
Joukiousmé. See Chokuyem.
Jukiusme
Jova. Taracahitian; Sonora, Chihuahua; extinct.
Joba
Jobal
Ova
Juaneño. Takic (Southern California Shoshoncan); 1 in California (1962).[180]
Gaitchim
Netela
Netēla
San Juan Capestrano
San Juan Capistrano
San Juan Capistrano Mission
Julime. Concho.
Jumano. Taracahitian; Chihuahua, Texas, New Mexico; extinct, 1 (1897).
Shuman
Suma
Kabo. Mosquito.
Kadohadacho. Caddoan; Texas, Arkansas, Louisiana; 300 to 400 Caddo in Oklahoma (1962).[181]
Kahi. See Northern Hokan (a).
Kaialigmiut. Eskimo.
Kaibab. Southern Paiute.
Kaivavwit
Kaigani. Haida.
Caiganee
Kaigan
Kygáni

[180] Swanton, *Tribes*, p. 494, calls Juaneño 'a variant of Luiseño'.
[181] Subdivisions: (1) Cahinnio (also called Tula), (2) Kadohadacho, (3) Nanatsoho, (4) Upper Nasoni, (5) Upper Natchitoches, (6) Upper Yatasi.

Kaiyuhkhotana. Koyukon.
Káiyuhkhatána
Kalapuya. Kalapuyan; perhaps 1 or 2 in Oregon (1962).
Ahantchuyuk
Atfálati
Calapooa
Calapooiah
Calapooya
Calapuya
Kalapooiah
Lúkamiute
Wapatu
Wapatu Lake
Willamet
Kalapuyan. Penutian. See Takelman.
Kalapooian
Kalispel. Interior Salish; Washington, Idaho, Montana; 500 to 1,000 in Montana and Washington (1962).[182]
Flathead
Kalispelm
Kulleespelm
Kullespelm
Pend d'Oreille
Pends d'Oreille
Ponderay
Pondéra
Kamchadal. Luorovetlan.
Kamchatka
Kamskadale
Kamtschadale
Kamtschatka
Kamtshatka
Kamia. Southern Diegueño; Imperial Valley, California.
Campo
Comeya
Comoyei
La Huerta
Quemayá
Tipai

[182] Divisions: (1) Chewelah (upper Colville Valley, Washington), (2) Upper Kalispel (also called Upper Pend d'Oreilles, in Montana), and (3) Lower Kalispel (also called Lower Pend d'Oreilles, Flathead, or Kalispel proper, in Washington).

Kanghiryuachiakmiut. Eskimo.
Kanghiryuarmiut. Eskimo.
Kangjulit. Eskimo.[183]
    Kángiulit
Kaniagmiut. Eskimo; S. Alaska; 1,154 (1890).
    Achkugmjuten
    Kadiac
    Kadiack
    Kadiak
    Kadjack
    Kadjak
    Kadjaker
    Kageagemut
    Kaniagmiout
    Kaniagmut
    Karyak
    Katmai
    Katmay
    Kodiak
    Koniagmut
    Koniágmūt
Kañianermiut. Eskimo.
Kanithlualukshuamiut. Eskimo.
Kanjobal. Kanjobalan.
    Kanhobal
    Subinha
Kanjobalan. Mayan.
    Kanhobalan
Kansa. Dhegiha; Kansas, Missouri; 10 to 100 in Oklahoma (1962).
    Hútañga
    Kansas
    Kanzas
    Kanzes
    Kau
    Kaw
    Konsa
    Konza
Karalit. A synonym of Eskimo.
    Kaladlit

[183] See Pilling, Nos. 1226a and 3551. In No. 3551, part of the reference is to Zagoskin's data on Kuskokwim Eskimo: the rest is to his data on Kwikhpak and Tshnagmjut.

Kālālik
Kalalit
Karaler

Karankawa. Cariban; Texas; extinct, after 1860.[184]
Clamcoets
Clamcoche

Karankawan. See Karankawa.

Karkin. Costanoan.
Carquin
Karquines
Korekins

Karok. Hokan-Siouan; 100 to 1,000 in California (1962).[185]
Ara
Arra Arra
Cahroc
Karakuka
Károk
Pehtsék
Pehtsik
Quoratean

Kashaya. Pomoan; 100 in California (1962).
Southwestern Pomo

Kaska. Athapaskan; 200 to 500 in British Columbia, Yukon, and Alaska (1974).
Caska
Dease River
Eastern Nahane
Espatodena
Frances Lake
Nelson Indians
Upper Liard

Kaskaskia. Illinois.

Kaskinampo. Muskogean (?); Tennessee; extinct, 500? (1725).
Casqui
Casquin
Icasqui

Kasuá. Chumashan.
Cieneguita
Kahsowah

[184] Names of tribes given by Swanton are (1) Coapite, (2) Coaque (also called Coco), (3) Karankawa, (4) Kohani, (5) Kopano. Perhaps also (6) Tiopane, (7) Tups, (8) Pataquilla, (9) Quilotes.
[185] Swanton gives Karakuka as a dialect of Karok.

Kathlamet. Chinookan; Washington; extinct, 58 (1849).
Cathlamet
Katmay. Kaniagmiut.
Katmai
Kato. Athapaskan; fewer than 10 in California (1962), 1 or extinct (1970).
Batem-da-kai-ee
Batemdakaice
Batemdakaii
Kaipomo
Laleshiknom
Tlokeang
Katzie. Halcomelem; 50 in British Columbia (1962).
Kaitze
Katezie
Katsey
Kaulits. See Cowlitz.
Kuwalitsk
Kavelchadom. Yuma type Yuman; Arizona; extinct. See Halchidom.
Cocomaricopa
Kaveltcadom
Opa
Kaviagmiut. Eskimo.
Kaviágmut
Kaviágmūt
Kawaiisu. Numic (Ute type Plateau Shoshonean); fewer than 10 in California (1962).
Kawchottine. See Hare.
Kawia. Tule-Kaweah Yokuts.
Waiktshumni
Waitshumni
Kechayi. Northern Foothill Yokuts.
Kekchi. Kekchian; mostly in Alta Verapaz department, Guatemala, with an enclave in S. British Honduras; 250,000 (1952).
Cacchi
Caché
Cachi
Caichi
Cakchi
Cakgi
Cechi
Kachice
Kahchi
Kakchi

Kekchí
K'ekchi'
Quecchi
Quekchi
Kekchian. Mayan.
Kekchom
Kekchom. Quichoid.
Kenai. Tanaina.
Kenesti. See Wailaki.
Keres. A general term, sometimes used ambiguously for the Keresan language of a particular, otherwise unidentified pueblo.
Queres
Keresan. Hokan-Siouan.[186]
Keres
Queres
Kern Lake. Yawelmani.[187]
Kern River. See Tubatulabal.
Kern River Shoshonean. See Sierra Nevada Shoshonean.
Ket. Western Paleosiberian.
Kevalingamiut. Eskimo.
Keyauwee. Siouan (?); North Carolina; extinct some years after 1761.
Khabenapo. Pomo.
Cabanapo
Habenapo
Kábinapek
Khwakhamaiu. See Chwachamaju.
Kiatexemut. Eskimo.[188]
Kichai. See Kitsai.
Kiche. See Quiche.
Kechi
Tiche
Kickapoo. Algonquian; Michigan, Illinois, Indiana, Kansas and elsewhere; some Kickapoo moved to Mexico about 1852; 500 in Oklahoma and Kansas and 500? in E. Chihuahua (1962).
Kikapoo
Kikapu

[186] Divisions: (1) Queres (or Eastern Keresan), with Cochiti, San Felipe, Santa Ana, Santo Domingo, and Zia, and (2) Sitsime (or Kawaiko or Western Keresan), with Acoma and Laguna.
[187] Pilling, No. 3098: numbers 1–10 taken from a Yawelmani by Powers, *CNAE* 3.392 (1877), identified by Kroeber, *BAE-B* 78.478–9 (1925), as puns or word-play, extravagant Yawelmani mimicry of Salinan numerals.
[188] Perhaps the Kiatagmiut, a division of the Aglemiut.

Kikkapoe
Kikkapoo
Kigiktagmiut. Eskimo.
Kiglinirmiut. Eskimo.
Kij. See Gabrieleño.
Kīj
Kizh
Kikima. Halyikwamai.
Kiksht. Term used by M. Silverstein for Upper Chinookan dialects, Clackamas, Wasco-Wishram, Cascades, and others, excluding Kathlamet.
Kiliwa. See Kiliwi.
Kiliwi. Yuman; 60 in N. Baja California (1955).
Kiliwa
Kiliwee
Yukaliwa
Killinirmiut. Eskimo.
Killinunmiut. Eskimo.
Kilusiktomiut. Eskimo.
Kimbaya. Cariban? Chibchan?
Kinai. See Tanaina.
King George's Island. Data lacking.[189]
Ile du Roi George
King George's Sound. See Chugachigmiut.
King Island. Eskimo; in Bering Sea 40 miles W. of Cape Douglas, Alaska.
Ukivok Island
Ukiwuk Island
Uviuvok Island
Kings River. Foothill Yokuts.
King River
King William's Land. Eskimo. See Gjoa Haven.
Kinomi. Data lacking.[190]
Kinugumiut. Eskimo.
Kiowa. Kiowa-Tanoan; Idaho, Wyoming, South Dakota, Oklahoma, Coahuila, Chihuahua, Durango and elsewhere; 2,000 in Oklahoma (1962).
Káyowē
Kiaway
Manrhoat (?)
Quichuan (?)
Tepda

[189] Pilling, No. 1101, numerals 1–10 in E. Duflot de Mofras, *Exploration* 2.401 (1844).
[190] Pilling, Nos. 537–8, vocabulary from Whipple, in J.C.E. Buschmann, *König. Akad. der Wiss. zu Berlin, Abhandlungen ... 1857*, pp. 299–301 (1858).

Tepki'nägo
Tideing Indians

Kiowa-Apache. Apachean; fewer than 10 in Oklahoma (1962).
Déna
Gattacka
Kiowa Apache
Pacer Apache
Prairie Apache

Kiowan. See Kiowa.

Kiowa-Tanoan. Aztec-Tanoan.
Tanoan-Kiowa

Kitamat. Kwakiutl; 100 to 1,000 in British Columbia (1962).
Haisla
Heiltsuk[191]

Kitanemuk. Takic (Southern California Shoshonean); California; extinct, fewer than 50? (1910).
Kikitamkar
Kikitanum

Kitsai. Caddoan; Texas, Oklahoma; extinct before 1940, 10 (1910).
Kichai
Kitsei
Quichais
Quidehais

Kitksan. See Gitksan.

Kittitas. Northwest Sahaptin.

Kittizoo. A Tsimshian division; British Columbia; extinct after 1907.
Kittistzu

Kiwai. Tanaina?[192]

Kiwomi. Santo Domingo.

Kizh. See Gabrieleño.

Klahuse. Comox.

Klallam. See Clallam.

Klamath. Lutuamian; 100 in Oregon (1962).
Máklaks

Klamath. Penutian.
Klamath-Modoc
Lutuami
Lutuamian

[191] Also used for Bella Bella.

[192] Pilling, No. 529, vocabulary in J.C.E. Buschmann, *König. Akad. der Wiss. zu Berlin, Abhandlungen ... 1855*, pp. 242–313 (1856). Perhaps a misprint for Kinai.

Klaokwat. Nootka; British Columbia; 241 (1904).
  Claoquat
  Clayoquat
  Hancock Harbor
  Hancock's Harbor
  Tlaoquatch

Klatskanai. See Clatskanie.

Klatsop. See Clatsop.

Kleo Lake. Southern Tutchone.

Klikitat. Northwest Sahaptin; Oregon, Washington; 10 to 20 in Washington (1962).
  Kalikclat
  Kleketat
  Klicatat
  Klickitat
  Klikatat
  Kliketat
  Roilroilpam
  Tlakatat

Kluane. Tutchone; S.W. Yukon at S. end of Kluane Lake.

Knistenaux. See Cree.
  Kalisteno
  Kenistenoag
  Killisteno
  Knisteneaux
  Knisteneux
  Kristinaux

Koasati. Eastern Muskogean; Alabama, Mississippi, Louisiana, Texas, Oklahoma; 100 to 200 in Louisiana and Texas (1962).
  Coassatte
  Coosada
  Coosauda
  Coosawda
  Coushatta
  Koassati
  Koosatis
  Louisiana Koasati
  Shati
  Texas Koasati

Kobuk River. Eskimo.
  Kuuvaŋmiitun

Kocheyali. Kings River Yokuts (?).

Kodiak. See Kaniagmiut.
    Kadiak
    Kadjak
    Konægan
    Konega
    Koniagmut
Kogloktogmiut. Eskimo.
Kohani. Karankawa.
Kohuana. Cocopa type Yuman; Arizona, California; extinct after joining the Maricopa, 36? with the Maricopa (1883).
    Cajuenche
    Cawina
    Coana
    Cutganas (?)
    Quokim
Koikhpagmiut. Eskimo.
Koksoakmiut. Eskimo.
Koltschane. See Upper Kuskokwim.
Koluschan. See Tlingit.
Komuk. See Comox.
Konega. See Kaniagmiut.
    Konægan
Koniagmut. See Kaniagmiut.
Konithlushamiut. Eskimo.
Konkow. See Maidu.
    Konkau
Konomihu. Shastan; California; extinct some years after 1850.
Koosatis. See Koasati.
Kopano. Karankawa.
Kopé. Patwin.
    Copeh
Kopogmiut. Eskimo.
Koroa. Gulf (?); Mississippi, Louisiana; extinct, 80? (1730).
    Coligua (?)
    Colima (?)
    Kúlua
Koryak. Luorovetlan.
    Koriak
    Koriaque
    Korjak
Kosalektawi. Achumawi.
Koskimo. Kwakiutl.

Koso. See Panamint.
Kot. Western Paleosiberian.
Kotow. Data lacking.[193]
Kotzebue Sound. Eskimo.
Kowagmiut. Eskimo.
Kowilth. See Wiyot.
Koyeti. Yokuts.
Koyukon. Athapaskan; 400 to 500 in Alaska (1962).[193a] Krauss gives 700 (1970).
    Coyukon
    Co-yukon
    Ingelete
    Káiyuhkhatána
    Kaiyuhkhotana
    Koyukan
    Koyukukhotana
    Nulato
    Ten'a
    Unakhatana
    Unakhotana
Ku. See Sumo.
Kuitsh. See Lower Umpqua.
Kukpaurungmiut. Eskimo.
Kulanapo. See Pomo.
    Kulanapan
Kumachisi. Poso Creek Yokuts (?).
Kumanagoto. Cariban.
Kungugemiut. Eskimo.
Kunmiut. Eskimo.
Kusa. See Coos.
    Kusan
Kuskatchewak. Kuskokwim.
    Kuscatchewan
    Kuskutshewac
Kuskokwim. Eskimo.
    Aglemiut
    Aglemoute
    Aglegmut

[193] Pilling, No. 3123, vocabulary in J.C. Prichard, *Researches* (1826), pp. 353–4.

[193a] David and Kay Henry, *Hadohzil-eeyah. We are reading* (Fairbanks, 1969), p. 2: 'This Athapaskan language is spoken in the following Indian villages located on the Yukon and Koyukuk Rivers of central Alaska: Allakaket, Hughes, Huslia, Koyukuk, Kaltag, Nulato, Galena, Ruby, Kokrines, Tanana, Rampart and Stevens Village. There are changes in the language in some of these villages.'

Agulmut
Inkalit
Inkalit Yugelmut
Kouskovimtsi
Kuscatchewan
Kuskatchewak
Kuskivigmut
Kuskokivim
Kuskokwimjut
Kuskowigmjute
Kuskutchewac
Kuskutchewak
Kuskutshewac
Kuskwogmiut
Kuskwogmut

Kuskwogmiut. See Kuskokwim.

Kutcha-kutchin. Athapaskan; 1,000 in Alaska (1964).[194]

Fort Indians
Ik-kil-lin
Itchali
Itkpe'lit
Itku'dliñ
Kotch-á-kutchen
Kutchákutchin
Lowland People
Na-kotchpô-tschig-kouttchin
O-til'-tin
Western Kutchin
Youkon Louchioux
Yukon Flats

Kutchin. Athapaskan. See Kutcha-kutchin, Nakotcho-kutchin, Natsit-kutchin, Takkuth-kutchin, Tatlit-kutchin, Tennuth-kutchin, Tranjik-kutchin, Vunta-Kutchin. Perhaps 900 in Alaska and 900 in Canada (1970).

Kutchan
Loucheux
Takudh
Tukudh

Kutenai. Algonquian-Wakashan; Alberta, later Idaho, Washington, Montana, British Columbia; 300 to 500 in Idaho, Montana and British Columbia (1962).

[194] R.J. Mueller, *Topical dictionary of Western Kutchin* (Fairbanks, 1964), p. 5, cites speakers of Western Kutchin 'in Arctic Village, Fort Yukon, Venetie, Chalkyitsik, Canyon Village, Birch Creek, and Circle City'.

Arc-a-plat
Cootonais
Counarrha
Cuttonasha
Flatbow
Kitunaha
Kitunahan
Koetenaice
Koetenay
Kootenai
Kootenay
Kootenuha
Kutänä
Kutanai
Kutenay
Kutnehä
Lower Kutenai
Skalza
Skalzi
Upper Kutenai

Kuuvaŋmiitun. Eskimo.
Kobuk River

Kwaiailk. See Upper Chehalis.

Kwakiutl. Wakashan; 1,000 in British Columbia (1962). See Kitamat, Hailtsuk.
Kagutl
Kwaiantl
Kwakiool
Quagutl
Quoquols

Kwakiutlan. See Kwakiutl.

Kwalhioqua. Athapaskan; Washington; extinct, 2 (1910).
Kivalhioqua
Kwaliokwa
Willapa
Willopah

Kwantlen. Halcomelem; 15 in British Columbia (1962).

Kwigpak. See Kuskokwim, Kangjulit.
Kwigpakjute
Kwikhpak

Kwinaiutl. See Quinault.
Kwenaiwitl

Queniult

Kwoneatshatka. Nootka.

Labrador. Eskimo.

Lacandon. Cholan; Chiapas. See Chol.

Chol Lacandon

Lacandon. Maya; formerly in Yucatan; 200? in Chiapas and Tabasco jungles (1970).

Lacandón

Lacandone

Maya Lacandon

Xoquinel

Yucatecan Lacandon

La Cimienta. Nahuatl; San Luis Potosi.[195]

Laguna. Keresan; more than 3,000 in New Mexico (1970).

Lagunero. Aztecoidan; Mexico; extinct.[196]

Laimon. Cochimi; Baja California; extinct.

Laymon

Laymon-Cochimi

Laymonem

Lake. Okanagon.

Lakes

Lake Laberge. Southern Tutchone.

Lake Miwok. Miwok; 8 in California (1965).

La Palma. North Pame.

La Purisima. See Purisimeño.

Lakota. See Dakota.

Lakus. Sumo; Nicaragua.

Lakweip. Athapaskan (Tahltan type); Portland Canal, Alaska; later on Stikine River headwaters, British Columbia (1910).

Lackweip

Lāq'uyî'p

Naqkyina

Lassik. Athapaskan; California; 100 (1910).

Las Vegas. Data lacking.[197]

Lassik. Athapaskan; California; 100 (1910), 1 or 2 or extinct (1970).

Rogue River

Upper Rogue River

Upper Takelma

195 Perhaps the same as La Pimienta in Hidalgo. See Bright, *HMAI* 5.31 (1967).

196 Subdivisions: (1) Ahomamas, (2) Alamamas, (3) Caviseras, (4) Daparabopos, (5) Hoeras, (6) Irritila, (7) Maiconeras, (8) Meviras, (9) Miopacoas, (10) Ochoes, (11) Paogas, (12) Vassapalles, (13) Yanabopos. Orozco y Berra used the name Irritila as the tribal name.

197 Pilling, No. 3069, manuscript vocabulary taken by J. W. Powell, Oct., 1873, at Las Vegas, Nevada.

Walumskni
Lathruunun. Yokuts.
Laurentian. Iroquoian (Huron type); extinct well after 1536.
Lauretano. See Concho (Guaycuran).
Loretano
Loretto
Lekwiltok. Kwakiutl; British Columbia; 218 (1904).
Lekwiltoq
Ucalta
Ukwulta
Yokultat
Yukulta
Lenape. See Delaware.
Lenape Trading Jargon. A jargon based on Delaware, used in the seventeenth century.
Lenca. Lencan; Honduras, El Salvador; nearly extinct (1952).[198]
Lencan. Misumalpan? Xinca-Lencan?
Lepitan. See Sahaptian.
Lillooet. Interior Salish; 1,000 to 2,000 in British Columbia (1962).
Chin
Liloeet
Lilowat
Loquilt
Stlā'tliumQ
Lipan. Apachean; New Mexico, Texas, Coahuila, Nuevo Leon, Tamaulipas; 10 in New Mexico (1962), down to perhaps 1 (1970).
Faraon
Lipanes Abajo
Lipanes de Arriba
Lipanjenne
Lipano
Yabipai Lipan
Lkungen. South Georgia Salish; British Columbia; 40 (1962).[199]
Etzāmish
Lkū'men
L'kungen

198 Dialects: in El Salvador, (1) Chilanga, (2) Guatijigua; in Honduras, (3) Guaxiquero, (4) Intibucat [extinct], (5) Opatoro, (6) Similaton. Conguaco was assigned here by Mason but was classed by Lehmann as Xincan. Swanton followed Lehmann.
199 Synonyms listed here are those of the Songish tribe, whose name for themselves is Lkungen. The Songish language (also called Straits and Lkungen) is used by the Clallam, Lummi, Saanich, Samish, and Semiahmoo, and was used by the extinct Sooke.

Lkungeneng
Songees
Songish
Straits
Tsong

Llanero. Name of the Jicarilla in Coahuila.

Lohim. Northern Paiute (?); Oregon; 114 (1870).
Willow Creek

Long Island. Algonquian; New York; extinct.

Loretano. See Lauretano.

Loretto. See Lauretano.

Loucheux. See particularly Kutcha-kutchin, Nakotcho-kutchin, Takkuth-kutchin, and Tatlit-kutchin, as well as Kutchin.
Louchieux
Louchioux

Loup. Algonquian. See Mahican. The unique Loup mentioned by Teeter may be the Pocomtuc, who moved from Massachusetts, arriving in Quebec about 1754.

Lower Chehalis. Olympic Salish; fewer than 10 in Washington (1962).
See Chehalis.

Lower Chinook. Chinookan.
Coastal Chinook

Lower Rogue River. Tututni?[200]

Lower Umpqua. Yakonan; Oregon; extinct, fewer than 10 (1930).
Coast
Kuitsh
Qū'ītc

Lowland Chontal. Tequistlatec.

Lowland Tzeltal. Tzeltal.

Lucayan. An extinct Arawakan group of the Bahamas.
Lucayo
Lukayan
Yucayo (?)

Luckiamute. Kalapuya; Oregon; extinct, 8 (1910).
Lakmiut
Lúkamiute

Luiseño. Takic (Southern California Shoshonean); 100 to 200 in California (1962).
Juaneño (?)
Reyano
Saint Louis Mission
San Luis Mission

[200] Pilling, Nos. 270, 272, vocabularies taken for the Smithsonian by W.H. Barnhardt.

San Luis Rey
San Luis Rey Mission
San Luiz Rey de Francia

Lummi. Lkungen; Washington, British Columbia; 150 in Washington (1962).
Há-lum-mi
Hookluhmic
Nooh-lum-mi
Nookluolamic
Nŭh-lum-mi
Nŭkh'-lum-mi
qtlumi

Luorovetlan. Eastern Paleosiberian.

Lutuamian. Sahaptian. See Klamath.
Lutuami

Macapiras. Undetermined; Florida; 24 near St. Augustine (1728).
Amacapiras

Machapunga. Algonquian; North Carolina; extinct, 30 (1761).

Mackenzie Flats. Kutchin.
Fort McPherson
Nakotcho

Mackenzie River. Eskimo.
Chiglit
Inuvik
KitiyaRyuŋmiut
Mackenzie Eskimo
Tuktoyartuk
UumaRmiut

Mackenzie River Delta. Eskimo. See KitiyaRyuŋmiut.

Macoyahui. Taracahitian; Sonora; extinct.
Macoague (?)
Macoyahuy

Macro-Algonquian. Group with Algonquian, Muskogean and Gulf.
Macro-Algonkian

Macro-Mayan. Macro-Penutian.
Mayan-Zoquean-Totonacan
Mexican Penutian

Macro-Otomanguean. Macro-Penutian.
Macro-Oto-Manguean

Macro-Siouan. Group with Siouan, Iroquoian and Caddoan.

Macultanguis. Northern Zapotecan.

Madesiwi. Achumawi.

Mag Readings. See Patwin.

Magemiut. Eskimo.
Maguana. Arawakan (?); Haiti, perhaps also Cuba; extinct.
Magua (?)
Maguano (?)
Mahican. Algonquian; New York, Massachussetts, Vermont, Connecticut; extinct.[201]
Akochakanen
Brotherton
Hikanagi
Housatonic
Loup
Macicanni
Mahicann
Mahikan
Moheagan
Moheakanneew
Moheakannuk
Mohegan
Mohican
Mohikan
Muhekaneew
Muhheconnuk
Muhhekaneew
Muhhekaneok
Muhkekaneew
Stockbridge
Maidu. Penutian. See Nisenan, Northeast Maidu, Northwest Maidu.
Digger
Holólupai
Konkau
Konkow
Maiduan
Meidoo
Michopdo
Nákum
Pujuni
Secumne
Sekumne
Tsamak
Yuba

[201] Subtribes: (1) Mahican, (2) Mechkentowoon, (3) Wawyachtonoc, (4) Westenhuck (also called Stockbridges), (5) Wiekagjok. The term Mahican sometimes refers to (1) the Mahican on the Hudson River in New York State, or (2) the Mohegan on the Connecticut River, Connecticut.

Yupu

Makah. Nootka; 500 in Washington (1962). See Ozette.

Cape Flattery Indians
Fuca Straits
Macaw
Mac-kaw
Nitinaht Sound
Nitteenat

Malecite. Algonquian; 600 to 700 in New Brunswick and Maine (1962).

Abnaki
Echemin
Etchemin
Etchimi
Etechemin
Etechemine
Mahnesheet
Malechite
Maliseet
Malisete
Malisit
Mareschet
Mareschit
Mareschite
Meeleeceet
Melicete
Melicite
Milicete
Milicite
Millicete
St. Jean
St. John
St. John's
Wlastukweek

Malemiut. Eskimo; Norton Sound, Alaska; 630 (1900).

Mahlemut
Máhlemūt
Malehmiout
Malemute
Malimoot
Tschuagmjuten
Ulúkuk

Malhommes. Menomini.

Malincheno. Unclassified; N. Mexico; extinct.

Mam. Mamean; Chiapas, W. Guatemala; 270,000? (1965).

Mame

Mem

Zaklapahkap

Zaklohpakap

Zaklopahkap

Mam. A Mosquito tribe of Honduras.

Mam-Aguacatec. Quichoid.

Mamean. Mayan.

Manahoac. Ohio Valley Siouan; Virginia; extinct, 350? (1654).

Mahock

Manche. Chol; Guatemala (?); extinct.

Mandan. Siouan; Lake Michigan to the Dakotas; 12 in North Dakota (1970).

Mawatani

Numakaki

Numangkake

Sepohskanumakahkee

Wahtani

Mangue. Chorotegan; Nicaragua.[202]

Chololteca

Choluteca

Chorotega

Chorotegan

Dirian

Mánkemo

Nagrandan

Manso. Tanoan; near Las Cruces, New Mexico until 1659; fewer than 10? near El Paso at Isleta del Sur, Texas, or Senecú del Sur, Chihuahua (1950).

Gorretas

Lanos

Maratino. Tamaulipecan; Tamaulipas; extinct.

Maratin

Martinez

Maribichicoa. Tlapanec.

Maribichicoa-Guatajigiala

Maribio

[202] Swanton lists two divisions: (1) Diria, and (2) Nagrandan (with Subtiaba). Rivet lists three extinct groups called Chorotega or Mangue: (1) Choluteca, (2) Orotiña, and (3) Mangue, with divisions as noted by Swanton. For Rivet, Subtiaba belongs here only, and he brands the use of 'Subtiaba' as a synonym for Hokan Maribio 'a mistake'. Brinton says Rocha's Mangue is the dialect of Masaya. Berendt got some variant forms in the villages of Masatepec, Niquindomo and Namotiva.

Maricopa. Yuma type Yuman; 500 in Arizona (1962).
Cocomaricopa
Opa
Marien. Arawakan; Santo Domingo and perhaps Cuba; extinct.
Marin. See Miwok.
Mascouten. Term for (1) the Peoria band of the Illinois or (2) the Prairie band of the Potawatomi.
Maskegon. Cree.
Cree of the Lowlands
Makegong
Mushkeag
Muskegon
Savanois
Swampy Cree
Massachusetts. See Natick.
Massachuset
Massachusett
Massaco. See Wappinger.
Massacoe
Masset. Haida.
Matagalpa. Matagalpan; Nicaragua, Honduras, El Salvador; extinct?[203]
Chondal de Nicaragua
Chontal of Nicaragua
Matagalpan
Popoluca de Matagalpa
Matagalpan. Misumalpan.
Matlame. Southern Otomian; Guerrero; extinct.
Matlapa. Nahuatl.
Matlatzinca. Southern Otomian; Mexico, Guerrero, Michoacan; 300 in Mexico (1952). See Pirinda, Ocuiltec.[204]
Maltlatzinga
Matalzinga
Matlacinga
Matlalsinken
Matlaltzinca
Matlalzinca
Matlalzinga
Matlanzinga
Matlazinca

[203] Matagalpa had two dialects in the sixteenth century, Matagalpa and Cacaopera.
[204] Pirinda was the variety of Matlatzinca spoken in Michoacan. Swanton gives the subdivisions of Matlatzinca as (1) Atzinca, (2) Quata, and (3) Ocuiltec. Rivet uses Atzinca as a synonym of Ocuiltec.

Matlazinga

Mattabesec. See Wangunk.

Mattole. Athapaskan; California; perhaps extinct by 1967.

Saia (?)

Saiaz (?)

Maya (Yucatec). Mayan; Yucatan, Campeche, Quintana Roo, Chiapas, Oaxaca, Tamaulipas, Zacatecas: 81,013 monolinguals (1960); several hundred thousand in Yucatan, Campeche, Quintana Roo, parts of British Honduras, and Peten department, Guatemala (1967).[205]

Itza

Itzae

Mayo

Mayu

Mopan

Peten

Punctunc

Putunc

Yucatan

Yucatana

Yucatanice

Yucatano

Yucatec

Yucateca

Yucateco

Yucatèque

Yucatese

Mayan.[206] Macro-Mayan. See Maya.

Mayan-Zoquean-Totonacan. See Macro-Mayan.

Mexican Penutian

Mayo. Taracahitian; Sonora, Sinaloa: 1,837 monolinguals (1960); Yaqui and Mayo in Sonora, 10,000 (1967).

Cáhita

Mazahua. Central Otomian; Mexico, Michoacan; 15,759 monolinguals in Mexico state (1960).

Maçahva

Mazahuatl

[205] Swanton's Maya subdivisions [all with speakers of Maya (Yucatec) except (3)]: (1) Icaiche (Yucatan), (2) Itza (N. Guatemala [Lake Petén], British Honduras, Yucatan), (3) Lacandon (Yucatan; Chiapas, Tabasco), (4) Maya, also called Yucatec (Yucatan, Tabasco), (5) Mopan, also called Moapan (S. British Honduras, Guatemala), (6) Santa Cruz (N.E. Yucatan). McQuown, *IJAL* 22.193–5 (1956), lists as Maya dialects: (1) Yucatec, (2) Lacandone, (3) Itza, (4) Mopan.

[206] Bright lists s.v. *Mayan* several vocabularies of Chiapas, and Schuller's Api: see Bright (1967).

Mazahui
Mozahui

Mazapil. Aztecoidan (Nahuatl?); Zacatecas.

Mazatec. Popolocan; mostly in N. Oaxaca, Puebla and Veracruz with some in Distrito Federal and Coahuila; 73,416 monolinguals (1960), 95,000 speakers (1970).[206a] See Huautla de Jimenez.
Matlazahua
Mazateco

Mazatec of Guerrero. Unclassified; Guerrero; extinct.

Mazatec of Jalisco. Unclassified; Jalisco; extinct.

Mazatec of Tabasco. Unclassified; Tabasco; extinct.

Mazatecan. Otomanguean.

Mazatlan de Flores. Mazatec.

McCloud River. Okwanuchu?[207]

Mecayapan. Nahuatl; Veracruz.

Mechan. Term coined by Swadesh in 1956 for Zoquean.

Meco. See Chichimec.

Mediotaguel. Unclassified; Sinaloa; extinct.

Mednovskie. Ahtena.
Mednofski
Midnooski

Meherrin. Iroquoian; Virginia, North Carolina; extinct, 80 (1701).
Maharineck

Melchora. Chibchan; Nicaragua.

Menomini. Algonquian; Michigan, Wisconsin; 300 to 500 in Wisconsin (1962).
Folle Avoine
Malhommes
Mennomonie
Menomanie
Menomene
Menomenee
Menomeni
Menomine
Menominee
Menomonee
Menomoni
Mnemones

[206a] Paul L. Kirk, "Dialect intelligibility testing: The Mazatec study," *IJAL* 36.205–11 (1970), identifies a maximum of eight dialect areas: (1) Ayautla, (2) Chiquihuitlan, (3) Huautla, (4) Ixcatlan, (5) Jalapa, (6) Mazatzongo, (7) San Jeronimo Tecoatl, (8) Soyaltepec.

[207] Pilling, Nos. 3761, 3762, California vocabulary by L. Stone in S.F. Baird, *Report* 2.198–200, 3.428–9 (1876), reprinted in *CNAE* 3.531–4 (1877).

Wild Rice Men
Menunkatuck. See Wappinger.
Mescalero. Apachean; 1,500 in New Mexico (1967).[208]
Faraon
Llanero
Pharaoh
Querecho
Vaquero
Metlatonac. Mixtec.
Guerrero Mixteco
Methow. Okanagon type Interior Salish.
Battle-le-mule-emauch
Chilowhist
Metztla. Nahuatl; Puebla.
Mexican. See Nahuatl.
Aztec
Mexicano
Mexican Diegueño. Diegueño.
Imperial Valley
La Huerta
Meztitlaneca. Nahuatl.
Mextitlaneca
Miahuatlan. Southern Zapotecan.
Miahuateco
Serrano de Mihuatlan
Sierra del Sur
Southern Mountain
Miami. Algonquian; Wisconsin, Michigan, Indiana, Ohio, Kansas; extinct, 287 in Oklahoma (1937).[209]
Piankashaw
Tawatawas
Twightwees
Wea
Michigamea. Illinois.
Michilimacknac. Chippewa.
Michelmack
Michilimackinac

[208] Querecho and Vaquero are terms applied by Spaniards to various Apachean groups, not just the Mescalero. Similarly, Llanero is applied to the Mescalero, the Jicarilla and, sometimes, the Comanche.

[209] Miami bands in French sources: (1) Atchatchakangouen, (2) Kilatika, (3) Mengakonkia, (4) Pepicokia, (5) Piankashaw, (6) Wea.

Michoacan. Tarascan.
Mechoacan
Mechuacā
Michuacan
Michoacan. Nahuatl; Michoacan.
Micmac. Algonquian; Nova Scotia, Capa Breton Island, New Brunswick, later, Newfoundland; 3,000 to 5,000 in Nova Scotia, Prince Edward Island, New Brunswick and Quebec (1962).
Gaspésien
Mickmak
Micmacensi
Mikemak
Mikmak
Mikmaque
Miquemaque
Sourikwos
Souriquois
Mictlantongo. Mixtec.
Middle Kuskokwim. Ingalik.
Migichihilinious. See Chippewa.
Eagle Eyed Indians
Migueleño. Salinan; California; extinct, 1,000? (1814).[210]
San Miguel
Mikasuki. Eastern Muskogean; a variety of Hitchiti. See Hitchiti, Chiaha.
Mekusuky
Miccosukee
Mikasuke
Seminole
Millbank. Hailtsuk (Bella Bella).
Millbank Sound
Millerton. Yokuts.
Milpa Alta. Nahuatl.
Miluk. See Coquille (Coos).
Mimbreño. Apachean; New Mexico; extinct.
Coppermine
Jano (?)
Miniconjou. Dakota (Teton).
Minneconjou
Minitari. See Hidatsa.

[210] Kroeber, *BAE–B* 78.546 (1925), calls San Antonio and San Miguel two dialects of one language. He calls Playano a second Salinan language.

Minqua. See Conestoga.

Minto. Central Tanana (but cf. note 303). See Ingalik.

Miskito. See Mosquito.

Missisauga. Chippewa; Ontario, New York; 810 in Ontario (1906).

Achsissaghecs
Aoechisacronon
Cheveux Relevez
Messisauga
Messisauger
Messisaugi
Mississaga
Mississage
Nation de Bois
Oumisagai
Wisagechroanu

Mississippi Valley Siouan. Siouan.

Missouri. Chiwere; Wisconsin, Iowa, Missouri, Nebraska, Kansas, Oklahoma; extinct, 13 (1910).

Missouria
Missourie

Missouri River Siouan. Siouan.

Misumalpan. Chibchan?

Mosumalpan

Mitla. Central Zapotecan.

Miwok. Penutian.

Bodega
Lekumne (?)
Marin
Meewoc
Mewoc
Miwoc
Miwokan
Mokélumne
Moquelumnan
Saclan
Saklan
San Raphael
Talatui
Talutui
Yosemite

Miwok-Costanoan. See Utian.

Mixco. Pocomam.
    Chinautla
    Palin
Mixe. Zoquean; mostly in Oaxaca and Veracruz; 34,687 monolinguals (1960).
    Ayook
    Guichiovian
    Mije
    Tapijualapane-Mixe
Mixe-Zoque. See Zoquean.
    Mixe-Zoquean
Mixtec. Mixtecan; mostly in Oaxaca, Puebla, and Guerrero, with some in Veracruz, San Luis Potosi, Coahuila and Colima; 106,545 monolinguals (1960).[211]
    Mistec
    Misteca
    Misteco
    Mistekic
    Mistèque
    Mixtecice
    Mixteca
    Mixteco
    Mixtekeu
    Mixtèque
    Miztec
    Mizteca
Mixtecan. Otomanguean.
Mixtepec. Southern Zapotecan.
    The Mixtepecs
Mizocuavean. Penutian.
M'mat. Yuman (Yuma type?).
Mobile. Muskogean (Choctaw type); Alabama; extinct, 100? (1758).[212]
    Mabila
    Mavila
    Mobilian

[211] Orozco y Berra (1864) listed eight dialects: (1) Mixteco de Nochiztlan, (2) Mixteco de Tlaxiaco, (3) Mixteco de Xaltepec, (4) Mixteco de Zamapilapa, (5) Mixteco de Mictlantongo, (6) Mixteco de Cuilapa, (7) Mixteca Baja, and (8) Mixteco de Jauhuitlan, all in Oaxaca, except for Mixteca Baja in Puebla and Guerrero. E.V. Pike and J.H. Cowan, "Huajuapan Mixtec phonology and morphophonemics", *AnL* 9/5.1–15 (1967), mention without subgrouping (1) Ayutla, (2) Huajuapan [pop. 5,000 (1967)], (3) Jicaltepec, (4) Metlatonac or Guerrero Mixteco, (5) San Esteban, (6) San Miguel, (7) Santa Tomás [sic].

[212] B.S. Barton, *New views* (1798), has a Mobilien vocabulary (Pilling, No. 298). I do not know if this vocabulary represents the Mobile language per se or the 'Mobile Jargon' which had a Choctaw or Chickasaw grammatical core.

Mobilien

Mocama. Timucua.

Mocorito. Taracahitian (Cahita?); Sinaloa; extinct.

Modoc. Klamath; Oregon, California; 10 to 100 in Oregon (1962).
See Lutuamian.
Lutuami
Modok

Mohave. Yuma type Yuman; California, Arizona; 1,000 in Arizona (1962).
Amojave
Hummock'havi
Iat
Jamajabs
Mahao
Mojave
Soyopas

Mohawk. Iroquoian; 1,000 to 2,000 in Ontario, Quebec and New York (1962).
Agnier
Canienga
Caughnawaga
Macquaic
Mahakuassica
Mahaqu
Mohaux
Mohogica (?)
Mohogice (?)
St. Regis

Mohegan. See Mahican.

Mohogica. Mohawk?
Mohogice

Moklasa. See Muklasa.

Molala. Penutian; Oregon; extinct.
Molale
Mólale
Molalla
Molele

Monacan. Siouan; Virginia; extinct, 100 (1669).
Rahowacah

Moneton. Siouan; West Virginia; extinct.

Mono. Numic (Plateau Shoshonean); 100 to 500 in California (1962). See Northern Paiute.

Montagnais. Algonquian; Labrador, Quebec; 5,000 in Quebec (1962).[213]
Montagnaise
Montagnais-Naskapi
Montagnar
Montagnards
Montagnie
Mountain Indians
Mountainee
Mountaineers
Mountainiers
Sheshapotosh
Sheshatapoosh
Sheshatapooshoish
Sheshatapooshoïsh
Montanyes. Mixtec; Guerrero.
Montañes
Montauk. Algonquian; New York; extinct, 6? (1869).[214]
Montaug
Montaucktt
Patchoag
Patchogue
Unachog
Unquachog
Monterey. See Rumsen.
Moose Cree. Cree.
Monsoni
Moose
Moose Factory
Moosehide. Kutchin at Dawson.
Mopan. Maya; 2,000 to 3,000 in Guatemala and British Honduras (1965).
Moapan
Moquelumnan. See Miwok.

[213] Tribes (Hodge, *Handbook* 1.933): (1) Astouregamigoukh, (2) Attikiriniouetch, (3) Bersiamite, (4) Chisedec, (5) Escoumains, (6) Espamichkon, (7) Kakouchaki, (8) Mauthæpi, (9) Miskouaha, (10) Mouchaouaouastiirinioek, (11) Naskapi, (12) Nekoubaniste, (13) Otaguottouemin, (14) Oukesestigouek, (15) Oumamiwek, (16) Papinachois, (17) Tadousac, (18) Weperigweia.

The Algonquian Montagnais should not be confused with the Athapaskan groups called Montagnais. See Mountain.

[214] Divisions: (1) Corchaug, (2) Manhasset, (3) Massapequa, (4) Matinecock, (5) Merric, (6) Montauk, (7) Nesaquake, (8) Patchogue (also called Unquachog or Unachog), (9) Rockaway, (10) Secatogue, (11) Setauket, (12) Shinnecock.

Jefferson, who took an Unquachog vocabulary from one of the last three speakers in 1791, reported that Unquachog, Shinnecock and Montauk were almost mutually unintelligible.

Moratok. Algonquian; North Carolina; extinct.
Mosan. Algonquian-Wakashan.
Mosopelea. See Ofo.
Mosquito. Misumalpan; Nicaragua, Honduras; 15,000 (1954).[215]
Miskito
Missquito
Moscan
Moskito
Waikna
Mosquitoan. Misumalpan (?).
Motozintlec. Mayan; S.E. Chiapas; 4,000? (1952).
Mochó
Motocintlec
Mototzintlec
Motozintleca
Motozintleco
Mount St. Elias. Chugachigmiut.[216]
Mountain. Athapaskan (Chipewyan type); in the region of Caribou Lake, Axe Lake and Brechet Lake, Canada; 900 (1906).[217]
Caribou Eaters
Etheneldeli
Montagnais
Mountain Cahuilla. Cahuilla.
Mountain Maidu. See Maidu.
Move. Chibchan (Guaymi); N.W. Panama; extinct.
Norteño
Valiente
Muca-Oreive. Unclassified; Sonora; extinct.
Muckleshoot. Southern Puget Sound Salish; Washington; fewer than 10? (1962).[218]
Mugulasha. Muskogean (Quinipissa?); Louisiana; extinct, 300? (1698).
Muite. Chibchan (Guaymi); Panama; extinct.
Muklasa. Alabama (?); Alabama; extinct by 1911, 120? (1792).

[215] Dialects: (1) Baldam, (2) Kabo, (3) Tāwira; (4) Mam, (5) Wanki.

[216] Pilling, No. 1231, 60 words in a Smithsonian manuscript, taken from 'the Indians near Mount St. Elias'.

[217] The term Mountain (especially in the form Montagnais) may refer to a type of Chipewyan or Yellowknife spoken on the N. shores and E. bays of Great Slave Lake, for which syllabary records are available. The term Mountain, however, has been applied also to groups speaking Beaver, Chipewyan, Kaska, Sarsi, Slave, Tsetsaut and Yellowknife. The judgments of Morice and Petitot have added to the confusion. Morice's Sekani includes Sarsi and groups which Morice called Mountain. Petitot's Montagnard refers to the Nahane (his cover term for the Tahltan, the Kaska and some Slave) and the Sekani.

[218] Bands: (1) Dothliuk, (2) Sekamish, (2) Skopamish [222 (1863)], (4) Smulkamish [183 (1870)].

Multnomah. Chinookan (Clackamas); Oregon; extinct perhaps by 1910, 800 (1806).[219]
Mathlanobs
Moltnomas
Mulknomans

Munsee. Delaware; New Jersey, New York, Wisconsin, Kansas, Oklahoma; 10 in Oklahoma (1910), fewer than 10 in Ontario (1962).
Christian Indians
Esopus
Minsi
Monsee
Muncey

Muoi. Chibchan (Guaymi); W. Panama; extinct.

Muran. Paezan.

Murire. Chibchan (Guaymi); S.W. Panama; extinct.
Bogota
Bonkota
Bukueta
Sabanero

Muskogean. Gulf.
Muskhogean

Muskogee. Eastern Muskogean; South Carolina, Georgia, Alabama, Florida; 10,000 in Oklahoma and Alabama and 300 called Seminole in Florida (1962).[220]
Creek
Crick
Crickice
Maskogi
Maskoke
Maskoki
Maskωke
Mukkogee
Muscogee
Muscoghe
Muscogulge
Muscoki
Muskhogee
Muskogh

[219] Divisions: (1) Cathlacomatup, (2) Cathlacumup, (3) Cathlanaquiah, (4) Clahnaquah, (5) Clanin-nata, (6) Kathlaminimin, (7) Multnomah, (8) Nechacokee, (9) Nemalquinner, (10) Shoto.

[220] Creek is (1) a synonym of Muskogee, or (2) a cover term for any of various allied tribes.

Muskoghe
Muskogulge
Muskohg
Muskohge
Muskohgee
Muskoke
Muskokee
Muskoki
Seminole

Musqueam. Halcomelem; 100 in British Columbia (1962).

Mutsun. Costanoan.
Esselen
Hluimen
Huelel
Karkin
San Juan Bautista
Tuichun (?)
Uhimen

Muutzicat. See Cora (Aztecoidan).

Naamirus. Western Aleut; on the islands of Tanaga, Iak, Kavalga, Unalga and perhaps Skagul; extinct (by 1950).

Nabesna. Athapaskan; 400 to 500 in Alaska (1962). [Hoijer's Nabesna =Tanana B.]
Upper Tanana

Nabiltse. See Hupa.

Nagailer. See Carrier.

Nagrandan. See Mangue.
Masaya
Nagranda
Subtiaba

Nagyuktogmiut. Eskimo.

Nahane. Athapaskan. See Mountain.[221]
Esbataottine
Espatodena

[221] The reference of Nahane is to 'outsiders', not to a single tribe. In consequence, ethnographers have attached the term to various tribes. Swanton, *Tribes*, p. 584, listed these bands or tribes as Nahane: (1) Esbataottine, (2) Etagottine, (3) Kaska, (4) Pelly River Indians [i.e., Tutchone], (5) Tagish, (6) Takutine, (7) Titshotina, (8) Tahltan, (9) Mountain (also called Tsethaottine). Others have equated Nahane with one or more of the following: Kaska, Mountain, Slave, Tagish, Tahltan, Teslin, Tsetsaut, Tutchone. Pilling has recorded under the rubric Nahane only three items — three Smithsonian manuscripts, two 180 word vocabularies, one by R. Kennicott, the other by R.B. Ross (Pilling, Nos. 2079, 3395), taken in the mountains N.W. of Fort Liard and on the Nehawney River in S.W. Mackenzie, and comparative study of these lists by F.L.O. Roehrig, done in 1874 (*BAE–B* 14.89 [1892]).

Nahani
Nahawney
Nahâwney
Nehawni
Nohannies

Nahua-Tanoan. See Aztec-Tanoan.

Nahuat. Nahuatlan; 40,000 to 75,000 in S. Veracruz (1960)
Isthmus Nahuat
Nauat
Pipil

Nahuatl. Aztecoidan; roughly 30,000 to 90,000 monolinguals in each of these states: Puebla, Hidalgo, Veracruz, Guerrero, and San Luis Potosi; the total of monolinguals in these states and Tlaxcala, Oaxaca, Mexico, Morelos, Durango, Distrito Federal, Zacatecas and Baja California was over 297,000 (1960).
Aztec
Azteca
Aztek
Aztekisch
Azteque
Culhua
Megicana
Megicano
Messicana
Messicanice
Mexica
Mexicaine
Mexican
Mexicana
Mexicane
Naguatl
Nahóa
Nahua
Nahúa
Nahual
Nahúal
Nahualt
Náhuatl
Nahúate
Nahúatl
Niquira
Niquiran

Nuhuatl

Pipil

Nahuatlan. Uto-Aztecan.

Nahuatlato. Aztecoidan; Nicaragua; extinct.

Nahuizalco. Nahuatl; El Salvador.

Nahyssan. Siouan; Virginia; extinct.

Monahassano

Monahassanugh

Yesa^{n}

Ñakipa. Yuman.

Nakota. See Dakota.

Nakotcho-kutchin. Kutchin; Mackenzie; 600 (1906).

Gens de la Grande Riviere

Loucheux

Mackenzie Flats

Nakotcho

Naloten. Carrier.

Nalotin

Nulaantin

Nulaautin

Nulaáutin

Naltunnetunne. Athapaskan; Oregon; extinct, 77 (1877).[222]

Noltanana

Nûltŏnät'-tĕne

Tututni

Nambe. Tewa; 200 in New Mexico (1967).

Nambé

Namoller. See Yuit.

Nanaimo. Halcomelem; 150 in British Columbia (1962).

Nanaimoo

Nanaimook

Snanaimoo

Snanaimuk

Snanaimux

Snonowas

Nanticoke. Algonquian; Maryland, Pennsylvania, Delaware; extinct, 30 (1792).

Doegs

Nanticok

Nentego

[222] Naltunnetunne, despite the reference to it by some as Tututni, was not the same as Tututni Naltunnetunne and Tututni were neighboring dialects of noticeable difference.

Taux
Toags
Unalachtigo
Unechtgo
Wiwash

Naolan. Taracahitian (?); S.W. Tamaulipas; extinct, 1,000? (1500).

Napochi. Muskogean (Choctaw type); Alabama; extinct, probably after joining the Chickasaw about 1699.

Narragansett. Algonquian; Rhode Island, Connecticut; extinct, 16 (1910).
Naraganset
Narraganset
Nousaghauset

Naskapi. Montagnais (Algonquian); Labrador, Quebec; 2,500 (1858).
Nascapee
Naskapee
Scoffie
Skoffi
Skoffie

Naskoten. Carrier.
Naskotin
Niscotins

Nass. See Niska.
Naas

Natchesan. Gulf.

Natchez. Natchesan; Mississippi, Alabama, South Carolina, Tennessee, Louisiana and elsewhere; extinct, possibly later than 1950, 300? (1836), 2 (1936).
Na'htchi
Natches

Natchez-Muskogean. See Gulf.

Natchitoches. Caddo; Louisiana; extinct, 150? (1831).
Yatchitoches

Natick. Algonquian; Massachusetts; extinct, 500 (1631). See Nauset.
Eastern Indians
Massachuset
Massachusett
Massachusetts
Natik

Natsit Kutchin. Athapaskan; 200? in Alaska (1970).
Chandalar River
Gens du Large
Natché-kutchin
Natsit

Natsit-kutchin
Neyetse-kutchi
Tpe-ttchié-dhidié-kouttchin

Naudowessi. See Dakota.

Naugatuck. See Wappinger.

Naukan. Central Siberian Yupik; fewer than 300 at Nunyagma and Pinakul, St. Laurence Bay (1970).
Navuqaq

Nauset. Algonquian (Natick?); Cape Cod, Massachussetts; extinct, 515 at Mashpee, mostly Nauset and Wampanoag (1698).

Navajo. Apachean; 140,000?, mostly in Arizona, New Mexico and Utah (1970).
Apaches de Navaio
Apaches de Navajo
Apaches de Navajox
Apaches Navajoes
Apachi Navajentes
Diné
Nabajo
Navaho
Navajoe
Yabipais Nabajay

Nawathinehena. Arapaho; 885 in Oklahoma (1906).
Nawunena
Nermonsinnansee
Southern Arapaho

Nawiti. Kwakiutl; British Columbia; 69 (1906).
Niwiti
Tlatlasikoala

Nayarit. See Cora, Huichol.

Nedlungmiut. Eskimo.

Negrito. Taracahitian (?); Tamaulipas; extinct, 1,000? (1500).

Nehelim. Tillamook; Oregon; extinct, 28 (1871).
Nehalem

Nehethawa. Cree.

Nejicho. See Nexitzo.

Nelson Indians. Kaska.

Nenitagmiut. Eskimo.

Nespelim. See Sanpoil.

Nestucca. Tillamook; Oregon; extinct, 46 (1881).
Nönstöki
Noustoki

Netcetumiut. Eskimo.
Netela. See San Juan Capistrano.
Netla. Slave.
Netlakapamuk. See Thompson.
    Neetlakapamuch
    Neklakapamuk
    Nitlakapamuk
    Ntlakyapamuk
Netsilingmiut. See Gjoa Haven.
Neusiok. Algonquian (?), Iroquoian (?); North Carolina; extinct, 60? (1709).
    Neuse
Neutral. Iroquoian; Ontario, New York, Ohio, Indiana (?), Michigan; extinct, 800 near Detroit (1653).
    Attiwandaronk
    Hatiwa^{n}ta-runh
Nevome. Pima Bajo.
    Nebome
New England. See Natick.
New Galicia. Data lacking.[223]
New Jersey. Algonquian (Delaware?).[224]
New Milford Indians. Algonquian refugees in Connecticut; 200? (1800).
New Netherland. Algonquian and Iroquoian.[225]
New River Shasta. Shastan.
New Stockbridge. Algonquian.[226]
New Sweden. Delaware.
Newittee. Nootka.
Nexitzo. Northern Zapotecan.
    Nejicho
    Nesicho
    Netzicho
    Nexitza
Nez Perce. Sahaptin (two dialects, Upper Nez Perce and Lower Nez Perce); Idaho, Washington, Oregon; 500 to 1,000 in Idaho (1962).
    Chopunnish
    Nez Percé
    Nez Percés
    Nùmípotitókĕń

[223] Pilling, No. 1538; remarks by H.R. Gil, *Soc. Geog. Mex. Bol.* 8.474-501 (1860).
[224] See Pilling, *BAE–B* 13.373 (1891), citing e.g. S. Smith, *History of ... New-Jersey* (1765), p. 137.
[225] Pilling, No. 352; E. Benson, *Memoir* (1817), Algonquian and Iroquoian names, pp. 5-17.
[226] Pilling, Nos. 1959–62; J. Tanner, *Narrative* (1830), numerals from Kao-no-mut, a woman from Fox River, 1827.

Numipu
Numípu
Saaptins
Sahapotins
Sahaptanian
Sahaptin

Niantic. See Eastern Niantic, Western Niantic.

Nicaragua. Data lacking.[227]

Nicarao. Aztecoidan; Nicaragua; extinct.
Niquisan

Nicola. Athapaskan; British Columbia; extinct, 150 (1780).[228]
Stuichamukh
Stuwihamuk

Nicoleño. Takic (Southern California Shoshonean);[229] San Nicolas Island, some 80 miles S.W. of Los Angeles, California; extinct since about 1865.

Nicoya. See Orotiña.

Nikolai. See Ingalik.
Nicolai

Nikutamuk. See Thompson.
Nicoutemuch
Nikutemukh

Nio. Taracahitian; Sinaloa; extinct, 1,000? (1500).

Nipissing. Algonkin; Ontario; 223 (1906).

Nipmuc. Algonquian; Massachusetts, Rhode Island, Connecticut; extinct in 1821, 142 (1774).
Nipmuck
Nipmunk
Nipnet

Niquiran. See Nahuatl.

Nisenan. Maidu; 12 in California (1962).
Neeshenam
Nishinam
Pujuni
Southern Maidu
Wapumni

Niska. Tsimshian; British Columbia, Alaska; 800 to 1,000? in British Columbia (1970).[230]

[227] Pilling, No. 2525, day names in the Nicaragua language [Nicarao?], B. Mayer, *Mexico* 2.174 (1852).

[228] Not to be confused with the Nicola band of the Thompson.

[229] Only four words are on record.

[230] Divisions: (1) Kithateh (also called Gitrhatin), (2) Kitgigenik (also called Gitwinksilk), (3) Kitwinshilk, (4) Kitanwilksh.

Naas
Nass
Nass River Indians

Nisqualli. Southern Puget Sound Salish; Washington; 62? (1937), 50 to 100 speakers of all varieties of Southern Puget Sound Salish, including Nisqualli and five other groups (1962).
Niskwalli
Niskwally
Nisqually
Skwale
Skwali
Squallyamish
Squallyomish

Nitinat. Nootka; British Columbia; 10 to 100 (1974).
Nettinat
Nitinaht

Niwiti. Nawiti

Noahonirmiut. Eskimo.

Noatagmiut. Eskimo.

Nochiztlan. Mixtec.

Nochpeem. See Wappinger.

Nomlaki. Wintun; fewer than 5 in California (1962).
Nome Lackee
Tehama
Tehema

Nongatl. Athapaskan; California; 100 (1910), language extinct.

Nooksack. Squamish; fewer than 10 in Washington (1962).
Mooksahk
Nooksahk
Nootsack
Nuksack
Nuksahk

Noonatarghmeutes. Eskimo.
Noona-targh-meutes

Nootka. Wakashan; 1,000 to 2,000 in British Columbia (1962). See Makah.[231]
Aht
Clayoquot
Hancock Harbor (?)
King George Sound

[231] The term Nootka may refer not only to Wakashan but in older works to Haida, Chimakuan, Salishan or Chinookan. For a list of 24 Wakashan subdivisions or tribes called Nootka, see Swanton, *Tribes*, p. 587.

Kwoneatshatka
Newittee
Nootka Sound
Nootkah
Noutka
Nutka
Tahkaht
Tlaoquatch
Tlaoquatsh
Vancouver Island
Wakash

Nootsack. See Nooksack.

Noowookmeutes. Eskimo.
Noowook-meutes

Noquet. Algonquian; Michigan; extinct some years after 1659.

Norfolk Sound. Sitka.

Norridgewock. Abnaki. See Canniba.
Caniba
Canniba
Norridgwog

Norteño. See Terraba and Move.

North Georgia Salish. Coast Salish.

North Pame. Otopamean; in the Sierra Gorda at Ciudad del Maíz, Alaquines, La Palma, Gamotes, and (in a divergent form) Santa María Acapulco.

Northeast Maidu. Maidu; fewer than 10 in California (1962).
Mountain Maidu
Northeastern Maidu

Northeast Sahaptin. Northern Sahaptin.

Northeast Yuki. See Yuki.

Northeastern Pomo. Pomoan; 1 in California (1962).
Salt Pomo

Northeastern Yavapai. Yavapai.

Northern Costanoan. Costanoan.

Northern Diegueño. Diegueño.
Mesa Grande

Northern Ępęra. Chocoan.

Northern Foothill. Foothill Yokuts.

Northern Hill Patwin. Patwin.

Northern Hokan (a). Term for Karok, Chimariko and Shastan (with Palaihnihan).
Kahi

Northern Indians. Data lacking.[232]

[232] Pilling, Nos. 539, 540 (Athapaskan), 1978a, 1610.

Indios del Norte

Northern Iroquoian. Iroquoian.

Northern Mixe. Mixe.

Northern Otomian. Otomian.

Northern Paiute. Numic (Bannock type Plateau Shoshonean); 2,000 in Nevada, California, Oregon and Idaho (1962).[233]

Monachi

Mono

Mono-Paviotso

Paiute

Paviotso

Snake

Northern Pomo. Pomoan; fewer than 40 in California (1962).

Northern Sahaptin. Sahaptin.

Northern Shoshoni. Numic (Shoshoni type Plateau Shoshonean); Idaho, Wyoming, Utah; part of the 5,000 speakers of Shoshoni (1962).

Aliatan

Gens du Serpent

Snake

Northern Sierra Miwok. Sierra Miwok; 20 to 30 in California (1962).

Northern Sumo. Sumo.

Northern Tepehuan. Tepehuan.

Northern Valley Yokuts. Valley Yokuts.

Northern Wintu. Wintu.

Northern Yaana. Yana.

Gari'i

Northeastern Yana

Northern Yana

Northern Yahi. Yahi.

Central Yana

Southern Yana

Northern Zapotecan. Zapotecan.

Northumberland Inlet. Eskimo.

Northwest Maidu. Maidu; 10 to 100 in California (1962).

Konkow

Northwestern Maidu

Northwest Sahaptin. Northern Sahaptin.

[233] Northern Paiute, in Swanton's usage, is the language of several tribes in W. Nevada, S.E. Oregon (including Powder River Valley and upper John Day River), S.W. Idaho, and a California strip E. of the Sierra Nevada to Owens Lake. Mono, however, should be distinguished from Northern Paiute or Paviotso. Powell in 1891 used the term Paviotso for part of the Nevada Shoshoneans. The term Snake, applied to the Northern Paiute of Oregon, is used of other Shoshonean groups as well, for example the Bannock and the Northern Shoshoni.

Norton Sound. Eskimo.
Norumbega. Data lacking.[234]
Nottoway. Iroquoian; Virginia; extinct, 47 (1825).[235]
    Mangoack
    Mangoak
    Mengwe
Ntlakyapmuk. See Thompson.
Ntsietshaw. See Tillamook.
    Ntsietshawus
Nueva España. Data lacking.[236]
Nueva Segovia. Data lacking.[237]
Nugumiut. Eskimo.
Nuksahk. See Nooksack.
Nukwalimuk. Data lacking.[238]
    Nuskiletemh
Numsu. Patwin.
Nunatogmiut. Eskimo.
Nunennumiut. Eskimo.
Nunivak. Eskimo.
    Nunivagmiut
    Nuniwok
    Nuniwok Island
Nuqua. Tlingit.
Nushagagmiut. Eskimo.
    Nushergagmut
    Nushergágmūt
Nusulph. See Cowlitz.
Nuvorugmiut. Eskimo.
Nuvugmiut. Eskimo.

[234] Pilling, No. 3842, Algonquian (Penobscot?) vocabulary in A. Thevet, *Cosmographie Universelle* 2.1008–13 (1575), reprinted in part by J.H. Trumbull, *Hist. Mag.* 7.239 (1870) and reprinted in *Mag. of Amer. History* 8.130–8 (1882).

[235] The term Nottaway (from an Algonquian epithet equating enemies with adders) applies also to (1) a group known in N. South Carolina, 1748–1754, belonging to the Meherrin or possibly the Susquehanna, and (2) the Eskimo.

[236] Pilling, No. 2870, words in G.F. de Oviedo y Valdés, *Historia* 4.593–607 (1855).

[237] Pilling, No. 2401, grammar and dictionary reputedly by Fr. Ambrosio de la Madre de Dios, listed by Beristain.

[238] Names from Pilling's Salishan index, derived from F. Boas, *BAAS–R* (1892), p. 409, where the spellings are Nuqálmukh and Nusk'életemh. See Pilling, *BAE–B* 16.5 (1893). Pilling had rough sledding with his Salishan names. In a letter to Wilberforce Eames, Nov. 3, 1891, pp. 1–2, Pilling wrote: 'Hope to tackle the Salishan [bibliography] next if I can get any order out of the chaos of Henshaw's synonymy cards. They gave me the headache yesterday and as for his Shoshonian —! I simply gave it up.'

Obispeño. Chumashan; California; extinct.
San Luis Obispo Mission
Ocale. Gulf (?); Florida; extinct.
Etocale
Ocala
Occaneechi. Siouan; Virginia, North Carolina; 150? (1709).
Botshenins
Patshenins
Saponi
Oconee. Muskogean; Georgia, Florida; extinct, 200? (1761).
Seminole
Ocoroni. Taracahitian; Sinaloa; extinct.
Ocotlan. Central Zapotecan.
Ocotopec. Zoque.
Ocuiltec. Southern Otomian; 300 in Mexico state (1952).
Atzinca
Ocuilteca
Ocuilteco
Yŭkak'o
Ofo. Ohio Valley Siouan; Ohio, Indiana, Tennessee, Kentucky (?), Mississippi, Louisiana; extinct, 1 (1908).
Chonque
Mosopelea
Mosoperea
Ossipe
Ouesperie
Ouispe
Ushpee
Oglala. Dakota.
Ogallah
Ogallala
Ohio Valley Siouan. Siouan.
Ohuera. Unclassified; Sinaloa; extinct.
Ojibwa. See Chippewa.
Okanagon. Interior Salish; Washington, British Columbia; 1,000 to 2,000 in Washington (1962).[239]
Okanagan
Okinakan
Okinaken
Okinagan

[239] Chafe (1962) under Okanagan lists Southern Okanagan, Sanpoil, Colville and Lake.

Wakynakane

Okelousa. Muskogean (?); Mississippi, Louisiana; extinct, 230? (1698).

Caluça (?)

Okmulgee. Eastern Muskogean (Hitchiti type?); Georgia, Alabama; extinct, 220 in Oklahoma (1822).

Okwanuchu. Shastan; California; extinct by 1925, 200? (1860).

McCloud River (?)

Olamentke. See Bodega.

Olamentko

Olive. Unknown; Texas, later S. Tamaulipas; extinct.

Olmeca. Nahuatl; Veracruz, Tabasco.

Olmec

Olomeca

Oluta. Zoquean; Veracruz

Popoluca of Veracruz

Olympic Salish. Coast Salish.

Omaha. Dhegiha; Minnesota, South Dakota, Nebraska; 1,000 to 3,000 in Nebraska (1962).

Maha

Mahaw

Omahaw

Omawhaw

Omohaw

Onatheaqua. Gulf (?); Florida; extinct.

Oneida. Iroquoian; 1,000 to 2,000 in Ontario, New York and Wisconsin (1962).

Oneidah

Oneider

Oneydoe

Onnoiout

St. Xavier

San Francisco Xavier Mission

Onondaga. Iroquoian; fewer than 1,000 in New York and Ontario (1962).[240]

Maqua (?)

Onondagaisch (?)

Onondago

Onondago County (?)

Onontager

[240] Materials for Onondaga by Zeisberger are suspect. Zeisberger's 'Onondaga or Maqua' represents a mixture, it seems, of Zeisberger's Onondaga and Zeisberger's Mohawk: see Chafe's remarks, *IUPAL* 25.2 (1970). For Zeisberger's 'Onondaga' bibliography see Pilling, Nos. 4296–300; Pilling, *BAE–B* 6.179–80 (1888); and Chafe, *loc. cit. supra.*

Onnontagué
Saint Jean Baptiste

Opata. Taracahitian; N.W. Mexico; extinct. See Eudeve.
Ópata
Opataice
Ore
Sonora
Teguima
Tegüima
Tequima
Ure

Opelousa. Tunican; Louisiana; extinct, 20 (1814).

Oregon Salish. Salishan.

Orisa. Chibchan (?).

Orosi. Orotiña; W. Costa Rica, S. of Lake Nicaragua; extinct.

Orotiña. Chorotegan; W. Costa Rica; extinct.[241]
Mangue
Nicoya
Orotina
Orotinan
Orotino
Orotinya

Osage. Dhegiha; Missouri, Arkansas, Kansas, Oklahoma; 100 to 400 in Oklahoma (1962).
Bone Indians
Osagen
Wa-sa-see
Wasawsee
Wazhazhe

Osochi. Timucuan (?); Florida (?), Alabama, Georgia, Oklahoma; extinct, 539? (1833).
Ossachile (?)
Uçachile (?)

Ostotitla. Nahuatl; Veracruz.

Ostuacan. Zoque.

Oto. Chiwere; Iowa, Nebraska, Missouri, Kansas, Oklahoma; 100 to 500 in Oklahoma (1962).
Che-wae-rae
Otoe

[241] Divisions: (1) Nicoya, (2) Orosi.

Otta
Otto
Ottoe
Uahtaktato
Wah-tok-ta-ta

Oto-Manguean. Macro-Otomanguean.
Otomanguean

Otomi. Otopamean (Central Otomian); 57,721 monolinguals mostly in Hidalgo, Mexico, Veracruz, Queretaro and Puebla (1960).
Heiang-Hyong
Hiā Hiū
Otetoes
Othomi
Othomiz
Othomy
Otomí
Otomita
Otomite
Otomitice

Otomian. Macro-Otomanguean.

Otopamean. Otomanguean.

Ottawa. Algonquian; Ontario, Ohio, Illinois, Indiana, Michigan, Wisconsin, Kansas, Oklahoma; fewer than 100 in Michigan and Oklahoma (1962).
Odahwah
Ottawwaw
Ottowa
Outaouak
Tawa

Ouachita. Caddo (?); Louisiana; extinct, 100? (1700).

Oyana. Cariban.

Ozette. Makah; Washington; extinct, 1 (1937).

Pacasa. Unclassified; Sonora, Sinaloa; extinct.

Pachera. Tarahumara; Chihuahua.

Pacific Chibchan. Chibchan.

Pacula. South Pame; in the Sierra Gorda; 1 (1967).

Padligmiut. Eskimo.

Padlimiut. Eskimo.

Paezan. Macro-Chibchan.

Paipai. Yavapai; Arizona, later N. Baja California; under 100 (1967).
Akwa'ala
Akwaʔala

Paiute. Numic (Plateau Shoshonean), but with ambiguous reference in regard to such terms as Northern Paiute, Southern Paiute or Western Paiute.
Pah-utah
Pah-ute
Pah-yutah
Paiuli
Paiulee
Pai-ute
Paiyute
Pa-uta
Payusitas
Payutes
Piede
Piute
Pi Ute
Pajalate. Coahuilteco.
Pakawa. Coahuiltecan.
Pala. Luiseño.
Palaihnihan. Hokan-Siouan.
Achomawan
Palaik. Palaihnihan.
Palaihnih
Palencano. Chol (?); Palenque, Mexico.
Palenke. Cariban.
Paleuyami. Poso Creek Yokuts.
Palmar. Jicaquean.
Palouse. See Peloos.
Palpenan. Wintun and Maiduan.
Pame. Northern Otomian; in the Sierra Gorda, Mexico, Queretaro, Guanajuato, Nuevo Leon, San Luis Potosi. See North Pame and South Pame.
Pamlico. Algonquian; North Carolina; extinct, 75 (1710).
Pampticough
Pamticoe
Pamticough
Pampuchin. Unclassified; Jalisco; extinct.
Pamunkey. Powhatan; Virginia; language extinct, 60? (1781).
Panamint. Numic (Shoshoni type Plateau Shoshonean); California, Nevada; 10 to 100 in California (1962).
Ke-at
Koso
Pantec. Unclassified; Guerrero; extinct.

Panteca

Papabuco. Chatino.

Papago. Pima Alto; 14,000 in S. Arizona and Sonora (1969).[242]

Papabicotan

Pápago

Papagol

Pima

Pima-Papago

Paparo. Choco; E. Panama.

Pascagoula. Muskogean (?); Mississippi, Louisiana, Texas; extinct, 100? (1832), 2? (1912).

Passamaquoddy. Algonquian; Maine, New Brunswick; 300 in Maine (1962).

Machias

Openango

Pasamaquoddice

Quaddie

Quoddy

Saint Croix

Scotuks

Unchechauge

Unquechauge

Patwin. Wintun; 10 to 100 in California (1962).

Colouse

Copeh

Kopé

Korusi

Mag Readings

Numsu

Suisun

Pauma. Luiseño.

Paviotso. See Northern Paiute.

Pawatin. See Saulteurs.

Pawnee. Caddoan; Wyoming, Nebraska, Kansas, Oklahoma; 400 to 600 in Oklahoma (1962).[243]

Grand Pawnee

[242] The Saxtons (1969) identify Papago dialects on reservations at Sells, San Xavier, Gila Bend and Ak Chin, as including (1) Totoguani, (2) Kokololodi, (3) Gigimai, (4) Huhhu'ula, (5) Huhuwash, (6) Ahngam, and (7) Ge Aji. The Saxtons identify Pima on reservations at Gila River and Salt River and map Kohadk, a Pima dialect, E. of (4) and N. of (6).

[243] Swanton sets the Skidi or Skiri Pawnee dialect in contrast with the single dialect of three other tribes, the Chaui or Grand Pawnee, the Kitkehahki or Republican Pawnee, and the Pitahauerat or Tapage Pawnee.

Kitka
Pahni
Pani
Pany
Pawne
Pawnee Picts
Pawni
Picts
Republican Pawnee
Toweahge

Pawokti. Muskogean (?); Florida, Alabama; extinct some years after 1799.

Paya. Classification uncertain: see Cariban and Misumalpan; N.E. Honduras; several hundred speakers in Dulce Nombre de Jesús, El Carbón, Santa María Tayaco, El Payal and Pusquira (1952).

Peš
Peška
Pahaya
Poya
Seco

Pecos. Towa; New Mexico; pueblo abandoned in 1838 by 17 who joined the Jemez; 10 (1910), extinct by 1952.

Old Pecos
Tamos

Peedee. Siouan (?); South Carolina; 600 (1600), extinct perhaps by 1810.

Peloos. Northeast Sahaptin, supposedly a Yakima offshoot; Washington, Idaho; 82 (1910).

Pallotepellows
Palouse
Palús
Peloose

Pend d'Oreille. See Kalispel.

Pennacook. Algonquian; New Hampshire, Massachusetts, Maine, Vermont; Canada and New York after 1675; 2,000 (1600); some of the 280 Saint Francis Indians reported in 1924 were Pennacook.[244]

Merrimac
Necheganset
Owaragees

[244] James Mooney in Hodge, *Handbook* 2.225 (1910), says [cavalierly, in the face of absence of linguistic data] that the Pennacook confederacy of Algonquian tribes spoke 'substantially the same language as the Massachusetts and Rhode Island Indians, and are generally classed with the Mahican'. Main tribes of the confederacy were (1) Agawam, (2) Wamesit, (3) Nashua, (4) Souhegan, (5) Amoskeag, (6) Pennacook, (7) Winnipesaukee.

Pennsylvania. Algonquian; Pennsylvania.[245]
Pensilvanie
Pensylvan
Pensylvania
Pensylvanie
Pensylvanien

Penobscot. Algonquian; fewer than 10 in Maine (1962). See Abnaki.
Penobscotice
Pentaguoet

Penonomeño. Chibchan (Guaymi); Panama.
Penomeño
Penonomenyo

Pensacola. Muskogean (Choctaw type?); Florida, Mississippi; extinct some years after 1764, 80? (1726).
Achuse (?)
Ichuse (?)
Ychuse (?)

Pentlatch. North Georgia Salish; E. Vancouver Island, British Columbia; extinct, 13 (1906).
Pentlash
Pentlatc
Puntlatch
Puntlatsh
Puntledge

Penutian. Macro-Penutian.

Penutoid. Term used by Swadesh in 1956 for twenty groups of languages. See Shipley's list, in the present volume.

Peoria. Illinois; N.E. Iowa, Illinois; fewer than 10 in Oklahoma (1962).[246]

Pequot. Algonquian (Mahican type); New York (?), Connecticut, Rhode Island; extinct, 66 (1910).
Sickenames

Pericu. Unclassified; Baja California; extinct. See Waïcurian.
Pericú
Pericù

Peshkwaus. See Piskwaus.
Peskwaus

Peten. Maya.
Itza

[245] Algonquian (Delaware?) vocabulary in *A letter from William Penn* (1683), on which see Pilling, *BAE-B* 13.388-92 (1891).

[246] Around 1867 or 1868 the term Peoria was extended to all Illinois in N.E. Oklahoma, mostly Peoria, Kaskaskia, Wea and Piankashaw.

Itzae

Piankashaw. Miami; Illinois, Indiana; in Kansas, 1832, and Oklahoma after 1866; extinct, 50? (1885). See Peoria.

Piankeshaw

Piato. Pima Alto; Sonora; extinct.

Picuris. Tiwa; 100 in New Mexico (1968).

Picoris

Piegan. See Blackfoot.

Paegan

Pilingmiut. Eskimo.

Pima. Pima Alto; 5,000 in Arizona and Mexico (1962). See Papago.

Papago

Pima-Papago

Pime

Pimeria

Pimo

Pina

Pima Alto. Piman.

Upper Pima

Pima Bajo Piman; Sonora, Sinaloa, Chihuahua.[247]

Cora

Lower Pima

Nebome

Nevoma

Nevome

Pima

Piman. Uto-Aztecan.

Pimic

Tepiman

Pinaleño. Apachean; Arizona, Mexico; perhaps merged with the San Carlos Apache.

Pingangnaktogmiut. Eskimo.

Pipil. Nahuatl (Nahuat type); enclaves in El Salvador, Guatemala, and Honduras; said to be extinct except in El Salvador.[248]

Izalco

Iztepeque

Pirinda. Matlatzinca; Michuacan; extinct.

Characo

Charense

Matlaltzinca de Michoacan

[247] Divisions: (1) Cocomacaque, (2) Nebome, (3) Ure, (4) Yécora.

[248] Izalco is a variety of Pipil spoken about Izalco, S. of San Salvador City, El Salvador.

Perindice
Pirinta

Piro. Towa (but Leap rejects assignment to Tanoan on the basis of grammatical dissimilarities); New Mexico and Chihuahua; 60 (1950), some speakers (?) 1970.
Senecu
Senecu del Sur

Piscataway. Conoy.
Maryland

Piskwaus. See Wenatchi.
Peshkwaus
Piskaus
Piskaws
Piskwau
Pisquous
Pisquow
Piskwaw

Pison. Unclassified; N. Mexico; extinct.
Pisone

Pit River. Achumawi.
Pit River Valley
Pitt River

Plains Cree. Cree.
Lowland Cree
Paskwawininiwug
River Cree

Plains Miwok. Miwok; 1 in California (1962).

Plains Salish. Interior Salish.

Plateau Shoshonean. Uto-Aztecan.

Playano. Salinan; California; extinct. See Migueleño.

Pochutla. Term for (1) a Nahuatl dialect in Oaxaca, or (2) a Zapotecan dialect.

Pocomam. Kekchian; Guatemala, El Salvador, Honduras; 25,000 in Guatemala, especially around Antigua and Jalapa (1952).
Pocoman
Pocomanice
Pokomam
Pokoman
Pokomane

Pocomchi. Kekchian; Alta Verapaz, Baja Verapaz, and Quiche, N. central Guatemala; more than 37,500 (1968).
Poconcham
Poconchi

Poconchice
Poconchine
Poconchini
Pokonchi

Pocumtuc. Algonquian (Wappinger type); Massachusetts, Connecticut, Vermont, later New York and Canada; extinct, 23? in Massachusetts (1910).

Pohoy. Timuquan; Florida; extinct, 300 (1680).
Oçita
Pojoy
Pooy
Posoy
Ucita

Point Barrow. Eskimo.

Pojoaque. Tewa; fewer than 10 (?) in New Mexico (1962).
Pojuaque
Pojuate

Polar Eskimo. See Ita.

Pómaro. Nahuatl; Michuacan.

Pomo. Pomoan; California. See Central Pomo, Eastern Pomo, Kashaya, Northeastern Pomo, Northern Pomo, Southeastern Pomo.
Ballo-kai-pomo
Cabanapo
Habenapo
H'hana
Kábinapek
Khabenapo
Khana
Kulanapan
Kulanapo
Ungieskie (?)
Venaambakaia
Venambakaiia
Yokaia

Pomoan. Hokan-Siouan.
Kulanapan
Pomo

Ponca. Dhegiha; South Dakota, Nebraska, Oklahoma; 100 to 1,000 in Nebraska and Oklahoma (1962).
Poncara
Ponka
Punca
Puncah

Punka

Pond Inlet. Eskimo.

North Baffin Island

Pond's Bay. Eskimo.

Popoloca. Term applied to several groups, sometimes with a place name added (such as Conguaco, Oaxaca, Puebla, Veracruz or Guatemala). See names listed below this entry.

Popoloc

Popoloco

Popoluca

Pupuluca

Popoloca. Mayan.

Pupuluca

Popoloca of Conguaco. See Conguaco (Xincan or Lencan?).

Popoloca of Guatemala. See Xinca.

Popoloca of Matagalpa. See Matagalpa.

Popoloca of Nicaragua

Popoloca of Oaxaca. See Chocho (Popolocan).

Popoloca of Puebla. See Chocho (Popolocan).

Popoloca of Veracruz. Zoquean. See Oluta, Sayula, Sierra Popoluca, and Texixtepic.

Popolocan. Otomanguean.

Popoloc

Popo-Mangean. See Otomanguean.

Popotecan. Otomanguean.

Popolocan-Mixtecan

Porepecha. See Tarascan.

Port des Français. Data lacking.[249]

Port de Français

Portlock Harbor. Data lacking.[250]

Portlock's Harbor

Poso Creek. Foothill Yokuts.

Potano. Timuquan; Florida; extinct, 160 (1675).

Potawatomi. Algonquian; Michigan, Wisconsin, Illinois, Indiana, Ohio, Kansas, and elsewhere; fewer than 1,000 in Oklahoma, Kansas, Wisconsin, Michigan, and possibly Ontario (1962).

Fire Nation

Mascouten

Podawahdmih

[249] Pilling, Nos. 28, 527–8, 1337, 2190, 2199a, 2202a. Numerals 1–100, in J.F. Gallup, Comte de La Pérouse, *Voyage round the world* (1801), p. 68.

[250] Pilling, Nos. 527–8, 3037–8. Vocabulary in N. Portlock, *Voyage round the world* (1789), p. 293.

Poodawahduhme
Potawatomie
Potawatomy
Potawattamie
Potawotami
Potawotamice
Potawotamie
Potewateme
Potewatemi
Potewatimi
Potewattomie
Potewotomi
Potiwattomie
Potowatome
Potowatomie
Potowotami
Potowotomie
Potrwatame
Potrwatome
Pottawatameh
Pottawatomi
Pottawatomie
Pottawotomie
Pottowotami
Pottowotamie
Poutouatomi
Poutouatomi
Putawatomie

Potlapiqua. Pima.
Potlapigu

Powhatan. Algonquian; Virginia; language extinct.[251]
Powhattan
Virginia
Virginiane
Virginice
Virginien

Prince William Sound. See Chugachigmiut.
Prince William's Sound

[251] Divisions: (1) Accohanoc, (2) Appomattoc (3) Chesapeake, (4) Chickahominy, (5) Pamunkey, (6) Potomac, (7) Powhatan, (8) Rappahannock, (9) Werowocomoco, (10) Wicocomoco, (11) Nansemond, (12) Mattapony, (13) Upper Mattapony.

Pshwanwapam. Northwest Sahaptin; Washington.
Upper Yakima
Psteni. Data lacking.[252]
Pueblo. Data lacking.[253]
Pueblo Shoshonean. Uto-Aztecan.
Hopi
Puget Sound Salish. See Southern Puget Sound Salish.
Toughnowawmish
Puivlirmiut. Eskimo.
Pujunan. See Maidu.
Pujuni
Pujūni
Punctunc. See Maya.
Putunc
Puntlatsh. See Pentlatch.
Pupuluca. Mayan.[254]
Purisimeño. Chumashan; California; extinct.
La Purisima
La Purisima Concepción
Puthlavamiut. Eskimo.
Putima. Unclassified; Sonora; extinct.
Puyallup. Southern Puget Sound Salish; fewer than 50 (?) in Washington (1962).
Pooyalawpoo
Qaernermiut. Eskimo.
Qarus. Western Aleut; on the Rat Islands, including Amchitka and Kiska; removed to Adak and Atka; extinct (after 1900?).
Qaumauangmiut. Eskimo.
Quahatika. Pima; S. Arizona.
Kohátk
Quapaw. Dhegiha; Mississippi, Arkansas, Louisiana, Texas, Kansas; fewer than 10 in Oklahoma (1962).
Akansa
Arkansas
Papikaha
Quappa
Quawpaw
Queen Charlotte's Islands. See Haida.

[252] Pilling, No. 1282a, words in H. Ferry, *La California* (Venice, 1851), pp. 186–7.
[253] Pilling, No. 1955c, names of 'Pueblo' chiefs in W.H. Jackson, *Descriptive catalogue of photographs of North American Indians* (1877).
[254] See W. Bright, *HMAI* 5.24 (1967), No. 164. The language of this wordlist otherwise unidentified is Mayan.

Queets. Olympic Salish; Washington; 82 (1936).
    Quaitso
Quelem. Term applied to (1) Tzeltalan, or (2) Tzotzil.
    Quélène
Quepo. Boruca.
Querecho. Term for Jicarilla and other Apache groups.
    Vaquero
Quiche. Quichean; Chiápas, Guatemala; over 300,000 (1965).
    Guatemala
    Guatemalteca
    Guatimaltec
    Kechi
    Kichai
    Kiche
    Kiché
    Qiche
    Queche
    Quiché
    Quixe
    Qviche
    San Miguel Chicah (Quiche de Rabinal)
    Tiche
    Utlateca
    Utlatecat
    Utlateco
Quichean. Mayan.
Quichil. Quichoid.
Quichoid. Mayan.
Quileute. Chimakuan; 10 to 100 in Washington (1962).
    Quillayute
Quinault. Olympic Salish; 10 to 100 in Washington (1962).
    Quinaietl
Quinigua. Coahuiltecan (?); N.W. Mexico; extinct.
    Borrados
Quinipissa. Muskogean (Choctaw type?); Louisiana; extinct, 300? (1698).
    Mugulasha (?)
Quinnipiac. See Wappinger.
Quiripi. See Connecticut.
Rabinal. See Achi.
Rae. Dogrib; in N. Mackenzie on the Rae River, which flows to Coronation Gulf.
Rama. Chibchan; S.E. Nicaragua.
Rama-Corobici. Chibchan.

Rankin Inlet. Eskimo; N.W. Hudson's Bay, Canada.
SaniŋayuRmiut
Rat. Term applied to (1) the Takkuth-kutchin, and (2) the Vunta.
Repulse Bay. Eskimo; N.W. Hudson's Bay, Canada.
Aiviliŋmiut
Rincón. Term for a dialect of (1) Luiseño, or (2) Northern Zapotecan.
Rio Sucio. Chocoan.
Rio Verde. Chocoan.
Ritwan. Algonquian-Wakashan.
River Indians. Term for (1) the Mahicans of the Hudson and the Housatonic, (2) Connecticut River groups including the Wangunk, Podunk, Mattabesett, Poquonnoc and Sicaogg, all identified by Swanton as Wappinger, or (3) the Mohegans of Connecticut.
Rock Creek. Columbia River Sahaptin.
Rocky Mountain Stoney Indians. Data lacking.[255]
Rocoroibo. Tarahumara; 10,000? in S.W. Chihuahua (1970).
Rogue River. Term applied to (1) the Tututni, and (2) the Takelma.
Rumsen. Costanoan; California; extinct.
Achastlien
Achastlier
Carmel
Carmel Mission
Carmelo
Monterey
Rumsien
Runsien
Runsiène
Ruslen
Russian River. Data lacking.[256]
Saanich. Lkungen; 200 in British Columbia (1962).
Sanetch
Sabagui. Pima.
Sabaibo. Taracahitian (Acaxee?); Sonora; extinct.
Sabanero. Murire.
Sabassa. Kwakiutl.[257]
Sebasa
Sac. See Sauk.

[255] Pilling, No. 3776, vocabulary from J.W. Sullivan in J. Pallisser, *Journal* (1863), pp. 210–12.
[256] Pilling, Nos. 217, 217a, 217b, vocabulary in H.H. Bancroft, *Wild tribes*.
[257] Hodge's Sabassa [Pilling's spelling is Sebasa] applies to Indians of Laredo and Principe Channels, British Columbia; Kane (1859) uses the term for Tsimshian and Kwakiutl alike.

Saclan. See Saklan.
Sacramento River. Data lacking.[258]
Saganaw. Chippewa.
    Saginaw
Sagdlirmiut. Eskimo.
Sahaptian. Penutian.
    Shahaptian
    Shapwaiilutan
Sahaptin. Sahaptian.
    Shahaptin
Sahehwamish. Southern Puget Sound Salish (Nisqually type); Washington; 50 to 100 in Washington for all tribes speaking Southern Puget Sound Salish (1962).
Saia. See Mattole.
    Saiaz
Saint Francis. Western Abnaki.
Saint John's. See Malecite.
    Wlastukweek
Saint Louis Mission. See Luiseño.
    San Luis Mission
Saint Michael. Eskimo.
Saixa. Chocoan.
Saklan. Miwok (?); California; extinct.[259]
    Saclan
Salinan. Hokan-Siouan; 2 or 3 in California (1962).[260]
Salinero. See Seri.
Salish. Salishan; Montana, Idaho, Washington; part of the 500 to 1,000 speakers of Salish, Pend d'Oreille and Kalispel in Montana and Washington (1962).
    Flathead
    Kettle Falls
    Selish
    Soaiatlpi
    Têtes-Plates
Salishan. Algonquian-Wakashan.
Salmon River. See Bella Coola.
Salteaux. See Chippewa.
Saluda. Shawnee (?); South Carolina; extinct.
Samachique. Tarahumara.

[258] Pilling, No. 2214, vocabulary in R.G. Latham, *Phil. Soc.* [*London*], *Trans.*, *1856*, pp. 79–80.
[259] See M. Beeler, *IJAL* 21.201–9 (1955), 25.67–8 (1959). Kroeber, *BAE-B* 78.463 (1925) lists Saklan under the rubric Costanoan.
[260] Divisions: (1) San Miguel Salinas or Migueleño, (2) San Antonio or Antoniano, (3) Playano (?).

Sambú. Chocoan.
Samish. Lkungen; 2 in Washington (1962).
San Agustín Oapan. Nahuatl; Guerrero.
San Andres. Tzotzil; in Chiapas at Larrainzar, Bochil, Soyaló, Jitótol, Pueblo Nuevo Solistahuacan, San Juan del Bosque and Simojovel; 35,000 (1964).
    San Andrés
San Antonio. See Antoniano.
San Blas. See Cuna.
San Buenaventura. See Ventureño.
San Carlos. Apachean; 3,000 to 4,000 in Arizona (1962).
    Pinaleño
San Carlos. Mission formerly having Esselenian and Costanoan speakers, in California.
San Cristóbal Verapaz. Pocomchi.
San Esteban. Mixtec.
San Felipe. Keresan; 1,000 in New Mexico (1962).
San Fernando. See Fernandeño.
San Francisco. Costanoan.
    San Francisco Bay
San Franciso Borja. See Borjeño.
San Francisco Xavier. See San Xavier.
San Ildefonso. Tewa; 250? in New Mexico (1967).
San Javier. See Cochimi.
San Jeronimo Tecoatl. Mazatec.
San Joaquin. See Cochimi.
San Jorge. Chocoan.
San José de Comondre Mission. See Cochimi.
    San Giuseppe di Comondu Mission
San Juan. Tewa; 1,000 in New Mexico (1967).
San Juan Bautista. Costanoan; California; extinct.
San Juan Capistrano. See Juaneño.
San Luis Jilotepeque. Pocomam.
San Luis Obispo. See Obispeño.
San Luis Rey. See Luiseño.
San Miguel. Mixtec.
San Miguel Soyaltepec. Mazatec.
San Pedro Tototepec. Nahuatl; Mexico.
San Rafael Mission. Coast Miwok.
    Joukiousmé
    San Raphael Mission
San Xavier. See Cochimi.
    San Francesco Saverio Mission

San Francisco Xavier (de Viggé-Biaundo) Mission
Sandia. Tiwa; 100 to 200 in New Mexico (1962).
Sanpoil. Okanagon; 202 (1913), part of 1,000 to 2,000 speakers of Okanagon in Washington (1962).
Nespelem
Nespelim
Sans Poil
Santa Ana. Keresan; 300 in New Mexico (1962).
Santa Anna
Santa Clara. Tewa; 500 to 600 in New Mexico (1962).
Santa Clara. Costanoan; California; extinct.
Santa Cruz. Costanoan; California; extinct.
Santa Cruz County
Santa Cruz Mission
Santa Cruz. Maya.
Santa Cruz Island. Barbareño.
Santa Gertrude Mission. See Cochimi.
Santa Gertrudis
Santa Ines Mission. See Ynezeño.
Santa Inez
Santa Ynez
Santa Maria. See Cochimi.
Santa Maria Mission
Santa Maria Acapulco. North Pame.
Santa Rosa Island. Chumash.
Santa [sic] Tomás. Mixtec.
Santa [sic] Tomas Mission. See Diegueño.
Santo [sic] Tomás
Santee. Dakota.
Isanti
Isauntie
Isayyati
Santee. Siouan; South Carolina; extinct, 85 (1715).
Seretee
Santiam. Kalapuyan; Oregon; extinct, 9 (1910).
Kalapuya
Mary's River
Santo Domingo. Keresan; 1,000 to 2,000 in New Mexico (1962).
Kiwomi
Santo Domingo. Nahuatl; Sonsonate, El Salvador.
Saponi. Siouan (Tutelo type); Virginia, North Carolina, later New York, Pennsylvania; extinct, 120? (1765).

Paanese

Sarsi. Athapaskan; 6? in Alberta (1970). See Mountain.

Castors des Prairies

Sarcee

Surcee

Sussee

Saskinar. Western Aleut; on Near Islands; language extinct; 100? (1745).

Sasuchan. Sekani.

Satsop. Olympic Salish; 12 in Washington (1936).

Saturiwa. Timuquan; Florida; extinct some years after 1680, 500 in missions (1602).

Sauk. Algonquian; Michigan, Wisconsin, Illinois, Missouri, Iowa, Kansas and elsewhere; 600? in Iowa, Oklahoma and Kansas (1962). See Fox.

Sac

Sack

Sahkey

Sakewi

Sakis

Sauki

Saukie

Sawk

Sawkee

Saulteurs. See Chippewa.

Cascade Indians

Fall Indians

Pawateeg

Pawatin

Pawating

Pawichtigouek

Salteaux

Sault Sainte Marie

Saulteaux

Saulteux

Saut

Sauteu

Sauteux

Shingwauk

Saumingmiut. Eskimo.

Sawokli. Hitchiti; Florida, Alabama, Georgia; extinct, 450 (1833).

Sabougla (?)

Sayula. Zoquean; on the N. side of the Isthmus of Tehuantepec, Veracruz, in most of the town of Sayula, etc.; 4,000 (1961).

Popoluca of Veracruz

Sayultec. Aztecoidan; in S. Jalisco and S. and S.W. of the Lago de Chapala; extinct.

Scatacook. Term used by De Forest for refugee Algonquians, including Paugusset, Unkawa and Potatuck Wappingers, at Scatacook, near Kent, Connecticut; extinct, 40? (1849).

Scaticook

Sebasa. See Sabassa.

Sechelt. North Georgia Salish; fewer than 100 in British Columbia (1962).

Seechelt

Seshalt

Sicatl

Sishiatl

Seco. Paya.

Sekani. Athapaskan; said to be a Beaver group driven into the Rocky Mountains by the Cree; 100 to 500 in British Columbia (1962).[261]

Cloud Lake

Rocky Mountain Indians

Sicani

Sicanni

Siccany

Sikani

Sikanni

Thekenneh

Tselone

Tseloni

Ts'ets'ā'ut[262]

Ware

Selawigmiut. Eskimo.

Sematuse. Salish (?); W. Montana; extinct.

Semiahmoo. Lkungen; Washington, British Columbia; 2 in British Columbia (1962).

Birch Bay Indians

Seminole. Eastern Muskogean; 300 in Florida (1962). See Muskogee.[263]

Seminolee

Seneca. Iroquoian; 2,000 to 3,000 in New York and Ontario (1962).[264]

[261] Morice extended the term Sekani to the Beaver, Sarsi and other Athapaskan groups.

[262] Name used by Skeena River and Nass River Indians for the Sekani, from a Niska term, used as a main entry word by Swanton, *Tribes*, p. 606, in the spelling Tsetsaut. As a synonym of Sekani Swanton uses miscopied 'T'set'sa'ut'.

[263] The term Seminole refers to Creeks in Florida from 1750. Of these perhaps two-thirds spoke Muskogee and one-third Hitchiti, Alabama or Yamasee. The term also covered some Yuchi. After 1842 most of the Seminole were removed to Oklahoma.

[264] The 'Seneca' of Oklahoma were composed of Erie, Huron, perhaps Conestoga, and certainly other Iroquoian groups.

Hodenosaunee
Mæchachtini
Senecka
Sinicker

Senecu. Piro.

Senijextee. Okanagon; British Columbia, Washington, Oregon; 342 on the Colville Reservation in Washington (1909).
Lake Indians

Seri. Serian; formerly on Tiburón Island, Gulf of California, as well as coastal Sonora; now on the Sonora coast.[265]
Ceri
Tiburón

Serian. Hokan-Siouan.
Seri

Serrano. Takic (Southern California Shoshonean); 2 or 3 in California (1962).
Meco
Takhtam
Vanyume

Serrano. Northern Zapotecan; Oaxaca.
Ixtlán
Serrano de Ixtepegi
Serrano de Ixtepexi
Sierra de Juarez
Sierra de Villa Alta

Serrano de Mihuatlan. See Miahuatlan.

Seshart. Nootka; S.W. coast of Vancouver Island, British Columbia; 124 (1909).
Seshat

Severnow. Data lacking.[266]

Sewee. Siouan (?); South Carolina; extinct some years after 1715, 57 (1715).
Xoxi (?)

Shakori. Siouan; North Carolina, Virginia, South Carolina; 500? (1600), extinct some years after 1716.
Chicora (?)
Schockoores
Sissipahaw (?)
Sugari (?)

Shapwailutan. Sahaptian.

Sharon Indians. Nineteenth-century terminology for a refugee Algonquian group in Connecticut, 1720-1780?; extinct, 10 (1774).

265 Extinct groups: (1) Guayma, (2) Salinero, (3) Tastioteño, (4) Tepoca, (5) Upanguayma.
266 Pilling, No. 2204, words in R.G. Latham, *Phil. Soc.* [*London*], *Proc.* 47–8 (1846).

Sharon and Salisbury Indians

Shasta. Shastan; California, Oregon; fewer than 10 in California (1962).[267]

Saste
Sasti
Shaste
Shasti
Shastie
Shastika
Shasty

Shastan. Hokan-Siouan.

Sastean

Shawnee. Algonquian; early in Tennessee, with groups ranging into Alabama, Georgia, Illinois, Indiana, Kansas, Kentucky, Maryland, Missouri, Ohio, Pennsylvania, South Carolina, Texas, Virginia and, especially from the 1850s and 1860s, Oklahoma; 300 to 400 in Oklahoma (1962).

Chawano
Savana
Savanahica (?)
Savanahice
Savanna
Sawano
Sawanwan (?)
Sawanou
Schawanese
Shavannice
Shawan
Shawanee
Shawanese
Shawannee
Shawanno
Shawano
Shawanoe
Shawanoese
Shawnese
Shawni
Shawnoe

Sheshapotosh. Montagnais (Algonquian).

Sheshatapoosh
Sheshatapooshoish

[267] Subdivisions: (1) Ahotireitsu, (2) Cecilville Indians or Haldokehewuk, (3) Iruaitsu, (4) Kahosadi, (5) Kammatwa or Wiruhikwairuk'a.

Shiwapmuk. Data lacking.[268]
Shiwapmukh
Schwapmuth
Shihwapmukh
Shoshonean. Uto-Aztecan.
Shoshoni. Numic (Shoshoni type Plateau Shoshonean); 5,000 in California, Nevada, Idaho, Oregon and Wyoming (1962).[269]
Schoschone
Schoshone
Shoshone
Shoshonee
Shoshonie
Snake
Tosauwihi
Wihinasht
Shuman. See Jumano.
Shuswap. Interior Salish (Lillooet type); 1,000 to 2,000 in British Columbia (1962).
Atna
Ahtena
Shooswaap
Shooswap
Shushwapumsh
Shyenne. See Cheyenne.[270]
Siberian Eskimo. See Yuit.
Siberian Yupik
Sicatl. See Sechelt.
Sidarumiut. Eskimo.
Sierra de Juarez. See Serrano (Northern Zapotecan).
Sierra Miwok. Miwok.
Sierra Nevada Shoshonean. Uto-Aztecan.
Kern River Shoshonean
Sierra Popoluca. Zoquean; Veracruz, Puebla and Oaxaca; 3,053 monolinguals in a total of 10,000 to 12,000 speakers (1960).
Popoloca
Popoloco of Puebla
Popoluca of Veracruz

[268] For references see Pilling, *BAE–B* 16.26–7 (1893).

[269] The Northern Shoshoni centered in E. Idaho, W. Wyoming, and N.E. Utah. The Western Shoshoni centered in Idaho, Utah, Nevada and California.

[270] Gallatin (1836) assigned the Shyenne language to his Sioux group on the basis of several names of 'Shyennes' who signed a treaty in July, 1825. The signers were possessed of Siouan, not Algonquian, names.

Sigua. Nahuatlan; Panama.
Sikosuilarmiut. See Fox Channel.
Siksika. Algonquian; a confederacy of the Siksika proper or Blackfeet, the Kainah or Bloods, and the Piegan, in Alberta and Montana. See Blackfoot.
Siletz. Oregon Salish; Oregon; extinct, 72 or less (1930).
  Silets
Similaton. See Lenca.
  Sinacantan. See Xinca.
Sinaloa. See Cahita.
  Cinaloa
Sinimiut. Eskimo.
Sinkaietk. Okanagon; Washington; part of 1,000 to 2,000 speakers of all varieties of Okanagon in Washington (1962).
  Lower Okanagon
  Lower Okanagan
Sinkakaius. Okanagon (?); Washington; a group composed mostly of Sinkaietk and Moses Columbia.
Sinkyone. Athapaskan; California; extinct, 35? (1910).
Siouan-Yuchi. Hokan-Siouan.
Sioux. See Dakota.
Sirenik. Yuit; Siberia; 10? (1970).
Sishiatl. See Sechelt.
Sisseton. Dakota.
Sissipahaw. Siouan (?); South Carolina (?), North Carolina; extinct, 800 (1600).
  Sauxpa (?)
  Shakori (?)
Sitka. Tlingit.
  Norfolk Sound
Siuslaw. Yakonan; 1 or 2 in Oregon (1962).
  Sayuskla
Siuslawan. A family rubric proposed by Frachtenberg in 1911 for the Kuitsh and Siuslaw languages. See Lower Umpqua.
  Siuslauan
  Siuslaw
Skagit. Southern Puget Sound Salish; 200 to 300 in Washington (1962).[271]
  Skaget
Skalza. See Kutenai.
  Skalzi
Skidegate. Haida.

[271] The Swinomish, listed as a separate tribe by Swanton (p. 446), had a village named Skagit on Whidbey Island.

Skilloot. Clackamas; Washington, Oregon; extinct, 200 (1850).
  Thlakalama
Skin. Northwest Sahaptin (Tenino?); Washinton; extinct, 1200? (1805).[272]
  Eneeshur
  Tapanash
Skitaget. See Haida.
Skitswish. See Coeur d'Alene.
  Schitsui
  Skitsuish
Skittagetan. See Haida.
Skokomish. See Twana.
Skoyelpi. See Colville.
  Schwoyelpi
  Shwoyelpi
Slave. Athapaskan; 3,000 in S.W. and S. central Mackenzie, N.E. British Columbia and N.W. Alberta (1962).[273]
  Awokanak
  Brushwood Indians
  Etchaottine
  Fort Liard
  Fort Norman
  Fort Providence
  Hay River
  Mountain
  Netla
  Slave Lake
  Slavi
  South Nahanni
Sliammon. A subdivision of the Comox on Malaspina Inlet; 500 to 600 in British Columbia (1962).
Snag. Tutchone; S.W. Yukon near the Tanana River.
Snake. See *inter alia* Northern Paiute and Shoshoni.
Snanaimuk. See Nanaimo.
  Snanaimoo
  Snanaimux
Snohomish. Southern Puget Sound Salish; S. Whidbey Island and lower Snohomish

[272] Hodge, *Handbook* 1.422, 2.691, equates Eneeshur and Tapanash and fixes the language as Tenino. Swanton supplies the name Skin.

[273] Swanton puts the Etchaottine mainly in the valley of the Mackenzie River between Lake Athabaska or Fort Norman, northwards to Great Slave Lake. He lists the Fort Norman band, in addition to bands listed by Petitot: (1) Desnedeyarelottine, (2) Eleidlinottine, (3) Etchaottine, (4) Etcheridiegottine, (5) Etechesottine, (6) Klodesseottine.

River, Washington.
Sneomus
Sneounis
Snoqualmie. Southern Puget Sound Salish; Snoqualmie River and Skykomish River, Washington.
Snuqualmie
Soacatino. Caddoan; N.W. Louisiana or N.E. Texas; extinct.
Xacatin
Sobaibo. See Sabaibo.
Sobaipuri. Piman (Papago?); S. Arizona and Sonora; extinct, 600 (1680).
Sabagui
Sobaipure
Soledad. Costanoan; California; extinct.
La Soledad
Soledad Mission
Solomec. Kanjobalan.
Soltec. Chatino.
Solteco
Songish. See Lkungen.
Sonoran. Uto-Aztecan.
Sooke. South Georgia Salish; S. Vancouver Island, British Columbia; nearly extinct, 28 (1909).
Achiganes
Sâ'ok
Sock
Tsohke
South Georgia Salish. Coast Salish.
South Pame. Otopamean; in the Sierra Gorda, at Jiliapan, Pacula and Tilaco; 6 or 7 (1967).
Southeastern Pomo. Pomoan; fewer than 10 in California (1962).
Lower Lake Pomo
Southeastern Yavapai. Yavapai.
Southern California Shoshonean. Uto-Aztecan.
Takic
Southern Diegueño. Diegueño.
Baron Long
Comoyei
Kamia
La Huerta
Tipai
Viejas
Southern Ępęra. Chocoan.

Southern Iroquoian. See Iroquoian.
Southern Mixe. Mixe.
Southern Otomian. Otomian.
Southern Okanagon. Okanagon.
Southern Paiute. Numic (Ute type Plateau Shoshonean); 1,000 to 3,000 in Utah, Arizona, Nevada and California (1962).
Diggers
Kaibab
Kaivavwit
Nüma
Shivwits
Southern Pomo. Pomoan; fewer than 40 in California (1962).
Gallinomero
Gallinoméro
Southern Puget Sound Salish. Coast Salish.[274]
Southern Sierra Miwok. Sierra Miwok; 20 in California (1962).
Yosemite
Southern Sumo. Sumo.
Southern Tepehuan. Tepehuan.
Southern Tutchone. Tutchone.
Southern Valley Yokuts. Valley Yokuts.
Southern Yaana. Yana; California; 40? (1925), fewer than 10 (1930).
Central Yana
Gata'i
Northern Yana
Southern Yahi. Yahi; California; extinct in 1916.
Southern Yana
Yahi
Southern Zapotecan. Zapotecan.
Miahuateco
Southwestern Pomo. See Kashaya.
Spokane. Okanagon (Spokane type); Washington, Idaho, Montana; 100 to 200 in Washington and Montana (1962).
Spokan
Tsakaitsitlin
Squamish. South Georgia Salish; 100 to 200 in British Columbia (1962).[275]

[274] Speakers of Southern Puget Sound Salish lived from just N. of Seattle down to the S. end of Puget Sound and up to the end of the Kitsap Peninsula on the W. shores of the Sound. The language was used by the (1) Duwamish, (2) Muckleshoot, (3) Nisqualli, (4) Puyallup, (5) Snoqualmie and (6) Suquamish. For these tribes Chafe reported 50 to 100 speakers in 1962. T.M. Hess, *IJAL* 32.350ff. (1966) adds (7) Snohomish and (8) Skagit, and uses the rubric Puget Salish for all eight tribes just named.
[275] Not to be confused with the Suquamish (Southern Puget Sound Salish). The Nooksack are an offshoot of the Squamish.

Skay-wa-mish
Squawmish
Squaxon. Nisqualli; North Bay, Puget Sound, Washington; 32 (1937).
Skwaksin
Skwaxon
Squakson
Squoxon
Stailakum. Nisqualli (?); Steilacoom Creek, N.W. Washington.
Steilacoom
Steilacoomamish
Steilakūmahmish
Stillacum
Stalo. See Tait.
Stikine. Tlingit.
Stockbridge. Mahican; Massachusetts, later New York and Wisconsin; extinct as a tribe some years after 1833.
Housatonic
Pootatuck
Stoney. Assiniboin.
Stony
Straits. See Lkungen.
Straits of Fuca. See Fuca.
Stuart Island. Eskimo.
Stewart Island
Stuart Lake. See Fort St. James.
Stupart Bay. Eskimo.
Stuwihamuk. See Nicola.
Subinha. Tzeltalan; Guatemala; extinct.[276]
Subtaino. Arawakan; Cuba; extinct.
Sub-Taino
Subtiaba. Supanecan; S.E. of the Bay of Fonseca, Nicaragua; extinct.
See Mangue.
Maribichicoa
Maribio
Nagrandan
Subtiabo
Subtiaba-Tlappanec. Supanecan.
Suerre. Talamanca; Costa Rica. See Guetar.
Sugeree. Siouan (?); South Carolina, North Carolina; extinct.
Suturees

[276] Rivet in *Les langues du monde* 2.1073 (1952) locates the Subinha as probably in Kanjobal country, but this does not mean that Subinha is Kanjobal or Mamean. N. McQuown in 1970 assured me that Subinha is distinct from but to be grouped with Tzeltal and Tzotzil.

Suisun. Patwin.
  Southern Patwin
Suk. Yupik.
  Pacific Eskimo.
Suma. See Jumano.
Sumas. Halcomelem; 60 in British Columbia (1962).
  Sumass
Sumo. Misumalpan; Nicaragua and Honduras.[277]
  Chondal de Nicaragua
  Chontal of Nicaragua
Supanecan. Hokan-Siouan.
  Supanec
Suquamish. Southern Puget Sound Salish; Washington; fewer than 50? in Washington (1962).
  So-qua-mish
  Susquamish
Surruque. Unclassified; Florida; extinct.
  Sorrochos
Susquehanna. See Conestoga.
Sutaio. Algonquian (Cheyenne type); Minnesota, South Dakota; merged with the Cheyenne about 1850.
  Chousa (?)
  Staitan (?)
Swallah. Coast Salish (Lummi?); Washington; spoken on the Lummi Reservation (1910).
  Swalash
Swampy Cree. Cree; Manitoba to Hudson's Bay and James Bay, N. Ontario. See Maskegon.
  Barren Ground Cree
  Fort Albany
  James Bay
  Kesagami Lake
  Sakawininiwug
  Woodland Cree
Swinomish. See Skagit.
Tacana. Mam.
Tacaneco. Mam.
Tacatacuru. Timucua; Florida; extinct.

[277] Divisions: (1) Bawihka, (2) Boa, (3) Coco, (4) Dudu, (5) Musutepes, (6) Panamaka (with the Karawala, Panamaka and Tunki), (7) Lakus, (8) Pispis, (9) Tawahka, (10) Wasabane, (11) Ku, and (12) Silam.

Tachi. Southern Valley Yokuts.
Tatché
Telame
Telami
Tacully. See Carrier.
Tadó. Chocoan.
Tadousac. A Montagnais-Naskapi tribe or band of Quebec.
Tadussak
Taensa. Natchesan (?); Louisiana, Alabama; extinct, 100? (1805).
Tagish. Western Canadian Athapaskan; fewer than 5 in Yukon (1970).
Tahgish
Tagishoten. Tahltan.
Tahltan. Athapaskan; 200? in British Columbia and Yukon (1970).
Tahue. Taracahitian (Cahita?); Sinaloa; extinct.
Tahueca
Taidnapam. See Upper Cowlitz.
Taitlnapam
Tait. Halcomelem; 250 in British Columbia (1962).
Cowichan of Fraser River
Halkome'lēm
Stalo
Tē'it
Takelma. Takelman; Oregon; extinct, 6? (1910).
Takilma
Takelman. Penutian.
Takilman
Takic. See Southern California Shoshonean.
Taku. Tlingit.
Takkuth-kutchin. Athapaskan; 150? in Alaska and Yukon (1960).
Dakaz
Dakkadhè
Deguthee
Klovén-kutchin
Louchieux
Nattsae-kouttchin
Porcupine River
Quarrelers
Rat
Takadhé
Upper Porcupine River Kutchin
Yukuth Kutchin

Talamanca. Chibchan; central Costa Rica.
Pueblo de Caché
Talamana
Talamenca
Talemenca
Telamanca
Terraba
Talatui. Miwok.
Talantui
Tali. Muskogean (Muskogee?); Tennessee (?), Alabama; extinct.
Talirpingmiut. Eskimo.
Taltaltepec. Chatino.
Taltushtuntude. See Galice.
Tamahú. Pocomchi.
Tamanak. Cariban.
Tamanaca
Tamaroa. See Illinois.
Tamathli. Muskogean; Georgia, Florida; extinct, 220 (1818).
Toa (?)
Toalli (?)
Tamaulipec. Classification uncertain; Tamaulipas, Nuevo Leon, Coahuila; extinct.[278]
Tamalipec
Tamaulipeco
Tamazulaxa. Mixtec.
Tanaina. Athapaskan; 400 in S. Alaska (1970).[279]
Bay of Kenai
Cook's Inlet Indians
Iliamna
Ilyamna
Inkalit-Kenai (?)
Kachemak Bay
Kenai
Kenaier
Kenáitená
Kenaïtses
Kenaizi
Kenay
Kinai

[278] Swadesh, *RMEA* 19.93–104 (1963), characterized Tamaulipec as an independent division within Uto-Àztecan. Others have suggested the rubric Coahuiltecan.
[279] Subdivisions: (1) Clark Lake, (2) Iliamna (Pedro Bay), (3) Lower Inlet (Kachemak Bay, Seldovia), (4) Middle Inlet, (5) Susitna, (6) Tyonek, (7) Upper Inlet, (8) Lime-Hungry-Stoney River.

Kinaïtze
Kiwai (?)[192]
Knaiakhotana
Kohtana
Ougagliakmuzi-Kinaia
Pedro Bay
Susitna
Taašnēi
Tašne
Tenahna
Tēnaina
Thnaina
Tinina
Tnac
Tnai
Tnaina

Tanana. Athapaskan; 300 in Alaska (1970).
Tananá
Tenankutchin (?)

Tenetze. Zapotecan.

Tangipahoa. Muskogean; Louisiana; extinct, 525? (1698).
Tangibao

Tano. Tewa; fewer than 5 (?) in New Mexico (1952).

Tanoan. Kiowa-Tanoan.

Taos. Tiwa; 1,200 in New Mexico (1967).

Tapachulane-Huastèque. Name of a family proposed by Charencey.

Tapachultec I. Zoque; on the border of Mexico and Guatemala; extinct.
Tapachula

Tapachulteca. Mixe; S. Chiapas, near the border of Mexico and Guatemala; extinct.[280]
Chiapas Mixe
Tapachultec II
Tapachulteco

Tapaliza. Data lacking.[281]

Tapijulapa. See Zoquean.

Taposa. Muskogean (Chickasaw?); Mississippi; extinct, 100? (1730).
Tacusas
Tapoosas
Tapousas

[280] See Longacre *CTL* 4.322 (1968).

[281] Pilling, No. 2296a, name of a language of Darien from a title sent by A. Pinart.

Tapoussas

Tapanash. See Skin.

Taquial. Mam.

Taracahitian. Uto-Aztecan.

Taracahitic

Tarahumara. Taracahitian; Chihuahua, Sonora, Durango; 10,478 monolinguals in Chihuahua and Sinaloa (1960), 50,000 in S.W. Chihuahua (1970).

Tarahumar

Tarahumare

Tarauhmarice

Taraumara

Tarrahumara

Tarascan. Tarascan; Michuacan, Guerrero, Guanajuato, Jalisco; 50,000 in Michuacan (1968).[282]

Mechoacan

Mechuacā

Michoacano

Michuacan

P'orepeča

Porepecha

Purepeča

Tala

Tarasca

Tarasco

Tarasken

Tatimolo. Totonac.

Tatlit-kutchin. Athapaskan; Mackenzie; 240? (1866).

Fon du Lac Loucheux

Peel River Kutchin

Sa-to-tin

Tpe-tliet-kouttchin

Tatsanottine. See Yellowknife.

Tawahka. Sumo.

Tawakoni. Wichita (?); Oklahoma, Texas; extinct, 1 (1910).

Touacara

Troiscannes

Tawasa. Timuquan; Alabama, Florida, Louisiana; extinct, 240? (1792).

Tawehash. Caddoan (Wichita type?); Oklahoma, Kansas; they merged with the Wichita after 1867.

Aijaos (?)

282 Pimentel (1874) proposed a Tarasca family with (1) Chorotega de Nicaragua, and (2) Tarasco.

Jumanos
Taovayas
Teguayos (?)
Toayas
Tawira. Mosquito.
Tebaca. Acaxee.
Tecaya. Acaxee.
Tecə. Mamean; 5,000 in S. Mexico and W. Guatemala on the border (1969).[283]
Teco. Aztecoidan (Nahuatl?); W. Michuacan and S. Nayarit; extinct.
Popoloco
Teca
Teco de Michoacan
Teco-Tecoxquin
Tecoxquin
Tecoripa. Pima.
Tecual. Aztecoidan; Nayarit; extinct.
Tecuexe. Cazcan.
Tecueshe
Tegüima. See Opata.
Tehuano. See Isthmus Zapotec.
Tehuantepec
Tehuantepecano
Tehueco. Cahita.
Tegueco
Thehuoco
Zuaque
Tejon Pass. Data lacking.[284]
Tekesta. Muskogean (?); Florida; extinct, 175? (1763).
Tequesta
Temecula. Luiseño.
Temori. Tarahumara; Chihuahua; extinct.
Ten'a. See Koyukon.
Tene. Unclassified (Apachean?); Jalisco; extinct.[285]
Tenino. Columbia River Sahaptin; 250 in Oregon (1962).
John Day
Tairtla

283 See T. Kaufman, *IJAL* 35.154–74 (1969).
284 Pilling, No. 3098, numbers 1–10 from Powers, *CNAE* 3.399 (1877).
285 Rivet, *Les langues du monde* 2.1085–6, follows Mendizábal and Jiménez Moreno in listing Tene as one of the extinct languages of Jalisco, spoken in the sixteenth century. Tiné (*The People*) is the Navajo tribal name, and I have wondered if the Tene of Jalisco might be a related Apachean group, ranging far to the south.

Tapanash
Tyigh
Warm Springs

Tennuth-kutchin. Athapaskan; N.E. Alaska along Birch Creek; 100 (1740), extinct in 1863.
Birch Creek
Birch River
Gens de Bouleaux

Teotitlan del Valle. Central Zapotecan.

Tepahue. Taracahitian (Cahita type); Sonora; extinct.

Teparantana. Unclassified; Sonora; extinct.

Tepecano. Southern Tepehuan; Zacatecas, N. Jalisco.
Tepecan

Tepehua. Totonacan; Hidalgo, N. Puebla, N. Veracruz; 4,000 (1952), 14,000 (1967).
Tepewa

Tepehuan. Piman; 1,766 monolinguals mostly in Nayarit, Chihuahua and Durango (1960).
Tepegua
Tepeguan
Tepeguana
Tepehua
Tepehuana
Tepehuane
Tepehuano

Tepetixtec. Unclassified; Guerrero; extinct.
Tepetixteca

Tepoca. Seri.

Tepuzculano. Mixtec.
Tepuzculula (?)

Tepuzteco. Unclassified; Guerrero; extinct.
Tlacote
Tlacotepehua
Tlacotepehua-Tepuztec

Tequesta. See Tekesta.

Tequistlatec. Tequistlatecan; S. Oaxaca; 9,000 (1967).
Chontal of Oaxaca

Tequistlatecan. Hokan-Siouan.
Chontal
Tequistlatec

Terraba. Talamanca; Costa Rica, Panama.
Brurán
Depso

Térraba
Teshbi
Tiribi (?)
Tishbi

Teslin. Tlingit.

Tesuque. Tewa; 200 in New Mexico (1967).
Tezuque

Tête de Boule. Cree; 2,000 in S. central Quebec, N. of Montreal.

Tetelcingo. Nahuatl; Morelos.

Tetiquilhati. Totonac.
Tetiquilhatí

Teton. Dakota.
Teeton

Teul. Piman (Tepecano type); Zacatecas; extinct.

Tewa. Kiowa-Tanoan; New Mexico, Arizona. See Hano, Nambe, Pojoaque, San Ildefonso, San Juan, Santa Clara and Tesuque.
Taowa
Tegua
Tehua
Telma
Tigua

Texixtepec. Zoquean; Veracruz.
Popoluca
Popoluca of Veracruz
Texistepec

Texome. Unclassified; Guerrero; extinct.

Tezcatec. Unclassified; Guerrero; extinct.
Tezcateca
Tezcateco

Tfalati. Kalapuyan.

Thlingchadinne. See Dogrib.

Thompson. Interior Salish; 1,000 to 2,000 in British Columbia (1962).
Neetlakapamuch
Neklakapamuk
Netlakapamuk
Nicoutemuch
Nikutamuk
Nikutemukh
Nitlakapamuk
Ntlakyapmuk
Thompson River Indians

Thule. See Ita.

Tiam. Unclassified; Jalisco; extinct.
Tikeramiut. Eskimo.
Tilaco. South Pame.
Tillamook. Oregon Salish; 1 in Oregon (1970).
  Kilamook
  Ntsietshaw
  Ntsietshawus
  Talamoh
  Tilamuk
Tilo. Mamean; S. Mexico, N. and W. of the Teco.
  Tiló
Timucua. Timuquan; Florida; extinct, 60? (1728). See Saturiwa, Tacatacuru.
  Florida
  Floridiana
  Timuacuana
  Timuquan
  Timuquana
Timuquan. Natchez-Muskogean, Hokan-Siouan (?).
  Timucuan
  Timuquanan
Tionontati. Iroquoian; Ontario, Wisconsin, Michigan; after merger with Hurons in Michigan, they were called the Wyandot, about 1748.
  Petun
  Tobacco Nation
Tinlinneh. Data lacking.[286]
  Tejon
Tinne. See Athapaskan.
Tiou. Tunican (?); Mississippi; extinct some years after 1731.
  Koroa
  Sioux
Tipai. See Campo.
Tiribi. Bribri.
  Rayado
Tisteco. Unclassified; Guerrero; extinct.
Tiwa. Kiowa-Tanoan; New Mexico, Arizona. See Isleta, Picuris, Sandia, Taos.
Tlacomulteco. Unclassified; Jalisco; extinct.
Tlacopan. Nahuatl.
Tlacotepehua. See Tepuzteco.
Tlahuiltoltepec. Mixe; Oaxaca.

[286] Pilling, No. 2678, numerals in F. Müller, *Grundriss* 2.429–39 (1882).

Tlaltempanec. Unclassified; Jalisco; extinct.
    Tlaltempaneca
Tlanepantla. Nahuatl; Puebla.
Tlaoquatch. See Nootka.
    Klahoquaht
    Tlaoquatsh
Tlapanec. Supanecan; 18,000 in Guerrero (1967). See Mangue.[287]
    Tlapaneco
    Tlappanec
Tlascalteca. Nahuatl. Also see Zia.
    Tlascala
    Tlaskalteke
    Tlatscalca
    Tlaxcala
    Tlaxcalla
Tlatiman. Mam.
Tlatskanai. Athapaskan; Washington, Oregon; extinct, 3 (1910).
    Clackstar
    Clatskanie
    Klatskanai
    Klatskenai
    Tlatskani
    Tlatskenai
Tlatzihuizteca. Unclassified; Guerrero; extinct.
    Tlatzihuizteco
Tlaxcala. See Tlascalteca.
Tlaxpanaloya. Nuhuatl; Puebla.
Tlatzihuiztec. Unclassified; Mexico; extinct.
Tlaxiaco. Mixtec.
Tlepanoten. Tahltan.
Tlingit. Na-Dene; 1,000 to 2,000 in S.E. Alaska, Yukon and British Columbia (1962).[288]
    Kalouche
    Klinkit
    Koljusch
    Koljuschen

[287] Rivet, *Les langues du monde* 2.1000 (1952), counts Tlapanec as a Coahuiltecan language spoken by (1) the Tlapanec of Guerrero, (2) the extinct Maribio (called Subtiaba *à tort*) once in Nicaragua S.E. of the Bay of Fonseca, and (3) the extinct Maribio called Maribichicoa, once near Ocotal, Nicaragua.
[288] Swanton, *Tribes*, pp. 541–2, gives prominence to: (1) Auk, (2) Chilkat, (3) Gonaho, (4) Hehl, (5) Henya, (6) Huna, (7) Hutsnuwu, (8) Kake, (9) Kuiu, (10) Sanya, (11) Sitka, (12) Stikine, (13) Sumdum, (14) Taku, (15) Tongass, (16) Yakutat.

Koljusck
Kolosch
Kolosche
Koluschan
Kolush
Kolusic
Koulischen
Lhiinkit
Sheetkah
Sitka
Sitka-kwan
Sitkawan
Skatkwan
Stakbin-kwan
Stakhin
Stakhinkwan
Takukwan
Thlingit
Thlinkit
Tlinkit
Tongas
Tongass
Tonguas
Yakutat

Tlotona. Sekani.

Toboso. Apachean; Coahuila, Durango, Nuevo Leon, Chihuahua; extinct.[82]

Cabezas (?)
Cocoyome (?)
Tobozo

Tochana. Data lacking.[289]

Tocobaga. Timuquan; Florida; extinct.

Amacapiras (?)
Macapiras (?)
Tompacuas (?)

Togiagmiut. Eskimo.

Toihicha. Kings River Yokuts.

Tohome. Muskogean; Alabama; extinct some years after 1772, 200? (1758).

Tojar. Terraba (?); Tojar Island, off the N. coast of Panama.

Tojolabal. Tzeltalan; 3,779 monolinguals in Chiapas (1960).

Toholabal

[289] Pilling, No. 1955b, names of Tochanas in W. H. Jackson, *Descriptive catalogue of the photographs of the United States Geological Survey of the Territories* (1874), pp. 69–83.

Tolimec. Unclassified; W. Guerrero; extinct.
  Tolimeca
Tolowa. Athapaskan; 3 or 4 in Oregon (1960).
  Haynarger
  Henagi
  Henaggi
  Lagoons
  Lopas
  Smith River
  Tahlewah
  Tahluwah
Toltec. Data lacking.[290]
  Tolteki
  Tulteca
Toltichi. Northern Foothill Yokuts (?).
Tomatec. Unclassified; Jalisco; extinct.
  Tomateca
Tongas. Tlingit.
  Tongass
Tonikan. See Tunican, Gulf.
Tonkawa. Tonkawan; Texas, Oklahoma; fewer than 10 in Oklahoma (1962).
  Kádiko
  Kariko
  Komkomé
  Konkoné
  Maneaters
  Toncawe
Tonkawan. Classification uncertain. Hokan-Siouan, Algonquian-Wakashan and Penutian have been suggested.
Tonto. Apachean; 500 at Camp Verde, Arizona (1962).[291]
Tonto. Yuman.[292]
Topilejo. Nahuatl; Distrito Federal.
Topiltepec. Nahuatl; Guerrero.
Toquart. Nootka.

[290] Pilling, Nos. 217, 217a, 217b, 1559, 1754, 3972, 3973. The non-mythical Toltecs came to Hidalgo from Jalisco or Zacatecas about 900 A.D. and were a power there until about 1250 A.D. But it may be that nineteenth-century references to Toltecs were in some cases pseudo-scientific.

[291] Divisions: (1) Southern Tonto, (2) Northern Tonto.

[292] Pilling, No. 1430, vocabulary by O. Loew and J.B. White published by Gatschet in *ZEthn* in 1877. The term Tonto may refer to various groups. Note particularly: (1) a group of Yavapai, Yuma, Maricopa and some Pinaleño who assembled on the Verde River Reservation, Arizona, in 1873 and moved to the San Carlos Reservation, Arizona, in 1875; (2) a group in Arizona descended mostly from Yavapai fathers and Pinaleño mothers.

Aht
Takaht
Tokoaat

Toquegua. Cholan (?); on the Gulf of Honduras, N.W. Honduras; extinct.
Loquehua

Totonac. Totonacan; 63,794 monolinguals mostly in N. Puebla and Veracruz, with a few in Hidalgo and Distrito Federal (1960).[293]
Ipapana
Naolingo
Natimolo
Tonaca
Totolaca
Totonac
Totonaca
Totonacca
Totonaco
Totonak
Totonaka
Totonaken
Totonaquæ
Totonaque
Totonicapan
Totonoco

Totonacan. Macro-Mayan.

Totorame. Aztecoidan; Sinaloa and Jalisco; extinct.
Pinome
Pinonuquia

Towa. Kiowa-Tonoan.

Towka. Data lacking.[294]

Tranjik-kutchin. Athapaskan; 200? in N. Alaska, S. of the Porcupine River and along the Black River (1962).
Black River Kutchin
Cache River People

Trinity River. Data lacking.[295]

Trique. Mixtecan; 4,000 in Oaxaca (1952).
Trike
Triqui

[293] Mason (1940): (1) Coast, (2) Papantla, (3) Sierra. Zembrano (1752): (1) Chacahuaxtli [in Xalpan and Pentepec], (2) Ipapana [in Augustine missions], (3) Tatimolo [in Noalingo], (4) Tetiquilhati [in the high sierras].

[294] Pilling, Nos. 217, 217a, 217b.

[295] Pilling, No. 1353, vocabulary by W.M. Gabb, *CNAE* 3.518–29 (1877).

Triquean. Otomanguean.
Trokek. Unclassified; Chiapas; extinct.
  Trogeg
Tsattine. See Beaver.
Tschukak Island. Eskimo.
Tseloni. See Sekani.
Tsetsaut. Athapaskan; early on Behm Canal, S. Alaska, extending to Portland Canal and inland into British Columbia; 1 or more (1970).
  Ts'ets'ā'ut
  T'set'sa'ut
Tshnagmjut. See Kuskokwim.
Tsihalish. See Chehalis.
Tsimshian. Tsimshian; 7,000 or more in British Columbia, including the Coast Tsimshian, the Niska and the Gitksan (1974).
  Chemmesyan
  Chimesyan
  Chimmesyan
  Chimsyan
  Coast Tsimshian
  Skeena Indians
  Spuch'-æ-lotz
  Tchim'-chæ-an'
  Tshimshean
  Tshimsian
  Tsimsian
Tualatin. See Atfalati.
Tubar. Taracahitian (Cahita?); Chihuahua; extinct.
Tubatulabal. Sierra Nevada Shoshonean; fewer than 10 in California (1962).[296]
  Kern River
  Tübatulabal
Tucurrike-Orisa. Chibchan.
  Tucurrique
Tuhohi. Buena Vista Yokuts.
Tukkuth. Kutchin.
  Takudh
  Tukudh
  Upper Porcupine
Tuktoyaktuk. Eskimo; Western Canadian Arctic. See Mackenzie River.
  KitiyaRuŋmiut
Tulamni. Buena Vista Yokuts.
  Tuolumne

[296] Subdivisions: (1) Bankalachi, (2) Palagewan, (3) Tübatulabal.

Tulapa. Nahuatl; Puebla.
Tule. Term for (1) a Central Zapotecan group, and (2) a Cuna group.
Tule-Kaweah. Foothill Yokuts.
Tunahe. Kutenai.[297]
Tunica. Tunican; Mississippi, Louisiana, Arkansas, Texas; extinct, 1 (1939).
Tunican. Hokan-Siouan (?).
    Tunica
Tuninirmiut. Eskimo.
Tununirusirmiut. Eskimo.
    Admiralty Inlet
    Agomiut
    Too-noo-nee-noo-shuk
Tupancal. Mam.
Turucaca. Boruca; Panama; extinct.
Tuscarora. Iroquoian; North Carolina, Pennsylvania, New York, Ontario; 100 to 300 in New York and Ontario (1962).
    Touscarora
    Tuskara
    Tuskarora
    Tuskeruro
Tuskegee. Muskogean (?); North Carolina, Tennesee, Alabama, Oklahoma; extinct, 250? (1830).
    Tasqui
    Tasquiqui
Tutchone. Athapaskan; 1,000 in S.W. Yukon (1974).
    Kluane
    Snag
    Southern Tutchone
    Upper Pelly River Indians
Tutelo. Ohio Valley Siouan; Virginia, North Carolina, Pennsylvania, New York, Ontario; language extinct in 1898.
    Kattera
    Shateras
Tutuapa. Mam.
Tututni. Athapaskan; 2 or 3 in Oregon (1970).[298]
    Loloten
    Rogue River
    Tootooten

[297] Mistakenly listed as an extinct Salishan tribe by Teit and Boas, *BAE–R* 45.23–396 (1930).
[298] Divisions: (1) Euchre Creek (Yukichetunne), (2) Joshua (Chemetunne), (3) Kwaishtunne (Khustenete), (4) Mikonotunne, (5) Pistol River (Chetleschantunne), (6) Sixes (Kwatami), (7) Tututni (Tututunne).

Tututen
Tututene

Tuxtec. Unclassified; Guerrero; extinct.
Tuxteca
Tuxteco

Twana. Hood Canal Salish; fewer than 10 in Washington (1962).
Skokomish
Toanhooch
Toanhuch

Tygh Valley. See Tenino.

Tzeltal. Tzeltalan; 55,951 monolinguals in Chiapas (1960).
Celdala
Celdale
Celtala
Cendal
Sendal
Tzendal
Tzental
Zendal

Tzeltalan. Mayan.
Quelem
Quélène

Tzinanteco. Tzotzil.
Cinanteco

Tzotzil. Tzeltalan; 57,235 monolinguals, about 65,000 total in Chiapas (1960). See San Andrés.
Chamula
Cinanteco
Quelem
Quélène
Tzinanteco
Zotzil
Zotzlem (?)
Zozil

Tzutuhil. Quichean; 25,000 S. and W. of Lake Atitlán, in Guatemala (1968).
Atiteca
Tzutohile
Tzutuchil
Tzutuhile
Zacapula
Zacatula
Zutugil

Zutuhil
Uchita. Waïcuri.
Uchiti
Ugalakmiut. Ambiguous term for Eyak or Eskimo groups.
Ougaljakhmoutzi
Ugalachmjut
Ugalachmut
Ugalachmutzi
Uglakmut
Ugalákmūt
Ugaliachmutzi
Ugaljachmutzi
Ugashachmüt
Ugalenzi. See Ugalakmiut and Eyak.
Ugalenzen
Ugashachmut. Eskimo.
Ukhotnom. Yuki.
Ukkusiksaligmiut. Eskimo.
Utkusiksaligmiut
Ulgatcho. Carrier.
Lower Carrier
Nētcāut'in
Ulua. Southern Sumo; 1,000 in Nicaragua (1952).[299]
Ulba
Ulva
Vulua
Walwa
Woolua
Woolwa
Wulwa
Ulúkuk.[300] See Malemiut and Ingalik.
Umatilla. Columbia River Sahaptin; 10 to 100 in Oregon (1962).
Umnak. Sėe Unalaska.
Umpqua. Athapaskan; Oregon; perhaps extinct about 1960, 43 (1937).[301]
Unaaliq. Eskimo.
Unakhotana. See Koyukon.
Unakhatana
Unalachtigo. Delaware.

299 Subdivisions: (1) Guanexico, (2) Prinzo, (3) Ulua.
300 The Athapaskan Ulúkuk are the Ulukakhotana, a division of the Kaiyuhkhotana on the Unalaklik River.
301 Not to be confused with Lower Umpqua or Kuitsh.

Unalaska. Aleut; part of the Alaskan Peninsula, and Fox Islands. Krauss counts 500 Eastern Aleut for Umnak, Unalaska, Peninsula, and Pribilof (1970).
    Eastern Aleut
    Fox
    Onalashka
    Onolaska
    Oonalaska Eskimo
    Ounalachka
    Umnak
    Unalaschka
    Unalaschker
    Unalashka
Unaligmut. Eskimo.
    Unaaliq
    Unaligmiut
    Unalígmūt
Unami. Delaware.
Unavamiut. Eskimo.
Uncpapa. See Dakota.
    Hunkpapa
Ungieskie. Data lacking.[302]
Unquachog. See Montauk.
    Unachog
Upanguayma. Seri.
    Upanguaima
Upland Arizona Yuman. Yuman.
    Arizona Yuman
    Highlands Yuman
    Northern Yuman
    Northwest Arizona Yuman
    Walapai Type Yuman
Upper Chehalis. Olympic Salish; fewer than 10 in Washington (1962).
    Chehalis
    Kwaiailk
Upper Chinook. Chinookan.
    Kiksht
    River Chinook
Upper Cowlitz. Northwest Sahaptin; Washington; extinct perhaps by 1907.
    Taidnapam
    Taitinapam
Upper Kuskokwim. Athapaskan; Kuskokwim headwaters, Alaska; 100 (1970).

[302] Pilling, No. 3413a, Russian name for two dialects at Fort Ross about 1825, according to A. Pinart.

See Ingalik.[303]
Galcäni
Galtzanen
Galzanen
Ingalik of Nikolai
Kaltschanen
Koltschane
Koltschanen
Koltschani
Kulchana
Kuskokwim
Nikolai

Upper Liard. Kaska.
Upper Nisqually. Northwest Sahaptin.
Upper Porcupine. Tukkuth.
Upper Sacramento. Data lacking.[304]
Upper Tanana. Athapaskan; 250 at Tetlin, etc. (1970). See Nabesna.
Upurui. Cariban.
Ure. Pima Bajo.
Uren. Chibchan.
Uru. Chipaya-Uru.
Uru-Chipaya. See Chipaya-Uru.
Uspantec. Quichean; 3,000 in central Guatemala, about 35 miles W. of Cobán (1952).
Uspanteca
Uspanteco

Ute. Numic (Ute type Plateau Shoshonean); Utah, Colorado, New Mexico and elsewhere; 2,000 to 4,000 in Utah and Colorado (1962).
Capote Uta
Ietan
Sampitche
Sanpet
Tabuat Ute
Uintah Ute
Uta
Utah
Weminuche

[303] I have assumed the identity of Hodge's Kulchana (Pilling's Koltschane) and Krauss's Upper Kuskokwim, from geographical clues only. Raymond Collins and Sally Jo Collins, *Upper Kuskokwim Athapaskan dictionary* (Fairbanks, 1966), p. [iii]: '[Upper Kuskokwim] is somewhat related to the Ingalik and Koyukon languages but is probably closest to the dialect spoken by the Lower Tanana people at Minto and Nenana, Alaska.' Krauss writes me, however, that the Kulchana are probably the Transitional Tanana.

[304] Pilling, Nos. 986, 1635, 1991, vocabulary from Dana originally in Hale, *Ethnography and philology* (1846), p. 630.

Yampa
Yuta
Yutah
Utian. Miwok and Costanoan.
Miwok-Costanoan
Utina. Timuquan; Florida; extinct, 60? (1728).
Utkiavinmiut. Eskimo.
Utlateco. See Quiche.
Uto-Aztecan. Aztec-Tanoan.
Utaztekan
Uto-Aztekan
Utukamiut. Eskimo.
Vacoregue. See Guasave.
Guazave
Valiente. Term for (1) the Bribri, and (2) the Move.[305]
Valle. Central Zapotecan.
Ocotlan
Valley
Valley Maidu. Maidu.
Valley Miwok. Sierra Miwok.
Valley Yokuts. Yokuts.
Valley Zapotecan. See Central Zapotecan.
Vanyume. Takic (Southern California Shoshonean); California; extinct by 1925, 65? (1776).
Vaquero. See Querecho.
Varohio. Tarahumara; Chihuahua and Sonora.
Chinipa
Varogio
Varohío
Voragio
Vasco-Dene. Term used by Swadesh in 1960 for a group with Basque, Na-Dene, and an assemblage of other language groups around the world.
Vasco-Déné
Vascodene
Vayema. Unclassified; Sonora; extinct.
Ventureño. Chumashan; California; extinct.
Alliklik
San Buenaventura
Veracruzano. Huastec.
Vera Paz. Data lacking.[306]
Viceita. Bribri.

305 See Pilling, No. 3617.
306 Pilling, No. 4021, manuscript vocabulary by F. Viana, according to Beristain.

Vizeita
Vigitega. Piman; Nayarit; extinct.
Vijana. See Bijano.
Villa Alta. See Northern Zapotecan.
Rincón
Villalteco
Sierra de Villa Alta
Yalálag
Virginia. See Powhatan.
Virginiane
Virginice
Virginien
Voto. Chibchan; N.W. Costa Rica.
Vunta-kutchin. Athapaskan; 200? in N. Alaska N. of the middle Porcupine River, including Old Cow Creek (1962).
Crow River Kutchin
Rat
Zjén-ta-kouttchin
Waccamaw. Eastern Siouan (?); South Carolina, North Carolina; extinct, 400? (1720).
Cape Fear (?)
Guacaya (?)
Woccon (?)
Waco. Caddoan (Wichita type?); Oklahoma, Texas; extinct, 5 (1910).
Huanchané (?)
Hueco
Houechas (?)
Wee-co
Wahkiakum. See Wakaikam.
Wahpeton. Dakota.
Waican. Chibchan.
Waïcuri. Waïcurian; Baja California; extinct.[307]
Cora
Guaicura
Guaicuri
Guajiquiro
Guaricuri
Uchitie
Vaicura
Waicura
Waicuri

[307] Divisions: (1) Aripa, (2) Cora, (3) Monqui, (4) Uchita (Utciti), (5) Waïcuri, (6) Edú, (7) Didú, (8) Ika.

Waikur
Waikura
Waikuri

Waïcurian. Hokan-Siouan (?).
Guaicura-Pericú

Waiilatpu. See Cayuse.
Willetpoos

Waiilatpuan. Sahaptian.
Waiilatpu

Wailaki. Athapaskan; California; 1 or extinct (1970).
Kenesti
Wailakki

Wakaikam. Lower Chinook; Washington; extinct some years after 1850.
Wackiacum
Wahaikan (?)
Wahkiakum
Wahkyecum
Waiwaikum (?)
Wa-kái-a-kum
Waikaíkam
Waqa-iqam

Wakanasisi. Chinookan; mouth of Willamette River, Oregon; extinct by 1910, fewer than 100 (1849).
Galakanasisi
Gatqstax
Waccanessisi
Waccanéssisi
Waccanessisí
Wakanakessi

Wakashan. Algonquian-Wakashan.

Wakichi. Valley Yokuts.
Millerton (?)

Wakynakaine. Data lacking.[308]

Walapai. Walapai type Yuman; 442 in Arizona (1962).
Hualapai
Jaguallapai
Matávěkě-paya

Wales. Eskimo; Seward Peninsula, Alaska; a similar dialect is found on Little Diomede Island, and on Big Diomede Island, U.S.S.R.
Imaklik

[308] Pilling, No. 3873, vocabulary from W.F. Tolmie, *CNAE* 1.247–65 (1877).

Walla Walla. Northeast Sahaptin; early in Washington, later on the Umatilla Reservation, N.E. Oregon; 100 to 200 in Oregon (1962).

Wampanoag. Algonquian; Rhode Island and Massachusetts, Martha's Vineyard, Nantucket; 1 or 2 in Massachusetts (1962).
Massasoits
Philip's Indians

Wanapam. Northeast Sahaptin; Washington; 175? (1910).
Lekulk
Lokulk
Priest's Rapids
Sokulk
Wanapum

Wangunk. See Wappinger.
Mattabesec

Wanki. Mosquito.

Wappinger. Eastern Algonquian; on E. bank of the Hudson River from N. of Manhattan to Poughkeepsie and E. to the Connecticut River Valley; extinct mostly by way of mergers with Nanticokes and Delawares; Potatuck, 2 (1774), Podunk, 50? (1774), Quinnipiac (including the Guilford Indians), 70? (1774), extinct in 1850, Tunxis or Sepous (including the Massacoe Indians, extinct about 1750), 56 (1774), 1 (1850).[309]
Hammonasset
Hammonassett
Massaco
Massacoe
Menunkatuck
Naugatuck
Nochpeem
Podunk
Quinnipiac
Quinnipiak
Quiripi

Wappo. Yukian; 1 in California (1970).[310]
Ashochimi
Soteomellos
Sotomieyos

[309] Divisions: (1) Hammonasset, (2) Kitchawank, (3) Massaco, (4) Menunkatuck, (5) Nochpeem, (6) Paugusset [with Algonquian "Naugatuck Indian" refugees at Naugatuck, 1720–1790], (7) Podunk, (8) Poquonock, (9) Quinnipiac, (10) Sicaog, (11) Sintsink, (12) Siwanoy, (13) Tankiteke, (14) Tunxis, (15) Wangunk, (16) Wappinger, (17) Wecquaesgeek. Scholars view the Wappinger language as perhaps a form of Munsee (Delaware).

[310] Divisions: (1) Central Wappo, (2) Lile'ek Wappo, (3) Northern Wappo, (4) Southern Wappo, (5) Western Wappo. Dialects surviving in 1964: (1) Geyserville, (2) Napa or Napa River.

Warao. Paezan.
Ware. Sekani.
Warm Springs. See Tenino.
Wasco. Upper Chinook; 10 in Oregon and Washington (1962).
    Wasko
Washa. Chitimachan; Louisiana; extinct some years after 1805.
    Ouacha
Washo. Washoan; 100 in California and Nevada (1962).
    Washoe
Washoan. Hokan-Siouan.
    Washo
Wateree. Siouan (?); South Carolina, North Carolina; extinct some years after 1750.
    Chickanee
    Guatari
Watlala. Clackamas; Washington, Oregon; extinct, 1,400 (1812).
    Cascade Indians
Waunana. Chocoan.
Wawyukma. Northeast Sahaptin; Washington. See Peloos.
    Wauyukma
Waxhaw. Siouan (?); South Carolina, North Carolina; extinct.
    Gueza (?)
    Weesock
    Wisacky
Wea. Miami; Illinois, Indiana, Kansas; extinct, 50? (1885).
    Weah
    Weaw
    Wee-ah
Weapemeoc. Algonquian (?); North Carolina; extinct, 180? (1700).
    Yeopim
    Pasquotank
    Perquimaw
    Poteskeet
Weminuche. Ute.
Wenatchi. Interior Salish; 200 in Washington (1962).
    Chelan
    Columbia-Wenatchi
    Peshkwaus
    Piskaus
    Piskaws
    Piskwau
    Piskwaus
    Pisquous

Pisquow
Piskwaw
Wenachee
Wenatchee

Wenrohronon. Iroquoian; New York, Pennsylvania; extinct (some years after 1673) after refugee groups of 1639 joined the Hurons and the Neutrals; 600 with Hurons (1639).
Ahouenrochrhonons
Cat Nation

Western Abnaki. Algonquian (Saint Francis; probably Pennacook, etc.).

Western Aleut. Aleut. The term is ambiguous, sometimes applying to dialects elsewhere called Central (Atka), sometimes only to Attu. Bergsland in 1959 included, as Western Aleut, speakers on the Andreanov Islands including Atka, the Niiruris, the extinct Naamirus, the Qarus on the Rat Islands, and the extinct Saskinar on the Near Islands, including Attu. Krauss counts 10 on Attu and 25 on Copper Island (1970).

Western Apache. Apachean.

Western Atakapa. Atakapa.

Western Canadian. An Athapaskan group with Tagish, Kaska, Sekani and Tahltan.

Western Chibchan. Chibchan.

Western Eskimo. Eskimo.

Western Kutchin. See Kutcha-kutchin.

Western Miwok. Utian.

Western Muskogean. See Muskogean.

Western Niantic. Algonquian; W. Connecticut; extinct, 85 (1761). See Eastern Niantic.
Western Nihantic
Western Nehantic

Western Paleosiberian. Paleosiberian.
Yeniseian

Western Shoshoni. See Shoshoni.

Western Yavapai. Yavapai.

Western-Southern Pomo. Pomoan.

Whilkut. Athapaskan; California; more than 50 (1910).

Whitehorse. Southern Tutchone.

White Mountain. Apachean; more than 4,000 in Arizona (1963).[311]
Coyotero

Wichikik. Yokuts.

Wichita. Caddoan; Oklahoma, Kansas, Texas; 100 to 200 in Oklahoma (1962).
Black Pawnee
Panis

[311] Bands: (1) Carrizo, (2) Cedar Creek, (3) Cibeque, (4) North Fork, (5) White River.

Quivira
Witshita
Wihinasht. See Shoshoni.
Wihinacht
Wikchumni. See Wükchamni.
Willamet. Kalapuya.
Willopah. See Kwalhioqua.[312]
Wind River. Numic (Shóshoni type Plateau Shoshonean); Wyoming.
Winnebago. Mississippi Valley Siouan; Wisconsin, Indiana, Iowa, Minnesota, South Dakota, Nebraska; 1,000 to 2,000 in Wisconsin and Nebraska (1962).
Hochangara
Nipegon
Puant
Winebago
Winnebagoe
Winnebagog
Wintu. Wintun, 20 to 30 in California (1962). See Nomlaki, Patwin, and Suisun.
Trinity
Trinity County
Wintun
Wintun. Penutian.
Copehan
Wintoon
Wintuan
Winyaw. Siouan (?); South Carolina; extinct, 35? (1715).
Yenyohol (?)
Wipukapaya. Yavapai.
Wishram. Upper Chinook; 10 in Washington (1962).
Echeloot
Nihaloitih
Nihaloth
Tlakluit
Wiyot. Algonquian-Wakashan; 1 in California (1962).
Humboldt Bay
Kowilth
Viard
Weeyot
Weiyot
Wischosk
Wishosk

[312] Not to be confused with the Chinookan Willopah, for whom no linguistic data are on record.

Wyot

Woccon. Eastern Siouan; North Carolina; extinct as a tribe after 1711, 480? (1709).
Waccamaw (?)
Waccoon

Woolwa. See Ulua.

Wrigley. Athapaskan (Hare? Slave?); S.W. Mackenzie on the Mackenzie River N. of Fort Simpson.[313]

Wükchamni. Tule-Kaweah Yokuts.
Wikchumni

Wyandot. Iroquoian; created by merger of Huron and Tionontati refugees in Michigan; fewer than 5 in Oklahoma and California (1962). See Tionontati.
Guyandot
Huron
Hurone
Wanat
Wandot
Weiondot
Wundat
Wyandote
Wyandott
Wyandotte

Wynoochee. Coast Salish; Washington.

Xalacapan. Nahuatl; Puebla.

Xaltepec. Mixtec.

Xaltianguis. Northern Zapotecan.

Xilotlantzinca. Unclassified (Uto-Aztecan?); S. Jalisco and W. Michoacan; extinct.
Tamazulteco
Xilotlanzinca-Tamazultec
Xilotlantzinco

Xinca. Classification disputed (Xinca-Lencan? Misumalpan?); 200?, mostly in Chiquimulilla and Guazacapan, Guatemala (1965).[314]
Popoloca of Guatemala
Sinca

Xincan. See Misumalpan.
Xinca

Xixime. Taracahitian; Durango and Sinaloa; extinct.[315]

Xochihuehuetlan. Nahuatl; Guerrero.

Xochixtlahuaca. Nahuatl; Guerrero.

[313] See remarks by Krauss in the present volume.

[314] Dialects: (1) Sinacantan, (2) Xupiltepec, (3) Xutiapa. Some add (4) Conguajo (?) assigned to Lencan by Juarros in 1824.

[315] Divisions: (1) Aibine, (2) Hine, (3) Hume.

Xocotec. Unclassified; Jalisco; extinct.
Xocoteca
Xoxocotla. Nahuatl; Morelos.
Yaana. See Yana.
Yadkin. Eastern Siouan (?); North Carolina; extinct some years after 1710.
Reatkin
Yattken
Yahi. Yanan. See Southern Yahi.
Yaitepec. Chatino.
Yakima. Northwest Sahaptin; 1,000 to 2,000 in Washington (1962).
Cutsahnim
Jaakema
Jakon
Pshawanwappam
P'shwan-wapam
Shanwappoms
Yakama
Yakoma
Yakonan. Penutian.
Yakutat Bay. Tlingit or Eyak.
Yalalag. Northern Zapotecan.
Yalálag
Yamacraw. See Yamasee.
Yamasee. Eastern Muskogean (?) (Hitchiti type?); Georgia, South Carolina, Florida, Alabama; extinct some years after 1825 (after joining the Seminole in Florida starting early in the eighteenth century).
Emusas
Ocklawaha Seminole
Yamacraw
Yemasee
Yumersee
Yamhill. See Kalapuya.
Yamel
Yampa. Ute.
Yana. Yanan; California; extinct, 9 (1930). See Southern Yahi.
Noje
Noze
Nozi
Yaana
Yahi
Yanan. Hokan-Siouan.
Yana

Yanhuitlan. Mixtec.
Yankton. Dakota; 1,000 to 2,000 in North Dakota, South Dakota and Montana (1962).
    Nakota
    Yancton
    Yanktong
Yanktonai. Dakota.
    Yanctonai
Yaqui. Taracahitian; 545 monolinguals in Sonora and Chihuahua (1960), 3,000 in Arizona (1967); 10,000 Yaqui and Mayo in Sonora (1967).
    Hiaki
    Hiaque
Yaquina. Yakonan; Oregon; extinct, 19 (1910).
    Iakon
    Jacon
    Killamuk
    Killemook
    Lower Killamuks
    Southern Killamuk
    Yacona
    Yakon
    Yakona
    Yakwina
    Youkone
Yatasi. Caddo; Louisiana, Oklahoma; extinct, 26 (1826).
Yatzachi el Bajo. Northern Zapotecan.
Yautepec. Zapotecan.
Yavapai. Walapai type Yuman; fewer than 600 in Arizona (1962).
    Apache
    Apache-Mojave
    Apache-Yuma
    Mohave-Apache
    Tonto
    Tulkepa
    Tulkepaia
    Yampai
    Yampaio
    Yavapai-Apache
    Yavape
    Yavepe Kutcan
    Yavipai
    Yuma Apache

Yavi. Data lacking.[316]
Yawdanchi. Tule-Kaweah Yokuts.
Yawelmani. Southern Valley Yokuts. See Kern Lake.
 Yauelmani
Yazoo. Tunica (?); Louisiana (?), Arkansas (?), Mississippi; extinct, 200? (1758).
Yecora. Pima Bajo.
 Yécora
Yellowknife. Athapaskan (Chipewyan type); 400 to 600 in Mackenzie (1962). See Mountain.
 Copper Indians
 Red Knife
 Tatsanottine
Ynezeño. Chumashan; California; extinct.
 Inezeño
 Santa Inez
 Santa Ines Mission
Yokod. Tule-Kaweah Yokuts.
Yokuts. Penutian; California. See Chukchansi.
 Lathruunun
 Mariposan
 Millerton (?)
 Nopthrinthres
 Tachi
 Tatché
 Telame
 Telami
 Wechikhit
 Wichikik
 Wi'-chi-kik
 Yocut
 Yokut
 Yokutsan
Yonkalla. Kalapuyan; Oregon; extinct, 11 (1910).
 Yamkallie
 Yoncalla
Yopi. Unclassified; Guerrero; extinct.
 Jope
 Yope
 Yoppi
Yoro. Jicaquean.

[316] Pilling, No. 2276, the Yavi word for 'head' in J. P. Lesley, *PAPS* 7.148–52 (1862).

Yosemite. See Miwok.
Yosemite Valley. Data lacking.[317]
    Yo-semite Valley
Yosko. Sumo; central Nicaragua; extinct.
    Yosco
Yscani. Wichita; Oklahoma; extinct, 360? (1782)
    Ascani
    Hyscani
    Ixcani
Yucatec. See Maya.
Yucayo. Data lacking.[318]
Yuchi. Hokan-Siouan; Tennessee, Kentucky, South Carolina, Georgia, Florida, Alabama, Illinois and elsewhere; 10 to 100 in Oklahoma (1962).
    Chisca
    Euchee
    Hogologe
    Rickohockans (?)
    Uche
    Uchee
    Uchi
    Utchee
    Yoochee
    Yuchian
Yui. Timuquan; S.E. Georgia (?), Florida; extinct, more than 1,000 (1602).
Yuit. Eskimo; 1,000 in N.E. Siberia, and 850 on St. Lawrence Island (1972). See Yupik.
    Asiatic Eskimo
    Chuklukmut
    Chū'klūkmūt
    Chūklū'kmut
    Chukohukmute
    Namoller
    Namolli
    Namollo
    Siberian Eskimo
    Siberian Yupik
Yuk. Central Yupik.
Yukaghir. Eastern Paleosiberian.

[317] Pilling, Nos. 1930, 2765 and 2766, place names in J. M. Hutchings, *Scenes* (1870), p. 169, and in C. Nordhoff, *California* (1872), p. 75, (1882), p. 58.
[318] Pilling, No. 2621, words from Haiti in Antonio del Monte y Tejada, *Historia de Santo Domingo* (1853), pp. 366–79.

Yuki. Yukian; 1 in California (1970).[319]
    Huchnom
    Northeast Yuki
    Redwoods
    Yukai
    Yuke
    Yukeh
Yukian. Hokan-Siouan.
    Yuki
Yukon River Eskimo. Eskimo.
Yukultas. Data lacking.[320]
Yuma. Yuma type Yuman; 1,000 in California and Arizona (1962).
    Cetguanes
    Chirumas
    Cuchan
    Kertchan
    Tonto
    Yumaya
Yuman. Hokan-Siouan.
    Cochimí
Yunca-Puruhan. Paezan.
Yunga. Yunga-Chipayan (?); Peru; extinct.[321]
    Yunka
Yupik. Eskimo; 13,000 to 14,000 S. of Unalakleet, Alaska and 900 Yuit in Siberia (1962); 20,000 Central, 1,000 Pacific, and 1,910 Siberian Eskimo (1970).
Yurok. Algonquian-Wakashan; 10 to 20 in California (1962).
    Euroc
    Weithspek
    Weitspeh
Yurumangui. Hokan-Siouan (?)
Yustaga. Timuquan; Florida; extinct, fewer than 1,000? (1675).
    Hostaqua
Zaachila. Central Zapotecan.
Zacapoaxtla. Nahuat.
Zacapula. See Tzutuhil.

[319] Dialects: (1) Yuki or Northeast Yuki, (2) Huchnom, (3) Coast Yuki.

[320] Pilling, No. 2960, Joseph Antonio Perez de la Fuente, *Cartilla Mexicàna, y Castellana*, unverified title of manuscript listed by Boturini.

[321] L.R. Stark, in a paper of 1968 [see abstract published by American Anthropological Association, *Bulletin* 1.133–4] proposed a node with Proto-Mayan and Yunga-Chipayan as branches, the latter with Yunga and Uru-Chipayan. Note that R.D. Olson, *IJAL* 30.313–24 (1964), had proposed a node labeled Proto-Mayan-Chipaya with Proto-Mayan and Chipaya as branches.

The term Yunga is ambiguous, as it refers to various groups of Peru.

Zacatula

Zacatec. Aztecoidan; S.W. Zacatecas, S.W. Durango; extinct.

Zacateco

Zamuco. A language of Paraguay.[322]

Zapaluta. Data lacking.[323]

Zapotec. Zapotecan; 78,763 monolinguals in Oaxaca, Veracruz, Puebla and Guerrero (1960).[324]

Çapoteca

Capotèque

Tehuantepec (?)

Tzapoteco

Zaapoteca

Zapoteca

Zapoteco

Zapoteken

Zapotèque

Zapotec of Jalisco. Unclassified; Jalisco; extinct.

Zapotecan. Otomanguean.

Mixteco-Zapoteco

Zapotlanec. Unclassified; Jalisco; extinct.

Zapotlaneca

Zayahuec. An extinct division of the Aztecoidan Cora.

Zayahueco

Zenzontepec. Chatino.

Zia. Keresan; 300 in New Mexico (1962).

Sia

Silla

Tlascalteca

Tlaskalteke

Tlatscalca

Tlaxcalla

Zinacanteco. Tzotzil.

Zoe. Taracahitian; Sinaloa, Chihuahua; extinct.[325]

Troe

Zongolica. Nahuatl; Veracruz.

322 Pilling, No. 2678.

323 Pilling, No. 2250b. Pilling found the name Zapaluta in the description of a manuscript owned by Joaquin García Icazbalceta, *Lenguas de Chiapas*, containing among other things a Confesonario en lengua Zapaluta.

324 There were, according to the census of 1940, 93,898 Zapotecan speakers in a total population of about 300,000.

325 The Zoe and the Baimena tribes are supposed by some to have shared the same language.

Zoque. Zoquean; 7,683 monolinguals (in a total of about 20,000?) in Chiapas, Oaxaca and Tabasco (1960).[326]
    Çoque
    Loque
    Soke
    Soque
    Troc
    Tzoc
    Zoc
    Zoke
Zoquean. Macro-Mayan.
    Mixe-Zoque
    Mixe-Zoquean
    Zoque-Mixe
Zoyatec. Unclassified; Jalisco; extinct.
    Zoyateca
Zuaque. See Tehueco.
Zuni. Macro-Penutian (?); 3,500 in New Mexico (1967).
    Ashiwi
    Zuñi

ADDENDUM

Michael Krauss offers the following classification as a substitute for that given under Athapaskan. I am grateful to him for his kindness in reviewing and improving proofs. I will be grateful also to any other correspondents who might want to suggest improvements. The text which follows is exactly as received from Krauss.

Athapaskan
    Northern
        The following is a brief summary of the Alaskan Athapaskan 'languages' as defined (in part arbitrarily) by Krauss as a result of his 1961–62 survey. Very rough estimates of numbers of speakers and indications of the age of the youngest speakers are also given.

Ahtena	A	Chitina, Tonsina, Copper Center, Glenallen, Tazlina, Louise-Tyone, Gulkana-Gakona, Denali-Cantwell
	B	Chistochina, Batzulnetas
	C	Mentasta
	ca. 250;	very few, if any, under 20.
Tanaina	A	'Inner': Knik, Eklutna, Susitna- Talkeetna, some Tyonek
	B	'Outer': Kenai, Ninilchik, Seldovia, some Tyonek, Iliamna, Nondalton, Lime-Hungry, Stoney River

326 Dialects: (1) Tapixulapan (or Tapijulapa or Tapijulapan), (2) extinct Tapachultec (or Tapachulteca or Tapachula or Tapachultec I), called Soconusca in sixteenth-century records.

ca. 400; very few, if any, under 20.

Ingalik A Kuskokwim: nearly extinct, except for a few individuals at Sleetmute, Stoney River, Aniak, all bilingual in Eskimo.

B Yukon: Anvik, Shageluk, Holy Cross

ca. 150; very few, if any, under 30.

Holikachuk (now moved to Grayling on Yukon; intermediate language between Ingalik and Koyukon)

ca. 50; very few, if any, under 30.

Koyukon A 'Outer': Kaltag, Nulato, Koyukuk, Ruby, Galena, Kokrines, Allakaket, Huslia, Hughes, some at Rampart

B 'Inner': 1. Tanana Village, Stevens Village, some at Rampart, few at Allakaket ('South Fork'); 2a. Crossjacket, Manley Hot Springs; 2b. Roosevelt-Minchumina (extinct), Bearpaw

ca. 700; very few under 30, except at Hughes, very few under 20.

Upper Kuskokwin: Nikolai, Telida (closely related to Tanana A, but separated by Koyukon B2b.)

ca. 150; including all children at Nikolai.

Tanana A 'Central': Minto, Tolovana, Toklat, Nenana, Wood River

ca. 150; very few under 35, probably none under 25.

B 'Transitional': Chena, Salcha, Goodpaster; Healy Lake, Tanacross

ca. 150; very few except at Tanacross, but including some children there.

Upper Tanana Tetlin, Northway, Nabesna, Scottie Creek

ca. 250; including all children at Tetlin, many at Northway.

Han Eagle (also Moosehide, near Dawson, Yukon Territory)

ca. 30 at Eagle, including perhaps some children.

Kutchin (dialects not defined) Circle, Ft. Yukon, Venetie, Arctic Village, Chalkyitsik, Birch Creek, Canyon Village, some at Beaver (also in Canada)

ca. 900 in Alaska (perhaps as many again in Canada); including all or most children in some locations, e.g. Arctic Village, some children at others, e.g. Ft. Yukon.

Tutchone (Northern and Southern)

Hare; Bear Lake, Dogrib, Mountain

Slavey

Chipewyan, Yellowknife

Kaska; Tagish

Tahltan

Tsetsaut [or should this be a separate branch of Athapaskan altogether?]

Sekani

Beaver

Sarsi
Carrier
Chilcotin; Nocola?
Kwalhioqua, Tlatskanai
Pacific Coast
Oregon
Upper Umpqua
Galice, Applegate; Chasta Costa, Coquille, Tututni, Chetco, Tolowa [Euchre Creek is one of several Tututni subdialects. Certainly all these are one language, mutually intelligible, according to V. Golla, probably also Galice-Applegate.]
California
Hupa, Chilula, Whilkut
Mattole, Sinkyone, Nongatl, Lassik, Wailaki, Kato
Apachean
Navajo, San Carlos, White Mountain, Chiricahua, Mescalero; Jicarilla; Lipan; Kiowa Apache (or Kiowa Apache may be a separate language)

SELECTED REFERENCES

ADLER, FRED W. 1961. A bibliographical checklist of Chimakuan, Kutenai, Ritwan, Salishan, and Wakashan linguistics. IJAL 27.198–210.

BRIGHT, WILLIAM, ed. 1964. Studies in Californian linguistics. UCPL 34.

——. 1967. Inventory of descriptive materials. HMAI 5.9–62.

BRIGHT, WILLIAM, and JANE HILL. 1967. The linguistic history of the Cupeño. Studies in southwestern ethnolinguistics, ed. by D. H. Hymes and W. E. Bittle, pp. 351–71. The Hague and Paris, Mouton.

CALLAGHAN, C. A. 1967. Miwok-Costanoan as a subfamily of Penutian. IJAL 33.224–27.

CHAFE, WALLACE L. 1962. Estimates regarding the present speakers of North American Indian languages. IJAL 28.162–71.

——. 1965. Corrected estimates regarding speakers of Indian languages. IJAL 31.345–46.

——. 1970. A semantically based sketch of Onondaga. IJAL 36/IUPAL 25.

ELMENDORF, WILLIAM W. 1969. Geographic ordering, subgrouping, and Olympic Salish. IJAL 35.220–25.

HAAS, MARY R. 1951. The Proto-Gulf word for *water* (with notes on Siouan-Yuchi). IJAL 17.71–79.

——. 1960. Some genetic affiliations of Algonkian. Culture in history, ed. by S. Diamond, pp. 977–92. New York.

——. 1968. Notes on a Chipewyan dialect. IJAL 34.165–75.

HAMMERICH, L. L. 1970. The Eskimo language. The Nansen Memorial Lecture, October 10th, 1969. Det Norske Videnskaps-Akademi i Oslo. Fridtjof Nansen Minneforelesninger VI. Oslo.

HODGE, FREDERICK WEBB, ed. 1907, 1910. Handbook of American Indians North of Mexico. BAE-B 30, Parts I and II. Republished by Rowman and Littlefield, New York, 1965.

HOIJER, HARRY. 1960. Athapaskan languages of the Pacific Coast. Culture in history, ed. by S. Diamond, pp. 960–76. New York.

HYMES, DELL H. 1967. Interpretation of a Tonkawa paradigm. Studies in southwestern ethnolinguistics, ed. by D. Hymes and W. Bittle, pp. 264–78. The Hague and Paris, Mouton.

JOHNSON, FREDERICK. 1940. The linguistic map of Mexico and Central America. The Maya and their neighbors, ed. by C. L. Hay et al., pp. 88–114. New York.

KROEBER, A. L. 1925. Handbook of the Indians of California. BAE-B 78. Republished by the California Book Co., Ltd., Berkeley, 1953.

LEHMANN, W. 1920. Zentral-Amerika. 2 vols. Berlin.

MASON, J. ALDEN. 1940. The native languages of Middle America. The Maya and their neighbors, ed. by C. L. Hay et al., pp. 52–87. New York.

MILLER, WICK R. 1967. Uto-Aztecan cognate sets. UCPL 48.

ORTH, DONALD J. 1967. Dictionary of Alaska place names. Geological Survey Professional Paper 567. Washington, D.C.

PILLING, JAMES CONSTANTINE. 1885. Proof-sheets of a bibliography of the languages of the North American Indians. Washington, D.C. Republished by Central Book Co., Inc., Brooklyn, N.Y., 1966.

——. 1887a. Bibliography of the Eskimo language. BAE–B 1.

——. 1887b. Bibliography of the Siouan languages. BAE–B 5.

——. 1888. Bibliography of the Iroquoian languages. BAE–B 6.

——. 1889. Bibliography of the Muskhogean languages. BAE–B 9.

——. 1891. Bibliography of the Algonquian languages. BAE–B 13. [Issued in February, 1892.]

——. 1892. Bibliography of the Athapascan languages. BAE–B 14.

——. 1893a. Bibliography of the Chinookan languages (including the Chinook Jargon). BAE–B 15.

——. 1893b. Bibliography of the Salishan languages. BAE–B 16.

——. 1894. Bibliography of the Wakashan languages. BAE–B 19.

POWELL, JOHN W. 1891. Indian linguistic families of America north of Mexico. BAE–R 7.1–142. [Issued in May or June, 1892.]

RIVET, PAUL, G. STRESSER-PÉAN, and Č. LOUKOTKA. 1952. Les langues de l'Amérique. Les langues du monde, ed. by A. Meillet and Marcel Cohen, 2.941–1097.

SAXTON, DEAN and LUCILLE. 1969. Dictionary. Papago and Pima to English... English to Papago and Pima..., pp. 183–89. Tucson.

SEBEOK, THOMAS A., ed., and ROBERT LADO, NORMAN A. MCQUOWN and SOL SAPOR-

TA, assoc. eds., Yolanda Lastra, asst. ed. 1968. Current Trends in Linguistics 4: Ibero-American and Caribbean linguistics. The Hague and Paris, Mouton.

SHIPLEY, WILLIAM. 1969. Proto-Takelman. IJAL 35.226–30.

SWANTON, JOHN R. 1952. The Indian tribes of North America. BAE–B 145. Republished by the Scholarly Press, Grosse Pointe, Mich., 1968.

THOMAS, CYRUS, and J. R. SWANTON. 1911. Indian languages of Mexico and Central America and their geographical distribution. BAE–B 44.

VOEGELIN, C. F., and F. M. 1965. Languages of the world: Native America, fascicle two. AnL 7/7, part I, 1–150.

ZISA, CHARLES A. 1970. American Indian languages; Classifications and list. Center for Applied Linguistics: ERIC Clearinghouse for Linguistics. Washington, D.C.

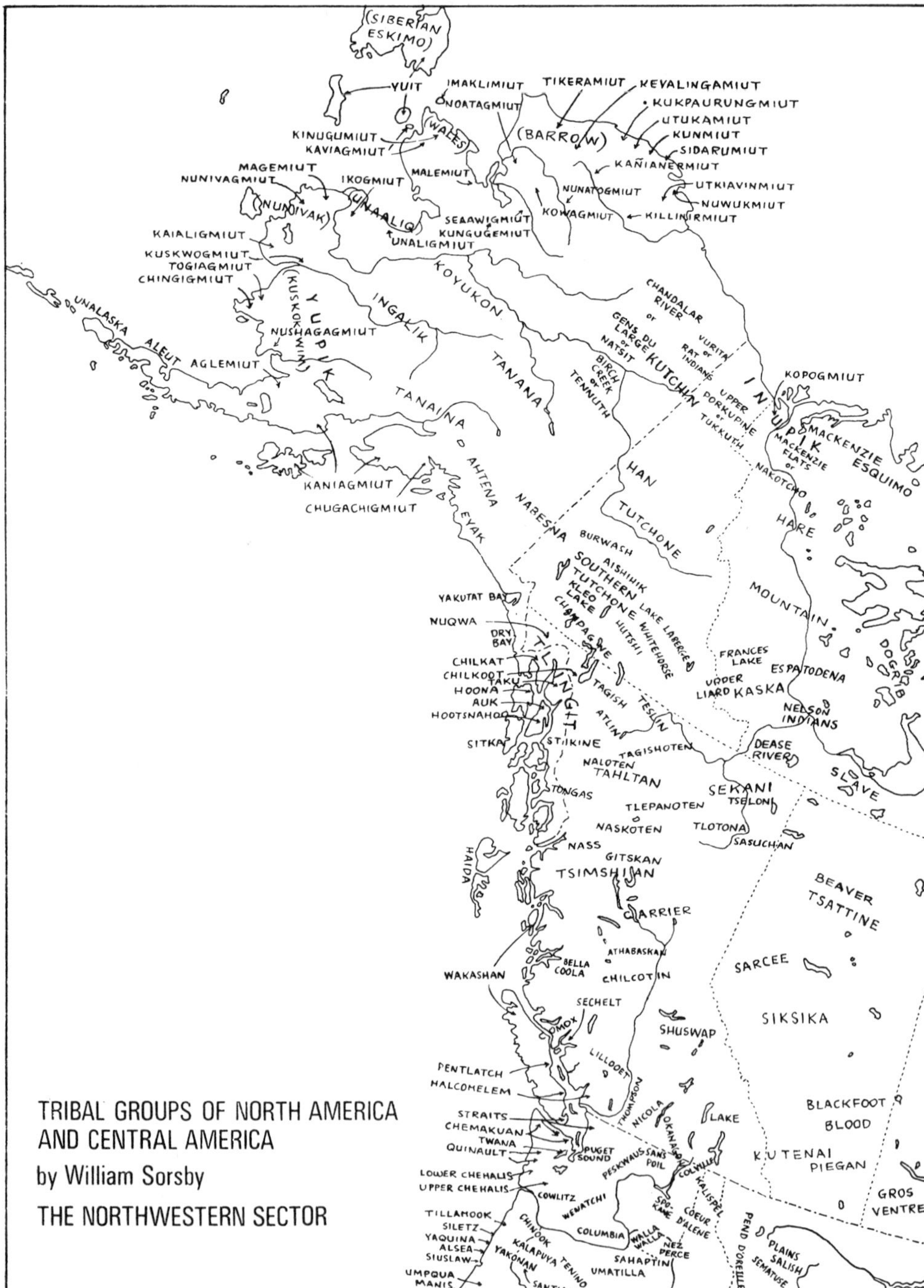
TRIBAL GROUPS OF NORTH AMERICA
AND CENTRAL AMERICA
by William Sorsby
THE NORTHWESTERN SECTOR
(SIBERIAN ESKIMO)
YUIT
IMAKLIMIUT
TIKERAMIUT
KEVALINGAMIUT
KUKPAURUNGMIUT
UTUKAMIUT
KUNMIUT
SIDARUMIUT
NOATAGMIUT
KINUGUMIUT
KAVIAGMIUT
(WALES)
(BARROW)
MAGEMIUT
NUNIVAGMIUT
IKOGMIUT
MALEMIUT
KAÑIANERMIUT
UTKIAVINMIUT
NUWUKMIUT
NUNATOGMIUT
KOWAGMIUT
KILLINIRMIUT
(NUNIVAK)
(UNALIQ)
SEAAWIGMIUT
KUNGUGEMIUT
UNALIGMIUT
KAIALIGMIUT
KUSKWOGMIUT
TOGIAGMIUT
CHINGIGMIUT
(KUSKOKWIM)
YUPIK
KOYUKON
UNALASKA
ALEUT
NUSHAGAGMIUT
INGALIK
AGLEMIUT
CHANDALAR RIVER or
GENS DU LARGE or NATSIT
VURITA or RAT INDIANS
KUTCHIN
BIRCH CREEK or TENNUTH
UPPER PORKUPINE or TUKKUTH
TANANA
TANAINA
INUPIK
KOPOGMIUT
MACKENZIE ESQUIMO
MACKENZIE FLATS or
NAKOTCHO
AHTENA
KANIAGMIUT
CHUGACHIGMIUT
EYAK
HAN
TUTCHONE
NARESNA
HARE
BURWASH
AISHIHIK
SOUTHERN TUTCHONE
KLEO LAKE
LAKE LABERGE
WHITEHORSE
HUTSHI
CHAMPAGNE
MOUNTAIN
YAKUTAT BAY
NUQWA
DRY BAY
CHILKAT
CHILKOOT
TAKU
HOONA
AUK
HOOTSNAHOO
SITKA
TLINGIT
TAGISH
TESLIN
ATLIN
FRANCES LAKE
UPPER LIARD
KASKA
ESPATODENA
DOGRIB
NELSON INDIANS
STIKINE
TAGISHOTEN
DEASE RIVER
NALOTEN
TAHLTAN
SEKANI
TSELONI
SLAVE
TONGAS
TLEPANOTEN
NASKOTEN
TLOTONA
SASUCHAN
HAIDA
NASS
GITSKAN
TSIMSHIAN
BEAVER
TSATTINE
CARRIER
ATHABASKAN
BELLA COOLA
WAKASHAN
CHILCOTIN
SARCEE
SECHELT
SIKSIKA
COMOX
SHUSWAP
LILLOOET
PENTLATCH
HALCOMELEM
THOMPSON
NICOLA
OKANAGON
LAKE
BLACKFOOT
BLOOD
STRAITS
CHEMAKUAN
TWANA
QUINAULT
PUGET SOUND
PESKWAUS
SANS POIL
COLVILLE
KUTENAI
PIEGAN
LOWER CHEHALIS
UPPER CHEHALIS
COWLITZ
WENATCHI
SPOKANE
KALISPEL
COEUR D'ALENE
PEND D'OREILLES
GROS VENTRE
TILLAMOOK
SILETZ
YAQUINA
ALSEA
SIUSLAW
UMPQUA
MANIS
CHINOOK
KALAPUYA
YAKONAN
TENINO
SANTIAM
COLUMBIA
WALLA WALLA
NEZ PERCE
SAHAPTIN
UMATILLA
PLAINS SALISH
SEMATUSE

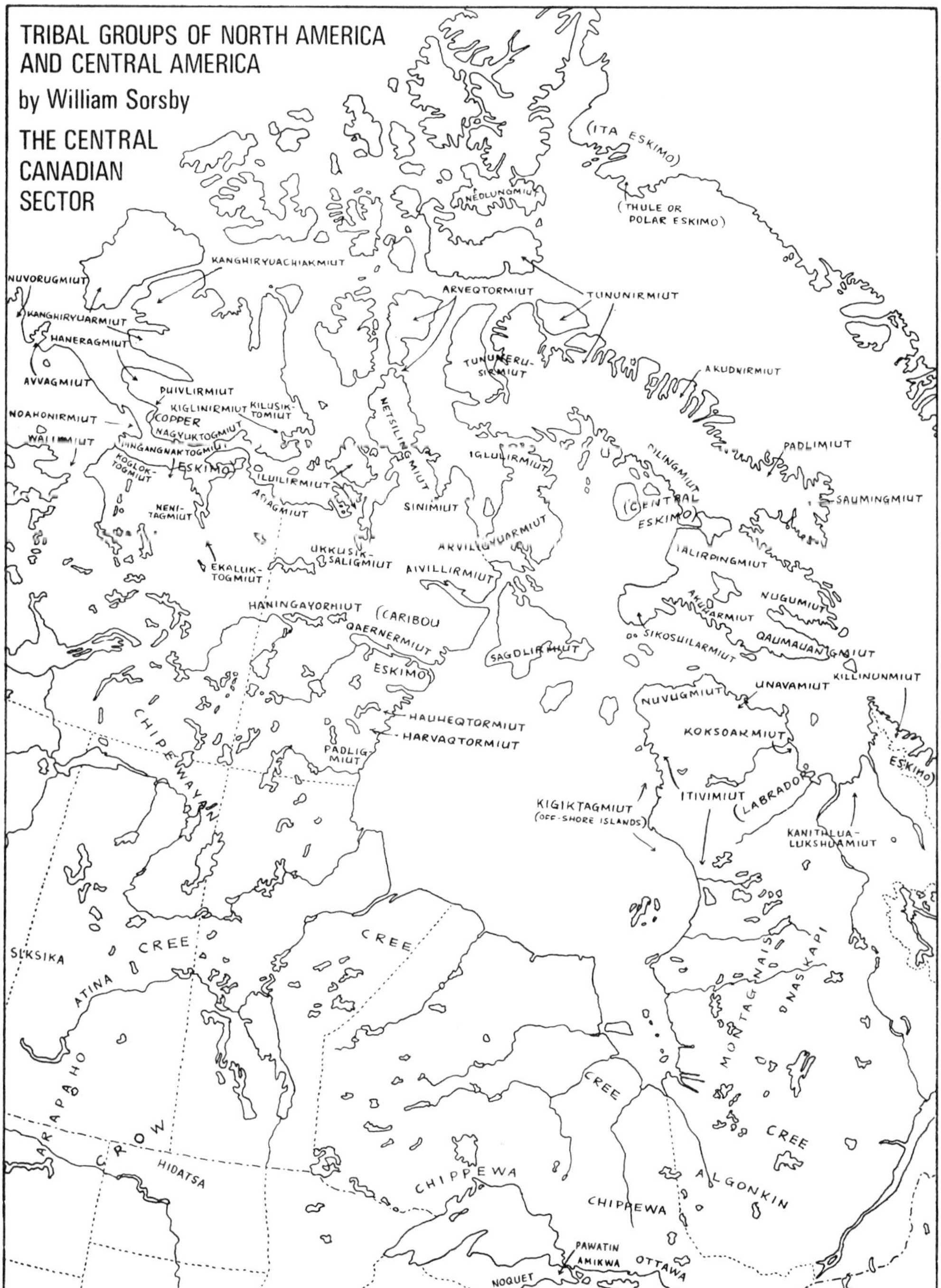
TRIBAL GROUPS OF NORTH AMERICA
AND CENTRAL AMERICA
by William Sorsby
THE CENTRAL
CANADIAN
SECTOR
(ITA ESKIMO)
(THULE OR POLAR ESKIMO)
NEDLUNOMIUT
KANGHIRYUACHIAKMIUT
NUVORUGMIUT
KANGHIRYUARMIUT
HANERAGMIUT
AVVAGMIUT
NOAHONIRMIUT
PUIVLIRMIUT
KIGLINIRMIUT
KILUSIKTOMIUT
COPPER
NAGYUKTOGMIUT
ESKIMO
KOGLOKTOGMIUT
NENITAGMIUT
ILUILIRMIUT
EKALLIKTOGMIUT
UKKUSIKSALIGMIUT
ARVEQTORMIUT
TUNUNIRMIUT
AKUDNIRMIUT
NETSILINGMIUT
SINIMIUT
IGLULIRMIUT
ARVILIGYUARMIUT
AIVILLIRMIUT
PADLIMIUT
SAUMINGMIUT
(CENTRAL ESKIMO)
IALIRPINGMIUT
NUGUMIUT
AKUHARMIUT
SIKOSUILARMIUT
QAUMAUANGMIUT
KILLINUNMIUT
HANINGAYORMIUT
(CARIBOU
QAERNERMIUT
ESKIMO)
SAGDLIRMIUT
UNAVAMIUT
NUVUGMIUT
KOKSOAKMIUT
HAUHEQTORMIUT
HARVAQTORMIUT
PADLIGMIUT
ESKIMO
(LABRADOR
ITIVIMIUT
KIGIKTAGMIUT
(OFF-SHORE ISLANDS)
KANITHLUALUKSHUAMIUT
CHIPEWAYAN
SIKSIKA
CREE
ATINA
CREE
MONTAGNAIS
NASKAPI
ARAPAHO
CROW
CROW
HIDATSA
CREE
CREE
CHIPPEWA
CHIPPEWA
ALGONKIN
PAWATIN
AMIKWA
OTTAWA
NOQUET

TRIBAL GROUPS OF NORTH AMERICA AND CENTRAL AMERICA
by William Sorsby
THE NORTHEASTERN SECTOR

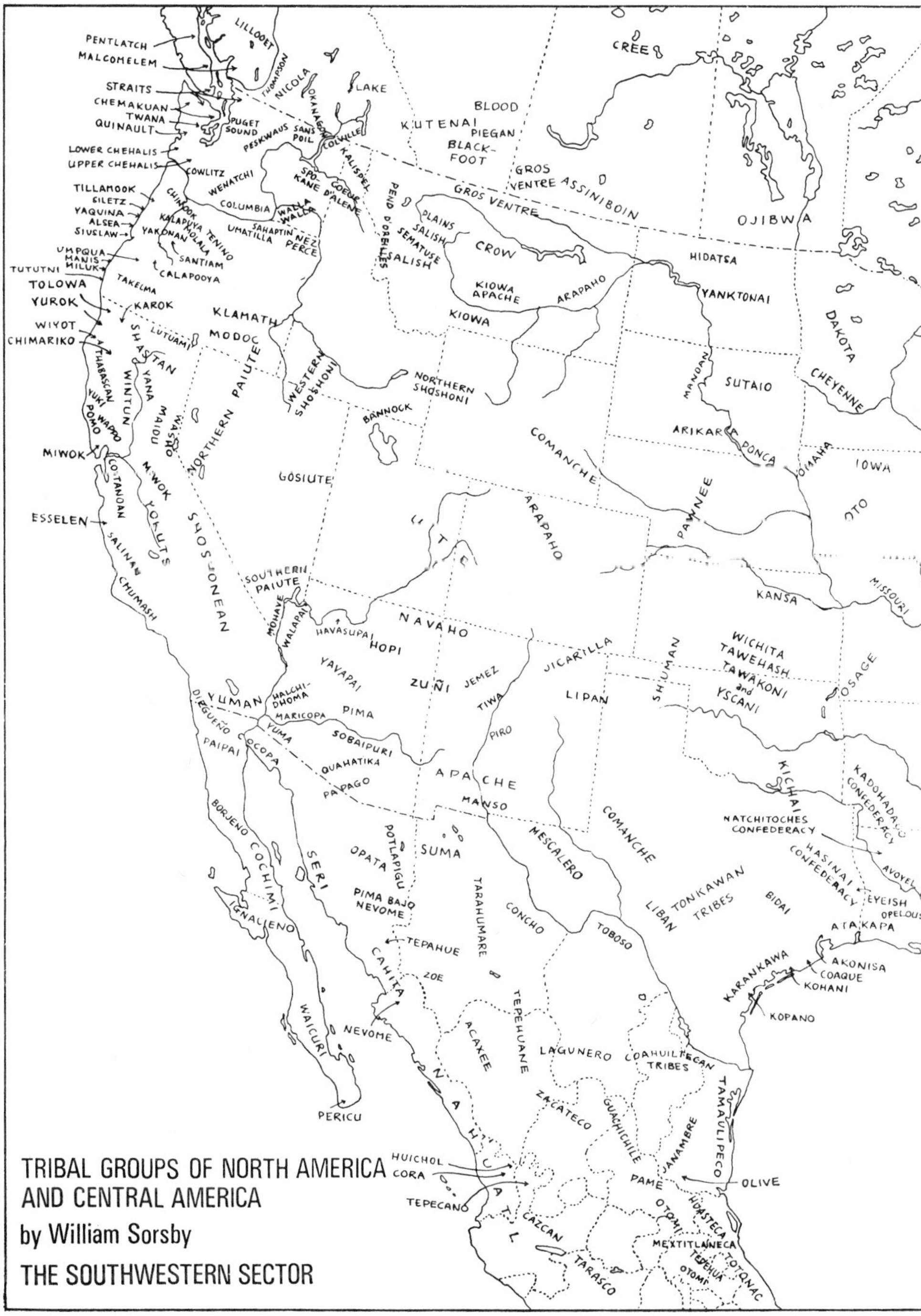

TRIBAL GROUPS OF NORTH AMERICA AND CENTRAL AMERICA
by William Sorsby
THE SOUTHWESTERN SECTOR

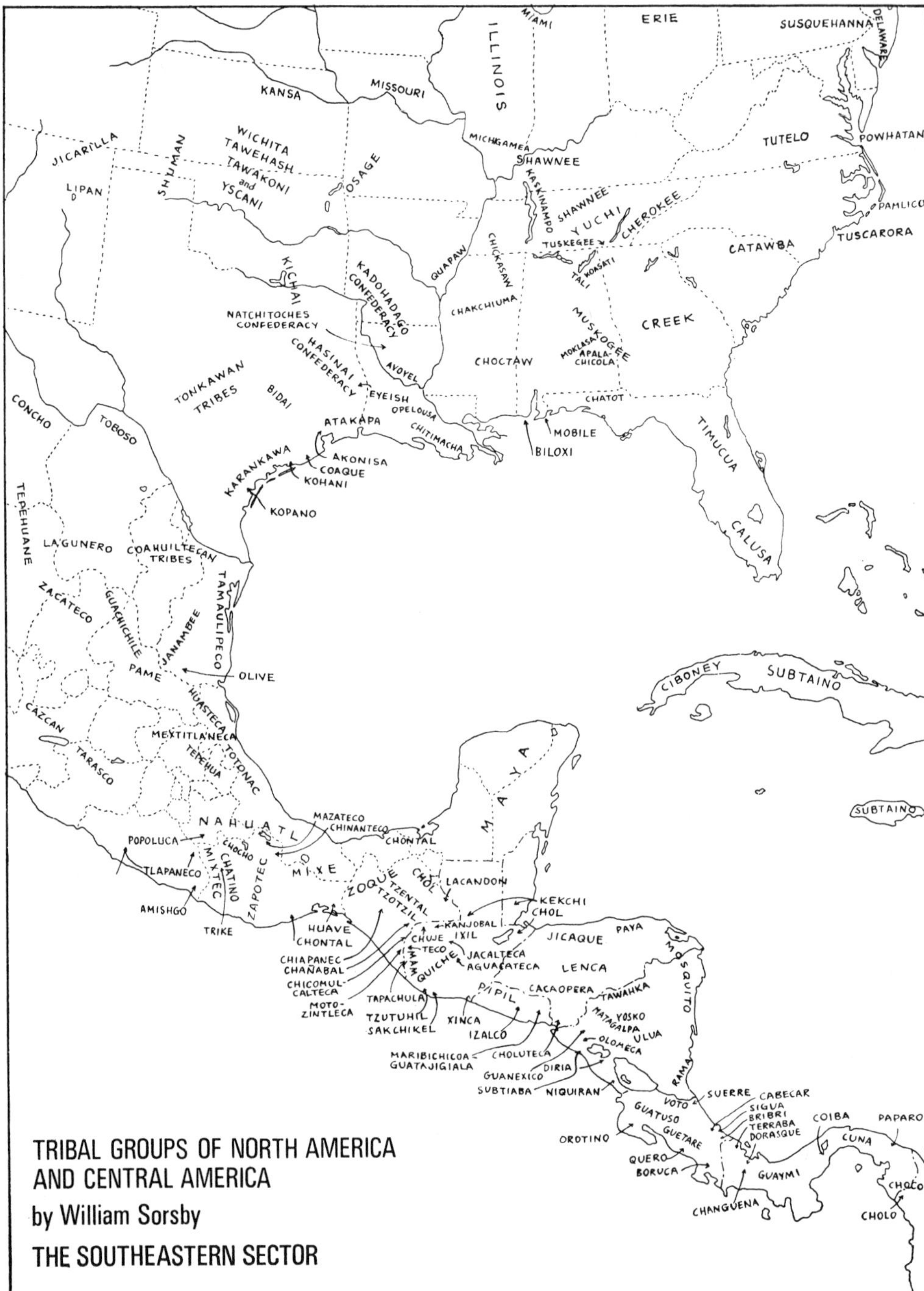

TRIBAL GROUPS OF NORTH AMERICA
AND CENTRAL AMERICA
by William Sorsby
THE SOUTHEASTERN SECTOR

SOUTH AND CENTRAL AMERICAN INDIAN LANGUAGES

HERBERT LANDAR

FOREWORD TO THE MAPS

Data from numerous maps have been consolidated for the maps in the present volume. The major contributions, however, have been those of Swanton for North America and the wall map of Loukotka for South America. It is hoped that the maps in the present volume will be found useful in spite of the deficiencies which plague attempts to include a great range of data in a relatively limited space. It has not been possible to put every single name of the map prepared for Loukotka's linguistic classification onto our South American maps, partly because abbreviations are used on Loukotka's map and names are spelled out on ours. For greater detail, the reader will have to consult Loukotka's map and maps available with articles in learned journals. (Loukotka's map is available with his classification from the Latin American Studies Center at the University of California, Los Angeles, or in unfolded form from the Association of American Geographers, 1146 Sixteenth St., N.W., Washington, D.C. 20036.)

Loukotka's map uses various colors and patterns to indicate language distributions and families. As a substitute we have used letters and numbers. The key (with a few minor changes in the spelling of names) follows:

Alacaluf	**38**	Cariban	A	Chono	a
Araua	q	Cariri	Q	Cofan	**19**
Arawakan	E	Catacao	12	Cucura	**35**
Atacama	e	Catuquina	7	Diaguit	d
Aymara	o	Cayuvava	**22**	Erikbaktsa	**27**
Baenan	**40**	Chapacura	U	Fulnio	18
Bora	aa	Charrua	i	Gamela	1
Bororo	R	Chechehet	b	Gennaken	**37**
Botocudo	k	Chibcha	B	Guaicuru	L
Cahuapana	t	Chimú	y	Guamo	34
Camacan	X	Chiquito	D	Guato	**33**
Canichana	**24**	Choco	13	Huari	8
Carajá	la	Cholon	z	Huarpe	c

Humahuaca	f	Múra	p	Timote	16
Iranche	**30**	Murato	w	Tinigua	11
Itonama	**25**	Nambicuára	n	Tucano	N
Jívaro	v	Opaie	**34**	Tucuna	**21**
Jirajara	14	Oti	**36**	Tupí	T
Kaingán	I	Otomac	9	Uarao	J
Leco	**31**	Pano	S	Uitoto	M
Lengua	g	Patagon	V	Uru	F
Lule	h	Piaroa	10	Vilela	j
Macú	K	Puquina	P	Yabuti	5
Macu	**28**	Puri	2	Yagua	G
Mapuche	W	Quechua	0	Yamana	**39**
Mashacali	Z	Sabela	17	Yanoama	Y
Mataco	H	Sechura	15	Yuracare	**32**
Matanawi	**26**	Shucurú	3	Yuri	**20**
Mayna	u	Tacana	r	Zamuco	6
Mosetene	s	Tarairiú	4	Záparo	x
Movima	**23**	Taruma	**29**	Žé	C

CARIB
CARACA
GUAIQUERI
PARIAGOTO
CAQUETIO
JIRAJARA
AJAGUA GOTO
CIPARI-
TAIRONA BONDA
COSINA
GUANACA
CHIMILA
CUNA
CUEVA
SENU
TOLU
URABA
TUCURA
CITARA
CATIO
CHAMI
BAUDO
PIJAO
MANIPO
ACHAGUA
CHIBCHA
TECUA
TUNEBO
LACHE
CARARE
OPONE
MUZO
COLIMA
GUAMOCO
CHIRICOA
YARURO
AMORUA
CABRE
SALIVA
GUAHIBO
PIAROA
MACO
TAMANACO
CALIÑA
INGARICO
ARECUNA
MACUSI
CASAPARE
WAICA
PUINAVE
YAVITERO
BANIVA
BARE
MANAO
SAMATARI
MAUACA
TARIANA
TUCANO
TUYUCA
MACU
ANODOVE
CABURICHENA
ARUAQUI
JAGUANAI
BAHUANA
YURI
JUMANA
TUCUNA
YAGUA
PEBA
COTO
CATUQUINA
CATAUISH
CATUQUINA
CATAUISHI
BURUE
MARUBA
MORIQUE
COCAMA
MAYNA
SHUARA
CANELO
ZAPARO
PIOJE
CUTINANA
AGUARUNA
CHACHAPOYA
SIPIBO
REMO
CASHIBO
CURINA
CANAMARI
IPURINA
PAUMARI
YUMA
PARINTINTIN
ARARA
PAMA
CARIPUNA
CHACOBO
CAYUVAVA
MOBIMA
MOJO
TACANA
LECO
MOSETENE
SIRIONO
GUARAYO
CHIQUITO
MIZQUE
CHANE
AYORE
CAUTARIE
OTUQUE
CHAPACURA
BAURE
ITONAMA
CANICHANA
URU
PUQUINA
COLLA
COLLAGUA
CAVANA
CAMANA
AREQUIPA
MOQUEGUA
NAZCA
ICA
SORA
CHOCORVO
CANCHI
QUECHUA
MACHIGANGA
CAMPA
AMUESHA
PIRO
AMAHUACA
CONIBO
CHOLONA
HIVITO
MUCHIC
CHIMU
CULLI
CAJAMARCA
SECHURA
COLAN
TUMBI
CALVA
PALTA
PUNA
CAÑARI
MANABI
CARANQUI
CARA
COFAN
COLORADO
YUMBO
QUIJO
PANZALCO
PASTO
MALABA
TAMA
OMAGUA
CAMANAWA
ARAONA
CAVIÑA
TOROMONA
PAUSERNA
APIACA
MUNDURUCU
AMANAJE
CHAYMA
PALENQUE
CUMANAGOTO
CHAPACUARE
QUIRIQUIRE
TOMUZA
GUAMONTE
GUAMO
GUIRE
GUARICO
PAYURE
COCAIMA
TORORO
OTOMACO
TAPARITA
CHAGUAN
WARRAU
MAKIRITARE
GUINAU
MAKU
CUNUANA
DECUANA
YECUANA
PAUDA
ARINAGOTO
ARMACOTO
CAMARACOTO
CACHIRIGOTO
UAICA
CALIANA
AUAKE
PURUCOTO
TAUREPAN
WAPISHANA
SAPARA
PAUXIANA
KARIME
ARDA
TIMBA
YOLO
SAIXA
WAUNANA
NOANAMA
QUIMBAYA
PANCHE
SUTAGAO
GUAYUPE
TAMA
AMARIZANA
CATARRO
CHUCUNA
TINIGUA
CHOQUE
YAPOOA
TAIGUANA
UMAUA
CARIJONA
ANDOQUE
WITOTO
OCAINA
BORA
MIRANHA
YAMAMADI
SEWACU
UAIMARE
CANAMARE
CHONTAQUIRO
PUCAPUCARI
MASHCO
INAPARI
TOYERI
ATSAHUACA
GUACANAHUA
GUARIZO
ARAZAIRE
LAPACHU
CHIRIGUANO
TAMACOSI
CHURAPA
POHENA
URACARE
MAXIENA
SARAVE
PAUNA
QUITEMO
NAPECA
PAICONE
CUSIQUIA
MANASI
TAO
MACURAP
KEPKIRIWAT
KOAIA
WAYORO
HURI
PALMELA
ITENE
CUJUNA
URUNAMACAN
MIALAT
PAWATE
URUPA
YAMARU
KAWAHYB
URUMI
RAMARAMA
ARIQUEM
CARITIANA
ARARA
TORA
MATANAWI
PIRAHA
YAMANI
MURA
IRURI
TOROARI
PURUPURU
YUMA
TAGUANA
CARAGUATA
CAPECHI
CAUAURI
ZURINA
AISUARE
YURIMAGUA
IBANOMA
MANAU
URANA
CRICHANA
YAUAPERY
UAIMIRI
ABACAUI
PAUCOSA
CARIAY
UIRINA
JABAANA
ARARAIBO
AMAMATI
CIPO
CUNIBA
MAMORI
ACAUA
CAUAMARI
TAWARI
BENDIAPA
TUCUNDIAPA
CUNIBA
MASARARI
UARAICU
TUXINAUA
CULINO
CATUQUINA
CAPANAGUA
SETEBO
SENSI
CHAMICURO
TABALOSO
CAHUAPANA
MURATO
SIMACO
ANDOA
ARDA
AUISHIRI
CAMUANO
IQUITO
CAUMARI
YAMEO
UPANO
ACHUAL
MALACATO
ALAUSI
PURUHA
CHIMBO
HUANCAVILCA
SIONA
TETETE
PECAYA
ICIEUENE
SABELA
ENCABELLADO
MACAGUAJE
AIFUE
CORECAJE
GUAQUE
QUILLACINGA
TOMACO
BARBACOA
PUBMATARI
ANDAQUI
CAMSA
CHEDUA
ALON
COGNOMONA
HUAMBO
HUAYLA
LAMBA
CASMA
CAJATAMBO
HUAMACHI
SUPE
HUACHO
CHANCAY
YAUJO
CAUQUI
LLAMISU
ATAVILA
HUANCA
CHINCHA
ANGARA
TANQUIHUA
CHUMBIVILCA
CHUNATAHUA
CHUN
TEPQUI
CARAPACHO
PANATAHUA
HUALLAGA
MONTOPAMPA
CUTERVO
HUAMBISA
AYAVACA
LACHIRA
TABANCALE
HUANCAPAMPA
SACATA
GUAYACUNDO
POCHE
KOSURAI
HUARI
SIRINEIRI
QUIRINEIRI
IMPETINERI
HUACHIPAIRI
MABENARO
GUARA
PACAGUARA
CAXARARI
CAPUIBO
SINABO
MALAWA
KAPISHANA
BOCAS PRETAS
MUCHOJEONE
PUBORA
TIATINAGUA
CHIRIGUA
MAROPA
COLLAHUAYA
CHAQUI
CHUNCHO

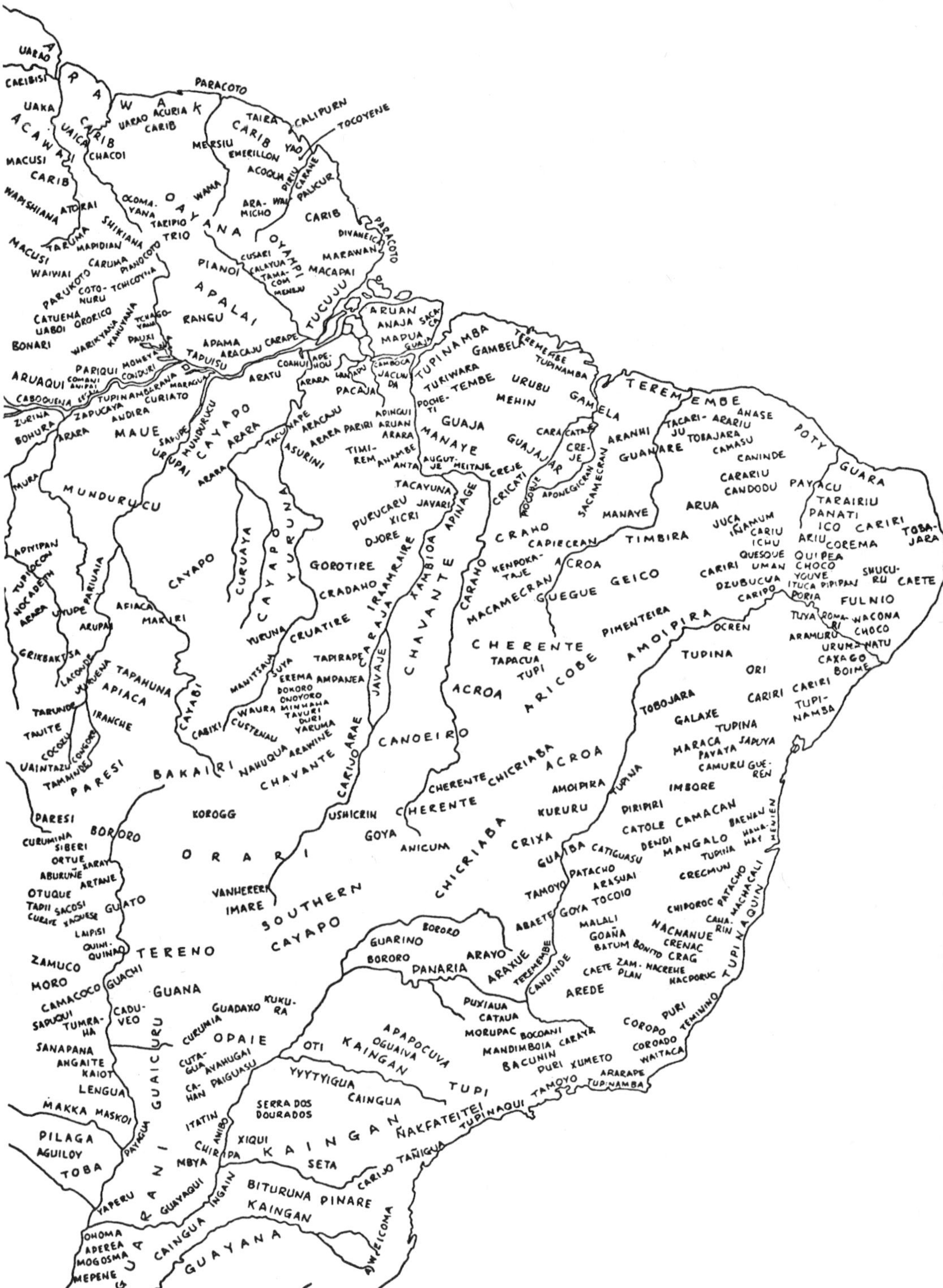
UARAO
ARAWAK
CARIBISI
UAKA
ACAWAI
UAICA
CARIB
CHACOI
MACUSI
CARIB
WAPISHIANA
ATORAI
PARACOTO
UARAO
ACURIA
CARIB
TAIRA
CALIPURN
TOCOYENE
CARIB
MERSIU
EMERILLON
YAO
ACOQUA
PIRIU
CARANE
PALICUR
OCOMA-YANA
WAMA
OAYANA
ARA-MICHO
WAI
CARIB
TARIPIO
TRIO
SHIKIANA
MAPIDIAN
TARUMA
MACUSI
WAIWAI
CARUMA
PIANOCOTO
PARUKOTO
COTO-NURU
TCHICOYNA
CATUENA
UABOI
ORORICO
BONARI
WARIKYANA
KAHUYANA
TCHAGO-YANA
PAUXI
PIANOI
CUSARI
CALAYUA
TAMA-COM
MENEJU
OYAMPI
DIVANEIC
PARACOTO
MARAWAN
MACAPAI
APALAI
RANGU
TUCUJU
ARUAN
ANAJA
SACA
MADUA
GUAJA
APAMA
ARACAJU
CARAPE
TAPUISU
MOHEYA
CONDURI
PARIQUI
ARUAQUI
COMANI
ANIPAI
CABOQUENA
TUPINAMBARANA
MARAGUA
ZAPUCAYA
CURIATO
ANDIRA
ZURINA
BOHURA
ARARA
MAUE
SAPUPE
MUNDURUCU
CAYADO
ARARA
URUPAI
ARARA
ARATU
COAHUI
APE-HOU
ARARA
PACAJA
CAMBOCA
JACUN-DA
TACUNAPE
ARACAJU
ASURINI
ARARA
PARIRI
APINGUI
ARUAN
ARARA
TIMI-REM
ANAMBE
ANTA
TUPINAMBA
GAMBELA
TURIWARA
TEMBE
POCHE-TI
GUAJA
MANAYE
AUGUT-JE
MEITAJE
TEREMEMBE
TUPINAMBA
URUBU
MEHIN
GAMELA
GUAJAJAR
CARA
CATAJE
CRE-JE
CREJE
CRICATI
TEREMEMBE
POTY
ANASE
TACARI-JU
ARARIU
TOBAJARA
CAMASU
ARANHI
GUANARE
CANINDE
GUARA
CARARIU
CANDODU
PAYACU
TARAIRIU
PANATI
ICO
CARIRI
TOBA-JARA
MURA
MUNDURUCU
APIYIPAN
TUPIOCON
NOCADETH
ARARA
UYUDE
PARIUAIA
ARUPAI
AFIACA
MAKIRI
CAYAPO
CURUAYA
CAYAPO
YURUNA
TACAYUNA
JAVARI
PURUCARU
XICRI
DJORE
GOROTIRE
CRADAHO
APINAGE
XAMBIOA
IRAAMRAIRE
CARAJA
CHAVANTE
CARAHO
CRAHO
CAPIECRAN
KENPOKA-TAJE
CROA
MACAMECRAN
GUEGUE
GEICO
APONEGICRAN
SACAMECRAN
MANAYE
TIMBIRA
ARUA
JUCA
IÑAMUM
CARIU
ICHU
QUESQUE
UMAN
ARIU
COREMA
QUIPEA
CHOCO
YOUVE
CARIRI
DZUBUCUA
ITUCA
PIPIPAN
SHUCU-RU
CAETE
CARIPO
PORIA
FULNIO
GRIKBAKTSA
LACONDE
JURUENA
TAPAHUNA
APIACA
YURUNA
CRUATIRE
MANITSAUA
SUYA
TAPIRAPE
EREMA
DOKORO
ONOYORO
MINHAHA
TAVURI
DURI
YARUMA
AMPANEA
JAVAJE
CHERENTE
TAPACUA
TUPI
ARICOBE
PIMENTEIRA
AMOIPIRA
OCREN
TUYA
ROMA-RI
WACONA
ARAMURU
CHOCO
URUMA
NATU
CAXAGO
BOIME
TUPINA
ORI
CARIRI
CARIRI
TUPI-NAMBA
ACROA
TOBOJARA
GALAXE
TUPINA
TARUNDE
IRANCHE
CAYABI
CABIXI
WAURA
CUSTENAU
TAUITE
COCOZU
CONCORE
UAINTAZU
TAMMINDE
PARESI
BAKAIRI
NAHUQUA
ARAWINE
CHAVANTE
CARIJO
ARAE
CANOEIRO
CHERENTE
CHICRIABA
ACROA
MARACA
PAYAYA
SAPUYA
CAMURU
GUE-REN
AMOIPIRA
TUPINA
IMBORE
PIRIPIRI
KURURU
CATOLE
CAMACAN
BAENAN
PARESI
BORORO
KOROGG
CURUMINA
SIBERI
ORTUE
XARAY
ABURUÑE
ARTANE
OTUQUE
TADII
SACOSI
CURAVE
XAQUESE
GUATO
LAIPISI
QUINI-QUINAO
USHICRIN
CHERENTE
GOYA
ANICUM
ORARI
VANHERERI
IMARE
SOUTHERN CAYAPO
CHICRIABA
CRIXA
GUAIBA
CATIGUASU
DENDI
MANGALO
HAHA-HAY
MENIEN
TUPINA
PATACHO
ARASUAI
CRECMUN
TAMOYO
GOYA
TOCOIO
PATACHO
MACHACALI
CHIPOROC
CAHA-RIN
NACNANUE
TUPINAQUIN
MALALI
GOAÑA
BATUM
BONITO
CRENAC
CRAG
CAETE
ZAM-PLAN
NACREHE
NACPORUC
AREDE
ABAETE
TEREMEMBE
CANDINDE
BORORO
GUARINO
BORORO
PANARIA
ARAYO
ARAXUE
ZAMUCO
MORO
TERENO
CAMACOCO
GUACHI
GUANA
SAPUQUI
TUMRA-HA
CADU-VEO
GUADAXO
KUKU-RA
PUXIAUA
CATAUA
MORUPAC
BOCOANI
MANDIMBOIA
CARAYA
BACUNIN
PURI
XUMETO
PURI
COROPO
TEMININO
COROADO
WAITACA
SANAPANA
ANGAITE
KAIOT
LENGUA
CURUMIA
OPAIE
CUTA-GUA
AVAHUGAI
CA-HAN
PAIGUASU
GUAICURU
OTI
KAINGAN
APAPOCUVA
OGUAIVA
TUPI
YVYTYIGUA
CAINGUA
SERRA DOS DOURADOS
TAMOYO
ARARAPE
TUPINAMBA
TUPINAQUI
MAKKA
MASKOI
PILAGA
AGUILOY
TOBA
PAYAGUA
ITATIN
ANIBO
CHIRIPA
XIQUI
KAINGAN
ÑAKFATEITEI
MBYA
SETA
CARIJO
TAÑIGUA
YAPERU
GUAYAQUI
INGAIN
BITURUNA
PINARE
KAINGAN
OHOMA
ADEREA
MOGOSMA
MEPENE
GUARANI
CAINGUA
GUAYANA
WEICOMA

AYMARA
CHIPAYA
URU
TARAPACA
TOMINA
YAMPARA
CHIRIGUANO
IZOCEÑO
SIRACUA
GUARANOCA
UGARAÑO
MORO
YANAYGUA
CHANE
KASKIHA
CHICHA
LIPE
TOMATA
CHURIMA
COCHINOCA
TAPIETE
SINTO
SAPUQUI
NOCTEN
TAYNI
CHOROPI
VEJOZ
KOMLEK
SANAPANA
CHOROTI
ASHLUSLAY
CHANGO
ATACAMA
CASAVINDO
HUMAHUACA
OJOTA
TEUTA
MATACO
GUISNAI
COLLAGA
SOTIRAI
MAKKA
MASKOI
TOBA PILAGA
OCLOYE
JUJUY
LULE
OMOAMPA
SINIPI
VILELA
PAYAGUA
ITATIN
ANIBO
CHIRIPA
XIQUI
KAINGAN
SETA
MBYA
TOBA
MAHOMA
CHALCHAGUI
TOLOMBON
TONOCOTE
ORISTINE
PASAIN
CARIJO
TAÑIGUA
BITURUNA
PINARE
KAINGAN
GUARANI
YAPERU
GUAYAQUI
INGAIN
SOLCO
TUCUMAN
MOCOVI
ANDALGALA
QUILME
HUALLIN
ANCASTI
MATARA
OHOMA
APEREA
MOGOSMA
MEPENE
CAINGUA
GUAYANA
ABAUCAN
PALCIPA
ABIPON
COPIAPO
CARI-ANGASTA
FAMATINA
SANAGASTA
INDAMA
EGUALO
KAINGAN
CARIJO
CAPAYANA
SANAGASTA
NOLONGASTA
SANAVIRON
QUELOEI
MALQUESI
MOCOVI
PAIRINDI
ARECHANE
MINUAN
BOHANE
MINUAN
TAPE
OLONGASTA
COMECHINGON
PICUNCHE
ALLENTIAC
BEGUA
CHANA
CHARRUA
QUERANDI
MILLCAYAC
TALUHET
OICO
CHANDRI
CHIQUIYAMA
DIHIHET
TUBICHAMINI
PEHUENCHE
PEGUENCHE
CHECHEHET
DIHIHET
VELICHE
GENNAKEN
POYA
TEHUELCHE
CHONO
TEHUESH
TSONECA
ALACALUF
SELKNAM
HAUSH
YAMANA

34
36
C
2
T
T
T
I
T
T
T
T
I
T
i
T
g
L
H
H
j
H
L
F
e
f
d
h
c
b
W
c
37
V
a
a
a
V
38
V
39

INTRODUCTION

It was with misgivings that I consented to prepare this checklist, partly because of the target date, partly because of the chaos of names and claims to be sorted and identified, partly because various scholars know much more about the matter than I do. In spite of everything, however, the assignment stimulated my interest. Beyond the drudgery lay something that would be useful not only to the compiler but also to members of the anthropological profession and others who might need a quick preliminary answer to the questions which a checklist is designed to answer.

There are limitations, then, on the quality of this checklist. My excuse for offering it with its faults included is mainly that it is not entirely worthless, once the reader has been advised about its nature, the kinds of data available to him here. As with any checklist, improvements are possible, and I hope that the present compilation will be extended and improved as the years go by.

Very little work of distinction has been done in the classification of South American languages. Requirements for work of distinction were spelled out by McQuown (1955) at the start of his checklist. Not everyone who has collected and assessed data on South American languages, of those with pretensions to academic excellence, has met these requirements, either because he was born too soon, or because his motives have been to move swiftly rather than carefully. At least, that is how it seems to me, dedicated as I am to patience on the one hand and skepticism on the other. In her review of Loukotka's final classification of South American Indian languages (1968), Wistrand (1971) has shown how easy it is to pose questions about checklist misinformation. Wilbert, in editing Loukotka's manuscript, did not reflect Summer Institute of Linguistics contributions of recent years, Wistrand points out. And these contributions are among the finest yet made in South American Indian linguistics. One limitation of the present checklist, surely, is that it captures mistakes of earlier compilers; but perhaps we can make a virtue of this fact, by giving the present checklist an historical function.

This is a checklist not simply of tribes and languages. It has been compiled partly as a guide to more substantial works, or to works with some value because they have a place in the history of native Ibero-American linguistics. Loukotka (1968) has been used as the basic element of the present checklist. (I am grateful to Mary Strayer, my assistant, for reducing Loukotka's data to literally thousands of file sheets.) But the first careful checklist, that of Brinton (1891), with over 700 names of stocks and languages, has not been neglected. Rivet and Loukotka (1952), with 108 units or groups, and Mason's survey for the *Handbook of South American Indians,* as well as other sources, have been partially indexed for the present study.

In the following section, I have listed the names of families in Mason's essay, with page references, as well as additions from Key and Key (1967). Brinton's more archaic determinations are identified by page references with preceding B. Other codes and references indicate the positions of Rivet and Loukotka (1952) and Loukotka (1968).

Consider, for example, these data:

(1) Calianan 254; Kaliána ~ Sape XL 1122
(2) Callahuaya
(3) + Camacan 295; Camacan (Tapuya) B239; Kamakán XLI 1122; Kamakan PC22 stock

The initial item comes from Mason, p. 254. The second item comes from Rivet and Loukotka, the source being indicated partly by the roman numeral: the preferred spelling Kaliána and the synonym Sape shown after the alternation sign (~) are followed by the family number, XL, and a reference to p. 1122. The second item comes from Key and Key (1967). It is lacking in the other sources. The third item indicates that Camacan is extinct (+ being the sign of extinction), that Mason discusses Camacan on p. 295, that Brinton, p. 239, assigned Camacan to his Tapuya stock, that Rivet and Loukotka have Kamakán as family XLI, p. 1122, and that Loukotka uses the spelling Kamakan for what he calls a stock. The P stands for Paleo-American, the C for the Central Brazilian division, and the 22 for the code number (in Loukotka's list of 117 languages and stocks). Loukotka's code will be given in detail below. Nothing is said about the quality of judgments which led to the categories shown; but the basis is provided for a rapid survey of such judgments, upon which critical commentary can be founded.

Greenberg's views are touched on in the checklist proper. Greenberg is still compiling data to support the quaternary reduction published in Steward and Faron (1959: 22). His plan of research is to test these major categories:

(1) Macro-Chibchan: (i) Chibchan, (ii) Paezan
(2) Andean-Equatorial: (i) Andean, (ii) Jivaro type, (iii) Macro-Tucanoan, (iv) Equatorial
(3) Ge-Pano-Carib: (i) Macro-Ge, (ii) Macro-Panoan, (iii) Nambicuara, (iv) Huarpe, (v) Macro-Carib, (vi) Taruma
(4) Hokan: including among others Jicaque and Yurumango

Several checklists have been compiled which use Greenberg's categories. That some readers will be misled by such efficiency will be apparent enough to perceptive scholars. With linguistic classifications perhaps it is true that the larger the category, the greater the uncertainty.

Wistrand (1971) has neatly criticized Loukotka's geographical biases, rooted in part, perhaps, in those of Brinton (1891). For historiographical reasons, however, we make record of them here. We use the code letters P, T, and A for the designations Paleo-American, Tropical Forest, and Andean. There are five groups, A through E, in the first, and four groups, A through D, in the second and third areas. Correcting an obvious editorial oversight, which failed to move group 15 into the Chaco division, the division names are shown thus:

PALEO-AMERICAN

A = Southern Division (1–7), B = Chaco Division (8–15), C = Division of Central Brazil (16–28), D = Northeast Division (29–38)

TROPICAL FOREST

A = North Central Division (45–74), B = South Central Division (75–80), C = Central Division (81–88), D = Northeastern Division (89–93)

ANDEAN

A = Northern Division (94–98), B = North Central Division (99–106), C = South Central Division (107–112), D = Southern Division (113–117).

Loukotka's classification is suggested here. Italic numbers correspond to the numbers in the preceding paragraph. A few minor changes have been made, and the stock names have been alphabetized.

Aksanás, *3*. Alacaluf, *2*. Andoque, *82*. Arawa, *88*. Arawak, *46*: (1) Island Arawak, (2) Guiana, (3) Central Arawak, (4) Mapidian, (5) Goajira, (6) Caquetio, (7) Maypure, (8) Baníva, (9) Guinau, (10) Baré, (11) Ipéca, (12) Tariana, (13) Mandauáca, (14) Manáo, (15) Uirina, (16) Chiriána, (17) Yukúna, (18) Resigaro, (19) Marawa, (20) Araicú, (21) Uainumá, (22) Jumana, (23) Cauishana, (24) Pre-Andine Arawak, (25) Ipurina, (26) Apolista, (27) Mojo, (28) Paresí, (29) Chané, (30) Waurá, (31) Marawan, (32) Aruan, (33) Moríque, (34) Chamicurò, (35) Lorenzo, (36) Guahibo. Atacama, *111*. Auaké, *92*. Auishiri, *60*. Aymara, *108*. Baenan, *21*. Bora, *84*. Boróro, *27*. Botocudo, *20*. Canichana, *74*. Capixana, *67*. Catacao, *102*. Catuquina, *87*: (1) Southern Catuquina, (2) Northern Catuquina. Cayuvava, *71*. Chapacura, *65*. Charrua, *15*. Chechehet, *6*. Chibcha, *94*: (1) Paleo-Chibchan, (2) Rama, (3) Guatuso, (4) Talamanca, (5) Dorasque, (6) Guaymi, (7) Cuna, (8) Antioquia, (9) Chibcha, (10) Chibchan Motilon, (11) Betoi, (12) Arhuaco, (13) Malibú, (14) Andaquí, (15) Paez, (16) Coconuco, (17) Barbácoa, (18) Sebondoy, (19) Mosquito, (20) Matagalpa, (21) Paya. Chimú, *106*: (1) Southern Chimú, (2) Northern Chimú. Chiquito, *13*. Chocó [Piancó River], *32*. Chocó, *97*. Cholona, *57*. Cofán, *100*. Copallén, *105*. Culli, *103*. Diaguit, *114*. Erikbaktsa ~ Canoeiro, *41*. Fulnio, *23*. Gamela, *38*. Gennaken, *5*. Gorgotoqui, *14*. Guaicuru, *8*. Guamo, *48*. Guató, *80*. Huarpe, *117*. Huari, *66*. Humahuaca, *115*. Idabaez, *98*. Iranshe, *43*. Itonama, *73*. Itucale, *61*. Jíbaro, *62*. Jirajara, *96*. Kahuapana, *55*. Kaigán, *16*: (1) Northern Kaingán, (2) Southern Kaingán. Kaliána, *93*. Kamakan, *22*: (1) Southern Kamakan, (2) Northern Kamakan. Karaib, *89*: (1) Western Karaib, (2) Eastern Karaib, (3) Trio, (4) Chiquena, (5) Waiwai, (6) Yauapery, (7) Pauishana, (8) Macusi, (9) Pemón, (10) Maquiritaré, (11) Mapoyo, (12) Panáre, (13) Tamanaco, (14) Yao, (15) Shebayi, (16) Motilon, (17) Pijao, (18) Opone, (19) Carijona, (20) Patagon, (21) Arára, (22) Palmela, (23) Pimenteira, (24) Xingú. Karajá, *28*. Katembri, *29*. Kiriri, *36*. Koaiá, *68*. Kukura, *25*. Leco, *112*. Lengua, *11*. Lule, *116*. Máku, *52*. Makú, *86*: (1) Western Makú, (2) Independent Tribes, (3) Central Makú, (4) Northern Makú. Mapuche, *113*. Mashakali, *19*: (1) Western Mashakali, (2) Eastern Mashakali, (3) Southern Mashakali. Mataco, *10*. Matanawí, *40*. Mayna, *58*. Mobima, *72*. Munichi, *56*. Múra, *39*. Murato, *59*. Mosetene, *79*. Nambikwára, *42*: (1) Eastern Nambikwára, (2) Central Nambikwára, (3) Western Nambikwára, (4) Northern Nambikwára. Natú, *34*. Opaie, *17*. Oti, *26*. Otomac, *47*. Pankarurú, *31*. Pano, *75*: (1) Northern Pano, (2) Yamináua, (3) Sensi, (4) Central Pano, (5) Eastern Pano. Patagon, *4*. Piaroa, *50*: (1) Eastern Piaroa, (2) Western Piaroa, Puquina, *109*. Puri, *18*: (1) Eastern Puri, (2) Western Puri. Purubora, *69*. Quechua, *107*: (1) Old or pre-Columbian Dialects, (2) Modern or post-Columbian Dialects. Sabela, *63*. Sanaviron, *7*. Sechura, *101*. Shukurú, *35*. Tabancale, *104*. Tacana, *76*. Tarairiú, *37*. Taruma, *49*. Timote, *95*. Tinigua, *51*. Toyeri, *77*. Trumai, *70*. Tucano, *81*. (1) Western Tucano, (2) Yahuna, (3) Yupua, (4) Coretu, (5) Cubeo, (6) Sära, (7) Erulia, (8) Desána, (9) Tucano. Tucuna, *53*. Tupi, *45*: (1) Tupi, (2) Guarani, (3) Guaranized languages, (4) Kamayurá, (5) Tapirapé, (6) Northern Tupi, (7) Pará, (8) Guiana, (9) Southern Tupi, (10) Amazonas, (11) Chiriguano, (12) Mawé, (13) Mundurucú, (14) Yuruna, (15) Itogapúc, (16) Arikém, (17) Macuráp, (18) Mondé, (19) Kepkeriwát. Tushá, *30*. Uarao, *91*. Uitoto, *83*: (1) Western Uitoto, (2) Eastern Uitoto. Umán ~ Huamoi, *33*. Uro, *110*. Vilela, *9*. Yabutí, *44*. Yagua, *54*. Yamana, *1*. Yanoana, *90*: (1) Casapare, (2) Sanema, (3) Waica, (4) Samatari. Yuracare, *78*. Yuri, *85*. Yurimangui, *99*. Zamuco, *12*: (1) Northern Zamuco, (2) Southern Zamuco. Záparo, *64*. Zé ~ Ge, *24*: (1) Timbira, (2) Krao, (3) Kayapó, (4) Central Zé, (5) Western Zé, (6) Eastern Zé, (7) Jeicó.

McQuown (1955) introduced the following classification, extending use of a code proposed by Trager in 1937. For the full list see McQuown (1955: 512–13). The section of the list which begins with the letter I is reproduced here. The language counts have been dropped, our concern being with the terminology which the reader may encounter, especially in writings of more conservative linguists.

I.	Macro-Chibchan	I.2.a.	Western Chibchan
I.1.	Misumalpan	I.2.a.α.	Talamanca
I.1.a.	Miskitoan	I.2.a.β.	Barbacoa
I.1.b.	Sumoan	I.2.a.β.(1).	Pastoan
I.1.c.	Matagalpan	I.2.a.β.(2).	Cayapan
I.1.d.	Unclassified Misumalpan	I.2.a.β.(3).	Guatusoan
I.2.	Chibchan	I.2.a.β.(4).	Cunan

I.2.b.	Pacific Chibchan
I.2.b.α.	Isthmian
I.2.b.β.	Colombian Chibchan
I.2.c.	Inter-Andine Chibchan
I.2.c.α.	Paezan
I.2.c.β.	Coconucoan
I.2.c.γ.	Popayanense
I.2.d.	Eastern Chibchan
I.2.d.α.	Cundinamarcan
I.2.d.β.	Arhuacoa
I.2.d.γ.	Central American Chibchan
J.	Cariban
J.1.	Northern Cariban
J.1.a.	Coastal Northern Cariban
J.1.a.α.	Insular Coastal Northern Cariban
J.1.a.β.	Mainland Coastal Northern Cariban
J.1.b.	Central Northern Cariban
J.1.c.	Amazon Northern Cariban
J.1.d.	Bonarian
J.2.	Southern Cariban
J.2.a.	Araran
J.2.b.	Xinguan
J.3.	Northwestern Cariban
J.3.a.	Cariban Maracaibo-Magdalena
J.3.b.	Chocoan
J.3.c.	Southwest Northwest Cariban
J.3.d.	Southeast Northwest Cariban
K.	Arawakan
K.1.	Northern Arawakan
K.1.a.	Insular Northern Arawakan
K.1.b.	Northwestern Arawakan
K.1.b.α.	Guajiroan
K.1.b.β.	Caquetioan
K.1.b.γ.	Guayupean
K.1.b.δ.	Piapocoan
K.2.	Northern Amazon Arawakan
K.2.a.	Arauan
K.2.b.	Palicuran
K.2.c.	Arawakan Rio Branco
K.2.d.	Arawakan Orinoco
K.2.e.	Arawakan Indeterminate
K.2.f.	Arawakan Rio Negro
K.3.	Pre-Andine Arawakan
K.4.	South Arawakan
L.	Macro-Ge
L.1.	Ge
L.1.a.	Northwest Ge
L.1.a.α.	Timbira
L.1.a.β.	Caiapo
L.1.a.γ.	Suia
L.1.b.	Central Ge
L.1.c.	Jeico
L.2.	Caingangan
L.3.	Camacanian
L.4.	Machacalian
L.5.	Purian
L.6.	Patacho
L.7.	Malali
L.8.	Coropo
L.9.	Botocudo
M.	Macro-Tupi-Guarani
M.1.	Tupi-Guarani
M.1.a.	Guaranian
M.1.a.α.	Guaranian Parana
M.1.a.β.	Guaranian Bolivian
M.1.a.γ.	Guaranian Araguaia
M.1.b.	Tupian
M.1.b.α.	Coastal Tupian
M.1.b.β.	Guianan Tupian
M.1.b.γ.	Southern Amazon Tupian
M.1.b.δ.	Upper Amazon Tupian
M.2.	Huitotoan
M.3.	Zaparoan
N.	Quechumaran
N.1.	Quechuan
N.2.	Aymara
O.	Catuquinan
P.	Tucanoan
P.1.	Eastern Tucanoan
P.2.	Western Tucanoan
Q.	Panoan
Q.1.	Central Panoan

Q.2. Southwest Panoan
Q.3. Southeast Panoan
R. Macro-Guaicuruan
R.1. Mataco-Maca
R.2. Guaicuruan
S. Araucanian
T. Chon
Z. Unclassified South American Languages
Z.1. Mocoa
Z.2. Cuica-Timote
Z.3. Yunca-Puruhan
Z.4. Chiquitoan
Z.5. Lule-Vilelan
Z.6. Arauan
Z.7. Tacanan
Z.8. Jirajaran
Z.9. Jivaroan
Z.10. Peba-Yaguan
Z.11. Omurano
Z.12. Sabelan
Z.13. Canelan
Z.14. Guarauan
Z.15. Chirianan
Z.16. Salivan
Z.17. Pamiguan
Z.18. Guahiban
Z.19. Puinavean
Z.20. Cahuapanan
Z.21. Munichean
Z.22. Aguanoan
Z.23. Mosetenan
Z.24. Yuracarean
Z.25. Chapacuran
Z.26. Huanhaman
Z.27. Mascoian
Z.28. Zamucoan
Z.29. Borotuque
Z.30. Nhambicuaran
Z.31. Muran
Z.32. Carajan
Z.33. Caririan
Z.34. Guaitacan
Z.35. Ataguitan
Z.36. Huarpean
Z.37. Comechingonan
Z.38. Alacalufan
Z.39. Single Unclassified South American Languages

INDEX OF CLASSIFICATIONS

Achagua (Arawak) B268
+ Aconipa 193; Akonipa ~ Tabankale I 1100; Tabancale AB104 isolated language
Acroa (Tapuya) B239
Agace (Payagua) B316
Aginara
Agoya ~ Mataguayo (Mataco) B316
+ Aguano 271
Aguantea (Omagua type Tupi) B289
Aguaruna (Jivaro) B284
Aguilote. See Mbocobi.
Aimore. See Botocudo.
Airico ~ Ayrica (Betoya) B273
Akavai ~ Accowoio (Carib) B257
Aksanás PA3 small stock
Alacaluf 311–12; Alikuluf ~ Alikuluf ~ Karaika B329, 331; Alakaluf ~ Alikuluf II 1100; Alacaluf PA2 isolated language
+ Allentiac 306; Allentiac (Guarpe) B325; Huarpe XXXV 1121; Huarpe [including Millcayac] AD117 stock
Almaguereño (Mocoa) B200
Alon 271–2
Amaguage (Betoya) B273
Amarapa (Arawak) B249
Amarizona ~ Amarisane (Carib) B264
Amasifuin 271–2
Amazona (Tupi) B235
Amniapé 240; Amniapé III 1101
Amorua (Arawak) B268
+ Amuesha 217–18; Amueša ~ Lorenzo IV 1101
Anambe (Tupi) B235
+ Andaki 181; Andaqui B199–200
Andoa (Zaparo) B279–82
Andoque 246–7; Andoke ~ Paţiače ~ Čo'oxe V 1101; Andoque TC82 isolated language
Angamarca ~ Colorados de Angamarca. See Colorado.
Anguagueda (Choco) B176
Anibali ~ Anaboli (Betoya) B273
Anti ~ Campa (Arawak) B242, 243, 249
Antipa (Jivaro) B284
Apalai (Carib) B257
Apiaca (Tupi) B235
Apiaca (Carib) B253, 257

Apina-gê (Tapuya) B239
+ Apolista 217; Apolista B303
Aponegi-Cren (Tapuya) B239
Araguagu (Tupi) B235
Araicu (Arawak) B249
Araua 216–17; Araua B292–3; Arawa TC88 stock
Araua ~ Araicu ~ Araó (Araua) B292–3
Araucanian 307–9; Aucanian ~ Araucanian ~ Pampas B322, 325–6; Araukan ~ Aukanian ~ -Che ~ Auka VI 1101–2; Mapuche AD113 stock
Araucano ~ Chilidungu (Aucanian) B325
Arauno (Tacana) B298
Arawak (Arawak) B249
Arawakan 208–25; Arawak ~ Maipure B241–50; Arawak ~ Maipure ~ Nu-Arask ~ Arowak VII 1101–8; Arawak TA46 stock
Arbaco B180
+ Arda 234–5; Arda B286
Arecuna (Carib) B257, 264
Aricapu 276; Loukotka puts this in Yabutí
Arigua (Carib) B264
Arikem ~ Ariqueme 240–41; Arikem ~ Uitáte ~ Ahôpovo VIII 1109
Aroaco ~ Aruac (Chibcha) B189
Aruá 240
Aruaca (Arawak) B264
Aruashí 276
Aruba (Carib?) B253
Atacama 302–3; Atacameño ~ Lican-Antais ~ Cunza B ; + Atakama IX 1109; Atacama AC111 small stock
Ataguitan 302–4
Atalan 195: Atalala (Mataco) B316; + Atal'an ~ Tal'an X 1109
Atene (Tacana) B298
Atorai ~ Dauri ~ Tauri (a Wapisiana Arawak group) B249
Ature (Saliva) B264ff.
Auakean (perhaps +) 253; Auaké ~ Arutani XI 1109; Auaké TD92 isolated language
Aucano ~ Auca (Aucanian) B325
Avaneni ~ Avane (?) (Arawak) B268
Awishira 252; Auiširi ~ Avixira ~ Aviširi ~ Abikira ~ Tekiráka XII 1109; Auishiri TA60 isolated language
Ayahuca (Kechua) B215
Aymara 200; Aymara (Kechua or a jargon based on Kechua and other languages) B216–17, 221; Aymará XIII 1109–10; Aymara AC108 stock

Aymoré XIV 1111; some see this under Botocudo
Ayore. See Zamucoan.
Ayuli (Jivaro) B284
Baenan PC21 isolated language
Bakairi (Carib) B257
Baniva ~ Maniva ~ Manitava (Arawak) B249, 268
Barbacoa 180–81; Barbacoa B198–9
Barbacoa (Barbacoa) B198
Barbudo (Urarina) B287
Barbudo (Pano) B291
Baré ~ Barré ~ Bare (Arawak) B250, 268
Baure (Arawak) 249
Bayano (Cuna) B
+ Betoi 181–2; Betoi ~ Betoya (Betoya) B273–6
Bora TC84 stock
Bororo. See Borotuke.
Borotuke ~ Bororo-Otuke 282–3; Bororo (Tupi) B235, Otuqui B304; Bororó XV 1111; Boróro PC27 stock
Boruca ~ Brunca (Talamanca) B189
Botocudo 298–9; Botocudo (Tapuya) B239; Botocudo PC20 stock
Bribri (Talamanca) B189
Buruburá ~ Huari (?) ~ Puruborá 240; cf. Purupuru (Araua) B292–3; Puruborá LXXXI 1139
Cabacaba (Arawak) B268
Cabecar (Talamanca) B189
Çabiune (Carib) B264
Cabre. See Cavere
Caca ~ Cacana (Catamareña) B320
Cacana B312
Cacana. See Calchaqui
Caccharari B294
Cadioéo (Guaycuru) B310, 315
Cafuana (Arawak) 268
Cahuapanan 261–2; Maina ~ Mayna ~ Cahuapana B279, 284–5; Kahuapana XXXVIII 1121; Kahuapana TA55 stock
Caimane B177–81
Caingang 291–3; Kaingán XXXIX 1121–2; Kaingán PC16 stock
Calchaqui ~ Cacana ~ Catamareño ~ Katamareño B319–20
Calianan 254; Kaliána ~ Sape XL 1122; Kaliána TD93 isolated language
Callahuaya
Calliseca (Pano) B291; later known as the Setibo.

+ Camacan 295; Camacan (Tapuya) B239; Kamakán XLI 1122; Kamakan PC22 stock
Camagura (Tupi) B235
Cambeva. See Omagua.
Camboca (Tupi) B235
Came (Botocudo jargon with African elements) B262
Campa (Arawak) B279
Cana (Kechua) B215
Cana (Aymara) B221
Canamirim (Arawak) B249
+ Cañari 195; Cañari (Kechua) B201; + Kañari XLIII 1122
Cañasgordas (Choco) B176
Canawary ~ Canamary B294
Canchi (Aymara) B221
Candoshi 191–2; Čirino XXI 1116–17
+ Canelo 251–2; Canelo ~ Yumbo (Kechua) B208
Canichana; Canichana ~ Canisiana B; Kaničana ~ Kanesi XLIV 1122; Canichana TA74 isolated language
Canoa 276 [not the same as Canoeiro in Guaranï]
Canoeiro s.v. Erikbaktsa PE41 isolated language
Capayo (Tapuya) B239
Capesaco (Tupi) B
Capishana 275; Kapišana XLV 1122–3; Capixana TA67 isolated language
Caquetio B177–81
Cara 184; Cara (Kechua) B207, 215
Caraca B177–81
Caracara (Tupi) B307
Caracata (Tupi) B235
Caraho (Tapuya) B239
Caraja 286; Caraja B260–2; Karajá ~ Karayá LXVI 1123; Karajá PC28 stock
Carajahi (Caraja) B262
Caramanta (Choco) B176
Caranca (Aymara) B221
+ Carangue 220
+ Carapacho 271–2
Carapato 302
Catataima (Carib) B264
Carera (Samucu) B301
Cariayo (Arawak) B249
Cariban 226–31; Carib B252, 255, 257, 264–5; Karib XLVII 1123–8; Karaib TD89 stock

Caribisi (Carib) B257
Carijona (Carib) 257
Cariniaco (Carib) B257
Caripuna (Pano) B292
Cariri 286–7; Cariri ~ Kiriri (Carib) B259; + Kariri LXVIII 1128; Kiriri PD36 stock
Carnijo ~ Fornio (Tapuya) B241
Carusana (Arawak) B268
Casamarca (Kechua) B215
Cascoasoa 271–2
Cashibo (Pano) B292
Catacoa ~ Catacao (Yunca) B226; Catacao AB102 small stock
Catamarca (Catamareño) B320
Catamareño (Araucanian?) B320
Catauxi B294; Katawiši ~ Hewadie XLIX 1128
Catembri s.v. Katembri PD29 isolated language
Catio B193
Catukina 277; Catoquina (a jargon) B262; Katukina L 1128–9; Catuquina TC87 stock
Catoxa ~ Cotoxo (a jargon) B262
Cauiri (Arawak) B268
Cauixana (Arawak) B249
Caumari (Peba) B286
Cauqui. See Yauyo.
Cauwachi (Peba) B286
Cavere ~ Cabre (Arawak) B268
Cavina (Tacana) B298
Cayapa (Barbacoan) B197–8
Cayova (Tupi) B235
Cayporotade (Samucu) B301
Cayuvavan 273; Cayubaba ~ Cayuvava B302, 306; Kayuvava LI 1129; Cayuvava TA71 isolated language
Chachapuya (Kechua) B215
Chaima ~ Chayma (Carib) B257, 264
Chaliva (Changuina) B175
Chami (Choco) B176
Chamicuro 271; Chamicuro (Pano) B292
Chana 305–6
Chanca (Kechua) B216
Chanco (Yunca) B226
Chane (Charrua) B317

Chon 310–11; Čon XXII 1117
Chono 309; + Chono ~ Chuno ~ Cuncone (Aucanian?) B235
Chontaquiro. See Piro.
Choroya (Churoya) B276
Choseoso (Anti) B243
Chuala. See Guana.
Chucunaco. Cuna.
Chumulu (Changuina) B175
+ Chunanawa 271–2
+ Chuncha (Anti?) B243
Chuncho. See Tuyuneri.
Chuncho. Listed by Key and Key (1967) as an unclassified language of Bolivia.
Chunipi ~ Chumipy ~ Ciulipi ~ Sinipi (Lule) B313, 316
+ Chupacho 271–2
Churumata (Guaycuru) B315
+ Chusco 271–2
Citarae (Choco) B176
Cobeu (Tucano) B240
Cocama (Tupi) B235
Cocamilla (Tupi) B235, 289
Cocanuca B196, 199
Coche 186–7; Mocoa ~ Engaño ~ Ingano B200–1; Kamsá ~ Mokóa ~ Koče XLII 1122
Cochivuina. See Mayoruna.
Coco. See Guck.
Coconuco (Cocanuca) B196
+ Coeruna 246
Cofan ~ Cofán ~ Cofane (Churoya) B276–7; placed by Rivet and Loukotka (1952) in Barbacoan; Cofán AB100 isolated language
+ Cognomona 271–2
Colane (Yunca) B226
Colla ~ Collagua (Aymara) 221
Colorado. Ambiguous term, "painted." See Saccha. B198
Colorado (Yunca) B226
Comaba B279
+ Comechingón 307
Conchuco (Cocanuca? B196; Kechua B216)
Coni (Yurucari) B298
Conivo (Pano) B292
+ Copallén 192–3; Kopal'én ~ Kopal'in LIII 1131; Copallén AB105 isolated language

Corabeca B303
Core (Carib) B252
Coretu (Tapuya) B239
Coroado. Ambiguous term, "crowned" with a certain haircut style, applied to peoples of S. Brazil and others, e.g., the Puris-Coroados (not Tapuyan).
Coroino (Samucu) B301
Coromocho B177–81
+ Coropó 298; Coropo (Goyotaca) B240
Correguage (Betoya?) B273–4
Cotoxo (Tapuya) B239
Covareca B303
Cren. See Botocudo. B239
Crichana (Carib) B252
Cuaiquere (Barbacoa) B197
Cuccivero (Carib) B265
Cuchi (Yurucari) B298
Cuchiuara (Tupi) B235
Cuculado (Samucu) B301
+ Cucurá 300; Chavante (Tapuya) B239; Kukurá ~ Chavante LIV 1131; Kukura PC25 isolated language
Culino (Pano) B292
Culli s.v. Kul'i ~ Kul'e LV 1131; Culli AB103 isolated language
Cumana (Carib) B252
Cumanacho (Goyotaca) B240
Cumanacho (Tapuya) B239
Cumanagoto (Carib) B252. Language used by the Chayma, Core, Cumana, Palenque, Paria, Quaca, and Varrigone.
Cunco (Aucanian) B325
Cuneguara (Carib) B265
Cunipusana (Bare) B250
Cuniba B279
Cunza. See Atacameño.
Curave B303
Curucaneca B303
Curuminaca B303
Cuzco (Kechua) B
Dace (Tucano) B240
+ Diaguita 303–4; Diaguita ~ Drachita (Catamareña) B320; + Diagit ~ Katamareño ~ Kalčakí XXIV 1117–8; Diaguit AD114 stock
Divieche (Aucanian) B325
Duit (Chibcha) B189

Enagua (Carib) B265
Encabellada (Zaparo) B281, 282
Eneté (Yurucari) B298
Engaño ~ Ingano (Mocoa) B200
Enimaga ~ Imaco ~ Inimaca ~ Mataguayo (Mataco) B316
+ Equari 220; Equari (Tacana) B298
Erikbaktsa. See Canoeiro.
+ Esmeralda 187; + Esmeralda XXV 1118
Etene ~ Estene (Yunca) B226
Fitita 246
Fulnio 301; Fulnio XXVI 1118; Fulnio PC23 small stock
Galibi (Carib) B257
+ Gamella ~ Akobu XXVII 1118; Gamela PD38 stock
Ge 289–91; Gê (Tapuya) B239; Že CVIII 1150–1; Ge ~ Zé PC24 stock
Gennaken. See Puelchean.
Goajiro (Arawak) B249
+ Gorgotoki ~ Korokotoki XXVIII 1118; Gorgotoqui PB14 isolated language
Goyotaca (Tapuya) B239
Guacará 208
Guachi ~ Guachagui (Guarani?) B233
Guachi (Guaycuru) B309–10, 315
Guacico (Chibcha) B189
Guague. See Quaqua.
Guaharibo. See Shirianan.
Guahiban 256–7
Guaicuru 204–5; perhaps here Brinton's Cuaiquere; Guaykurú XXXIII 1119–20; Guaicuru PB8 stock
+ Guaitacá 300–1
Gualaca (Changuina) B175
Gualacho (Guarani) B233
Gualea ~ Yumbo (Kechua) B208
Guamaca (Aruac) B189
Guamo 256; Guama (Tupi?) B264; + Guamo XXX 1119; Guamo TA48 small stock
Guambiano. See Moguex.
Guana (Arawak) B249
Guanero (Carib) B264
Guanuco (Cocanuca) B196
Guaque (Carib) B257
Guarani (Tupi) B235
Guaranoca (Samucu) B271, 301

Guaratagaja 240
Guarauno. See Warrauan.
Guarayo. Ambiguous term, "savage," used for various tribes.
Guarayo (Tupi) B235
Guarayo (tribe on Rio Ituxy, 1885) B294, 295
Guaripeni (Arawak) B268
Guariquena (Bare) B250
Guarive (Carib) B265
Guarpe (Aucanian) B325
Guatoan 281–2; Guato ~ Vuato (Tapuya?); Guató XXXII 1119; Guató TB80 isolated language
Guayana (Tupi) B235
Guayba. See Guahibo.
Guaycarú 276
Guayco (Cocanuca?) B196
Guaycuru B315
Guaycuru ~ Payagua (Guaycuru) B309, 315
Guaymi B184, 189
Guaymi (Guaymi) B189
Guaypunavi ~ Guipunavi (Arawak) B268
Guayqueri (Carib) B258, 264
Guayquira (Carib) B258, 264
Guayue (Churoya) B276
Guck ~ Coco. A false construct or "stock" of Martius based on koko-type words for uncle. The areal distribution of koko-type words for kinsmen is uncharted but will involve North as well as South America.
Guenoa (Charrua) B317
Guinau (Arawak) B249
Guipunabi (Arawak) B278
Gujajara (Tupi) B235
Haitian, See Taino.
Hautanary B295
Herisebocona B306
Het 309–10. See Querandí.
+ Híbito 192; Hibito ~ Xibito ~ Chuncho of the Sierra B288
Huacrachucu (Kechua) B216
Huamachucu (Kechua) B216
Huambisa (Jivaro) B284
Huanca (Kechua) B216
Huancapampa (Kechua) B216
Huancavillca (Kechua) B216

Huari 275; Huari ~ Masaka ~ Corumbiara XXXIV 1120–1; Huari TA66 small stock
Huarpe. See Allentiac.
Huemul (Ona) B331
Huiliche ~ Huilliche (Aucanean) B323, 325
Hyuma B295
Ibiraya (Samucu) B301
Idabaez AA98 isolated language
Indama B321
Iebera ~ Tiputini ~ Tibilo (Zaparo) B279, 281
Inca (Kechua) B216
Ingano. Name of the Quechua-speaking Mocoa.
Intag ~ Yumbo (Kechua) B208
Ipotwat 240
Ipurucoto. See Purigoto.
Iranshe PE43 isolated language
Iquichano (Kechua) B216
Iquito (Zaparo) B281
Iscuande (Barbacoa) B196. See Saccha.
Isistine ~ Ysistine (Lule) B312, 316
Isuiama (Tacana) B298
Ite ~ Guarayo ~ Itene B303
Itonama 272; Itonama ~ Mačoto XXXVII 1121; Itonama TA73 isolated language
Itucalean 270–1 (probably +) Urarina B279; Ssimaku ~ Čimaku ~ Urarina ~ Oruaríña ~ Singakučuska ~ Arukuye ~ Itukale ~ Čambira ~ Huambisa LXXXVIII 1141; Itucale TA61 isolated language
Jabaana (Bare) B249, 250
Jabotifed 240
Jacunda (Tupi) B235
Jama (Betoya) B273
Jamuda (Tupi) 236
Jaruri. See Yaruro.
Jauamery ~ Waimiri B252, 258
Jauna (Tucano) B240
Javahai (Caraja) B262
Jinori (Zaparo) B281
Jirara (Betoya?) B275-6
Jirajara 221–2; Xiraxara CI 1149; Jirajara AA96 stock
Jivaro 222–4; Jivaro ~ Givaro ~ Xivaro B282–4; Xíbaro ~ Xívaro ~ Šiwora ~ Šuāra C 1148–9; Jíbaro TA62 stock
Jucuna (Arawak) B249

Jumana (Arawak) B249
Jupua (Tucano) B240
Jupurina ~ Hypurina B294
Juri ~ Yuri (Arawak) B249
Juri (Lule) B316
Kaingán. See Caingang.
Kamakan. See Camacan.
Karaika (Alikuluf) B331
Katamareño. See Chalchaqui.
Katembri. See Catembri.
Kechua B215–16. See Quechua.
Kechua (Kechua) B216
Kechumaran 196–200
Kiriri. See Cariri.
Kepikiriwat 240, 276
+ Kijo 184. Language extinct, replaced by Quechua.
+ Kikidcana 271–2. Language extinct, replaced by Quechua.
Konió TA68 isolated language
Köggaba (Aruac subtribe, Chibcha) B183, 189
Kustenau (Arawak) 249
Laiana. See Guana.
Lamano ~ Lamisto (Kechua) B216
Leco 274; Leco (Tacana?) B298; Leko ~ Ateniano LVI 1132; Leco AC112 isolated language
Lengua. Ambiguous term, in Mason's view, for various groups including Cachaboth and Mascoi; Lengua (taken as a stock) B316; Lengua PB11 stock, with Mascoy, Lengua, etc.
Lingoa Gêral 237; Lingua Geral (Tupi jargon of the Amazon and the Brazilian coasts) B229–30
Lojano (Jivaro) B284
Lokono ~ West Indies (Arawak)
Lucumbia B279
Lule. Ambiguous term applied to the Diaguita, Vilela, and others.
Lule 207; Lule B316; + Lule ~ Lule de Machoni LVII 1132; Lule AD116 stock (sans Vilela)
Lule ~ Tonicote (Lule) B311, 316
Lule-Vilelan ~ Lulela 206–8
Lupaca (Aymara) B221
Macá (in Mason's Macro-Guaicurú) 203; perhaps here Maco (Churoya) B276
Macoa. Ambiguous term for Chaké as well as Mapé (both Motilón).
Macro-Ge 287–99

Macro-Guaicuruan 201–8
Macro-Tupí-Guaranían 236–50
Macuan 253; Máku LVIII 1132; Máku TA52 isolated language. Máku LVIII should be distinguished from Puinave Makú of Rio Negro and Rio Yapura, Saliva Máku of the Ventaurí, and Cófan, i.e., Chibchan, Mako of Lake Cuyabeno.
Macueni (Arawak) B268
Macuni (Goyotaca) B240
Macurap 240; Makuráp LIX 1132
Macusi ~ Macuchi (Carib) 252, 258
Magdaleno (Mosetena) B298
Mage (Yurucari) B298
Maina ~ Mayna B279, 284–5; + Mayna LXV 1134; Mayna TA58 small stock
Maina. See Cahuapana.
Maina (Maina) B285
Maipure (Arawak) B249, 269, 284. Term applied by Gilii to various Orinoco tribes: (1) Avane, (2) Meepure, (3) Cavere ~ Cabre, (4) Parene ~ Pareni, (5) Guipunave ~ Guaypunavi, (6) Chirupa.
Malaba (Kechua) B216
+ Malalí 275; Malali (Tapuya) B239
MMalbala ~ Malbalai (Guaycuru) B315
Manacica (a Chiquito band) B295–6
Manao (Arawak) B249
Manatenery (Arawak) B249
Mandauaca (Bare) B250
Maniquie (Mosetena) B298
Manitsaua (Tupi) B236
Maniva. See Baniva
Manivi (Barbacoa) B199. See Saccha.
Mansiño (Yurucari) B298
Manta (Kechua) B207
Maopityan. See Taruma.
Mapuche. See Araucanian.
Mapuya (Carib) B264
Maqueritari (Carib) B258. Placed on Rio Branco; perhaps the same as the Maqueritari of the Orinoco, B379, ~ Maquiritari.
Maranho (Arawak) B249
Mariate (Arawak) B249
Mariche B180
Maritzi (Saliva) B267
Maropa (Tacana) B298

Martidane (Charrua) B317
Masáca 275; Masaca (Bare) B250
Masacara (Tapuya) B239
Mascoian 279–80; perhaps here Brinton's Enimaga (see above); Maskoi ~ Machicui ~ Muscovi ~ Enimaga LXI 1132–3
+ Mashacalí 295; Masăkali LX 1132; Mashakali PC19 stock
Mashibi 275–6; Mašubi ~ Meken LXII 1133; Loukotka's Mashubi, s.v. Yabutí
Mataco 202–3; Mataco B316; Mataco PB10 stock
Mataco-Macú 202–4; Matako-Maká LXIII 1133–4, with Mataguayo, etc.
Mataguayo. Ambiguous term for groups of Guaycurus and Matacos (Agoyas, Enimagas, Palomos): B314.
Mataguayo 203; Mataguayo (Mataco) B316
Mataguayo Churumata (Guaycuru) B310, 315
Matanawí 285; Matanawí LXIV 1134; Matanawí PE40 isolated language
Matano (Carib) B265
+ Matará 208; Matara (Lule) B316
Maxoruna (Pano) B292
Maue (Tupi) B236
Mawakwa (Arawak) B249
Mayonggoong (Carib; Brinton has Saliva, following Hartmann, 1886) B267
Mayoruna (Pano) 292
Mbaya ~ Payagua (Guaycuru) B315
Mbegua (Tupi) B236
Mbocobi ~ Bocobi (Guaycuru) B310–1, 315
Menien (Tapuya jargon with African elements, used in E. Brazil) B262
Merigoto B180
Mesaya (Omagua) B200, 233
Mialat 240
Minuane (Charrua) B317
Miranyan 243–4
Mocoa. See Coche.
Mocoa (Mocoa) B200–1
Mogana. See Natixana.
Moguex ~ Guambiano (Cocanuca) B196
Moluche ~ Manzanero (Aucanian; Pampean) 324
Monoxo (Goyotaca) B240
Morcote (Chibcha) B189
Moré-Iten
Morochuco (Kechua) B216
Moroqueni (Arawak) B269
Morotoco (Samucu) B301

Morropa (Kechua) B197
Morrope (Yunca) B226
Morua (Arawak) B269
Mosetenan 274; Mosetena B298; Moseten LXVII 1134; Mosetene TB79 small stock
Motilon 229; Motilone (Carib) B255, 258
Movima 273; Movima ~ Mobima B303–4, 306; Mobima ~ Movima ~ Moyma LXVI 1134; Mobima TA72 isolated language
Moxo (Arawak) B249
+ Moyopampa 271–2. Language extinct, replaced by Quechua.
Muco (Carib) B265
Muchani (Mosetena) B298
Muchic s.v. Mučik LXVIII 1134–5
Mucuru (Carib) B264
Muenane 246
Muku. See Timote.
Mundurucu (Tupi) B236
Muniche 262; Muniche B279; Muniče ~ Muniči LXIX 1135; Munichi TA56 stock
Muoi (Guaymi) B189
Muran 285; Mura (Tupi) B232, 236; Múra LXX 1135; Múra PE39 small stock
Murato (Jivaro) B284; Murato TA59 stock
Murindoe (Choco) B176
Muro ~ Mura (Tupi) B306
Muysca. See Chibcha.
Nambicuaran 283–5; Nambikwára LXXI 1135–6; Nambikwára PE42 stock
Nanegale ~ Yumbo (Kechua) B208
Napo ~ Yumbo (Kechua) B208
Natixana ~ Natica B321
Natú 302; Natú LXXII 1136; Natú PD34 isolated language
Necodade (Choco) B176
+ Nindasu 271–2. Language extinct; replaced by Quechua.
Nnehengatu B266
Noanama (Choco) B176
+ Nomona 271–2. Language extinct, replaced by Quechua.
Nonuya 245
Nutabe B193
Ochosuma 225
Oje (Carib) B264
Ocole (Mataco) B316
Ocorona ~ Rocorona (?) B306. Mason 278 puts this under Chapacuran.
Omagua (Tupi) B233, 236

Omapacha (Kechua) B216

+ Omawaca 303; + Humaguaka ~ Omaguaka XXXVI 1121; Humahuaca AD115 stock

Omurano 250–1

Ona (Patagonian if not a separate stock) B329, 331

Onote B177–81

Opayé 300; Opaie ~ Opaie-Šavánte LXXIII 1136; Opaie PC17 isolated language

Orejón 246

Oristine (Lule) B312, 316

Oromo (Yurucari) B298

+ Otí 299; + Oti ~ Šavante LXXIV 1136, not to be confused with Kukurá Šavante or Ge Šavante; Otí PC26 isolated language

+ Otomaco 255–8; Otomaco ~ Otomaca (Otomaco) B264, 269; Otomak LXXV 1136; Otomac TA47 small stock

Otuqui B304. See Mason's Borotuke.

Ouayéoué. See Waiwai.

Oyampi (Tupi) B236

Pacaguara ~ Pacavara (Pano) B290, 292

Pacaja (Tupi) B236

Pacasa (Aymara) B221

Pacimonaria (Bare) B250

Paiconeca ~ Paunaca (Arawak) B244–5, 249

Pacaya (Peba) B286

Paiura (Carib) B264

Palenque. Ambiguous term for (1) a N. Carib language, B264, or (2) a S.E. Carib language, Patángoro.

Palmella 235; Palmella (Carib) B258

Palomo ~ Mataguayo (Mataco) B316

Pama ~ Purupuru (?) (Araua) B292–3

Pamana B295

+ Pamigua 255

Pammary ~ Pamary ~ Pammana (Araua) B292–3

Pana B279

Panare (Carib) B265

Panca (Tapuya) B239

Pancarãrú 301; Pankarurú LXXVI 1136–7; Pancarurú PD31 isolated language

Panhame (Goyotaca) B240

Paniquita B190

Pano (Pano) B292

Panoan 262–71; Pano B289; Pano LXXVII 1137–8; Pano TB75 stock

+ Pantahua 271–2. Language extinct, replaced by Quechua.

Panzaleo 184
Paparo (Choco) B176
Paranawat 240
Paravilhana (Carib) B258
Pareca (Carib) B265
Parene ~ Pareni (Arawak) B249, 269
Parentintim (Tupi) B236
Pari. See Mundurucu.
Paria (Carib) B252
Parisi (Arawak) B249
Passé (Arawak) B249
Pastuzo (Mocoa) B200
Patacho (Goyotaca) B240
Patagonian B328–9; Patagón PA4 stock
Patashó 296–7; Patašo LXXVIII 1138
Patia (Mocoa?) B200–1
Patoe (Choco) B176
Paudacoto (Carib) B265
Paunaca. See Paiconeca.
Pauti (Jivaro) B284
Payacú 302
Payagua B316
Payagua (Payagua) B314–5
+ Payanso 271–2. Language extinct, replaced by Quechua.
Peban. See Yagua. Brinton 286 counted Peba as independent or tied to Omagua, hence Tupi.
Penoquie (Chiquito) B296
Peschere ~ Ire (Ona) B331
Pianagoto (Carib) B258
Piapoco (Arawak) B249, 269
Piaroa (Saliva) B264; 277; Piaroa TA50 stock, with Sáliva as a W. branch
Pilcosumi (Anti) B243
Pimenteira 236; Pimenteira (Carib) B258
Piñoco (Chiquito) B
Pioje (Betoya?) B273–4
Pira B279
Piro (Arawak) B249
Pituruna (Tupi) B236
Polindara (Cocanuca) B196
Poté ~ Poton (Tapuya) B239
Poturero (Samucu) B301

Poya ~ Peyyuy (Patagonian?) B329
Pubenano. See Guanuco.
Puelchean 309; Puelche, a geographical term for Aucanian tribes of the N. Pampas, B323; Puelče ~ Künnü ~ Tehelkünnü ~ Tehuelhet ~ Tehuelče ~ Tuelče ~ Pampa ~ Tehuiliče ~ Gennaken ~ Toelče ~ Gününa-küne LXXIX 1139; Gennaken PA5 isolated language
Puinahua (Omagua type Tupi) B289
Puinavean 257–8; Puinavi ~ Poignavi (?) B278; Puináve LXXX 1139
Pukapakari ~ Toromona (?) ~ Tuyu ~ Tuyumiri (Tacana) B298
Puquina 224–5; Puquina ~ Huno ~ Ochozoma ~ Uro ~ Uru B218, 222; Puquina AC109 small stock
+ Puri 295–6; Puri (Tapuya) B239; perhaps here + Coroado XXIII 1117; Puri PC18 stock
Purigoto ~ Ipurucoto (Carib) B252, 258
Purubora 275; cf. Purupuru (Araua) B292–3; Puruborá LXXXI 1139; Purubora TA69 isolated language. Cf. Buruburá.
+ Puruhá 195; + Puruhá LXXXII 1139
Purupuru (Araua) B292–3
Quaca (Cumanagoto type Carib) B252
Quaqua ~ Guague (Arawakan) B264
Quaquaro. See Guama.
Quechua 197–9; Kechua ~ Quechua ~ Quechua B215–6; Kičua ~ Runa-Simi LII 1129–31; Quechua AC107 stock
Querandí 305; Querandi (Aucanian) B323, 326; + Čečehet ~ Het XVIII 1112; Chechehet PA6 small stock. See Het.
Quevacu (Saliva) B267
Quilifaye (Betoya) B273
Quillagua (Aymara) B221
Quilme (Catamareña) B320
Quiniquinao (Guaycuru) B243
Quiniquinaux (Guaycuru) B311, 315
Quiriquiripa ~ Quiri-Quiripá (Carib) B265
Quitu (Kechua) B206–7, 216. See Yumbo.
Quiva (Carib) B265
Ranquele (Aucanian) B323
Remo (Pano) B292
Resigero 247
Reyes ~ Reyyuy (Patagonian?) B329
Rio Verde (Choco) B176
Rocorona. See Ocorona and Herisebocona.
Roucouyenne (Carib) B253

Rucana (Kechua) B216
+ Sabela 251; Ssabela ~ Tuey LXXXVII 1141; Sabela TA 63 small stock
Sabuya (Cariri type Carib) B259
Saccha ~ Colorado ~ Manivi B196, 198
Saliva ~ Saliba (Saḷiva) B264, 267
Sálivan 254–5; Saliva B264, 267; Sáliba ~ Sáliva ~ Sálliba ~ Sáliua LXXXIII 1139, including Sáliba, Piaróa, and Máku
+ Samachuane 220
Sambo (Choco) B177
Samucu. See Zamucoan.
Sanamaica 240, 276
+ Sanavirón 307; Sanavirona B321; Sanaviron PA7 isolated language
Sapibocona (Tacana) B298–9
Saraveca (Arawak) B249
Sarigue (Payagua) B316
Satieno (Samucu) B301
Sebondoye (Mocoa) B200–1
+ Sec 196
Sechura (Yunca) B226; Sechura AB101 small stock
Senci (Pano) B292
Sepaunabo (Anti) B243
Setibo (Pano) B292
Shavanté 299–301. An ambiguous term: see Opayé and Otí.
Shirianan 254; Guaharibo (Carib) B252, 258; Širianá LXXXV 1140
Shocó 301; Šokó LXXXVI 1140
Shucurú 301–2; + Šukuru LXXXIX 1141; Shucurú PD35 stock
Simigae ~ Semigae (Zaparo) B279, 282
Simirenci. See Piro.
Sinipi. See Chunipi.
Sinsiga (Chibcha) B189
Sipibo (Pano) B292
Siquisique (Aruac?) B183
Siriono (Tupi) B236
Situfa (Betoya) B273
Solosto (Yurucari) B298
Suya (Tapuya) B239
Tabancale. See Aconipa.
Tacana 218–21; Tacana B298–300; Tacana TB76 stock
Tacana (Tacana) B298
Tado (Choco) B177
Tahami B193

Taino ~ Haitian (Arawak) B249
Taipö-Shishi B240
+ Tairona 187–8; Tayrona (Chibcha) B189
Takanika ~ Kenneka (Yahgan) B332
Takwatib 240
Talamanca (Chibcha), cf. B184
Tama (Betoya) B273
Tamanaca (Carib) B258, 265
Tamano (Catamareña) B320
Tamoyo (Tupi) B236
Tao (Chiquito) B
Tapauna (Tupi) B236
Tape (Tupi) B231, 236
Tapio (Samucu) B301
Tapirape (Tupi) B236
Tapuya (stock with Tapuya, Goyotaca, Tucano) B221–2, 236–41
Tarairiu 302; + Tarairirú XC 1141; Tarairiú PD37 stock
Tarapita. See Otomaco.
Tariano ~ Turiana (Barc) B250
Tariano ~ Javi B266
Tarumá 218; Taruma (Arawak) B246, 250; Taruma XCI 1141; Taruma TA49 isolated language
Taunie ~ Tayuni (Mataco) B316
Tehuelche 310; Tehuelche ~ Chonek ~ Choonke ~ Inaken ~ Patagonian ~ Tzoneca (Patagonian) B328. Cf. Puelchean.
Telembe. See Saccha.
Teluskie (Changuina) B175
+ Tepqui 271–2. Language extinct, replaced by Quechua.
Teremembé 302
Tereno (Guaycuru) B244, 310, 315
Terraba (Talamanca) B189
Teuta (Mataco) B316
Timote 188–91; Timote B179–80; Timote ~ Muku XCII 1141; Timote AA95 stock
+ Tingan 271–2. Language extinct, replaced by Quechua.
Tinigua 255; Tinigua XCIII 1142; Tinigua TA51 small stock
Tirribi (Talamanca) B189
Tirripi (Chibcha?) B177–81
Tiverigoto (Carib) B258
Toba (Guaycuru) B315
+ Tonocoté 208; Tonocote (Lule) B316. See Lule.
+ Torococy 220

Toquistine (Lule) B312, 316
Toromona ~ Macarani (Tacana) B298
Totoro (Cocanuca) B196
Toyeri TB77 isolated language
Tricagua ~ Zapara (Timote) B180
Trio (Carib) B258
Trumai 286; Trumai XCIV 1142; Trumai TA70 isolated language
Tuapoco (Carib) B265
Tucanoan 258–61; Tucano B240; Tukáno ~ Betoya XCV 1142–3; Tucano TC81 stock
Tucumafed 240
Tucuna 218; Ticuna ~ Orejone (?) ~ Tecuna ~ Tucuna B287–8; Tucuna TA53 isolated language
Tucupi (Mosetena) B298
Tucura (Choco) B177
Tucurrique (Talamanca) B189
+ Tulumayo 271–2. Language extinct, replaced by Quechua.
Tumupasa (Tacana) B298
Tunebo (Betoya) B273
Tunebo (Chibcha) B189
Tuparí 240, 276
Tupí-Guaranían 236–43; Tupi ~ Guarani ~ Carai B235–6; Tupi-Guaraní XCVI 1143–7; Tupi TA45 stock
Tura (Tupi) B232, 236
Turbaco (Chibcha?) B177–81
Tushá 302; Tušá XCVII 1148; Tushá PD30 isolated language
Tuyumiri (Tacana) B298
Tuyuneri 221
Uainambeu (Arawak) B250
Uainuma (Arawak) B250
Uambisa (Jivaro) B284
Uaupe (Arawak?) B269
Ugarono (Samucu) B301
Uirina (Arawak) B250
Umán PD33 isolated language
Urarina. See Itucalean.
Uru 224–5; Uro AC110 small stock
Uyapa (Tupi) B236
Vaiyamara (Carib) B258
Valiente (Guaymi) B189
Varrigone (Carib) B252

Vayamano (Carib) B265
Vejoso (Mataco) B316
Vilela 207; + Vilela ~ Lule XCVIII 1148; Vilela PB9 small stock
Voyavai (Carib) B258
Waimiri. See Jauamery.
Waiwai ~ Ouayéoué (Carib) B257
Wapisiana ~ Wapiana (Arawak) B250
Warrauan 252; Guarauno ~ Guarauna ~ Warrau (Guarauno) B264; 272; Guarauno ~ Uarao ~ Uarauno ~ Warrau XXXI 1119; Uarao TD91 small stock
Wayoró 240
West Indians. B250 for Lokono.
Witotoan 244–7; Witóto XCIX 1148; Uitoto TC83 stock
Xolote (Mataco) B316
Yagua 233–4; Yagua ~ Yahua ~ Yegua (Peba) B286
Yahgan 311; Yahgan B329, 332; Yahgan ~ Yámana CIII 1149; Yámana PA1 isolated language
Yahgan ~ Yapoo (Yahgan) B332
Yamaci B193
Yameo ~ Lama ~ Lamista ~ Llameo ~ Yamea B279, 285
Yanoama TD90 stock
Yao (Carib) B258, 265
Yapitalagua ~Pitilaga (Guaycuru) B310–1, 315
Yaputi 276; Yabutí CII 1149; Yabutí PE44 stock
Yaro (Charrua) B317
Yaruro 255–6; Jaruri ~ Japurin ~ Yarura B264, 271; Yaruro ~ Pume ~ Yuapín CIV 1149
Yauyo (Kechua) B216
Yaviteri (Arawak) B269
Yocuno (Carib) B265
Yoe (Mataco) B316
Yuma 235
Yumbo ~ Yumbo de Guerra. Ambiguous term for tribes around Quito in the nineteenth century, unconquered, usually speaking Quechua; of tribes using Quechua B406 lists (1) Canelo, (2) Gualea, (3) Intag, (4) Nanegale, (5) Napo.
+ Yunca 194; Yunca ~ Chimu B224–6; Chimú AB106 stock
Yunca-Puruhán 193–6
Yuracare 175; Yurucari ~ Yurucare B296–8; Yurakáre ~ Yuruxure ~ Yurukare ~ Kuči ~ Enete CV 1149; Yuracare TB78 isolated language
Yuri 235–6; Yuri ~ Yuría ~ Tukano-Tapuya CVI 1149–50; Yuri TC85 isolated language

Yurimagua 240
Yurumanguí 188; Yurimangui AB99 small stock
Yuruna (Tupi) B236
Zamora (Jivaro) B284
Zamucoan 280–1; Key and Key s.v. Ayoré; Samucu ~ Zamuco B301; Samuku LXXXIV 1139–40; Zamuco PB12 stock
Záparoan 247–50; Zaparo ~ Jebero ~ Xebero B280–2; Záparo CVII 1150; Záparo TA64 stock
+ Zapazo 271–2. Language extinct, replaced by Quechua.
Zurumuta. A Macusi subtribe. B259

CHECKLIST

Abbreviations include + (extinct), * (unclassified), R. (river). Unless otherwise noted, the primary reference is Loukotka (1968).

Aarufi.*; Colombia.
Aba. See Canoeiro.
Abacatiara. Kiriri; R. São Francisco, Pernambuco; +.
Abaeté. Tupi; Bahia on R. Abaeté; +.
Abane ~ Avani. Maypure; R. Auvana and R. Tipapa; +.
Abañéem ~ Guarani ~ Karani. Guarani; Paraguay and Corrientes province, Argentina.
Abañeéga ~ Tupi. Tupi; R. Amazon mouth and coast of Brazil; +.
Abatipó. *; R. Matipú, Minas Gerais; +.
Abaucan ~ Tinogasta. Diaguit; Abaucan valley, Catamaraca; +.
Aberiana. Maquiritaré; upper R. Orinoco; +.
Abibe. Antioquia; Sierra de Abibe; +.
Abipon ~ Callaga ~ Yaucaniga ~ Escusgina. Chaco; between R. Paraná and R. Salado, Chaco province; +.
Abiquira ~ Auishiri ~ Tequiráca ~ Ixignor. Auishiri; R. Curaray mouth, Loreto, Peru.
Abira. Panare; R. Manapiare; +.
Abiseta. See Viceyta.
Abitana. Wañàm; R. São Miguel.
Aboba. Huari; R. Guajejú; +.
Aboninim. Mashakali; Serra Geral do Espinhaço, Minas Gerais; +.
Aburuñe. *; Xarayes Lagoon, Bolivia; +.
Acarabisi. See Pomeroon.
Acarapi. *; R. Parimé, R. Branco area, Brazil; +.

Acariana. Maquiritaré; R. Orinoco; +.
Acaroa. See Cauyari.
Açawai ~ Capong. Pemón; R. Moruca, R. Cuyuni, R. Acarabisi, and R. Pomeroon, Guyana.
Acáyaca. See Katapolítani.
Acé. See Guayaquí.
Achagua. Caquetio; R. Apure and R. Arauca, Colombia.
Achipaya. See Shipaya.
Achirigoto. Pemón; R. Caura, left bank; +.
Achote. See Nonuya.
Achual ~ Achuara. Jíbaro; R. Mazal and R. Pastaza, Ecuador.
Acobu. See Gamela.
Aconan ~ Wakona. *; Lagoa Comprioa and Penedo; +.
Aconipa. See Tabancale.
Acoqua. Karaib; R. Approuague and R. Camopi, French Guiana; +.
Acriú. Tarairiu; R. Acaraná, left bank; +.
Acroá ~ Coroá. Eastern Zé; R. Parnaíba and R. Paranaíba, Bahia; +.
Acuria. Karaib; R. Nickerie and R. Coppename, later R. Berbice, Guyana.
Acuriyo. Trio; R. Tapanahoni source, Dutch Guiana.
Adyána. See Adzáneni.
Adzáneni ~ Adyána ~ Izaneni. Baré; R. Caiarí and R. Apui sources, border of Brazil and Colombia.
Agatá. Pijao; R. Magdalena, Cundinamarca; +.
Agavotocueng. Waurá; R. Curisevú and R. Culuene.
Agaz ~ Magach. Guaicuru; R. Paraná and R. Paraguay; +.
Aguachile. See Apolista.
Agual. Chocó; Roldanillo; +.
Aguano ~ Awáno. Chamicuro; R. Huallaga lower course; +.
Aguaricoto. Pemón; R. Caura lower region; +.
Aguaruna ~ Awahun. Jíbaro; R. Marañon and R. Nieva, Amazonas, Peru.
Aguilot. Guaicuru; R. Bermejo, Chaco; +.
Aharaibu. Waica or Yanomamö; N.W. Brazil at the Venezuelan border near R. Cauaboris; 500? (1953). [Not in Loukotka (1968).]
Ahôpovo. See Arikém.
Aí. See Pilagá.
Aicana. See Masaca.
Aifue. Uitoto; Caquetá near Orteguasa.
Aikamteri. Yanoama; R. Parima, R. Branco area.
Aimoré. See Botocudo.
Aipats. Xingú; R. Curisevú; probably +.

Aipé-Chichi. See Raipé-Sisi.
Airassú. See Bora.
Airico. Betoi; R. Manacasia sources; +.
Airuan. *; Serra Ibitipoco, Minas Gerais, and near Barbacena; +.
Aiwaterí. Yanoama (Casapare group); R. Totobí and R. Mapuluan, R. Branco.
Aiyo. See Vejoz.
Aizuare. Amazonas; between mouths of R. Japura and R. Juruá; +.
Ajagua. Caquetio; R. Tocuyo, Venezuela; +.
Ajajú. Carijona; R. Ajajú, Amazonas; +.
Ajie. Pijao; region of R. Losada, R. Tagua and R. Meta; +.
Ajuano. See Uainumá.
Ajujure. See Arára.
Ak'aro. See Cauqui.
Akaroa. See Aricobé.
Akenóini. See Iquito.
Aksanás. See Kaueskar.
Akuän. See Xavante.
Akwẽ. See Xavante.
Alacaluf ~ Halakwalip ~ Pesherah ~ Hekaine. Andean [Greenberg]; Concepción Channel to Dawson Island, Chile.
Alarua. *; R. Auatí-Paraná and R. Japurá, Amazonas; +.
Alausí. Paez; village of Alauxí, Chimborazo, Ecuador; +.
Albauin. See Sumu.
Alile. Goajira; R. Guasape, Zulia, Venezuela; +.
Allentiac. See Huarpe.
Allouage. See Eyeri.
Almaguero. Quechua; Almaguer and Sibundoy villages, Colombia.
Alon. *; R. Huambo, San Martín, Peru; +.
Amacacore. See Iquito.
Amachi. Antioquia; San Bartolomé valley; +.
Amage. See Amoishe.
Amaguaje ~ Encabellado ~ Rumo. Tucano; R. Aguarico, Loreto, Peru; +.
Amahuaca ~ Sayaco ~ Impetineri. Pano; R. Ucayali and R. Urubamba, Loreto, and R. Perus and R. Juruá, Acre.
Amaicha. Diaguit; Sierra de Aconquija, Tucumán; +.
Amamati. Arawa, R. Mucuim N. of the Pamanas; +.
Amaná. Diaguit; Amaná, La Rioja; +.
Amanaye. See Manaxo.
Amani. Pijao; W. of Pantagoras, Caldas.
Amariba. Central Arawak; R. Tacutu and R. Rupununi, Guyana; +.
Amarizana. Caquetio; R. Aguas Blancas and R. Vera, Meta; +.

Amasifuin. *; R. Huallaga, left bank; +.
Amatsenka Ashaninka. Campa.
Amaygua. See Maiba.
Ambargasta. See Inoama.
Amboré. See Imboré.
Amhó. Kaingán; Riacho Ivitoracái, Paraguay; +.
Amicuan. Karaib; R. Marouini sources, French Guiana; +.
Amisha. See Amuesha.
Amniapé. Arikem; R. Mequéns sources.
Amoeca. *; R. Moraro; Amazonas; +.
Amoipira ~ Anaupirá. Tupi; R. Grande mouth to Cabrobo, Bahia; +.
Amoishe. See Amuesha.
Amoquebit. See Mocovi.
Amorúa. Guahibo; R. Bita.
Ampaneá. Tapirapé; R. Tapirapé sources, Mato Grosso; +.
Amuescha. See Amuesha.
Amuesha ~ Amoishe ~ Amísha ~ Amuescha ~ Amage ~ Lorenzo. Pre-Andine Arawakan (?); R. Palcazú region, Peru; 3,000? (1971).
Amuimo. *; R. Nhamundá, Amazonas; +.
Amulalá. See Matará.
Anabali. Betoi; S. Atabaca region.
Anacaioury. See Yao.
Anajá. Pará; Marajó Island, R. Anajá; +.
Anambé. Para; R. Tocantins, left bank, near Rebojo de Guariba; +.
Anapurú. Gamela; R. Parnaiba, right bank; +.
Anasé. Tarairiú; Ceará, R. Acaraú, right bank.
Anáukwá. See Nahukwá.
Anaupirá. See Amoipira.
Anauyá. Uirina; R. Castaño, Amazonas, Venezuela.
Ancash ~ Cheqyan-simi. Quechua; Ancash.
Ancasti. Diaguit; Sierra de Ancasti, Catamarca; +.
Ancutere. See Angotero.
Andagueda. Chocó; R. Quibdó; +.
Andalgala. Diaguit; Andalgala, Catamarca; +.
Andaquí. Andaquí; R. Magdalena, San Agustin, Colombia; later Pueblo Viejo and Belén de Andaquí, Caquetá.
Andirá. Mawé; S. of Tupinambarana Island, R. Amazon; +.
Andoa. Záparo; R. Morona and Pastaza, Andoas; few (1968).
Andoas. Quechua; Andoas, Loreto, Peru.
Andoque ~ Cho'oje ~ Patsiaehé. Classification disputed; middle R. Caquetá, Curiplaya to La Pedrera, Caquetá, Colombia.

Andoquero ~ Miraña-Carapana-Tapuyo. Uitoto; Araracuára mouth, R. Caquetá, Amazonas, Colombia; +.
Anetine. *; Mojos, Bolivia; +.
Angaité. Lengua; between R. Verde and R. Galbán, Chaco, Paraguay.
Angara. *; Angara, Ayacucho, Peru; +.
Angotero ~ Ancutere ~ Pioje. Western Tucanoan; R. Napo, R. Tarapoto, and R. Aguarico, Loreto; 160 (1960) [Johnson and Peeke (1962), p. 78.]
Aniba. Manáo; Saracá Lagoon and R. Aniba; +.
Anicun. *; sources of R. Dos Bois and R. Uruhu; +.
Ankwet. Botocudo; Serra dos Aimorés; perhaps +.
Anodöub. Makú; R. Teia.
Añonolá. See Nonuya.
Anserma ~ Humbra ~ Umbra. Antioquia; Anserma, R. Cauca; +.
Ansus. See Ichú.
Anta. Pará; Igarapé do Bacurí and Cachoeira de Itaboca areas; +.
Anti. See Campa.
Antimilene. See Timirem.
Antioquia. Group with Abibe, etc.; +.
Antipa. Jíbaro; R. Santiago.
Anũja. See Ocaina.
Anunze ~ Soálesu. Nambikwára; R. Papagaio and R. Camararé, Mato Grosso.
Aona. See Ona.
Aoniken ~ Tsoneca. Patagon or Tshon; Chubut and Santa Cruz, S. Patagonia, Argentina; +.
Apacachodego. Guaicuru; R. Apa and R. Jejui; +.
Apairandé. R. Gi-Paraná and R. Maiçi.
Apalai ~ Aparai. Karaib; middle R. Parú de Leste and upper R. Maicurú.
Apalaquiri. See Kalapalo.
Apama. Guiana Tupi; R. Maecurú, Pará; few (1968).
Apáñekra. See Aponegicran.
Apanto. See Apoto.
Aparai. See Apalai.
Apapocúva. Guarani; R. Anambai and R. Dourados; later R. Itaparé, São Paulo; +.
Aparono. See Moṣetene.
Apehou. Pará; R. Xingú; +.
Apeiaca. See Apingi.
Aperea. *; Santiago Sánchez, Corrientes, Argentina; +.
Apiacá. Southern Tupi; upper R. Ronuro and R. São Manoel, Mato Grosso.
Apiacá de Tocantins. See Apingi.
Apichum. Macuráp; location uncertain.

Apinagé. Timbira; R. Araguaia and R. Tocantins.
Apingi ~ Apeiaca ~ Apiacá de Tocantins. Arára; R. Jacunoá and R. Tocantins, Pará; few (1968).
Apirú. See Yaperú.
Apiteré. Guarani; R. Anambaí and R. São Joaquin, Mato Grosso.
Apitupá. *; R. Aquitipi, Bahia; +.
Apiyipán. *; R. Aripuaña, Amazonas.
Apolista ~ Lapachu ~ Aguachile. Apolista; Apolobamba mission, La Paz, Bolivia; +.
Apon. See Chaque.
Aponegicran ~ Apáñekra. Timbirá; R. Corda sources.
Aponteño. Quechua; Aponte, Nariño.
Apoto ~ Apanto. Waiwai; R. Nhamundá, S. of Uaibois; +.
Apque-Sepque. See Enimaga.
Apurimã. See Ipurina.
Arabela. Zaparoan.
Aracadaini. *; R. Aroá and R. Corodoá, R. Cunhuá tributaries, Amazonas; +.
Aracajú ~ Uaraguazú. Tupi elements; R. Parú de Leste and R. Gurupatúba, Pará; +.
Aracapa. Kiriri; Aracapá Island, R. São Francisco, Pernambuco; +.
Arachane ~ Arechane. Guarani; Lagoa dos Patos, Rio Grande do Sul; +.
Arae. *; R. Araguaia, left bank, S. of Bananal Island; +.
Araicú ~ Waraikú. Araicu; R. Jandiatuba sources and R. Juraí, right bank, Amazonas; +.
Aramagoto. Trio; R. Parú de Oeste and R. Parú de Leste upper courses, Pará.
Aramayana. Trio; S. of Aramishos.
Aramayu. *; R. Oiapoque, Amapá, Brazil; +.
Aramihoto. Trio; upper R. Coeroeni, Dutch Guiana.
Aramisho. Trio; upper R. Parú de Leste, Pará.
Aramurú. *; R. São Francisco, Sergipe state; +.
Aranãa. Botocudo; R. Aranãa, Minas Gerais; few (1968).
Aranawa. Yamináua; between R. Liberadade and R. Humaitá.
Arañí. Gamela; between R. Itapecurú and R. Parnaíbaand; +.
Araona. Tacana; R. Manuripi and R. Madre de Dios; perhaps +.
Araote, See Uarao.
Arapaso ~ Koréa. Tucano; R. Yapú, Amazonas, Brazil; +.
Arapico. Jíbaro; Arapico village.
Arapiyú ~ Aripuana. Mawé; R. Arapiuns mouth; +.
Arapoá. *; Jaboatão, Pernambuco; +.
Arara. Itogapúc; R. Prêto mouth, R. Gi-Paraná, to R. Madeira.
Araraibo. Samatari; R. Cauabori, Amazonas.

Ararandeuára. See Manajé.
Ararape. Tupi; R. Paraíba, Rio de Janeiro state; +.
Ararau. *; R. Jatapú, Amazonas.
Arari ~ Ariari. Botocudo; R. Arassuaí and R. Jequitinhonha range; +.
Arariú. *; Meroca on R. Acatajú, Ceará; +.
Arasa. Tacana; Arazaire tribe on R. Arasa and R. Marcopata.
Arasairi. See Toyeri.
Arasi. * (possibly Puri?); Minas Gerais, Serra Ibitipoca and Barbacena.
Araticum. See Aticum.
Aratú. Para; R. Curuá mouth; +.
Araua. Central Pano; R. Chiva, Colonia, Bolivia.
Arauá. See Aráwa.
Arauaqui. Manáo; R. Uatuma and R. Negro range; +.
Araucano. See Mapuche.
Aravirá. Bororo; R. Sipotuba and R. Cabaçal, Mato Grosso; +.
Arawa ~ Arauá. Arawa; R. Chiué and R. Chiruan, and Lake Jaíruan, Amazonas, Brazil; +.
Arawak ~ Aruaqui ~ Luccumi ~ Locono. Arawakan; Guianas.
Arawak. Guiana Arawak: Eastern Arawak; R. Oyapoque and R. Curipi, French Guiana.
Arawak. Guiana Arawak: Western Arawak; British Guiana.
Arawiné. Kamayurá; Rio 7 de Setembro, Mato Grosso.
Araxó. Central Zé (?); Araxá, Minas Gerais; +.
Araxué. Central Zé (?); Serra Canastra and Mata de Coroa; +.
Arazaire. Central Pano; R. Marcapata.
Arbaco. Tamanaco; Victoria, Aragua; +.
Arbi. Chocó; sources of R. Perillo, R. Carino, R. Guali, and R. Miel; +.
Archidona. Záparo; Archidona village, Loreto, Peru; +.
Arda. *; R. Nanay and upper R. Mazán, Loreto, Peru; +.
Aré. See Shetá.
Arebato. Pemón; Cuchara, R. Caura, Bolivar; perhaps +.
Arechane. See Arachane.
Arecuná ~ Arecuna. Pemón; R. Paragua and R. Caroní sources, Bolivar, Venezuela.
Aredé. * (possibly Puri?); Itabirito and Espinhaço; +.
Arequipa. *; Arequipa department; +.
Areviriana. Maquiritaré; E. of Ihuruánas; +.
Ariari. See Arari.
Aricagua. Caquetio; Mérida, Venezuela; +.
Aricapú. Yabuti; R. Branco.
Aricarí. Karaib; lower R. Calçoene; +.

Aricobé ~ Akaroa. Eastern Zé; R. Prêto and Serra das Figuras, Bahia; +.
Arihini. See Baré.
Arikém ~ Uitáte ~ Ahôpovo ~ Ariquemes. Arikém; R. Jamarí and R. Ariquemes, Mato Grosso.
Arina. Manáo; middle R. Marauiá, Amazonas; +.
Arinagoto. Pemón; R. Paragua, Bolivar; perhaps +.
Aripiado. *; Serra da Araponga, Minas Gerais; +.
Aripuana. See Arapiyú.
Ariquemes. See Arikém.
Arití. See Parecí.
Ariú ~ Peba. Kiriri; R. Sabugí and R. Piranhas, Paraíba; +.
Arma. Antioquia; R. Pueblanco; +.
Armacoto. Pemón; between R. Merevari and R. Paragua; +.
Aroã. See Aruan.
Aroásene. *; sources of R. Nhamundá, Amazonas.
Arsario. See Guamaca.
Artane. *; Xarayes Lagoon, Bolivia.
Aruan ~ Aroã. Aruan; N. Marajó Island, Pará; later R. Uacá, Amapá territory; +.
Aruaqui. See Arawak.
Aruáshi. Mondé; sources of R. Branco, near the Tuparis.
Arucuaya. See Itucale.
Aruma. See Yaruma.
Arupai ~ Urupaya. Mundurucú; R. Xingú S. of Yurunas; +.
Arutani. See Auaké.
Asaruntoa. Záparo; R. Asaruntoa; +.
Asepáng. Macusi; S. of Keserumas.
Ashaninka. Campa.
Ashlusláy ~ Etehua ~ Chulupí ~ Sowuash. Eastern Mataco; San José de Esteros and López de Filipis, R. Pilcomayo, Paraguay.
Assek. See Sintó.
Asurini. Para; upper R. Xingú and R. Freso and R. Pacajá.
Atabaca. Betoi; +.
Atacama ~ Cunza ~ Lican Antai. Atacama; Atacama desert, Chile; later Peine, Bolivia.
Atacama. Atacama; Potosí province, Bolivia, and Antofagasta province, Chile; few (1968).
Atacama. Peine; Peine village, Antofagasta province, Chile; few (1968).
Atacamez. See Tacame.
Ataguate. Kahuapana; R. Aipena and Lake Atagua; +.
Atalalá. See Vilela.

Atalán. See Tallan.
Atanque ~ Campanaque ~ Busintana ~ Buntigwa ~ Kalkuama. Arhuaco; Atanquez, Sierra Nevada de Santa Marta.
Atapaima. Guamo; R. Guanaparo mouth, Guárico, Venezuela; +.
Atature. Jirajara; between R. Rocono and R. Tucupido, Portuguesa; +.
Atavila. *; Canta, department of Lima; +.
Ateniano. See Leco.
Aticari. Jirajara; R. Tocuyo, Lara; +.
Aticum ~ Araticum. *; near Carnaubeira, Pernambuco; +.
Atorai ~ Attaraye ~ Daurí. Central Arawak; R. Cuyuwimi and R. Rupununi, Guyana.
Atroahi. See Yauapery.
Atsahuaca ~ Chaspa. Central Pano; R. Carama.
Attaraye. See Atorai.
Atunseta. See Tunceta.
Ature. Piaroa; Ature falls, R. Orinoco, Venezuela; +.
Atzíri. See Campa.
Auacachi. Pará; R. Auacachi mouth; +.
Auaké ~ Oewacu ~ Arutani. *; Maracá Island, R. Branco, Brazil; later, sources of R. Uraricapara, along the frontier of Brazil and Venezuela.
Auca. See Mapuche and Sabela.
Aueiko. *; R. Paranaiuba, Mato Grosso; +.
Auetö. See Awití.
Augutjé. See Menren.
Auishiri ~ Abiquira ~ Tequiráca ~ Ixignor. Macro-Tucanoan, Andean-Equatorial [Greenberg]; R. Curaray mouth, Loreto, Peru.
Aunale. Záparo; R. Curaray and R. Tigre, Concepción mission; +.
Auwáwiti. Xingú group; R. Curisevú; few (1968).
Auyama. See Tororó.
Avahuguai. Guarani; R. Dourados, Mato Grosso.
Avani ~ Abane. Maypure; R. Tipapa and R. Auvana, Amazonas, Venezuela; +.
Avaza. See Pinche.
Aviamo. Caquetio; R. Uribante, Táchira; +.
Avis. *; R. Pajeú valley, Pernambuco; +.
Avurrá. Antioquia; Aburrá valley; +.
Awahun. See Aguaruna.
Awakachi. Amazonas Tupi; R. Auacachi mouth; +.
Awáno. See Aguano.
Aweicoma ~ Bugres ~ Owaikománg ~ Xocren. Kaingán; Blumenau, Palmas and Itajaí, Santa Catarina state.
Aweti. See Awití.

Awití ~ Auetö ~ Aweti. Kamayurá; R. Culiseú, Mato Grosso.

Axata Darpa. *; Gran Chaco, Paraguay.

Ayacore. *; R. Curaray, Loreto, Peru; +.

Ayacucho ~ Chanka-simi. Quechua; Ayacucho.

Ayahuaca. Chimú; Ayabaca, Piura, and R. Quiros; +.

Ayavaka. Quechua; Ayabaca, Piura, Peru.

Ayaya. See Guajá.

Aymara ~ Colla. Aymara; S. Peru and S.W. Bolivia.

Ayomán; Jirajara; Siquisique village, Lara; +.

Ayoré. Zamuco; R. Paragua and R. Grande, Bolivia.

Azumara. See Wayumara.

Babui. See Uaiboí.

Bacaery. See Bacairí.

Bacairí. Xingú Karaib; between R. Curisevú and R. Batouí; later, R. Paranatinga, and Posto Simões Lopes, Mato Grosso; few families (1968).

Bacuen ~ Bocué. Botocudo; R. Mucuri near Imburana; +.

Bacunin. *; near Valença and R. Preto; +.

Baenan. Isolated language; R. Pardo and R. Cahoeira, Bahia; later, Posto Paraguaçú; few (1968).

Baguaja. See Tiatinagua.

Bahuana. Manáo; R. Araçá and R. Padauarí.

Bahukíwa ~ Bahuna. Cubeo; originally on R. Cuduiarí, speaking Arawak.

Bahuna. See Bahukíwa.

Bailadores. See Mucutu.

Baixóta. *; no data; +.

Bakuen. See Bacuen.

Bakurönchichi. *; R. Branco, Rondônia.

Baldam. Mosquito; Sandy Bay and near Bimuna.

Balomar. Charrua; Entre Rios province; +.

Balsapuertiño. See Munichi.

Baníva. Baníva; San Fernando de Atabapo and other villages, R. Orinoco, Amazonas, Venezuela.

Baniva del Rio Içana. See Ipéca.

Bará ~ Pocanga. Tucano; R. Tiquié sources, Colombia.

Barasano. See Tucano.

Barauána. See Chiriána.

Barbácoa ~ Colima. Barbácoa; R. Patia and R. Iscuandé, Nariño, Colombia; +.

Barbados. See Gamela.

Barbudo. See Umutina.

Baré ~ Ihini ~ Arihini. Baré; R. Casiquiare, Amazonas, Venezuela, and upper R. Negro, Amazonas, Brazil.

Barinagoto. Pemón; R. Caroní mouth, Bolivar, Venezuela; +.
Barira ~ Cunaguasáya. Motilon; R. Oro Rincón and R. Lora.
Bascherepo. See Gauchí.
Batachoa. See Botocudo.
Baticola. Guarani; Serra Anambaí, Mato Grosso; +.
Batum. Mashakali; between R. Conceição and R. Doce; +.
Baturité. See Itañá.
Bauá. *; R. Corneg and R. Motum, Amazonas; +.
Baudó ~ Nuqui. Chocó; Baudó R. and in Nuqui.
Baure ~ Chiquimiti. Mojo; R. Blanco by Baures city.
Bavan. Botocudo; near Teófilo Otoni, R. Mucuri; +.
Bawihka. Mosquito; R. Banbana.
Bayano. See Cuna.
Beakeo ~ Beutuebo. Guaicuru; Miranda, later Lalima village, Mato Grosso.
Becaba. *; Loreto near San Miguel, on R. Putumayo; +.
Begua. See Chaná-Mbegua.
Belenista. See Guaicuru.
Belsano. See Cumbazá.
Benoiapa. Catuquina; R. São José.
Betoi ~ Guanero ~ Isabaco. Betoi; R. Apure, R. Cravo, and R. Casanare, Arauca territory, Colombia; +.
Beutuebo. See Beakeo.
Bikutiakap. *; R. Pimenta Bueno, right bank.
Bintucua ~ Ijca ~ Ika ~ Iku ~ Machaca ~ Vintukva. Arhuaco; San Sebastián.
Biriboconé. See Boróro.
Bisanigua. See Churuya.
Bituruna. Guarani; R. São Antonio, R. Chopim, and R. Peixe, Paraná, Brazil; +.
Bixarenren. *; R. Tiucunti, tributary of R. Jamachiua, Rondônia.
Boanari. See Bonari.
Bobure. See Bubure.
Bocas Pretas. See Dawahib.
Bocayú. *; R. Pomba; +.
Bocoani. Central Zé; between R. Prêto and R. Turvo, Minas Gerais; +.
Bocué. See Bacuen.
Bogota. See Murire.
Bohane. Charrua; near Maldonado, Uruguay; +.
Bohurá ~ Buxwaray. Múra; R. Autaz, Amazonas.
Boimé ~ Poyme. *; near Aracajú, R. São Francisco; +.
Bolbo. See Sobolbo.
Boliviano. Quechua; Cochabamba, Bolivia.
Bolona. Jíbaro; Zamora, Ecuador; +.

Bonama. See Ibanoma.

Bonari ~ Boanari. Waiwai; R. Uatumá, Amazonas; perhaps +.

Boncota. See Murire.

Bonda ~ Matuna. Arhuaco; R. Santa María and R. Bonda; +.

Bonitó. Mashakali; R. Suassuí Grande near Peçanha and Bonito; +.

Bora ~ Meamuyna ~ Miraña ~ Airassú ~ Miranha Oira-Assútapuya. Bora; R. Jacaré and R. Cahuinari, and Sierra Iutahy, Amazonas, Colombia.

Boróro ~ Bororo ~ Coroados ~ Biriboconé. Boróro; R. Jaurú and R. Cabaçal, Mato Grosso; +.

Boróro, Eastern. See Orari.

Boruca. See Brunca.

Borun. See Gueren.

Botocudo ~ Aimoré ~ Batachoa. Botocudo is an ambiguous term for Ivaparé ~ Are ~ Sheta ~ Ntobotocudo, a Tupi group, or for the Macro-Ge Caingang of Santa Catarina state, or for a group called Macro-Ge by Greenberg (1959), synonyms for which include, from Mason, Aimbore ~ Borun, in Minas Gerais and Espíritu Santo, apparently the same as Loukotka's Botocudo.

Bracamoro ~ Papamuru. *; near Jaén, Cajamarca, Peru; +.

Brancararú. See Pankarurú.

Bribri ~ Lari. Talamanca; R. Tarire and R. Coca, Costa Rica.

Brunca ~ Boruca ~ Turucaca. Talamanca; R. Grande and in Boruca region, Costa Rica; +.

Brurán. See Terraba.

Brusela. See Guetar.

Bubure ~ Bobure. Karaib Motilon; Bobures and Gibraltar, Zulia; +.

Bucan. *; between Funil and Itacolumí, near Mariana, Minas Gerais; +.

Bucobu. See Piokobjé.

Bucueta. See Murire.

Buga. Chocó; near modern Buga; +.

Bugres. See Aweicoma.

Buhágana ~ Karawatana. Sära; R. Piraparana, Colombia.

Bultrin, Kiriri; Serra Borborena, Paraíba; +.

Bungá. Arhuaco; R. Santa Clara; +.

Buntigwa. See Atanque.

Burede. Karaib Motilon; R. Socuy sources, Zulia; +.

Burgua. Caquetio; near San Camilo, R. Burgua, Santander, Colombia; +.

Buritaca. Antioquia; R. Sucio sources; +.

Buritiguara. *; R. Manso and R. Araguaia, Mato Grosso; +.

Buruá. Catuquina; R. Jutaí and Biá.

Burubora. See Puruborá.

Busintana. See Atanque.

Busquipani. Pano; R. Alacrán, Loreto; +.
Buxwaray. See Bohurá.
Bwihá. See Mbyhá.
Caapina. *; between R. Jarí and R. Maicuru, Pará; +.
Cabahyba. See Kawahyb.
Cabanaé. See Arára.
Cabanatit. See Mascoy.
Cabecar. Talamanca; R. Moy, Costa Rica.
Cabere ~ Cabre. Caquetio; R. Zama and R. Teviare, Vichada territory; +.
Cabixi. *; R. Steinen, Mato Grosso.
Caboquena. Manáo; R. Urubú, Amazonas; +.
Cabre. See Cabere.
Caburichena. Manáo; R. Negro, right bank; +.
Cabuyarí. See Cauyari.
Cacan. See Calchaquí.
Cacaopera. Matagalpa; Cacaopera and Lislique, El Salvador.
Cacataibo. See Cashibo.
Cachi. See Viceyta.
Cachináua ~ Caxinaua ~ Huñikui. Pano; range of R. Embira, R. Liberdade and R. Tarauacá, Amazonas.
Cachipuna. *; Puna de Quillpaco, Lima; +.
Cachirigoto. Pemón; S. of Camaracotos, Bolivar; +.
Cachoarí. See Cachuena.
Cachuena ~ Kaxihuâna ~ Casiana ~ Cachoarí. Chiquena; R. Cachorro mouth; few families (1968).
Cadaupuritani. See Katapolítani.
Cadupinapo. Mapoyo; S. of Achirigotos; +.
Caduveo ~ Kadiueo. Guaicuru; between R. Tereré and R. Nabileque, Serra Bodoquena, Mato Grosso, Brazil; later, Miranda, Mato Grosso.
Caeté ~ Caité. Tupi; mouth of R. Paraíba to mouth of R. São Francisco; +.
Cafuana. *; R. Japurá S. of Waríwas; +.
Cágaba ~ Köggaba ~ Kaugia ~ Koghi. Arhuaco; San Andrés, San Miguel, San José, Santa Rosa, and Pueblo Viejo, Sierra Nevada de Santa Marta.
Cahan. *; R. Espocil and R. Iguatimí, Mato Grosso; +.
Cahicahi ~ Caicaze ~ Caicai. Tupi; lower R. Itapecurú, Maranhão; +.
Cahuapana ~ Chuncho. Kahuapana; R. Cahuapana, Loreto, Peru; Quechua is favored now (so Loukotka, 1968).
Cahuarano ~ Moracano. Záparo; R. Pucacuro.
Cahumari. See Caumari.
Cahuyana. Chiquena; middle R. Trombetas.
Cahygua. See Mbyhá.

Caicai. See Cahicahi.
Caicaze. See Cahicahi.
Caicuchiana. Karaib; S. of Parabaianas, French Guiana; +.
Caicusiana. Chiquena; S. of Salumás, R. Tunúru.
Caimbé. *; Masacara village, near Mirandela, Bahia; +.
Caimito ~ Káimö. Uitoto; Puerto Montclar, Amazonas, Colombia.
Caingang. See Kaingán.
Caité. See Caeté.
Caitoporade. See Tunacho.
Caiua. See Mbyhá.
Cajamarca ~ Qahamarka-simi. Quechua; villages at Cajamarca.
Cajatambo. *; Cajatambo, Lima; +.
Cajaurun. See Pejaurún.
Cajurú. See Cararú.
Calabaça. Kiriri; R. Salgado, Ceará; +.
Calamari. Malibú; coast S. of Cartagena to Covenas; +.
Calayua. Guiana Tupi; R. Inipucú sources, Pará; +.
Calchaqui ~ Calchaquí ~ Cacan ~ Tocaque. Diaguit; Quimivil valley and Santa María valley, Salta; +.
Calian ~ Mocalingasta. Diaguit; Guadacol valley; +.
Calinago. See Caraib.
Caliponau. Arawak; Lesser Antilles.
Calipurn. See Caripuna.
Caliseca. See Carapacho.
Callaga. See Abipon.
Callahuaya. See Pohena.
Calva. Chimú; N. of Ayahuacas, Loja, Ecuador; +.
Camachire. See Suerre.
Camamu. Tarairiú; R. Acaraú, Ceará; +.
Camana ~ Maje. *; R. Majes, Arequipa; +.
Camanawa. Pano; R. Moa.
Camaniba. See Maniba.
Camaracoto. Pemón; Bolivar, Venezuela, R. Paragua and R. Caroní.
Camarapim. Pará; R. Pacajá mouth; +.
Camaraxo. *; between Serra dos Aimorés and Ilhéus, Bahia; +.
Camaré. *; R. Camoó, tributary of R. Trombetas, Amazonas; +.
Camasú. Tarairiú; R. Acaratí-guasú sources, Ceará; +.
Camayura. See Kamayurá.
Camba. See Chiriguano.
Cambi. See Yalcon.
Cambioá. *; Serra Negra, Pernambuco; +.

Camboca. Pará; between R. Tocantins mouth and R. Jacundá mouth; +.
Camé. See Kaingán.
Camiare. Huarpe, S. dialect of Comechingon; Sierra de Córdoba, Córdoba, Argentina; +.
Campa ~ Anti ~ Atzíri ~ Thampa ~ Kuruparia. Pre-Andine Arawak; R. Urubamba and R. Ucayali, Cuzco, Peru; Wistrand (1971), pp. 109–10, lists divisions as (1) Ashaninka, (2) Amatsenka Ashaninka, (3) Nomatsiguenga. She specifies the Campa area as R. Pachitea S. to 40 miles S. of the confluence of R. Apurimac and R. Mantaro, and from the Peruvian border at Puerto Pardo to the Andes foothills at the west.
Campanaque. See Atanque.
Campaz. See Colorado.
Campueua. See Omagua.
Camsa. A language of Colombia.
Camuchivo. See Yameo.
Cana. Aymara; between R. Ayaviri and R. Tinta, Cuzco; +.
Cañacure. *; R. Mamoré, Bolivia; +.
Canamari. Southern Catuquina; R. Jurua, Amazonas.
Canamirim. See Kanamaré.
Cañarí. Northern Chimú; Canar, Ecuador; +.
Canarin. Eastern Mashakali; R. Mucurí and R. Caravelas, Espirito Santo; +.
Canawari. Northern Pano; R. Rixalá and R. Curumaha, Acre, Brazil; +.
Canchi. Ayamara; Vilcanota Valley, Cuzco, Peru; +.
Candindé. Central Zé; Itapecerica Valley near Divinopólis, Minas Gerais; +.
Candodú. Tarairiú; near the Caratiú, Jucá, and Quixetó.
Canduashi. See Murato.
Canella. See Krenkatajé.
Canelo ~ Penday. Jíbaro; R. Canelos; +.
Canelos. Quechua; R. Canelos, Oriente, Ecuador.
Canesi. See Canichana.
Canichana ~ Canesi. Isolated language; R. Machupo and R. Mamoré, Beni, Bolivia.
Canindé. Tarairiú; R. Chorro sources, Ceará; +.
Canoê. See Kanu:a.
Canoeiro. Ambiguous term, used as a synonym of Erikbaktsa, or for a Guarani dialect (see next entry).
Canoeiro ~ Aba ~ Tiäbezä. Kainguá dialect in Guarani group of Tupi; part of Bananal Island, R. Tocantins banks, and R. Peixe and R. Crixás mouths, Goiás.
Capacho. Opone; Capacho village, Táchira, Venezuela; +.
Capaheni. See Capechene.

Capaná. See Yamamadí.

Capanagua. Northern Pano; R. Blanco and R. Tapiche, Loreto.

Caparo. Caquetio; R. Caparo, Santander, Colombia; +.

Capayana. See Cupayana.

Capechene ~ Capaheni. *; R. Rosiano and R. Xapurí, Acre, Brazil.

Capinamari. See Yamamadí.

Capixana ~ Kanoe. Isolated language; R. Guarajú sources, Rondônia.

Capong. See Acawai.

Capoxo. See Kaposho.

Capua. *; R. Rolim de Moura, Rondônia.

Capueni. *; between R. Ixié and R. Amazon, Amazonas; +.

Capuibo. Sensi; R. Biata; +.

Caquetio. Caquetio Arawak; R. Apure, R. Portuguesa, and R. Yaracuy, Venezuela, island of Curaçao and Aruba near coast of Venezuela; +.

Cara ~ Caranqui ~ Imbaya. Barbácoa; R. Guallabamba and province of Imbabura, Ecuador; +.

Carabinani. See Yamamadí.

Caraca. Tamanaco; around Caracas, Venezuela; +.

Caraçatan. *; R. Manhuaçú and R. Caratinga, Minas Gerais; +.

Caraguara. *; between Lake Anama and R. Amazon; +.

Caraib ~ Calinago ~ Karib. Western Karaib; northern South America and Antilles.

Caraib. Insular Karaib; Lesser Antilles. Loukotka (1968) reports a few individuals on Dominica, but these surely are Arawakan, not Cariban, speakers. See Caraib ~ Kaliña below.

Caraib ~ Kaliña ~ Garina ~ Galibi. Western Karaib; Guyana and Dutch and French Guiana.

Caraib ~ Caribisi ~ Acarabisi. Western Karaib; R. Macarani and R. Pomeroon.

Carajá. See Karajá.

Caramanta. Antioquia; city of Antioquia; +.

Caramonan. *; R. Manhuaçú and R. Caratinga, Minas Gerais; +.

Caranariú. Marawan; R. Urucauá; +.

Caranbú. Pará; near the Anambés.

Carane. Western Karaib; São Paulo d'Oiapoque mission, Amapá; +.

Caranga. Aymara; from Lake Coipasa to R. Desaguadero, Bolivia; +.

Caranqui. See Cara.

Carapocho ~ Caliseca. Pano; R. Carapacho; +.

Carapana-tapuya. See Möxdöá.

Carapeuara. Eastern Karaib; R. Maicurú S. of Apamas, Pará; +.

Carapoto. Fulnio; Serra do Comonati; later Porto Real de Colégio, Alagoas; perhaps +.

Caraque. Paleo-Chibchan; Caráquez Bay, Manabi, Ecuador; +.
Carára. *; R. Jatapú sources, Amazonas; +.
Carare. Opone; R. Carare, Santander; a few speakers (1968).
Carari. See Omagua.
Cararú ~ Cajurú. *; Soroabé Island, R. São Francisco, Pernambuco; +.
Caras Pretas. See Tacumandícai.
Carate. Opone; Ocaña, Norte de Santander; +.
Caratiú. Tarairiú, R. Triá valley and sources of R. Potí; +.
Carauau. See Karaho.
Caravare. See Kuruáya.
Carayá. Central Zé (?); N. area of R. Paraíba, Minas Gerais; +.
Carcarañá. Charrua; R. Carcarañá, Santa Fe, Argentina; +.
Carendie. See Querandí.
Cariachil. Arhuaco; between R. Fonseca and R. Molino; +.
Cariay ~ Carihiahy. Mandauáca; region of R. Padauarí, R. Araçá, and R. Negro, Rio Branco territory, Brazil; +.
Caribe. Western Karaib; Plains of Barcelona, Monagas and Anzoátegui states, Venezuela; +.
Caribisi. See Pomeroon.
Carif ~ Moreno. Western Karaib according to Loukotka, this dialect is really Arawakan, the Island Carib or Central American Carib of British Honduras, Guatemala on Gulf of Hunduras, and Roatan Island.
Cariguano. Chiquena; R. Panemá; +.
Carihiahy. See Cariay.
Carijó. See Cariú.
Carijona ~ Kalihóna. Carijona; R. Caquetá, Caquetá territory; a few speakers (1968).
Cariña. See Tabare.
Caringasta. Diaguit; Anguco Valley, San Juan; +.
Cariniaco. Western Karaib; R. Caura mouth, Bolivar, Venezuela; +.
Carinuaca ~ Kurushikiána ~ Orechicano. Mapoyo; R. Biehita sources; a few speakers (1968).
Caripó ~ Curupehe. *; R. São Francisco near Boa Vista, Pernambuco; +.
Caripuna ~ Calipurn. Guiana Tupi; R. Curipi, Pará.
Caripuna ~ Jaunavô ~ Shakáre ~ Éloe ~ Yacariá. Eastern Pano; R. Madeira and R. Beni sources; later in a village at the R. Mutum-paraná mouth, in Rondônia.
Caripurá ~ Karipuere. Marawan; Amapá territory, R. Urucauá.
Cariquena. Pijao; R. Cariquena, Táchira, Venezuela; +.
Cariri. See Kariri.
Caritiana. Arikém; R. Candeias, Rondônia.

Cariú. Kiriri; between Bastiões and R. Cariú, Ceará; +.

Carnijó. See Fulnio.

Carrapa. Chocó stock; R. Tapia, R. Chilona, and R. Honda, Caldas; +.

Carruacane. See Curucane.

Cartama. Antioquia; Cartama city; +.

Carútana ~ Corecarú ~ Yauareté-tapuya. Baré; R. Içana, on the frontier of Colombia and Brazil.

Casapare ~ Shirianá ~ Shirishana ~ Quirishána. Casapare; R. Uraricapara and R. Uraricoera, Rio Branco, Brazil.

Casavindo. Humahuaca; Casavindo city, Jujuy; +.

Cascoasoa. See Chasutino.

Casharari. Ipurina; between R. Ituxí and R. Abuña and on tributaries Curequeta and Iquirí, Acre.

Cashibo ~ Cacataibo ~ Caxivo ~ Hagueti. Pano; R. Aguaytía, R. Pisqui, and R. Pachitea, Loreto, Peru.

Cashingui. Arhuaco; R. Palomino; +.

Casiana. See Cachuena.

Casigara. *; R. Juruá mouth; +.

Casma. Chimú; R. Casma, Ancash; +.

Casota. *; Santa Lucia mission, Corrientes; +.

Catacao. Catacao; Catacaos city, Piura, Peru; +.

Catamarca ~ Cusco ~ Cuzco. Quechua; Catamarca, Argentina. Spoken by Diaguites.

Catarana. Botocudo; Arassuaí city; +.

Catarro. Guahibo; Meta territory on R. Yucavo, and San Miguel de Salivas mission.

Catathoy. See Kutasho.

Catauxi ~ Catosé ~ Hewadie ~ Katawishi ~ Quatausi. Catuquina; between R. Purus and R. Madeira; a few families (1968).

Catiana. Arawa; R. Iaco, Acre; +.

Catiguasú. Eastern Mashakali; between R. São Francisco and R. Jequitinhonha, Minas Gerais; +.

Catio. Antioquia; Dabaiba, Colombia; +.

Catío. Chocó stock; sources of R. Sucio, R. Murri, R. Tugurico, middle R. Cauca, Dabeiba.

Catolé. Kamakan; valleys of R. Verde and R. Pardo, Minas Gerais; +.

Catongo. Pre-Andine Arawak; R. Tambo.

Catoquina do rio Gregorio. See Waninâua.

Catosé. See Catauxi.

Catrimbi. See Katembri.

Catuena. See Totocumu.

Catuquina ~ Wiri-dyapá. Northern Catuquina; R. Jutai, Amazonas, Brazil.
Catuquinarú. Southern Tupi; R. Embira, Amazonas; used by a Tupinized Katukina tribe.
Cauaborí. Makú; R. Cauaborí, Amazonas, Brazil.
Cauacaua ~ Kawakawa. *; R. Japuré; +.
Cauauri. *; S. of Curanaves in Amazonas; +.
Caucau. See Chono.
Cauishana ~ Kayuishana ~ Noll-hína. Cauishana; R. Tonantins, Lake Mapari, Amazonas; a few families.
Caumari ~ Cahumari. Yagua; R. Guerari, tributary of R. Napo, Loreto; +.
Cauni. *; S. of the Guanarús.
Caupuna. *; R. Purus; +.
Cauqui ~ Ak'aro ~ Haqearu ~ Kawki. Aymara; Tupe and Huantan villages, Yauyos, Peru.
Cautarie ~ Kareluta ~ Quie. Zamuco; R. Quie or Cautarie, Chaco, Bolivia.
Cautario. See Kumaná.
Cauyari ~ Acaroa ~ Cabuyarí. Tariana; R. Cananari and middle R. Apaporis, Amazonas, Colombia; perhaps +.
Cavana. *; middle R. Majes, Arequipa; +.
Caviña ~ Cavineña. Tacana; R. Beni, R. Madidi, and R. Cavinas; probably +.
Cavineña. See Caviña.
Caxago. *; R. São Francisco, Sergipe; +.
Caxinaua. See Cachinaua.
Caxine. *; between R. Paraíba and R. Preto, near Valença, Minas Gerais; +.
Caxinití. Paresí; R. Sucuriú, R. Sepotuba, and R. Sumidouro, Mato Grosso, Brazil.
Caxivo. See Cashibo.
Cayápa ~ Nigua. Barbácoa; R. Cayapas, Esmeralda, Ecuador; a few families (1968).
Cayapó do rio Pau d'arco. See Iraamráire.
Cayapó do Xingú. See Gorotiré.
Cayú. *; R. Pimenta Bueno left bank, Rondônia.
Cayuvava. Isolated language; R. Mamoré at Exaltación village, Beni, Bolivia.
Ceño. See Siona.
Central Uitoto. Western Uitoto; El Encanto, Carapaná and La Chorrera villages and environs, Amazonas, Colombia. Spoken by the Búe, Mekka and Yaboyano.
Cenufara. See Sinufana.
Ceococe. *; Serra Pão de Açúar and São Pedro, Pernambuco; +.
Chacamecran. See Sakamekran.
Chacanta. Caquetio; R. Mucuchachi, Mérida; +.

Chachapoya. *; Chachapoya city, Amazonas, Peru; +.

Chacobo. Eastern Pano; Lake Rogoaguado, Beni, Bolivia.

Chacoi. Western Karaib; between R. Essequibo and R. Berbice, Guyana; a few speakers (1968).

Chaguan. Uarao; Laguna de Asfalto, Monagas.

Chama. See Guacanahua.

Cháma ~ Manava ~ Chipeo ~ Setebo ~ Shipibo ~ Puinahva. Northern Pano; R. Ucayali N. of Canibos.

Chamacoco. Southern Zamuco; R. Paraguay near Forte Olimpo.

Chamacoco bravo. See Tumrahá.

Chamaygua. Tamanaco; Sucre, near Cumanagotas; +.

Chambira. See Itucale.

Chamí. Chocó stock; R. Marmato, Antioquia.

Chamicuro. Chamicuro; R. Chamicuro, Loreto, Peru.

Chaná. Charrua; R. Paraná-Guazú and R. Uruguay; +.

Chaná-Mbegua ~ Begua. Charrua; R. Paraná near Crespo and Victoria, Entre Rios province; +.

Chancay. *; R. Chancay, Lima, +.

Chanchamayo. Pre-Andine Arawak; R. Perené.

Chanco. Chocó stock; middle R. Cauca left bank; +.

Chancumakkeri. See Uro.

Chandri ~ Yarri. Guarani; Martín Gracía Island and Martín Chico region, Argentina, and on coast near San Lázaro, Paraguay; +.

Chanduy. Northern Chimú; Sierra Chanduy, Guayas, Ecuador; +.

Chané. See Izozo.

Chané ~ Izoceño. Chané; R. Itiyuro, Salta, Argentina; the Arawakan language is reserved for religious ceremonies, and Tupi is spoken otherwise.

Chango. Uro; Chilean coast from Huasco to Cobija, Antofagasta; now Araucanized.

Changuena. Dorasque; R. Changuena and Panama; +.

Chanka-simi. See Ayacucho.

Chantari. Sanema; R. Ugueto, Amazonas.

Chapacuare. Tamanaco; Pascua valley, Guárico; +.

Chaparro. See Shapáru.

Chaque ~ Apon. Yupe dialect of Karaib Motilon; R. Apon, Zulia.

Charca. Aymara; near Oruro, N.E. of Lake Poopó, in Oruro province, Bolivia.

Charrua. Charrua; S. of R. Ibicuy, Uruguay and along R. Yapexú, Argentina; +.

Charúma. See Salumá.

Chaspa. See Atsahuaca.

Chasutino ~ Cascoasoa. Munichi; R. Huallaga, at Chasuta; +, replaced by Quechua.

Chauquéz. See Chilote.

Chavante. See Otí.

Chawiyana. Waiwai; upper R. Nhamundá right bank, Amazonas.

Chayavita ~ Tsaawí. Kahuapana; R. Paranapura sources, Loreto.

Chayma ~ Guarapiche ~ Sayma. Tamanaco; R. Guarapiche, Anzoátegui, Venezuela; +.

Chechehet. Chechehet stock; Sierra Ventana, Buenos Aires province, Argentina; +.

Cheoua. *; R. Huambo, San Martín; +.

Cheqyan-simi. See Ancash.

Chesquío. Coconuco; R. Sucio; +.

Chewache. See Téuesh.

Chibcha ~ Muisca ~ Mosca. Chibcha stock; Bogotá and Tunja plateau, Cundinamarca, Colombia; +.

Chicha. *; Cordillera de Chorolque, Potosí, Bolivia; +.

Chicluna. Chamicuro; E. of Aguanos; +.

Chicoana ~ Pulare. Diaguit; Lerma Valley, Salta; +.

Chicriabá. See Xakriabá.

Chikaõ. See Ticaõ.

Chikrí ~ Xicri. Kayapó; between R. Pardo and R. Macacheira, S. of R. Itacaiuna, Pará.

Chilote ~ Chauquéz. Mapuche; Chauquéz Island and Chiloé Island; few speakers (1968).

Chimane ~ Chumano ~ Nawazi-Moñtji. Mosetene; R. Maniqui and R. Rapulo, Beni.

Chimila ~ Shimizya. Malibú; R. Frio and between Sierra Nevada de Santa Marta and R. Magdalena; a few speakers (1968).

Chimú ~ Yunga ~ Chincha ~ Quingnam ~ Muchic ~ Mochica. Chimú stock; N. Pacific coast, Peru—or so Loukotka, whose views on Uro (Uru), Chipaya and Chimú (Yunga) have been superceded by those of L. Stark and others who connect these languages with Mayan.

Chimú. Chimú stock; Trujillo, Peru; +.

Chinato. Opone; upper R. Zulia, Norte de Santander, at Cúcuta; +.

Chincha. *; R. Chincha, Ica; +.

Chinchaysusyu ~ Tampish. Quechua; R. Macará to Cerro de Pasco, Peru.

Chinchipe. *; R. Chinchipe, Cajamarca; +.

Chingo. See Jinotega.

Chipaya. Uro; Lake Poopó, Oruro, Bolivia; later Panza Island, N. bank of Lake Coipasa, and Panza Lake. Beuchat and Rivet saw Uru-Chipaya as Arawakan; Loukotka saw Uro as a stock; but Stark and others have revised these views: see Chimú.

Chipeo. See Cháma.

Chiquena ~ Shikiana. Chiquena; R. Panemá sources, Pará, and R. Apiniwau, Guyana.

Chiquimiti. See Baure.

Chiquito ~ Tarapecosi. Chiquito; language of early missions in N. Chaco, Santa Cruz de la Sierra, Bolivia. Dialects: Tao, Piñoco, Penoqui, Cusiquia, Manasi, San Simoniano, and Churápa.

Chiquiyama. Huarpe; Mendoza city, and R. Barranca; +.

Chira ~ Lachira ~ Tangarará. Catacao; R. Chira, Piura; probably +.

Chiránga ~ Siriána. Desána; R. Paca-igarapé, Colombia.

Chiriána ~ Baraúna. Chiriána; between R. Demeni and R. Marari, Rio Branco.

Chiricoa. Guahibo; R. Lipa and R. Ele, Arauca, R. Cravo and R. Arauca, Arauca territory, Colombia, and in Apure, Venezuela, on R. Arichuna, R. Capanaparo, R. Cinaruco and R. Cinaruquito.

Chiricum. Pemón; Rio Branco territory. W. of Taurepáns; +.

Chirigua ~ Shiribá. Tacana; Santa Buenaventura mission, Beni; +.

Chiriguano ~ Camba. Chiriguano; Serraniá de Aguarugüe, Bolivian Andes, and W. Chaco, Sara province and upper R. Bermejo, Bolivia; later, in Carandaiti Valley and around Tarabuco.

Chirino. Murato; Cordillera del Condor on R. Chirino, Cajamarca, Peru; +.

Chiripá. Guarani; R. Acaray, Paraguay, and R. Iguasú mouth, Argentina.

Chiripó. Talamanca; R. Chiripó and R. Matina, Costa Rica.

Chiripuno. Záparo; R. Chiripunos.

Chiriwiyana. Waiwai; upper R. Nhamundá right bank, Amazonas.

Chirú. *; S.W. of Coibas, Panama; +.

Chita. See Sinsiga.

Chitarero. Chibcha; at Pamplona, Santander; +.

Chiuppa. See Suerre.

Choarana. See Echoaladí.

Chocama. See Waunana.

Chocaz. See Chocó.

Chochama. Cuna; R. Suegro, Panama; +.

Chocó ~ Xocó ~ Chocaz. Isolated language; R. Pianco, Pernambuco; later, outside Pôrto Real de Colégio, Alagoas.

Chocó ~ Cholo ~ Emperá. Choco stock; mainly Colombia on Pacific Coast.

Chocorvo. See Chucurpu.

Chocue ~ Choque. Caquetio; R. Herorú and R. Guayabero, Meta; +.

Cholo. See Chocó.

Cholona ~ Seeptsá. Cholona; R. Huallaga near Uchiza, Peru; a few speakers (1968). Chongo. *; near Jauja, Junín; +.

Chongón. Northern Chimú; R. Jama mouth to Galera, Ecuador coast; +.

Chono ~ Caucau. Aksanás; Aisén territory on Chonos and Taitao, Chile; +.
Chonqui. See Péeneken.
Chontal. See Matagalpa.
Chontaquiro. Pre-Andine Arawak; R. Chandless, R. Cathé and R. Yaco, Acre, Brazil.
Cho'oje. See Andoque.
Choque. See Chocue.
Chori. See Siriono.
Choropi ~ Churupí. Eastern Mataco; R. Pilcomayo near Tartagal, Argentina.
Choroti ~ Solote ~ Yofuaha ~ Moianek. Eastern Mataco; Chaco, Paraguay, on confluence of R. Pilcomayo and R. Caruas.
Chuchure. Mosquito; Nombre de Dios, Panama; +.
Chucuna. Caquetio; between R. Vichaoa and R. Manacacia, Meta and Vichada, Colombia; +.
Chucurpu ~ Chocorvo. *; R. Churchinga sources, Huancavelica; +.
Chukahamai. See Metotíre.
Chulupí. See Ashlusláy.
Chumano. See Chimane.
Chumbivilca. Aymara; Chumbivilca city, Cuzco, Peru; +.
Chumulu. Dorasque; Potrero de Vargas, Panama; +.
Chunatahua. Lorenzo; R. Chinchao, Huánuco, Peru; +.
Chuncho. See Cahuapana. Also see Tiatinagua.
Chunupi. Vilela; confluence of R. Bermejo and R. San Francisco, near La Encrucijada, Valtolema, Ortega, Laguna Colma and Esquina Grande; +.
Chupacho. *; R. Chinchao and R. Monzón, Huánuco; +.
Churápa. Chiquito; R. Piray, Santa Cruz, Bolivia.
Churima. *; mission of San José de Maharenos, Beni, Bolivia; +.
Churumata. Humahuaca; N.W. of Humahuacas; +.
Churupí. See Choropí.
Churuya ~ Bisanigua. Guahibo; R. Güejar and in El Piñal; +.
Chusco. Lorenzo; near Huánuco; +.
Ciaman. Choco stock; R. Cuaca at Ciaman; +.
Ciparigoto. Tamanaco; R. Aroa and R. Yaracuy, state of Yaracuy; +.
Cipo. See Sipó.
Citara, Chocó stock; R. Sucio mouth, on R. Atrato.
Cituja. See Situfa.
Coaní. Pará; R. Xingú mouth; +.
Coanoa ~ Guanoa. Malibú; R. César; +.
Coaque. Northern Chimú; Jama mouth to Galera, Ecuador coast; +.
Coatí-tapuya. See Kapité-Mínanei.
Cocaima. Caquetio; between R. Matiyure and R. Setenta, Apure Venezuela; +.

Cocama. Amazonas Tupi; R. Ucayali left bank and near Nauta, Peru.
Cocamilla. Amazonas Tupi; lower R. Huallaga, Peru.
Cochabot. See Enimaga.
Coche. See Sebondoy.
Cochinoca. Humahuaca; city of Cochinoca, Jujuy; +.
Cockorack. See Cucra.
Cucoloth. See Lengua.
Coconuco. Coconuco; R. Cauca sources, Cauca, Colombia; a few families (1968).
Cocto. See Coto.
Coeruna. Eastern Uitoto; R. Caritaia and R. Miritíparana at São Antonio de Maripi and São João do Principe, Amazonas, Brazil; +.
Cofán ~ Cofane ~ Cofan. Isolated language; in eight regions of Ecuador and Colombia along the border. The Ecuadorian dialect is used on R. Aguarico, with 75 speakers at Dureno village (1960). The mutually intelligible Colombian dialect is used on R. San Miguel, R. Guamués and R. Putumayo.
Cognomona. *; upper Huallaga; +.
Coiba. Cuna; R. Chagre, Panama; +.
Colan. Catacao; city of Catacaos, Piura, Peru; +.
Colastiné. Charrua; Santa Fe, near Colastine; +.
Colima. Pijao; R. Magdalena right bank and R. Negro and R. Pacho, Cundinamarca; +.
Colima. See Barbácoa.
Colima. Barbácoa; middle R. Daule, Guayas; +.
Colime. See Colorado.
Colla. See Aymara.
Collagá. See Karraim.
Collagua. See Qollawa-simi.
Collagua. Aymara; R. Colca, Arequipa; +.
Colonche. Northern Chimú; R. Colonche, Guayas, Ecuador; +.
Colorado ~ Tsáchela ~ Chono ~ Campaz ~ Satxíla ~ Colime. Barbácoa; R. Daule, R. Vinces and R. Esmeralda, Pichincha and Los Ríos, Ecuador.
Comanahua. *; Huánuco near Tepquis; +.
Comaní. *; N. of Lake Saracó, Pará; +.
Comayana. See Ocomayana.
Comechingon. Huarpe; Sierra de Córdoba, Córdoba province, Argentina; +.
Conobo ~ Univitsa. Northern Pano; R. Unini and R. Inua; +.
Conambo. Záparo; R. Conombo.
Conamesma. See Sapuqui.
Conchuco. *; Pomabamba, Ancash; +.
Conchucu. See Huaylas.
Conduri. Chiquna; R. Nhamundá mouth, +.

Conibo ~ Cunibo ~ Curibeo. Northern Pano; R. Ucayali.
Contanáwa. Yamináua; upper R. Tarauaca and R. Humaitá.
Copallén. Isolated language; villages of Llanque, Las Lomas, and Copallén, Cajamarca, Peru; +.
Copiapó. Diaguit; city of Copiapó, Atacama, Chile; +.
Coquibacoa. See Cosina.
Corbago. Opone; Magdalena department, in Sierra de Mene; +.
Corbesi. See Corobisi.
Corecarú. See Carútana.
Coreguaje. Western Tucano; R. Caquetá sources; Cauca, Colombia.
Corema. Kiriri; R. Piancó, Paríba; +.
Coretu ~ Kueretú. Coretu; R. Mirití-paraná, Amazonas, Brazil.
Coritanahó. *; R. Ajubacábo, tributary of R. Trombetas, Pará; +.
Coroá. See Acroá.
Coroado. See Kaingán.
Coroado. Eastern Puri; R. Chipoto, Serra da Onça, near Ubá, Rio de Janeiro and Minas Gerais states; +.
Coroatá. Gamela; R. Itapecurú, Maranhão; +.
Corobisi ~ Corbesi ~ Cueresa ~ Rama de rio Zapote. Guatuso; R. Zapote, Costa Rica; a few speakers (1968).
Coroino. See Moro.
Coronado. Hee Hichachapa.
Coronáwa. Northern Pano; Acre territory.
Corondá. Charrua; Corondá city, Santa Fe, Argentina; +.
Corumbiara. See Huari.
Cosina ~ Coquibacoa. Goajira; Serranía Cosina, Goajira Peninsula, Colombia; +.
Cospique. Malibú; Bolivar department (?); +.
Coto ~ Cocto. Talamanca; between R. Grande and R. Coto sources, Costa Rica; +.
Cóto ~ Payoguaje. Western Tucano; R. Napo mouth, Loreto, Peru.
Cotoguéo. See Kotogéo.
Cotonúru. Waiwai; between R. Cachorro and R. Cachorrinho.
Cotoxo. See Kutasho.
Coussani. See Cusari.
Covare, Boróro; Santa Ana de Chiquitos mission, Bolivia; +.
Coyaima ~ Tupe. Karaib Motilon; R. César, Magdalena; +.
Coyone. Jirajara; R. Portuguesa sources, Portuguesa state; +.
Crenaque ~ Crenac ~ Krenak. Botocudo; R. Doce left bank; +.
Crixaná ~ Crichana ~ Quirixana. Yauapery; between R. Curiauaú and R. Yauapery middle courses; probably +.
Cuacá. See Itucá.

Cuaiquer ~ Koaiker. Barbácoa; R. Cuaiquer.
Cubeo ~ Kobéua ~ Kaniwa ~ Hahanana. Cubeo; R. Cuduiarí and R. Caiarí, Amazonas, Brazil.
Cuchi. See Yuracare.
Cucra ~ Cockorack. Mosquito; R. Siqui and R. Escondido.
Cueresa. See Corobisi.
Cueta. See Mâm.
Cueva ~ Darien. Cuna; R. Atrato mouth, Colombia; +.
Cuiapopihibi. Guahibo; R. Tomo, Vichada territory.
Cuiba. Jirajara; near Aricagua, Lara and Portuguesa states; +.
Cuica ~ Chontal. Timote; R. Boconó and R. Motatán, Trujillo; +.
Cuicuro. See Kuikutl.
Cuiloto. Guahibo; R. Cravo and R. Cuiltoto, Arauca, Colombia.
Cuite. Coquetio; R. Cuite, Santander, Colombia; +.
Cuiva. Guahibo; R. Meta, Vichada, Colombia.
Cujuna. Chapacura; N. of Kumanás; perhaps +.
Culaycha. *; mission of Santa Lucia, Corrientes; +.
Culino. Northern Pano; area of R. Jandiatuba, R. Javari and R. Jutaí, Amazonas; +.
Culli ~ Ilinga. Isolated language; villages of Bologna and Pallazca, Huaylas, Peru; perhaps +.
Cumanagota. Tamanaco; Cabo, Codero and near Cumaná, Sucre, Venezuela; +.
Cumanaxo. See Kumanasho.
Cumayari. *; R. Purús mouth (?).
Cumbazá ~ Belsano. *; between Yanaycu and Santa Catalina, San Martín; +.
Cuna ~ Bayano ~ Tule ~ Mandingo ~ San Blas ~ Karibe-kuna ~ Yule. Chibcha; R. Bayano in San Blas, and N. coastal islands, E. Panama.
Cunaguasáya. See Barira.
Cuniba. Pre-Andine Arawak; between R. Jutaí and R. Juruazinho and on R. Mapuá, Amazonas; +.
Cunibo. See Conibo.
Cunipúsana. Mandauáca; R. Siapa, Amazonas; +.
Cunuaná ~ Kunuhana. Maquiritaré; R. Cunucunuma sources.
Cunza. See Atacama.
Cupayana ~ Capayana. Diaguit; San Juan and La Rioja provinces; +.
Cupelobo. See Tapirauha.
Curanave. *; W. of R. Negro, Amazonas; +.
Curasicana ~ Kurushikiána ~ Orechicano. Mapoyo; R. Biehita sources; a few speakers (1968).
Curaso. See Guarañoca.
Curave ~ Ecorabe. Boróro; Santo Corazón mission, Bolivia; +.

Curi. *; S. of Parianas; +.
Curia. Pre-Andine Arawak; R. Embira and R. Murú, Acre; perhaps +.
Curiane. *; N.E. division of Tropical Forest, exact location unknown.
Curiato. Mawé; R. Maricauá mouth; +.
Curibeo. See Conibo.
Curicuriai. Western Makú; R. Curicuriai, Amazonas, Brazil.
Curierano. *; R. Orinoco sources, Amazonas, Venezuela; +.
Curina ~ Kulina ~ Kólö. Arawa; R. Juruá right bank, R. Mararí, upper R. Tapauá, R. Gregorio, R. Erú, R. Murú left bank, Acre, Brazil.
Curinsi. Gamela; near Vianna; +.
Curipaco. Ipéca; R. Guriniá, Amazonas, Venezuela.
Curivere. See Kuruáya.
Curizeta. *; R. Cosanga, Loreto, Peru; +.
Curuapa. See Kuruáya.
Curuaya. See Kuruáya.
Curubianan. *; R. Jatapú and R. Urubú, Amazonas; +.
Curucane ~ Carruacane. Boróro; San Rafael mission, Bolivia; +.
Curucuane. Western Karaib; lower R. Casipore, S. of Itutans; +.
Curumaní. Karaib Motilon; S. of R. Tucui, Magdalena.
Curumiá. *; R. Brilhante sources, Mato Grosso; +.
Curumina. Boróro; Casalvasco mission; +.
Curupehe. See Caripó.
Cururi. Gamela; near Uruatis; +.
Curuzirari. *; between R. Tefé mouth and R. Juruá mouth; +.
Cusari ~ Coussani. Guiana Tupi; upper R. Araguarí, Amapá; +.
Cusco. See Catamarca.
Cushitineri. See Kushichineri.
Cusiquia. Chiquito; N. of Penoquis; +.
Custanáwa. Northern Pano; upper R. Purus, near R. Curanja mouth, Loreto.
Cutaguá. *; R. Dourados, Mato; +.
Cutervo ~ Huambo. *; R. Chancay sources, Junín.
Cutinana. Moríque; R. Samiria, Loreto; +.
Cutriá. *; middle R. Branco, Rondônia.
Cuximiraíba. *; R. Aripuaña, Amazonas.
Cuxiuára. *; R. Purus right bank near mouth; +.
Cuyanáwa. Northern Pano; R. Moa.
Cuzqueno. See Qosqo-simi.
Dace. See Tucano.
Dagseje. See Tucano.
Dajseá. See Tucano.
Dallus. See Maruba.

Daminivá. *; R. Igarapé do Pacú, tributary of R. Caratirimani, and in Serra do Urubú, Rio Branco.

Dapatarú. Manáo; between R. Urubú and R. Uatuma and on Saracá Island, Amazonas; +.

Dapicosique. See Toba.

Darien. See Cueva.

Dätuana. Yahuna; R. Apoporis.

Dawahib ~ Bocas Pretas. Kawahyb, Southern Tupi; R. Anarí, Rondônia.

Dawainomol. *; Gran Chaco, Paraguay.

Dazaro. Guamo; R. Guanare at Zamora; +.

Decuána ~ Deukwana ~ Maquiritaré. Maquiritaré; R. Caura, R. Ventuari, R. Auari and R. Merevari, Bolivar, and Amazonas, Venezuela, and between R. Majori and R. Cotinga, Rio Branco, Brazil.

Demacuri. *; R. Caburi near São Pedro, Amazonas.

Dendi. Southern Kamakan; Serra Geral de Condcúba, on borders of Bahia and Minas Gerais; +.

Depso. See Terraba.

Dequaca. See Oa.

Desána ~ Wina ~ Uina. Desána; between R. Caiarí and R. Tiquié, Colombia and Brazil.

Deukwana. See Decuána.

Diaguit. Diaguit; Catamarca, Argentina; +.

Diáu. See Trio.

Digüt. Mondé; R. Machado left bank.

Divihet. *; R. Chico, R. Sauce, and R. Colorados, La Pampa, Argentina; +.

Djiporoca. See Xiporoc.

Djupá. *; R. Jiparanã, Rondônia.

Dobocubí ~ Motilon ~ Barira ~ Mapé ~ Motilone. Chibchan Motilon; R. Tarra and Atacarayo mission, Norte de Santander, Colombia.

Dokoro. *; R. Paranaiuba, Mato Grosso; +.

Dóu. Makú; R. Ducupixí-igarapé.

Doxcapura. See Tuyuca.

Ducaiya. See Ocaina.

Duit. Chibcha; R. Tundama and R. Tunja; +.

Duludi ~ Northern Cayapó. Kayapó; R. Jaraucu near Moz, R. Xingú, Pará.

Duri. *; R. Paranaiuba, Mato Grosso; +.

Durina ~ Sokó. Yupua; R. Carapato, Amazonas, Colombia.

Dyuremáwa ~ Yiboia-tapuya. Cubeo; R. Querarí, Amazonas.

Dzáse. See Piapoco.

Dzubucua. See Kiriri.

Dzyoré. Kayapó; R. Cuxura sources, Pará.

Eastern Kaingán ~ Ñakfáteitei ~ Yakwändatéye ~ Guayana de Paranapamena. Dialect of the Northern Kaingán language called Kaingán; R. Paranapamena, São Paulo; perhaps +.

Ebidoso ~ Ishirá. Southern Zamuco; Puerto Diana, Paraguay.

Echoaladí ~ Choarana. Chané; Mato Grosso; +.

Echoja. See Tiatinagua.

Ecorabe. See Curave.

Ecusgina. See Abipon.

Eduria. See Erulia.

Eenslit. See Mascoy.

Egualo. *; Santiago Sánchez mission, Corrientes, Argentina; +.

Eidum. See Tacuñapé.

Eimi. *; R. Napo, Loreto.

Einslet. See Lengua.

Ele. Betoi; R. Ele.

Eliáng. Macusi; S. of Asepángs.

Eloe. See Caripuna.

Elotasu ~ Waiklitisi. Central Nambikwára; R. Utiariti, Mato Grosso.

Emejeite. See Imihitä.

Emereñon. See Emerillon.

Emerillon ~ Teko ~ Emereñon ~ Marêyo. Guiana Tupi; R. Araoua, R. Approuague, R. Camopi, R. Coureni, and R. Inini, French Guiana; a few families (1968).

Emischata. *; Santa Lucia mission, Corrientes, Argentina; +.

Emok. See Toba-michí.

Emperá. See Chocó.

Encabellado. See Amaguaje and Macaguaje.

Enete. See Yuracare.

Enimaga ~ Lilei ~ Cochabot ~ Apqe-Sepqe. Mataco; R. Verde sources, Chaco, Paraguay; +.

Eno. Western Tucano; R. San Miguel mouth, Caquetá, Colombia; a few speakers (1968).

Enslet. See Lengua.

Envuelto. *; Quebrada de Jirijirima, Caquetá, Colombia.

Eochavante. See Otí.

Eperigua. Caquetio; R. Güejar sources and near San Juan de los Llanos, Meta; +.

Epetineri. Pre-Andine Arawak; R. Pijiria, tributary of R. Urubamba, Peru; +.

Epineo. See Puináve.

Equiniquinao. See Quiniquinao.

Erema. *; R. Paranaiuba, Mato Grosso; +.

Erikbaktsa ~ Canoeiro. *; R. Juruena, Mato Grosso.

Erulia ~ Paboa ~ Eduria. Erulia; R. Piraparana, Colombia.
Escoria. *; at Santiago, Panama; +.
Escuque. Timote; R. Motatán left bank.
Ese'ejja. See Guacanahua.
Esmeralda. Paleo-Chibchan; R. Esmeralda, Esmiralda province, and in Sierra de Cojimies, Manabi, Ecuador; +.
Espino. Northern Pano; R. Curumaha.
Esquegua. See Urraca.
Estrella. Talamanca; R. Estrella, Costa Rica; +.
Etaboslé. See Makká.
Etagl. Xingú; Etagl village.
Etehua. See Ashlusláy.
Eten. Southern Chimú; Eten and Monsefú villages, Lambayeque, Peru; a few speakers (1968).
Eteteguaje. See Tetete.
Etwet. Botocudo; R. Manhuaçú sources; +.
Eurpari. See Upar.
Eye. Panáre; R. Cuchivero sources, S. W. of Panáres; +.
Eyeri ~ Allouage. Island Arawak; Lesser Antilles; +.
Eyibogodegi. Guaicuru; R. Branco, Mato Grosso; +.
Ezeshio. See Kamakán.
Fa:ai. Bora; Sierra Iutahy.
Famatina. Diaguit; La Rioja in Famatina Valley; +.
Faranakaru. Waiwai; R. Mapuera sources, S. of Waiwais.
Faranauaru. Waiwai; R. Mapuera left bank.
Faraute. See Uarao.
Fitita. Eastern Uitoto; R. Fititas.
Foklása. *; Serra dos Cavalos, Pernambuco; +.
Fórnio. See Fulnio.
Frentones. See Toba.
Fulnio ~ Fórnio ~ Carnijó ~ Iaté ~ Yathé ~ Fornió. Macro-Ge [Greenberg, 1959]; upper R. Moxotó; later, city of Aguas Belas, Pernambuco.
Funucuna. Chocó stock; W. of R. Buritica, Chocó territory.
Gaamadi. See Yamamadí.
Gadio. *; Espirito Santo, locality unknown; +.
Galache. *; near Macaubas, Bahia; +.
Galibi. See Caraib.
Gambéla. *; near São José and Ourem, Maranhão; +.
Gamela ~ Acobu ~ Barbados. Gamela; R. Pindaré, R. Turiaçú, and R. Itapucurú; +.
Garañun. Shukurú; Serra dos Garanhuns; +.

Garina. See Caraib.
Garú. See Gaurú.
Gaula. See Ulua.
Gavião. See Kaapor.
Gaviões. See Menren.
Gay. See Simigae.
Gayón. Jirajara; R. Tocuyo sources, Lara; +.
Ge. See Zé.
Gekoinhalaák. See Lengua.
Genipapo. Tarairiú; R. Chorro; +.
Gennaken ~ Puelche ~ Pampa ~ Gününa-küne. Huarpean in Ge-Pano-Carib [Greenberg]; R. Negro and R. Colorado, C. Patagonia; +.
Giriguana. See Upar.
Goajira ~ Uáira. Goajira; Goajira Peninsula, Colombia and Venezuela.
Goaña. Mashakali; R. Correntes and R. Guanhães; +.
Goguez ~ Guegué. Eastern Zé; between R. Gurgueia and R. Tocantins, Piauí; +.
Goma. Uitoto; R. Igra-paraná mouth, Amazonas.
Gopujegual. Goajira.
Gorgotoqui. Isolated language; R. Guapay, Santa Cruz, Bolivia; perhaps +.
Gorone, Chocó stock; at La Cumbre, Valle de Cauca; +.
Gorotiré ~ Cayapó do Xingú. Kayapó; between R. Pau d'arco and R. Xingú.
Goyá. Eastern Zé; R. Vermelho sources, Goiás; +.
Goyana. *; lower R. Branco, Rio Branco territory; +.
Goytacaz. See Waitaka.
Gradaú. See Kradahó.
Great Tobas. See Toba-guazú.
Gritones. See Sinabo.
Guaca. Chocó stock; lower R. Atrato.
Guacanahua ~ Chama ~ Ese'ejja. Tacana; R. Undumo and R. Madidi, La Paz, Bolivia.
Guachí ~ Guaxarapo ~ Bascherepo. *; R. Miranoa sources, Mato Grosso, Brazil. Language extinct; replaced by Guaicuru (?).
Guachí. Opaie; R. Vaccaria; +.
Guachipa. Diaguit; Guachipa Valley, Salta; +.
Guacurure. See Pilagá.
Guadaxo. *; upper R. Anhanduí, Mato Grosso; +.
Guaharibo. See Sanemá.
Guahibo. Guahibo; R. Orinoco, R. Vichada, R. Meta, and R. Arauca, Colombia and Venezuela.
Guahuara. See Kuruáya.

Guaiba. Eastern Zé; Guaiba Island, R. São Francisco near São Romão, Minas Gerais; +.
Guaica. See Waica.
Guaicuru ~ Gwaikuru ~ Mbayá ~ Belenista. Guaicuru; Gran Chaco, Paraguay; +.
Guaimute. *; near falls of Salto Grande, Espirito Santo; +.
Guaipuño. See Puináve.
Guaiquiraré. Charrua; Entre Ríos province on Arroyo Guaiquiraré; +.
Guajá ~ Guaxara ~ Wazaizara ~ Ayaya. Northern Tapirapé; between lower R. Gurupá and R. Capim, Maranhão.
Guajajára. Northern Tupi; R. Mearim and R. Itapecurú sources; later, R. Grajaú and R. Pindaré, Maranhão.
Gujarapo ~ Guasaroca. *; at Villa Maria and Santa Ana de Chiquitos, Santa Cruz, Bolivia; +.
Guajejú. Huari; R. Jamarí and R. Candeia sources; +.
Guajiro. See Goajira.
Gualaca. Dorasque; R. Chiriquí, Panama; +.
Gualachí. See Guayana.
Gualaquiza. Jíbaro; village of Gualaquiza.
Guamaca ~ Níbela ~ Sanha ~ Arsario. Arhuaco; villages of El Rosario, Potrerito and Marocaso, Colombia.
Guambiana ~ Silviana ~ Silviano. Coconuco; villages of Cucha, Ambató and Silvia, Colombia.
Guamo. Guamo; R. Santo Domingo, R. Masparo, R. Portuguesa, and R. Paoviejo, Portuguesa, Venezuela; +.
Guamoco. Antioquia; at Zaragoza; +.
Guamontey. Guamo; R. Zarate mouth to R. Apure; +.
Guaná ~ Layano. Chané; R. Galván and R. Yacaré; later, R. Miranda, Mato Grosso.
Guaná de Chaco. See Kaskihá.
Guanáca ~ Guanuco. Coconuco; Plata Vieja village; +.
Guanano. Data lacking; Colombia; see Wistrand (1971), p. 110.
Guanare. Gamela; between R. Parnaíba and R. Itapecurú; +.
Guanarú. *; R. Juruá, N. of Marawas, Amazonas, Brazil; +.
Guanavena. *; between R. Jatapú and R. Urubú, Amazonas; +.
Guane. Opone; Santander at R. Tarare sources; +.
Guanebucán. Goajira; R. Hacha, Magdalena, Colombia; +.
Guanero. See Betoi.
Guanguí. See Micay.
Guanhanan. See Guayana.

Guanoa. See Coanoa.
Guanoco. Uarao; Laguna de Asfalto, Monagas.
Guanuco. See Guanáca.
Guapi. Barbácoa; R. Guapi, Cauca; +.
Guaque ~ Huaque ~ Murcielaga. Carijona; R. Inganos, Caquetá, Colombia; +.
Guaquiri. Mapoya; N. of Curasicanas; +.
Guaraní ~ Karani ~ Abañéem. Guarani; interior of Paraguay and Corrientes province, Argentina.
Guarañoca ~ Curaso ~ Laant. Northern Zamuco; Salina de San José, Bolivia; perhaps +.
Guarapiche. See Chayma.
Guaratégaja ~ Mequen. Macuráp; R. Mequéns and R. Verde sources.
Guarauno. See Uaroa.
Guaraxué. *; between Ouro Preto, Mariana and Piranga; +.
Guarayo. Chiriguano; R. Blanco sources and R. San Miguel, missions of Yotáu, San Pablo and Yaguarú, Santa Cruz, Bolivia.
Guarena. See Haerena.
Guariba. See Wariwa.
Guárico. Guamo; R. Guárico, R. Apure and R. Portuguesa; +.
Guarino. *; middle R. Tijuco, Mato Grosso; +.
Guariteré. *; Mato Grosso, exact location unknown; +.
Guarizo. Tacana; Reyes and San Antonio de Isiama missions; +.
Guarú. *; S. of Pitás, state of Rio de Janeiro; +.
Guarú ~ Garu. Yakúna; R. Meta, R. Mamura, and R. Cuama, Caquetá, Colombia.
Guassaroca. See Guajarapo.
Guatiedéo ~ Uettidiáu. Guaicuru; Albuquerque, Mato Grosso; +.
Guató. Isolated language; Uberabá; Uberabá Lagoon, R. São Lourenço, in Bolivia and Brazil.
Guatuso. Guatuso; R. Frio, Costa Rica; perhaps +.
Guaxara. See Guajá.
Guaxarapo. See Guachí.
Guaxina. Gamela; R. Itapecurú mouth; +.
Guayabero ~ Guyaverun. Guahibo; R. Guayabero, Meta.
Guayana ~ Wayana ~ Gualachí ~ Guanhanan. Southern Kaingán; between R. Paraná and R. Uruguai, Rio Grande do Sul, Brazil; +.
Guayana de Paranapamena. See Eastern Kaignán.
Guayapi. See Oyampi.
Guayaquí ~ Acé. *; Cordillera de Villa Rica, Paraguay. Language extinct, replaced by Guarani (?).
Guayami. Guayami; Panama.

Guayqueri. Tamanaco; R. Paoviejo, Cojedes; +.
Guayuno. See Pariagoto.
Guayverun. See Guayabero.
Guazuzú. Antioquia; Sierra de San Jerónimo, Antiquia, Colombia; +.
Guegué. See Goguez.
Guenoa ~ Minuan. Charrua; Entre Ríos province from Arroyo Hernandarias to R. Paraná, and on R. Minuanes, Rio Grande do Sul, Brazil; +.
Guenta. *; Huila, Colombia; +.
Guentuse. Eastern Mataco; near R. Verde source, Paraguay; +.
Gueren ~ Borun. Botocudo; R. Paruhipe; later, near Olivença, Bahia; perhaps +.
Guetar ~ Brusela. Guatuso; R. Grande, Costa Rica; +.
Guicurú. See Kuikutl.
Guimara. See Wayumara.
Guimpejegual. Goajira.
Guinau ~ Inao ~ Guniare ~ Temomeyéme ~ Quinhau. Guinau; R. Merevari and R. Caura sources, Bolivar, Venezuela; perhaps +.
Guire. Guamo; R. Guaritico, R. Orituco and R. Tiznados, middle courses, Guárico; +.
Guisnai. Western Mataco; R. Itiyuro, near San Andrés.
Guniare. See Guinau.
Gününa-küne. See Gennaken.
Guratégaja ~ Mequen. Arikém; sources of R. Mequéns and R. Verde.
Guti Krag. See Uti Krag.
Guyarabe. *; between R. Auatíparaná and R. Amazon, Amazonas; +.
Guyaverun. See Guaybero.
Gwaikuru. See Guaicuru.
Haauñeiri. See Yamiaca.
Hacaritama. Opone; city of Hacaritama, Santander; +.
Haerena ~ Guarena. Tamanaco; between R. Guarenas and R. Guatire, Anzoátegui; +.
Hagueti. See Cashibo.
Hahaháy. Eastern Mashakali; R. Cachoeira, Bahia.
Hahanana. See Cubeo.
Hairúya ~ Jairuia. Western Uitoto; R. Tamboryacu and R. Putumayo Peruvian bank.
Halakwalip. See Alacaluf.
Hamno. Kawahyb; S. of Paranawáts.
Haqearu. See Cauqui.
Harateri. See Sanemá.
Harritiahan. *; middle R. Matapi, Amapá territory; +.
Haush. See Mánekenkn.

Haveniken. See Péeneken.
Hehénawa. Cubeo; R. Cuduiarí.
Hekaine. See Alacaluf.
Henia. Huarpe, N. dialect of Comechingon; Sierra de Córdoba, Córdoba, Argentina; +.
Here:kere. Botocudo; R. Jequitinhonha; +.
Herisebocon. Chapacura; R. Rapulo near San Borja mission; +.
Hevejico. Antioquia; Evejico Valley and Tonusco Valley; +.
Hewadie. See Cutauxi.
Hiánocoto. See Umáua.
Hiauahim ~ Javaim. *; middle R. Tapajós, Pará, Brazil; +.
Híbde-Nehern. See Húbde.
Hichachapa ~ Coronado ~ Ipapiza. Záparo; R. Bobonaza mouth and R. Pastaza; +.
Hirka-simi ~ Junín. Quechua; Junín department.
Hishcariana ~ Ishkariyána ~ Tucano. Waiwai; middle R. Nhamundá.
Hiupiá. See Yupua.
Hivito ~ Xibitoana. Cholona; R. Huamo, N. of Cholonas; nearly +.
Hobacana. See Yabaána.
Hohodene ~ Huhúteni. Baré; R. Cubate, Amazonas.
Hohoma. See Mahoma.
Holcotian. See Oico.
Hölöua. Cubeo; R. Cuduiarí; perhaps +.
Hon-dyapa. See Parawa.
Horihi. See Musuraqui.
Hório. Southern Zamuco; near Puerto Mihanovich, Paraguay.
Huanchi. See Chapacura.
Huachipairi ~ Huachpairi. Pre-Andine Arawak; R. Pilcopata and R. Cosñipata, Madre de Dios; +. A dialect of Mashco.
Huacho. *; at Huacho, Lima; +.
Hualfin. Diaguit; Hualfin Valley, Catamarca; +.
Huamachi. *; Chongo Alto, Junín; +.
Huamachuco. *; R. Condebama, Libertad; +.
Huamalí. Quechua; at Huamalí, Huanuco.
Huamalí, *; R. Panáo, Huánuco; +.
Huamanga. *; Peru; +.
Huambisa. Jíbaro; R. Santiago and R. Morona, Loreto, Peru.
Huambo. See Cutervo.
Huambuco. *; R. Chinchipe, Amazonas; +.
Huamoi. See Umán.
Huanca ~ Wanka. *; R. Mantaro, Junín. Language extinct, replaced by Quechua.

Huancamarca ~ Wankamarka-simi. Quechua; Huancavelica.

Huancavilca. Northern Chimú; R. Yaguachi, R. Daule, and around Guayaquil, Guayas province; +.

Huancayo ~ Huancay ~ Wanka-simi ~ Mantaro. Quechua; Jauja.

Huánuco ~ Wanuku-simi ~ Xalqa. Quechua; Huänuco.

Huanyam. See Wañám.

Huaque. See Guaque.

Huarani. See Sabela.

Huarayo. See Tiatinagua.

Huari ~ Corumbiara. Huari; between R. Guarajú and R. Corumbiara, Rondônia, Brazil.

Huarpe ~ Allentiac. Huarpe; Laguana Huanacache, Mendoza province, Argentina.

Huatama ~ Otanavi. Munichi; villages of Otanahui and San José de Sisa. Language extinct, replaced by Quechua.

Huayla. *; middle R. Santa, Ancash. Language extinct, replaced by Quechua.

Huaylas ~ Conchucu ~ Waylas. Quechua; Huaylas, Huaraz department.

Húbde ~ Híbde-Nehern. Western Makú; R. Yapú-igarapé.

Hueshuo. See Vejoz.

Huhúteni. See Hohodene.

Huiliche ~ Veliche. Mapuche; Valdivia province, Chile, to Lake Nahuel Huapi, Argentina.

Huitoto. See Uitoto.

Humahuaca ~ Omaguaca. Humahuaca; Tilcará Valley and Humahuaca Valley, Jujuy, Argentina; +.

Humbra. See Anserma.

Hunacabamba. *; R. Chamaya, Piura; +.

Huñikui. See Cachináua.

Hunurana. See Omurana.

Iaté. See Fulnio.

Ibabi Aniji. *; Peru.

Ibanoma ~ Bonama. Amazonas Tupi; R. Juruá mouth to R. Purus mouth along right bank of R. Amazon; +.

Ibirayára. See Kayapó.

Ica. *; R. Ica, Ica department; +.

Icaguate. Western Tucano; R. Putumayo and R. Caucaya, Putumayo territory, Colombia; +.

Ichikile. See Shukurú.

Ichú ~ Ansus. Kiriri; R. Salgado sources, Ceará; +.

Icó. Kiriri; R. Salgado, R. Piranhas and R. Peixe area; +.

Icozinho. Kiriri; confluence of R. Salgado and R. Jaguaribe, Ceará; +.

Idabaez. *; Cape Marzo to Bahía Solano, Pacific coast of Colombia; +.
Ificuene. Western Tucano; R. Aguarico to R. Gúepi, Loreto.
Igapuitariara. Mawé; R. Curauaí sources; +.
Ignaciano. See Mojo.
Ihini. See Baré.
Ihuruána. Maquiritaré; R. Ventuari sources, Amazonas, Venezuela.
Ijca. See Bintucua.
Ika. See Bintucua.
Iku. See Bintucua.
Ilinga. See Culli.
Imaré. *; R. Taquari, Mato Grosso; +.
Imató. Botocudo; R. Doce; +.
Imbaya. See Cara.
Imboré ~ Amboré. Southern Kamakan; R. Gongoi sources, Bahia; +.
Imburú. Botocudo; R. Jequitinhonha and R. Doce; +.
Imihitä ~ Emejeite. Bora; R. Jacaré.
Imono. See Tunacho.
Impetineri. See Amahuaca.
Ina. *; R. Paranaíba, Mato Grosso; +.
Inabishana. See Uainumá.
Iñacoré. See Southern Kaingán.
Iñajurupé. *; Gracioso mission, Goiás; +.
Iñamum. Kiriri; Inhamum Island, R. São Francisco, Pernambuco; +.
Inao. See Guinau.
Inapari ~ Mashco Piro. Pre-Andine Arawak; between R. Amigo and R. Tacutimani, Madre de Dios; perhaps +.
Indama ~ Ambargasta. Diaguit; N. of Salinas Grandes, Santiago del Estero; +.
Inga. See Quechua.
Ingahiva. See Nhengahiba.
Ingain ~ Tain. Southern Kaingán; Misiones province, Argentina; +.
Ingano. See Quechua.
Ingaricó. Pemón; N. of Mount Roroima, border area of Brazil and Venezuela.
Ingarüne. Chiquena; R. Panemá sources and tributaries.
Inkata. Quechua; R. Huallaga near Yurimagua, Loreto.
Iñuru. See Shapra.
Ipapiza. See Hichachapa.
Ipëca ~ Kumada-mínanei ~ Baniva de rio Içana. Ipéca; near San Pedro, on R. Içana, border area of Brazil and Colombia.
Ipoteuate. Kawahyb; R. Gi-Paraná.
Ipuricoto. See Taurepän.

Ipurina ~ Apurimã ~ Kangiti. Impurina; R. Sepatiní mouth to R. Yaco mouth, along R. Purus, Amazonas.

Iquito ~ Akenóini ~ Amacacore ~ Quiturran. Záparo; R. Amazon near Iquitos, Loreto, Peru.

Iraamráire ~ Meibenokre ~ Mekubengokrä ~ Cayapó do rio Pau d'arco. Kayapó; R. Pau d'arco and R. Arraida, Pará; probably +.

Iranshe ~ Iranché ~ Münkü. Classification disputed: Mason listed Iranché under Paressi, one of five main groups of South Arawakan; in 1942 M. Schmidt said that Iranshe is not Arawakan, and this determination was accepted by Loukotka (1968); right bank of R. Cravari, Mato Grosso, Brazil.

Irapa. Karaib Motilon; E. of Shiquimus.

Ira-tapuya. See Mapanai.

Iroca. Karaib Motilon; R. Casacará, Magdalena.

Irrá. Chocó stock; R. Upirama mouth, Caldas.

Iruri. *; between R. Aripuanã and R. Maiçí on R. Madeira right bank, Amazonas; +.

Isabaco. See Betoi.

Iscuandé. Barbácoa; R. Iscuandé, +.

Ishirá. See Ebidoso.

Ishkariyána. See Hishcariana.

Isiama ~ Ydiama. Tacana; R. Unduma and around Ydiama.

Isistiné. Lule; R. Salado near San Juan de Valbuena, Chaco; +.

Itañá ~ Baturité. Tarairiú; Serra de Baturité, Ceará; +.

Itatin. Guarani; S. of R. Apa, Paraguay; later, on R. Brilhante, Mato Grosso, Brazil; a few families (1968).

Itene ~ Moré. Chapacura; R. Mamoré, R. Azul, and R. Guaporé, Beni, Bolivia.

Itipuna. *; between R. Juraí and R. Juruá; +.

Itoehebe. See Parintintin.

Itogapúc ~ Ntogapyo. Itogapúc; R. Machadinho, Mato Grosso; perhaps +.

Itonama ~ Machoto. Isolated language; R. Itonama and Lake Itonama, Beni.

Itoreauhip. Capacura; between R. Azul and R. Guaporé.

Itoto. See Ocanopán.

Ituarupa. See Urupa.

Itucá ~ Cuacá. *; Serra Negra, Pernambuco. Language extinct, replaced by Portuguese.

Itucale ~ Simacu ~ Oruarina ~ Urariña ~ Arucuaya ~ Chambira ~ Singacuchusca. Isolated language; R. Chambira, Loreto, Peru; a few families (1968).

Itutan. Western Karaib; lower R. Casipore and Serra Lombard, Amapá; +.

Iuruty-tapuyo. See Patsoca.

Ivitiiguá. See Yvytyiguá.

Ivitorocái. See Amhó.

Ixignor. See Auishiri.

Iyäine ~ Kumandene ~ Yurupary-tapuya. Tariana; N. of Tarianas; +. Language replaced by Tucano.

Izaneni. See Adzáneni.

Izoceño. See Chané.

Izozo ~ Chané. Chiriguano; R. Itiyuro, Campo y Durán, and R. Parepetí, Chaco.

Kaapor ~ Urubú ~ Gavião. Northern Tupi; R. Tuiassú, R. Guama, and R. Gurupi, Maranhão; perhaps +.

Kabishiana. Macuráp; between R. Verde and R. Corumbiara, Rondônia.

Kabixi. Chapacura; between R. Prêto and R. São Miguel; perhaps +.

Kâbô. Mosquito; coast of Nicaragua.

Kadekili-dyapa. See Tawari.

Kadiueo. See Caduveo.

Kaduveo. See Caduveo.

Kadyrukré. See Kaingán.

Kaguan. *; Santiago Sánchez mission, Corrientes, Argentina; +.

Kahuapana. See Cahuapana.

Káimö. See Caimito.

Kaingán ~ Caingang ~ Camé ~ Taven ~ Kaingygn ~ Coroado ~ Kadyrukré. Northern Kaingán; Central Kaingán between R. Tiquié and R. Ivaí, Paraná, Brazil; Southern Kaingán ~ Iñacoré, around Nonohag and Cáceres, Rio Grande do Sul; Eastern Kaingán, q.v.; and Northern Kaingán, R. Tietê, São Paulo, +, form one of four groups listed by Mason. Though the classification of this language is disputed, Greenberg (1959) sees it in Macro-Ge.

Kainguá ~ Painguá ~ Montese. Guarani; R. Jejui, Paraguay, and R. Igatimí and R. Aracaí, Paraná.

Kaingygn. See Kaingán.

Kaiotugui ~ Menaie. Lengua; R. Gonzales, Paraguay.

Kalapalo ~ Apalaquiri. Xingú; Kalapalo village, R. Culuene.

Kaliána ~ Calianá ~ Sapé. Isolated language for Loukotka but Macro-Tucanoan (in Andean-Equatorial) for Greenberg (1959); R. Paraua, Bolivar, Venezuela.

Kalihóna. See Carijona.

Kaliña. See Caraib.

Kalkuama. See Atanque.

Kamakán ~ Ezeshio. Southern Kamakan; R. Pardo, R. Contas, and R. Ilheos, Bahia; +.

Kamayurá ~ Camayura. Kamayurá; R. Ferro, Xingú basin, Mato Grosso.

Kamsá. See Sebondoy.

Kamurú. Kiriri; R. Pardo and Pedra Branca; +. Survivors on R. Gongoí speak Portuguese.

Kanakateyé. Timbirá; R. Farinha, Maranhão; +.

Kandoshi. See Murato.

Kangiti. See Ipurina.

Kaniwa. See Cubeo.

Kano:e. See Capixana.

Kanu:a ~ Koaratira ~ Canoê. Macuráp; middle R. Verde and valley of R. Apidia, Rondônia.

Kapiekran. Krao; R. Balsas, Maranhão; +.

Kapité-mínanei ~ Coatí-tapuya. Ipéca; R. Içana sources, Vaupés territory, Colombia.

Kaposho ~ Capoxo. Western Mashakali; R. Arassuaí; +.

Karaho ~ Carauau. Timbirá; Serra do Estrondo, Goiás; +.

Karaib. Spelling used by Loukotka for Carib or Cariban, a stock given by Mason in three geographical rather than linguistic groups, Northern, Southern, and Northwestern, the latter including Chocoan. Greenberg (1959) has Carib, including Pimenticra and Palmela, as a branch of Macro-Carib and Chocó as belonging in Paezan of Macro-Chibchan. For a list of tribes and review of classifications, including that of Landar of Cariban as Hokan, see Landar (1968), pp. 241–47.

Karajá. Karajá; middle R. Araguaia, Goiás; later only N. Bananal Island.

Karákatajé. Timbirá; S. of Kreapimkatajés of middle R. Grajaú; +.

Karani. See Guaraní.

Karawatana. See Buhágana.

Kareluta. See Cautarie.

Karib. See Caraib.

Karibe-Kuna. See Cuna.

Karime ~ Shauari. Waica; R. Caratirimani, Rio Branco, Brazil.

Karipuere. See Caripurá.

Kariri ~ Quipea ~ Cariri. Kiriri; Serra dos Velhos, Paraíba; later, Missão Nova, Missão Velha, Milagres, Crato, and other missions in states of Paraíba, Pernambuco and Ceará. Language extinct, replaced by Portuguese.

Kiriri de Mirandela. See Katembri.

Karraim ~ Collaga. Guaicuru; R. Pilcomayo near Paso de las Tobas, Chaco, Argentina.

Kárro. Ipéca; R. Puitaná, Amazonas.

Kaskihá ~ Guaná de Chaco. Lengua; R. Salado, Paraguay.

Katágua. Central Zé; R. Jequirica, Minas Gerais; +.

Katapolitani ~ Acayaca ~ Cadaupuritani. Baré; R. Içana village of Tunuhy, Brazil.

Katawian. See Parucoto.

Katawishi. See Catauxi.

Katembri ~ Catrimbi ~ Kariri de Mirandela. Isolated language; Saco dos Morcegos mission; later, Mirandela, Bahia.

Katukina. See Catuquina.

Káua-tapuya. See Máulieni.

Kaueskar ~ Aksanás. Aksanás; along the coast of Chile from Gulf of Penas to Concepción Channel.

Kaugia. See Cágaba.

Kawahíwa. See Kawahyb.

Kawahyb ~ Cabahyba ~ Kawahiwa. Southern Tupi; W. of upper R. Tocantins; later, R. Marmelos and R. Gi-Paraná, Pará.

Kawakawa. See Cauacaua.

Kawki. See Cauqui.

Kaxiuâna. See Cachuena.

Kayabí ~ Parua. Southern Tupi; lower R. Verde and R. Paranatina.

Kayamó. See Xavante.

Kayapó ~ Ibirayára. Kayapó; interior of Goiás; later, between R. Tapajoz and R. Araguaia, Pará. Dialects listed by Loukotka are Iraamráire, Gorotiré, Chikrí, Duludi, Kuben-Kran-Keñ, Dzyoré, Purucaru, Metoíre, Kruatire, Krinkatíre, Kren-Akárore, Mek-kran-noty, Kradahó and Ushikrin.

Kayarára. See Tawari.

Kayuishana. See Cauishana.

Kenpokatajé. Timbirá; R. Manuel Alves Grande to R. Manuel Alves Pequeño; +.

Kepkeriwat ~ Quepi-quiri-uate. Kepkeriwat; R. Pimenta Bueno right bank.

Keseruma. Macusi; R. Tacutú.

Klechuwa. See Quechua.

Kiapüre ~ Quiapyre. *; R. Mequéns, Rondônia; +.

Kilmaharats. See Kilyetwaiwo.

Kilyetwaiwo ~ Kilmaharats ~ Toba. Lengua; R. Mosquito, Paraguay and near Puerto Casado, Paraguay; +.

Kiriri ~ Cariri ~ Kariri ~ Kairiri ~ Cairiri ~ Kayriri ~ Kirirí ~ Cayriri. An independent stock for Mason and Loukotka, the group has been called Cariban by Gillin in 1940 and Equatorial by Greenberg (1959).

Kiriri ~ Dzubucua ~ Quiriri. Kiriri; R. São Francisco islands near Cabrobó, Pernambuco; +.

Koaiá ~ Quaiá. Isolated language; R. Pimenta Bueno left bank and on Igarapé São Pedro.

Koaiker. See Cuaiquer.

Koaratíra. See Kanu:a.

Kobéua. See Cubeo.

Köggaba. See Cágaba.

Koghi. See Cágaba.

Kokakañú. See Siona.

Kokakôre. *; R. Tocantins, Mato Grosso; +.

Kokozú ~ Uaindze ~ Ualixere. Central Nambikwára; R. 12 de outobro, left bank.

Kólö. See Curina.

Komiuveido. See Uitoto.

Komlék ~ Toba de Bolivia. Guaicuru; near Fortín Orbigny and Fortin Creveaux, Gran Chaco, Bolivia.

Komokare. *; Goiás, exact location unknown.

Kongore: Central Nambikwára; R. Buriti, Mato Grosso.

Koréá. See Arapaso.

Koróge. *; R. Pogúbe, Mato Grosso; +.

Koropó. Western Puri; R. Pomba, Minas Gerais and Rio de Janeiro states, +.

Koshurái. *; lower R. Jiparanã, Amazonas.

Kotédia. See Uanána.

Kotogéo ~ Cotoguéo ~ Ocotegueguo. Guaicuru; R. Branco sources, Mato Grosso; +.

Kotsuñ. See Uro.

Kozarini ~ Parecí-Cabixi. Paresí; R. Juruena, R. Burití, R. Papagaio, R. Verde, R. Guaporé, R. Jaurú, R. Cabaçal, and R. Júba, Mato Grosso.

Kradahó ~ Gradaú. Kayapó; between R. Sororó and R. Araguaia, Pará; perhaps +.

Krahó ~ Krao. Krao; between R. Balsas and R. Macapá, and in Serra das Alpercatas, Maranhão.

Kraik-mús. See Krekmun.

Kreapimkatajé ~ Krepúnkateye. Timbirá; middle R. Grajaú.

Krekmum ~ Kraik-mús. Botocudo; R. Jequitinhonha right shore, Minas Gerais; +.

Kren-Akárore. Kayapó; Mato Grosso.

Krenjé. Timbirá; R. Gurupi sources.

Krenkatajé ~ Canella. Timbirá; Suridade, R. Alpercata; +.

Krepúnkateye. See Kreapimkatajé.

Krikatajé. See Krikati.

Krikati ~ Krikatajé. Krao; between R. Grajaú and R. Tocantins to R. Pindaré sources, Maranhão.

Krinkatíre. Kayapó; Mato Grosso.

Krixá. Eastern Zé; between R. Paracatú and R. Urucuia, São Marcos valley, Minas Gerais; +.

Kruatire. Kayapó; R. Liberdade right bank, Pará.

Kuben-Kran-Keñ. Kayapo; Ambé near Altamira, Pará.

Kueretú. See Coretu.
Kuikutl ~ Guicurú ~ Cuicuro. Xingú; Cuicuro village, R. Culuene.
Kukoekamekran. Timbira; lower R. Grajaú, Maranhão; +.
Kukura. Isolated language; middle R. Verde, Mato Grosso; +.
Kulina. See Curina.
Kumada-mínanei. See Ipéca.
Kumaná ~ Cautario. Chapacura; between R. Guaporé and R. Cautario, Rondônia.
Kumanasho ~ Cumanaxo. Western Mashakali; R. Suassuí Grande, Minas Gerais; later, R. Gravatá sources, Bahia; +.
Kumandene. See Lyäine.
Kumayena. See Ocomayana.
Kunuhana. See Cunuaná.
Kupẽ-rob. See Tapirauha.
Kuruáya ~ Caravare ~ Curivere ~ Guahuara ~ Curuapa. Mundurucú; R. Curua; perhaps +.
Kurukurú. See Paumarí.
Kurukwá. See Tapieté.
Kurumro. *; Chaco, Paraguay.
Kuruparia. See Campa.
Kururu. *; R. Carinhanha, Mato Grosso; +.
Kurushikiana. See Curasicana.
Kushichinerí ~ Cushitineri. Pre-Andine Arawak; R. Curumaha, Acre.
Kushiita. Yupua; R. Apoporis mouth, Amazonas, Brazil; perhaps +.
Kustenau. Waurá; R. Jatobá and R. Batoví, Mato Grosso.
Kutasho ~ Cotoxo ~ Catathoy. Southern Kamakan; R. Contas and R. Pardo region; +.
Laant. See Guarañoca.
Lache. Chibcha; R. Chicamocha and Sierra de Chita, Boyaca; +.
Lachira. See Chira.
Laconde:. Northern Nambikwára; R. Castanho (or Roosevelt) right bank.
Laipisi. Northern Zamuco; R. San Rafael.
Lama ~ Lamista. Munichi; R. Moyobamba; +.
Lamano. Quechua; R. Mayo, San Martín.
Lambi. *; R. São Miguel and R. Branco region, Rondônia; +.
Lamista. See Lama.
Lampa. *; R. Pativilca, Ancash; +.
Lañagashik. Guaicuru; R. Pilcomayo near mouth, Formosa territory; +.
Lanapsua. See Sanapaná.
Lapachu. See Apolista.
Lapalapa. See Leco.
Lapuna. See Puná.

Larecaja. Aymara; city of Larecaja, La Paz.

Lari. See Bribri.

Latacunga. See Panzaleo.

Layano. See Guaná.

Leco ~ Lapalapa ~ Ateniano. Isolated language; R. Yuyo, R. Mapiri, R. Tipuani and R. Beni, La Paz, Bolivia; a few speakers (1968).

Lengua ~ Enslet ~ Paisepto ~ Gekoinhalaák ~ Einslet ~ Cocoloth. Lengua; between R. Araguay-gúazú and R. Verde, Chaco, Paraguay.

Lican antai. See Atacama.

Lichagotegodí ~ Xaguetío. Guaicuru; lower R. Apa; +.

Lilei. See Enimaga.

Lili. Yurimangui; around Cali; +.

Limoncocha. Ecuadorian Lowland Quichua; Limoncocha, lower R. Napo, Ecuador. [The spelling Quichua is preferred for Ecuadorian Quechua.]

Lingoa geral. See Nheéngatu.

Lipe ~ Olipe. Atacama; S. of Salar de Uyuni, Potosí, Bolivia; +.

Llameo. See Yameo.

Llamish. *; Lima department, Cordillera de Huantan; +.

Llepa. See Pinche.

Lobatera. Karaib Motilon; at Iobatera, Táchira; +.

Locono. See Arawak.

Lolaca. Betoi; R. Chitage and R. Arauca confluence; +.

Lôpo ~ Rôpo. *; Serra de Abrecampo, Minas Gerais; +.

Lorenzo. See Amoishe.

Loushiru. See Otuque.

Lucaya. Arawak; Bahamas Islands; +.

Luccumi. See Arawak.

Lule. Lule; R. Salado and R. Sali and near San Esteban de Miraflores, Chaco, Argentina; +.

Lupaca. Aymara; Lake Titicaca, Peru and Bolivia.

Maba. Huari; R. Guajejú, Brazil; +.

Mabenaro. Tacana; R. Manuripi.

Macaguaje ~ Encabellado ~ Siona ~ Sioni. Western Tucano; Loukotka noted a few families for R. Caucaya and R. Mecaya, and around Puerto Restrepo; there were two villages, in 1961, El Tablero and El Hacha, 15 and 25 miles down the Putumayo from R. San Miguel, with Macaguaje, Cofan and Witoto residents.

Macamasu. *; a N.E. Paleo-American area language, exact location unknown; +.

Macarú. *; Brejo dos Padres village; +. A few survivors speak Portuguese (1968).

Machaca. See Bintucua.

Machicui. See Mascoy.

Machiganga ~ Ugunichire ~ Mashigango. Pre-Andine Arawak; R. Paucartambo, R. Urubamba, R. Apurimac, R. Mantaro, Cuzco.
Machiringa. Pre-Andine Arawak; R. Ene and R. Apurimac.
Machoto. See Itonama.
Maco. Eastern Piaroa; R. Cunucunuma and R. Ventuari, Amazonas.
Macoa. Karib Motilon; R. Negro and R. Yasa, Zulia.
Macomita. Vilela; W. of R. Juramento, Santiago del Estero, Argentina; +.
Maconcuji. Botocudo; near Santa Clara do Mucuri; +.
Macu. Ambiguous term used by Loukotka (1968) for two stocks, No. 52, Máku, which Mason refers to as Macuan, supplying synonyms Macu ~ Mahku ~ Sope, and No. 86, Makú ~ Macú, with four subgroups, one of which is represented by Puináve. See Macuan in the Index of Classifications above. Mason locates the Macu of his Macuan stock on R. Uraricoera but Loukotka locates them elsewhere: see Máku below.
Macuani. *; R. Oiapoque, Amapá territory; +.
Macuarê. *; R. Pimenta Bueno, left bank, Rondônia.
Macuja. *; R. Poré, Amazonas.
Macuma. Jíbaro; Ecuador.
Macuna. Sära; R. Apoporis mouth, Colombia.
Macuráp. Macuráp; R. Colorado sources, Rondônia.
Macurendá. See Mocoreta.
Macuruné. *; R. Mucunis, Minas Gerais; +.
Macusi ~ Makushí. Macusi; R. Rupununi, Guyana, and R. Tacutú sources, middle R. Branco, territory of Rio Branco, Brazil.
Madiha. Arawa; R. Erú near Bom Jardim, Amazonas.
Magach. See Agaz.
Magdaleno. See Mosetene.
Mage. Yuracare; Bolivia; +.
Mague. See Mawé.
Mahibarez. See Parecí.
Mahoma ~ Hohoma. Guaicuru; R. Bermejo near Laguna Blanca, Argentina; +.
Mahotoyana. Carijona; R. Macaya, Vaupés.
Maiba ~ Amaygua. Otomac; between R. Capanaparo and R. Cunaviche; +.
Maimbari. See Parecí.
Maipuridjana. Trio; R. Sipaliwini, Dutch Guiana.
Mairajiqui. *; Bahia de Todos os Santos, Bahia; +.
Maje. See Camana.
Majigua. Tinigua; R. Ariari, Meta; +.
Majubim. Kawahyb; R. Gi-Paraná and R. Pimenta Bueno confluence.
Makamekran ~ Pepuxi. Timbirá; R. Manuel Alves Pequeño; +.
Makirí, Southern Tupi; R. São Manoel mouth.

Makká ~ Nimacá ~ Toósle ~ Towothli ~ Etaboslé. Mataco; R. Montelindo and R. Confuso sources, Chaco, Paraguay.

Makoni. Western Mashakali; R. Caravelas and near Alto dos Bois; perhaps +.

Makú. Loukotka (1968) assigns to Makú, his stock No. 86, (1) Western Makú, with one language, used by members of a tribe subjected by Tucano tribes, (2) Makú of independent tribes, (3) Central Makú, and (4) Northern Makú, with one language, Puináve. Tax (1960) charts Macu of Brazil and Colombia as Macuan and Puinave of Colombia as Puinave, both subfamilies being in the Puinavean family of the Macro-Tucanoan stock in Greenberg's Andean-Equatorial phylum.

Máku. Isolated language; confluence of R. Parima (or Uatatás) and R. Auari, frontier areas of Brazil and Venezuela.

Makushí. See Macusi.

Malaba. Barbácoa; R. Mataja; +.

Malacato. Jíbaro; Piedras, El Oro, Ecuador; +.

Malacaxi. Western Mashakali; between Urupuca and Malacaheta; +.

Malali. Southern Mashakali; R. Suassuí Pequeño and Serra Redonda, Minas Gerais; +.

Malbalá. Western Mataco; R. Valbuena near Fortín San Fernando; +.

Malla. See Sindagua.

Malonde:. Western Nambikwára; Mato Grosso, exact location unknown.

Malquesi. *; Laguna Porongos W. shore, Córdoba, Argentina; +.

Mâm ~ Cueta. Mosquito; R. Coco left bank, Honduras.

Mamayaná. Pará; S. of R. Anapú mouth; +.

Mamori. *; R. Cunhuá.

Manabi ~ Manta. Northern Chimu; Manabí province; +.

Manajé ~ Ararandeuára. Northern Tupi; R. Bajarú sources and R. Ararandéua and R. Mojú, Maranhão.

Manamabobo. Northern Pano; R. Pachitea; +.

Manáo ~ Oremanao ~ Manoa. Manáo; at Manáus on R. Negro, Amazonas, Brazil; +.

Manare. Chibcha; R. Manare.

Manasi. Chiquito; San Francisco Xavier and Concepción missions, Santa Cruz, Bolivia; +.

Manastara. Karaib Motilon; R. Becerril, Zulia.

Manaure. Karaïb Motilon; lower R. La Paz left bank, Magdalena.

Manava. See Cháma.

Manaxo ~ Amanaye. Northern Tupi; lower R. Mearim near São Bento, Maranhão. +.

Manchineri. Piro; R. Acre and R. Iaco, about 200 miles E. of the Piro at Acre, Brazil.

Mandauáca ~ Maldavaca. Mandauáca; R. Pasimoni, R. Capabury, and R. Baria, Amazonas, Venezuela.
Mandimbóia. Central Zé (?); R. Sapucai-guasú and R. Verde, Minas Gerais.
Mandingo. See Cuna.
Mánekenkn ~ Haush. Patagon; extreme E. Tierra del Fuego; +.
Manesono ~ Mopeseano. *; San Francisco Borja mission, Beni, Bolivia; +.
Maneteneri. Pre-Andine Arawak; R. Aracá, R. Purus, R. Aquiri and R. Caspatá, Acre; +.
Mangaló ~ Mongoyo ~ Monshoko. Southern Kamakan; lower R. Pardo near frontier of Minas Gerais and Bahia states; +.
Mangeroma. See Tucundiapa.
Maniba ~ Camaniba. Caquetio; middle R. Guaviare, Vaupés, Colombia.
Manipo. Pijao; R. La Plata mouth; +.
Manitsauá ~ Mantizula. Yuruna; one village, R. Manitsau-missú, tributary of R. Xingú.
Manoa. See Manáo.
Manoutas. See Mayna.
Mansiño. See Yuracare.
Manta. See Manabi.
Mantaro. See Huancayo.
Mantizula. See Manitsauá.
Manyã. See Menien.
Maotityan. See Mapidian.
Mapanai ~ Ira-tapuya. Baré; R. Içana near Cachoeira Yandú, Amazonas.
Maparina. Chamicuro; lower R. Ucayali and Santiago mission; +.
Mape. Chibcha Motilon; R. Agua Blanca and R. Catatumbo, Zulia, Venezuela.
Mapidian ~ Maotityan. Mapidian; R. Apiniwau sources, Guyana; perhaps +.
Mapoxo. Western Mashakali; R. Suassuí Grande; +.
Mapoyo ~ Nepoyo. Mapoyo; between R. Paruaza and R. Suapure, Bolivar, Venezuela.
Mapruan. Marawan; R. Oiac, Amapá; +.
Mapua. Pará; Marajó Island, R. Mapuá; +.
Mapuche ~ Araucano ~ Auca. Mapuche; R. Bío-Bío to R. Toltén, Chile; later, in Bío-Bío, Maule, Arauco, Cautin, Nuble and other Chilean provinces.
Maquinuca. Eastern Mashakali; R. Jequitinhonha near Salto Grande; +.
Maquiritaré. See Decuána.
Maraca. Karaib Motilon; R. Machique sources and R. Maraca, Magdalena.
Maracá. Botocudo; Serra do Espinhaço, Bahia; +.
Maracáni. See Tamupasa.
Maracano. *; C. Maracá Island, Rio Branco, Brazil.
Marachó. Chiquena; middle R. Cuminá.

Maragua. See Marawa.
Maraguá. Mawé; R. Amazon right bank S. of Condurís; +.
Marahan. Independent Maku; R. Marahan, Amazonas, Brazil.
Maraon. See Marawan.
Marapaña. *; R. Uaimberê right bank, above R. Pimenta Bueno, Rondônia.
Marawa ~ Maragua. Marawa; between R. Juraí and R. Juruá in the nineteenth century; later, one village, R. Juruá mouth, Amazonas.
Marawan ~ Maraon. Marawan; R. Curipi and R. Oiapoque, Amapá territory.
Marêyo. See Emerillon.
Margaya. See Tupiniquin.
Mariaté ~ Muriaté. Uainumá; R. Iça mouth; +.
Mariche. Tamanaco; Baruta valley, Miranda; +.
Maricoxi. *; R. Branco sources, Rondônia; +.
Maricupi. *; lower R. Montoura, Amapá; +.
Mariman. *; R. Riozinho, tributary of R. Cunhuá.
Marináwa. Northern Pano; R. Furnaya, Loreto.
Maripá. *; R. Tonantins, Amazonas; +.
Mariusa. Uarao; Macareo and Cocuina branches, R. Orinoco delta.
Maromoni. Tupi; São Bernabé mission, Rio de Janeiro state.
Maropa. Tacana; lake Rogoaguado, Beni; probably +.
Maruba ~ Maxuruna ~ Mayoruna ~ Pelado ~ Dallus. Northern Pano; R. Maruba and R. Jandiatuba, Amazonas.
Maruquevene. *; R. Auatí-paraná mouth to R. Japurá mouth; +.
Masa. *; Santiago Sánchez mission; +.
Masaca ~ Aicana. Huari; R. Corumbiara left bank.
Masacará. Northern Kamakan; S. of Juázeiro and in Saco dos Morcegos mission, Bahia; +.
Masamae ~ Mazan ~ Parara. Yagua; R. Mazan, Loreto.
Masarari. *; S. of R. Juraí, Amazonas; +.
Masaya. *; R. Caguán sources, N. of Guaques; +.
Mascoy ~ Cabanatit ~ Machicui ~ Eenslit. Lengua; S. of R. Confuso, Paraguay; a women's language, the men's counterpart being Toba.
Mashakali ~ Mashacari ~ Maxacari. Western Mashakali; R. Jucurucú and R. Marucí, Minas Gerais; later, R. Belmonte; +.
Mashco ~ Sirineiri ~ Moeno. Pre-Andine Arawak; R. Pilcopata, Madre de Dios, Peru. Dialects are identified by Wistrand (1971), p. 109, as Mashco, Huachpairi and Toyeri.
Mashco Piro. See Inapari.
Mashigango. See Mashiganga.
Mashubi. Yabutí; R. Mequéns, Rondônia; perhaps +.
Masinga. Arhuaco; R. Bonda; +.

Maspo. Northern Pano; R. Maniparboro and R. Taco; +.

Mastele. Barbácoa; R. Guaitara left bank near mouth, Nariño; +.

Mastináhua. Northern Pano; R. Purus.

Mataco ~ Mataguayo. Western Mataco; R. Bermejo near Embarcación, Puerto Irigoyen and Las Lomitas, Salta, Argentina.

Matagalpa ~ Chontal ~ Populuca. Matagalpa; R. Olama to R. Tumo, Nicaragua; +.

Mataguayo. See Mataco.

Matanawí ~ Mitandu ~ Moutoniway. Matanawí; R. Madeirinha and R. Castanha, Amazonas; probably +.

Matapí. Yakúna; near Campoamor, Amazonas.

Matará ~ Amulalá. Lule; near Matará, R. Salado; +.

Mataua. Chapacura; W. part of R. Cautario.

Mateiros. See Sakamekran.

Matipú ~ Matipuhy. Xingú; Matipú village, R. Curisevú right bank.

Matipuhy. See Matipú.

Matisana. See Wapishana.

Matuana. See Bonda.

Máua. See Umáua.

Mauhé. See Mawé.

Mauitsi. Pemón; R. Paragua sources; +.

Máulieni ~ Káua-tapuya. Baré R. Aiarí, Amazonas.

Mawakwa. Mapidian; R. Mavaca, Venezuela; +.

Mawé ~ Mauhé ~ Mague. Mawé; R. Tracuá, R. Arichi, R. Arapium, R. Maué-assú, R. Tapajós and R. Mataura, Pará; later R. Uicurapá.

Maxacari. See Mashakali.

Maxiena ~ Ticomeri. *; Mojos Plains, W. of Trinidad mission, Beni, Bolivia; +.

Maxuruna. See Maruba.

Mayasquer. Barbácoa; Mayasquer and Pindical, Carchi, Ecuador. Language extinct, replaced by Quechua.

Mayé. Western Karaib; R. Casipore, Amapá, Brazil; +.

Mayna ~ Rimachu. Mayna; area of R. Pastaza, R. Chambira and R. Nucuray, Loreto, Peru. Language extinct, replaced by Quechua, or by Spanish.

Mayongcong. See Yecuaná.

Mayoruna. See Moríque.

Maypure. Maypure; Maipures, Vichada, Colombia. Language extinct, replaced by Spanish.

Mayu. *; R. Jaquirana, tributary of R. Javari, Amazonas.

Mazan. See Masamae.

Mbayá. See Guaicuru.

Mbyhá ~ Jeguaká ~ Tenondé ~ Bwihá ~ Caiua ~ Cahygua. Guarani; R. Monday, Paraguay.

Meamuyna. See Bora.

Mehín. Timbirá; Araraparituya village, R. Gurupi right bank, Maranhão; perhaps +.

Mehináku ~ Meinacu ~ Mináko. Waurá; between R. Curisevú and R. Botouí.

Meibenokre. See Iraamráire.

Meinacu. See Mehináku.

Meitajé. Timbirá; N.E. of Itupiranga, Maranhão; a few speakers (1968).

Mejepure. Maquiritaré; lower R. Ventuari left bank; +.

Mek-kran-noty. Kayapó; R. Iriri, Pará.

Mekmek. Botocudo; R. Lages; +.

Mekubengokrä. See Iraamraíre.

Melchora. Rama; R. San Juan Melchoras, Nicaragua; +.

Menacho. See Monoxo.

Menaie. See Kaiotugui.

Menejou. *; middle R. Jari, Amapá; +.

Menien ~ Manyã. Southern Kamakan; R. Jequitinhonha sources; +.

Menımehe. Yahuna; R. Caquetá and R. Mirití-paraná mouths.

Menren ~ Gaviões ~ Augutjé. Timbirá; between R. Tocantins and R. Surubiú, Pará.

Mepene. Guaicuru; Corrientes province, Argentina; +.

Mepuri. *; S. of Barés, middle R. Negro, Amazonas; +.

Mequen. See Guaratégaja.

Meregoto. Tamanaco; Lake Valencia W. shore, Aragua; +.

Merrime. See Remkokamekran.

Mersiou. Western Karaib; R. Aua, R. Inini and R. Aratye; +.

Metotíre ~ Chukahamai. Kayapó; R. Culuene near Falls of Von Martius, and R. Jarina, Mato Grosso; a few speakers (1968).

Mialat. Southern Tupi; middle R. Machado.

Miarigois. See Tobajara.

Micay ~ Guangui. Chocó stock; R. Micay, Cauca.

Michilenge ~ Puntano. Huarpe; Conlara valley, San Luiz; +.

Miguelheno. See Uómo.

Migurí. Timote; village of Acequias; +.

Millcayac. Huarpe; San Luiz, Argentina; +.

Mináko. See Mehináku.

Miñan-yirugn. Botocudo; between R. Doce and R. São Mateo; later, Posto Pancas, Espirito Santo; a few speakers (1968).

Miñari. Tarairiú; R. Apodí valley, Rio Grande do Norte; +.

Minhahá. *; R. Paranaiuba, Mato Grosso; +.
Minuan. See Guenoa.
Miquirá ~ Shuensampi. Kahuapana; one village on R. Paranapura; +.
Miraña. See Bora.
Miraña-Carapana-tapuyo. See Andoquero.
Miranha Oira Assú-tapuya. See Bora.
Mirapác. See Morupak.
Mìrripú. Timote; village of El Morro; +.
Mishara. See Yagua.
Mishorca. Karaib Motilon; R. Tucuco sources near Pariris.
Mískito. See Mosquito.
Mitandua. See Matanawí.
Mitua. See Piapoco.
Miyuse. Karaib Motilon; R. Tucani and R. Mucujepe, Mérida; +.
Mizque. *; R. Mizque, Cochabamba, Bolivia. Language extinct, replaced by Quechua.
Moakañi. Mashakali; R. Panado near Conceição; later R. Caravelas; +.
Mobima ~ Moyma ~ Movime. Mobima; R. Rapulo, R. Yacumá and R. Mamoré, Beni, Bolivia.
Mocalingasta. See Calian.
Mocana. Malibú; E. of Cartagena, Bolivar, Venezuela; +.
Mochica. See Chimú.
Mochica. Chimú; coast of department of Libertad; +.
Mochobo. Northern Pano; between R. Guarimi and R. Guanie; +.
Mocoa. See Sebondoy.
Mocochí ~ Mucuchíe ~ Torondoy. Timote; Lagunillas, Mérida; +.
Mocolete. See Mocoreta.
Mocoreta ~ Macurendá ~ Mocolete. Charrua; R. Mocoreta, Entre Ríos province; +.
Mocoví ~ Amoquebit ~ Moscovítica. Guaicuru; R. Salado to R. Bermejo, Argentina; colony of Aé-garrás, near Belém Novo, Rio Grande do Sul, Brazil; later, Colonia Domingo Matchu and Quitilipí, Chaco, Argentina.
Moeno. See Mashco.
Mogosna ~ Natixana ~ Mogoznana. Guaicuru; Santiago Sánchez mission, Corrientes, Argentina; +.
Mogoznana. See Mogosna.
Moguex. Coconuco; Quisgó village and part of Silvia village.
Moheyana. *; between R. Acapú and R. Erepecurú, Pará.
Mohino. See Tiatinagua.
Moianek. See Choroti.

Mojo ~ Ignaciano ~ Morocosi. Mojo; R. Mamoré and Plains of Mojos, Beni, Bolivia.

Moluche ~ Nguluche. Mapuche; from Lake Nahuel Huapi to Limay, Argentina.

Mompox. Malibú; at Mompos, Bolivar; +.

Monachobm. See Monoxo.

Mondé. Mondé; R. Ouro, tributary of R. Pimenta Bueno, Rondônia.

Mongoyo. See Mangaló.

Monoicó. Macusi; R. Cotinga, Brazil.

Monoxo ~ Monachobm ~ Menacho. Western Mashakali; R. Itanhaen; later, R. Posto Paraguaçú, Bahia.

Monshoko. See Mangaló.

Montese. See Kainguá.

Moperecoa. See Pauserna.

Mopeseano. See Manesono.

Moquegua. *; Moquegua, Peru; +. Aymara dialect?

Moracano. See Cahuarano.

Morcote. Chibcha; R. Tocaría and village of Morcote.

Moré. See Itene.

Morcno. See Carif.

Moríque ~ Mayoruna. Moríque; R. Javarí, border of Peru and Brazil.

Moriquito. *; lower R. São Francisco, Alagoas; +.

Moriwene ~ Sucuriyú-tapuya. Baré; Seringa Upita village, R. Içana, Amazonas, Brazil.

Moro ~ Morotoco ~ Takrat ~ Coroino. Northern Zamuco; Chaco, Bolivia; once at San Juan mission.

Morocosi. See Mojo.

Morononi. Maquiritaré; R. Ventuari; +.

Morotoco. See Moro.

Morua. *; R. Japurá S. of Maruquevenes; +.

Morupak ~ Mirapác. Central Zé; between R. Jaguari and R. Sapocaiguasú, Minas Gerais; +.

Mosca. See Chibcha.

Moscovítica. See Mocoví.

Mosetene ~ Rache ~ Magdaleno ~ Muchan ~ Tucupi ~ Aparono. Mosetene; R. Quiquive and R. Bopi, Beni, Bolivia; a few speakers (1968).

Mosquito ~ Mískito. Mosquito; Caribbean coast of Nicaragua and Honduras, Central America, supposedly Macro-Chibchan.

Motilon. See Dobocubí and Yupe.

Moutoniway. See Matanawí.

Move ~ Valiente. Guaymi; R. Guaymi and Veragua Peninsula.

Movime. See Mobima.

Möxdöá ~ Carapana-tapuya. Tucano; between R. Caiary and R. Papury, Colombia.

Moxotó. Western Mashakali; R. Suassui Pequeño and R. Suassuí Grande near Peçanha; +.

Moyma. See Mobima.

Moyobamba. *; city of Moyobamba, San Martín. Language extinct, replaced by Quechua.

Muchan. See Mosetene.

Muchic. See Chimú.

Muchojeone. Mojo; El Carmen mission, Beni, Bolivia; +.

Mucuchíe. See Mocochí.

Mucutu ~ Bailadores. Timote; R. Mucuties and village of Bailadores; +.

Mudzyetíre. Pará; Igarapé Sororosinho; +.

Muellama. Barbácoa; Muellama village; +.

Muinane. Eastern Uitoto; Sejerí and Piñuna Negra villages, Amazonas, Colombia.

Muisca. See Chibcha.

Mundurucú ~ Paiquizé ~ Pari ~ Weidéñe. Mundurucú; R. Tapajós; later, R. Maué-assú and R. Urariá, Amazonas.

Munichi ~ Balsapuertiño. Munichi; Balsapuerto village, Loreto, Peru; a few families (1968).

Münkü. See Iranshe.

Muoi. Guaymi; Miranda Valley; +.

Múra. Múra; R. Manicoré and R. Mataurá; later, R. Paraná Mamorí and R. Tefé, Lake Saracó, and elsewhere, Amazonas.

Murato ~ Kandoshi ~ Canduashi ~ Roamaina. Murato; between R. Pastaza and R. Morona, Peru.

Murcielaga. See Guaque.

Mure. Chapacura; R. San Martín; +.

Muriaté. See Mariaté.

Murire ~ Bucueta ~ Boncota ~ Bogota. Guaymi; Serranía de Tabasara; a few families (1968).

Muriva. *; R. Jamachim mouth to R. Tapajós, Pará, Brazil; +.

Musitian. Diaguit; Sierra de los Llanos, La Rioja; +.

Musuraqui ~ Horihi. Northern Zamuco; R. Aguas Calientes.

Mutuan. Chiquena; lower R. Nhamundá; +.

Mutun. Botocudo; Mutum Valley, Espirito Santo; +.

Muzapa. *; near Cognomonas, in department of San Martín; +.

Muzo. Pijao; R. Carare sources and Paima Valley, Cundinamarca; +.

Nábela. See Guamaca.

Nabudib. Sanema; R. Ventuari sources, Amazonas, Venezuela.

Nacai. *; R. Aquitipi, Bahia; +.

Nacrehé. Botocudo; R. Manhuaçú sources.

Nahukwá ~ Naucuá ~ Anáukwá. Xingú; between R. Culuene and R. Curisevú.

Nakazetí. See Parintintin.

Ñakfáteitei. See Eastern Kaingán.

Naknanuk ~ Nakyananiuk. Botocudo; area of R. Jequitinhonha, R. São Mateo and R. Mucurí.

Nak-Ñapma. Botocudo; between R. Pancas and R Mutum; +.

Nakpie. See Uti Krag.

Nakporuk. Botocudo; R. Guandú right bank; +.

Nakyananiuk. See Naknanuk.

Nambikwára ~ Nhambicuara. Tax (1960) following McQuown and Greenberg shows Ge-Pano-Carib as the phylum, with Nhambicuran having three families, Nhambicuara, Pseudo-Nhambicuara, and family "c". The family Nhambicuara has Northeast Nhambicuaran with Anunze, Cocozu, Congore, and Nene (Brazil), and Southwest Nhambicuaran with Cabichi, Tagnaní, Tauite and Uaintazu (Brazil). The Pseudo-Nhambicuara family has Pseudo Nhambicuara (Brazil). Family "c" has Nhambicuara (Brazil). Loukotka (1968) has four branches: Eastern Nambikwára (Tagnaní, Tamaindé, Nene: Tarunde), Central Nambikwára (Kokozú, Anunze, Elotasu, Kongore:, Navaite, Tadutè), Western Nambikwára (Tauité, Uaintasú, Mamaindé, Uamandiri, Tauandé, Malonde:, Unetunde:, Tapóya), and Northern Nambikwára (Sabané, Jaiá, Laconde:).

Nambu. *; R. Guapay, Santa Cruz, Bolivia; +.

Namiwó. Sanema; Amazonas territory.

Naparina. Arawak; Island of Trinidad; +.

Nape. Chapacura; Lake Chitiopa; +.

Napeño. Quechua; R. Napo, Loreto, Peru.

Naperú. See Yaperú.

Napipi. Chocó stock; R. Salaqui, R. Napipi and middle R. Atrato.

Naravóto. See Naravute.

Naravute ~ Naravóto. Xingú; R. Curisevú.

Nasayuwä. Paez; village of Pitayo.

Natá. *; Parita Bay, Panama; +.

Natixana. See Mogosna.

Natú ~ Peagaxinan. Isolated language; R. Ipanema, Pernambuco; later, suburb, Cariri, Pôrto Real do Colégio, Alagoas.

Naucuá. See Nahukwá.

Nauna. *; R. Juraí S. of Marawas; +.

Naura. Pijao; N. of Muzos; +.

Nauta. See Mayna.

Navaite. Central Nambikwára; R. Dúvida, Mato Grosso.
Nawazi-Moñtji. See Chimane.
Nazca. *; R. Grande mouth, Ica; +.
Ñeéngatu. See Nheéngatu.
Nehanáwa. Northern Pano; R. Jordão, Acre.
Neimade. Western Uitoto; lower R. Yari, Caquetá, Colombia.
Neiva. Pijao; at Neiva, Huila; +.
Nene:. Eastern Nambikwára; confluence of R. Juruena and R. Juína, Mato Grosso.
Ñeozé. Chiriguano; R. Mamoré and R. Grande.
Nepnep. Botocudo; between R. São Mateo and R. Mucuri; +.
Nepoyo. See Mapoyo.
Nepuya. Arawak; E. part, Island of Trinidad.
Ngúd-Krág. See Uti Krag.
Nguluche. See Moluche.
N'gverá ~ Ngvera. Chocó stock; R. San Jorge, Antioquia.
Nheéngatu ~ Ñeéngatu ~ Niangatú ~ Lingoa geral. Tupi; R. Amazon. Used as a trade jargon or lingua franca, as well as for colonial missionary work.
Nhengahiba ~ Ingahiva. Tupi; S. Marajó Island, Pará; +.
Niangatú. See Nheéngatu.
Nigua. See Cayápa.
Nijamvo. See Peba.
Nimacá. See Makká.
Ninaquigila. See Poturero.
Nindaso. Munichi; R. Huallaga N. of Zapasos; +.
Nitaino. See Taino.
Nixináwa. Yamináua; R. Jordão, Acre.
Noanáma. See Waunana.
Nobenidze. Western Uitoto; Quebrada Peneya and Quebrada Idoromaní.
Nocadeth. *; R. Aripuanã, Amazonas.
Nocamán. Northern Pano; R. Chesco sources, Loreto.
Nocten ~ Oktenai. Western Mataco; Cordillera de Pirapo.
Nodöbö. Independent Makú; R. Jurubaxí, Amazonas, Brazil.
Noll-hína. See Cauishana.
Nolongasta. Diaguit; Chilecito Valley, La Rioja; +.
Nomatsiguenga. Campa.
Nomona. Munichi; R. Saposoa left bank; +.
Nonamá. See Waunana.
Nonuya ~ Añonolá ~ Achote. Eastern Uitoto; upper R. Igara-paraná, Loreto.
Norac ~ Norag. Western Karaib; R. Approuague, French Guiana; later, R. Anotari; +.

Norag. See Norac.

Norek. Botocudo; near Teófilo Otoni, R. Noreth; +.

Norockwajé ~ Ñurukwayé. Timbira; R. Tocantins, S. of Apinagés; perhaps +.

Norteño. Guaymi; N. coast of Panama; perhaps +.

Northern Uitoto. Western Uitoto; Puerto Boy and other villages, Caquetá, Colombia.

Notobotocudo ~ Pihtadyouai. Guarani; R. Iguasú sources and R. Uruguai sources, Santa Catarina; +. A Guaranized language.

Noyene. Eastern Karaib; R. Cuc, Pará; +.

Ntocowit. See Toba.

Ntogapyd. See Itogapúc.

Nucuini ~ Remo ~ Rheno. Northern Pano; R. Javari sources and R. Ipixuba and R. Moenalco, Amazonas.

Nulpe. Barbácoa; R. Nulpe; +.

Ñumasiara. *; R. Canamari and R. Giraparaná.

Nuqui. See Baudó.

Ñurikwayé. See Norokwajé.

Nutabé. Antioquia; San Andrés valley; +.

Oa ~ Dequaca. Záparo; R. Arrabina, tributary of R. Bobonaza; +.

Oayana. See Waiana.

Oayca. See Waica.

Ocaina ~ Ducaiya ~ Anũja. Eastern Uitoto; R. Igara-paraná, Loreto, Peru.

Ocanopán ~ Itoto. Arhuaco; at Cerro Pintado; +.

Ochozuma. See Uro.

Ochucuyana. See Tarairiú.

Ocloya. Humahuaca; R. Normente, Jujuy and near Necay; +.

Ocole. Vilela; between Lacangayá and Laguna Colma; +.

Ocomatairi. Casapare; R. Muri sources and R. San Rafael sources, Bolivar, Venezuela.

Ocomayana ~ Kumayena ~ Comayana. Trio; R. Coeroeni sources, Dutch Guiana, and R. Oronoque sources, Guyana.

Ocomesiane. Maquiritaré; R. Padamo; +.

Ocotegueguo. See Kotogéo.

Ocren. *; R. São Francisco, Bahia, near Salitre; +.

Ocro. *; R. Santa sources, Ancash; +.

Oewacu. See Auaké.

Ofaie-Chavante. See Opaie.

Oguaíva. Guarani; Mato Grosso; later, R. Paranapamena, São Paulo.

Ohoma. *; near Homa or Ohoma mission, Corrientes, Argentina; +.

Oico ~ Holcotian. Huarpe; Mendoza province in Diamante Valley; +.

Oivaneca. *; R. Tartarugal, Amapá, Brazil; +.

Ojota. Western Mataco; between R. Centa and R. Bermejo; +.
Okoshkokyéwa. Paez; village of La Peña.
Oktenai. See Nocten.
Oldwaw. See Ulua.
Olipe. See Lipe.
Olongasto. Huarpe; near Allentiacs, La Rioja; +.
Omagua ~ Campeua ~ Carari. Amazonas Tupi; R. Juruá mouth to R. Napo mouth, along R. Amazon; a few villages (1968).
Omaguaca. See Humahuaca.
Omarí. See Romarí.
Omasuyo. Aymara; La Paz province, E. of Lake Titicaca.
Ömöa. Sära; R. Tiquié sources, Colombia.
Omoampa. Vilela; from Miraflores to Ortega; +.
Omurana ~ Hunurana. Mayna; R. Nucuray, Loreto; a few speakers (1968).
Ona ~ Selknam ~ Aona. Patagon; N.E. Tierra del Fuego.
Onicoré. *; between R. Marmelos mouth and R. Manicoré mouth, Amazonas; +.
Onoto. Goajira; between Lake Maracaibo and R. Palmar, Zulia, Venezuela; +.
Onoyóro. *; R. Paranaiuba, Mato Grosso; +.
Opaie ~ Ofaie-Chavante. Isolated language; R. Nhanduí, R. Pardo and R. Ivinhema, Mato Grosso; a few speakers (1968).
Opaina. See Tanimuca.
Opinadkóm. See Arára.
Opone. Opone; R. Opone, Santander, Colombia; +.
Orari ~ Eastern Boróro ~ Orarimugodoge. Boróro; R. Madeira, R. Garças, and R. Valhas, Mato Grosso.
Orcoyan ~ Oscollan. Huarpe; S. Mendoza province; +.
Orechicano. See Curasicana.
Orejón. Term, "big ear" (from large earplugs), used ambiguously for speakers of Witoto (Uitoto), Tucano (cf. the Western Tucanoan Orejón of Johnson and Peeke (1962), p. 78, 160 speakers, 1960), and other languages. Loukotka (1968) for Orejone has Eastern Uitoto; R. Ambiyacu, Loreto, Peru; +.
Oremanao. See Manáo.
Orí. *; R. Vasa Barris and R. Itapicurú, Bahia; +.
Oristine. Lule; R. Salado; +.
Orocoto. Waiwai; R. Jatapú and R. Urubú; +.
Oromina ~ Zeremoe. Antioquia; S. of Urabá Bay, Antioquia, Colombia; +.
Oromo. See Yuracare.
Ororicó. Waiwai; upper R. Cachorrinho.
Orosi. See Viceyta.
Ortue. *; Xarayes Lagoon, Bolivia; +.
Oruarína. See Itucale.

Oscollan. See Orcoyan.
Otanavi. See Huatama.
Otecua. *; R. Sucumbio, Loreto.
Otegua. *; Huila, Colombia; +.
Otí ~ Chavante ~ Eochavante. Isolated language; R. Peixe and R. Pardo and in Campos Novos, São Paulo; +.
Otomac. Otomac; between R. Meta and R. Orinoco, and R. Cinaruco and R. Arauca, Apure, Venezuela; +. In Greenberg's classification, as in Tax (1960), Otomaco and Taparita form the Otomaco-Taparita family in the Equatorial stock of Andean Equatorial.
Otuque ~ Loushiru. Boróro; Santo Corazón mission, Chaco, Bolivia; a few speakers (1968).
Owaikománg. See Aweicoma.
Oyampi ~ Wayapí ~ Guayapi. Guiana Tupi; lower R. Xingú; later, R. Oiapoque, Amapá, French Guiana; later, R. Maroni.
Oyaricule. See Tliometesen.
Paboa. See Erulia.
Pacabuey. Malibú; Zapatoza Lagoon; +.
Pacaguara. Eastern Pano; between R. Abuña and R. Beni; probably +.
Pacahanovo ~ Uari Wayõ. Chapacura; R. Pacas Novas.
Pacanáwa. Northern Pano; R. Embira sources, Acre.
Pacarará. *; Serra Cacaréa and Serra Arapuá, Pernambuco; +.
Pacasa. Aymara; between Lake Callapain and R. Desaguadero, La Paz, Bolivia.
Pacimonari. *; lower R. Siapa, Amazonas, Venezuela; +.
Pacioca. See Tolombon.
Pacu-tapuya. See Payualiene.
Paez ~ Paisa. Paez; R. Paez, Huila.
Paguana. Amazonas Tupi; R. Cafua mouth to R. Tefé mouth, along R. Amazon; +.
Paguara. *; R. Tefé; +.
Paicone. Mojo; R. Paragua sources, Santa Cruz, Bolivia; +.
Paiguasú. Guarani; R. Curupaiña, Mato Grosso.
Paikipiranga ~ Parixi. Guiana Tupi; R. Maracá sources, Pará.
Paiquizé. See Mundurucú.
Pairindi. Charrua; from Corrientes to R. Feliciano, Entre Rios; +.
Paisa. See Paez.
Paisepto. See Lengua.
Pakidái. Samatari; R. Demeni, Rio Branco territory.
Palanc. Eastern Karaib; middle R. Yaroupi, middle R. Apima, and R. Unani, French Guiana; +.
Palänoa. Erulia; middle R. Piraparana.

Palenque. Tamanaco; between R. Tamanaco and R. Unare, Guárico; +. Also see Pantagora.

Palicur ~ Parikurú. Marawan; middle R. Calçoene and upper R. Cassipore; later, R. Urucauá, Amapá. Also on R. Oiapoque, French Guiana. Speakers are 500 (1971).

Palmela. Palmela; R. São Simão mouth, R. Guaporé, Rondônia; +.

Palta. Jíbaro; at Xoroca, Cajamarca, Peru and in Loja, Ecuador; +.

Pama ~ Pamainá. Eastern Pano; R. Caldeirão, Rondônia.

Pamana. Arawa; R. Mucuim and R. Ituxí, near Lake Agaam; probably +.

Pamari. See Paumarí.

Pamdabeque. Kahuapana; R. Paranapura and R. Aipena, Loreto; +.

Pamigua. Tinigua; San Concepción de Arauca mission, Meta; +.

Pamöá ~ Tatú-tapuyo. Tucano; R. Papury sources and on Tuyigarapé, Colombia.

Pampa. See Gennaken.

Pampam. Botocudo; R. Pampam; +.

Panahi. Tarairiú; near the Miñaris, Rio Grande do Norte.

Panamaca. Mosquito; area of R. Bocay, R. Waspuc and R. Pispis.

Pañáme. Western Mashakali; R. Suassui Poqueno, Minas Gerais; +.

Panao-simi. Quechua; R. Panáo, Huánuco.

Panáre. Panáre; R. Cuchivero sources, Bolivar, Venezuela.

Panariá. Central Zé; near Uberaba, Minas Gerais; +.

Panatahua. Lorenzo; R. Huallaga right bank between Coyumba and Monzón; perhaps +.

Panatí. Tarairiú; Serra Panatí and near Villaflor, Paraíba; +.

Panau. Northern Pano; Seringal Barão Rio Branco, Acre; a few families (1968).

Panche. Pijao; R. Fusagasuga, R. Magdalena, R. Seco, R. Villeta, R. Coella, R. Guarinó, R. Mariquita, and R. Gualí, Cundinamarca; +.

Panga. Barbácoa; near Sotomayor, Nariño; +.

Pangoa. Nomatsiguenga.

Paniquita. Paez; a few villages, including Paniquita.

Pankarurú ~ Brancararú. Isolated language; between R. Pajeú and R. Moxotó, Pernambuco; later, villages of Tacaratú and Brejo dos Padres.

Pano ~ Pánobo. Northern Pano; Contamana, R. Ucayali, Loreto, Peru.

Pánobo. See Pano.

Panpa-simi. See Santiagueño.

Pantagora ~ Palenque. Pijao; between R. San Bartolomé and R. Guarinó, Caldas, Colombia; +.

Panzaleo ~ Latacunga ~ Quito. Paez; Pichincha, Cotopaxi and Tunguragua provinces, Ecuador; +.

Pao. *; R. Pao, Monagas, Venezuela; +.

Papale. Malibú, R. Fundación; +.

Papamiän. *; R. São Simão, Rondônia.
Papamuru. See Bracamoro.
Papana. *; between R. Jequitinhonha and R. Doce, Minas Gerais; +.
Papare. Chocó stock; R. Puero and R. Sapa, Panama; +.
Papateruana. Pará; part of Tupinambarana Island, R. Amazon; +.
Papury. Western Makú; R. Papury, Vaupés, Colombia.
Paquí. See Puri.
Paquirí. See Paraitirí.
Para. See Paraujano.
Parabaiana. Western Karaib; middle R. Marouini, French Guiana; +.
Paracoto. Western Karaib; R. Araguarí mouth, Amapá and R. Mana mouth, French Guiana; +.
Paragoaru. *; R. Capó; +.
Paraguayan Chaco. *; language with unknown name, interior of Chaco, Paraguay, indexed in Loukotka (1968), p. 64, under Paraguayan Chaco.
Paraíba. *; R. Bonito, Rio de Janeiro state; +.
Paraitirí ~ Paquirí. Waica; R. Caratirimani sources, Rio Branco territory.
Parakanã. Pará; between R. Pacajá and R. Tocantins.
Paramonga. Southern Chimu; R. Fortaleza, Ancash; +.
Paraná Boá-boá. Independent Makú; R. Paraná Boá-boá, Amazonas, Brazil.
Paranawát. Kawahyb; R. Muqui mouth.
Paran-náwa. Yamináua; R. Murú, Acre.
Paraparixana. *; between R. Aninde and R. Manicoré, Amazonas; +.
Paraparucota. Pemón; between R. Cuchivero and R. Caura, Bolivar; +.
Parapicó. *; Serra Comonati, Pernambuco; +.
Parapiti. See Tapieté.
Parara. See Masamae.
Paratió ~ Prarto. Shukurú; R. Capibariba; later, in Cimbres; a few speakers (1968).
Paraucan. See Paraujano.
Paraugoaru. Chiquena; R. Capó, tributary of R. Trombetas; +.
Paraujano ~ Paraucan ~ Parawogwan ~ Para. Goajira; Lake Maracaibo, Zulia, Venezuela.
Paravilhana. See Paraviyana.
Paraviyana ~ Paravilhana. Macusi; between R. Caratirimani and R. Tacutú, Rio Branco; +.
Paravori. Samatari; R. Orinoco sources, Amazonas, Venezuela.
Parawa ~ Hon-dyapa. Southern Catuquina; R. Gregorio near Santo Amaro.
Parawogwan. See Paraujano.
Paraxim. Western Mashakali; R. Suassuí Pequeno; +.
Pareca. Mapoyo; W. of R. Cuchivero; probably +.

Parecí ~ Arití ~ Maimbari ~ Mahibarez. Paresí (Arawak); see under these dialects: Caxenití, Kozariní, Uariteré, and Waimaré.
Pareci-Cabixi. See Kozariní.
Pareni. See Yavitero.
Pari. See Mundurucú.
Pariagoto ~ Guayuno. Tamanaco; Paria peninsula, Sucre; +.
Pariana. Cauishana; middle R. Marauia; +.
Pariana. *; R. Auatí-paraná mouth, Amazonas; +.
Parikurú. See Palicur.
Parimitari. Casapare; R. Uraricoera.
Parintintin ~ Nakazetí ~ Itoehebe. Kawahyb; between R. Maiçí and Madeira, Pará.
Paripazo. See Yolo.
Pariquí. Waiwai; between R. Negro mouth and R. Uatumá mouth; +.
Parirí. Kariab Motilon; S. of R. Apon.
Parirí. Arára; R. Arataú sources, R. Jacundá sources and R. Pacajá sources, Pará; perhaps +.
Pariuaia. Southern Tupi; R. Barati sources.
Parixi. See Paikipiranga.
Pariza. Guaymi; Veragua peninsula; +.
Parua. See Kayabí.
Parucoto ~ Katawian. Waiwai; middle R. Mapuera and between sources of R. Cachorrinho and R. Acarí.
Paru-podeari. See Yaruna.
Pasain. Vilela; near Macapillo, Chaco, Argentina; +.
Pasipa. Diaguit; Vicioso Valley, Catamarca; +.
Passé ~ Pazé. Jumana; area of R. Içá, R. Japurá and R. Negro. Language extinct, replaced by Portuguese.
Pasto. Barbácoa; at Pasto, Nariño, Colombia and in Carchi province, Ecuador; +.
Patagon. Karaib Patagon; villages of Bagua, Paco and Olipanche, and at Jaén, Cajamarca, Peru; +.
Patagon ~ Tshon ~ Chon. Loukotka (1968) has Téuesh, Poya, Péeneken or Tehuelche, and Aoniken or Tsoneca as one of two Patagon groups, "Languages of Patagonia." Ona or Selknam and Mánekenkn or Haush form the other group, "Languages of the Island." Mason has Chon (not Chona of the coast of Chile) with Chon or Tehuelche having two groups, Tehuelche and Ona. Rivet, in various articles of 1925 through 1927 tied Chon to Australian languages. Mason counted Téuesh (Tä'uüshn ~ Tewesh), Northern Tehuelche (Payniken ~ Pä'änkün'k) with Poya, and Southern Tehuelche (Inaken ~ Ao'nükün'k) as three varieties of Tehuelche; his Ona has Haush ~ Manekenkn and Sheknam (two varieties, Northern and Southern). Mason points to

ambiguity in the use of the name Tehuelche, as it refers to the Chon just noted or the Küni ~ Northern Tehuelche (probably Puelche). Tax (1960) has Araucanian, Ona, Tehuelche, Alacalufan, and a fifth subfamily (with Puelche and Yahgan) in a family called Araucanian-Chon, of the Andean stock of the Andean Equatorial phylum.

Patamona. Pemón; R. Ireng and R. Potaro, Guyana.

Patasho. Eastern Mashakali; between R. São Francisco and R. Jequitinhonha, Minas Gerais; later, R. Jequitinhonha right shore, in Espirito Santo; +.

Patia. Coconuco; between R. Guachicono and R. Timbío; +.

Patiti. *; R. Mequéns, Rondônia; +.

Patoco. Sebondoy; R. Caquetá sources; +.

Patsiaché. See Andoque.

Patsoca ~ Iuruty-tapuyo. Tucano; R. Apoporis and R. Abio, Colombia; +.

Pauana. *; R. Cafua, Amazonas; +.

Pauaté. Kawahyb; R. Zinho sources; +.

Paucara. Chocó stock; Pacora Valley; +.

Paucosa. Waica; between R. Taboti and R. Demeni, Amazonas, Brazil.

Paudacoto. Pemón; R. Aro sources, Bolivar; +.

Pauishana. Pauishana; between R. Branco and R. Catrimani, Rio Branco, Brazil.

Paumarí ~ Pamari ~ Kurukurú. Arawa; R. Jacaré mouth to R. Maroiá mouth, along R. Purus, Amazonas.

Pauna. Mojo; R. Baures sources, Santa Cruz, Bolivia; +.

Pauserna ~ Moperecoa ~ Warádu-nëë. Chiriguano; R. Tarbo and R. Paragua, Bolivia; later, R. Verde, tributary of R. Guaporé, Mato Grosso; a few speakers (1968).

Pauxi ~ Pawiyana. Chiquena; middle R. Erepecurú (or Cuminá) right bank; perhaps +.

Pawiyana. See Pauxi.

Pawumwa. See Wañám.

Paya ~ Poyuai ~ Seco. Paya; R. Guayupe and between R. Sico and R. Patuca, Honduras.

Payacu. Tarairiú; Serra do Coité, Serra do São Bento and Serra Calabouço between R. Apodí and R. Jaguaribe, Rio Grande do Norte; +.

Payaguá ~ Sarigué ~ Tacumbú. Guaicuru; rivers of Paraguay and Asunción; later, Colonia Capitán Bado, Paraguay.

Payanso. *; R. Chipurana, Loreto; +.

Payaya. Southern Kamakan; R. Canamu, Bahia; +.

Payo. See Poya.

Payoariene. See Payualiene.

Payoguaje. See Cóto.

Payualiene ~ Payoariene ~ Pacu-tapuya. Ipća; R. Arara-paraná.

Payure. Guamo; R. Guárico mouth; +.

Pazé. See Passé.

Peagaxinan. See Natú.

Peba. See Ariú.

Peba ~ Nijamvo. Yagua; Peba village, Loreto.

Pedraza. Chibcha; R. Pedraza.

Péeneken ~ Tehuelche ~ Chonqui ~ Haveniken. Patagon; between Cordillera Central and the Atlantic Ocean, Chubut territory, Argentina.

Peguenche non-araucano. *; Neuquén province, Argentina; +.

Pehuenche. Mapuche; from Valdivia to Neuquén.

Peine. Atacama; Peine village, Antofagasta, Chile; a few speakers (1968).

Pejaurún ~ Cajaurun. Botocudo; R. Doce; +.

Pelado. See Maruba.

Pemeno. Karaib Motilon; R. Escalante mouth, Zulia; +.

Pemón. See Taurepän.

Penday. See Canelo.

Penonomeño. Guaymi; Penonemé village; +.

Penoqui. Chiquito; San José mission; +.

Pepuxi. See Makamekran.

Pequi. Antioquia; Pequi region; +.

Peria ~ Poria. *; Rodelas, Bahia; +.

Perovosan. *; S. of Xarayes Lagoon, Bolivia; +.

Pesatupe. Western Mataco; near the Taños, between 61°–62°; +.

Pesherah. See Alacaluf.

Petigaré. See Potiguara.

Péua. See Tacuñapé.

Pezacó. Macusi; S. of Eliángs.

Pianocoto. Trio; R. Jamunda and R. Trombetas sources; later, R. Marapi mouth, Parú de Oeste, Pará.

Pianoi. Trio; R. Citaré sources and upper course, Pará.

Piapai. *; between Irirí and R. Jamachim, Pará; +.

Piapoco ~ Mitua ~ Dzáse. Caquetio; R. Guaviare, Vaupés, Colombia.

Piaroa. Eastern Piaroa; R. Ventuari, R. Sipapo and R. Orinoco, Amazonas, Venezuela.

Picara. Chocó; R. Frisolera sources and R. Pozo sources; Caldas; +.

Pichobo. Northern Pano; R. Paguamigua mouth; +.

Picunche. Mapuche; R. Bío-Bío to Coquimbo, Chile.

Pihtadyouai. See Notobotocudo.

Pijao ~ Pinao. Pijao; R. Magdalena, R. Aipe, R. Tetuán, R. Tuamo, R. Otaima and R. Luisa; later, Ortega, Coyaima and Natagaima, Tolima, Colombia.

Pilagá ~ Yapitilaga ~ Aí ~ Guacurure. Guaicuru; near Fortin Descanso and Estero Patiño, Chaco, Argentina.

Pile. See Puscajae.
Pillku-simi. Quechua; Huánuco, Ambo and Pachitea valleys, Huanuco.
Pimenteira. Pimenteira; Lake Pimenteira, R. Sant' Anna sources, and between R. Piauí and R. Gurgueia, in Piauí, Brazil.
Pinao. See Pijao.
Pinaré. Northern Kaingán; R. Uruguay, left shore, in Rio Grande do Sul; +.
Pinche ~ Llepa ~ Uchpa ~ Avaza. Murato; R. Corrientes.
Piñoco. Chiquito; San José mission; +.
Pioje. See Angotero.
Piokobjé ~ Bucobu ~ Pukobje. Krao; R. Grajaú sources.
Pipipan. *; lower R. Moxotó, Pernambuco; +.
Pirahá. Múra; R. Maiçi and R. Branco, Amazonas.
Pira-tapuya. See Waikína.
Piriou. Western Karaib; middle R. Oyapoque; +.
Piripiri. Southern Kamakan; R. Gorotuba and R. Verde valleys, Minas Gerais; +.
Piritú. Tamanaco; at Puerto Piritú, Anzoátegui; +.
Piro ~ Simirinche. Pre-Andine Arawak; R. Inuya, Loreto. Also Acre, Brazil.
Pisa-tapuya. See Uasöna.
Pishauco ~ Pshavaco. Maquiritaré; Serra Tepequem, Rio Branco territory; +.
Pitá. *; R. Bonito, Rio de Janeiro; +.
Pius. Barbácoa; Laguna Piusbi; +.
Pocanga. See Bará.
Pocheti. Northern Tupi; R. Mojú and R. Araguaia; +.
Pocoana. *; Lake Maracaparu to R. Amazon; +.
Pocosi. Guatuso; at Puerto Limón and on R. Matine, Costa Rica; +.
Pocra. *; Peru; +.
Pohena ~ Callahuaya. Puquina; at Tipuani and on R. Camita, La Paz, Bolivia; probably +.
Pojichá ~ Pozyichá. Botocudo; R. Todos os Santos; +.
Pontá. Jeicó; on an island in R. São Francisco, near Quebrobó, Pernambuco; +.
Popayan. See Puben.
Popoluca. See Matagalpa.
Porcá. *; Várgea Island in R. São Francisco, Pernambuco; +.
Poria. See Peria.
Porokun. Botocudo; R. San Mateo; +.
Porú ~ Procáze. *; Serra Nhumarana and Serra Cassuca; later, on Várgea Island and Nossa Senhora de O Island in R. São Francisco; probably +.
Poruntun. Botocudo; R. São Mateo; +.
Poté ~ Potun. Botocudo; Teófilo Otoni near Poté; +.
Poti. See Puti.
Potiguara ~ Petigaré. Tupi; R. Parnaíba mouth to R. Paraíba mouth; later, Baía do Traição, Paraíba; a few families (1968).

Potun. See Poté.

Poturero ~ Ninaquigila. Northern Zamuco; R. Otuquís and R. San Rafael near Santa Ana, Chaco, Bolivia.

Poya ~ Payo. Patagon; near Lake Nahuel Huapí, Rio Negro, Argentina; +.

Poyanáwa. Yamináua; R. Moa.

Poyme. See Boimé.

Poyuai. See Paya.

Pozo. Antioquia; R. Pacova and R. Pozo; +.

Pozyichá. See Pojichá.

Prarto. See Paratió.

Prehnoma. Chiquena; W. of Pianocotos.

Procáze. See Porú.

Progoto. See Purucotó.

Prohyana. Trio; Eilerts de Haan Gebergte, Dutch Guiana.

Pshavaco. See Pishauco.

Pshicacuo. Karaib Motilon; W. of the Tucucos.

Puben ~ Pubenano ~ Popayan. Coconuco; Plains of Popayán, Cauca; +.

Pucapucari. Pre-Andine Arawak; R. Tunquini and R. Camisia, Peru; +.

Puçá-tapuya. See Uantya.

Puelche. See Gennaken.

Puelche algarrobero. See Tuluyame.

Puinahua. See Cháma.

Puináve ~ Guaipuño ~ Uaipí ~ Épined. Northern Makú; R. Inirida, Vaupés, Colombia.

Puipuitene. Maquiritaré; R. Ventuari near the Decuanás; +.

Pukobje. See Piokobjé.

Pulare. See Chicoana.

Pumé. See Yaruro.

Puná ~ Lapuna. Northern Chimú; Puná Island, Ecuador; +.

Puncuri. Pre-Andine Arawak; R. Puncuri, Acre.

Puntano. See Michilenge.

Puquina. Puquina; E. coast of Lake Titicaca; +.

Puracé. Coconuco; Laguna de las Papas and Puracé volcano; +.

Purekamekran. Timbirá; R. Grajaú source; +.

Puri ~ Telikóng ~ Paquí. Eastern Puri; R. Braço Sul do Jucu, R. Itapemirim, and R. Itabapoana, Espirito Santo; +.

Puruborá ~ Burubora. Isolated language; R. Manoel Correia, Rondônia.

Purucaru. Kayapó; between R. Itacaiuna sources and R. Fresco.

Purucotó ~ Progoto. Macusi; R. Uraricapará, Rio Branco.

Puruguai. See Puruhá.

Puruhá ~ Puruguai. Northern Chimú; Chimborazo and Bolivar provinces, Ecuador; +.

Purupurú. Arawa; lower R. Purus; +.

Pusarakau. Waica; hills W. of Karimes, Rio Branco.

Puscajae ~ Pile. Yurimangui; R. Dagila left bank; +.

Puti ~ Poti. Gamela; R. Poti mouth; +.

Puxacáze. Huari; R. Guajejú, Brazil; +.

Puxiauá. Central Zé; near the Katáguas of R. Jequirica, Minas Gerais.

Puyo Pongo. Ecuadorian Lowland Quechua; E. Ecuador.

Qahamarka-simi. See Cajamarca.

Qheshwa. See Quechua.

Qollawa-simi ~ Collagua. Quechua; Abancay department.

Qosqo-simi ~ Cuzqueno ~ Quechua-imperial. Quechua; Cuzco department.

Quaiá. See Koaiá.

Quaqua. Mapoyo; N. of the Mapoyos; +.

Quatausi. See Catauxi.

Quechua ~ Quichua ~ Qheshwa ~ Inga ~ Runa-simi ~ Khechuwa ~ Kechua. Quechua; Peru.

Quechua-imperial. See Qosqo-simi.

Quelosi. *; E. of Mar Chiquita, Córdoba, Argentina; +.

Quenagua. Karaib Motilon; Espíritu Santo Valley, Zulia; +.

Queniquea. Caquetio; R. Pereño, Colombia; +.

Quenoloco. Macusi; R. Cotinga sources.

Quepi-quiri-uate. See Kepkeriwát.

Quepo. Guatuso; R. Pacuar, Costa Rica; +.

Quequexque. See Terraba.

Querandi ~ Carendie. Chechehet; R. Salado and near R. de la Plata mouth; +.

Querarí. Central Makú; R. Querarí, Amazonas.

Quesque. Kiriri; R. Pajeú, Pernambuco; +.

Quiambioá. *; Serra Negra, Pernambuco; +.

Quiapyre. See Kiapüre.

Quichua. See Quechua.

Quidquidcana. *; Magdalena Valley, Huánuco; +.

Quie. See Cautarie.

Quijo. Barbácoa; R. Coca and R. Napo, Oriente, Ecuador; +.

Quijos. Quechua; R. Quijos, Oriente.

Quilifay. Betoi; near the Lolacas; +.

Quilla. Coconuco; Almaguer, Santiago and Milagros villages; +.

Quillaca. Aymara; S.E. of Lake Poopó, Oruro.

Quillasinga. Sebondoy; R. Guaitara and R. Caquetá; +.

Quilme. Diaguit; Quilmes, Catamarca; +.

Quiloaza. Guaicuru; R. Salado sources, Santa Fe; +.

Quimbaya. Chocó; middle R. Cauca, from R. Chinchiná mouth to R. La Paila mouth, Valle de Cauca; +.

Quingnam. See Chimú.
Quinhau. See Guinau.
Quiniquinao ~ Equiniquinao. Paresí; near Albuquerque; later, Posto Cachoeirinha near Miranda, Mato Grosso; a few families (1968).
Quinó. Caquetio; Lagunillas, Mérida, Venezuela; +.
Quipiu. See Yabutí.
Quirineri. Pre-Andine Arawak; R. Manu and R. Paucartambo, Cuzco.
Quiriquire. Tamanaco; R. Misoa and R. Tuy, Miranda; +.
Quiriquiripa. Pemón; R. Caura left bank; +.
Quiriri. See Kiriri.
Quirishaná. See Casapare.
Quirixana. See Crixaná.
Quitemo. Chapacura; R. Uruvaito, Santa Cruz, Bolivia; +.
Quiteño. Quechua; around Quito and elsewhere in Ecuador.
Quito. See Panzaleo.
Quiturran. See Iquito.
Quixelu. Kiriri; R. Jaguaribe, Ceará; +.
Quixexeu. Kiriri; R. Jaguaribe, Ceará; +.
Qurigmã. *; São Salvador Bay, Bahia; +.
Rabona. Murato; Santiago de las Montañas, Loja, Ecuador; +.
Rache. See Mosetene.
Raipé-Sisi ~ Aipé-Chichi. Southern Tupi; between R. São Manoel and R. Arinos; +.
Rama. Rama; Bluefields Lagoon and R. Rama, Nicaragua.
Rama de rio Zapote. See Corobisi.
Ramarama ~ Ytangá. Itogapúc; R. Prêto, R. Branco, and R. Machadinho sources, Mato Grosso.
Rangú. Trio; R. Parú de Oeste sources, Pará.
Ranquelche. Mapuche; La Pampa plains; later, R. Colorado and Chalileo, General Acha, Argentina.
Rayado. See Tirub.
Remako-Kamékrere. See Remkokamekran.
Remkokamekran ~ Remako-Kamékrere ~ Merrime. Timbirá; R. Alpercata and R. Cordas, especially at Ponto village.
Remo. See Nucuini.
Resigaro ~ Rrahanihin ~ Rosigaro. Resigaro; R. Igaraparaná near Casa Arana; a few families (1968).
Rheno. See Nucuini.
Riama. Carijona; area of R. Vaupés, R. Apoporis and R. Yari; in Caquetá and Vaupés.
Rimac. *; at Lima, Peru; +.

Rimachu. See Mayna.
Roamaina. See Murato.
Rocorona. Chapacura; R. San Martín; +.
Romarí ~ Omarí. *; Serra de Pão de Açúar, Pernambuco; +.
Rôpo. See Lôpo.
Rosigaro. See Resigaro.
Rrahanihin. See Resigaro.
Ruanagua. Northern Pano; R. Corjuania, Loreto.
Rucana. *; near Andamarca, Ayacucho; +.
Rucuyene. Eastern Karaib; R. Lawa; +.
Rumo. See Amaguaje.
Runa-simi. See Quechua.
Sabané. Northern Nambikwára; R. Juruena Mirim and R. Ananáz, Mato Grosso.
Sabanero ~ Savaneric ~ Valiente. Dorasque; plains S. of Serrania de Tabasara; +.
Sabela ~ Auca ~ Huarani. Sabela; R. Tiwaeno and nearby rivers, Ecuador.
Sabril. See Yapreria.
Sabuya. See Sapuyá.
Sacaca. Aruan; E. Marajó Island; +.
Sacurú. *; R. Paraíba, Rio de Janeiro; +.
Sacata. Murato; Socota on R. Chota, Cajamarca; +.
Saccha ~ Colorado ~ Manivi. South Barbacoan Chibcha; around Santo Domingo de los Colorados, N.W. Ecuador; 600 (1960).
Sacopé. See Sapupé.
Sacosi. *; Puerto de los Reyes, Bolivia; +.
Sacracrinha ~ Sequaquirihen. *; near R. Salitre mouth in R. São Francisco, Bahia; +.
Sacuya. Northern Pano; between R. Tamaya and R. Juruá, Acre; +.
Sae. Caquetio; near the Guayupes; +.
Saha ~ Tsahatsaha. Carijona; between R. Yarí and R. Cuemaní, Caquetá.
Saija ~ Saixa. Chocó; R. Saija.
Sakamekran ~ Chacamecran ~ Mateiros. Timbirá; R. Flores and R. Codo.
Salamay. See Sanamaica.
Sáliba. See Sáliva.
Salumá ~ Charúma. Chiquena; area of upper courses of R. Tanúru, R. Uanabé, and R. Trombetas, Pará.
Samatari ~ Shamatairi. Samatari; Serra Parima and R. Demeni, Rio Branco.
Sambú. Chocó; R. Sambú, Panama and Serranía del Darien, Colombia.
Samuco. See Zamuco.
Sanagasta. Diaguit; Sierra de Velasco, La Rioja; +.
Sanamaica ~ Salamay. Mondé; R. Pimenta Bueno left bank.

Sanapaná ~ Lanapsua. Lengua; R. Galbán, Paraguay.
Sanaviron. Isolated language; near Salinas Grandes, Córdoba; +.
San Blas. See Cuna.
Sanemá ~ Harateri ~ Guaharibo. Sanema; R. Orinoco, R. Siapa and R. Yatua, Amazonas, Venezuela.
Sanenäre. Kawahyb; S. of the Paranawáts.
Sanha. See Guamaca.
Saninàwa ~ Shaninàua. Yaminàua; R. Humaitá, R. Liberdade and R. Valparaiso, Acre.
Sañogasta. Diaguit; Sañogasta Valley, La Rioja; +.
Sansa-simi. Quechua; R. Apurimac in department of Apurimac.
San Simoniano. Chiquito; Sierra de San Simón and R. Danubio, Beni, Bolivia.
Santiagueño ~ Panpa-simi. Quechua; Santiago del Estero, Argentina.
Sapai. Western Karaib; R. Mana, French Guiana; +.
Sapará. See Zapara.
Sapeiné. *; R. Napo, Loreto.
Sapiboca. Tacana; Reyes mission, Beni, Bolivia; +.
Sapupé ~ Sacopé. Mawé; R. Bararatí; +.
Sapuqui ~ Conamesma. Lengua; R. Galbán sources, Chaco, Paraguay; perhaps +.
Sapuyá ~ Sapuya ~ Sabuya. Kiriri; Serra Chapada; later, Caranguejo, Bahia; +.
Sära. Sära; between R. Tiquié and R. Piraparana, Vaupés, Colombia.
Sarave ~ Zarabe. Paresí; R. Paragua and R. Verde, Santa Cruz, Bolivia; perhaps +.
Sąrigué. See Payaguá.
Sarrakong. See Serecong.
Satxíla. See Colorado.
Savaneric. See Sabanero.
Sayaco. See Amahuaca.
Sayma. See Chayma.
Sebondoy ~ Mocoa ~ Sibundoy ~ Kamsá ~ Coche. Sebondoy; R. Iça sources, Putumayo territory, Colombia; later, partly in villages of Mocoa and Las Casas.
Sec. See Sechura.
Sechura ~ Sec. Sechura; desert of Sechura, Piura, Peru; +.
Seco. See Paya.
Secoya ~ Secoya-Gai. Western Tucano; in small groups along R. Aguarico tributaries, R. Putumayo, and R. Napo, N.E. Ecuador, and in adjacent parts of Peru and Colombia; 160 (1960).
Seden. Manáo; between R. Negro and R. Uatuma; +.
Seeptsá. See Cholona.
Selknam. See Ona.

Sensi. Sensi; R. Chanuya and R. Huanachá, Loreto, Peru.
Senú. See Zenú.
Sequaquirihen. See Sacracrinha.
Serecong ~ Sarrakong. Pemón; R. Mahú sources; +.
Sereu. Chiquena; E. of R. Cachorro sources.
Serra dos Dourados. Guarani; Serra dos Dourados, Paraná.
Setebo. See Cháma.
Sewacu. Arawa; R. Pauiní; later, R. Purus left bank opposite R. Seaptini mouth.
Shakáre. See Caripuna.
Shamatairi. See Samatari.
Shanináua. See Saninâwa.
Shapáru ~ Chaparro. Karaib Motilon; W. of the Paririś, Zulia.
Shapra ~ Iñuru ~ Zapa. Murato; R. Pusaga.
Shauari. See Karime.
Shebayi ~ Supaye. Yao; Guianas; +.
Shenabu. See Sinabo.
Shetá ~ Aré ~ Yvaparé. Guarani; R. Ivaí, Paraŋá; +.
Shikiana. See Chiquena.
Shimikae. See Simigae.
Shimízya. See Chimila.
Shipaya ~ Achipaya ~ Jacipoya. Yuruna; R. Curua and R. Irirí; probably +.
Shipibo. See Cháma.
Shiporok. See Xiporoc.
Shiquimu. Karaib Motilon; S.W. of the Shapárus, Zulia.
Shirishána. See Casapare.
Shiribá. See Chirigua.
Shirishána. See Casapare.
Shiulik. Guaicuru; Laguna Blanca; +.
Shiwila. See Jebero.
Shomana. See Jumana.
Shuara. See Jíbaro.
Shuensampi. See Miquirá.
Shukurú ~ Xucuru ~ Ichikile. Shukurú; Serra de São José on R. Taperoá, R. Capibariba and R. Meio, Pernambuco and Paraíba states; later, in Cimbres city and in Serra Ararobá, Pernambuco.
Shuor. See Jíbaro.
Siaviri. See Simigae.
Siberi. *; Xarayes Lagoon, Bolivia; +.
Sibundoy. See Sebondoy.
Sicuane. Guahibo; R. Tuparro, Vichada, Colombia.
Silviano. See Guambiana.

Simacu. See Itucale.

Simigae ~ Shimikae ~ Gay ~ Siaviri. Záparo; area of R. Bobonaza, R. Napo, R. Curaray and R. Tigre. Language is being replaced by Quechua.

Simirinche. See Piro.

Simou. See Sumu.

Sinabo ~ Shenabu ~ Gritones. Eastern Pano; R. Mamoré near Los Almendrales, Beni; +.

Sindagua ~ Malla. Barbácoa; R. Patia, R. Tapaje, R. Mamaonde and R. Iscuande, Nariño, Colombia; +.

Singacuchusca. See Itucale.

Sinipi. Vilela; R. Bermejo near Lacangayá; +.

Sinsiga ~ Chita. Chibcha; R. Chisca and village of Chita.

Sintó ~ Assek ~ Upsuksinta. *; Gran Chaco, Paraguay, N. of the Chorotis.

Sinufana ~ Cenufara. Chocó; between R. Magdalena and R. Nechi, Bolivar; +.

Siona ~ Zeona ~ Ceño ~ Sioní ~ Kokakañú. Western Tucano; spanning part of the E. border of Colombia and Ecuador along upper R. Putomayo. Of 200 speakers of both dialects, (1) Siona (150 speakers) and (2) Macaguaje (50 speakers), in 1961 there were 50 in Ecuador and 150 in Colombia.

Sipisipi. *; Peru; +.

Sipó ~ Cipo. Arawa; R. Tapauá N. of Yuberís; +.

Siracua ~ Tsirákua. Northern Zamuco; R. Parapití, Bolivia.

Siriána. See Chiránga.

Sirineiri. See Mashco.

Siriono ~ Chori. Chiriguano; R. Ichillo and R. Grande, between R. Yapacuñí and R. Blanco, between R. Quimore and R. Ivari, between upper R. Ivari and R. Grande, between R. Itonama and R. Piray, and between R. Mamoré and R. Beni, Bolivia.

Situfa ~ Cituja. Betoi; R. Casanare; +.

Siusí ~ Ualíperi-dákeni ~ Uereperidákeni. Baré; lower R. Içana and lower R. Caiarí, and middle R. Aiarí, Amazonas, Brazil.

Smus. See Sumu.

Soálesu. See Anunze.

Sobolbo ~ Bolbo. Northern Pano; R. Cohengua; +.

Socomba. Karaib Motilon; between R. Tucui and R. Maraca; formerly also on R. Buenavista, Magdalena.

Socorino. *; Bolivia; +.

Socorpa. Karaib Motilon; N. of Maracas.

Sokó. See Durina.

Solco. Diaguit; Tucumán province N. of Tucumanes; +.

Solote. See Choroti.

Sora. *; R. Pampas, Apurimac; +.

Soropalca. Aymara; around Soropalca city, Potosí.

Sotegraic. See Sotsiagay.

Sotirái. See Sotsiagay.

Sotsiagay ~ Sotegraic ~ Sotirái. Eastern Mataco; between R. Pilcomayo and R. Curvas, Paraguay.

Southern Kaingán ~ Iñacore. Northern Kaingán; around cities of Nonohag and Cáceres, Rio Grande do Sul.

Southern Uitoto. Western Uitoto; R. Putumayo, Amazonas, Colombia and in Méria, R. Igara-paraná, Amazonas, Brazil. Spoken by the Menekka, Eraye, Meresiene, Xúra and Seueni.

Sowuash. See Ashlusláy.

Stanatevogyet. *; Chaco, Paraguay.

Suberiono. Mojo; W. of R. Guapay and R. Mamoré, Bolivia; +.

Suchichi ~ Suriche. Munichi; Tarapoto village in R. Moyobamba region; +.

Sucuriyú-tapuya. See Moriwene.

Suerre ~ Camachire ~ Chiuppa. Guatuso; R. Tortuguero, Costa Rica; +.

Suhín ~ Sújen. Eastern Mataco; R. Seco and R. Yabebirí, Chaco, Paraguay.

Sújen. See Suhín

Sumu ~ Simou ~ Smus ~ Albauin. Mosquito; R. Prinzapolca, Nicaragua.

Sunesua. Karaib Motilon; Espíritu Santo Valley, Zulia, S. of Quenagas; +.

Supaye. See Shebayi.

Supe. *; R. Huaura, Lima; +.

Supeselo. *; Santa Lucia mission, Corrientes; +.

Surára. Samatari; R. Demeni, near the Pakidáis.

Suriche. See Suchichi.

Surucosi. *; Bolivia; +.

Suruim. *; R. Machado right bank, Rondônia.

Susa. Karaib Motilon; central Sierra de Perijá, Magdalena.

Sutagao. Caquetio; R. Sumapaz and R. Pasca, Meta; +.

Suva ~ Tsúva. Xingú; R. Curisevú right bank; a few speakers (1968).

Suyá. Western Zé; R. Suiá-missu mouth on R. Xingú; later, N. of this area.

Tabajari. Mapoyo; R. Erebato left bank, Bolivar, probably +.

Tabaloso. Munichi; Tabalosa on R. Mayo, Loreto.

Tabancale ~ Aconipa. Isolated language; Aconipa village, Cajamarca, W. Ecuador; +.

Tabare ~ Cariña. Western Karaib; Tapaquire, Bolivar, Venezuela and El Guasey, Cachipo, Cachama and San Joaquín de Parire or Mapicure, Anzoátegui.

Tacame ~ Atacamez. Northern Chimú; Pacific coast, Esmeralda province; +.

Tacana. Greenberg (1959) calls Tacana-Pano a Macro-Panoan language. Tax (1960) shows Tacanan as a family of Macro-Panoan in Greenberg's Ge-Pano-Carib phylum. Loukotka (1968) regards Tacana as a stock. Girard (1971) reduces the chaos, showing, p. 145, the possibility of relating Panoan and Tacanan (his Takanan). He suggests, p. 172, connections with Mayoruna (which may be Panoan but between Panoan and Tacanan somehow). He allows that Tucanoan may belong with Panoan-Tacanan. See Girard (1971), p. 41, for details of the subgrouping of (1) Tacanic (Tacana, Sapibocona [Sapibocona, Guariza, Maropa, Reyesano], Araona), (2) Mabenaro, (3) Cavinic (Cavineño), (4) Chamic (Chama ~ Tiatinagua ~ Huarayo ~ Eseʔejja; Guarayo ~ Warayo ~ Tambopata-Guarayo ~ Tiatinagua ~ Huarayo, etc.).

Tacana. Tacana; R. Beni, R. Tuichi, and R. Tequeje, Colonia, Bolivia; a few families (1968).

Tacarigua. Tamanaco; Lake Valencia, Miranda.

Tacarijú. Gamela; R. Longa, Piauí; +.

Tacarua. See Tacarúba.

Tacarúba ~ Tacarua. *; Soroabé Island, R. São Francisco, Pernambuco; +.

Tacayuna. Pará; R. Tacaiuna; +.

Táchira. Karaib Motilon; R. Táchira, Táchira state; +.

Tacuatepe. See Takwatíp.

Tacumandícai ~ Caras Pretas. Pará; lower R. Xingú.

Tacumbú. See Payaguá.

Tacuñapé ~ Eidum ~ Péua. Pará; R. Novo and R. Iririru; +.

Tacunbiacu. *; between R. Guapay and Chiquitos Plains, Bolivia; +.

Tadó. Chocó; middle R. San Juan and R. Sipi.

Tadutė. Central Nambikwára; R. Dúvida near Navaites.

Taga. See Tawihka.

Tagare. Tamanaco; Gulf of Cariaco coast, Sucre; +.

Tagnaní. Eastern Nambikwára; R. Castanho (or Roosevelt), Mato Grosso.

Taguari. Waiwai; between R. Ipitinga and R. Mapuera; +.

Taguaylen. *; Santa Lucia mission, Corrientes; +.

Tahami. Antioquia; R. Magdalena and R. Tora; +.

Taiguana. *; Sierra Araracuára. Caquetá, Colombia.

Tain. See Ingain.

Taino ~ Nitaino. Island Arawak; Cuba, Haiti, Puerto Rico and Jamaica; +.

Taira. Western Karaib; R. Iracoubo.

Tairona ~ Teyuna. Arhuaco; R. Frío and Caribbean coast, Magdalena, Colombia; said to be secret language of priests, Cágaba tribe.

Tajé ~ Timbirá. Timbirá; Bacurí village, R. Mearim right bank, Maranhão.

Takacuá. Eastern Zé; middle R. Somno, Goiás; +.

Takrat. See Moro.

Takshik. Guaicuru; S. of Toba-guazú; +.

Takuñapé. See Tacuñapé.

Takwatíp ~ Tacuatepe. Kawahyb; confluence of R. Pimenta Bueno and R. Gi-Paraná.

Tallan ~ Atalán. Sechura; Piura department; +.
Taluhet. *; Plains of province of Buenos Aires; +.
Tama. Western Tucano; R. Caguán and R. Yarú, Caquetá, Colombia; perhaps +.
Tamacom. Guiana Tupi; middle R. Jarí and R. Maracá sources, Pará; +.
Tamacosi. *; R. Guapay near La Barranca, Santa Cruz, Bolivia; +.
Tamindé. Eastern Nambikwára; R. Papagaio and R. Marquez de Sousa, Mato Grosso.
Tamanaco. Tamanaco; R. Caroní mouth to R. Cuchivero mouth, along R. Orinoco, Bolivar, Venezuela; +.
Tamaní. *; Quebrada de Tamaní, Caquetá, Colombia.
Tamaquéu. *; confluence of R. Salitre and R. São Francisco, Pernambuco; +.
Tamararé. *; R. Galera and R. Juruena sources, Mato Grosso; +.
Tambakori. Botocudo; R. Itambacuri; +.
Tambaruré. *; R. Apaxoná mouth, Rondônia; +.
Tambopata-Guarayo. See Tiatinagua.
Tame. See Tunebo.
Taminani. *; R. Uaçá and R. Curupi, Amapá territory; +.
Tamoyo. Tupi; Cabo de São Tomé to Angra dos Reis, Rio de Janeiro; +.
Tampish. See Chinchaysusyu.
Támud. Caquetio; N.E. of R. Sagamoso; Santander, Colombia; +.
Tangarará. See Chira.
Tangwera. See Tawira.
Tanimuca ~ Opaina. Yahuna; R. Guacayá and R. Popeyaca, Amazonas, Colombia.
Taño. Western Mataco; near Fortín San Rafael; +.
Tanquihua. *; at Ayacucho city, department of Ayacucho; +.
Tañyguá. Guarani; R. Dourados, Mato Grosso; later, R. Aguapeí, São Paulo; +.
Tao ~ Yúnkarirsh. Chiquito; San Rafael, Santa Ana, San Miguel, San Ignacio, Santo Corazón, Concepción and San Juan missions, Bolivia; +.
Tapacura. See Chapacura.
Tapacurá. *; R. Tapacurá-assú, Pará; +.
Tapajó. Pará; R. Tapajós mouth; +.
Tapano. Karaib Motilon; between Lake Motilon and Lake Onia, Mérida; +.
Tapañuna. Southern Tupi; between R. Tapanhuna and R. Peixe, Mato Grosso; +.
Taparita. Otomac; between R. Apure and R. Orinoco, Apure, Venezuela; +.
Taparito. Mapoyo; middle R. Caura; +.
Tape. Guarani; Serra Geral, Rio Grande do Sul; +.
Tapicari. Waiwai; R. Mucajaú.
Tapieté ~ Kurukwá ~ Yanaygua ~ Parapiti. Chiriguano; upper R. Pilcomayo and on R. Parapití, Chaco, Paraguay.
Tapii. Boróro; Santiago de Chiquitos mission, Bolivia; +.
Tapirapé. Tapirapé; R. Naja and R. Tapirapé, Mato Grosso.

Tapirauha ~ Cupelobo ~ Kupẽ-rob ~ Jandiaí. Pará; R. Igarapé do Bacurı and W. of Cachoeira de Itaboca; a few speakers (1968).

Tapoaya. Chapacura; R. Cautario sources.

Tapóya. Western Nambikwára; upper R. Dúvida.

Tapuisú. *; R. Maicuru mouth, Amapá; +.

Tarairiú ~ Ochucuyana. Tarairiú; between R. Apodí and R. Assú, Rio Grande do Norte; +.

Taramembé ~ Tremembé ~ Taramembé. *; coast between R. Chorro mouth and R. Monim mouth, Ceará.

Tarapaca. *; Tarapaca province, Chile; +.

Tarapecosi. See Chiquito.

Tariana ~ Yavi. Tariana; Yauareté and Ipanoré on R. Caiarí, Vaupés, Colombia.

Tarimoxi. *; N. of Guratégajas, Rondônia.

Taripio. *; border areas of Brazil, state of Pará, and Dutch Guiana, N. of the Rangús.

Tarma. Tamanaco; near Maracay, Aragua; +.

Tarmatampu. Quechua; at Tarma city, Junín.

Taruma. Isolated language; near Manáus, Amazonas, Brazil; later, R. Essequibo sources, Guyana; a few families (1968). Mason thought that Tarumá was probably Arawaken. Greenberg (1959) assigned Taruma to Ge-Pano-Carib, and in Tax (1960) Taruma is grouped with Cucura, Palmela and Pimenteira as comprising a Macro-Carib family in the Ge-Pano-Carib phylum.

Tarunde. Eastern Nambikwára; R. 12 de outubro.

Tatú-tapuyo. See Pomöá.

Tauandé. Western Nambikwára; R. São Francisco Bueno, Mato Grosso.

Táuaxka. See Tawihka.

Tauira. See Tawira.

Tauité ~ Tawite. Western Nambikwara; R. Camararé, Mato Grosso.

Taulepa. See Ulua.

Taulipáng. See Taurepän.

Taurepän ~ Taulipáng ~ Ipuricoto ~ Pemón. Pemón; between Mount Roroima and R. Uraricuena to R. Caroní, border zone of Brazil and Venezuela.

Täuüshn. See Téuesh.

Taven. See Kaingán.

Tavúri. *; R. Paranaiuba, Mato Grosso; +.

Tawari ~ Kadekili-dyapa ~ Kayarára. Southern Catuquina; N. of Bendiapas.

Tawihka ~ Táuaxka ~ Twaca ~ Taga. Mosquito; R. Prinzapolca and R. Coco.

Tawira ~ Tauira ~ Tangwera. Mosquito; R. Prinzapolca.

Tawite. See Tauité.

Tayaga. Guamo; between R. Apure and R. Arauca, Apure; +.

Tayni. Western Mataco; S. of Teutas; +.

Tchagoyána. *; between R. Acapú and R. Erepecurú, Pará.
Tchicoyna. *; R. Cuátari, Pará.
Tchili. *; Cimbres, Pernambuco; +.
Tecua. Caquetio; R. Lengupa and in Teguas, Boyacá, Colombia; +.
Tegría. Chibcha; R. Tegría, Boyacá.
Tehuelche. See Péeneken.
Teiuana. See Tsölá.
Teko. See Emerillon.
Telembi. Barbácoa; R. Télembi; +.
Telikóng. See Puri.
Tembé. Northern Tupi; upper R. Pindaré; later, R. Acará Poqueno and R. Capim, Maranhão.
Tembecua. Guarani; near the Ivitiigúas.
Temimino. Tupi; Espiri to Santo coast; +.
Temomeyéme. See Guinau.
Tenetehara. Northern Tupi language with two dialects; see Guajajára and Tembé.
Tepqui. *; R. Santa Maria, Huánuco, Peru; +.
Tequenica. See Yámana.
Tequiráca. See Auishiri.
Terraba ~ Depso ~ Quequexque ~ Brurán. Talamanca; R. Telorio, Costa Rica; +.
Teremembe. Central Zé; R. Sapucai-guasú, R. Paraopeba, and R. Paranaíba Grande, Minas Gerais; +.
Terena. Chané; R. Jijui and R. Miranda, Mato Grosso.
Tetete ~ Eteteguaje. Western Tucano; R. Güepi sources, Loreto; +.
Téuesh ~ Täuüshn ~ Chewache. Patagon; Comodoro Rivadavia and Chubut territories, Argentina, in the Cordillera Central; +.
Teuta. Western Mataco; R. Teuco sources and vicinity; +.
Tevircacap. *; R. Pimenta Bueno, right bank, Rondônia.
Teweia. Macusi; R. Cotinga.
Teyuna. See Tairona.
Thampa. See Campa.
Tiäbeza. See Canoiero.
Tiatinagua ~ Mohino ~ Chuncho ~ Huarayo ~ Baguaja ~ Tambopata-Guarayo ~ Echoja. Tacana; R. Tambopata, border to Peru and Bolivia. Girard (1971), p. 41, has this language in his Chamic subgroup; see Tacana.
Tibilo. Chamicuro; R. Samiria; Loreto; +.
Tiboi. *; Bolivia.
Ticaõ ~ Tonore ~ Chikaõ. *; R. Culiseú, tributary of R. Xingú, Mato Grosso.
Ticomeri. See Maxiena.
Tikúna. See Tucuna.

Timaná. Andaquí; R. Guarapas and R. Magdalena at Timaná; +.
Timaóna. Southern Tupi; R. Peixe.
Timba. Yurimangui; R. Canambre, Valle de Cauca department; +.
Timbío. Coconuco; R. Timbío; +.
Timbirá. See Tajé.
Timbirá ~ Eastern Timbirá. Jeicó; between R. Parnaíba and R. Itaim, Piauí; +.
Timbú. Charrua; R. Carcarañá sources and near Gaboto, Sante Fe, Argentina; +.
Timirem ~ Antimilene. Arára; R. Agua de Saúde, Pará.
Timote. Timote; Cordillera de Mérida and Trujillo states, Venezuela; +.
Tingán. *; R. Monzón mouth, Huánuco.
Tinigua. Tinigua; R. Guayabero mouth, Meta, Colombia; a few families (1968).
Tinogasta. See Abaucan.
Tiquié. Western Makú; R. Tiquié, Amazonas, Brazil.
Tirandá. Timote; R. Motatán right bank.
Tiribi. See Tirub.
Tirinié. Chiriguano; R. Momoré.
Tirió. See Trio.
Tirub ~ Rayado ~ Tiribi. Talamanca; R. Virilla, Costa Rica; +.
Tivericoto, Tamanaco; coast of Monagas, Venezuela; +.
Tiwituey ~ Tuei. Sabela; R. Napo and upper R. Curaray.
Tliometesen ~ Oyaricule. Trio; between R. Tapanahoni and R. Litani, Dutch Guiana; a few speakers (1968).
Toba ~ Tocoit ~ Ntocowit ~ Frentones ~ Dapicosique. Guaicuru; between R. Bermejo and R. Pilcomayo, Chaco, Bolivia and Argentina.
Toba. See Kilyetwaiwo.
Tobachana. *; beteen R. Jurí and R. Jurúa, Amazonas, S. of Itipunas; +.
Toba de Bolivia. See Komlék.
Toba-guazú ~ Great Tobas. Guaicura; R. Pilcomayo, Argentina.
Tobajara ~ Miarigois. Tupi; R. Camocim, Ceará; +.
Toba-michí ~ Emok. Guaicuru; R. Pilcomayo area; Argentina.
Tocana. See Tucano.
Tocaque. See Calchaquí.
Tocoit. See Toba.
Tocoyene. Marawan; R. Uanarí, Amapa; +.
Tocoyó. Eastern Mashakali; R. Arassuaí valley and near Minas Novas de Fanado, Minas Gerais; later, R. Jequitinhonha right bank, Espirito Santo; +.
Tohazana. *; Venezuela; +.
Tolombon ~ Pacioca. Diaguit; Tolombon Valley, Tucumán; +.
Tolú. Choco; Tolú and Covenas areas; +.
Tomaha. See Tumrahá.
Tomata. *; near Tupiza, Potosí, Bolivia; +.

Tomina. *; between R. Pilcomayo and R. Mizque, Chuquisaca, Boliva. Language extinct, replaced by Quechua.
Tomuza. Tamanaco; between R. Piritú and R. Chico, Miranda and Anzoátegui; +.
Tonocoté. Lule; R. Bermejo near Concepción, Chaco; +.
Tonore. See Ticaõ.
Toósle. See Makká.
Topare. Guarani; near San Gabriel, Uruguay; +.
Toquistiné. Lule; R. Salado near Miraflores; +.
Torá ~ Tura. Chapacura; R. Paricá and R. Marmelos, Amazonas; later, Posto Cabeça d'anta, Amazonas; a few speakers (1968).
Toréjicana. Western Mashakali; between R. Fanado and R. Arassuaí; +.
Toromaina. Tamanaco; R. San Pedro, Federal district of Venezuela; +.
Toromona. Tacana; area of R. Madre de Dios, R. Madidi and R. Beni; perhaps +.
Torondoy. See Mocochí.
Tororí. *; R. Madeira right bank, Amazonas, N. of Parintintins; +.
Tororó ~ Auyama. Caquetio; San Cristóbal, Táchira; +.
Tostó. Timote; R. Boconó.
Totocumu ~ Catuena. Waiwai; between R. Acarí and R. Ipitinga.
Totoró. Coconuco; Totoró and Polindara villages
Towothli. See Makká.
Toyeri ~ Tuyoneiri ~ Arasairi ~ Huachipairi. Mashco; R. Inambari, Cuzco, Peru.
Tramalhy. See Trumai.
Tremembé. See Teremembe.
Trio ~ Diáu ~ Tirió. Trio; R. Palumeu, R. Corentijn and R. Tapanahoni, Dutch Guiana, and area of sources of R. Parú de Leste and Parú de Oeste, Pará.
Trumai ~ Tramalhy. Isolated language; one village on R. Culiseú, tributary of R. Xingú, Mato Grosso, Brazil. Greenberg (1959) counts Trumai as a member of the Equatorial stock of Andean-Equatorial.
Tsaawí. See Chayavita.
Tsáchela. See Colorado.
Tsahatsaha. See Saha.
Tshon. See Patagon.
Tsirákua. See Siracua.
Tsölá ~ Teiuana. R. Piraparana and R. Tiquié, Colombia.
Tsölöa. Erulia; R. Piraparana.
Tsoneca. See Aoniken.
Tsúva. See Suva.
Tubichaminí. Chechehet; R. Tubichaminí, Buenos Aires Province; +.
Tucano. Loukotka (1968) has nine divisions, (1) Western Tucano, (2) Yahuna, (3) Yupua, (4) Coretu, (5) Cubeo, (6) Sära, (7) Erulia, (8) Desána, and (9)

Tucano. Mason's classification is ultra-geographic; his two divisions, Eastern Tucano and Western Tucano, would seem to comprehend respectively Loukotka's groups (2) through (9), and group (1). Some writers keep the geographical designation and assign to Eastern Tucanoan two languages formerly lumped together as Barasano: (1) Southern Barasano, on R. Piraparaná and lower R. Caño Colorado, and (2) Northern Barasano. Greenberg (1959) has Macro-Tucanoan with two divisions, (1) Puinave, (2) Tucano type, with Tucano (*cum* Awishira), Catukina, Ticuna, Muniche, Auaké, Caliana, Macú, Canichana and Móvima. The arrangement of Tax (1960) shows Tucanoan as a subfamily of Catuquinean-Tucanoan, which, with Puinavean and Simacu, belongs to the Macro-Tucanoan stock of Andean-Equatorial. There were perhaps 10,000 Tucanoan speakers in 1948.

Tucano-tapuya. See Yuri.

Tucanuçú. Eastern Mashakali; S. of R. Jequitinhonha near Campos de Caatinga; +.

Tucuco. Karaib Motilon; R. Tucuco sources, Zulia.

Tucujú. Marawan; R. Jarí, Amapá; perhaps +.

Tucuman ~ Tukma. Diaguit; at Tucuman city; +.

Tucumanduba. *; upper R. Canacau, tributary of R. Cunhuá, Amazonas; +.

Tucuna ~ Tikúna ~ Tikuna ~ Ticuna ~ Tecuna ~ Orejone (?). Isolated language; R. Iça mouth near São Paulo de Olivença and Tabatinga, Amazonas, Brazil, and near Leticia, Amazonas, Colombia, as well as in Peru. Wistrand (1971), p. 109, reports 500 speakers at Cushillococha, Loreto, Peru. Rivet, a student of Arawakan, thought that Tucuna was a very much altered form of Arawakan. Loukotka saw Mura and Tucano loans. Tax (1960) shows Tucuna in the Catuquinean-Tucanoan family of Macro-Tucanoan, Andean-Equatorial phylum.

Tucundiapa ~ Mangeroma. Southern Catuquina; R. Itecoaí.

Tucupi. See Mosetene.

Tucura. Chocó; R. Verde and R. Sinú, Bolivar.

Tucurina. Pre-Andine Arawak; R. Igarapé Cuchicha, tributary of R. Chandless, Acre; a few speakers (1968).

Tucurrique. See Viceyta.

Tucushmo. Karaib Motilon; Magdalena, N. of Irocas.

Tuei. See Tiwituey.

Tukma. See Tucuman.

Tukumaféd. Kawahyb; middle R. Machado.

Tukurá. See Tucura.

Tule. See Cuna.

Tulumayo. *; R. Aguaytia, R. Azul and R. Muna, Huánuco; +.

Tuluyame ~ Puelche algarrobero. Huarpe; Calamuchita Valley, Mendoza; +.

Tumaco. Barbácoa; at Tumaco, Nariño; +.
Tumanaha. See Tumraha.
Tumbez. See Tumbi.
Tumbi ~ Tumbez. Northern Chimú; R. Naranjal and R. Tumbez, Tumbez department, Peru; +.
Tumrahá ~ Tumanahá ~ Tomaha ~ Chamacoco bravo. Southern Zamuco; R. Salado, Chaco, Paraguay, S. of Chamacocos.
Tumupasa ~ Maracáni. Tacana; R. Uchipiamona.
Tunacho ~ Imono ~ Caitoporade. Northern Zamuco; near San Ignacio mission; +.
Tunayana. Chiquena; between middle R. Tunúru and middle R. Panemá.
Tunceta ~ Atunseta. Chocó; R. Dagila right bank, Valle de Cauca; +.
Tunebo ~ Tame. Chibcha; E. of the Chibcha tribe.
Tunía. Coconuco; R. Ovejas and R. Tunía; +.
Tupari ~ Wakaraü. Macuráp; upper R. Branco (or São Simão); probably +.
Tupe. See Coyaima.
Tupi ~ Abañeénga. Tupi; coast of Brazil and inland from R. Amazon mouth to 30° Latitude.
Tupi do rio Machado. See Wiraféd.
Tupijó. *; near the Maracás, Bahia; +.
Tupina. Tupi; Bahia interior; +.
Tupinamba. Tupi; coast from R. São Francisco mouth to Camamu; later, coast of Maranhão.
Tupinambarana. Tupi; on Tupinambarana Island in R. Amazon; +.
Tupiniquin ~ Margaya. Tupi; coast from Camamu, Bahia, to Espirito Santo; +.
Tupiokón. *; R. Paxiuba, Mato Grosso.
Tura. See Torá.
Turiguara. See Turiwára.
Turucaca. See Brunca.
Tushá. Isolated language; R. São Francisco near Gloria; later, village of Rodelas, Pernambuco.
Tutura. *; at Totora, Cochabamba, Bolivia. Language extinct, replaced by Quechua.
Tuxináua. Northern Pano; R. Humaitá and R. Embira, Acre.
Tuyoneiri. See Toyeri.
Tuyuca ~ Doxcapura. Tucano; R. Papury and R. Tiquié in Brazil and Colombia.
Twaca. See Tawihka.
Twahka. See Tawihka.
Uaca. Samatari; R. Ocamo.
Uacambabelté. See Vilela.
Uaia. *; R. Içá, W. of Passés; +.

Uaíana. Tucano; R. Caiary, Colombia.
Uaiboi ~ Babui ~ Uaiboí ~ Wabou. Waiwa; middle R. Nhamundá.
Uaica ~ Waica. Pemón; R. Cuyuni and R. Yuruari, Bolivar; a few families (1968).
Uaikana. See Waikína.
Uaimiri ~ Wahmirí. Yauapery; R. Curiauaú sources, Amazonas.
Uainamari ~ Wainamarí. Arawa; R. Inauní, tributary of upper R. Purus; +.
Uainamby-tapuya. See Uainuma.
Uaindze. See Kokozú.
Uaintasu ~ Waintazú. Western Nambikwára; R. Pimenta Bueno right bank, Mato Grosso.
Uainumá ~ Ajuano ~ Wainumá ~ Inabishana ~ Uainamby-tapuya ~ Uaypi. Uainumá; R. Upi, tributary of R. Icá, Amazonas; +.
Uaipí. See Puináve.
Uaiquire. See Wökiare.
Uáira. See Goajira.
Uairua. *; R. Juruá and R. Jaracui; +.
Ualapiti. See Yaulapíti.
Ualíperi-dákeni. See Siusí.
Ualíxere. See Kokozú.
Uamandiri. Western Nambikwára; between R. Corumbiara and R. Cabixi.
Uanána ~ Wanána ~ Kotédia. Tucano; R. Caiari near Cachoeira dos Araras, Brazil.
Uanapú. Pará; R. Anapú; +.
Uantya ~ Puçá-tapuya. Tucano; R. Macú-igarapé, Colombia; +.
Uapixana. See Wapishana.
Uaraguazú. See Aracajú.
Uaranacoacena. Manáo; area of R. Araçá, R. Negro and R. Branco, Amazonas; +.
Uarao ~ Guarauno ~ Waraw ~ Faraute ~ Araote ~ Warrau ~ Warau ~ Worrow ~ Uarow ~ Guarau ~ Uarauno ~ Waraweti ~ Tivitiva. Loukotka's Uarao includes Uarao, Guanoco, Chaguan and Mariusa. Greenberg (1959) identifies Warrau as Paezan (Macro-Chibchan) and Tax (1960) includes as Guarauan four families, Mariusa, Chaguan, Guaiqueri, and Guarau. Guarauan is taken by Tax as a stock of the Macro-Chibchan phylum.
Uarao ~ Guarau ~ Guarauno ~ Waraw ~ Faraute ~ Araote. Uarao; R. Orinoco delta, Amacuro, Venezuela, and parts of Guyana nearby.
Uárema. See Pubmatari.
Uarequena. Baré; R. Guainia, Vaupés, Colombia.
Uariteré. Paresí; R. Pimenta Bueno, Rondônia.
Uariua. See Waríwa.
Uari Wayõ. See Pacahanovo.

Uasaí. Waiwai; R. Jatapú and R. Urubú, Amazonas.
Uasamo. Karaib Motilon; Zulia N. of Shapárus.
Uasöna ~ Pisa-tapuya. Tucano; R. Caiary, Colombia.
Uatanari ~ Watanarí. Arawa; R. Ituxí and R. Sepatini; perhaps +.
Uauarate. *; R. Juraí N. of Catuquinas; +.
Uayeué. Chiquena; R. Mapuera and tributary R. Urubú de Silves.
Uaypi. See Uainumá.
Ubina. Aymara; R. Tambo, Arequipa, Peru.
Ucayali. Quechua; R. Ucayali, Loreto, Peru.
Uchpa. See Pinche.
Uchumi. See Uro.
Uereperidákeni. See Siusí.
Uettidiáu. See Guatiedéo.
Ugaraño. Northern Zamuco; San Ignacio mission, Bolivia; +.
Ugunichire. See Machiganga.
Uina. See Desána.
Uiquina. See Waikína.
Uirina. Uirina; R. Marari sources, Rio Branco; +.
Uitáte. See Arikém.
Uitoto ~ Witóto ~ Huitoto ~ Komiuveido. The stock has been called Macro-Carib by Greenberg (1959); Loukotka (1968) identifies two branches, (1) Western Uitoto (Uitoto [Northern Uitoto, Central Uitoto, Southern Uitoto, Caimito, Nobenidze, Aifue, Goma], Neimade, Hairúya) and (2) Eastern Uitoto (Muinane, Orejone, Ocaina, Nonuya, Fitita, Andoquero, Coeruna). Some speakers live in Macaguaje areas in Ecuador (see Macaguaje); others live in Colombia, Brazil, and Peru. Wistrand (1971), p. 109, extends the coverage of Loukotka in mentioning the Ecuadorian Witotos and those in Peru, on R. Amazon sources from Iquitos to Colombia, N. of the Amazon, where about 80 families live, including some speakers of Muinane.
Uitoto. Name of a language in Loukotka's Uitoto stock. See above under Western Uitoto and under individual names of dialects.
Ulabangui. Arhuaco; R. Negro; +.
Ulua ~ Wulwa ~ Gaula ~ Oldwaw ~ Taulepa. Mosquito; R. Carca and R. Ulúa, Nicaragua.
Umán ~ Huamoi. Isolated language; between R. Pajeú and R. Moxotó and in Serra Umán, Pernambuco.
Umaquena. Karaib Motilon; R. Umaquena, Zulia; +.
Umáua ~ Hiánocoto ~ Máua. Carijona; R. Apoporis sources, Caquetá.
Umbra. See Anserma.
Umutina ~ Barbudo. Boróro; between R. Bugres and R. Paraguai, Mato Grosso; a few families (1968).

Uncasica. Chibcha; Sierra Librada.
Unetunde. Western Nambikwára; upper R. Dúvida.
Univista. See Comobo.
Uómo ~ Miguelheno. Chapacura; R. São Miguel.
Upano. Jíbaro; R. Lhaipa.
Upar ~ Eurpari ~ Giriguana. Arhuaco; R. César; +.
Upsuksinta. See Sintó.
Upurui. Eastern Karaib; upper R. Jarí; later, R. Parú de Leste sources, Pará, Brazil; a few speakers (1968).
Uraba. Chocó; Urába Bay, Antioquia.
Uranaju. *; middle R. Araguari, Amapá; +.
Urariña. See Itucale.
Uro ~ Chancumakkeri ~ Ochozuma ~ Uchumi ~ Kotsuñ. Uro; Peru and Bolivia; mostly at Ancoaqui and Iruito, La Paz, Bolivia, Aymarized, at the present time. For connections with Macro-Mayan see Chipaya and Chimú.
Urraca ~ Esquegua. *; N. of Cañaza, Panama; +.
Uruati. Gamela; R. Monim mouth, Maranhão; +.
Urubú. See Kaapor.
Urubu-tapuya. Tucano; R. Caiary sources, Colombia; +.
Urucuai. *; R. Corumbiara, Rondônia; +.
Urucuyana ~ Urucuyena ~ Waiano. Trio; R. Parú de Leste, left bank, Pará.
Urufu. Botocudo; E. of Bacuenes; +.
Urukú. Itogapúc; R. Lourdes.
Uruma. *; R. São Francisco, Sergipe; +.
Urumí. Itogapúc; R. Tarumã, Mato Grosso.
Urunamacan. Chapacura; N. of Wañámes, Rondônia, Brazil.
Urupá ~ Ituarupa. Chapacura; R. Urupá, Rondônia, Brazil.
Urupaya. See Arupai.
Urupuca. *; R. Urupuca, Minas Gerais; +.
Ururi. *; Mato Grosso, Brazil; +.
Ushikrin. Kayapó; R. Vermelho, Goiás, S. of Carajás; +.
Usnus. Botocudo; R. Jequitinhonha right bank; +.
Uti Krag ~ Nakpie ~ Guti Krag ~ Ngúd-Krág. Botocudo; between R. Pancas and R. Dole; later, Colatina, Espirito Santo; a few speakers (1968).
Valiente. See Move.
Vanherei. *; R. Piquirí sources, Mato Grosso; +.
Vejoz ~ Aiyo ~ Hueshuo. Western Mataco; R. Piquirenda.
Veliche. See Huiliche.
Viatan. Tupi; Pernambuco, Brazil; +.
Viceyta ~ Abiseta ~ Cachi ~ Orosi ~ Tucurrique. Talamanca; R. Tarire, Costa Rica; +.
Vilela ~ Atalalá ~ Uacambabelté. Vilela; R. Bermejo from San Bernardo to

Esquina Grande and near Fortín Garrití and Lacangayá; later, Napalpí near Quitilipí, Chaco, Argentina; +.
Vintukva. See Bintucua.
Vocoin. Western Mashakali; between R. Jequitinhonha and R. Arassuaí; +.
Voto. Guatuso; R. San Juan mouth, Costa Rica; +.
Vouve. *; R. Piancó, Pernambuco; +.
Wabou. See Uaiboí.
Wahmiri. See Uaimiri.
Wai. Western Karaib; R. Tamouri; perhaps +.
Waiana ~ Oayana. Eastern Karaib; R. Lawa and R. Palumeu, Dutch Guiana and Surinam, and R. Parú and R. Jarí, Pará, Brazil; formerly between R. Maroni and R. Marouni, French Guiana.
Waiano. See Urucuyana.
Waica. See Uaica.
Waica ~ Guaica ~ Oayca. Waica; between sources of R. Orinoco and R. Uraricoera, Amazonas.
Waikína ~ Uiquina ~ Uaíkana ~ Pira-tapuya. Tucano; R. Papury, Colombia.
Waiklitisi. See Elutasu.
Waimaré. Paresí; R. Timalatía and R. Verde, Mato Grosso.
Wainamarí. See Uainamari.
Waintazú. See Uaintasú.
Wainumá. See Uainumá.
Waitaka ~ Goytacaz. *; R. São Mateo and near Cabo de São Tomé, Rio de Janeiro; +.
Waiwai ~ Woaywai. Waiwai; R. Essequibo sources, Guyana and R. Mapuera sources, Pará, Brazil.
Wakaraü. See Tupari.
Wakona. See Aconan.
Walêcoxô. *; Ceará.
Wama. Trio; R. Oelemari sources, Dutch Guiana.
Wañám ~ Huanyam ~ Pawumwa. Chapacura; between R. São Domingo and R. São Miguel, Rondônia, Brazil.
Wanána. See Uanána.
Waninâua ~ Catoquino do rio Gregorio. Yaminâua; R. Gregorio.
Wanka. See Huanca.
Wankamarka-simi. See Huancamarca.
Wanka-simi. See Huancayo.
Wanki. Mosquito; R. Coco and Cabo Gracias a Dios.
Wanuku-simi. See Huánuco.
Wapishana ~ Matisana ~ Wapityan ~ Uapixana. Central Arawak; R. Tacutu, R. Mahú, R. Surumú, Rio Branco, Brazil and neighboring parts of Guyana.
Wapityan. See Wapishana.

Warádu-nëe. See Pauserna.
Waraikú. See Araicú.
Waraw. See Uarao.
Waríkyana. Chiquena; lower R. Trombetas; +.
Wari-simi. See Huari.
Waríwa ~ Guariba ~ Uariua. Independent Makú; R. Japurá right bank.
Waruwádu. *; between R. Erebato and R. Ventuari, Bolivar, Venezuela.
Watanarí. See Uatanari.
Wau. *; R. Coca, Loreto.
Waunana ~ Noanáma ~ Nonamá ~ Chocama. Chocó; R. San Juan.
Waurá. Waurá; R. Batoví, tributary of Xingú, Mato Grosso.
Wayana. See Guayana.
Wayapí. See Oyampi.
Waylas. See Huaylas.
Wayoró ~ Wyarú. Macuráp; R. Colorado and R. Terevinto sources, Rondônia.
Wayumara ~ Azumara ~ Guimara. Macusi; between R. Mucajaí and R. Uraricoera and on part of Maracá Island.
Wazaizara. See Guajá.
Weidéñe. See Mundurucú.
Wína. See Desána.
Wiraféd ~ Tupi do rio Machado. Kawahyb; R. Machado.
Wiri-dyapá. See Catuquina.
Witóto. See Uitoto.
Woaywai. See Waiwai.
Wökiare ~ Uaiquire. Mapoyo; R. Paro.
Wulwa. See Ulua.
Wyarú. See Wayoró.
Xacuruina. *; R. Sangue, Mato Grosso; +.
Xaguetío. See Lichagotegodí.
Xakriabá ~ Chicriabá. Eastern Zé; between R. Corumbá and R. Palma, Goiás; +.
Xalqa. See Huánuco.
Xambioa. Karajá; R. Pau d'arco mouth; +.
Xamixumá. *; R. Doce, Minas Gerais; +.
Xanindáua ~ Xanináwa. Northern Pano; R. Riozinho, Acre.
Xaquese. *; Puerto de los Reyes, Bolivia; +.
Xaranáwa. Northern Pano; R. Curanja, Loreto.
Xaraó. Eastern Zę; Pedro Afonso village, R. Tocantins; +.
Xaray. *; Xarayes Lagoon, Bolivia; +.
Xauwiyana. Waiwai; near Hishcarianas.
Xavante ~ Akwẽ ~ Akuän ~ Kayamó. Eastern Zé; Serra do Roncador and between R. Araguaia and R. Tocantins in Serra dos Chavantes, Mato Grosso.

Xerente. Eastern Zé; area of R. Urucuaí, R. Somno and R. Tocantins, Goías.
Xevero. See Jebero.
Xibata. *; Ceará.
Xibitoana. See Hivito.
Xicri. See Chikri.
Xingú. See Yanumakapü.
Xipará. *; between R. Jatapú and R. Urubú, Amazonas; +.
Xipináwa. Yamináua; between R. Liberdade and R. Valparaiso.
Xiporoc ~ Djiporoca. Botocudo; R. São Mateo near Pepinuque; +.
Xiqui. Northern Kaingán; R. Piquiri and R. São Francisco, Mato Grosso; +.
Xirara. See Jirara.
Xiriguana. Opone; Cordillera de Lebaja, Santander; +.
Xocó. See Chocó.
Xocren. See Aweicoma.
Xonin. Western Mashakali; area of R. Doce, R. Figueira and R. Peçanha; +.
Xónvúgn. Botocudo; between R. Aranaa and R. Mutum; +.
Xópxóp. Botocudo; R. Doce near Resplendor; +.
Xoró. Tarairiú; R. Apodí, Rio Grande do Norte; +.
Xubiri. See Yuberí.
Xucuru. See Shukurú.
Xumeto. *; Serra Mantiqueira, Rio de Janeiro; +.
Xurúpixuna. See Yuri.
Yabaána ~ Jabâ-ana ~ Hobacana. Uirina; R. Cauaboris and R. Marauia, Rio Branco.
Yabarána. See Yauarána.
Yabutí ~ Quipiu. Yabutí; R. Branco sources, Rondônia.
Yacariá. See Caripuna.
Yaghan. See Yámana.
Yagua ~ Mishara. Yagua; R. Napo, R. Nauta, and R. Nahua, Loreto, Peru; later, E. of Iquitos in Peru, and in enclaves strung out from Colombia to Brazil.
Yaguai. Caquetio; R. Arichuna, Apure, Venezuela; +.
Yaháhi. Múra; R. Branco, Amazonas.
Yahgan. See Yámana.
Yakwändatéye. See Eastern Kaingán.
Yalcon ~ Cambi. Andaquí; between R. La Plata and R. Magdalena; +.
Yamamadí ~ Carabinani ~ Gaamadi ~ Capaná ~ Capinamari. Arawa; R. Pauiní, R. Purus, R. Juruá, R. Chiruan and R. Tapauá; perhaps +.
Yámana ~ Yahgan ~ Yagan ~ Yaghan ~ Tequenica. Isolated language; S. extreme of Tierra del Fuego; 20? (1948). Mutually intelligible dialects were (1) Eastern (Navarin, Gabler, Nueva and Lennox Islands), (2) Central-Western with Central (Punta Davide, Mascart and Ushuaia, Tierra del Fuego) and

Western (Punta Davide to Brecknock), (3) Southern (Bahia Cook and Milne Edwards), (4) Southwestern (Wallaston Island). Greenberg (1959) has Yahgan as Andean; Tax (1960) has Yaghan and Puelche as an unclassified subfamily of Araucanian-Chon, an Andean family of the Andean-Equatorial phylum.

Yamarikuná. Xingú; R. Curisevú.

Yamarú. Chapacura; R. Jamarí; +.

Yamaye. Island Arawak; Jamaica; +.

Yameo ~ Llameo ~ Camuchivo. Yagua; R. Tigre and R. Nanay, Loreto.

Yamesi. Antioquia; R. Porce and R. Nechi mouth; +.

Yamiaca ~ Haauñeiri. Central Pano; R. Yaguarmayo, Madre de Dios, Peru.

Yaminaua. Yamináua; R. Tarauaca sources, Acre.

Yamorai. Kahuapana; R. Sillai, Loreto.

Yampará. *; middle R. Pilcomayo, Chuquisaca, Bolivia; +.

Yamu. Guahibo; R. Ariari right bank, Meta.

Yanaygua. See Tapieté.

Yandé. Chiriguano; R. Mamoré.

Yanumakapü ~ Nahukwá. Nahukwá; between R. Culuene and R. Curisevú. Dialects are (1) Aipats, (2) Auwáwiti, (3) Etagl, (4) Kalapalo, (5) Kuikutl, (6) Naravute, (7) Matipú, (8) Suva, (9) Yamarikuná, and (10) Yanumakapü, all classified as Nahukwá, which is one of three Xingú Karaib languages, the other two being Bacairí and Yaruna.

Yao ~ Anacaioury. Yao; W. part of Trinidad and R. Cau and R. Ivaricopo, French Guiana; +.

Yapacoye. Eastern Karaib; R. Itany left bank, French Guiana; +.

Yapel. Chocó; near Ayapel, Bolivar; +.

Yaperú ~ Naperú ~ Apirú. *; near Asunción, Paraguay; +.

Yapitilaga. See Pilagá.

Yapóoa. Western Makú; R. Papury and R. Caiary.

Yapreria ~ Sabril. Karaib Motilon; R. Palmar sources, Zulia.

Yariguí. Opone; R. Sogamoso and in Barranca Bermeja; +.

Yaro. Charrua; between R. San Salvador and R. Negro, Uruguay; +.

Yarri. See Chandri.

Yarú. Chapacura; R. Yarú; a few families (1968).

Yaruma ~ Aruma. Xingú; R. Paranaiúba sources, Mato Grosso; perhaps +.

Yaruro ~ Pumé ~ Yuapín. Chibcha; R. Capanaparo plains, Apure, Venezuela; +.

Yathé. See Fulnio.

Yauapery ~ Atroahi. Yauapery; middle R. Yauapery, Amazonas.

Yauarána ~ Yabarána. Mapoyo; R. Manapiare.

Yauareté-tapuya. See Carútana.

Yauarí. Samatari; R. Igarapé Apiauú and between R. Mocajaí and R. Caratirimani.

Yauavo. Northern Pano; between R. Aturia and R. Tejo, Acre; +.

Yaucaniga. See Abipon.

Yauei. *; R. Madeira left bank facing R. Aripuanã mouth, Amazonas; +.

Yaulapífi ~ Yawarapiti ~ Ualapiti. Waurá; between R. Curisevú and R. Meinacu, Mato Grosso.

Yauyo. *; R. Huaco and R. Mala, Lima, Peru; +.

Yavi. See Tariana.

Yavitano. See Yavitero.

Yavitero ~ Pareni ~ Yavitano. Baníva; Yavita village, R. Atabapo.

Yawanáwa. Yamináua; upper R. Jordão, Acre.

Yawani. Samatari; R. Uesete, Amazonas, Venezuela.

Yawarapiti. See Yaulapiti.

Ydïama. See Isiama.

Yecoamita. Vilela; N.W. of R. Teuco, Formosa; +.

Yecuaná ~ Mayongcong. Maquiritaré; R. Caura S.W. of Arecunas, Bolivar, Venezuela.

Yehúbde. Western Makú; S. of R. Querarí, Amazonas, Brazil.

Yenmu. *; R. Curè, Amazonas, Colombia.

Yeral. *; Colombia; +.

Yeté. Amazonas Tupi; R. Tiputini, Loreto, Peru; +.

Yiboia-tapuya. See Dyuremáwa.

Yocabil. Diaguit; Yocabil Valley, Catamarca; +.

Yoemanai. *; R. Purus right bank and mouth, Amazonas, Brazil; +.

Yofuaha. See Choroti.

Yolo ~ Paripazo. Yurimangui; R. San Joaquín, Valle de Cauca; +.

Yoriman. See Yurimagua.

Yosco. Mosquito; R. Bocay and R. Tumo.

Ytangá. See Ramarama.

Yuapín. See Yaruro.

Yuberí ~ Xubiri. Arawa; middle R. Purus facing R. Mamoriá mouth and around Lake Abunini; later, lower R. Tapauá.

Yufiua. *; R. Japurá S. of Coerunas; +.

Yukúna ~ Yucuna. Yukúna; R. Miritíparaná, Amazonas, Colombia.

Yule. See Cuna.

Yúma. Arára; R. Ituxí and R. Jacaré, Rondônia; +.

Yumanáwa. Yamináua; R. Muruzinho, Acre.

Yumbo. Barbácoa; Cordillera de Nanegal and Cordillera de Intag, Pichincha, Ecuador. Language extinct, replaced by Quechua.

Yuminahua. Yamináua; R. Tarauaca, Acre.

Yunga. See Chimú. Yunca, Yunga, Mochica or Chimu has been tied to various groups—Chibcha, Uro, Quechua, Zapotec, and Maya. Greenberg (1959) suggested Paezan in Macro-Chibchan; Tax (1960) kept Macro-Chibchan but specified the Yunca-Puruhan stock with Atalan and Yuncan as families.

Yúnkarirsh. See Tao.

Yupe ~ Motilon. Karaib Motilon; Serra de Perijá, Zulia, Venezuela and Magdalena department, Colombia, in numerous dialects.

Yupua ~ Hiupiá. Yupua; R. Coca, tributary of R. Apoporis, Colombia.

Yura. Northern Pano; R. Piqueyaco, Loreto; +.

Yuracare ~ Yurujure ~ Cuchi ~ Enete. Isolated language; R. Secure sources and R. Chimore and R. Cháparo, Cochabamba, Bolivia; +. Dialects were Mansiño ~ Oromo to the W., and Mage and Soloto to the E.

Yuri ~ Xurúpixuna ~ Tucano-tapuya. Isolated language; R. Puré, Amazonas, Colombia and between R. Japurá and R. Içá, Amazonas, Brazil; perhaps +.

Yurimagua ~ Yoriman. Amazonas Tupi; R. Purus mouth to R. Jutai mouth; later, city of Yurimaguas; a few speakers (1968).

Yurimangui. Yurimangui; R. Yurimangui, Valle de Cauca, Colombia; +.

Yurujure. See Yuracare.

Yuruna ~ Paru-podeari. Yuruna; middle R. Xingú.

Yurupary-tapuya. See Iyäine.

Yuaparé. See Shetá.

Yvytyiguá. Kainguá Guarani; Serra do Diabo, Mato Grosso.

Zamirua. Malibú; R. Ariguani; +.

Zamplan. Southern Mashakali; R. Doce and R. Piracicaba sources; +.

Zamuco ~ Samuco. Northern Zamuco; San Ignacio mission, Chaco, Bolivia; +.

Zapa. See Shapra.

Zapara ~ Sapará. Macusi; central and E. Maracá Island.

Záparo. Záparo; R. Tigre, Loreto, Peru; later, E. Ecuador. Spoken by old people as a private language, the public language now being Quichua, the jungle trade language.

Capaso. Munichi; R. Saposoa; +.

Zapucaya. Pará; between R. Paraná do Uraria and R. Amazon; +.

Zarabe. See Sarave.

Zé ~ Zyé ~ Ge ~ Tapuya ~ Cran ~ Gueren ~ Nac-Nanuc. Loukotka (1968) lists main divisions as (1) Timbirá, (2) Krao, (3) Kayapó, (4) Central Zé, (5) Western Zé, (6) Eastern Zé, and (7) Jeicó. Tax (1960) preserves Mason's division into (1) Northwest Ge, (2) Central Ge, and (3) Jeicó, and shows Ge as a family of the Macro-Ge stock of Ge-Pano-Carib.

Zendagua. Chocó; between R. Magdalena and R. Cauca; +.

Zenú ~ Senú. Chocó; between R. Sinú and R. San Jorge, Bolivar; +.

Zeona. See Siona.

Zeremoe. See Oromina.

Zorca. Opone; San Cristóbel Valley; +.

Zuana. *; R. Amazon S. of R. Cafuá mouth, Amazonas; +.
Zurina. *; R. Mamorí mouth, Amazonas; +.
Zurumata. Chiquena; village of Zurumata, upper R. Trombetas, Pará; probably +.
Zyé. See Zé.
Zyeikó. See Jaicó.
Zyuimakane. Arhuaco; R. Volador; +.

SELECTED REFERENCES

BRINTON, DANIEL GARRISON. 1883. Aboriginal American authors and their productions; especially those in the native languages. A chapter in the history of literature. Philadelphia.

——. 1891. The American race: A linguistic classification and ethnographic description of the native tribes of North and South America. New York. [Translated into Spanish by Alejandro G. Perry as La raza americana (Buenos Aires, 1946).]

GIRARD, VICTOR. 1971. Proto-Takanan phonology. UCPL 70.i-x, 1–209. [Classification history, pp. 11–16; discussion of synonyms, pp. 16–20; annotated bibliography, pp. 177–206: all Panoan and Tacanan languages.]

GREENBERG, JOSEPH H. 1960. The general classification of Central and South American languages. Men and cultures, Selected papers of the Fifth International Congress of Anthropological and Ethnological Sciences, A.F.C. Wallace, ed., pp. 791–4. Philadelphia. [See also Steward and Faron (1959).]

JIJÓN y CAAMAÑO, JACINTO. 1940–45. El Ecuador Interandino y Occidental antes de la conquista Castellana. Quito. 4 vols. [Vol. 1, 1941; vol. 2, 1941; vol. 3, 1943; vol. 4, Apéndices a la primera parte, 1945 (issued 1947). Vol. 1 has language specimens, sources, history of linguistic and ethnographic studies, and place names. Vol. 2 has linguistic data. Vol. 3 includes "Las Lenguas del sur de Centro América y el norte y Centro del oeste de Sud-América," pp. 390–654, with tribal names, bibliography, and territory, for Colombia, Ecuador and other places. The back pocket of vol. 3 has maps and a pamphlet of eight pages with 396 map code numbers and names of languages.]

KEY, HAROLD, and MARY KEY. 1967. Bolivian Indian tribes: Classification, bibliography and map of present language distribution. Summer Institute of Linguistics Publications in Linguistics and Related Fields, No. 15. Norman.

LEHMANN, WALTER. 1920. Zentral-Amerika. Die Sprachen Zentral-Amerikas. Berlin. 2 vols.

LOUKOTKA, ČESTMIR. 1942. Klassifikation der südamerikanischen Sprachen. Zethn 74.1–69. Berlin.

——. 1950. Les langues de la famille Tupi-Guarani. Universidade de São Paulo,

Faculdade de Filosofia, Ciências e Letras, Boletim 104, Ethnografia e Lingua Tupi-Guarani, No. 16, São Paulo. [Reviewed by N. P. Smith, IJAL 17.193–5.]

——. 1968. Classification of South American Indian languages, ed. by Johannes Wilbert. Latin American Center, UCLA, Reference Series Vol. 7. Los Angeles.

MANSUR, GUÉRIOS. 1948–49. Dicionário das tribos e línguas indígenas da América meridional. Museu Paranaense, Publicações avulsas, No. 6. Tomo I, A, pp. 1–63; Tomo II, B-Cax, pp. 65–141. Curitiba. [Reviewed by Z. Salzmann, IJAL 17.192–3 (1951).]

MASON, J. ALDEN. 1950. The languages of South American Indians. BAE-B 143, Pt. 6, pp. 157–317. Washington, D.C.

MCQUOWN, NORMAN A. 1955. The indigenous languages of Latin America. AmA 57.501–70.

——. 1967. Handbook of Middle American Indians, Vol. 5. Austin.

MEILLET, ANTOINE, and MARCEL COHEN. 1924. Les langues du monde. Paris.

O'LEARY, TIMOTHY J. 1963. Ethnographic bibliography of South America. New Haven.

OROZCO y BERRA, MANUEL. 1864. Geografía de las lenguas y carta ethnográfica de México, precedidas de un ensayo de clasificación de las mismas lenguas y de apuntes para las inmigraciones de las tribus. Mexico.

PILLING, JAMES CONSTANTINE. 1885. Proof-sheets of a bibliography of the languages of the North American Indians. Washington, D.C. [Reprinted by Central Book Co., Brooklyn, N.Y., 1966.]

PIMENTEL, FRANCISCO. 1862–65. Cuadro descriptivo y comparativo de las lenguas indígenas de México. Tomo Primero [Segundo]. Mexico.

——. 1875. Cuadro descriptivo y comparativo de las lenguas indígenas de Mexico, o tratado de filología Mexicana. Mexico.

RIVET, PAUL, and GEORGES DE CRÉQUI-MONTFORT. 1951–56. Bibliographie des langues aymara et kičua. Travaux et Mémoires de l'Institut d'Ethnologie, 51. Paris. [Vol. 1, 1540–1875; Vol. 2, 1876–1915; Vol. 3, 1916–40; Vol. 4, 1941–55.]

RIVET, PAUL, and ČESTMIR LOUKOTKA. 1952. Langues de l'Amérique du Sud et des Antilles. Les langues du monde, ed. by A. Meillet and Marcel Cohen, rev. ed. 2.1099–1160.

SALZMANN, ZDENĚK. 1970. Review of Classification of South American Indian languages, by Čestmir Loukotka. IJAL 36.70–2.

STEWARD, JULIAN H., and LOUIS C. FARON. 1959. Native peoples of South America. New York. [Greenberg's classification, p. 22.]

SWANTON, JOHN R. 1952. The Indian Tribes of North America. BAE-B 145. [Republished by the Scholarly Press, Grosse Pointe, Michigan, 1968.]

TAX, SOL. 1960. Aboriginal languages of Latin America. Current Anthropology 1.430–6. Chicago.

TOVAR, ANTONIO. 1961. Catálogo de las lenguas de América del Sud; Enumeración, con indicaciones tipológicas, bibliografía y mapas. Buenos Aires.

VOEGELIN, C. F., and F. M. VOEGELIN. 1964. Languages of the world: Native America fascicle one. AnL 6(6).1–149.

——. 1965. Languages of the world: Native America fascicle two. AnL 7(7).1–150.

——. 1966. Index of languages of the world. AnL 8.i–xiv, 1–202.

WISTRAND, LILA M. 1971. Review of Classification of South American Indian languages, by Čestmir Loukotka. Linguistics 75.106–13.

ZISA, CHARLES A. 1970. American Indian languages; classifications and list. Center for Applied Linguistics: ERIC Clearinghouse for Linguistics. Washington, D.C.

INDEX OF NAMES